# CASEWORK

Third Edition

# CASEWORK

## A Psychosocial Therapy

**FLORENCE HOLLIS**
and
**MARY E. WOODS**

*Random House*  *New York*

Third Edition

9  8  7  6  5

**Library of Congress Cataloging in Publication Data**

Hollis, Florence.
    Casework, a psychosocial therapy.

    Bibliography: p. 28
    Includes index.
    1. Social casework.  2. Psychotherapy—Social
aspects.  I. Woods, Mary E., 1930-   .  II. Title.
HV43.H58  1981     361.3'2     80-29399
ISBN:  0-394-32368-8

Manufactured in the United States of America

To Rosemary Reynolds

" . . . so warm hearted and generous and open-eyed and peaceful,
indeed so much all of a piece. . . ."
—excerpt, letter from a friend, E. Y.

# Preface

*Casework: A Psychosocial Therapy* is designed to give a clear presentation of the psychosocial approach to casework by discussing both its principles and its applications to practice. It deals with the "hows" and "whys" of clinical social work practice in the treatment of psychological, interpersonal, and social problems. The early chapters of the book describe the development of the approach, including its roots in casework practice, the personality theory on which it operates—ego psychology in a Freudian context—and the many concepts from other social and psychological theories upon which it draws—systems theory, family therapy, communication and role theories, plus other pertinent social science concepts and data. Throughout, theory is closely related to practice. Detailed illustrations are included to demonstrate long- and short-term cases, individual, marital, and family therapy, environmental treatment, work with different age groups, and different clinical conditions.

This new edition describes many developments in clinical practice over the last ten years and demonstrates how they can be assimilated by the psychosocial approach. An extensive discussion of the theory and practice of family therapy, new material on environmental treatment, recent concepts related to the client-worker relationship, mutuality, discussions of time and treatment, and the contract are now included. Attention has been given to new thinking about the diagnosis and treatment of personality disorders. Case examples are from recent clinical work and reflect current problems and treatment techniques.

Many of the new emphases in this edition are primarily the work of my co-author, Mary E. Woods. Chapters 10 and 11, on family treatment, have been written entirely by her; and she is largely responsible for the new content and focus of Chapters 8 and 9, on environmental treatment, and Chapter 12, on the client-worker relationship. Equally important is the new case material that she has secured from a number of sources and presented in Chapters 3, 9, 11 and 19.

This third edition documents one more step in the growth of an approach to casework practice that has been developing for many years. In working on this revision I have been impressed again by the soundness of psychosocial casework as a theoretical system. It is obviously an open system, constantly incorporating new ideas as well as corrections of old ideas, constantly expanding. But it also has a "skin"—as the systems theorists say—that is tough and resistant to new ideas that have not been tested in practice or that are incompatible with the principles of the system. Change is therefore gradual, through assimilation rather than by assault. Comparison of the three editions of this book will clearly demonstrate this process.

In this edition we have included in our first chapter a brief history of the development of the psychosocial approach from the "diagnostic" or "differential" approach, which preceded it, and have also given more attention than in previous editions to its empirical base. Effort has also been made to refer to other approaches to casework, wherever appropriate, especially to show overlap and compatibility where those exist, as they often do.

The principles of the diagnostic-differential point of view continue to be basic to psychosocial casework, but their interpretation and application in practice have changed in many ways and have been greatly expanded.

As in the previous editions, this book is addressed to a variety of readers. Advanced workers and doctoral students, we hope, will find thinking about theory in general clarified, increased understanding of conflicts and problems that have recently come to the fore, and a view of how a number of new developments in theory can be assimilated into psychosocial work.

Students in masters' programs, who are training for direct service to clients, will find the book a basic text and resource for understanding and preparing to practice the psychosocial approach. Instructor leadership and full class discussion will enrich and clarify the content. Obviously, casework is a skill that cannot be learned from books alone, but must be acquired through practice. For this, competent field instruction is essential.

Previous editions of the book have also been found useful in undergraduate work, especially when accompanied by field instruction. Some chapters are better suited than others to this beginning phase of preparation. In our view, one needs to be careful not to overload students with theory and controversy before they have had substantial experience with practical work.

Many students in other countries have also made use of this book. Obviously, it must be read and used with due regard to differences in thought, customs, psychology, and personal environmental needs in different parts of the world.

# Acknowledgments

I feel extremely fortunate in having been able to enlist an experienced and skillful practitioner—Mary E. Woods—to co-author this edition. Since I have now been retired from the field for almost ten years, it would have been difficult to give a sound, convincing, modern presentation of psychosocial casework without her contribution of both ideas and material.

Mary Woods' experience includes seven years in protective work, and eleven in the Family Consultation Service of Eastchester, New York, where as a clinician she worked with individuals, families, and groups. She entered part-time private practice in 1969 and went into full-time practice five years ago. While in Eastchester she also served as field instructor, training director and program developer. In the latter capacity she planned and supervised a store-front program for "hard-to-reach clients." In addition to her private practice, she is a consultant to other clinicians and to several social agencies and from time to time conducts workshops, institutes, and seminars.

In addition to the chapters that she has written and those she has revised, Mary Woods has made many helpful suggestions in the rewriting of the rest of the book. In preparation for the new edition I read widely, of course, but stood in need of a colleague with whom to exchange thinking on material with which I was no longer able to deal through active practice and teaching. Together we have discussed each chapter in advance of writing, have exchanged ideas about content, and have read each draft critically. Thus the book as a whole is definitely a joint product, not simply a series of chapters by two different people.

I am also grateful to Helen Pinkus who was consulted at the outset. Characteristically, she was generous in making exceedingly helpful suggestions. It is a great loss to social work that this vigorous, straightforward, clear thinker and leader has died at so early an age.

During the writing of this edition my mind has frequently gone back to the many people who have shared in the building of psychosocial casework. Only a few, with whom I have been directly associated, can be acknowledged here. In early years as a student and caseworker,

I was first exposed to new ideas about casework by Betsey Libbey, then case supervisor at the Philadelphia Family Society. She was a doer and teacher rather than a writer and therefore is not as well known today as she should be. She conducted agency and regional seminars in which many who have contributed to casework practice and theory learned to examine case material both critically and appreciatively. She also encouraged staff members to study and write and to move to leadership posts in other communities, thus spreading the new ideas.

Then there were Virginia Robinson and Jessie Taft who might be surprised to see themselves referred to in this context. It was from them that many of us, who disagreed with the Rankian psychology on which they based their approach, nevertheless first learned the value of "acceptance" and "self-determination."

My mind has also gone back repeatedly during the writing to what I think of as those good years in Cleveland during the thirties. We were a group of young enthusiasts. Florence Day was then on the Western Reserve faculty. Rosemary Reynolds during the first years was heading a large district in the Cleveland public assistance agency and later was case consultant to that agency. I was running a district office of the family service agency. Rosemary Reynolds and I were both invited to do some part-time teaching at Western Reserve University. The new concepts concerning acceptance, self-determination, empathy, listening, and helping clients to think for themselves were exciting and liberating. We were beginning to assimilate psychoanalytic theory, with its explanations of the causes of mental stress, the value of ventilation, and the possibility of alleviating anxiety and reducing hostility. Along with other staff members we worked together to build these ideas into our casework courses. We kept notes on our teaching and cases and studied them together. When we wrote papers, Florence, Rosemary, and I worked especially closely together, exchanging ideas and criticizing each other's writings. In the two agencies with which we were associated—one public, one private—there were young practitioners enthusiastic about experimenting with new methods. Their practice not only provided source material for teaching and writing but also a continuous opportunity for observing results and reshaping practice. Helen Hanchette and Florence Waite, executives of the Associated Charities in Cleveland, contributed much to that period by their willingness to take the risk of allowing their young staff members to experiment with new ideas and to write about them. It was a very exciting time and a process which must have been paralleled in other schools and communities.

In the early years Gordon Hamilton, well known for her many writings contributing to the diagnostic or differential approach, and

Bertha Reynolds promoted these ideas in other settings. In the forties and fifties, as a colleague of Gordon Hamilton at Columbia University, I was fortunate in being part of a dynamic group of casework teachers who wrestled with and exchanged new concepts and teaching material. Gordon Hamilton was the natural leader of this casework faculty group. She, Lucille Austin, Isabel Stamm, and other colleagues ranged widely in their reading, often introducing new ideas for discussion. We all worked together to assimilate new content with the best of what we already knew.

Associations with Annette Garrett at the Smith College School for Social Work and Charlotte Towle of the University of Chicago, both personally and through their writings, also added greatly to my understanding of the theory this book describes. The beginnings of the first edition of this book included early conversations with Florence Day, then Director of the Smith College School for Social Work, and Annette Garrett, her associate. They both wanted the book to be written, and contributed to that initial impetus which sets a project going. In addition, Annette Garrett helped in the location of suitable agencies from which to secure case material for that first edition. It was a great pleasure to have Charlotte Towle, another of the builders of modern casework, consent to write the preface to the first edition and to have had her express her response to the book in such generous terms.

Many psychoanalysts too have been influential in the development of psychosocial casework. My own primary associations have been with Dr. Alan Finlayson during the Cleveland years, Dr. LeRoy Maeder during the forties when crucial theoretical differentiations were being shaped, Dr. B. Mildred Evans, and Dr. George Wiedeman during the Columbia years.

The third edition has drawn again upon the wisdom and generosity of my friend Rosemary Reynolds. As in the first and second editions, she has shared her professional knowledge, acted as critical reader, worked on the index, and given constant encouragement to the undertaking. In fact, it is she, with her realistic base in practice, who has constantly enriched my understanding and kept my sometimes abstract thinking close to the ground of reality by contributing her direct knowledge of psychosocial casework in practice. I am most grateful to her.

Appreciation goes finally to the many Masters and Doctoral students who have helped to reshape psychosocial casework. Seeking, challenging, restless, determined to do things better than we have done, they have forced us constantly to modify practice and augment it with the flow of new experience and new ideas they so eagerly grasped in their urgent quest for answers. Without apology for my own generation of caseworkers, I respect and value the contributions of these younger colleagues and fervently hope they will continue to push forward our knowledge of how to overcome our ever more pressing human dilemmas.

*August 1980*

Florence Hollis

Words cannot adequately express my appreciation to Florence Hollis for inviting me to share in the writing of this third edition. Always challenged, often exhilarated, occasionally frustrated, we have worked together for over two years, hammering out our perspective, sharing our ideas, surprised and pleased at how a meeting of the minds or new realizations often emerged from initially divergent slants on a particular question.

My thanks go to Flo Hollis not just for giving me the opportunity to work with her, but for the spirit of mutuality and openness that she brought to our joint endeavor. Part of her uniqueness derives from the fact that she seems not to need to "prove" herself. She is always interested in the ideas of others. Similarly, she sees her contribution to casework as a step in a process, giving full credit to those who came before her and, even in "retirement," she avidly seeks understanding of new formulations or strategies that may enhance clinical practice. Justifiably proud of casework's heritage, she is equally committed to rigorous inquiry into the effectiveness of our methods of helping—always insistent that the principles on which we operate have demonstrable merit. Where research is wanting, she prefers experience-based "practice wisdom" to ungrounded theory-spinning. The accumulation of abstract knowledge has little meaning to her if it cannot be used to guide us in truly helping the troubled people who turn to us for help.

Florence Hollis' example seems especially important in an era when new fads and untested "cures" spring up in the social work and mental health fields with disturbing regularity, when brand new labels get pinned on old ideas, when the word "traditional" too often is used pejoratively—as somehow opposite to "relevant"—and when casework itself is periodically under fire. While she strongly urges that we preserve casework principles and knowledge of the past that have proved their value, for fifty years she has also been in the forefront of those who developed a theoretical approach designed to systematize and assimilate consonant new ideas, data, and theory as these evolved. As a practitioner, educator, and researcher and, equally important, as a woman of integrity and caring, Florence Hollis' contribution to modern-day clinical social work is beyond measure. I am among many others who are grateful to her.

My part in this book is the culmination of many influences in my life, professional and personal. Unfortunately, it is impossible to acknowledge each person who has touched me or helped to shape my ideas. However, among those on the top of the list are the hundreds of clients I have seen over the years: the many courageous people through whom I learned so much about the painful human condition and about the imaginative ways that can be found to struggle against personal miseries and environmental assaults. And, had I not learned these elsewhere, my clients surely would have taught me the value of listening, of mutuality, of tailoring each piece of work to the uniqueness of the person and his or her circumstances, and of humility. Sometimes the very "demanding" or "recalcitrant" clients taught me the most.

I am also grateful to those students whose fresh thinking, inquisitive minds, and eagerness to find ever better ways to help people, stimulated some exciting explorations and insights; teaching has been the most rewarding in an atmosphere of give-and-take.

Of those most immediately helpful to me with my chapters, I mention first my friend and colleague, Dorothy Kitchell, who carefully read each one of them and offered useful suggestions; her encouragement during inevitable moments of uncertainty was invaluable. I am also indebted to Juliene Berk who, in a generous act of friendship, loaned her keen eye and blue pencil to several sections of the manuscript; her advice led to tighter, clearer text.

Others who freely gave their support and help and/or were instrumental in directing me to case materials include Jane Bloomer, Avra Mark, Julie Patton, the late Helen Pinkus, Nina Shilling, and Susan Solomon. I cannot thank them enough.

I do want to mention at least the following few among many people who significantly influenced my thinking at various stages of my professional development: the late Lucille Austin, Andrew Ferber, Thelma Samson, and Maurice Shilling. The impressions they made have endured and in one form or another found their way into the writing of this book.

And last, but far from least, my thanks to Elmeta Phillips, who took over the typing of the final manuscript, lovingly and cheerfully adjusting her life to accommodate to deadlines.

*Fall 1980*

Mary E. Woods

# Epilogue

Rosemary Reynolds died on September 18, 1980. In the interlude of
convalescence between a severe heart attack and what we had hoped
would be restorative heart surgery, she continued to work on the index,
completing it—characteristically—the day before she reentered the
hospital. She had read the final text and expressed her ever valuable
reactions. The book in a very real way represents her thinking as well
as that of the two authors. Rosemary was a gentle, warm, creative friend
and colleague. Many friends, members of her staffs of former years, and
students of long ago are grateful for having known and worked with
her.

# CONTENTS

# PART ONE

# The Theoretical Framework

# Chapter 1

# A Developing Practice

The concern of this book is the description and analysis of the psychosocial approach to casework. Its ultimate purpose is to contribute to the improvement of the quality of casework treatment offered to troubled individuals and families facing social dilemmas in their lives with which they are not fully able to cope. These dilemmas may have to do with their situations, their personal relationships, their individual functioning, or some combination of these elements. We will endeavor to analyze the dynamics of treatment procedures in such a way that the essential principles underlying them are sufficiently clear to enable readers to enhance their own treatment skills.

We will begin this chapter with a discussion of recent developments in psychosocial casework practice and knowledge. This will be followed by a presentation of some relevant historical background, designed to give the reader an understanding of some of casework's roots, and specifically of the context from which the psychosocial approach emerged and evolved. A final section of this chapter will be devoted to considering the empirical base of casework on which theory is built and treatment processes and results may be studied; some problems in research are described.

## RECENT DEVELOPMENTS

In the period between the original publication of this book and its present third edition, many of the treatment methods that were more or less experimental in the earlier periods have matured in form and are now widely used. Some of these have developed into approaches that are alternatives to psychosocial casework. Others are expansions of the approach itself. Together, they provide workers with many new tools with which to assist individuals and families to cope with their dilemmas and move forward toward their own goals.

3

The psychosocial approach to casework described in this book is an open system of thought. It has been able to assimilate many of these extensions of the knowledge and practices of earlier years. This growth of the caseworker's range of knowledge creates a large learning task for all practitioners—those with experience and those just entering the field. Relatively little that the worker knew and used three decades ago has become obsolete. Instead, the knowledge base has been expanded, built upon, and enriched, so that today there is much more to learn than in earlier years and a wide range of approaches to study before the worker finds his or her own treatment emphases and preferences for specialization in practice.

The psychosocial approach includes in its methodology and in its applicability help with concrete practical problems and with interpersonal and intrapersonal difficulties. Naturally, different types of personal difficulty call for different emphases and treatment procedures, but the central principles apply across the board. The approach was developed primarily in work with clients who either voluntarily sought help or who, if referred by others, became voluntary clients when in the course of initial interviews, they came to understand enough of treatment or the "helping process" to want it. Work with involuntary and "hard to reach" clients is less well developed, though many efforts have been made in recent years to find ways to give service to people who either do not recognize a need for help as perceived by others or who do not trust the caseworker as a potential helper.

We will endeavor throughout to demonstrate the operational meaning of concepts by references to actual cases, with fictitious names, of course, ranging from brief illustrations to fairly detailed case summaries. We believe that such concrete illustrations have the value of enhancing understanding of how principles and concepts are applied, and of suggesting ways in which casework can be skillfully practiced.

## Terminology

A comment about some of the terminology used in this edition is necessary. Although the term "casework" is considered outmoded by some, because of its long history as the designation for service to individuals by social workers, we have chosen to keep it as part of the title of this book and to use it in the course of our writing. We also use the recently developed designation "clinical social work." Whether or not this term will eventually supplant that of "casework" is one of many current unknowns. At present, the field defines "clinical social workers" in various ways. The writers prefer to use the term to refer to workers who have had a concentration in the study of direct treatment in graduate school, including substantial work in interpersonal problems, and who have subsequently had some years of professionally supervised practice in direct service. These workers contrast with "generalists" who have opted for broader training, and who therefore have not had sufficient time to acquire a high degree of skill in direct treatment. Similarly, those with only undergraduate professional training have just started to study casework and could not yet have mastered the complexities of clinical knowledge and practice. In this book, we are using the term "clinical social work" to refer to that more complicated part of casework for which generalist and undergraduate training can only begin to prepare.

The psychosocial approach is by no means identical with clinical social work. A number of other approaches are also used in clinical work. Rather, it represents a particular set of principles that can be followed by workers at various levels of competence in casework study and practice. In clinical social work practice, full use can be made of the entire system. Naturally, a high degree of skill can be reached only by years of both practice and study. All aspects of the approach cannot be mastered at once. Fundamentals of psychosocial practice are being taught in many schools at the undergraduate level, and also in the preparation of generalists at the graduate level.

Different terms are also in use in referring to the casework and clinical social work processes—"treatment," "the helping process," "intervention," "therapy," and "service." Each has its own claim to particular appropriateness, although they are often used interchangeably. We are using the word "treatment" in its general dictionary sense of "dealing with" or "acting or behaving toward another person in some specified way." The word has a sufficiently broad meaning to cover most casework activities, but it is generally not used to refer to work in cases in which practical problems per se are the major concentration. Some social workers dislike this term because to them it implies "sickness," seeming to put the blame for any distress or dilemma upon the client rather than on social conditions. When the term "treatment" is used in this book, it distinctly is not intended to carry any such connotation. "Helping" or the "helping process" or "service" are used even more broadly than "treatment" to cover all forms of casework practice including work on practical problems. We have used "therapy" in this book and in its title to refer to work in which social and psychological means are used to enable troubled individuals (singly or in family or formed groups) to cope with environmental, interpersonal, and/or intrapsychic dilemmas that are causing personal distress. The term "intervention" is preferred by some as a rather general term. It is commonly used by family therapists, in work with formed groups, in the behavior modification approach, and often in research. It is also preferred by others to whom the terms treatment and therapy seem to imply sickness in the client, or the idea that in some way the client is mainly responsible for his or her own problems. To the authors, the term "intervention" has a somewhat mechanistic and intrusive flavor, but nevertheless we have employed it as an alternative general term because of its wide use in the field.

## New Trends in Practice

There have been many new trends in theories and practices in clinical social work in recent years. The psychosocial approach has been expanded by the addition of concepts from these new developments. Chief among these is family group treatment and the joint interviewing of a couple or of several other members of a family. Social workers have made substantial contributions to the family therapy movement. However, in 1962, when the first edition of this book was being written, casework with clients was primarily limited to individual interviews.

At that time, we referred to joint interviews of married couples and family interviewing as "promising new trends" not covered by the data on which the book was based. In the second edition, a chapter on theoretical aspects of family treatment was introduced. It is now clear that interviewing couples and treating families as a whole are powerful tools for developing understanding of intrafamilial relationships and bringing change in these relationships. Sometimes the entire contact consists of family interviews. Often, on the other hand, both individual and group interviewing are used in the same family, each form of work having its own purpose and value. In the present edition, we are including discussion of a psychosocial form of family treatment, and of how family concepts and concepts derived from the psychodynamic study of the individual can be combined.

Crisis treatment, task-centered, planned-time-limited, and agency-limited services have been used extensively by social workers in recent years. Historically, brief services have comprised a large portion of casework practice. Budget problems, rising costs, and increased concern with accountability have given added impetus to interest in setting time limits on services and in clearly defining the goals of treatment. Especially when clients' difficulties are narrow in range or confined to areas that the client at once recognizes as problematical, planned short-term treatment is now widely recognized as appropriate. It can often bring relief more quickly and sometimes more effectively than "open-ended" procedures. It enables more individuals and families to be served without long periods of waiting for help to become available. Not infrequently, of course, the problems of people and their situations are too complex for abbreviated treatment, requiring more than a few interviews to unravel, define, and resolve. The brief service approach has contributed to more effective work even in these complex situations, however, by highlighting the importance of keeping treatment well focused.

One sees well-focused short-term service most clearly in task-centered casework, which has evolved from experimentation in the late sixties with planned-short-term treatment.[1] This approach has helped to eliminate aimless "drifting" or unnecessarily exhaustive explorations in interviews with clients. Similarly, the contract—which makes explicit the mutual working agreement between client and worker, when flexibly implemented—is helpful in maintaining a clear direction in treatment.

The use of the small group as a means of treatment by clinical social workers has grown steadily in importance in the last three decades. Discussion of work with groups has not been included in this book, but this does not signify any desire to underrate this form of treatment. Work with groups varies in theory and practice just as widely as does work with individuals and families. Clinical social workers seeking an approach to group treatment compatible with psychosocial theory can find it in the writings of others who are experts in practice with formed groups.[2] Increasingly, in clinical social work, the practitioner is expected to become proficient in both individual interviewing and work with groups.

## Knowledge from Other Disciplines

New understanding is also coming into the field from psychology, and other social sciences. Recent studies and clinical observations of individuals with personality or character problems are adding to casework knowledge. Promising new understandings of the diagnosis and treatment of clients with borderline and narcissistic personality disorders are of great value when working with individuals handicapped by these developmental disturbances. Differential approaches to schizophrenia, spurred on in part by advances in psychopharmacology and by the deinstitutionalization and return to the community of many mentally ill patients, have been important to casework treatment over the past decade.

Communication theory is currently of great interest to clinicians working with individuals, groups, families, and collaterals. The attention this theory attracts to the importance of nonverbal and paraverbal communication and to the "slippage" in communication that occurs when symbols are not given the same meaning by individuals who are

attempting to communicate is of particular value to any caseworker. In
many ways, it contributes to the understanding of barriers that often
prevent effective discussion between individuals.

In many disciplines, the approach to knowledge known as systems
theory has proved a useful tool for helping the mind to deal with the
complexities of modern knowledge. Psychosocial casework has found
this mode of thought most congenial for dealing conceptually with the
multiplicity of psychological, familial, and social forces at work in the
human situation. As early as 1941, Gordon Hamilton,[3] in a major paper,
used the term "organismic" to characterize the psychosocial approach
and referred to its use by Henry A. Murray in *Explorations in Personal-*
*ity.* Murray, in describing an organism, said: "The organism is from the
beginning a whole, from which the parts are derived by self-differentiation. The whole and its parts are mutually related; the whole being as
essential to an understanding of the parts as the parts are to an understanding of the whole."[4] He also referred to human beings as adapting,
integrating, and differentiating "within a changing environmental matrix." Systems theory adds to Murray's early conception the transactional concept of the relationships between the individual and his or her
environment. When viewed from a systems outlook, the "case" of an
individual or family includes the situation and is seen as a system of
interrelated, reciprocal forces that dovetail and reinforce one another.
Systems concepts, which will be discussed in greater detail in the chapters that follow, have been found extremely useful in clarifying aspects
of the person–situation gestalt so central to the psychosocial approach.

As a careful study of casework history will show, the importance of
the environment and of the interrelationships between people and
their milieu has never been denied in casework theory. Practice in this
area has always been carried on.[5] However, during the period when we
were absorbing and applying knowledge of the dynamics of personality
functioning, for a time interest swung away from the environment to
the personality. Environmental work was seen as more or less self-
evident, while understanding of the personality and of interviewing
techniques seemed to be the really challenging aspects of casework.

Systems theory contributed to increased recognition of the complexity and importance of the environment in the person–situation
gestalt, adding to caseworkers' understanding of the impact of modifications in the client's physical and social milieu on his or her emotional
life and behavior.

Greater attention is also being paid, again, to the need to link
people with institutional resources, services, and opportunities. Systems
theory has directed attention to the complexity of agency and other
institutional operations, the interlocking of policy, administration, and
staff personalities, and it has helped caseworkers in carrying out their

responsibility for modifying and humanizing institutional functioning. There is increased recognition of the importance of locating caseworkers in institutions and agencies where they can make themselves available in imaginative ways—in prenatal clinics, day care centers, communities of older people, cancer hospitals, and so on—thus becoming enablers in the client's immediate "life space." Concepts from systems theory can be particularly useful in analyzing the client–situation interplay, thus contributing to greater understanding of what can be done to alleviate tensions and stress in the gestalt.

Closely related to concepts from general systems theory are concepts derived from the ecological perspective in sociology, which deals especially with the interdependence of men and their institutions. The ecological approach introduced into casework by Germain and Gitterman has focused attention on the complex intertwining of the person and his or her milieu. This aspect of ecology both parallels and contributes to the increased understanding of the nature of person–situation transactions and to the place of the environment in treatment, as these have been developing within the psychosocial point of view.[6]

Casework requiring emphasis upon the treatment of environmental factors has never constituted a separate form of casework, but it has been and is one of many different clusters of casework procedures within the general matrix of therapeutic and interventive processes that constitute the field of casework. When the problem is chiefly one of disturbed relationships or personality disturbance, certain procedures of treatment necessarily receive greater emphasis; when problems are due primarily to external pressure or disequilibrium between the person and his or her environment, other procedures are stressed. Obviously, all types of procedures are not needed in every case.

## Casework and Changing Times

The current social scene and changing concerns and aspirations that clients bring to treatment have also contributed to changes in the practice of casework. With growing social acceptance of a wide range of lifestyles, a specific case situation frequently involves consideration by client and worker of new kinds of choices. Decreased support from family, church, and stable neighborhoods has given impetus to a search for "self-realization." As social values and standards for behavior have become less clearly defined, both men and women often come to treatment to "find" themselves. Some seek to learn how to be more effectively "assertive."

Marital problems continue to be a major focus of treatment, with the changing roles of men and women of great concern. As has been true for many years, improvement in the marriage is not the only acceptable goal—separation may be the best ultimate solution in many cases. Second marriages—now more prevalent than ever—often require complex adjustments, especially when children are involved. Homosexual pairs are bringing their relationship problems to treatment. Unmarried couples also ask for help in living together, and sometimes in deciding whether or not to live together. Individuals who are divorced or separated often seek help in recovering from the blow and in rearranging their lives.

The movement for women's rights presents the social worker with a new pervasive dimension in social living. Women are more actively demanding equality at home, on the job, and in the community. Male–female roles in marriage are now flexible, and hence more decisions are involved than formerly, when custom settled many matters that now rest on personal preference and require mutual agreement. Changing social mores also mean that young people more often choose to be sexually involved before marriage than was true in the past; it is not uncommon for unmarried couples of all ages to decide to live together. Contraception is now readily accessible: for some clients, abortion has become a real option. Single parents are often so by choice rather than as victims of circumstance. In all walks of life, awareness of the importance of clear communication has increased. Value is placed on the open expression of feelings and ideas among people who are living or working closely together. Far more often than even a few years ago, the realities of terminal illness and death are frankly discussed; the dying patient and those who will survive him or her are freer to share their grief with each other.

Caseworkers, along with other social workers, continue to be outspoken advocates of the poor, the elderly, Blacks, Puerto Ricans, American Indians, Chicanos, Asian Americans, and others who are discriminated against and feel powerless in American society. The aspirations and needs of people trapped and debilitated by ghetto and slum life are more widely understood than formerly, though most caseworkers learned long ago how erroneous it is to "blame the victim" of social injustice. Many questions are now raised about the oversimplified concept of the "culture of poverty." The great variations in both personality and circumstance among people who have in common the experience of poverty are again being stressed. This is increasing the possibility of individualizing service to persons and families in this group.

Understanding of cultural differences continues to be emphasized, but recognition grows of the rich variations to be found among people of the same culture. Wider and more sophisticated use is now being made of the knowledge contributed by the social sciences on ethnic, class, and regional factors in personality and social functioning. Study of role behavior, social interaction, family structure, and other related matters continues to deepen understanding of variations in both personality and life experience.

Fundamental to an understanding of all these new developments and changing needs, with their many variations, is a solid foundation in the basic knowledge and theory of casework practice. The task of evaluating the new emphases and enlarging the knowledge and understanding of the caseworker so that he or she can use them in practice, when appropriate, may seem formidable. It is made somewhat easier, however, because many new trends represent additions to already well established casework treatment methods, rather than anything diametrically opposed to them. Rather than tearing down an erroneous or grossly inadequate frame of reference, in the main the task is one of expanding the framework, sometimes with new methods and procedures, at other times with methods and procedures that have been underemphasized, although they were theoretically provided for in the overall scheme.

A clear understanding of fundamental principles is never more needed than when theory is being expanded, and choices must be made between what is to be retained and what discarded of both the new and the old. It is, therefore, perhaps especially timely for caseworkers to formulate as clearly as possible the nature of their basic frame of reference. Treatment will become more effective only when what is potentially sound and useful in the new is admitted to the main body of principles whose value has already been demonstrated. Knowledge-building should be a cooperative enterprise in which one reformulates, refines, and adds to existing knowledge and theory, accrediting the value of what has gone before in the certain realization that in due time others will have their turn at reshaping what now seems so clear to us.

## RELEVANT HISTORICAL BACKGROUND

During the Great Depression of the thirties, social casework was just beginning to outgrow its technical school, apprenticeship phase. In increasing numbers, schools of social work were moving toward affiliation with universities, and graduate schools were becoming the preferred method of education for entry into the emerging profession of social work. During that same period, the literature grew rapidly as the field became increasingly conscious of its methodology and of differences in point of view among practitioners. Prior to 1930 the writings of Mary Richmond, whose first book, *Friendly Visiting Among the Poor: A Handbook for Charity Workers*,[7] appeared in 1899, provided the major basis for casework practice theory. For many years, beginning in 1905, Richmond was associated with the production of teaching materials, including many case histories printed by the Field Department of *Charities and Commons,* and from 1909 on by the Charities Organization Department of the Russell Sage Foundation. From 1910 through 1922, the one-month summer institutes—led by Richmond—for secretaries (as workers were then called) and other paid workers were a principal source of leadership in case work practice. Richmond's 1917 book, *Social Diagnosis,* [8] was based on cases drawn from children's agencies, medical settings, and the family field. It also reflected her many years of study, discussion, and teaching. This volume was very widely used in schools and agencies throughout the country during the 1920s.

As is well known, Richmond's great contribution—in an age when poverty was thought to be predominantly the result of innate character defects—was to stress the effect of social relationships on the individual and his or her problems. In *Social Diagnosis,* she emphasized the need to study thoroughly the client's immediate social environment— present and past—to understand a case. Intervention in the client's environment was one of her two treatment methods and was later called "the indirect treatment method." *Social Diagnosis* presented and discussed many resourceful and imaginative illustrations of work in the environment designed to lessen pressure on the family or individual, to increase opportunities, and in various ways to favor the positive or healthy development of the client. In this respect, her point of view directly reflected the new developments in sociology of her period, which saw personality as shaped primarily by the social experiences of the individual.

Richmond added to this, however, a second category—direct treatment, the influence "of mind upon mind." [9] Under this category, Richmond stressed the development of a strong, trusting relationship through which a worker could influence a client toward activities and decisions that would be in his or her best interests. Suggestion and persuasion were predominant techniques, but there was also discussion of the need for frankness and honesty in the relationship and on the client's participation in decision making, which seems to suggest rational discussion, though this term was not used.

The decade following the publication of *Social Diagnosis* was one in which psychology was flourishing. The major impetus to social work's turn to psychological theories came from the association of social workers with psychiatrists during World War I, followed by the establishment of the specialty in psychiatric social work at the Smith College School of Social Work, the special department of mental hygiene at the

New York School of Social Work, and the course in social psychiatry at
the Pennsylvania School of Social Work.[10] During most of the twenties,
various psychologies of that period were introduced into social work at
different times and in different places. Robinson, in her chapter, "Working Psychologies in Social Case Work, 1920–1930," in *A Changing Psychology in Social Casework,* referred to the influence of John Dewey,
H. A. Overstreet, William A. White, William Healy, Bernard Glueck,
Marion Kenworthy, Jessie Taft, Ernest Groves, and others.[11] She wrote
that Healy, in his influential *Reconstructing Behavior in Youth,* listed
five sources of the "new psychology": 1. The Behavioristic School, 2.
Thomas's View, 3. The Adlerian School, 4. The Freudian School, 5. The
Jung [sic] School."[12] Of this period, Robinson wrote: "But these various
and often conflicting viewpoints are frequently used indiscriminately,
and nowhere has there been any attempt by a caseworker to organize
or originate any psychological principles of interpretation."[13] In other
words, social work was in a period of examination and ferment seeking
greater understanding of the personality than Richmond had been able
to provide when social influences, heredity, physical makeup, and variations in intelligence were the main explanatory variables offered by
psychology and psychiatry.

In 1930, with the publication of Robinson's book, a strong new
influence entered the field—that of Otto Rank. Three years later, under
the leadership of Taft and Robinson and their associates at the Pennsylvania School of Social Work, "functionalism" became a focused, distinc-
tive approach to social casework. Functionalism not only brought
Rankian psychology into the field, but also found itself in strong disagreement with the Richmond approach and its successors. For the
functionalist, treatment revolved around agency services and the
client's responses to these services. Rank's concept concerning the will
took a central position. Past history was considered irrelevant. Diagnosis was deemphasized. Time limitations were used as a means of stimulating the client to act upon his or her problem. The terms functional,
Rankian, and Pennsylvania School were used to refer to this point of
view.

Meanwhile other schools, especially the other leading eastern
schools—Smith, Simmons, New York, and Cleveland—and practitioners in agencies affiliated with them, were moving toward Freudian
theory as the psychology yielding the most convincing explanations of
the human personality as well as contributions to treatment methodology.[14] This approach, like Richmond's, required careful history-taking,
including information about the relevant past. This continued to be
called a social study, although it had already become distinctly psychosocial—an effort to arrive at facts upon which a diagnosis could be

based and a tentative treatment plan could be formulated. The terms diagnostic, differential, and Freudian were used to refer to this point of view.

Concurrently, the social climate was becoming less authoritarian, the concept of self-determination was widely discussed, and Dewey's theories of education were receiving increased acceptance. On the issue of self-determination, the two schools of the thirties in actuality were not far apart. The functional school, under the leadership of Robinson and Taft, put great emphasis on this concept and there was much ferment, as though a real difference on this principle were at issue.

Hamilton, for many years the leading exponent of the differential approach, stressed in her writings the individual's "right to be himself," the uniqueness of the client's goals and objectives, and the movement away from authority and manipulation, as early as 1937.[15] In her 1940 book, *Theory and Practice of Case Work*,[16] widely used as a text in all parts of the country, she reiterated these points. Another early representative of the differential school wrote in 1939, "The final choice of the pattern he (the client) wants his life to take in matters large and small is his and not the worker's to make. . . . This principle is one of the most widely held in the field of casework. Its acceptance was greatly accelerated by its defense in Virginia P. Robinson's *A Changing Psychology in Social Case Work;* under the name of the client's right of 'self determination' it was also discussed by Bertha C. Reynolds in *Between Client and Community;* it is either stated explicitly or implied in almost all the writings by caseworkers listed in the Bibliography."[17] This bibliography included writings of about forty of the leading nonfunctionalist caseworkers of the day. Actually, both functional and diagnostic schools had departed from the earlier directiveness, and from the assumption that the worker would know what was best for the client in managing his or her own life.

It is not necessary here to go into all the differences between the two points of view. Gradually, the differential or diagnostic point of view developed far beyond its Richmond predecessor. The social part of the history became less extensive, but continued to put great emphasis on family influences. As the newer psychology with emphasis on ego functioning developed, more effort was made to observe the client's functioning both directly within the interview and indirectly, as he or she described encounters with others. The old directive techniques still common in the twenties, gave way to efforts to help individuals think for themselves and base decisions on their own judgment. The nature of history-taking changed markedly with recognition of the fact that treatment begins immediately, and that facts are gathered and observed more selectively and less formally than Richmond had advised.

While diagnostic thinking changed radically in response to increased understanding of personality, the idea that one must try to understand a person whom one is trying to help and that current functioning is influenced by past as well as by present events continued to be regarded as basic to differential, individualizing treatment. Richmond's two major treatment modes—treatment through change or use of the environment and treatment through direct work with the client —were also carried over into the differential point of view. They were considered, as Richmond considered them, interlocking components in treatment.

By the end of the thirties, except for the functional school, Freudian psychology was widely accepted by caseworkers as the most useful basis for understanding personality. The major theoretical task of the forties was to define the ways in which psychoanalytic understanding could be used by caseworkers, what factors distinguished casework treatment from psychoanalysis, and what different kinds of work with clients existed within the broad methodology of differential casework. As answers to these questions began to take form, the further problem of developing guiding principles for the relationship of diagnosis to treatment emerged. These issues will be explored further in later chapters.

Until the mid-fifties, the functional and the diagnostic or differential approaches were the only generally recognized points of view in case work. Functionalism continued to be sponsored chiefly by the Pennsylvania School, the University of North Carolina school, and a few other schools. Its influence was felt strongly in a number of agencies in the East. The diagnostic school was more widely accepted as the main body of casework thought.

At about this time, a sudden spurt occurred in the growth of theory and practice within the diagnostic group. Most important of all was the increasing assimilation by caseworkers of the new understanding of the ego developing in the psychoanalytic field. Several efforts were also made in the late fifties to bridge diagnostic and functional thinking.[18] Out of one of these, Perlman's "problem solving" approach developed. Experimentation also began with seeing both partners jointly in problems of marriage relationships. Then, beginning in the early sixties came family group treatment, crisis treatment, planned short-term treatment, and task-oriented treatment. The usefulness for our field of a number of other theoretical approaches has been, or is being, explored—Horney and Sullivan have been influential, the Rogerian approach (later called the client-centered system) is favored by some, behavior modification has many adherents, and others under study in recent years include cognitive theory, transactional analysis, the existential approach, and, most recently, the "life model," or ecological, approach.

In 1962, when the first edition of this book went to press, a number of these new approaches had been introduced. Many of these seemed, for the most part, to be variations in emphasis and areas of growth within the diagnostic–differential approach, with little or no basic incompatibility with that approach. When the term "psychosocial" was first used by Hollis in the subtitle of this book, it was a descriptive term, chosen to emphasize the fact that the diagnostic–differential approach was characterized by concern for both social and psychological aspects of life. Hamilton had used the term as early as 1941 in stressing the fact that all problems are to a degree both emotional and social.[19] The term was originally suggested in 1930 by Hankins, a sociologist, then teaching at the Smith School for Social Work.[20]

In 1969, a symposium was held in Chicago in memory of Charlotte Towle for the purpose of securing clear statements about the approaches then in operation in the casework field. Functional, problem solving, behavioral modification, and "psychosocial" were chosen as "general" approaches; family group treatment, crisis-oriented brief treatment, and adult socialization were seen as "middle-range approaches" addressed to specific groups within the general client population but having utility for wider application. In the publication of *Theories of Social Casework,* based on this series of discussions, the term "psychosocial casework" was used to designate the approach represented by the diagnostic–differential point of view.[21] Since then, "psychosocial" has been widely used as the designation for an approach described in publications by many writers as well as in this book. In both theory and practice, this point of view has now expanded considerably beyond the diagnostic–differential approach on which it was originally based. It is important to recognize that many elements now included in the psychosocial approach are by no means exclusive to it. When likenesses and differences between points of view are examined, it becomes apparent that there is indeed a considerable degree of agreement among most approaches on certain fundamental points which, as we see it, comprise a common core of casework practice.[22]

In this book, then, we are including both this common core of casework practice and concepts that are specifically components of the psychosocial approach.

## THE EMPIRICAL BASE

Psychosocial casework is a blend of concepts derived from psychiatry and the social sciences with a body of empirical knowledge developed within the casework field itself. The direct empirical basis of the approach rests upon the continued systematic study of treatment, focusing upon client response to the procedures employed.

Fortunately, the major outlines of the diagnostic–differential type of practice developed during a period when detailed process case recording was common, especially in the family agency and psychiatric social work settings in which this approach developed. Supervision was also customary, with weekly conferences of several hours held regularly for discussion of complicated and baffling cases. Agency seminars for group study of cases recorded in detail were common, as were also regional seminars, reports at state and national conferences, and published papers based upon case studies.

The term "practice wisdom," sometimes used to describe this empirical basis, does not sufficiently convey the continuous study process through which practice was observed and examined, both case by case, and in groups of cases. As in any other healthy profession, practice theory was built upon widely debated premises derived from scrutiny of actual experience. Practice concepts were constantly modified, as well as expanded as new evidence appeared. In later chapters, reference will be made to some of these changes in both practice and theory.

The first steps in the development of any body of knowledge or theory is that of close accurate observation of the phenomena under study. This usually begins informally and proceeds to the collection of data based on increasingly systematic study. Formulation of concepts and hypotheses and experimental testing of these in small-scale studies are usually the next steps in the development of theory. Such experimental testing can be only as informative as the accuracy of the observed data on which it rests. Techniques are now being developed for recording, defining, and organizing data for detailed study of actual practice, which will greatly increase the accuracy of future experimental case studies.

This is essentially the way in which the psychosocial approach has been built. Many of the early reports analyzed a single case. A number of others were based on study of a few cases, and a few were derived from systematic study of 50 to 100 or more cases.[23] For the most part, they were studies and articles based on practice designed to build, confirm, or demonstrate theory. They described, examined, and experimented, but did not test or attempt to prove either theory or practice. Control groups were almost never used.

Currently, attention is being given to the improvement of systematic observation and to techniques for experimental work with single cases and small groups of cases. Techniques now developing for recording, defining, and organizing data for detailed study of actual practice will greatly increase the accuracy of future experimental case studies.

At the time this book is being written, casework is just emerging from a period of experimentation and adaptation of a type of research methodology derived largely from the social sciences. The field was not ready for this type of research. Beginning in the sixties, interest in evaluative studies that attempted to measure the successfulness of programs and methods was high. Caseworkers were naively optimistic and researchers were equally naive about the fallacies inherent in applying certain methodologies, then in wide use in academic sociology, to a field in a relatively early stage of both knowledge and research development. Control and comparative group designs were emphasized with high reliance on probability statistics for relatively small samples. Emphasis was not on theory building but on outcome testing. Such evaluative studies depend upon the ability to prove that a particular form of treatment is either better than no treatment at all or better than a second form of treatment. In order for this to be accepted as probably so, the differences between the two groups have to be sufficiently large that one can be reasonably sure that reported findings are not due to chance. This level of certainty has usually been set at .05. This means that the chances are 95 to 5 (or 19 to 1) that the findings are not due to chance.

To the dismay of caseworkers, many of the studies reported between 1965 and 1972 failed by this standard to demonstrate good results. Many social workers concluded from this that casework was indeed ineffective. The control group statistical analysis type of research was so popular and highly respected during this period that the value of studies using methods more suitable to clinical work was greatly underestimated, and the notion grew that there was no empirical basis for the casework practice of the day. Two useful by-products of this otherwise discouraging situation were interest in newly emerging approaches to casework and new developments in the psychosocial approach.

The significance of many of these control studies is now in dispute. Fischer,[24] for instance, claims that nine of eleven studies he considers adequate in evaluating casework show it to be ineffectual. But Geismar,[25] who has done many respected studies, disagrees. Examining thirteen studies that he considers well designed, Geismar finds only four with no statistically significant positive findings, two with mixed results, and seven on which findings support the study's major hypothesis or are in the direction of the desired objectives.

Crane,[26] in a statistically astute and persuasive article examining many of the same pieces of research, argues that "research evidence as to the effectiveness of case services in social work is much less clearcut than has often been assumed." He examined twenty-five findings in evaluative control or contrast group studies in which the significance level was set at .05 to protect against the possibility of what is known statistically as a type I error; that is, the error of reporting as positive a finding that is merely due to chance differences between experimental and control groups. Crane is concerned about what he sees as an equally serious error—a type II error. In this type of error, a genuine difference in results between experimental and control or contrast groups fails to be recognized or reported. This often occurs because of overcaution against a type I error. These two errors are in a sense reciprocal. Statistical steps taken to guard against one of them increases vulnerability to the other.

Crane points out that in most of the studies of casework using the .05 criterion, the probability of type II errors is eight to fifteen times greater than the probability of type I errors. The significance of this is that in many, if not most, casework studies of the control group type using the .05 criterion, there is a very strong probability that even when results in the treatment group were better than in the control group, this difference was falsely attributed to chance and not favorably reported.

Crane states further that it has long been known that routine use of the .05 criterion has no scientific or logical justification, arguing that at the present stage of casework research the risk of type I and type II errors should be set at the same level.

Another statistical weakness of many of these studies lies in the fact that safeguards have not been taken against coding in the "treated group" many cases in which the problem under consideration was never treated and in all probability did not even exist. The failure to recognize this means that such studies have been unintentionally further loaded against the possibility of positive findings.

For instance, outcome studies comparing a group of standard public assistance cases with a similar group receiving additional casework service sometimes test differences between the two groups in a series of problem areas including unemployment, marriage adjustment, child rearing practices, health care, household management, and the like. Indeed, in an experimental group of 100 such cases, very few of the problems under study will have existed and been treated in all cases. The need for financial assistance in such a sample would be present in all cases, but even unemployment of an employable person may not have existed in more than half the sample. Other problems are likely to have been present in only 10 to 30 of the cases studied. Yet all 100 experimental cases are sometimes coded as if there had been treatment in all cases in all problem areas. In the smallest categories—say, those in which the problem had actually been treated in only 10 to 15 of the 100 cases—even if 8 of the 10 or 12 of the 15 cases had improved, the improvement *rate* would have appeared to be only 8 or 12 percent

instead of the actual 80 percent, and would have been rejected as due
to no more than chance.*

Many other important things have been learned from the research
of this earlier period about research methodology itself: the importance
of specifying goals that theory would lead one to expect were attain-
able, the need to monitor treatment procedures to ascertain that the
procedures under study were actually used, guarding against the use of
measuring scales and other procedures that are only marginally appropriate for the cases under study, among others. Perhaps most important
of all, writers are warning—as caseworkers have for many years—
against the dangers of overgeneralizing from a specific experiment or
demonstration to casework as a whole.[27]

This is by no means to say that the findings of all early control group
statistical analysis research are without value. On the contrary, a few
studies were very well designed and executed and brought important
changes in psychosocial practice. A good illustration of a study of major
significance to the field is reported in *Brief and Extended Casework* by
Reid and Shyne.[28] This study demonstrated the value of shorter treatment combined with certain new techniques. The Reid–Shyne study
also demonstrated enormous variability in the work of different practitioners who were presumably following the same basic approach.

Another excellent example of the control group statistical analysis
design is that of Weissman[29] et al., who studied casework treatment of
106 depressed women patients, primarily diagnosed as neurotic depres-
sives. Favorable changes were reported at the .05 or .01 level in five
areas—improved work performance, reduced interpersonal friction,
freer communication, reduced anxiety, and better overall adjustment.
It was further found that though medication alone reduced anxiety it
did not affect social adjustment. On the other hand, casework treatment
did not reduce symptomatology. The authors pointed out that this demonstrates that if studies do not distinguish between social adjustment
and symptomatology in measuring the effects of psychotherapy, but
wrap them up in the same measuring bundle, the results may well be
inconclusive, obliterating the favorable outcome on social adjustment
alone.

As the fallibility of tests and constructed scales for measuring behavior are becoming more apparent, there is greater willingness among
researchers to add the views of clients themselves (whose satisfaction
with treatment, after all, is of paramount importance) and even of

*Some researchers with whom the writer has discussed this problem claim that since
there would probably also be only 10 to 15 cases in the contrast group having such a
problem no bias has been introduced. This fails to recognize that this condition, which
magnifies the "no change" factor in both groups, automatically works in favor of the null
hypothesis.

caseworkers to the sources of evidence. The Beck and Jones[30] study, *Progress on Family Problems,* using such data, produced many significant findings.

A very important trend that should aid greatly in the study of casework practice and theory building is that of the "individual-control/applied-analysis" strategy.[31] Introduced to social work by researchers in the behavior modification approach, this type of research is now being adapted to other approaches. Essentially, it is a highly systematic way of studying individual cases or accumulations of such cases. Like the observational studies, which throughout casework history have steadily contributed to casework development of practice, it relies upon observations of cases. But it is far more methodical and exact than the early studies. It makes it possible to examine casework methodology in detail so that researchers know what treatment procedures have actually been used, and to examine observed or directly reported changes without reliance on scales only tangentially related to the phenomena under study. Specific and real goals acceptable to the client and deemed feasible by the worker can be articulated for each case, with results examined in relation to these goals. Such cumulative individual case study data can provide evidence upon which generalizations can be made convincingly. This type of research strategy also makes possible analysis of the direct connection between treatment step and hypothesized effect.

At the present time, the behavior modification approach has made the most systematic and successful use of this research strategy with impressive evidence of its ability to achieve the kind of effect it seeks.* Task-oriented casework is also making good use of this type of research. It shows promise of being of great value to the psychosocial approach in the period ahead for both building theory and monitoring results.

In Chapter 2 we will turn to detailed discussion of some elements of the theoretical framework of psychosocial practice. We shall begin by attempting to clarify and elaborate on the nature of the interaction between inner psychological and outer social components in the individual's development and functioning. The theoretical framework of psychosocial casework has long embraced both of these components and their interactions, providing a meeting ground for psychodynamic theory and theories dealing with the environment and with the impact of the transactions between people and their social environments.

---

*The writers' preference for the psychosocial approach rests, among other things, on value preferences and on the acceptance of broader goals of treatment that require different procedures from those to which behavior modification theoretically confines itself, not on doubt that behavior modification can often achieve the limited goals it sets itself.

## NOTES

1. See William J. Reid and Ann W. Shyne, *Brief and Extended Casework* (New York: Columbia University Press, 1969); and William J. Reid and Laura Epstein, *Task-Centered Practice* (New York: Columbia University Press, 1977). Or, for a shorter presentation, see William J. Reid, "Task-Centered Treatment," in Francis J. Turner, ed., *Social Work Treatment* (New York: Free Press, 1979), pp. 479–498.

2. See especially Helen Northen, *Social Work with Groups* (New York: Columbia University Press, 1969); and Helen Northen, "Psychosocial Practice in Small Groups," in Robert W. Roberts and Helen Northen, eds., *Theories of Social Work with Groups* (New York: Columbia University Press, 1976), pp. 116–152.

3. Gordon Hamilton, "The Underlying Philosophy of Social Case Work," *The Family*, 22 (July 1941), 139–148.

4. Henry A. Murray, *Explorations in Personality* (New York: Oxford University Press, 1938), pp. 38–39.

5. Gordon Hamilton, "Basic Concepts of Social Case Work," *The Family*, 18 (July 1937), 147; and Gordon Hamilton, "Psychoanalytical Oriented Casework and Its Relation to Psychotherapy," *American Journal of Orthopsychiatry*, 19 (1949), 209.

6. Carel B. Germain and Alex Gitterman, "The Life Model of Social Work Practice," *Social Service Review*, 50 (December 1976), 601–610.

7. Mary E. Richmond, *Friendly Visiting Among the Poor: A Handbook for Charity Workers* (New York: Macmillan, 1899).

8. Mary E. Richmond, *Social Diagnosis* (New York: Russel Sage Foundation, 1917).

9. Mary E. Richmond, *What Is Social Casework?* (New York: Russell Sage Foundation, 1922), pp. 101–102.

10. Virginia Robinson, *A Changing Psychology in Social Case Work* (Chapel Hill: University of North Carolina Press, 1930), p. 54.

11. Ibid., pp. 81–93.

12. Ibid., p. 83.

13. Ibid., p. 81.

14. Contrary to popular opinion, psychoanalysis was not a major force in casework in the 1920s. Shirley Hellenbrand, in her careful study of this period, *"Main Currents in Social Casework, 1918–36"* (doctoral dissertation, Columbia University School of Social Work, 1965), found very little mention of Freudian thinking in the literature or teaching materials of that period. Rather, it was gradually assimilated during the thirties, and by the end of that decade was a major component of the diagnostic or differential position.

15. Gordon Hamilton, "Basic Concepts upon Which Case Work Practice Is Formulated," *Proceedings of the National Conference of Social Work* (Chicago: University of Chicago Press, 1937).

16. Gordon Hamilton, *Theory and Practice of Case Work* (New York: Columbia University Press, 1940), pp. 29, 32.

17. Florence Hollis, *Social Casework in Practice: Six Case Studies* (New York: Family Welfare Association of America, 1939), p. 5.
18. See Herbert H. Aptekar, *The Dynamics of Casework and Counseling* (Boston: Houghton Mifflin, 1955); and Helen Harris Perlman, *Social Casework: A Problem-Solving Process* (Chicago: University of Chicago Press, 1957).
19. Hamilton, "Underlying Philosophy of Social Case Work," p. 141.
20. Frank Hankins, "Contributions of Sociology to Social Work." *Proceedings of the National Conference of Social Work* (Chicago: University of Chicago Press, 1930), p. 534.
21. Robert W. Roberts and Robert H. Nee, eds., *Theories of Social Casework* (Chicago: University of Chicago Press, 1970).
22. Turner deals well with this question. See his Chapter 21 in Turner, *Social Work Treatment,* pp. 535–546.
23. It may be useful to cite a few illustrations. Among the small studies, ranging from nine to 12 cases, in chronological order are: Marian F. Lewis, "Alcoholism and Family Casework," *The Family,* 18 (April 1937), 39–44.
Rosemary Reynolds and Else Siegle, " A Study of Casework with Sado-Masochistic Marriage Partners," *Social Casework,* 40 (December 1959), 545–551.
Joanne Geist and Norman Gerber, "Joint Interviewing: A Treatment Technique with Marriage Partners," *Social Casework,* 41 (February 1960), 76–83.
Miriam Jolesch, "Casework Treatment of Young Married Couples," *Social Casework,* 43 (May 1962), 245–251.
Richard D. Prodie, Betty L. Singer, and Marian R. Winterbottom, "Integration of Research Findings and Casework Techniques," *Social Casework,* 48 (June 1967), 360–366.
Among the larger studies, ranging from 75 to several hundred cases, are (in chronological order):
Gordon Hamilton, *Psychotherapy in Child Guidance* (New York: Columbia University Press, 1947).
Florence Hollis, *Women in Marital Conflict* (New York: Family Welfare Association of America, 1949).
Lilian Ripple, Ernestina Alexander, and Bernice Polemis, *Motivation, Capacity, and Opportunity* (Chicago: University of Chicago Press, 1964).
Leontine R. Young, *Wednesday's Children: A Study of Child Neglect and Abuse* (New York: McGraw-Hill, 1964).
Margaret Bailey, "Casework Treatment of the Alcoholic and His Family," in *Alcoholism and Family Casework* (New York: Community Council of Greater New York, 1968), pp. 67–108.
Catherine M. Bitterman, "The Multimarriage Family," *Social Casework,* 49 (April 1968), 218–221.
Pauline C. Cohen and Merton S. Krause, *Casework with Wives of Alcoholics* (New York: Family Service Association of America, 1969).
24. Joel Fischer, "Is Casework Effective? A Review," *Social Work,* 18 (January 1973), 5–20.

25. Ludwig L. Geismer, "Thirteen Evaluative Studies," in Edward J. Mullen, James R. Dumpson et al., eds., *Evaluation of Social Intervention* (San Francisco: Jossey-Bass, 1972).

26. John A. Crane, "The Power of Social Intervention Experiments to Discriminate Differences Between Experimental and Control Groups," *Social Service Review,* 50 (June 1976), 224–242.

27. For further discussion of these points, see Florence Hollis, "Evaluation: Clinical Results and Research Methodology," *Clinical Social Work Journal,* 4 (Fall 1976), 204–222.

28. William J. Reid and Ann W. Shyne, *Brief and Extended Casework* (New York: Columbia University Press, 1969).

29. Myrna M. Weissman et al., "Treatment Effect on the Social Adjustment of Depressed Patients," *Archives of General Psychiatry,* 30 (1974), 771–778.

30. Dorothy Fahs Beck and Mary Ann Jones, *Progress on Family Problems* (New York: Family Service Association of America, 1973). The generally positive findings of this study were challenged by John R. Schuerman in a critical essay review, "Do Family Services Help?", *Social Service Review,* 49 (September 1975), 363–375. Interested readers will want to study the Beck response and Schuerman's further comments in *Social Service Review,* 50 (June 1976), 312–331.

31. See discussion of this in Michael W. Howe, "Casework Self-Evaluation: A Single-Subject Approach," *Social Service Review,* 48 (March 1974), 1–23.

# Chapter 2

# The Psychosocial Frame of Reference

In this chapter we are seeking to sketch the frame of reference upon which psychosocial casework rests. Certain basic values of casework form the first component of that framework. Psychosocial casework is characterized by its direct concern for the *well being* of the individual. It is not its purpose to bring the individual into conformity with society and thus rid society of the social hazard presented by the discontented, unsatisfied, rebellious individual. On the contrary, casework came into being as a response to the needs of human beings for protection against social and natural deprivations and catastrophes. Historically, it represents a turning away from the laissez-faire doctrines that followed the unhappy combination of Malthusian thinking with Darwin's emphasis on the development of strength through the survival of the fittest. From its inception casework has stressed the value of the individual, and for the past fifty years it has consistently emphasized the right of each person to live in a unique way, provided that he or she does not infringe unduly upon the rights of others.[1] This emphasis upon the innate worth of the individual is an extremely important, fundamental characteristic of casework. It is the ingredient that makes it possible to establish the relationship of trust that is so essential for effective treatment. From it grow the two essential characteristics of the caseworker's attitude toward a person coming for help; first, *acceptance,* and second, respect for the client's right to make his or her own decisions—often referred to as *self-determination.*

By acceptance we mean the maintaining of an attitude of warm good will toward the client, whether or not his or her way of behaving is socially acceptable and whether or not it is to the worker's personal liking. This is without doubt the main ingredient in the development of a therapeutic or helping relationship. At the beginning of treatment, the client is often distrustful of the worker's interest and desire to help and may also have feelings of helplessness, and lack of self-esteem or fear of criticism. Uncritical acceptance by the worker lessens these fears and begins the building of a client–worker relationship in which the client feels support and can talk freely. It is true that in actual practice we cannot always live up to the ideal of warm good will in the face of hostility or coldness from the client, or of destructive behavior. This is sometimes especially difficult in family group treatment, where one is often caught in the crossfire between angry destructive family members, and impartiality is essential. But the greater the acceptance, the greater the likelihood that whatever understanding we achieve can be put to use in constructive communication with the client.

Acceptance is not to be confused with refraining from *evaluating* the appropriateness or usefulness of the client's ways of functioning. But even accurate and perceptive evaluation is of little use if it is accompanied by feelings of condemnation or hostility toward the client. The essence of acceptance is the maintaining of a constant caring feeling for the client.

*Self-determination*[2] is perhaps not too felicitous a term; it is too absolute in its implications. What is really meant by this concept from a psychosocial perspective is that self-direction, the right to make one's choices, is a highly valued attribute of the individual. The more a client can exercise autonomy, making decisions and directing his or her own life the better, and the less the caseworker tries to take over these responsibilities, the better. No one in this world can continually do exactly as he or she wants, but a person can make individual decisions about how to find a way among the limitations and opportunities presented by external reality.

In order to make sound decisions, the client sometimes simply needs better information; at other times, help is needed from the caseworker in understanding various aspects of a dilemma. Not infrequently, the client's ego is to varying degrees impaired in its capacity for accurate perception or judgment, or its functioning is distorted by the operation of mechanisms of defense, so that the problem becomes one of helping the person to develop greater capacity for decision making. The objective of such work is to increase the ability to make decisions, not to make them for the client. In extreme situations, where there is danger of real harm to others or to the self, or where the client is incapable of carrying this responsibility, the caseworker must take over and make decisions for the client. But this is done only where the necessity for such action is clear.

A belief in the value of self-determination does not mean that the caseworker plays a passive role with clients. On the contrary, change is promoted in clients' functioning when it is believed that this will enable them to meet their needs more effectively. But the means the worker chooses to bring about change must ever be consistent with the goal of increasing the client's capacity for self-direction—his or her autonomy. Thus the relationship is consistently an honest one, the worker showing respect for the wishes and goals of the client and sometimes offering suggestions and advice—not, however, as directives but as opinions that the client is free to accept or reject.

A worker sometimes offers suggestions about *how* to reach a goal that the client desires. Obviously, this is entirely different from becoming directive about *what* goal or decision is to be chosen. In reaching decisions and moving toward the realization of an objective, the worker's role is to help the client clarify thinking. In other words, whenever possible—and this is most of the time—clients are helped to reason things through for themselves, to correct their own misconceptions, and to accept the maximum responsibility of which they are capable for formulating their own ideas. Where more active guidance is needed, either because the client lacks knowledge, as is sometimes true in child-rearing problems, or because of limitations in education or in intellectual capacity, more active guidance may need to be given. But even in these circumstances, every effort is made to promote the client's self-directive ability. Strong emphasis is therefore placed on techniques for drawing out the client's own reasoning capacities.

## THE PERSON-IN-HIS-SITUATION

Casework has always recognized the interplay of both internal psychological and external social causes of dysfunctioning, and endeavored to enable individuals who seek help to meet their needs more fully and to function more adequately in social relationships.[3] Throughout its history, it has drawn continuously from other scientific fields as they uncovered data and developed theory that promised to throw light upon either the psychological or the social side of human problems. Psychology and psychiatry, cultural anthropology, sociology—especially its role theory, family theory, and group dynamics—systems theory, and communication theory have been the major sources of knowledge from other disciplines.

Central to psychosocial casework is the notion, as Hamilton so often phrased it, of "the-person-in-his-situation" as a threefold configuration consisting of the person, the situation, and the interaction between them. The terms "internal pressure" and "external pressure" are often used to describe forces within the individual and forces within the environment as they impinge upon or interact with each other. External pressure is sometimes referred to as *press* and internal pressure as *stress.*

Casework recognizes this interaction as highly complex. The external press is immediately modified by the way in which the individual perceives it. Depending upon their individual natures, upon their needs, or internal stress, individuals will react to their perceptions of press in their own peculiar ways. Furthermore, since the term "situation" most often implies a human situation—family, friends, employer, teacher, and so on—the situation is as complicated as the "person" who confronts it. The individual's family is seen as a fundamental component of this "situation." Therefore, the interactions occurring in the family system in both past and present are of high salience. When the person reacts to an external press, this reaction in turn becomes a press upon some other human being, who then responds with his or her own set of perceptions and needs. Hence, understanding of the person-in-his-situation requires varying degrees of understanding of the psychology of all the people involved in the gestalt. For the situation is never just one person, but a multiplicity of persons (to the sociologist, a *role network*) having varying degrees of importance in the life of the client.

## Concepts from Systems Theory

This whole gestalt can well be regarded as a system, and many concepts from general systems theory are useful in describing characteristics of the various systems involved in the person-in-his-situation constellation.[4] We know that the individual is in constant interaction—or *transaction*—with other members of the immediate family; with other relatives; with a network of friends and acquaintances, including neighbors; with an employment system, when working; and so on through all social relationships. Through spouse and children there may be either direct or indirect interaction with other systems, such as the school system. The unit of attention in casework goes beyond the client to include those systems that appear to be of salient importance to the problem for which the individual has sought help, and to others that later become the focus of treatment.

A primary characteristic of any system is that all its parts are in transaction, so that whatever affects one part of the system affects all parts to some degree. If a child in a family becomes seriously ill, this is certain to affect the father and mother to some degree, whether because of concern over the child, because of direct involvement in the child's care, or because of the time and attention that must be devoted to the child. This in turn may influence many other systems in which each is involved, such as the extended family system and the employment system. For instance, if a parent is unable to make a customary weekly visit to an elderly mother, he or she not only disappoints her but also may interfere with plans a sister, with whom the parent lives, made to enjoy time freed by the expected visit. The child's illness may also cause the husband or wife to be irritable at work, which may contribute to increased tensions with fellow workers or superiors. When two systems are in interaction because they have a common member, occurrences in one system will, to a greater or lesser degree, affect the other system. This is sometimes referred to as *input* from one system to another, or as *transactions* between systems. If the child's illness continues, there may well be repetitions of this kind of input from the original nuclear family system to the extended family and employment systems. Depending upon the importance of the part played by either spouse, both of these other systems may be seriously disrupted in their functioning by the changes in the father's or mother's behavior.

Another characteristic of interacting or transacting systems is the constant *feedback* among systems. The sister may begin to put pressure on the parent to resume regular visits, which may in turn cause tension between husband and wife. A foreman may be critical; talk about this at home may also worry the other spouse; consequently, tension may be increased to the point that both parents are irritable with other children in the family. This may lead to changes in their work at school. The school problem may then increase the stress felt by both father and mother, adding to the tension between them and increasing their difficulty in performing normally at work. Thus, the feedback from one system to another intensifies the tension in the family and causes other family members to behave differently in still other systems of which they are a part. Obviously, the possible chain of events is endless, and the individual who is being influenced by many forces at the same time has to arrive at some resolution within himself or herself—some equilibrium within the personality system—that ultimately determines how he or she will act.

This resolution is by no means entirely accounted for by the various pressures to which a person is exposed. By no means is this a billiard-ball type of reaction between the individual and the environment. Such an analogue would overlook the nature of the individuals who make up any social system.

When one individual says or does something to another, the second person's response is seldom simple and direct. First, the action is filtered through each individual's perceptive faculties, which may distort what actually happened. Then the perception is often worked upon by other ego and superego or ego ideal processes. The ego may react according to its notions about the other person's intent, about the reasons behind the action. The reaction will be influenced by the mood of the recipient, other pressures at the time, and general feelings toward the first person. Inevitably, it will also depend upon various aspects of the recipient's total personality: the quality of the capacity for relationships with others, the intensity of various drives and needs, standards, and ideals, the capacity of the ego for impulse control, the ability to express feelings adequately, the ways in which the ego defends against anxiety, and so on. The personality is itself a system with various and sometimes conflicting forces within and every action, every response, is shaped by these internal forces as well as by the presses and gratifications (either experienced or anticipated) from others with whom the individual is in interaction or transaction.

This realization that human beings are themselves systems of a very complicated and subtle nature radically modifies the application of systems theory to human transactions. If this is overlooked, the use of systems concepts becomes simplistic. Only by combining social systems concepts with adequate knowledge of the nature of human personality, can one productively understand the person–situation gestalt.

## PERSONALITY AND SOCIAL FUNCTIONING

The emphasis of this book is upon psychosocial procedures used by clinical social workers to bring about change in the individual's social functioning, and particularly in interpersonal relationships. This is not the whole of casework, but it is an extremely important part of the whole and is carried on by all clinical social workers under whatever auspices they work. Although the data on which this book is based derive primarily from family, medical, and psychiatric settings, the principles presented hold for casework in any setting in which interpersonal relationships are a treatment concern.

Before we can comprehend the dynamics of this type of social work treatment, however, we must have a clear picture of what the caseworker understands by personality and its social functioning. Social functioning represents the interplay between the two major variables —the social environment and individual—each of which, in turn, is a composite of various forces. The environment offers opportunities and gratifications, frustrations and deprivations. It consists not only of concrete realities—such as the availability of food, clothing, shelter, medical care, employment opportunities, physical safety, recreational opportunities, educational opportunities—but also of sociopsychological realities expressed through interpersonal relationships. For human beings need social relationships as much as they need food and shelter. We know that a baby can die when deprived of mothering.[5] Studies of young chimpanzees have demonstrated that even they are profoundly affected by the absence of warm care by the mother chimp.[6] An individual must rely on the environment to provide opportunities for social relationships of all sorts—parents, brothers and sisters, extended family relationships, marriage partners, lovers, friends, acquaintances. The quality of these relationships is to no small degree determined by forces independent of the individual's own efforts and choices.

Socially determined psychological realities also exert profound pressures, particularly in the areas of values and perceptions. Ethnic, class, race, regional, and role factors influence standards of behavior, aspirations, and perceptions of others and of self. At first these influences are transmitted primarily through the parents, later through other social relationships. The total environment, then, as experienced by any individual, is a complex set of interacting forces impinging upon the person simultaneously from many different directions and interacting with an equally complex set of forces within his or her own personality.[7]

## Personality Development

Psychosocial workers have found in the work of Freud and his followers a valuable frame of reference for the understanding of the individual.[8] In recent years, attention has been given particularly to the understanding of the ego as developed by such psychoanalytic theorists as Anna Freud, Hartmann, Kris, Erikson, Rapaport, White, and others.[9] Without attempting a detailed review of Freudian theory and modern ego theory as developed in psychoanalysis, we should like to comment on certain features of importance for understanding their use in clinical social work.[10]

First, psychoanalytic theory postulates that the individual from birth onward is characterized by certain sets of drives, libidinal and aggressive in nature, which originate in the part of the personality called the *id*. These drives vary in both absolute and relative strength in different individuals, constituting a continuing and unique demand upon the environment.

Moreover, the personality from birth onward includes a set of adaptive qualities, known in composite as the *ego*. These also vary in strength and quality in different individuals. In early Freudian theory, the ego was thought to develop out of the id and to be in a sense dependent on the development of the drives. Later theory sees the ego as independent, and potentially much stronger than was formerly believed in its ability to deal with drives and move toward goals of its own selection.

The ego controls and regulates the energies of the id, the impulse life, and mediates between the id and the environment—delaying the discharge of libidinal and aggressive impulses. The ego acts as a synthesizer of these drives, of thought processes, and of other functions of the individual's personality and experience; it serves as the reality tester of external events. The personality proceeds in its development under two major influences: internal biologically determined stages of maturation in both the drives and the ego, and interaction between the individual and the environment—especially one's family. Under these combined influences the drives change their form of demand and expression during the familiar oral, anal, oedipal, and genital stages of growth; the ego moves from primary to secondary modes of thought, builds its mechanisms of defense, adapts its perceptions and judgments to reality, and strengthens its capacities for direction and control.

The *superego* and *ego ideal*—or conscience formations of the ego —are comprised of internalized parental prohibitions, values, and ideals, social and moral standards derived from the world around the individual. The superego/ego ideal contains the "do's and don'ts," the ethical views and aspirations of the individual's personality; it can be punitive and guilt inducing; it can be destructively self-critical, as well as idealistic and self-approving. Some psychoanalytic writers use the terms superego and ego ideal interchangeably. In theory, the *superego* represents the part of the conscience that is absorbed primarily from the parents by parental dictation or by identification with parents in early childhood. It is often severe and not always functional. Its components are often unconscious. The *ego ideal* is for the most part a later development representing identifications with nonparental figures as well as with later perceptions of parents. It contains ideals of later childhood, adolescence, and later life. It is more apt to be consciously acquired and subject to ego evaluation.

As the individual grows and the ego matures, the libidinal drive proceeds from its early narcissistic stage, forming first oral dependent relationships, then moving to adult object relationships. Sexual feelings develop and are gradually sorted out for their special function in the range of libidinal feelings: love, affection, and less intense positive responses. The aggressive drives differentiate into hostility and constructive aggression harnessed to the job of mastering the environment and the self. Erikson described this maturation process as the achievement of basic trust, autonomy, and initiative.[11]

## Ego Theory

Early analytic theory was greatly concerned with the instincts, or drives, and their power, seeing the ego often as a rather weak instrument, a compromiser, buffeted between the superego, the id, and the outside world. In the late 1930s the development of ego theory began to enter casework thinking. The English translation of Anna Freud's *The Ego and the Mechanisms of Defence* was available in 1937.[12] As the theory of the autonomous development of the ego subsequently took over in analytic circles in the 1950s, caseworkers also began to see the ego as both stronger and far more differentiated than in earlier years.

The new ego psychology gave a better theoretical underpinning for the results that could be achieved by those caseworkers who stressed working with the "strengths" of the personality rather than emphasizing understanding of early causative factors. Combined with crisis theory, it led to the development of shorter treatment methods for certain types of difficulties. It also threw light upon the various forms of character disorder that in recent years seem to have become more prevalent than the neuroses.

Unfortunately, the term "ego theory" has been very loosely used in behavioral science. There is a tendency to think of it as a substitute for theory about the role of instinctual forces, or drives, in personality development, or by some writers as a substitute for all psychoanalytic theory. Actually, ego psychology has been developed primarily by psychoanalysts and is an extension of their earlier theory, sometimes correcting and sometimes enriching earlier concepts about the ego itself.

## Freudian Theory and the Environment

Because Freud elaborated more upon the needs and responses of the individual than upon the impact of the environment, it has become popular to regard Freudian theory as a theory of the instincts or a biological theory and to accuse it of disregarding environmental influences.[13] But the truth is that Freud strongly emphasized the influence of both intra- and extra-familial life experiences. Indeed, one of his major departures from predecessors such as Janet and Charcot, who regarded neurosis as a manifestation of constitutional weakness, was to see neurosis in terms of human relationships. The person with a hysterical paralysis, for example, in psychoanalytic theory is believed to be using this symptom as protection from something feared in relationships with other people. Although Freudian theory sees neurosis as a way of resolving conflicts among inner drives, the superego, and the ego, it also recognizes that such conflicts themselves emerge from the interactions between the child and parents or other parent figures. Freud's theory definitely rests upon social interaction as well as upon intrapsychic factors. It is therefore harmonious with the long standing psychosocial orientation of casework, and can be part of a total frame of reference that includes whatever data the social sciences can provide to illuminate the nature of the environment and the social forces with which the individual interacts.

This dual orientation lends itself very well to the systematizing of casework findings. Since the social worker's laboratory is the common everyday world, there is ample opportunity to observe the interplay between inner and outer forces. Social workers have repeatedly seen people change for better and for worse under the impact of benign and traumatic environments. We have observed people of diverse classes, ethnic origins, and regions and are well aware that adult behavior varies not only from group to group according to group norms, but also within each group in accordance with the individual personality differences and life experiences of its members. Because traditionally social workers have dealt with family units, we are particularly aware of the interplay among family members and of the profound influence of parents as well as other members of the family upon the development of the child's personality.

On the other hand psychoanalytic theory stoutly maintains that human beings are not merely products of their environments, clay upon which social influences leave their imprint. It insists, and rightly, that individuals make their own demands upon their environment. This assertion of the individual's role in shaping his or her interaction with the environment carries with it the corollary implication that even if it were possible to provide exactly the same environment for two different babies the resultant adult personalities would differ.

The foregoing may seem highly theoretical, but it has major practical implications. It puts emphasis upon *interaction,* particularly upon the individual's part in that interaction. In cases of marital adjustment, it guards the worker against seeing the partner with whom the interview is being held as merely the victim in the relationship. In parent–child disorders, it leads to a balanced examination of both what the parent is doing to the child and what the child is doing to and demanding of the parent. In general, it leads to the assumption that the individual can almost always do *something* about a problem and that the worker's task is to enable the client to develop greater capacity to do so. This by no means, however, precludes recognition of realistic environmental pressures where they exist, nor does it deny the responsibility of the caseworker to work with and for the client to ameliorate such pressures.

## Contributions of Sociology and Anthropology

The caseworkers' understanding of the influences and pressures of the environment on social functioning came not only from observation and case-by-case direct experience, but also from the fields of sociology and cultural anthropology. These have been drawn upon extensively over the years to describe and explain the nature of the environment. Beginning with the work of Benedict[14] and Mead,[15] the field was alerted in the thirties to the great differences between cultures and to the extent to which even such central matters as child rearing, marriage, and sex behavior not only differ among cultures but are regulated by customs that are themselves a form of social agreement. Kardner's[16] work studying cultural influences on behavior was a "bridging" contribution between culture and personality theory. Casework writers such as Boie[17] and de la Fontaine[18] demonstrated the use of these concepts in the understanding of family and personality problems. Later, the effects of differences in social class and of specific racial and ethnic origins on cultural differences became very important in understanding social influences on personality.

During and following the depression of the thirties, studies of the social effects of unemployment[19] on individuals and families gave social workers new understanding of the pressures created by this social condition. As marriage counseling developed in family agencies in the forties, studies of marriage and divorce, from a psychological and psychiatric standpoint, became important.[20]

The fifties and sixties brought further understanding of the strong effects on personality and behavior of the lack of opportunities for education, employment, and recreation, combined with the presence of opportunities for various kinds of deviant behavior, such as the use of hard drugs, participation in drug traffic, and delinquent behavior of other sorts.[21]

During this same period, studies of differentials in the treatment of psychiatric patients in both hospitals and clinics demonstrated the neglect and discrimination suffered by the poor in general, and by Blacks and Puerto Ricans in particular, alerting the field to this factor in the life of minority groups of the population.[22]

An important bridging concept between social influences and personality development was made by role theorists in the sixties. A number of role concepts are particularly useful in understanding the way in which the superego and ego ideal are shaped by social influences, and the part played by such influences in the judgment and decisions of the ego.

## INTERACTIONS BETWEEN INDIVIDUAL AND ENVIRONMENT

As noted earlier, the individual does not react to the environment as it exists but rather as he or she sees it, and a host of internal factors influence these perceptions. Among these are the remains in adult life of the distortions of thought that existed in early childhood when the mental processes were still under the sway of what psychoanalysis regards as the *primary process.* This is an early stage of development in which logical, rational thinking has not yet developed.[23] Wishes are imbued with magical power. Hence when a child has wished that a parent or brother or sister would get hurt, and some mishap subsequently occurs, the child may feel that he has actually caused it, and therefore fear retaliation. When someone close has died, the child may regard this as an act of purposeful abandonment and resent it accordingly. Children cannot always distinguish their own thoughts and feelings from the thoughts and feelings of others; when angry, a child may believe others are angry at him. Contradictory ideas exist side by side in the mind, and no need is felt to reconcile them. When crossed, a young child may feel anger that is not tempered by the good things experienced from the same source that is now frustrating. The child generalizes indiscriminately, often expecting all grown-up men to be like Father, all women like Mother. These misperceptions cause the child to react in a way that actually affects the response of the environment to him. Hence, he is already to a degree creating his own environment.

## Mechanisms of Defense

These early distortions would not be quite so serious a matter if childish things were always left behind, but unfortunately the adult to a greater or lesser extent continues these infantile thought processes. They become important ingredients in certain ego defense mechanisms.[24] These are devices the ego uses to ward off anxiety aroused by the individual's reactions to actual situational occurrences. In the mechanism known as *projection,* the individual's own thoughts and feelings are attributed to others. In *displacement,* a person will transfer feelings and thoughts that refer to one person to a different one. This is possible either because of superficial similarities between them or because they both occupy the same role in relation to the displacer. In *isolation,* different parts of experience are separated from each other, especially events or memories and the feelings associated with them, so that matters that are actually interrelated appear not to affect one another. Misapprehensions about other people are often not corrected, although contrary evidence is readily at hand. In *denial,* a person may deny to himself or herself as well as to others the existence of an emotion or thought—anger, love, jealousy—although his or her behavior clearly indicates its presence. *Reaction formation* is another common defense of the ego. It goes beyond denial in substituting another emotion or attitude for the one actually operating—for example "of course I don't love him, in fact, I hate him." Sometimes an unwanted emotion is turned against the self. This is particularly true of anger, where the person becomes angry at the self when the logic of the situation would seem to require anger at another. If realization of this outwardly turned anger would cause too much anxiety, the emotion is sometimes experienced as feelings of self-criticism, that is, as anger *turned against the self.* Another very common and sometimes socially useful defense is *avoidance,* where pains are taken simply to avoid a potentially anxiety arousing situation. The most pervasive defense of all, of course, is *repression.* By this the anxiety producing thoughts, feelings, or memories are forgotten—pushed or drawn into the unconscious. It is this unconscious content, especially of early childhood, that is the center of attention in psychoanalysis. *Suppressed* material is more likely to be dealt with by the clinical social worker. In this mechanism, the anxiety arousing mental content is pushed—sometimes consciously—only partly below the surface of the mind, where it can be retrieved with relative ease. It is a commonly used and sometimes useful mechanism— "After a good night's sleep I'll forget all about it."

Indeed, the individual's whole perception of the external world is a combination in varying degrees of what is actually there and what is expected. We often do not see what we do not look for, but we create for ourselves what we seek to find. The person who anticipates that someone else will be hostile may read into the other person's behavior belligerent meanings whether or not they exist, and by his or her own responses may very well give rise to hostility in the other person. In so doing, the individual has to a high degree created his own environment —a form of self-fulfilling prophecy. Fortunately, clients can be helped to become aware of dysfunctional ways of ego functioning, sometimes in individual instances and sometimes as patterns of behavior.

## Social Components in Perceptions and Expectations

Misperceptions are not entirely a matter of individual psychology. A child learns that a radiator is hot not only by direct experience but also by being told so by a person whose words are trusted; unfortunately, too, when trust exists, a false statement will be believed as readily as a true one. Indeed if it is "everybody" who holds something true, it becomes extremely difficult for even the good adult mind to have a contrary opinion. How many generations saw sails disappearing over the horizon and continued to believe the world was flat? Belief is often so strong that the believer is cut off from even the opportunity of testing it. Race stereotypes are a cardinal example. Not only do whites have many misperceptions about blacks, but blacks also have them about whites. Similarly, the "generation gap" is based to no small degree on stereotypes that often cause people on both sides of the magic dividing line to react according to distorted beliefs and misunderstandings rather than realities. Conflict caused by realistic competition of interests between different economic or cultural classes and groups is compounded by misinformation and distortions, sometimes newly created and sometimes handed down from one generation to another. The element of expectation that is part of one's perception of one's environment is a joint product of actual experience, individual distortion growing out of faulty thought processes, ideals incorporated from the idiosyncrasies of close associates, and ideas learned by personal contact but actually the product of group opinion—class, ethnic, racial, regional, occupational, religious, political, and so on. Certain ideas are commonly held in the West but not in the East, in the North but not in the South, in cities but not in rural areas, in the Soviet Union but not in the United States, among white-collar workers but not among industrial workers, among whites but not among blacks, among women but not among men, in poverty-stricken city areas but not in suburbia, and so on.

Role expectation is a form of group opinion especially significant for social work. Specific ways of behaving are commonly accepted as appropriate or necessary for the individual in certain areas of functioning—for example, as parent, as husband or wife, as employer—and he or she is perceived in terms of the way this role performance conforms to the norms held by the group. For instance, a man's perception of whether or not his wife loves him depends upon quite different cues in different groups. In some cultures, the wife's housekeeping tasks are deemed so important that the husband would see her subordination of them to interest in a job as personal neglect and evidence of lack of love. This perception would be reinforced by the opinions of his friends, before whom he would be disgraced. Similarly, a parent's view of a child depends very greatly upon the extent to which the child behaves according to group-influenced expectations. The ways in which an adult is expected to fulfill obligations to elderly parents, teacher-pupil relationships, interrace relationships, the roles of priests, rabbi or pastor, and congregational member—all these are in part culturally defined.

ROLE THEORY. Especially useful in understanding this interplay of person and situation is role theory.[25] It points out that the individuals who surround the child from birth onward, both singly and as an aggregate, hold certain behavioral expectations. These vary with one's position in life—one's "status," in sociological terminology. In any culture, for instance, a child is expected to act in many specific respects quite differently from an adult, a professional person from an unskilled worker, and so on. The same person is also expected to act differently under different circumstances. Ways of behaving acceptable at a football game are considered highly inappropriate if they occur in the course of professional functioning—and so on. In many respects, that is, the behavior of the individual is shaped by social expectations—by the society in which one lives.

However, many of these role expectations, while widespread, are by no means held identically by everyone. And herein lies the basis for much interpersonal tension. Sometimes one individual expects another to behave in a certain way because of his or her status and the second person defines the role behavior required in a different way. A very simple example of this occurs to men and women traveling in countries where the sex definition of who goes through a doorway first differs from that in the home country!

This is an illustration of another feature of role behavior. Much of it is complementary. For its exercise, the role performance definition for one status may require reciprocal performance by another. So if one fails, the other is frustrated. A priest cannot act as a confessor if the parishioner does not come to confession. A husband who defines his role behavior as including management of the budget is frustrated in carrying out this role if his wife, disagreeing with this definition, independently runs up charge accounts.

One of the major complications of life today is the rapidity with which culturally determined role expectations in all types of interpersonal relations are changing. Today, for instance, it very often happens that conflict in a marriage derives from the changing roles of men and women. This is particularly true when different definitions exist concerning decision making in general, and concerning the distribution of household tasks when a woman is working. It is sometimes easier, too, for a woman to claim her own expanded role than to be comfortable with a man's equally logical desire to be freed of some of the responsibilities that he accepted when he saw himself as head of the family and the sole wage earner. Changing role definitions are also causing considerable inner turmoil for the young person. The adolescent girl or young woman may be uncertain about what kind of woman she wants to be —dependent, sweet and girlish, competent loving mother and wife concentrating entirely on her family, self-reliant working woman, competent loving *working* mother and wife—or what have you! Needless to say, complementary role problems also face the adolescent boy and young man.

Similarly, the client will have certain expectations of how the caseworker will act, and these will vary according to personal and social experience. If the worker is to convey the same impression of good will, objectivity, and competence to clients of varying life experience, he or she will need to be aware of their preconceptions and of the different interpretations they will make of his or her actions. The worker will need to be more "friendly" with some, more "professional" with others. With the"hard to reach," much generous "doing for" may be necessary to overcome the stereotype of the caseworker as an interfering hostile do-gooder.

## Communication

Recent years have seen great advances in our understanding of the processes of communication and of the various ways in which misunderstandings can aise arise.[26] Some of these findings especially pertinent to clinical social work will be discussed in later chapters, but brief references to the communication factor is needed at this point.

When we think of the person–situation gestalt as a social system, faulty perception by the ego is seen as a major component in faulty communication among different members of a family or of any other social system. Preconceptions can cause people not to listen to each other at all or to hear something different from what has been said. Distortions in the way intonation is heard make great differences in interpretation of meaning. Internal elaborations and attributions of intent by the receiver can cause endless misunderstandings.

Distortions of the ego's perceptions resulting from earlier experiences and from the ego's patterned defenses against anxiety are among the internal factors accounting for failures in accurate reception of communications.

There are, however, other equally important factors that have to do with other aspects of the communication process. One very important influence arises from the fact that most communication takes place through symbols—both verbal and nonverbal. For accurate communication, these symbols must be commonly understood by sender and receiver. The meaning of gestures, posture, intonation, and even words of the same language differs markedly among people of different educational backgrounds, different social classes, and different ethnic or racial groups. Symbols of courtesy and discourtesy that are so basic to interpersonal relationships are particularly vulnerable to such misinterpretation.

## INTERACTING SOURCES OF DISTRESS

When clients come to a clinical social worker for assistance because there has been a breakdown in their social adjustment, this breakdown has three possible interacting sources:

1. Infantile needs and drives left over from childhood cause individuals to make excessive demands upon their world or to express inappropriate hostility.
2. A current life situation exerts excessive pressure.
3. Faulty ego and superego/ego ideal functioning. The degree to which each of these is present varies with different people. Sometimes all three contribute to the client's dilemma.

*Overly strong infantile needs and drives* persisting in adult life may lead to exaggerated narcissistic needs, excessive dependence or hostility, fixations on early family figures, fear of separation with resulting anxiety or timidity, which makes individuals require excessive protection and prevents them from assuming adult responsibilities, excessive aggression, and underdevelopment of the capacity for loving human relationships. Although it is sometimes possible for people to find social situations in which infantile needs can be gratified, for the most part this does not occur. The individual is then left with a constant sense of frustration and characteristically behaves in a way that creates antagonism in the social environment, cutting off gratifications that might otherwise be received.

Common among *current life pressures* are those of economic deprivation, lack of opportunity for employment, marginal working conditions, poor housing and neighborhood conditions, substandard educational opportunities, racial and ethnic hostility, illness, and loss of love by death or separation. To these must be added innumerable individual life experiences that arouse anger provoking frustration or feelings of inadequacy or guilt. They may occur in family relationships, when the needs of one individual conflict in a major way with those of another.

For example, the need to care for a retarded child or chronically ill family member may conflict with the vocational aspirations of a mother who is tied to the home by these circumstances. Such frustrations also exist when employment and living conditions are realistically very irritating and demanding, even though not substandard. And they certainly occur when general social conditions, such as racial discrimination, create constant environmental pressure of major proportions.

Frustration is frequently the major component in a circle of deteriorating interaction. It can set up circular responses both in the situational interaction and within the personality. Externally, expression of the individual's anger and other behavior often further alienates sources of satisfaction in a reverberating pattern. Internally, the deprivation may increase the need for love or appreciation, or self-expression, and may increase feelings of lack of worth. These, in turn, increase need for the very reassurance and gratification already lacking in the external world.

*Faulty ego functioning* includes distorted perception of either the outside world or the self, poor judgment, excessive anxiety, insufficient ability to control impulses or to direct behavior, poor reality testing, and inappropriate uses of ego defenses. Faulty superego and ego ideal functioning may be of several kinds. Sometimes the superego is so primitive that the individual has not incorporated much in the way of standards at all. The person just doesn't care about "right and wrong." More frequently, there is concern, but his or her standards and self-requirements are too high, too low, or otherwise out of harmony with the environment.

Faulty ego and superego functioning adds substantially to the environmental pressures felt by the individual. If an individual's ego misperceives pressures, the stress actually experienced in response to the distorted version of reality may be more severe than would have been appropriate to the actual life pressures. Such faulty functioning may also lead to actions that are self-defeating, depriving a person of satisfactions that would otherwise be available, unnecessarily exposing the individual to rejection. This, in turn, may cause the person to seek associates who confirm his childish distortions of the world, reinforcing the tendency to faulty general functioning.

Faulty ego and superego functioning is often combined with excessive or inappropriate infantile needs. When this is so, the individual who is already weak in the ability to control impulses or deal with anxiety also feels unusually strong inner urges that may be unrealistic and even harmful, but that he or she lacks the strength and ability to control or handle. Cases discussed in the next chapter will show the interplay of these three elements in personal difficulties.

The clinical social worker can be particularly effective in dealing with the second and third types of factors contributing to interpersonal adjustment problems. Excessive need—the first factor—can often be reached by entering the circle at the point of reducing external frustration and enabling the person through better ego functioning to secure more personal gratification. Freed from some of these self-created pressures, the individual may be able to find in life sufficient satisfaction of basic needs to maintain a fairly comfortable equilibrium, even though many childish needs and reactions remain untouched. The ego has amazing innate powers of maturation. If helped to overcome inhibiting ties and misperceptions, it may become able to resume the natural process of growth.

# REDUCING ENVIRONMENTAL PRESS

When a major part of the cause of the client's discomfort is in the environment, it is sometimes possible for the caseworker to modify the pressure or deficiency directly. Sometimes attitudes of individuals who are creating difficulties for the client can also be modified by casework contact; when such modification is required, environmental intervention becomes psychological in nature. Some services—child placement is a prime example—can be extremely complicated in the treatment required. Environmental services rarely stand alone. They are often accompanied by work directly with the client, in which his or her reactions become the focus of attention. The public assistance client may not understand or respond realistically to the eligibility process. The hospital patient may be unwilling to undergo the recommended medical procedures. The child may not be ready to use the educational or recreational services that have opened up. Much preparation involving both the resource and the client may be required before environmental pressure can be relieved.

Often, instead of relieving environmental pressures directly, the worker may help clients to bring about the necessary changes themselves, thereby reinforcing their feelings of competence. The nature of environmental work—more complex than it may seem at first—will be discussed in detail in chapters 8 and 9. Obviously, environmental changes brought about solely for the purpose of removing unusual pressures or deficiencies need not involve an effort to change the individual. A person may function more comfortably as a result of such change, but the inner balance may remain the same. On the other hand, at times improvement requires that client and worker address themselves also to the ego problem of misinterpretation of events in the environment or dysfunctional reactions to pressures that do exist.

# Treatment of Personality Factors through Environmental Work

To whatever extent the major causative factors in the client's problem lie either in too great a residue of infantile desires and needs or in faulty ego and superego functioning, change in the person himself becomes a potential goal of treatment. Such treatment may range from attempts to bring about lasting changes in the client's personality or way of functioning to temporary adjustments of behavior during a period of stress.

Environmental change can sometimes become the means through which such changes in personality are brought about. With children especially, lasting personality change occurs rather readily in response to environmental change, and this is the predominant method of casework treatment used with children.

Major personality changes in the child—particularly the young child—can often be brought about by various forms of substitute parental care: adoption, foster home care, day care centers, and so on. Less extensive changes may be promoted by modifications in the school environment or by the provision of recreational and other group experiences such as camping, bringing a "big brother" into the situation, and so on. Because the child's personality is still so fluid, environmental changes profoundly affect his or her view of the world and the extent to which infantile strivings remain a part of the later adult personality, identifications, ability to bear frustration, and in general the quality of ego functioning.

Often, we try to bring about changes in the parents' attitudes and behavior. Family group treatment (see chapters 10 and 11) can be one of the most effective means of altering a child's environment and also of promoting personality changes. For example, a mother may be encouraging her son's babyishness and excessive dependence on her. In family therapy, it may be revealed that her overinvolvement in her son's life is a compensation for her husband's emotional remoteness. If changes in the marriage can be effected that result in greater satisfactions in the relationship between husband and wife, the family environment can thereby become one more likely to support the boy's greater independence and maturity. When environmental changes are impossible or are not sufficiently effective, direct casework with the child may either accompany environmental modification or become the major form of treatment.

Sometimes a change of jobs will bring about a better fit between work and personality, leading to greater personal comfort and improved functioning. A woman may become less tense, less hostile, and more able to give love to her children when she is working outside the home and having others care for her children during the day than when she devotes her full time to their care. If the caseworker helps her to recognize this and to arrange her life so that she can take a job, there may be marked improvement in her functioning. A radical change in environment will sometimes bring about a lasting personality change in adults as, for example, when a particularly fortunate choice of marriage partner leads to a long period of satisfying living that seem to undo the effects of earlier misfortune and brings about a real reorientation to life. The phenomenon of religious conversion is another well known means of major adult personality change.

# DIRECT WORK WITH THE INDIVIDUAL

Intrapsychic factors causing personal difficulties for adults are usually modified primarily through work with the individual directed toward modification of the dysfunctioning aspect of the personality. (This approach is also used with children, but usually in combination with whatever situational changes can be achieved.) Casework uses for this purpose current reactions and behavior and sometimes memories that are either immediately accessible to consciousness or else suppressed, unverbalized, or uncomprehended, but not repressed or so remote from consciousness that only such means as free association, hypnosis, or therapy under drugs can bring them to the surface (see Chapter 13).

## Balance of Forces

To understand how work that does not reach the deeper layers of the personality can be effective, we must appreciate the various ways in which the personality system is a balance of forces. We referred earlier to the Freudian concept of the personality as consisting of id, ego, and superego/ego ideal. It is also useful to consider the balance of forces *within* each of these components, looking at this balance from the vantage point of social functioning. The residual, immature, or unusual needs within the id, to which we earlier referred, may be balanced by more mature needs and drives harmonious with the needs of others, and by considerable capacity for giving and receiving love. The ego and superego are also a balance of socially functional and dysfunctional tendencies. The ego does not always perceive and understand realistically. Certain defenses may obscure and distort the events of life. Self-confidence may be weak, guilt may be too strong, general lack of integration may impede action. The early and restrictive superego may still be so strong that certain actions are inhibited in unnecessary ways. On the other hand, these weaknesses are usually balanced by other tendencies toward personally and socially realistic functioning. The latter include the ability to make accurate appraisals of others, of the self, and of the external world, and responses likely to bring gratifications to the individual, to contribute to meeting the needs of associates, and to contribute to the harmonious functioning of the social systems of which a person is a part.

These opposing tendencies (whether within or between the personality components), in a sense, struggle with each other at any given moment and the resultant action often depends on whether strengths or weaknesses predominate. When certain inner drives push the individual toward socially unwise or self-destructive behavior, the healthy part of the ego says "No". When the irrational part of the ego distorts reality by projection or magical beliefs or when other unconscious or primitive thought processes cause distortions, the healthy part of the ego corrects this and keeps the irrational tendencies in check. It is often nip and tuck as to which side will win, depending upon the relative strength the two sets of forces can bring to bear in any particular situation. "If she had said just one more thing, I would have thrown the hammer at her." That is, "If I had been just a little more angry, nothing my ego was telling me would have been enough to keep me in control."

An interesting aspect of this balance of forces is that while the decision to act may hang upon a hair's weight of difference either in the opposing intrapsychic forces or in the nature and force of the pressure from the rest of the interpersonal system, the action that this slight difference triggers may be of major proportions and have extensive consequences.

For instance, anger left over from a family fight may tip the scales in the decision of an employee to respond to criticism at work by throwing down tools and walking off the job. The reverberations of this action in personal and family life may be enormous, but the action itself resulted from slight changes in balance in the employee's ego's capacity to control the anger. A series of such transactions can combine to make a pattern of considerable strength and significance.

## MODIFYING THE BALANCE OF FORCES

It is not the strength of a drive, such as a tremendously strong impulse, or the degree of a tendency toward distortion, that alone determines whether action is to be taken. These may be opposed by an equally strong counterforce, in the form of capacity for reality testing and ability to control impulses. Insofar as the opposing strengths are almost equally balanced, a relatively small amount of improvement in ego functioning may be enough to enable the individual to make significant changes in total social functioning. This is one of the answers to the oft-repeated question: "When the infantile demands and distortions are not modified, how can there be any real change?" The demands and distortions may remain untouched, but the person may handle them differently in interpersonal relationships if the ego is functioning better. Indeed, it is belief in these positive capacities of the human being that provides the main incentive for the treatment process.

Furthermore, all formative influences do not occur in infancy, nor are they all unconscious. If unresolved oedipal rivalries have made a daughter see her mother as hostile, the daughter's feeling may be reinforced by experiencing actual hostility from her mother in the later years of growth, or it may be somewhat lessened by experiences of a contrary nature. In the latter instance, not only is the original tendency not reinforced, but the ego is given a means by which to counteract the effect of the original distortion. In the former instance, when the mother's later behavior reinforces the daughter's belief that enmity must exist between them—a belief that may affect her attitude toward other women—there are several possible modes of treatment that do not involve an effort to uncover and correct the original infantile content.

In one approach, the client is encouraged to ventilate her feelings about the events she spontaneously remembers or can recall with the help of "eductive" interviewing techniques. For a person who has not previously been able to express her anger toward her mother, eliciting it may have a useful cathartic effect, reducing the amount of suppressed hostility pressing for displacement on current female figures in the client's life. If there has been guilt over the angry feelings, the worker's acceptance of these feelings as natural may reduce the guilt and subsequent need to use defenses such as projection, or turning against the self. If the anger has been displaced on a female child or on other adult women, it may be possible to enable the client through reflection to recognize and to stop behavior that provokes counterhostility and is thus causing her to experience constant repetitions of her original unhappy experience with a woman.

Another approach is to provide the client with an opportunity for a "corrective relationship."[27] By allowing a relationship to develop in which the client regards the worker as a mother figure, it may be possible to counteract the earlier bad mother–daughter experience by enabling the client to see, through the new experience, that the characteristics of her mother that caused her unhappiness are peculiar to her mother and not general characteristics of all women. This may also tend to undo some of the attitudes about herself, sex, marriage, child raising, and so on, that she acquired in her early relationship with her mother.

Another alternative is for client and worker to look carefully at current personal interactions in which the woman's unconscious attitudes have contributed to her responding unrealistically. One can examine details of the interaction to see if the responses were warranted by what the other person did, correcting unnecessary dysfunctional responses bit by bit by the use of current realities. This can greatly strengthen the person's ability to correct misperceptions and restrain impulsive actions. Still another approach is to enable the client to review her conscious and preconscious or near-conscious early memories of her experiences with her mother. By seeing their effects on her personality and current reactions to life, she may free herself to a degree from these childhood and adolescent reinforcements of her oedipal distortions and, in turn, reduce the degree of distortion with which her adult ego must now deal. Along with this reduction of the force of her childhood experiences, she may be helped to recognize her tendency to carry over feelings from her childhood to her current relationships, and may learn to improve these relationships by careful testing of her own reactions against the realities of other people's behavior. In actual practice, as will be discussed in later chapters, sometimes all of these approaches are used, sometimes even in the same interview. Characteristically, several are continuously used together.

None of these procedures will have touched directly the infantile core of the client's trouble. She will still have in her unconscious whatever hostilities and distortion tendencies and whatever components of infantile oedipal rivalry were there before the treatment. But the effect of some of the later childhood experiences that reinforced the earlier ones may have been reduced, the ego may have been strengthened in its efforts to correct and control destructive behavior, and the tendency to create repetitive hostile life experiences may have been lessened. Such changes in the balance of forces within the individual may well bring about marked improvement in functioning and constitute an internalized change in adaptive patterns.

All these approaches are built upon the assumption that even in adulthood the ego is open to influence and capable of growth and change. In systems terms, the assumption is that personality comprises an "open system," one that constantly changes in response to exchanges with the outside world, including situational changes that can be brought about by the caseworker and interaction with the worker in the process of treatment. They are also built upon the assumption that the individual is constantly evolving, that there is some individual initiative within each person, unique to himself or herself, that acts upon others as well as receives from others. Some central core influences the receptivity to the outside, even the reaching out for it, and the selective use of what others, including the caseworker, offer.

## Directive Versus Reflective Therapies

Psychosocial casework is a form of treatment that relies heavily upon reflective, cognitive measures embodied in a matrix of a sound, helping, or therapeutic relationship. It does, however, as indicated earlier, make use of directive techniques like suggestion, advice, and persuasion when diagnosis indicates that the client is unlikely to respond to measures that rely upon his or her own active thinking. This may be the case when one is so overwhelmed by pressing happenings in life—sickness, death, desertion—that one is unable to make use of one's usual reflective powers, or when one is severely handicapped in doing so by the severity of ego impairment. In other instances, when advice is given about such things as child rearing, job hunting, or how a client might obtain a goal, it is usually accompanied by explanations that supply understanding of the advice given.

In truly directive therapies, the therapist prefers to take a very active part in advising the client, relying primarily upon the weight of "professional authority" and upon the positive relationship to modify the client's, or patient's, responses. Psychosocial casework differs markedly from such therapies. It never uses directive procedures in isolation from cognitive measures and employs them only when the client is not ready or able to use reflective procedures. Even in the case of the very severely disturbed or inadequate person, with whom methods of "direct influence" may need to play a relatively large part in treatment, such methods would never constitute the sole ingredient. As we noted earlier, self-determination is not an absolute value. Whereas it requires that every effort be made to increase the client's capacity for self-direction, it also recognizes that clients vary in this capacity and that a limited amount of directiveness in treatment is sometimes advisable.

Some writers recognize only two ways of influencing behavior: one characterized by the bringing of unconscious factors under the control of the ego, the other by methods that rest essentially on the therapist's authority and the influence of the transference. They maintain that the latter types result only in unstable changes in functioning, because such changes are not truly built into the personality but remain a reflection of the continuing relationship with the therapist.

The first method referred to, psychoanalysis, attempts to modify infantile drive derivatives and needs that have partly become unconscious, cause intrapsychic conflict in the individual, and interfere with the adaptive functioning of the ego and superego. By inducing a strongly regressive transference in the patient, it enables his adult ego to relive and reevaluate early life experiences so that infantile attachments and fantasies can truly be relinquished and infantile misconceptions corrected. Psychoanalysis does in many instances bring about profound changes in personality. These changes often give promise of being permanent, though they are not necessarily so. In clinical social work, we find a kind of treatment that differs from both of those just described. It is clearly not psychoanalysis, but neither is it mainly manipulative. Like analysis it sometimes uses techniques of influence, and it does so to a greater degree than is true in analysis. It is, however, by no means primarily a directive therapy relying on the worker's professional authority to persuade the client to change behavior in a given direction. Rather, it seeks to engage the client's *ego*—the capacity to think, to reflect, to understand—in a reevaluation of himself-in-his-situation. It engages clients as fully as possible in their own treatment, endeavoring not only to preserve but to enhance reliance upon the self and the extent to which they are able to guide their actions by realistic understanding.

In addition to improvement in external functioning, such treatment, we maintain, can bring about such internalized modifications as improvement of the ego's perception and reality-testing ability, shifts in the use of defenses, changes in the demands, or in the reaction to the demands, of the superego, lasting reductions in the strength of destructive character traits such as chronic latent hostility and dependence, reduction of the strength of parental ties, and sometimes even a degree of maturation in the instinctual life. Such shifts are built into the personality and enable individuals to function better even when confronted by circumstances identical or essentially similar to those under which functioning was previously impaired. It is reasonable to expect that such changes will continue after treatment has ended.

In summary, then, when casework is employed to help the client achieve better social functioning, it can become a form of psychosocial therapy. Such treatment relies mainly on reflective procedures augmented by methods of direct influence and by direct efforts to bring about environmental changes when diagnosis indicates that these will be effective. Of paramount importance in such treatment is the relationship upon which it is based. The worker's acceptance of the client and wish to respond to the client's needs is constant. This worker attitude is expressed in varying ways, depending upon the client's wishes and needs but always characterized by honesty and basic supportiveness. Focus is always upon the person–situation gestalt, which is seen as an interacting balance of forces between the needs of the person and the influence upon him or her of the environment. Individual functioning is the end result of a complicated series of interactions between different parts of the personality highly susceptible to outside influences. In psychosocial therapy, influence is brought to bear on either the environment or the personality or both. When it is directed toward the personality, it can reduce the force of destructive trends in the individual by decreasing the force of earlier life experiences and by increasing the capacity of the ego and superego to handle current life experiences more realistically. Thus, the work strengthens clients in their ability to achieve the goals they set for themselves.

## NOTES

1. For a fuller discussion of casework values, see Herbert Bisno, *The Philosophy of Social Work* (Washington, D.C.: Public Affairs Press, 1952). See also

Harriett Bartlett, *The Common Base of Social Work Practice* (New York: National Association of Social Workers, 1970), pp. 63–69; William Gordon, "Knowledge and Value: Their Distinction and Relationship in Clarifying Social Work Practice," *Social Work,* 10 (July 1965), 32–35; Florence Hollis, "Principles and Assumptions Underlying Casework Practice," *Social Work* (London), 12 (1955), 41–55; Katherine Kendall, ed., *Social Work Values in an Age of Discontent* (New York: Council on Social Work Education, 1970); and Charles S. Levy, *Social Work Ethics* (New York: Human Services Press, 1976).

2. An excellent series of articles on this subject is to be found in F. E. McDermott, ed., *Self Determination in Social Work* (London: Routledge and Kegan Paul, 1975).

3. Gordon Hamilton and many other writers have stressed this point of view. See her *Theory and Practice of Social Work,* rev. ed. (New York: Columbia University Press, 1951).

4. Ludwig von Bertalanffy, *General Systems Theory: Foundations, Development, Application* (New York: Braziller, 1968), is a basic reference on systems theory; William Gray, Frederick J. Duhl, and Nicholas D. Rizzo, eds., *General Systems Theory and Psychiatry* (Boston: Little, Brown, 1969), is also useful as a general reference; Ervin Lazlo, ed., *The Relevance of General Systems Theory* (New York: Braziller, 1972), has excellent articles discussing the relevance of general systems theory to various disciplines.

   Werner A. Lutz, in his *Concepts and Principles Underlying Social Casework Practice* (Washington, D.C.: National Association of Social Workers, Medical Social Work Section, 1956), first introduced the systems theory approach to casework; articles from casework, psychiatry, and psychology increasingly recognized its usefulness; for example, see Gordon Allport, "The Open System in Personality Theory," *Journal of Abnormal and Social Psychology,* 61 (November 1960), 301–310; William Gordon, "Basic Constructs for an Integrative and Generative Conception of Social Work," in Gordon Hearn, ed., *The General Systems Approach: Contributions Toward a Holistic Conception of Social Work* (New York: Council on Social Work Education, 1969); and Florence Hollis, " 'And What Shall We Teach?': The Social Work Educator and Knowledge," *Social Service Review,* 42 (June 1968), 184–196.

5. For a comprehensive review of the findings concerning the effects of maternal deprivation, see John Bowlby, *Maternal Care and Mental Health,* 2nd ed., World Health Organization Monograph Series No. 2 (Geneva: World Health Organization, 1952); and Mary D. Ainsworth, "The Effects of Maternal Deprivation: A Review of Findings and Controversy in the Context of Research Strategy," in *Deprivation of Maternal Care: A Reassessment of Its Effects* (Geneva: World Health Organization, 1962). See also Selma Fraiberg, *Every Child's Birthright: In Defense of Mothering* (New York: Basic Books, 1977).

6. Jane van Lawick-Goodall, *In the Shadow of Man* (Boston: Houghton Mifflin, 1971).

7.  A rich literature exists pertinent to the social worker's understanding of the nature of the social component in the person–situation interaction. The following, in addition to items cited elsewhere, are among the useful readings: Andrew Billingsley, *Black Families in White America* (Englewood Cliffs, N.J.: Prentice-Hall, 1968); John A. Brown, "Clinical Social Work with Chicanos: Some Unwarranted Assumptions," *Clinical Social Work Journal,* 4 (Winter 1979), 256–266; Jerome Cohen, "Social Work and the Culture of Poverty," *Social Work,* 9 (January 1964), 3–11; Louis A. Ferman, ed., *Poverty in America,* rev. ed. (Ann Arbor: University of Michigan Press, 1968); Alejandro Garcia, "The Chicano and Social Work," *Social Casework,* 52 (May 1971), 274–278; Paul and Lois Glasser, eds., *Families in Crisis* (New York: Harper & Row, 1970); Elizabeth Herzog, "Is There a Breakdown of the Negro Family?", *Social Work,* 11 (January 1966), 3–10; Florence Hollis, "Casework and Social Class," *Social Casework,* 46 (October 1965), 463–471; Camille Jeffers, *Living Poor* (Ann Arbor, Mich.: Ann Arbor Publishers, 1967); Maurine LaBarre, "The Strengths of the Self-Supporting Poor," *Social Casework,* 49 (October 1968), 459–466; Hylan Lewis, "Child Rearing Among Low-Income Families," in Louis A. Ferman, ed., *Poverty in America* (Ann Arbor: University of Michigan Press, 1965), pp. 342–353; Elliot Liebow, *Tally's Corner* (Boston: Little, Brown, 1967); Eleanor Pavenstedt, ed., *The Drifters: Children of Disorganized Lower-Class Families* (Boston: Little, Brown, 1967); Norman A. Polansky, "Powerlessness Among Rural Appalachian Youth," *Rural Sociology,* 34 (June 1969), 219–222; Frank Riessman, Jerome Cohen, and Arthur Pearl, eds., *Mental Health of the Poor* (New York: Free Press, 1964; *Social Casework,* 51 (May 1970), the entire issue on black experience by black authors; Francis J. Turner, "Ethnic Difference and Client Performance," *Social Service Review,* 44 (March 1970), 1–10; Eileen Younghusband, "Intercultural Aspects of Social Work," *Journal of Education for Social Work,* 2 (Spring 1966), 59–65.

8.  For comments on this, see Annette Garrett, "Modern Casework: The Contributions of Ego Psychology," in Howard J. Parad, ed., *Ego Psychology and Dynamic Casework* (New York: Family Service Association of America, 1958), pp. 38–52; Gordon Hamilton, "A Theory of Personality: Freud's Contribution to Social Work," in Parad, *Ego Psychology and Dynamic Casework,* pp. 11–37; Eleanor B. Weisberger, "The Current Usefulness of Psychoanalytic Theory to Casework," *Smith College Studies in Social Work,* 37 (February 1967), 106–118; Katherine Wood, "The Contribution of Psychoanalysis and Ego Psychology to Social Casework," in Herbert S. Strean, ed., *Social Casework* (Metuchen, N.J.: Scarecrow Press, 1971).

9.  See Anna Freud, *The Ego and the Mechanisms of Defense* (New York: International Universities Press, 1946); Heinz Hartmann, *Ego Psychology and the Problem of Adaptation* (New York: International Universities Press, 1958); Heinz Hartmann, Ernst Kris, and R. Loewenstein, "Comments on the Formation of Psychic Structure," in Ruth S. Eissler et al., eds., *The Psychoanalytic Study of the Child,* vol. 2 (New York: International Universities Press, 1946), pp. 11–38; Ernst Kris, "Notes on the De-

velopment and on Some Current Problems of Psychoanalytic Child Psychology," in Ruth S. Eissler et al., eds., *The Psychoanalytic Study of the Child*, vol. 5 (New York: International Universities Press, 1950), pp. 24–46; Erik Erikson, *Identity and the Life Cycle* (New York: International Universities Press, 1959); David Rapaport, *Organization and Pathology of Thought* (New York: Columbia University Press, 1951); Robert W. White, *Ego and Reality in Psychoanalytic Theory* (New York: International Universities Press, 1963). For a general discussion of the "structural theory," see Jacob Arlow and Charles Brenner, *Psychoanalytic Concepts and the Structural Theory* (New York: International Universities Press, 1964), pp. 103–113. For casework use of "ego psychology," see Parad, *Ego Psychology and Dynamic Casework*; Howard J. Parad and R. Miller, eds., *Ego-Oriented Casework: Problems and Perspectives* (New York: Family Service Association of America, 1963); and Isabel Stamm, "Ego Psychology in the Emerging Theoretical Base of Casework," in Alfred J. Kahn, ed., *Issues in American Social Work* (New York: Columbia University Press, 1959), pp. 80–109.

10.  The first three chapters written by George Wiedeman in George Wiedeman, ed., *Personality Development and Deviation* (New York: International Universities Press, 1975), pp. 1–39, comprise an excellent review of psychoanalytic personality theory.

11.  Erikson, *Identity and the Life Cycle*, p. 54.

12.  Anna Freud, *Ego and the Mechanisms of Defense* (New York: International Universities Press, 1946). Other writers have dated the beginnings of the use of ego theory by caseworkers considerably later on the assumption that Anna Freud's book did not reach us until this 1946 edition. Actually, the 1937 edition published by Hogarth Press was read by many caseworkers. See discussion of ego defense mechanisms in Florence Hollis, *Social Casework Practice: Six Case Studies* (New York: Family Welfare Association of America, 1939), pp. 269–272.

13.  See Wiedeman, *Personality Development and Deviation*, pp. 2–3.

14.  Ruth Benedict, *Patterns of Culture* (Boston: Houghton Mifflin, 1934).

15.  Margaret Mead, *Sex and Temperament in Three Primitive Societies* (New York: Morrow, 1935).

16.  Abram Kardiner, *The Individual and His Society* (New York: Columbia University Press, 1939).

17.  Maurine Boie, "The Case Worker's Need for Orientation to the Culture of the Client," *Proceedings of the National Conference of Social Work* (Chicago: University of Chicago Press, 1937), pp. 112–123.

18.  Elise de la Fontaine, "Cultural and Psychological Implications in Case Work Treatment with Irish Clients," *Cultural Problems in Social Case Work* (New York: Family Welfare Association of America, 1940), pp. 21–37.

19.  See especially Robert C. Angell, *The Family Encounters the Depression* (New York: Scribner's, 1936); Ruth Shonie Cavan and Katherine Howland Ranck, *The Family and the Depression* (Chicago: University of Chicago Press, 1938); and Mirra Komarovsky, *The Unemployed Man and His Family* (New York: Dryden Press, 1940).

20. Edmund Bergler, *Unhappy Marriage and Divorce* (New York: International Universities Press, 1946); Ernest W. Burgess and Leonard S. Cottrell, Jr., *Predicting Success or Failure in Marriage* (New York: Prentice-Hall, 1939); Lewis N. Terman, *Psychological Factors in Marital Happiness* (New York: McGraw-Hill, 1938); and Willard Waller, *The Old Love and the New* (New York: Liveright, 1930).

21. See, for example, Richard A. Cloward, "Illegitimate Means, Anomie and Deviant Behavior," *American Sociological Review*, 24 (April 1959), 164–176; and Gregory Bateson, Don D. Jackson, Jay Haley, and John H. Weakland, "Toward a Theory of Schizoprenia," *Behavioral Science*, 1 (October 1956), 252–264.

22. See Louis A. Ferman, ed., *Poverty in America* (Ann Arbor: University of Michigan Press, 1965); Hylan Lewis, *Culture, Class and Poverty* (Washington, D.C.: Cross Tell, 1967); and Henry S. Maas, "Socio-cultural Factors in Psychiatric Clinic Services for Children," *Smith College Studies*, 25 (February 1955), 1–90.

    The Hollingshead–Redlich study on the greater prevalence of certain types of mental illness in lower socioeconomic classes aroused great interest and led to examination of the question of how prevalence was related to class-related differences in treatment. See August B. Hollingshead and Frederick C. Redlich, *Social Class and Mental Illness* (New York: Wiley, 1958).

23. Ways of thinking and feeling characteristic of the young child are vividly portrayed in the studies of Jean Piaget and Susan Isaacs. See especially Jean Piaget, *The Child's Conception of the World* (New York: Harcourt, Brace, 1929), and Susan Isaacs, *Social Development in Young Children* (New York: Harcourt, Brace, 1937). For less detailed but useful descriptions, see Erik Erikson, *Childhood and Society* (New York: Norton, 1950); and Selma Fraiberg, *The Magic Years* (New York: Scribner's, 1959); John Flavell, *The Developmental Psychology of Jean Piaget* (Princeton, N.J.: Van Nostrand, 1963), deals with Piaget's work as a whole.

24. Wiedeman, *Personality Development and Deviation*, pp. 29–39.

25. Herbert S. Strean offers a full discussion of role theory, its sources, and application in his chapter "Role Theory" in Francis J. Turner, ed., *Social Work Treatment*, 2nd ed. (New York: Free Press, 1979).

26. The importance of the subject of communication is receiving increasing recognition by caseworkers. Lotte Marcus, in Chapter 1 of "The Effect of Extralinguistic Phenomena on the Judgment of Anxiety" (doctoral dissertation, Columbia University School of Social Work, 1969), surveys the pertinent literature and provides an excellent bibliography. Other references of value are Starkey Duncan, "Non-verbal Communication," *Psychological Bulletin*, 72 (1969), 118–137; Lotte Marcus, "Communication Concepts and Principles," in Turner, *Social Work Treatment*, pp. 409–432; Judith C. Nelson, *Communication Theory and Social Work Practice* (Chicago: University of Chicago Press, 1980); Norman A. Polansky, *Ego Psychology and Communication* (New York: Atherton Press, 1971); Virginia Satir, *Conjoint Family Therapy*, rev. ed. (Palo Alto, Calif.: Sci-

ence and Behavior Books, 1967); and Brett A. Seabury, "Arrangement of Physical Space in Social Work Settings." *Social Work,* 16 (October 1971), 43–49.

27. For discussion of a "corrective relationship" see Lucille N. Austin, "Trends in Differential Treatment in Social Casework," *Journal of Social Casework,* 29 (June 1948), 207.

# Chapter 3

# Examples of Clinical Social Work Practice

Before we proceed with further discussion of theory, some case illustrations may be of value in demonstrating the use in actual practice of the concepts presented in the previous chapter. All of the four case examples that follow illustrate situations in which serious breakdowns in social adjustment led the clients to seek clinical social work assistance. In each case, the problems in social functioning reflected—to one degree or another—the three types of causation described in Chapter 2. The dynamics of the treatment process by which the clients were enabled to achieve better functioning demonstrate clearly many of the points made there.

These cases were selected to show competent casework practice and treatment that resulted in significant gains for the clients. Of course, even the most experienced worker sometimes must face the fact that a particular piece of work has not been as helpful as was hoped. But these cases are representative of many in which workers and clients together are able to ameliorate person–situation disturbances.

Each case illustration will include a discussion of the three interacting factors that contributed to the clients' difficulties. The following questions will be discussed: (1) To what extent did residual infantile needs or weaknesses in libidinal and aggressive functioning affect the clients' problems? (2) What current deprivations and pressures interfered with client functioning? (3) Which ego or superego functions were faulty or nonadaptive? Particular attention will be given to appraising the clients' personality strengths and environmental supports.

While studying the case material, it may be helpful for the reader to try to identify the ways in which these factors interacted to affect the clients and their problems: How did the treatment process bring about a change in the person–situation gestalt? Specifically, how did casework intervention help to shift the balance of forces within the individual, or between the personality of the individual and the pressures from the environmental or interpersonal situation? Was the change in balance

56

achieved by strengthening or altering a specific aspect of the person–situation configuration, or did treatment address all three contributing factors?

In general, the quality of the relationship between worker and client is seen by psychosocial caseworkers as crucial to the effectiveness of treatment. Basic to a good therapeutic alliance is the positive attitude of the worker toward the client. In these case presentations, attention will be given to the treatment relationship and how it varies according to the needs and personalities of the clients. Occasional mention will be made of the concept of *transference.* This phenomenon will be examined in greater detail in Chapter 12; suffice it to say for now that when we use this term here we are referring to feelings and attitudes (positive or negative) that the client brings to the worker from other (often early family) experiences in relationships. When the client develops a strong positive transference to the worker, trust and treatment are often enhanced, providing the client with temporary supports needed to mobilize resources sufficiently to cope with or resolve his or her difficulties. On the other hand, negative transference reactions, when discussed openly, can be important in helping a client develop self-understanding. As the reader will see, for some clients, transference reactions have little bearing on treatment; this is true when the worker is viewed realistically—primarily as an expert in treating problems of social functioning.

## A MARITAL CRISIS

The case of Dick and Susan Jones* is of particular interest because it illustrates how clinical social work can sometimes help clients bring about substantial changes very quickly. The worker's understanding of individual and interpersonal dynamics, and the couple's motivation for change, led to an improved marital relationship in eleven joint therapy sessions held over a period of three months.

Susan Jones, age thirty, telephoned a family service agency stating that her marriage of seven years was at the "crossroads." She was afraid of her husband who, she said, had become an "angry man." They were arguing constantly. Although reluctantly, her husband Dick, age thirty-two, was willing to participate in marital counseling.

During the first meeting, the caseworker learned that the open conflict was precipitated a month earlier when Dick discovered that Susan was having an affair with her boss. Although the very short affair ended before marital therapy began, Dick was still enraged, distrustful,

*All case material in this book is disguised and fictitious names are used throughout.

and frightened that he would lose Susan, in spite of Susan's reassurances that she wanted their marriage to work. They reported that they had considered terminating the marriage, but they wanted to keep the family together for the sake of their three "delightful" and "normal" children: Charles, age six, and twins Ann and Andy, age five.

Both Dick and Susan were from large, stable, two-parent, working-class families. Dick's parents were characterized as more rigid and emotionally aloof than Susan's, whom they portrayed as warmer and more communicative. Although Dick was black and Protestant and Susan was white and Jewish, neither of their families had strongly disapproved of their courtship and marriage. Both sets of grandparents enjoyed their grandchildren and visited with the Joneses quite regularly; they were close but not intrusive and good in-law relationships had been established early in the marriage.

Since high school graduation, Dick had worked for the electric company as a mechanic. Susan worked for several years before her marriage and, a year prior to her affair, had taken a secretarial job. Although the extra income was important, Susan's motivation to work again was in large part based on feeling trapped, bored, and isolated from adults when she was at home all day with the children. They lived in a rural area with very few opportunities for casual socializing, and Susan was afraid of becoming "nothing more than a housewife"; she spoke of needing to find her own "identity." Since Dick worked the evening shift, he had agreed to take on many of the child care and household functions. Although the division of roles was worked out comfortably between them, as treatment progressed, it became clear that he had been afraid from the beginning that Susan would find the outside world so attractive she would lose interest in him and in their home. He did not, however, resent sharing the duties (he even took pride in their vegetable garden and in doing canning and preserving), and he knew that she, like he, thoroughly enjoyed the children.

Neither Dick nor Susan evidenced severe personality difficulties. However, although Dick was conscientious in work, fond of his home, and caring in his relationships with the children, he tended to be passive and emotionally remote with Susan; generally, he let her take the lead. Susan, on the other hand, was a more expressive person who in many ways had been the pursuer of the relationship with her husband. Nevertheless, over the years she had not confronted Dick with her disappointment about the fact that he rarely initiated affectionate moments or sexual relations between them. By the same token, she had not encouraged him to share his dissatisfactions with her. Instead, she slowly but steadily began to withdraw. Although aware of the distance that was developing between them, Dick, too, took no steps to rekindle the intimacy they had enjoyed early in marriage. When Susan went back to work, she was flattered by her employer's attentions and briefly, albeit guiltily, yielded to them. Her remorse, she said, would not have allowed the affair to continue very long even if Dick had not discovered it.

Although it was Susan who initiated treatment, Dick joined the first session with more apparent motivation for self-understanding than she did. He was concerned about his inability to control his temper since discovering Susan's unfaithfulness to him; he found himself shouting at her on the slightest provocation. Furthermore, he disliked his distrust of Susan when his "reasonable mind" believed the affair was over. He said he wanted to make changes in himself and recognized that these would be important to the marriage. Susan, on the other hand, insisted that now that she was no longer involved with her boss, the rest of the problem was up to Dick. She had tried over the years to bring excitement to their life together, but nothing "set a fire under Dick." Contrary to Susan's expectations, however, Dick was quickly able to recognize the roots of the passivity about which she complained. As the youngest of seven children, with four older sisters who catered to him and yet dominated him, he had little chance to take the initiative in his relationship with them. He began to understand how he had carried this pattern of unassertiveness to his marriage.

By the third session, they were arguing less. Dick recognized that his anger had been in reaction to the blow to his self-respect, and his feelings of helplessness in the face of Susan's betrayal. Tentatively, at first, he began to take the initiative in moving closer to Susan. Now it was Susan who maintained an aloof reserve; she was barely responsive to Dick. At first she explained this by saying that she was still afraid of his temper and felt safer at arm's length from him. As the worker pressed her to explore her feelings further, Susan acknowledged that because she had been angry with Dick for such a long time she now felt like "giving him a taste of his own medicine." Beyond that, and more to the point in the long run, she was keeping her tender feelings for him in check for fear that she would "fall" for his overtures, after which she expected he would revert to his remote and passive ways. Fortunately, Dick was not deterred and continued to risk being affectionate and open with Susan, with the result that Susan recognized the need to examine her own reactions.

As Susan developed greater awareness of the part she played in the problem, she explored some of the roots of her behavior. She was the second of four daughters and believed that her father preferred her older sister, Anita. As hard as Susan tried to please him, her father always seemed to find Anita smarter, prettier, and more talented than she. When she realized that much of her current resignation and anger at Dick were displaced feelings about her father, she began to take the chance and accept the changes Dick was making. Within a few weeks, their relationship grew warmer and more trusting—more like it used to be, they both said.

When treatment began, the caseworker and the couple had "contracted" for ten sessions with the understanding that the therapy could be extended, if necessary, after an evaluation at that time. During the tenth session they reported that they were feeling much more hopeful about their marriage, and both Dick and Susan had maintained an awareness of how each had participated in bringing about the crisis that had developed between them. They rarely resorted to blaming each other, but each took responsibility for working to make the relationship better. They decided to come for a final, eleventh meeting in which they were able to summarize and reinforce the good work they had done. Almost a year later they sent a Christmas card to the caseworker on which Susan wrote: "We are recommending marriage counseling to all our friends! We learned a lot and everything is going well."

What were the factors that contributed to threatening this marriage? In most respects, Dick and Susan were psychologically healthy. Yet both brought to their relationship some unresolved emotional issues and personality features that played into the difficulties. Dick's lack of assertiveness in personal relationships was, in part, derived from his childhood experiences with his older sisters who were managerial and indulgent. Since they had expected little in return for their love—except compliance—Dick did not learn well enough how to take the initiative to get what he wanted when it was not naturally forthcoming. Also, he was not used to expressing openly his deeper feelings about anything. Therefore, when faced with the threat of losing Susan, he withdrew, feeling helpless and angry. Susan, for different reasons, also tended to despair in the face of withdrawn affection; since she felt she had never been fully appreciated and loved by her father—in spite of the fact that she came from a warm, essentially nurturing family—she could easily lose hope about ever having a man who truly treasured her.

In this case, then, some unfulfilled childhood needs and ego weaknesses interfered with adult adjustment. However, for both Dick and Susan, the damage was not pervasive and the deficiencies were less disabling than they are for many clients. In this marriage, each partner was able to bring good reality testing and an "observing ego" to the situation; both had the capacity to reflect on the aspects of their own personalities that led to the difficulties. They both functioned well in most areas, were able to take pride in their accomplishments, and were capable of enjoying life. Dick had the capacity to understand how his passivity had contributed to Susan's sense of isolation and subsequent willingness to engage in an extramarital affair. Because he was determined to save the marriage, he quickly learned to take initiative. Susan's sense of values (ego ideal and superego) helped her to recognize that her sexual relationship with her boss was no solution to her problems; her capacity for reality testing enabled her to understand that unless they worked on their marriage it would continue to deteriorate. She realized that by withdrawing from Dick she, too, had taken a passive role in the marital interaction.

The marital problems that the Jones couple experienced were not simply a product of the weaknesses of each. In interaction with one another, their separate vulnerabilities were aggravated and reinforced, resulting—as often occurs in marital and family relationships—in a sort of negative complementarity. As discussed in Chapter 2, one of the primary characteristics of a system is that the parts transact—acting and reacting one upon the other. The marital treatment, therefore, focused not only on the personalities of each partner, but also on the reciprocal dynamics—the circular interactions—between Dick and Susan. As their actions and reactions changed, the climate of the relationship improved and the unhappiness each was experiencing was alleviated. Because each brought many strengths, and because the marriage had been gratifying at an earlier point, it took relatively little work or time to resume a positive balance and achieve renewed satisfaction.

The therapeutic relationship was important in that the worker's competence, objectivity, and wish to help enabled Dick and Susan to trust her and reveal themselves. But, in contrast to many clinical cases, the worker did not need to make extensive use of sustaining procedures. Relatively little time was required for ventilation of feeling. The transference aspects of the treatment were negligible; primarily, the worker helped Dick and Susan to reflect on their situation, on their patterns of interaction, and on some aspects of their past lives that contributed to their marital problems. Once they understood the dynamics, between sessions they were able to bring about many improvements in their situation.

Although of relatively minor importance, it is worth noting that environmental influences—beyond those of the marital system itself—played a part in this couple's situation. In a general atmosphere in which the women's liberation movement was advocating greater assertiveness, Susan's eagerness to have a life outside of her home was supported. Unlike many marital pairs, however, Dick and Susan had the flexibility to redefine "male" and "female" roles in order to accommodate Susan's wish. Also, again in contrast to many other couples, the Joneses had a supportive extended family network in which the in-laws showed interest, but did not interfere or take sides. This was especially impressive since the marriage was interracial. With a minimum of outside pressure, efforts to resolve the marital difficulties were enhanced.

## SOME PROBLEMS OF AGING[1]

Clients often come to social workers at a time of crisis—when there has been illness, the loss of a loved one, a change in employment or financial circumstances, or when new living arrangements are needed. Sometimes, as in the Jones case, a crisis occurs in reaction to a problem that has erupted in a family relationship. Any of these events can affect a person's self-esteem or sense of well-being. For the aged—who constitute a greater proportion of our population than ever before—disruptions in their lives are practically inevitable. It is often at these times that casework intervention is sought.

It should go without saying that the needs of older people have much in common with those of every age group. For the elderly as well as for the young, certain essentials are required in order to live with full dignity: an acceptable home, economic security, social status and recognition, a meaningful purpose in life. As difficult as it is for many people of all ages to fulfill the conditions necessary for optimum adjustment, the aged often have the hardest time of all.

Sometimes, when working with aged clients, there is a tendency to think in terms of "limited goals." Indeed, in some cases where there has been extreme physical or mental deterioration, the caseworker's efforts may have to be circumscribed. But there are large numbers of older people—starting with those in their sixties—who may have ten, twenty, or even thirty fulfilling years ahead of them. For clients in this group, substantial gains are often possible. The case illustration that follows is one in which the aim of therapy was to help the client, Mr. Kennedy, to reduce the impact of changes in his circumstances and to aid him to find satisfactory replacements for several losses he had endured. Had the young caseworker viewed Mr. Kennedy solely as an old man whose best years were behind him, she would have overlooked the possibilities for helping him as she did, in which case her client might well have rapidly declined into a state of hopelessness, poor health, and dependency.

Miss Kennedy, age twenty-seven, was referred by her psychiatrist to the geriatric service of an outpatient mental health clinic; she was seeking help for her sixty-seven-year-old father. An elementary school teacher, she had lived with her father until recently. Her mother had died of alcoholism thirteen years before. Mr. Kennedy, a construction worker, had been retired for two years and was maintaining himself with social security benefits and odd jobs as a handyman. His daughter portrayed him as a man who had always been active and an independent thinker; for many years he was an officer in his union local. He had lived in his neighborhood for thirty years, was well known, and was considered something of a "streetcorner politician," devoting much time to agitating for social causes.

Six months previously, Miss Kennedy had moved to an apartment of her own, against her father's wishes. Since then Mr. Kennedy had become depressed, and had given up his part-time work. He was blaming his daughter for leaving him alone in the apartment they had shared, with the entire rent to pay. He had two sons who lived at a distance and from whom, for all intents and purposes, he was estranged. Miss Kennedy said he had always been domineering and possessive of her. Leaving him had not been easy, but she felt she had to take this step for the sake of her own "sanity." She knew that if she stayed, her father would interfere in her relationship with a man in whom she was interested. She felt very guilty when he accused her of betraying him; she confided that sometimes she wet her bed after an explosive argument with him.

The worker explored the possibility of joint meetings between father and daughter, but Miss Kennedy adamantly refused. She further indicated that her psychiatrist, with whom she was in intensive treatment, had encouraged her to minimize her contacts with her father at this time. Since Miss Kennedy's therapy was expensive, she was not in a position to offer her father much financial help, even though she had recently given him a little money after he angrily demanded it. Miss Kennedy had spoken with her father about the clinic and believed he would be willing to meet with the worker, but she herself preferred no further involvement.

When the worker telephoned Mr. Kennedy, he agreed to come in to speak with her. He spent much of the first session berating his mother (who had left his father when he was a child); his wife, who had been a heavy drinker for many years; the Catholic Church, toward which he felt very bitter for various reasons; and, above all, his daughter. They had all mistreated him—"a good man"—and, in his view, the result would be an "early grave" for him. He had loved and cherished his daughter, he said, and now she was treating him like this—leaving him sick and penniless. He did not care whether he ate or worked. Actually his physical health was good, but he felt ill and listless. If only his daughter could come back to share the rent and keep him company, he was sure he would be all right again. Nothing else would help.

Without exploring alternatives at first, the worker recognized his loneliness and made evident her interest in helping. She expressed understanding of how difficult the recent changes had been for him. She voiced her confidence that, together, they might be able to find some answers. Fortunately, Mr. Kennedy took to the worker quickly, and there were several long interviews within a period of a month.

They began to talk over steps he might take to improve his situation. Usually the worker followed the client's lead, but occasionally she offered some suggestions of her own. Gradually but consistently, Mr. Kennedy's feelings of hopelessness diffused and he began taking on new or renewed interests: He became attached to a puppy a neighbor gave him and took it with him everywhere he went. He solved a complex oil burner problem for his landlord for which he was paid. He began visiting with friends again. He resumed his interest in political affairs. Sometimes between meetings he would call the worker and tell her about the things he was doing.

It is important to note that in an early session with Mr. Kennedy, the worker (who was placed as a graduate student at the clinic) informed him that they would be working together for only a three-month period, after which she would be leaving the service. In view of Mr. Kennedy's strong reaction to losing the companionship of his daughter, it was especially important for the worker to give him as much advance notice of her plans as possible. She also reassured him that, if necessary, another worker (her supervisor) would be available to him after she left. Initially annoyed and unsettled by the worker's impending departure, he nevertheless was able to talk about his feelings easily; he asked about her plans, some of which she explained to him. He said he thought it was good that she was "bettering herself" by getting more training, and added that he was proud his daughter had gotten a better education than either he or his wife had had.

Often an important indicator of a client's strengths (or weaknesses) can be found in the quality of the therapeutic relationship he or she is able to establish. The basic soundness of the personalities of Dick and Susan Jones was evidenced by the way they realistically related to their caseworker and quickly utilized her expertise to help them resolve their difficulties. Mr. Kennedy, who was feeling so bereft, needed the worker to temporarily fill a place that his daughter had left by moving out. By keeping in close touch with the worker, he was able to find the help his daughter no longer provided; he could become dependent (although certainly not blindly compliant!) until he was able to remobilize his own inner resources. Another area of strength was perceived immediately by the worker: although he was clearly depressed and shaken, in the first meeting he had come in fighting; he was neither withdrawn nor totally dispirited. With the worker's help, Mr. Kennedy was able to redirect his belligerent energies and utilize them in the service of more satisfying ends.

In their next-to-last session, the worker asked her supervisor—who would be the new worker available to Mr. Kennedy—to join them. While talking over his situation, the supervisor offered information about a nearby apartment building in need of a superintendent. He applied immediately and was accepted; in return for services, he was given a rent-free apartment. On several counts, it was fortunate indeed that the agency could direct him to this opportunity. Since it was the supervisor who gave him the information, the transition to the new worker was facilitated. Furthermore, since one of the most profound but frequent insults to the aged is the loss of feelings of usefulness and respect, the job served to reestablish these. Also highly important was the financial relief the job provided.

In the final meeting with the worker, Mr. Kennedy reported that his daughter was planning marriage, adding, "It's about time!" He was able to say that it had meant a lot to have someone to talk to, but that he was doing much better now. He wasn't sure he would need frequent appointments any more, but he liked the supervisor and would keep in touch with her. He concluded by wishing the worker good luck in her career and, interestingly, advised her to get married and have children because he was sure she would make a good mother! Before the worker left, Miss Kennedy telephoned to thank her and say that, although she still felt guilty about leaving her father, he was no longer blaming her. He seemed more like his "old self" again.

With older clients, as with every client, it is important to take an individualized approach. One cannot generalize about "good planning." In this case, the worker was optimally helpful because she assessed the family situation, Mr. Kennedy's many strengths, and the resources available to him. For example, by knowing even as little as she did about Miss Kennedy's complicated involvement with her father, it was evident that he (unlike some elderly clients) would not be able to solve his problem by living with her. Eventually, the worker realized, he would have to accept this. Also, it was clear that Mr. Kennedy was not a man for whom hobbies, or many of the activities provided by the local senior citizens center, would have sufficed; he would have seen them as "busy work," an indication of his loss of status. What he needed was the very personal interest of the worker and an opportunity to feel purposeful and economically secure.

The effect of the worker-client relationship was by no means the only dynamic in treatment but, temporarily, it played a large part. This worker was really "there" for Mr. Kennedy when he was feeling rejected and needed someone to understand. The fact that it was a warm, yet very professional, relationship, permitted the remarkably easy shift to the new worker. There has been a tendency to belittle "transference cures." Some distrust of such cures is well based. When nothing more is done than to use suggestion as a way of directly removing symptomatic behavior, it is extremely likely that a new form of symptom will arise. Not infrequently, it will be a more harmful symptom than the one originally chosen by the client. If, however, the transference relationship is used to remove or lessen the effect of the factors contributing to the maladjustment, as it was for Mr. Kennedy, it is an entirely different situation. Had the worker used her influence directly to induce her client to make certain decisions, this would have been "symptomatic" treatment. Very likely the improvement would then have been only temporary; experience would lead us to believe that when the worker left the clinic, he might have reverted to looking to his daughter to provide emotional supplies, as he had for so many years, and fallen into despair when she refused him. Instead, the relationship provided Mr. Kennedy with the support he needed to mobilize his strengths and seek his own solutions. As it turned out, he visited the new worker only a few times over a period of months, and the gains he had made were maintained.

Finally, it is important to note that in the treatment of Mr. Kennedy, a principle of economy was followed. Although the worker surmised that many of the difficulties he was experiencing had their roots in the traumas of his childhood, or in past family relationships, practically no attention was paid to this material in the actual treatment. His relationship with his daughter, for example, may well have been a reflection of earlier unfilled needs, or grief over his unhappy marriage. When viewed in the framework of psychoanalytic theory, it is conceivable that there were unresolved oedipal issues. But, wisely, the worker made no effort to explore these more remote matters when it became clear that positive results could be achieved in the context of the present.

The reader might well ask at this point what the outcome of casework treatment would have been if Mr. Kennedy had been too ill to work, or had not had so many well developed ego functions on which to build. Under such circumstances, would he have been able to regain his self-esteem? Suppose he was forced to accept financial aid, or had to be moved to a health-related facility? Surely these are situations many elderly clients face. Sometimes, it is true, solutions are at best compromises. But the case of Mr. Kennedy illustrates the fact that older clients in crisis are not necessarily on an irreversible downhill road. Even caseworkers can sometimes lose sight of the fact that many aging clients—including some who evidence a degree of physical or mental deterioration—*can* make changes and enjoy a dignified style of life.

## AN "ACTING OUT" ADOLESCENT

It is well known that adolescence, far more often than not, is a time of change and turmoil—for the young person *and* his or her family. Striving to overcome childhood dependency, faced with the emergence of genital sexuality, in uncertain and often angrily rebellious ways the adolescent seeks to separate from parents and establish his or her own identity—his or her own set of standards. Strident expressions of loyalty to peers (whose acceptance can be so important to the adolescent), combined with various acts of nonconformity to family values, can bring about feelings of helplessness in parents, and sometimes harsh retribution.

Adolescents, perhaps more than any other age group, have the fluidity of personality that can make it difficult to assess the true situation. Conflict with the family or apparent inner distress may be related to the adolescent's developmental phase, or it may be a sign of more profound disturbance. Often unpredictable, egocentric, belligerent, on the one hand, and idealistic, loving, generous, on the other, teenagers can baffle parents, teachers, and even clinicians who then sometimes exaggerate the severity of adolescents' problems. Conversely, the young person who conforms and does not challenge authority at all actually may be harboring more difficulties than unsuspecting but grateful adults can detect.[2]

Betty Kovacs, age fourteen, was referred to a clinical social worker in private practice by a school psychologist in whom the girl had confided. She was the youngest of three children. Her father, born in Hungary, was very successful professionally; he held a responsible position in an import-export firm and traveled extensively. Her mother, American born, had been a free-lance writer for many years and had recently begun working part time in an advertising agency. Both parents were in their fifties. Betty's brother Jim, age twenty-six, had been a college dropout following a schizophrenic episode several years before. He had since managed to make a marginal adjustment and was living with an older woman in a small New England town where he did odd jobs and studied ceramics. A sister Doris, age twenty-four, was a law school graduate who lived away from home; she had recently been hired by a prestigious law firm.

Treatment for Betty lasted eight months, terminating when the family moved to another state. For the most part Betty was seen individually, once or twice weekly. Six sessions were held with Betty and her parents together. The worker made one home visit to see Mr. Kovacs. Occasionally, Betty and her mother were seen together. There were also two joint meetings with Betty and her boyfriend, Allan.

The immediate situation leading to the referral for help was that Betty's father had had a mild heart attack two months previously and, while recuperating at home, had begun "prowling around," as Betty put it, during the day. He had gone through her bureau drawers and had come upon her diary, from which he learned that she was regularly having sexual relations with eighteen-year-old Allan, and that they had experimented with illegal drugs. Mr. Kovacs was inflamed. Even before he confronted Betty with his discoveries, he telephoned Allan's parents and told them he was forbidding his daughter to see their son. When Betty was told this, she was enraged that her privacy had been violated. Her father declared that as long as she lived "under the same roof" she had no right to secrets. Betty's mother, to whom both father and daughter spoke more often than they spoke to each other, attempted to mediate. She told her husband that she thought he was too harsh and would permanently alienate Betty, and she told Betty that her father was only taking the stand he did because he loved her and wanted to protect her.

Betty was a tall, attractive, bright, and articulate young person who had been an excellent student until recently. At this point her grades were barely passing. In the first meeting, at which her mother was present, Betty told the worker that she could no longer live in the same house with her father, who called her a "whore" and an "addict." She said freely that she wanted to "kill" him—that he deserved to die. On the other hand, she was afraid of exploding at him for fear he really would "drop dead"; she could not stand the guilt if that happened. What she did, therefore, was to evade and ignore him and use her mother as the "whipping boy" for her outrage; she had been yelling at her mother a lot since all this trouble started.

She spoke at length about Allan, with whom she said she was very much in love. She did not think having sexual relations with someone she cared about so much was wrong. Her father should be grateful, she thought, that she was not like some other girls she knew who "slept around" with lots of boys. As for the drugs, she said that she had experimented with marihuana and pills, but she was no longer doing this. In fact, she was trying to persuade Allan to stop using them too.

In Betty's view, largely confirmed by her mother, her father had always preferred her sister Doris, who had many intellectual interests in common with him. As far back as she could remember, her mother had paid special attention to her brother Jim, who had always had problems. As a result, Betty felt that as she was growing up she had never come first with either of her parents. Only when she was a very small child could she remember feeling close to her father. By the time she started school, he was away a great deal or, when at home, he was either reading or involved in serious discussions with Doris—sometimes they would talk for hours. Occasionally, Betty's father teased her, but she found his humor "silly" and unpleasant. On the whole, she approached life in an emotional way and was interested in the arts, while her father concerned himself with politics, law, and history.

The worker's first impression of Mrs. Kovacs was that she was a conscientious but extremely obsessive woman. When she talked about the family situation, she often went into such minute detail that the point she was making got lost. In contrast to Betty, who expressed herself passionately, Mrs. Kovacs seemed colorless, burdened, and tired. She clearly wanted to do the best she could for Betty, but felt at a loss about how to help.

By catering to Betty, by yielding to her demands for "freedom," for new clothes, and so on, she tried to "make up" for what she viewed as Mr. Kovacs' rejection. The mother described herself as the "switchboard" whom the family members "plugged into" to complain about one another. As the worker listened, she sensed that Mrs. Kovacs was so invested in the personalities and demands of other members of the family, that she was rather undefined herself; she vacillated in the face of their pressures and seemed to have very few clear-cut opinions of her own. However, when recently she went to work part time, she did so against the wishes of her husband, who had a "European view" of the woman's role. It was shortly after this that her husband had his heart attack; she feared that her independent stand may have contributed to it. She liked her job but felt guilty about not living up to her husband's expectations. She had considered quitting, but for the first time she had something in her life that was her "own" and, with trepidation, she had decided not to give it up.

After three meetings with Betty, the worker made a home visit to see Mr. Kovacs who was still convalescing. In a session that lasted two hours, he told the worker he was interested in anything she had to say, but first he wanted to tell her how he felt. With sadness, he said he knew he'd neglected his daughter because his business affairs had taken him away so much during her formative years. He blamed himself for some of her current problems. He recalled how much love she used to show him when she was a very small child. She had been "beautiful" then, he said, but as she grew older, he had found her "artistic temperament" and emotionalism difficult to understand. Now he was enraged by her "loose" and "despicable" behavior. It was unbelievable that a daughter of his could behave so brazenly. As he spoke, the worker clearly showed understanding of his distress.

Once he had vented his remorse and bewilderment, this very intense, dignified man relaxed enough to ask the worker what she thought. He wanted her to be frank with him, he said. Taking his lead, the worker asked if he understood exactly why Betty was so furious with him. He said she thought he had violated her privacy, but he felt that he had no choice. He had suspected she was sexually involved with Allan and it was his responsibility to find out for certain and put a stop to it. Currently, he was opening her mail and monitoring her telephone calls. He loved her and did not want her to do any more harm to herself. The worker wondered whether he thought he could really stop Betty from seeing Allan. She also asked whether Betty might not be more open to his guidance and affection if she did not feel so "spied upon." Given Mr. Kovacs' traditional European view, the worker was surprised by the thoughtful consideration he gave to her questions. He was able to say that he was probably being too "hard-headed." He seemed genuinely appreciative of the worker's interest and said he would think over her suggestion about being less intrusive. The worker went on to say that, despite the fact that Betty was very angry with him, it was her view that his approval was very important to her. Certainly, she recognized, it was hard for him to approve of her recent behavior, but perhaps he could find other ways to let her know he loved her. In the course of their talk, Mr. Kovacs readily acknowledged that he found his older daughter much easier to understand because she was so level-headed and reasonable.

The worker did not assume that Mr. Kovacs would make any abrupt shifts in his approach to Betty, but he did seem to want to try. Intellectually, he could understand that his actions were contributing to the very behavior he wanted to prevent. Although his strong sense of values was deeply offended, a beginning had been made. Shortly after the session with Mr. Kovacs, Betty reported she had come home late from school one day and her father, who suspected she had been with Allan, began to berate her but suddenly stopped himself and walked away. He was also refraining from reading her mail and interfering with her telephone calls.

In her sessions, Betty was very preoccupied with Allan, the most important person in the world to her, she said. She was very upset about the fact that he would be graduating from high school and going to an out-of-town college the following year. She also talked about her failing school work, but efforts to improve were half-hearted. Her energies were being consumed by anger at her father and her relationship with Allan.

When the family met in sessions, the worker attempted to help the mother refrain from being the family "switchboard" in order to foster direct communication between father and daughter. Gradually, the father became more supportive and less critical, but Betty emphatically repelled his overtures. In family sessions, the mother made the greatest effort to change. Not only did she do less mediating, but she became less overprotective of Betty. She no longer sided with her against her father and she catered less to her demands.

Four months after treatment began, Betty learned she was pregnant. In discussion with the worker, she was able to become aware of some of her motives for having allowed this to happen. She and the worker had previously talked about birth control, and she knew she could have prevented pregnancy. But, first of all, she recognized that nothing she could have done would have been more hurtful to her father; her pregnancy was an expression of her rage at him. Second, and from Betty's standpoint even more important, she desperately wanted to hold on to Allan and to test his allegiance to her. In a family meeting during this period, because she was frightened and also more self-aware, she accepted her parents' care and comfort. Her father told her he was sorry she felt she had to do what she did, but he loved her and would stand by her. Both parents were willing to help her through an abortion.

Although her feelings were mixed, Betty had a strong wish to have the baby. If she did, she thought, Allan would go to college locally and therefore be with her the next year. In two joint meetings with Betty, Allan told her that he would not go away if she had the baby, but that he would feel very angry about being "forced" to stay. His college plans were made and he wanted to go through with them. After this, during several sessions scheduled closely together, Betty reflected on what course she should take. The worker neither pressured her toward a particular decision nor criticized her; she did, however, encourage her to look closely at her alternatives and to try to understand why she leaned toward one choice more than another. Finally, Betty decided to have an abortion after all. She realized that her relationship with Allan would deteriorate if he felt coerced; she also admitted that she was afraid to go through with the pregnancy and was really not yet prepared to care for a baby.

Following the abortion, Betty was in therapy for only three more months. For health reasons, her father decided to retire from his demanding business and move to another state. However, in this short time Betty worked very hard on herself. She expressed sadness about the abortion, but was pleased with herself for making a decision she believed was wise. She also realized she had been trying to control Allan in the misguided belief that she could hold on to him by doing so. She saw she was trying to dominate Allan as her father had tried to dominate her. This awareness led her to soften her attitude toward her father. She could see that his actions had truly derived from concern for her. She further realized that she was like him in some ways, particularly in her self-centeredness and demanding expectations of other people, especially her mother and Allan. Betty reported that in general she felt calmer than ever, less overcome by anger or excitement, and better able to measure her actions and reactions.

What were the early or unresolved childhood issues reactivated for Betty during these months of crisis? It seems likely that she had harbored feelings of being less important than her brother in her mother's eyes, and unable to compete with her sister for her father's attention. From the worker's point of view, there was every evidence that Betty's very early nurturing had been good: Mrs. Kovacs thoroughly enjoyed all of her babies and Mr. Kovacs had delighted in Betty as an infant. However, the mother had overindulged her children, in part as a reaction to the rather distant relationship with a husband whom she felt was too intellectual, emotionally remote, and authoritarian. On the other hand, as the worker saw it, the father, who had had a deprived childhood, was in competition with the children for his wife's caretaking and, when his needs were not met, took his anger out on them, particularly Jim and Betty. In the face of this, Betty's relationship to Allan represented far more than the ordinary adolescent expression of emerging sexuality or the wish to shed childhood dependency on her parents. Betty seemed to the worker to be compensating for longstanding feelings of not being loved enough by her father. Her outrage at his betrayal, although in some measure realistically based, also reflected unresolved oedipal disappointments stemming from his withdrawal from her. These early feelings had reemerged in adolescence, and Betty had acted them out through angry and sexual behavior.

There were also external pressures aggravating Betty's difficulties. Her father's traditional values about sexuality in a changing culture created special stresses. Even two decades ago, Betty's sexual behavior or experimentation with drugs—in and of themselves—would have been seen as seriously deviant. The sexual revolution, however, has touched every strata of American life, perhaps particularly the middle class. The women's liberation movement, the availability of contraceptive devices and legal abortions, the frank handling of sexual information by the mass media have all contributed to greater relaxation about sexual matters. In Betty's suburban school, with a student body primarily from affluent families, discussions about sexual activity and drugs—particularly marihuana—were common. The seemingly unconflicted sexual permissiveness among many young people has led some parents —more "enlightened" than Betty's—to encourage their daughters to practice contraception. In this sense, then, Betty was torn—more than some of her friends were—between her father's very strict views and the more relaxed "modern" climate of her peer culture.

The situation was further complicated by the fact that the mother, who had few defined opinions of her own, was unable to provide Betty with a model of solid values to emulate during this period. It was the worker's view, furthermore, that the mother's vagueness and vacillations about most issues influenced the father to take an even more drastic stance than he otherwise would have. Finally, the remote (although not altogether uncaring) relationship between the parents did not provide Betty with a very positive example of a loving heterosexual relationship, which would have been helpful to her at this stage of her development.

Certainly, Betty had many positive ego qualities. She was bright, had been a competent student, and was capable of self-awareness. In situations in which she was not too stressed, she could show good judgment and a sense of balance. Only in the face of strong impulses did her controls give way and her judgment fail, and she became self-destructive.

Unlike many adolescents, Betty was not evasive with the worker. She related easily to her from the beginning and, as time went on, viewed her as a very important person in her life. She told her that her "vision had been enlarged" by speaking with her; she learned she had many more options in her life than she had realized. For example, she discovered that when she behaved differently toward her father, he had more to offer her than she had thought. She realized that since her father was so dogmatic and her mother so "wishy-washy' she had tried to find her own way, which had sometimes hurt her badly. She trusted the worker to be objective, to give honest feedback, and to like her "no matter what." In her own way, Betty was aware that the worker had given her a "corrective" experience, one her parents had been unable to offer.

In the final family session, the improved relationship between father and daughter was evident, although there was still some tension between them, particularly over Allan. However, the mother had almost totally abandoned her "go-between" role and thus Betty and Mr. Kovacs had a better opportunity to work out their relationship, which, although far from perfect, had come a long way over the course of eight months of casework treatment.

Certainly, Betty's behavior reflected far more serious problems than those that arise during the course of a "normal" adaptation to the changes of adolescence. However, the fact that she was able to make very important gains in a relatively short time was a good prognostic sign, an indicator of her developing strengths and her potential for effective functioning. It was unfortunate that this therapy was prematurely terminated when the family moved, but the worker felt sure that Betty would enter treatment again. She was planning to study psychology—an interest she had had before treatment, probably reinforced by positive identification with the worker—and therefore she had an additional stake in developing self-understanding.

## EARLY DEPRIVATION

Some people need more extended and intensive treatment than was required by the clients thus far described in this chapter. Donna Zimmer, whose case we will now discuss, was in therapy for four years. In

the view of the writers and the worker who treated her, a brief casework contact would have been, at best, of minimal value. Clinical experience has repeatedly demonstrated that when developmental
deprivations have been severe and healthy ego organization has been
significantly interrupted, improved adjustment usually takes considerable time to achieve. This case is representative of many cases seen by
clinical social workers for which such long-term treatment is necessary.
It also illustrates the three types of causation mentioned earlier, and the
complexity of the interactions among these factors. Treatment that
addressed life history, early needs, ego development, and current environmental pressures was vital to the successful outcome.[3]

Referred by her physician, Mrs. Zimmer, age thirty-three, applied
to a family service agency. She had numerous somatic complaints that
her doctor believed were primarily psychogenic. During her first appointment, she sobbed continually, said her stomach ached unbearably,
and complained about being unfairly treated by her mother, her ex-
husband, and others. Over and over she said she might as well die, that
she was "good for nothing." Although an attractive woman—petite,
casually but tastefully dressed—her face was contorted, there were
dark circles under her eyes, and during much of the interview she
hugged her knees to her chest and rocked as she wept. In this initial
meeting, and in many that followed, she evidenced intense, pervasive
anxiety and despair; she wanted help because she was afraid of "falling
apart."

Mrs. Zimmer was seen at least once and often twice weekly during
her four years of therapy. From time to time there were family meetings with her and her children. There were also several sessions held
jointly with her mother. In early sessions with the worker, Mrs. Zimmer
was able to provide relevant information freely about her current situation and background. In contrast to her chaotic emotional condition,
her approach to factual material was intelligent and well organized.

Mrs. Zimmer was clearly frightened about the extreme rage she
often felt toward her children—Sonia, age eleven, and Michael, age
eight—since her recent separation from her husband. Although she had
ended her tempestuous marriage, she was reacting with strong feelings
of anger and depression, as if she had been the one to be rejected and
abandoned. Easily set off by even minor external pressures, she described herself as numb or empty when not in the grip of torment or
rage. She characterized her husband as an angry man, otherwise emotionally remote, who could not fulfill his responsibilities. During their
twelve years of marriage, he had worked only now and then and provided sporadic financial support for the children.

Following her separation, Mrs. Zimmer had enrolled in a secretarial school. In spite of her emotional distress, she was able to concentrate

enough to complete an accelerated course. But she was worried about finding a job during an economic recession, and afraid she could not earn enough money to support herself and her children. Although her mother lived in the same city, she could not give financial help. Furthermore, Mrs. Zimmer felt her mother had little else to offer; frequently, she would make promises to drop by and then cancel at the last minute. No other relative lived within visiting distance.

The current situational pressures on Mrs. Zimmer were obvious. She was having to take full responsibility for the care of her children. She had few friends or people to whom she could turn. She was forced to try to enter a tight labor market with newly acquired skills and no previous work experience. Furthermore, the children were reacting negatively to the breakup of the marriage and were more likely to vent their anger at her than at their father for fear that even his occasional visits would end. Much of Mrs. Zimmer's distress, then, was realistically based.

But what residual infantile needs and drives did Mrs. Zimmer bring to her already troubled circumstances? The oldest of five children in a Jewish lower middle class upwardly mobile family, she was placed at age three in a children's home for several weeks while her mother was hospitalized for post-partum depression. Mrs. Zimmer remembered this event vividly, and with intense fury; for her, it symbolized a general feeling of abandonment by her mother (a gentle, listless, guilt-ridden, self-effacing woman who seemed ineffectual and indecisive to her daughter). In addition to this separation from her family, when she was an infant Mrs. Zimmer herself was hospitalized several times for operations to correct a malformed eyelid. There were, then, many breaks in her early nurturing.

Furthermore, Mrs. Zimmer believed that by the age of seven or eight her mother had depended on her, the only girl, to be the "little mother" to her brothers. Her needs came last. As she saw it, any wish of hers was met with guilt-provoking responses that led her to feel undeserving. If she got what she wanted, other family members reacted with jealousy and anger. The worker surmised that Mrs. Zimmer's experience with early relationships had led her to believe that she would either be abandoned or "used" in the service of the needs of others. She never felt that she was loved freely for being herself.

Mrs. Zimmer still raged at her mother about the fact that on the same day she graduated from high school (at age sixteen with honors), one of her brothers was graduating from elementary school and her parents attended his ceremony and not hers. She recalled that when she complained, her father told her that education was much more important for boys than for girls. Like the man she married, she described her father as an angry, critical person who could not express loving feelings;

her timid mother, she said, cowered and cringed in the face of his dominating personality. At the time her father died when she was seventeen, Mrs. Zimmer felt she had to take over as head of the household until she "escaped into marriage" at twenty-one.

During the first year of treatment, the extreme oscillations in her view of herself and others was striking. At times she railed at her parents and her husband, seeing them as "all bad" and herself as the "good" one who had been unappreciated and victimized by them. Then, abruptly, often within the same treatment session, she would shift to the opposite view and become convinced that she was the "bad" one, and she would see this as the reason for having been treated so "shabbily" by her family. When she experienced these negative feelings toward others or herself, her hostility and infantile aggressive feelings would consume her. She would often act impulsively. Angry feelings would then be displaced onto her children, particularly her son Michael, whom she came close to abusing physically, and whom she was afraid one day she would "kill in anger." Her longstanding rage—which the worker saw as deriving from early emotional deprivation, reinforced by later experiences—was often aimed at Michael, because she felt he ridiculed her as her father had. All of her personal relationships were fraught with conflict and vacillation; her behavior toward her mother and various men in her life was impulsive and erratic. On several occasions, Mrs. Zimmer had explosive encounters with friends when she felt that they were trying to take advantage of her or that they were unsympathetic to her problems. A flood of emotion would lead directly to uncontrolled action: rage led her to strike out aimlessly; when she felt lonely or despairing, she became clinging or demanding.

In considering the effects of Mrs. Zimmer's early experiences, it is important to avoid the simplistic view that her parents' inadequacies, or the early separations, had "caused" her adult difficulties. To do so would overlook the contributions of her innate endowments, of her experiences in interaction with her family and the wider world, and of the ways in which she used later events both to compound and correct the effects of unfulfilled early needs. This point leads us to a discussion of the interplay of her drives and her ego development.

Faulty ego functioning was apparent in her frequently distorted evaluation of herself and others—as "all good" or "all bad." Since anything less than "perfect" was judged by her to be "terrible," her "all bad" reactions predominated. Her ego's ability to regulate and control infantile impulses was seriously impaired, causing her to create more environmental pressures on herself. Her intellect, good judgment, and reality testing—evident in the less emotional aspects of her life—were very vulnerable when strong impulses were stimulated. Flawed ego organization was evident in her inability to balance positive and negative feelings. In effect, the memory of a pleasurable feeling could not be retained when negative ones (despair, rage, fear) arose; good and bad experiences could not be integrated; she often had difficulty differentiating one feeling from another. Her defensive functioning—her heavy reliance on projection and denial—provided evidence of the depth of her difficulties and also contributed to many of her interpersonal problems. During the early months of treatment, only rarely could she admit that her negativism and provocative behavior created difficulties for her.

Apparently, her parents had taken little delight in her accomplishments and therefore she, too, could not realistically appraise or enjoy them. Nor could she take pride in the achievements of her children. Superego development was apparent in her conscientiousness, ethical values, and consistent ability to deal honestly with others in practical matters; on the other hand, her superego was severe and, for the most part, unforgiving. When self-critical (for example, about her frequent anger at her son), she became overwhelmed with such remorse that she had little energy for self-understanding.

Some ego functions were far better developed than others. On the positive side, she functioned competently (but rarely without anxiety) in the routine aspects of her life. She learned and could master new skills quickly. She consistently attended to the physical, educational, and even cultural development of her children. Her strengths and her good intelligence were of primary importance to her motivation for therapy and to its successful outcome. (It was not until the final months of therapy, however, that Mrs. Zimmer could say that she had kept coming to sessions because she had some hope that she could "get well." To have admitted that earlier, she said, would have made her feel vulnerable—afraid that the worker would try to "take away" her belief in herself, as she felt her parents had tried to do. But the regularity with which she kept appointments and participated in them gave evidence to the worker that there was a healthy part of Mrs. Zimmer that wanted change.)

The aim of treatment, then, was to help her to repair the damage while affirming her adaptive qualities. Specifically, the worker's treatment approach for the first year was in large measure supportive. During this time, Mrs. Zimmer poured out a great deal of rage, hopelessness, and despair. Alternately, she idolized and furiously distrusted her worker; on some occasions, she would try to cling to her physically and see her as her only "lifeboat," while at other times— often in an abrupt switch—she would accuse her of condemning her and wanting to be rid of her. Patiently and kindly, over and over again, the worker conveyed her understanding of how deprived of genuine caring Mrs. Zimmer felt she had always been, and acknowledged that, indeed, some early experiences had been hurtful to her. At the same time, the worker expressed confidence that now that Mrs. Zimmer was an adult—although it would probably take time—there was every reason to believe that she could grow to feel better and improve her life. When Mrs. Zimmer begged the worker to hold and rock her—or to prolong the treatment hour—the worker assured her that she recognized that these requests stemmed from deep unhappiness, but gently yet firmly explained the realities of what she could and could not do.

It would have been futile for the worker to make early efforts to help Mrs. Zimmer deal directly with her problems of impulse control, even though these were contributing to her many difficulties. For example, advice about how to handle her impulsivity would probably have been ineffective; in the worker's view, Mrs. Zimmer's controls were not yet sufficiently developed to change her reactions to stress. Efforts to persuade her to act differently when she could not, might have reinforced her profound feelings of failure. On the other hand, when Mrs. Zimmer occasionally did complain about her inability to control her temper, the worker caringly agreed that her intense hostility *did* create many problems for her—working against her own wish to be a good parent, to have friends, and to have a better relationship with her mother. False reassurance could have played into Mrs. Zimmer's tendency to blame others for her troubles. In general, however, the worker's approach at this stage was not to press Mrs. Zimmer to examine her behavior per se, but rather to encourage her to try to understand the feelings that stimulated it.

After about a year of therapy, Mrs. Zimmer was feeling slightly better and realized—at least intellectually—that her caseworker would not abandon her. Her security about this was undoubtedly enhanced by the fact that the worker saw to it that the agency fee was adjusted during periods in which Mrs. Zimmer was financially pressed, and sometimes extra appointments and telephone reassurance were offered when Mrs. Zimmer was in acute distress. During the worker's summer vacation, she sent Mrs. Zimmer weekly postcards as a reminder of her ongoing interest, since separations to this client were synonymous with abandonment. All of this was indisputable proof of the worker's caring —difficult for Mrs. Zimmer to deny, even when she felt distrustful. Beyond this, the worker's ability to accept and remain unprovoked by Mrs. Zimmer's negative feelings—including those toward the worker herself—served to reduce them, relieve her anxiety, and foster greater trust. Negative responses the worker occasionally felt in the face of angry outbursts or of clinging, demanding behavior were tempered by her awareness of the depth of Mrs. Zimmer's pain and unhappiness.

From the onset, and throughout treatment, the worker avoided being drawn into debates with Mrs. Zimmer. The importance of this approach was demonstrated by an event that occurred after about eighteen months of therapy: Mrs. Zimmer telephoned to say she wanted to stop coming. The worker, although surprised by this sudden move, did not argue. Rather, she said that perhaps a vacation from therapy might have some value, but suggested that they meet at least once again. Mrs. Zimmer agreed. As they discussed her wish to terminate, without pressure the worker asked if Mrs. Zimmer thought she might not make further progress if she continued. On the other hand, the worker went on, perhaps Mrs. Zimmer's wish to conclude therapy was an indication of her wish to "try her wings on her own" for a while —an indication of how far she had come. Taken aback but apparently relieved, Mrs. Zimmer said that she really *did* want to continue her sessions. She explained that she had been afraid the worker would insist that she stay, and that expectation had made her feel "used"—as she felt she had been used by her family, to whom she felt acceptable only if she did things the way they wanted her to.

As it developed, this session was a turning point for Mrs. Zimmer; she had asserted her independence—in and of itself a sign of growth. Furthermore, the worker supported her in this by not arguing or holding on to her, attitudes early experiences had led Mrs. Zimmer to anticipate from others. Rather than assuming that Mrs. Zimmer was just being hostile or resistant, the worker believed her move also reflected healthy strivings to grow up (self-assertion was replacing angry aggression). And, of utmost importance, this session firmly established for Mrs. Zimmer that it was *her* motivation that brought her to sessions, *not* the worker's need to possess or manipulate her. From this point on, Mrs. Zimmer became increasingly aware of the ways in which she distorted reality to conform to old expectations, thereby depriving herself of opportunities available to her in the present. Needless to say, the handling of Mrs. Zimmer's request to terminate required skill and delicacy, without which the client might have interpreted the worker's response as a rejection.

Now that a solid relationship had been established, the worker was able to confront Mrs. Zimmer and help her reflect on the contradictions between her feelings and her intellect and between her values and her behavior. To have done so earlier would probably have angered or frightened Mrs. Zimmer and might well have jeopardized the therapeutic relationship. But when it was possible, together they explored sudden reversals, such as when Mrs. Zimmer shifted from idealizing her children, her friends, and her caseworker to disparaging them. The worker challenged her unwillingness to entertain any other attitude than hatred toward her mother; Mrs. Zimmer was helped to tap other feelings, including sadness, longing, affection, and empathy. (Her mother's kindness as well as her blandness and dependency were apparent in joint therapy sessions, which gave the worker an opportunity to help Mrs. Zimmer take a more balanced and realistic view.) Similarly, when the client raged about how she wished her son had never been born, the worker expressed understanding of anger at his disobedience, but wondered if Mrs. Zimmer could remember that she had just spoken lovingly about him during the previous session. Asking her to think about this encouraged continuity of feeling and synthesis of "good" and "bad" feelings and experiences.

Mrs. Zimmer (and many clients with significant ego deficits and infantile residuals) often expressed her feelings in global terms—that is, it was hard for her to differentiate one feeling from another. Therefore, when she said she felt "awful," the worker urged her to get a better sense of what was wrong: was she feeling lonely, self-critical and guilty, hurt, abused, or just what? Often this was hard for her, but it was one of the important ego-building techniques employed by the worker that, over time, undoubtedly led to greater self-awareness.

By the time Mrs. Zimmer had been in treatment for two years, improvement in all of her relationships could be noticed. Most of the time she was able to relate civilly to her ex-husband about the children and financial support. To her surprise, Mr. Zimmer became somewhat more consistent in sending payments and in visiting the children, and she could recognize that some of his hostile attitudes had been provoked by hers. Although at times still impulsive, her aggressive behavior toward the children was less extreme and less frequent; no longer did she feel in danger of physically attacking her son Michael. More often than before, she began to take what she called "the middle road" in regard to her feelings and behavior; her emotions were no longer "all-or-nothing." When she was angry with someone, she was also able to maintain some awareness of her warm feelings. She was less likely to either idolize or denigrate her worker; more frequently, she saw her as a helpful person who was also human.

During the third year of treatment, Mrs. Zimmer worked to achieve further stability within herself and in her relationships. Her improvement was strongly tested by Sonia, who by this time was fourteen and in angry rebellion most of the time. (During this period, Sonia was seen by another clinical social worker for about six months.) In spite of repeated fluctuations and regressions, Mrs. Zimmer was able to maintain a balance of feeling and behavior toward her daughter, recognizing that she, too, was having "growing pains." In other relationships she was able to react more appropriately, tactfully, and warmly than she had. She saw it as a milestone in her therapy when, during a session with her mother, she was able to hug her and tell her that she very much wanted them to become closer than they had been; with occasional backsliding, their relationship improved substantially because Mrs. Zimmer had grown to accept her love for her mother, even though she disliked certain of her qualities. Opposite feelings could now coexist.

But she was still having difficulty reaching out for new friends, even though she very much wanted them. She was afraid of rebuff and of her own volatility. During this period of loneliness, the worker's constant interest, her confidence in the changes that had occurred and in the possibilities for more, were very supportive. Mrs. Zimmer was afraid that the worker (like her mother who tended to be suspicious of outsiders) would try to discourage her from friendships. Instead, without pressure, the worker shared some ideas about how Mrs. Zimmer might meet new people, and was helpful to her by talking over the ways she was handling new relationships. By the end of this third year of work, Mrs. Zimmer had made several woman friends on her job and at her temple.

With little direct help from the worker, Mrs. Zimmer established herself vocationally. Once she completed her secretarial course, she located a job with a small firm where she was immediately successful; she then returned to school part time to take bookkeeping, for which she had a natural aptitude. Within six months of completing her course, she was given a promotion and, by the time treatment ended, she had advanced to the position of full-charge bookkeeper. She was now better able than before to value her abilities and, by doing so, to bolster her self-esteem.

The final year of treatment focused intensively on her relationships with men. She had always been afraid of her sexual feelings (which, as she recalled, her father had directly discouraged); she realized she had married her husband partly because she was not attracted to him. Her sexuality was as frightening to her as her hostility had been. After separation from her husband, her only sexual encounters were those she called "vindictive"; she would have relations once with a man for whom she had contempt and then refuse to see him again, delighting in the fantasy that she had punished him for "taking advantage" of her. Here again, the worker helped Mrs. Zimmer examine contradictions. For example, the worker asked whether expending so much energy "getting back"—through these men—at the people who had deprived her so long ago, served her present wish to have positive relationships. The worker's attitude toward sex, as a natural and potentially rewarding adult experience, undoubtedly also gave Mrs. Zimmer "permission" to be less frightened and guilty about the possibility of enjoying it.

As her unbridled aggression subsided, and as good feelings became more available to her, slowly and tentatively, she reached the point of wanting "a person of my own to love." She began to date men she respected. She delayed becoming sexually involved until she grew to care deeply for one man whom she dated for several months during this phase of treatment. Before terminating therapy, she brought him to a session for the worker's "approval"; they were discussing marriage but neither she nor he wanted to rush into it.

The termination phase required careful handling on the worker's part.[4] The thought of leaving treatment excited Mrs. Zimmer but also stimulated old feelings of fear and anger. On the one hand, she was able to take justifiable pride in her hard-earned attainment of greater maturity and stability; on the other hand, she would sometimes feel outraged by the fact that she had had to work so hard to overcome the deprivations of her early years while, as she saw it, "normal" people could simply "sail" through life. Thoughts that perhaps the worker had wanted to get rid of her all along were activated as they talked about ending their work together. Separation fears were profound as Mrs. Zimmer began to say goodbye to her worker who had, indeed, nurtured her through tumultuous times. Never before had Mrs. Zimmer experienced an intimate relationship in which her growth toward independence and adulthood was unambivalently encouraged. While she was realistically grateful for this, the final phase of therapy also stirred a sense of loss associated with her childhood. When the worker helped her to examine and sort out her reactions, Mrs. Zimmer was able to distinguish which were projections or old feelings about herself as a "bad" person, and which were genuine feelings of sadness aroused by termination. In the final session, Mrs. Zimmer presented the worker with a Hummel figurine of a smiling, robust child that symbolized for her the "second chance" she had been given to grow up "the right way."

In analyzing the case of Mrs. Zimmer, we see that treatment was slow, turbulent, marked by periods of stalemate and regression. Mrs. Zimmer's conflicted, vacillating relationship with her worker tended to replicate old relationships, reflecting inner turmoil and ego deficiencies. The worker's patience, consistency, caring, and optimism were important dynamics of treatment. Fortunately, she neither retaliated when Mrs. Zimmer denounced her, nor was she countertransferentially seduced by excessive praise. Instead, Mrs. Zimmer was provided with a sustained experience of closeness without being hurt, "used," or abandoned.

However, it is important to note that the relationship was more than "corrective" (in the sense of providing parental support that she had not had). When the timing was right—always gently, sometimes firmly—the worker prodded her to reflect on distortions, contradictions, and oscillations; repeated discussions of current realities and of her feelings and behavior helped to strengthen ego functions of perception, judgment, and impulse control. Previously dissociated feeling states became better integrated as the balance between aggressive and libidinous drives was achieved. When she attained success in one area of life, her increased self-esteem served to help her make further gains. Based on the worker's diagnosis, little attempt was made to explore directly early life experiences that had contributed to this client's difficulties; many of these had occurred before there could be any memory of them. But treatment that worked with the residuals, later memories, and current issues—in the context of a positive relationship—resulted in significant personality change and improved functioning for Mrs. Zimmer.

In conclusion, we add that it was fortunate that Mrs. Zimmer was referred to an agency that had the flexibility to accommodate long-term, often twice-a-week therapy. We believe that efforts to abbreviate treatment would probably have failed, might have been experienced by Mrs. Zimmer as rejection, and perhaps would have discouraged her from seeking other therapy.

The four cases presented in this chapter illustrate clinical social work practice approached from the psychosocial point of view. In the chapters to follow, the theory and dynamics of the treatment process will be discussed in further detail.

## NOTES

1.  See Robert J. Havinghurst, "Social and Psychological Needs of the Aging," *The Annals,* 279 (January 1952), 11–17; Margaret Milloy, "Casework with the Older Person in the Family," *Social Casework,* 45 (October 1964), 450–456; E. Palmore, ed., *Normal Aging* and *Normal Aging II* (Durham, N.C.: Duke University Press, 1970, 1974); Charlotte Towle, *Common Human Needs,* rev. ed. (New York: National Association of Social Workers, 1957), 68–72; and the entire issue of *Journal of Social Welfare,* 5 (Spring 1978), in which several articles discuss various aspects of the aging process and problems encountered by the aging.

2.  See Peter Blos, *The Adolescent Passage* (New York: International Universities Press, 1979); Gerald Caplan and Serge Lebovici, eds., *Adolescence: Psychosocial Perspectives* (New York: Basic Books, 1969), for an excellent compilation of papers; and Group for the Advancement of Psychiatry, *Normal Adolescence,* 68 (New York: GAP, February, 1968).

3.  Mrs. Zimmer's clinical condition was diagnosed as "borderline personality organization" by the worker who treated her. For readings on this phenomenon, including theoretical discussions of faulty ego development and implications for practice, see the following writers who share some common views but also have definite differences in emphasis: Gertrude and Rubin Blanck, *Ego Psychology II* (New York: Columbia University Press, 1979); Janet Bintzler, "Diagnosis and Treatment of Borderline Personality Organization," *Clinical Social Work Journal,* 6 (Summer 1978), 100–107;

Otto Kernberg, *Borderline Conditions and Pathological Narcissism* (New York: Aronson, 1975); Otto Kernberg, "The Structural Diagnosis of Borderline Personality Disorganization," in Peter Hartocollis, ed., *Borderline Personality Disorders* (New York: International Universities Press, 1977), pp. 87–121; Heinz Kohut, *The Restoration of the Self* (New York: International Universities Press, 1977); and James F. Masterson, *Psychology of the Borderline Adult* (New York: Brunner/Mazel, 1976).

4. The importance of careful and sensitive handling of the termination of treatment is discussed in Evelyn Fox, Marion Nelson, and William Bolman, "The Termination Process: A Neglected Dimension in Social Work," *Social Work,* 14 (October 1969), 53–63; and Hilliard L. Levinson, "Termination of Psychotherapy: Some Salient Issues," *Social Casework,* 58 (October 1977), 480–489.

# CHAPTER 4

# Classifications of Casework Treatment

Logic might dictate that we move into detailed discussion of the casework process by way of chapters first on psychosocial study, then on diagnosis and treatment planning, and finally on treatment procedures. But in order to understand what information we should seek in the psychosocial study and what type of diagnosis will be useful in treatment planning, we first need further understanding of the nature of treatment itself as it has evolved in psychosocial casework.

Treatment of whatever persuasion is a goal-directed process. Different means are used by various approaches to bring about an intended effect. There are many ways of classifying these means. We have found it useful to base classification on the dynamics a treatment step is intended to bring into play.

Suppose our client is a widow who is afraid of an operation, partly because she is too sick to work out plans for the care of her children during her absence from home, partly because she is going to a strange doctor and is uncertain about the outcome of the operation, and partly because unconsciously she fears punishment for her hostile attitudes toward her mother, who had a similar illness and became a permanent cripple following an operation that the client erroneously assumes was similar to the one she is about to undergo. Many different dynamics can be employed to help this woman reduce her anxiety.

One alternative, among others, is the environmental one of providing for the care of the children during her absence. This can have a double effect: it will relieve her of that part of her anxiety caused by a realistic concern for the welfare of her children; and it will demonstrate to her that others care for her welfare and are ready to come to her assistance when she is weak and unable to manage her own affairs. We know that in serious illness regression may lead to a state of intense dependence. It is extremely important at such a time for the patient to feel that someone with strength will take care of her. The way in which plans for the children are made will also be of importance. If relatives or friends toward whom the patient has warm feelings can care for them, so much the better. If agency care must be sought, the degree of relief from anxiety felt by the patient will vary with the amount of confidence she has in the good will and competence of the caseworker who makes this arrangement.

A second possible mode of help consists of encouraging her to express her fears about the operation, showing understanding of her anxiety, indicating that it is a natural reaction, not a sign of childishness on her part. Not infrequently, it is possible to reassure a patient that the doctors are interested in her and are skillful. If the operation is not a dangerous one, this reality can also be used to allay fears *once they have been adequately expressed.*

A third way of reducing the anxiety would be to help the patient understand more fully the facts about the operation itself. Arrangements could be made for her to talk in detail with the doctor. Subsequently, she might again go over the facts with the caseworker, clarifying her understanding of what the doctor had told her.

If needed, client and worker can turn to a fourth alternative, that of the client's seeking to gain understanding of the relationship between her hostility to her mother, her mother's illness, and the possibility that her current fears about her own illness are related in part to her guilt about these hostilities. Naturally, the use of this alternative is dependent upon the client's willingness to explore her feelings and her ability to make connections between these and current medical fears.

These procedures all have a common aim—to reduce anxiety—but the dynamics involved in each are different. In one instance, some of the stimuli for the anxiety are removed by environmental measures; in another, reassurance is given, a procedure that depends for its effectiveness upon the client's confidence in the worker; in the third, the patient is encouraged to understand her situation more realistically; and in the fourth, she is helped to understand prior emotions involving interpersonal relationships and their consequences as these affect her current reactions.

It was in an effort to seek a more orderly understanding of diagnostic–differential casework that Hollis developed the classification of treatment procedures used in the first edition of this book. As noted in Chapter 1, the approach, now called psychosocial casework, developed from the diagnostic–differential framework with some modifications and many additions and expansions of the original approach as new knowledge came into the field.

Before discussing this typology, we should like to review the general development of classifications in diagnostic–differential theory. Changes in classification reflect growth of knowledge. Each new typology was built upon former ones and attempted to define the scope of casework treatment, as well as to describe the procedures in use at different periods.

## CLASSIFICATIONS REFLECTING GROWTH

There have been a number of classifications of casework treatment methods. Mary Richmond, as noted earlier, made only the very simple distinction in 1922 between "direct" and "indirect" treatment. By the former, she meant those processes that take place directly between the client and the worker—the "influence of mind upon mind"—and by the latter, changes the worker brings about in the client's human and physical environment.[1]

Despite the many changes that took place in casework in the thirties, it was not until 1947 that new classifications began to appear, reflecting the preceding years of growth in understanding of what Mary Richmond had called "direct treatment." By then, psychoanalytic concepts had not only been found useful in understanding psychological and emotional elements in personal problems, but had also contributed to interviewing processes. It was clear, of course, that caseworkers were not conducting psychoanalyses, and that there was a large part of casework only tangentially touched by psychoanalysis. However, since certain techniques had been borrowed from psychoanalytic methodology, it was important to define in what specific ways the two treatment methods did or did not overlap. The question of the extent to which caseworkers dealt with the unconscious was of special concern. A paper in 1947 by Grete Bibring,[2] a psychoanalyst who had worked closely with caseworkers for a number of years in Boston, mentioned five groups of technical procedures used by all types of therapists, including caseworkers. These were suggestion, emotional relief, immediate influence (or manipulation), clarification, and interpretation. It was her impression that interpretation was used sparingly in casework, and chiefly in dealing with preconscious rather than unconscious material, but she did not altogether rule out interpretation of unconscious material. Her major distinction was between interpretation, which she characterized as having as its goal insight development (a principal objective of psychoanalysis), and the other techniques, for which insight development was not a goal.

Bribring's classification represented a distinct elaboration of the earlier direct treatment method and reflected the influence of psychoanalysis in enriching the caseworker's understanding of the ways in which psychological forces can be used in treatment. Suggestion, emotional relief, and manipulation, though not recognized in these terms, were undoubtedly a part of early casework methodology, as was also a technique not specifically designated by Bibring—that of helping the client to reason his way through to a favorable solution of his problems. Clarification, in the sense of helping the client to separate objective reality from distortions of the external world, was, like insight development, the result of the incorporation of analytic concepts, and played little part in casework until the 1930s and 1940s.

Also in 1947, Hollis suggested another classification of treatment methods.[3] These were environmental modification (corresponding to the earlier indirect method) and psychological support, clarification, and insight development (representing subdivisions of direct treatment). This classification and Bibring's were similar in that both attempted to group techniques according to the psychological dynamics by which they operated. Bibring's suggestion, emotional relief, and manipulation corresponded to different aspects of the Hollis psychological support; insight development was similar in the two classifications. But Hollis was using the word "clarification" in a different sense than did Bibring, covering by that term the general encouragement of a reasoning approach to problems and to certain aspects of the separation of objective reality from distortions of external events. It was encouraging that there was so much basic similarity between the thinking of representatives of two different professions whose pertinent experience had been in completely different geographical locations—Cleveland and Boston.

## The Austin Classification

In this same period, Lucille Austin also proposed her widely used classification.[4] She specified two main divisions: social therapy and psychotherapy, dividing the latter into (1) supportive therapy, having the aim of preventing further breakdown, (2) insight therapy, having the aim of achieving a change in the ego and increasing its ability to deal with difficulties, and (3) experiential therapy, seen as intermediate in its goals between the first two. Social therapy involved environmental change, psychological support, and a rational approach to the solution of reality problems. Turning to the three forms of psychotherapy, supportive therapy relied heavily on psychological support and might often also include the techniques used in social therapy. In *insight* therapy, emphasis was placed on the emotional experience in the transference situation, interpretive techniques concerning feelings and unconscious motivations, and relevant childhood memories. In *experiential therapy*, the central focus was on the development and use of the relationship as a corrective emotional experience. In varying degrees, techniques used in the other two types of psychotherapy could be drawn upon, except that genetic interpretations concerning the relationship between developmental experiences and current behavior would not be emphasized.

Austin recognized that, although her supportive treatment was designed primarily to maintain present strengths, psychological improvement often occurred, with the ego gaining strength to handle immediate situations, and the experience of more adequate functioning becoming itself a growth process. Similarly, in the experiential form of treatment, Austin wrote that "in certain cases maturation already under way is carried through to completion." She further maintained that the objectives of experiential treatment "are mainly loosening restrictive ties to figures in the past, redirecting emotional energies, and promoting growth through increased satisfactions in living."[5]

All three writers helped to clarify what caseworkers were doing in the forties and fifties. All established tentative boundaries between casework and psychoanalysis, holding that casework does not reach deeply unconscious material but may deal with content that, though not conscious, is relatively accessible. They also spelled out specific techniques distinguishing casework from psychoanalysis. These will be discussed further in Chapter 13. Understanding of these issues set in motion a process of study to examine more closely the dynamics of the casework process.

## The Issue of Support Versus Clarification

In 1953, a committee of the Family Service Association of America studied some of these issues and published a report based in part on reading a series of cases from family service agencies.[6] This report proposed a simple classification of casework into two types based on the *aim* of the treatment. It designated type A, or "supportive casework," as "treatment aimed at maintaining adaptive patterns," and type B, or "clarification," as "treatment aimed at modification of adaptive patterns." The first type of treatment was described as resting upon the use of such techniques as Bibring's "manipulation of the environment, reassurance, persuasion, direct advice and guidance, suggestion, logical discussion, exercise of professional authority and immediate influence."[7] The second was characterized mainly by its use of the technique of clarification (in the Bibring sense) in addition to the other techniques. The committee also reported that it had decided not to include a category corresponding to the insight development or insight therapy included in preceding classifications, because it found that this type of treatment was used in very few agencies.

Five years later, in 1958, this classification was further developed by a committee of the Community Service Society of New York in a document entitled *Method and Process in Social Casework*,[8] which described in more detail the techniques used in the "supportive treatment method" and the "modifying treatment methods," limiting the latter to modification of "selected ego mechanisms of defense."[9]

These two reports played an important part in illuminating several issues concerning casework treatment. Their specificity was a distinct improvement over earlier efforts. Three issues were identified and spelled out in a way that led to further study: (1) To what extent is "insight therapy" undertaken by caseworkers? (2) Are changes in adaptive patterns dependent upon the use of clarification as a predominant treatment technique? (3) Is casework correctly conceptualized as a dichotomous process having two distinct treatment modes, one in which clarification is the predominant technique and one in which this technique is either absent or plays a minor role?

## PERSONALITY CHANGES AND TREATMENT TECHNIQUES

The first of these issues to be examined systematically was that of the relationship between changes in adaptive patterns and treatment method. Sidney Berkowitz,[10] in a paper given at the National Conference of Social Work in the spring of 1955, challenged the FSAA committee findings, taking the position that clarification is not the only way in which adaptive patterns can be modified. He maintained that, in his experience, such patterns could also be changed through a process of ego influence with little or no reference to—or clarification of—the relation of the past to the present.

This was an important question, because there was a tendency for caseworkers to put a sort of "halo" around "clarification" and to belittle all other work as "just" supportive. Berkowitz and many other practitioners believed the type of casework the committee named supportive to be of great value and not incapable of bringing changes in adaptive patterns. They feared that "nonclarifying" work was in danger of being used in a very oversimplified way because of this downgrading. Thus, much help that could be given without clarification would be lost.

To understand this question, we need to consider what is meant by a change in adaptive patterns.

A change in adaptive patterns is one that is internalized, built into the personality. It results in an improvement in functioning that cannot be fully accounted for by improved circumstances, the passing of a crisis, or the influence of the worker during the period of treatment; rather, it constitutes a change in the client's way of functioning that will enable him or her to respond differently even when the external situation has not changed and when the worker is not part of the client's current life. The individual will have learned to act differently and will respond to the same or similar life events more appropriately than he or she did before treatment.

Improvement in functioning without a change in adaptive patterns might be said to occur in situations such as the following. A man has been quarreling with his wife because of anxiety about his business. In discussions with the worker, he comes to understand the cause of his irritability, transfers to another position in which he is under less pressure, and subsequently is more even tempered at home. A widow, depressed because of the loss of her husband, is unable to care adequately for her children. She is helped during this period of grief, and as the grief subsides, is able to function normally again in relation to the children. A construction worker loses a leg in an accident and is told he will no longer be able to continue in his line of work. He loses interest in life, does not try to obtain a prosthesis, and retreats to dependent, whining, childlike behavior, to the despair of his formerly dependent wife. After a good deal of skillful work, including some development of understanding of his current responses, he regains his former stability and finds a new work adjustment. In none of these cases have "new adaptive patterns" necessarily been established.

It was generally agreed that such improvements in *functioning* often occurred in response to supportive treatment methods and constituted a very important type of recovery from a period of strain or disaster that might otherwise result in permanent impairment of functioning. But could the other type of improved functioning, that which does rest upon modification of *habitual patterns* of behavior, be brought about without treatment in which clarification in the Bibring sense was a predominant technique?

A paper by Hollis[11] in 1956 described a small preliminary study of this question that supported Berkowitz's point of view. Hollis had asked workers in a family service agency in her community for illustrations simply of good supportive treatment. Ten cases were submitted, but one of these turned out to be a type B case and so could not be used. The nine remaining cases yielded six in which a change in adaptive patterns appeared to have taken place in response to supportive procedures. This, of course, was no indication of the *frequency* with which this ordinarily happens. Workers probably submitted their "best" supportive cases, though they did not know the purpose for which the cases were to be used. What these six cases did show, however, was that it is not at all *impossible* to bring about changes in adaptive patterns in supportive work—the point at issue. A brief description of a few of the cases in which this appeared to be so will illustrate the point.

Mrs. Knight, an exceedingly immature young woman still in her teens, was married to a man old enough to be her father. At first he thoroughly enjoyed her dependence, but soon he became irritated by her inability to manage his home and be an adequate mother to the two children of his former marriage. Mrs. Knight sought help "in growing up" from the caseworker. The approach was one of guidance and support, with reliance on elements in the relationship, on considerable logical discussion, on extensive use of a visiting homemaker and of a nurse who educated the client in matters concerning her own and the children's health. With the ego strengthened by increased knowledge and skill, the maturation that had been arrested when Mrs. Knight was overwhelmed by demands beyond her ability to meet began again to take place, with marked improvement in her functioning as a wife and mother. There was every reason to believe that the improvement in adaptive patterns had been internalized and would be lasting.

Mrs. Landers, the mother of five children, was driven by a strong need to succeed, which showed itself in the form of perfectionistic demands upon the children and excessive self-criticism when difficulties arose in her own relationship with them. The worker became the "good mother" and on the basis of this relationship was able to help Mrs. Landers to handle the children more realistically and to reduce the severity of the demands of her superego upon the children and upon herself. Mrs. Landers became able to set up more lenient goals for her family and to see at a number of points that she was overreacting in holding herself so completely responsible for their behavior. Once again, a nurse was used for discussion of health problems; better housing plans were worked out; camp opportunities were provided for the children. Mrs. Landers learned new ways of handling her children and incorporated less demanding standards for herself and her family.

Mr. Ingersol, a married man of thirty-five, was repeatedly in trouble because of impulsive behavior at work and with his wife. Periodic drinking complicated the problem. The aim of treatment was to help him control his impulsiveness and his drinking. For a long time, Mr. Ingersol denied that his drinking was a problem and that his own behavior contributed to his quarrels with his wife. After treatment had advanced to a point where Mr. Ingersol trusted the caseworker, it was possible again and again to get him to go over the details of what happened between himself and his wife when he had been drinking excessively, to recall exactly how many drinks he had had and exactly what he did and said during the course of an evening. Gradually, he came to see that after a certain number of drinks he said things he would not otherwise have said, and that his behavior on such occasions precipitated certain responses from his wife that she would not otherwise have given. When he became able to admit to himself that his drinking really did cause trouble, he began to make a real effort to control it and succeeded in reducing it to a marked extent. A pattern of greater ego control was established, not by bringing suppressed material to consciousness or by seeking causative understanding of his drinking beyond current provocations, but by the effect of close examination of present realities.

Another factor at work in Mr. Ingersol's progress was the client–worker relationship itself. Mr. Ingersol was a dependent person who had greatly admired his father. He developed similar feelings toward his caseworker, whom he wanted to please as he had wanted to please his father. The worker did not interpret the transference but instead made use of it, giving Mr. Ingersol credit and appreciation when he showed understanding of the effects of his behavior and when he tried to modify it. His efforts to change were further fortified by the satisfaction he secured during periods of better relationship with his wife.

Logical discussion, advice, approval, and encouragement were all used in the effort to enable him to improve the quality and strength of his ego controls. At several points in this case clarification was very briefly used, but it was by no means the predominant technique. Considerable improvement in adaptive patterns seems to have occurred in this case, although one could not be wholly optimistic about the permanence of the new patterns.

In each of these cases, it appeared that changes in adaptive patterns occurred in response to techniques defined as "supportive." This gave further substance to the belief that the response to treatment was more fluid than the FSAA dichotomizing hypothesis maintained.

## Diverse Approaches to Changes in Personality

Why are we so concerned about this question? Because a change in adaptive patterns makes it more possible that whatever improvement in functioning has occurred will continue not only in the immediate circumstances but in other vicissitudes which the individual may meet. A better method of functioning will have been learned and become part of the personality. What, then, are some of the ways in which changes in adaptive patterns can be achieved?

First, there is the basic personality change, often called "structural change" in psychoanalytic terminology. This includes and goes beyond changes in adaptive patterns. It occurs when some of the decisive formative experiences of life are reached and relived in treatment and undergo reevaluation. This is a psychoanalytic process involving the bringing to consciousness and understanding of material that was previously unconscious or repressed, such as memories, thoughts, or fantasies representing infantile destructive and sexual impulses and wishes, and reactions and distortions growing out of very early life experiences. Many of the early feelings are revived in the transference in which the patient temporarily regresses to childhood. Structural change can be brought about by psychoanalysis and sometimes by less extensive psychotherapy carried on by therapists trained in psychoanalysis.

It was earlier pointed out, however, that irrational and inappropriate responses are also often based on *preconscious* influences, on events that at most have been *suppressed* rather than repressed and, hence, can be brought to the surface of the mind by the type of interviewing techniques used in casework. Indeed, many early influences are not even suppressed. Sometimes they are well remembered, but the client needs to recognize the connection between these childhood experiences and his or her current responses in order to see their irrationality. Experiences of adolescence and early adulthood may also be of great importance. The ego defenses, in particular, often operate on a preconscious level. Not infrequently, a person can become aware of and will modify defense patterns on seeing their irrationality or their harmfulness without needing to look back to factors that influenced the development of such patterns. That is, the dynamic may be understood independently of origins. Recognizing the influence of conscious and preconscious early life experiences and becoming aware of defenses are both forms of *clarification* in the FSAA use of the term and constitute a second way in which adaptational patterns can be modified.

A third way of bringing about changes in adaptive patterns consists of helping the individual to deal more effectively with current life relationships and problems. Better understanding of other people, thoughtfulness about the effects of one's ways of relating to others, fuller awareness of one's feelings and actions and of the effect of others on oneself, will lead first to better functioning in the immediate current life, or at least a sector of current life. As individual incidents pile up, the adaptive patterns themselves may be modified, even though they have not been discussed as such. This form of change parallels natural life experience. Without the help of any type of therapy, the relatively healthy individual repeatedly learns from experiences as he or she seeks to develop more effective ways of mastering the vicissitudes of life. A similar process occurs in treatment, but the individual's efforts need to be augmented by professional help.

A fourth way in which change occurs in adaptive patterns is in the context of a strong positive relationship to another person who is accorded a leadership or pattern-setting role in some area of living. In such a relationship, the individual either identifies with and imitates the worker, or subscribes to the worker's values, or accepts his or her assessment, suggestions, and advice. The "corrective relationship" described by Austin as an important aspect of "experiential" treatment can bring change in this fourth way. Again, treatment parallels a process common in natural life experience.

A fifth way in which adaptive patterns can change is in response to more favorable life experiences. As noted earlier, these are relatively easy to arrange for children. Adults can often be helped to make such changes for themselves—a new marriage, a better or more suitable job, completion of educational plans, and so on. Again, similar processes occur in natural life.

A sixth way in which personality change comes about is through the positive reinforcement that results from more effective and satisfying functioning. Sometimes this reinforcement is in the form of verbal or nonverbal communications from the worker. More often, it arises in subsequent life experiences. When temporary change in functioning is rewarded by positive experiences in interpersonal relationships or in other important areas of functioning such as work, a powerful incentive is given to continue the new ways until they constitute a new adaptive pattern. This too commonly occurs in life.

Several of these ways of bringing about change usually take place together in work with one individual or family. It appears that treatment is actually a blend of many influences that in combination are designed to bring about more effective and satisfying functioning. In the opinions of many experienced practitioners, casework is not best conceptualized as a dichotomous process leading to two quite different outcomes. Rather, a more fluid model must be sought that would readily permit us to think in terms of a blend of procedures flexibly adapted to the complex set of needs brought by individuals and families.

## DEVELOPING A TYPOLOGY

What sort of classification would be useful in relation to this revised understanding of the casework process? In 1958, Hollis began the process of devising a classification of treatment procedures in which the means by which treatment is carried out would be separated from treatment goals. This would permit workers and researchers to examine what procedures were actually used when changes occurred. It might also result in clearer thinking about the essential nature—the dynamics —of treatment procedures.

When work on such a classification, or typology, was begun, it was soon discovered that it is no simple matter to formulate a logical and useful classification of casework treatment, especially if this formulation was to be rich enough in its dimensions to make conceptually worthwhile distinctions, and yet not so elaborate as to be impractical.

It was important also to think about what purpose would be served by a treatment classification. Would it merely enable us to describe casework in a more orderly way in writing and teaching? This is one important use of classification; the very need for such clarity constitutes a strong impetus toward developing one. Would it provide agencies with a systematic way of grouping cases for reports of accountability, work distribution, evaluation, and the like?

Yes, but there was a more fundamental purpose—that of studying casework itself. Many questions needed to be answered in order to use casework effectively. For what configuration of personality tendencies and problems and what sorts of social problems is a particular treatment method or technique appropriate? What other factors—such as the client's wishes and responses, time available, worker skill, agency function, and so on—influence treatment choices? What is the result of using this or that technique under such and such circumstances? What alternative means are available to the end that client and worker have in mind? Under what circumstances is one means more likely to serve the purpose than another?

Before answers could be found to these questions, the numerous variables involved would have to be separated. In the end, ways would have to be found to identify and classify not only treatment procedures but also personality characteristics, types of problems and situational factors, outcomes, and relationships among these variables. Treatment procedures would be a good starting point.

It was particularly important that the *aim* of treatment and the *methods used* be examined as separate variables. Only by so doing could we hope to test the relationship of one to the other and examine the conditions under which specific techniques can lead to specific results.

A small preliminary study undertaken in 1958 was fruitful in pointing up the problems involved in classification and in providing material for experimentation with a series of classifications, each successively introducing modifications designed to fit the interview material more exactly and completely.

This was followed in 1959 by a study of 25 cases of not less than 12 interviews each, drawn from six agencies representing family service agencies, child guidance clinics, and psychiatric clinics in three different communities (Boston, Hartford, and New York). Interviews were examined line by line in an effort to characterize each recorded happening in each interview. Various groupings of techniques were tried in an effort to arrive at meaningful and essential distinctions between different processes. The tackling of each new case became a testing of the system worked out on previous cases and frequently involved modifications in the system to accommodate the new material. Further changes were made in the typology during this study, and as a result of two subsequent testings of the classifications by students at the Smith College School of Social Work in 1960 (15 interviews)[12] and at the New

York School of Social Work (now Columbia University) in 1961 (50 interviews).[13] Later, Hollis and her colleagues[14] analyzed over 100 interviews from four family service agencies in three cities in different parts of the country (Cincinnati, Cleveland, Philadelphia). A reliability study was completed and some hypotheses tested (see Chapter 14).

Each agency participating in the 1959 study had been asked to submit examples both of supportive treatment and of treatment in which the technique of clarification was used, including an example of a case representing the greatest depth in treatment carried on in the agency. It was soon discovered that workers differed enormously in their interpretation of this request. Cases of a type considered clarification by one worker would actually involve less use of the technique of clarification than cases classified as supportive by another worker. Troublesome as this confusion was, it led to the very useful observation that there seemed to be *no sharp dividing line* between supportive and clarification cases. The subsequent study of 100 cases confirmed the fact that casework can best be described as a continuum, beginning with cases in which no clarification whatsoever was used, going on to those in which snatches of it were used from time to time, proceeding to others where it played a considerable part in treatment. Furthermore, it also became clear that in most cases treatment moved through phases in which the balance between supportive work and clarification was constantly changing.

The typology that finally emerged dealt primarily with the interviewing process. It is essentially a classification of the communications that take place between client and worker, or collateral and worker. The typology has demonstrated its value in a number of research projects. Some of these will be described in Chapter 14. The typology has been particularly useful as a tool for clarifying what goes on in psychosocial casework and it will provide a framework for the discussion of treatment in this book. Obviously, it is not in any way the empirical base upon which psychosocial casework rests. Rather, it is a tool for studying this approach and for describing it. It allows us to follow the flow of each interview and can be used either in informal analysis or in more rigorous research. As had been hoped, it makes possible examination of the *dynamics* of treatment, and exploration of such questions as: In what way does a given procedure affect a client? What are the relationships of client personality factors to choice of treatment method? What is the relationship between problem and treatment steps? What factors in the client's response in a particular interview indicate the advisability of using a particular procedure? What procedures in early interviews are most likely to encourage the client to remain in treatment? And so on. As was pointed out earlier in illustration of the different ways in which anxiety can be reduced, a given result can be achieved by a variety of procedures, ranging from direct reassurance to full understanding of the intrapsychic cause of the anxiety. Under different circumstances and with different individuals, one approach will be more effective than another. This question of which means is most useful under different conditions is central to any study seeking to understand and improve casework methodology, and is therefore a particularly useful central dimension for a classification of casework.

The classification also distinguishes sharply between the means employed and its actual effect. For example, the caseworker's expression of interest in and appreciation of a client's situation or feelings is a means generally thought to promote perception of the worker as someone who is interested and who is capable of understanding him or her. This strengthens the feeling that here is someone who will help or take care of the client. By this means, it is hoped, anxiety will be lessened and, consequently, functioning will be improved. A paranoid person, however, may interpret this same response on the caseworker's part as a kind of magic mind reading, an effort to bring the person under some obscure influence, and the technique will not have the desired effect. Nevertheless, in the typology proposed, if a worker, however unwisely, used this technique it would be classified as a "sustaining procedure," the term used for this type of *potentially* reassuring technique. Such a separation of the means employed from the outcome puts us in a position to examine the actual effect of a treatment step, to study the circumstances under which it does not have the desired effect, and thereafter to use it more appropriately; or, if by research we find it rarely has the effect we theoretically thought it should have, we are in a position to correct our theory.

A classification of this sort is not static: it can be modified as research and study constantly correct our theories and can also lend itself well to expansion as new techniques are developed.

## THE MAIN DIVISIONS OF THE CLASSIFICATION

With these preliminaries, we may proceed to a brief description of the classification. Detailed discussion of the specific technical procedures included under the main divisions of the classification will be found in immediately following chapters. The major dimensions of the classification will be presented in this chapter, together with specific illustrations used only to clarify the meaning of the main categories; thus, we will be able to discuss certain general theoretical questions before going extensively into details of procedures.

# Client–Worker Communications

For the moment, let us set aside the question of treatment through the environment—Richmond's indirect treatment—and deal only with those procedures that take place directly between worker and client—Richmond's direct treatment. When working directly with clients—whether singly or in pairs, or in family group treatment—it was found that the caseworkers' techniques can be placed in six major groupings. The first two of these derive their force or influence from the relationship that exists between client and worker, from the way in which the client regards the worker and the degree of influence the client accords the worker or permits in his or her life. The third draws its strength from ventilation, the description of stressful events and the expression of feelings that are causing distress. The fourth, fifth, and sixth groups rest primarily upon various kinds of reflective considerations promoted within the client.

The first group of procedures dealing with *sustainment* include such activities on the worker's part as demonstration of interest, desire to help, understanding, expressions of confidence in the client's abilities or competence, and reassurance concerning matters about which the client has anxiety and guilt.

Sustaining techniques are used in varying degrees in all cases. Much of this type of communication takes place through nonverbal or paraverbal means—nods, smiles, an attentive posture, murmurings. In the early interviews, no matter what else is done, the worker usually tries, by giving the client a sympathetic hearing and by other sustaining techniques, to lessen anxiety and give the client the feeling that he or she is in a place where help will be forthcoming. Subsequently, cases vary in the extent to which sustaining techniques are needed, with fluctuations from time to time in the same case. Remarks such as "You are looking well today." or "I can understand how difficult that must have been" or "Such feelings are natural" are illustrative.

The second group of procedures dealing with *direct influence* include a range of techniques among which suggestion and advice are most frequently used. They involve in one form or another the expression of the worker's opinion about the kind of action a client should take —with such comments as "it might be better to do so-and-so," or "I think you ought to———," or "No, I don't think that will work; you had better——," and so on.

Procedures of direct influence are far less universally used than sustaining techniques, but, particularly in their more subtle forms, constitute a recognized part of casework treatment. One usually finds that where these procedures are being extensively used in the psychosocial approach there is also emphasis upon sustainment. Their effectiveness depends to a high degree upon the existence of a strong positive relationship between client and worker, which in turn is promoted by sustaining procedures.

The third group deals with *exploration, description,* and *ventilation*. It consists of communications designed to draw out descriptive and explanatory material from the client and to encourage the pouring out of pent-up feelings and description of emotionally charged events. This material, first of all, helps the worker to understand the person and his or her problems. In addition, considerable relief from tension is often felt by the client as a result of this outpouring. Quite frequently, this relief obtained by verbalization is supported by sustaining procedures that further reduce the accompanying anxiety or guilt. At other times, the content of the ventilating process is picked up for the purpose of promoting reflective consideration of it: "Yes, tell me more about it," or "Yes, yes—go on," or "What about your job? How do things go there?"

The fourth grouping consists of communications designed to encourage reflective consideration of the person–situation configuration. It is designated *person–situation–reflection* and refers to reflection upon current and relatively recent events, exclusive of early life material. This broad category can be subdivided according to another dimension, that of the type of subject toward understanding of which the communication is directed. The areas of understanding may be: (1) perception or understanding of others, of one's own health, or of any aspect of the outside world; (2) understanding of one's own behavior in terms of its actual or potential outcome or its effect on others or on the self; (3) awareness of the nature of one's own behavior; (4) awareness of causative aspects of one's own behavior when these lie in the interactions between the person and others; (5) evaluation of some aspect of the client's own behavior, in the sense of self-image, concepts of right and wrong, principles, values, or preferences; (6) awareness and understanding feelings about the worker and the treatment process. Note that in the first of these subdivisions attention is directed outward, in the second it is partly outward and partly inward, and in the last four it is directed inward to some aspect of the person's own feelings, thoughts, or actions—that is, toward a form of self-understanding that depends entirely upon reflection about specific interactions and reactions in the person–situation gestalt. To illustrate: (1) "Can you think of anything else that might be making your wife so nervous lately?" (2) "When you say things like that, how does it work? What happens?" (3) "You sound as though you were very angry." (4) "What actually happened that could have made you so angry—what do you think it was?"

(5) "Somehow you sound as though you feel very uncomfortable about doing that." (6) "Do you still think I am siding with John?"

It is impossible to imagine a case in which some of these types of person–situation reflection would not be used. The type of problem brought by the client is one of the important determinants of where the emphasis will be. The more realistic and external the problem, the greater the likelihood that interviews will emphasize procedures from the first two subdivisions; the greater the subjective involvement in the problem, the more likely it is that they will draw upon the third, fourth, and fifth subdivisions. These procedures of person–situation reflection are combined in varying degrees with sustaining techniques and may be accompanied to some degree also by direct influence. They are techniques that are also always an important part of the treatment process when other types of reflective consideration are in action.

The fifth main treatment category also relies upon reflective discussion. It consists of procedures for encouraging the client to think about the psychological patterns involved in his or her behavior and the dynamics of these patterns and tendencies. This category can be referred to as *pattern-dynamic reflection.* The client is helped to reflect upon some of the internal reasons for responses and actions, and encouraged to look at the dynamics of his or her behavior by studying the relationship between one aspect of this behavior and another. The client goes beyond thinking about a specific distortion of reality or inappropriate reaction toward consideration of the operations of the intrapsychic component itself: "I wonder whether you don't often think other people dislike you when underneath you are critical of them"; "Have you noticed how often that happens? You take it out on Mary when you're really mad at your wife."

The sixth treatment category, also a type of reflective discussion, includes procedures for encouraging the client to think about the development of his or her psychological patterns or tendencies—again, a subjective area. This is designated *developmental reflection.* Here, the client is helped to deal with early life experiences that are important because, although they occurred in the past, they have been internalized to such a degree that they are now part of his or her responses to current situations. As in pattern-dynamic reflection, treatment revolves around consideration of the relationship of one facet of behavior, one reaction, to another; this time, however, in historical terms: "You always talk about how wonderful your father was . . . sort of a superman. I should think that would be pretty hard to live up to. . . . How was it?", and later, "Maybe that has something to do with your underrating yourself now."

## Environmental Treatment

In the years following the Great Depression of the thirties until the development of poverty programs in the sixties, social work did not give the same quality of attention to indirect as to direct work. This neglect tended to downgrade environmental treatment in the worker's mind, as though it were something one learned to do with one's left hand, something unworthy of serious analysis. Furthermore, we tended to think of direct work as psychological and indirect as nonpsychological, or "social." This is, of course, a false assumption. Environmental work also takes place with people and through psychological means. We cannot physically make a landlord, teacher, or anyone else—even the representative of a public agency—do something for the benefit of our client. We have to talk with a *person* about it, and in the process we must use psychological procedures of one sort or another. Broadening our view of casework in this way helps us to narrow the distance that seems so often to separate direct from indirect work.

Recognition of the extent to which environmental deficiencies contribute to the woes of individuals and families has in recent years led to increased attention to the importance of environmental or milieu work. One can think in terms of treatment *through* the environment and of modification *of* the environment. The former makes use of resources and opportunities that exist or are potentially available for the benefit of the client in the total situation. The latter deals with modifications that are needed in a situation in order to lessen pressures or increase opportunities and gratifications. A clear example of treatment through the environment would be a worker's enlisting the help of a warm friendly relative to provide companionship and practical assistance for a woman experiencing postoperative depression. Work upon the environment is illustrated by a worker's intervening to bring change in a situation where a child is badly placed in a school system or a landlord is failing to make necessary repairs.

The increased attention given environmental work in recent years has suggested additional types of classification not developed in the original typology study. Therefore, we will introduce some new categories rather than confine ourselves to the early classification used in the first edition of this book. One can think of three general ways of looking at and classifying environmental work, each of which has its values and uses. First, it is sometimes useful to organize one's thinking about milieu work in terms of the *type of resource* one is trying to employ. A primary source of such help is the employing social agency itself. One thinks immediately of the child-placing agency where the workers are themselves responsible for making resources of the agency available, such as foster homes and adoptive homes. A second type closely related to the first is the employing agency or institution in which social work is not the sponsoring profession, but one of several services offered—for example, a hospital with a social service department. Here the worker is identified in the client's mind with the medical care and is in a good position to influence certain aspects of the medical service but, naturally, not to the same extent as would be true in the agency administered by social workers.

A third type of resource is the social agency of which the worker is *not* a staff member. A fourth type consists of non–social work organizations of which the worker is not a staff member.

Two additional types of environmental resource involve two sets of *individuals* in the milieu: (1) those who have an "instrumental" or task-oriented relationship to the client, such as employers and landlords, and (2) those who have an "expressive" or feeling-oriented relationship, such as relatives, friends, neighbors. Many differences exist in milieu work, depending upon which of these six types of situational contacts is involved. These will be discussed in chapters 8 and 9.

One can also analyze environmental or milieu work from the viewpoint of the *type of communications* used. All milieu work takes place through some form of communication, regardless of whether it is verbal. Indeed, paraverbal and nonverbal communication is often of great importance. The type of classification presented in the preceding section on communications between worker and client is also of value in studying communications between worker and collateral. (*Collateral* is a term commonly used in casework to refer to contacts with individuals other than the client.) Environmental treatment makes use of the first four groups of procedures described for direct work with the client but does not use the fifth and sixth. One does not discuss with any collateral —be it a teacher, doctor, landlord, friend, or relative—the dynamics of his or her attitudes or behavior, or its development. It is only when a relative or sometimes a friend enters treatment himself that this type of reflection would become appropriate. On the other hand, each of the other four types of communication procedure *is* used in environmental work. There are times when the techniques of sustainment are important in building the relationship necessary to involve the collateral constructively—or less destructively—in the client's affairs. One does sometimes use direct influence–suggestion or advice. Exploration, description, and ventilation are of great importance. Indeed, encouragement of ventilation is often the key to a relationship that will permit cooperative work. The fourth group of procedures, person–situation reflection, almost always occurs in collateral work as the worker describes or explains a client and his or her needs. Through such discussion, the worker hopes to modify or enlarge the collateral's understanding of the client and his needs or to work with the collateral in seeking to understand the client and how to help him. These four categories can be very useful in analyzing samples of work with collaterals. Reasons for the success or failure of efforts to help the client through the milieu can often be located by so doing.

Environmental work can also be classified by *type of role*—that is, in terms of the role a worker may be assuming when working with a collateral individual or an agency. First, one may be the *provider* of a resource. This is true when one is the vehicle through which one's own agency's services are given. Second, one may be the *locator* of a resource, as when one seeks and finds a resource that gives promise of meeting the client's need. Third, one's role may be that of *interpreter* of the client's need to a collateral. Fourth, in more difficult situations, one may become a *mediator* for the client with an unresponsive or poorly functioning collateral. Finally, in extreme situations, where an agency is clearly failing to carry its responsibilities or an individual is violating the client's rights, the worker may need to carry out a role characterized by *aggressive intervention.* We are giving increasing recognition to the importance of the two latter roles as we come to realize the extent to which clients do not receive services for which they are eligible—especially public assistance, health care, housing, appropriate educational resources. The term "advocacy" describes activities through which the worker strives to secure for clients services to which they are entitled, but which they are unjustly denied or unable to secure by their own efforts.

In summary, then, this chapter offers a classification of treatment procedures that starts with the Richmond suggestion of separating casework into direct work with the client and indirect work with the environment on his or her behalf, and then goes on to pick up the component parts of more recent classifications, arriving at a new arrangement that uses as its logical foundation the major dynamics employed by clinical social work in its effort to enable the client to move toward his or her goals.

Accordingly, six categories of direct treatment and three types of classification of environmental treatment are delineated. The six categories of client–worker communications are:

A.  Sustainment
B.  Direct influence
C.  Exploration, description, ventilation
D.  Person–situation reflection concerning:
    1.  Others, outside world in general, client's own health
    2.  The effects of own behavior on self and others
    3.  The nature of own behavior
    4.  Causative factors that lie in interactions of self with others or in situational provocation

     5.  Self-evaluation

     6.  The worker and treatment process

E.  Pattern-dynamic reflection (discussion of dynamics of response patterns or tendencies)

F.  Developmental reflection (discussion of developmental aspects of response patterns and tendencies)

The types of environmental procedures can be classified by:

1.  Type of resource
   a.  Worker's own social agency
   b.  A non–social work organization in which worker is employed
   c.  Another social work agency (i.e., not worker's own)
   d.  A non–social work organization that
      (1)  employs social workers but where worker is not employed
      (2)  does not employ social workers at all
   e.  Individuals who are in
      (1)  an instrumental relationship with client
      (2)  an expressive relationship to client

2.  Type of communication (parallel to first four client–worker categories)

3.  Type of role
   a.  Provider of resources
   b.  Locator of resources
   c.  Interpreter of client to milieu person
   d.  Mediator between client and milieu person
   e.  Aggressive intervener between client and milieu person

According to this system, the treatment of any case as a whole is seen as a constantly changing blend of some or all of these treatment procedures. The nature of the blend will vary with the needs of the case and with the nature of the client's personality, his or her problem, and a number of other variables.

In Chapter 14 we will describe research that has been carried on subsequently concerning the first half of this typology, communications between client and worker. Before turning to this research, however, we will discuss in detail the use of the six sets of client–worker procedures and the three types of classification of environmental procedures in psychosocial casework.

### NOTES

1.  Mary E. Richmond, *What Is Social Casework? An Introductory Description* (New York: Russell Sage Foundation, 1922), p. 102. Other references of interest are Virginia P. Robinson, "An Analysis of Processes in the

Records of Family Case Working Agencies," *The Family,* 2 (July 1921), 101–106; and *Social Casework, Generic and Specific: An Outline. A Report of the Milford Conference* (New York: American Association of Social Workers, 1929).

2.  Grete L. Bibring, "Psychiatry and Social Work," *Journal of Social Casework,* 28 (June 1947), 203–211.

3.  Florence Hollis, *Casework in Marital Disharmony* (doctoral dissertation, Bryn Mawr College, 1947); microfilmed (Ann Arbor, Mich.: University Microfilms, 1951). A similar classification is available in "The Techniques of Casework," *Journal of Social Casework,* 30 (June 1949), 235–244.

4.  Lucille N. Austin, "Trends in Differential Treatment in Social Casework," *Journal of Social Casework,* 29 (June 1948), 203–211

5.  Ibid., p. 207. In a later article, "Qualifications for Psychotherapists, Social Caseworkers," *American Journal of Orthopsychiatry,* 26 (1956), 47–57, Austin suggests giving up the term "insight therapy" as an inaccurate designation, since insight is a quality or experience that may result from different procedures.

6.  *Scope and Methods of the Family Service Agency,* Report of the Committee on Methods and Scope (New York: Family Service Association of America, 1953).

7.  Ibid., p. 19.

8.  See *Method and Process in Social Casework, Report of a Staff Committee, Community Service Society of New York* (New York: Family Service Association of America, 1958).

9.  Ibid., p.15.

10.  Sidney Berkowitz was the first writer to raise questions about this issue. See his "Some Specific Techniques of Psychosocial Diagnosis and Treatment in Family Casework," *Social Casework,* 36 (November 1955), 399–406.

11.  Florence Hollis, "Analysis of Two Casework Treatment Approaches," unpublished paper, read at Biennial Meeting of the Family Service Association of America, 1956.

12.  Teresa P. Domanski, Marion M. Johns, and Margaret A. G. Manly, "An Investigation of a Scheme for the Classification of Casework Treatment Activities" (master's thesis, Smith College School for Social Work, Northampton, Mass., 1960).

13.  Jacqueline Betz, Phyllis Hartmann, Arlene Jaroslaw, Sheila Levine, Dena Schein, Gordon Smith, and Barbara Zeiss, "A Study of the Usefulness and Reliability of the Hollis Treatment Classification Scheme: A Continuation of Previous Research in this Area" (master's thesis, Columbia University School of Social Work, New York, 1961).

14.  Florence Hollis, *A Typology of Casework Treatment* (New York: Family Service Association of America, 1968). (A reprint of four articles published in 1967 and 1968 in *Social Casework.*)

# PART TWO

# TREATMENT: AN ANALYSIS OF PROCEDURES

# Chapter 5

# Sustainment, Direct Influence, and Exploration– Description–Ventilation

Having discussed the skeletal outline of a new classification of casework treatment, we shall try in this and the following chapters to put flesh on its bare bones.

Although in the reality of treatment there is a fluid mixture of procedures as interviews proceed, in order to understand their nature one has to pull them apart and examine them separately. From time to time, nevertheless, we will have to shift from discussion of one to another in order to see some of their relationships to each other.

## SUSTAINMENT

Sustaining procedures are those designed to reduce feelings of anxiety, lack of self-esteem, or self-confidence by a direct expression of the worker's confidence or esteem for the client or confidence that some external threat is not as dangerous as it seems, or by conveying interest in the client, acceptance of the person and desire to help. In such work, the relief comes not from self-understanding, but because the worker in whom the client has placed confidence has said in effect that it is not necessary to be so worried. The dynamic is not one of reasoning but of faith, dependent upon the client's confidence in the worker's knowledge and good will.

Sustaining procedures are perhaps the most basic and essential of all psychosocial casework activities, for without them it would be extremely difficult even to explore the nature of the client's difficulties. When a person must seek help from someone else, discomfort and anxiety frequently arise. One is admitting to oneself as well as to others one's inability to handle one's own affairs. There is uncertainty about revealing oneself and one's affairs to another person. Have I come to the right place? What will the caseworker think of me? Will the worker try to get me to do something I don't want to do? Is the worker competent

—truly interested and ready to help? Will the worker be honest and frank? or will this stranger try to "con" me? Even when a person turns to a clinical social worker as a sounding board—to sort out issues related to important life decisions, or to explore avenues for personal growth —some of these questions may occur. Experience has repeatedly shown that clients will be able to give more complete and less distorted information if initial tension is relieved and they feel safe enough to discuss their situations frankly.

In problems that involve interpersonal adjustment, some anxiety typically continues, although with variations in level, throughout the whole period of treatment. Often, the anxiety is itself one of the main problems in the individual's adjustment. Sometimes it is a general sense of incompetence or of inability to carry on life's activities adequately; sometimes it is acute concern about some external situation by which the client is confronted—an operation, a new and challenging job, a set of examinations; it may be a traumatic threat, such as the possible breakup of a marriage; sometimes it is fear of inner impulses, aggressive or sexual; sometimes it is fear of the superego or conscience, expressing itself as a sense of guilt.

In general, it can be said that the greater the client's anxiety or lack of self-confidence either initially or during the course of treatment, the more need there will be for the use of sustaining techniques. Chief among these is interested, sympathetic listening, which conveys to the client the worker's concern for his or her well being. This skill comes naturally to most caseworkers, for it is usually an interest in people and their affairs that has brought them into social work in the first place. Nevertheless, workers do vary in their receptiveness and in their ways of showing it. Receptiveness can be indicated by a subtle set of techniques, often not adequately recorded, for the necessary attitude is often expressed more in the worker's bodily behavior than in words. Facial expression, tone of voice, even a way of sitting as one listens, convey the worker's interest as much as does choice of words. The client is not seeking avid curiosity or oversolicitude on the worker's part, but neither does he or she want cold detachment.[1] An attitude of interest is essential throughout treatment. Special pains must be taken to communicate it to clients whenever their anxiety is high unless, as we shall see later, there is some special therapeutic reason for allowing tension to remain unrelieved.

Another component in the atmosphere between client and worker that can have sustaining value is the sense of mutuality. This is not an authoritative encounter in which a superior relates, however benevolently, to a weak inferior. It is an undertaking in which two people will work together on a problem. They have mutual respect and a mutual interest in improving the client's well-being. Frankness and openness contribute to a feeling of mutuality. Ideally, the worker brings this to the task. Sometimes for the client it cannot exist immediately, but grows as the work proceeds.

Some of the most powerful sustaining procedures are not conveyed by specific words so much as by the worker's total behavior and demeanor. These reveal certain underlying attitudes of the worker toward the client that tend to relieve anxiety and increase the client's self-respect and self-confidence.

## Acceptance

A sustaining procedure that goes beyond expressing the basic attitude of interest, concern, and mutuality is that of conveying acceptance to a client.[2] This is a constant component of all treatment. It will be remembered from Chapter 2 that acceptance refers to the worker's continuing good will toward the client, whether or not the worker approves of the client's opinions and actions. It is particularly important that this positive, understanding attitude be conveyed to a client who is feeling guilty or for some reason hostile or afraid. It is possible for a worker to communicate this attitude even while expressing the opinion that the client was mistaken or even hurtful in his or her action.[3] Acceptance is not an expression of opinion about an act but an expression of good will toward the actor.

## Reassurance

A further step in the sustaining process consists of reassurance about the client's feelings of guilt and anxiety. For instance, a mother who has great difficulty in recognizing feelings of hostility may in the course of treatment become aware of considerable anger toward her child. The worker may seek to reassure her by expressing understanding of the feeling and recognition of the provocation. This technique must be used with delicacy and discrimination. Yielding to the temptation to overuse reassurance in an attempt to build up a relationship or because the worker cannot endure the client's anxiety may merely leave the client with the feeling that the worker does not fully comprehend the reasons for guilt or anxiety, or that the worker is deficient in moral discrimination and therefore is not a person whose judgment matters. Moreover, when the client is ready to explore the reasons for actions, the worker needs to be particularly careful not to give reassurance so readily that the client is made completely comfortable and feels no need to seek understanding of troublesome behavior.

In the illustration in the previous paragraph, for example, it was important to reassure the mother at first because she had unusually high guilt and could acknowledge her feelings only with great reluctance. But after a period of the client's increased ability to talk about her angry feelings toward her child, the worker no longer needed to be reassuring; instead, she agreed that the feelings were unusually strong, and shifting to procedures for developing understanding, suggested seeking out some of the causes of this excessive irritation. Reassurance must be justified by reality, or the client will almost always sense falseness and at best get only temporary comfort. It certainly does no good to tell a man he need not fear an exploratory operation that he already knows may reveal the presence of cancer. Instead, one may want to go into procedures for reflective discussion of his fears in the light of the real situation. This too would lessen anxiety, but by a dynamic different from that of sustainment. If the client is panicky about the operation, the worker's calm consideration with him of its possible outcomes will in itself be a reassuring process. If the client is overreacting, either anticipating certain discovery of cancer when this possibility is not realistically justified, or ignoring the possibility of medical help for the condition, even though it might be found to be malignant, reflective discussion combined with reassurance may clarify the realities of the patient's condition. Bringing to his attention the reality of a possible positive outcome of the operation and of the fact that cure may be possible even if cancer is found, may reduce his anxiety considerably. If the worker already has the confidence of the client, further reassurance of the sustaining type could be offered by an expression of confidence in the doctors, when this is justified, to increase the client's trust in them.

If an individual is afraid of his or her own drives, reassurance that he or she can control them is sometimes helpful, but only if the worker has a factual basis for believing that the client really is able to handle destructive impulses and wants to do so. Usually such reassurance must be accompanied by other procedures, especially forms of reflection where the dynamic is increased knowledge and understanding, thus giving the client reason to believe that greater control can be achieved and is worth achieving. The worker can refer to similar situations in which the client has been able to exercise control. Sometimes the worker goes into the dynamics of behavior, pointing out that an acknowledged impulse can be more easily held in check than a hidden one; or, the client may be helped to consider some of the unrealistic factors contributing to the drive. All these approaches can be strengthened by concurrent sustaining communications that convey the worker's understanding of the drive and acceptance of the individual even when the effort is to dissuade the client from unwise actions.

Obviously, except at the very beginning, sustaining procedures are usually preceded by exploration, description, and ventilation. One can scarcely react in a sustaining way until the client has talked about the matters that are causing feelings of inadequacy or anxiety. It is sometimes true, however, that a person is blocked from talking about these things. Then the worker's verbal and nonverbal indications of interest, concern, and desire to help are of value in overcoming the hesitation.

## Encouragement

A similar process takes place when the worker expresses confidence in a client's abilities, recognizes achievements, shows pleasure in successes, and so on. Encouragement is especially important in work with children, and it is also effective with adults who lack self-confidence and are faced with especially difficult tasks, or who are going through a period of anxiety in which their normal self-confidence is weakened. There is a great difference, of course, between honest appreciation and false praise or flattery. The very fact that people are insecure often makes them extremely sensitive to hollow insincerity, and their confidence in the worker evaporates if they suspect encouraging comments are merely a technique meant to inject courage into their personalities.

When expressing confidence in the client's ability to handle some task or situation, it is important that the worker be realistic about the client's capacity but also sensitive to the client's own perception of his or her abilities. Too ready reassurance, even when realistically justified, causes the client to bottle up anxiety, which may then reappear in full force at the very moment that whatever self-confidence he or she possesses is most needed. If the lack of self-confidence is very great, other procedures in addition to sustainment may be called for. Initial ventilation may be followed by whatever help the client is able to gain from reflective consideration of the situation that is causing so much fear.

One further caution concerning procedures of encouragement: they tend to arouse in the client a feeling that he or she should live up to the worker's expectations. Particularly if there is a possibility that the client will fail, it is important to deal in advance with the anxiety that this may create by making it clear that the worker will not be upset by failure, will continue to feel interest and confidence in the client, and will help the client to deal with disappointment and to find another solution. Other sustaining techniques of conveying acceptance and reassurance often need to accompany encouragement.[4]

## Reaching Out

At times the client's need for sustainment is so strong and distrust or anxiety is so great that something more concrete than words is needed to demonstrate the worker's concern and wish to help. We are most familiar with the use of such techniques with children who, it has long been recognized by practitioners, need concrete evidence of the worker's good will. Small gifts have always been part of the worker's way of building up a positive relationship with children, especially young children. A coke or some cookies often help. It is also customary for the worker to express liking or fondness directly and, with small children, to convey it physically, by holding a child on one's lap, putting an arm protectively around an upset youngster, and the like.

A comparable process is sometimes needed with adults. The early literature on the "hard to reach" emphasized the importance of winning the client's confidence partly by doing concrete things for his or her benefit,[5] such as working out difficult situations with a landlord or with the department of welfare, arranging for camp for the children, taking the children to busy clinics when the mother cannot do this herself, or even providing money for various household needs. These are, of course, important services in their own right, but they also symbolize to the client the worker's interest and concern, and thus act as emotionally sustaining factors.

Bandler[6] found that in order to get certain needful mothers to allow their children to go to nursery school, it was necessary to set up groups for the gratification of the mothers themselves because their own needs were so great. Sometimes when the contact has usually been in the office, the "reaching out" is a visit to the client at home in a period of stress; sometimes it is the arranging of an extra interview, or merely the giving of extra time in a regular interview. Sometimes it is securing information or making a phone call. Whenever the worker's action is designed *especially* to convey to the client concern and a desire to help, it represents this form of sustaining work. Again, it would not be the only procedure employed, but it might either accompany or be a necessary prelude to other techniques. In work with adults, such concrete demonstrations are not universally needed, and in any case they must be used with great discrimination based on sound diagnostic thinking. They should not, of course, grow out of the worker's enjoyment of the client's gratitude or out of the worker's need to encourage a dependent relationship.

## Nonverbal Sustainment

As noted earlier, much sustainment is given by paraverbal and nonverbal means. Workers do not listen to clients impassively. Rather, there is often a series of sympathetic "umms," facial and bodily expressions of complete listening, facial changes and gestures that respond to, and sometimes mirror, what the client is saying or feeling. Brief verbal comments such as "yes," "I know," "I see," and repetition of the last word or two of a client's sentence are all used to show continuing attentiveness. As a matter of fact, the very way in which a client is received in an office can have either a reassuring effect or the opposite. Is the receptionist courteous? Is the waiting room pleasant? How does the worker greet the client? Interaction begins at once.

Workers differ in their nonverbal expressiveness. Through the use of one-way viewing screens, film, and video tapes, we are now in a position to study this illusive quality and its bearing upon successful work.

## Secondary Sustainment

After some experience with the typology in both teaching and research, it became clear that there is both direct and indirect or secondary sustainment. Sustainment, that is, can be a by-product of procedures used primarily for the encouragement of reflection or even of exploration or direction. For instance, it not infrequently happens that we do not understand what a client is trying to say. One may then simply make comments such as "I don't quite know what you mean," and ask for further explanation until the communication is clear. This procedure is primarily a part of the process of exploration or ventilation, but it can also have the side effect of communicating to the client the worker's interest and constant attentiveness. In this sense, it is a secondary type of sustainment. A study by Boatman[7] of 76 tape-recorded interviews with 30 clients found that, in general, 10 percent of the communications that were classified as primarily something other than sustainment nevertheless carried this as a secondary probable effect.

It has been noted, in studying interviews, that workers differ greatly in the extent to which they insert sustaining words and phrases into their reflective communications when there is a possibility that these communications may arouse anxiety.

A special problem arises with sustaining procedures in joint or family interviews. Comments that could easily be made in an individual interview have to be seen in the light of the effect they will have on other clients who will also hear them. Sympathy with the hurt feelings

of one marital partner may convey disapproval to the other who caused
the suffering. Or sustainment of one person may arouse the jealousy of
another. This factor probably accounts for the findings of a study by
Ehrenkranz,[8] who in a content analysis comparing individual and joint
interviews in marital counseling cases found significantly less sustainment when husband and wife were seen together than when seen
separately.

## DIRECT INFLUENCE

The second set of procedures, those designated direct influence, includes the various ways in which the worker tries by the force, in
varying degrees, of his or her opinion to promote a specific kind of
behavior on the client's part. For example, a worker may give advice
or make suggestions about dealing more advantageously with an employer, consulting a doctor, going through with a medical recommenda-
tion, handling the children in a certain way, and so on.[9]

For many years, this type of activity has been suspect in casework.
In the days of innocence, prior to the 1930s, when workers were universally thought to be wiser and better informed than clients, advice was
one of the "visitor's" chief stocks in trade. Through bitter experience
caseworkers gradually learned that the wife who took the worker's
advice and separated from her alcoholic husband more often than not
took him back again, despite her fear of the visitor's disapproval; that
the mother who let herself be guided by the visitor's child-rearing
theories somehow managed to demonstrate that they did not work with
her Johnnie; and that the housewife who let herself be taught how to
make up a set of budget envelopes did not simultaneously learn how to
keep her fingers out of the wrong envelope when the installment man
came to the door. Out of such experiences came considerable healthy
reluctance about telling the client how to run his or her life. To a certain
extent, the official position of casework on this matter has often been
more extreme than actual practice. Workers have probably intuitively
recognized that there continues to be some need for guidance of some
clients.

There is some evidence—and we would expect this to be so—that
in parent–child problems workers are more likely to give advice than
in marital work. Davis[10] reported a study of seventeen mothers and five
fathers in which the general level of advice-giving (less than 8 percent
of all worker comments) was about twice as high as that found in studies
of casework with marital problems. Upon follow-up, eleven months
later, eleven of the seventeen mothers expressed satisfaction with the

amount of advice given, none wanted less, and six would have liked more.

It is often said that clients with little education in lower income groups come to agencies expecting to be given advice and are dissatisfied when the worker gives very little. A study by Reid and Shapiro[11] gave some support to this hypothesis. Using the Hollingshead and Redlich Class I to Class V scale of socioeconomic position, they found that only one of thirty-one clients in the two upper categories objected that too little advice had been given. Almost a fourth of the 151 clients in classes III to V, however, did object to this. Note, however, that three-fourths of the clients in these lower groups did *not* express such an objection.

This, of course, is only one aspect of the issue of how much advice is helpful. There are also questions such as: To what extent, when advice is given, is it used? To what extent has advice proved beneficial in the situation for which it was given? Then there is the hardest question of all to answer: In the long run, is it more helpful for the client to follow advice or to be helped to think things through for himself? Or, Is it better to follow advice, or more helpful to become aware of what contributes to one's doing things that are not wise?

## Degrees of Directiveness

Direct influence consists of a graduated set of techniques of varying degrees of directiveness. As one works with these procedures, one discovers that they constitute a range of processes that form a continuum. In the middle of the continuum, one may place the giving of advice— definitely stating an opinion or taking a stand concerning actions that the worker thinks the client should take. The worker may point out to a child's mother that Mary knows her way to school, is careful about crossing streets, and will have more chance to play with other children if her mother does not accompany her. Or the worker may comment to a man who is hesitating to ask for a seemingly deserved raise that several other men in his office have been given a raise, and that the only way to find out if he can get one is to ask for it.

A less forceful way of presenting these same ideas might be for the worker to make a suggestion. One might comment to Mary's mother, "It's only two blocks to the school; my guess is that Mary is old enough now to go that far with her friends." Or, one might comment to a second client, "Sometimes people just ask for a raise." The solution is raised in the client's mind in a way that conveys the worker's inclination toward it, but leaves the client with the alternative of rejecting the idea without feeling that he or she is going contrary to the worker's definite opinion.

A still milder form of influence is that of simply underlining, giving emphasis to, a course of action the client is already contemplating. A mother thinks it might be a good idea to let six-year-old Mary walk to school alone; the worker agrees it would be worth trying. Or the client says he is thinking of asking the boss for a raise, and the worker nods approvingly. Even if this client eventually decides against the step, there is very little likelihood that he will feel he has gone against the worker's opinion, for it was his own idea in the first place. When the client does go ahead with an idea and it works, the client takes the credit; if it fails, the edge is taken off the failure, since the worker also made the mistake of thinking it would work.

Toward the other end of the continuum is urging or insisting, putting a certain forcefulness behind the advice that is offered. The worker tells the mother that it is *essential* for her to take Mary to school, even though the child is frightened. Such pressure is sometimes necessary in treatment of a true school phobia, when the mother's own need to keep the child close to her is contributing to the difficulty. Treatment of the child cannot wait upon a slow change in the mother's attitude, which might take months to bring about, for in the interim school problems may have been added to the initial phobia to such a degree that a permanent learning problem may ensue.[12]

Or the worker might tell the man he thinks it would be *very unwise* for him to ask for a raise when he is on such bad terms with his boss, that such an action might very well result in his being fired. When there is a possibility of severe consequences of an impulsive, ill-considered action, or when sufficient time is not available to help the client think a matter through rationally, such active persuasion may be worth trying. Sometimes it saves the client from unfortunate consequences. But if the client does not take the advice and suffers the predicted result, the worker must by all means avoid anything that can be construed as an "I told you so" attitude. Properly handled, with the client able to express disappointment and to feel that the worker, too, regrets this disappointment, the failure may open the way to reflective consideration of what was involved and possibly ward off its repetition.

Most extreme of all the directive techniques is actual intervention in the client's life by such measures as removing a child from a home in which the child is subjected to cruelty or to a high degree of neglect, or taking a psychotic client to the receiving ward of a hospital. Such forceful interventions must rest on two conditions: first, one must be convinced that the step is fully justified and not motivated by some overreaction on one's own part; second, one must have thorough knowledge of the community resources involved in the plan of action and of the extent to which they will support it. For if the effort fails, one may well have lost constructive contact with the client and made the situation worse. In the first illustration given, the worker must know the conditions under which a court would uphold the action in custody proceedings; in the second, the worker must have sound clinical knowledge of the probable nature of the client's illness and of the procedures of the hospital to which the patient is to be taken. In both instances, the action must be carried out with skill. Firmness and kindness are needed. The probability of the client's acceding to the action with a minimum of resistance and disturbance is enhanced if in the first instance the worker is devoid of punitive motivation, and in the second the worker's anxiety is sufficiently under control that the client does not sense it. In both instances, it is important for the worker to feel sufficiently confident of ability to carry through the action that the client will sense this strength and therefore reject the temptation to test it.

Although in general it is best for a client to arrive at decisions by way of his or her own thinking, as understanding brings the individual to a possible solution, it is sometimes helpful for the caseworker to give support to the conclusions. In most situations, preference should be given to the most gentle form of influence that can be employed successfully, either putting ideas in the form of suggestions or reinforcing the client's own ideas.

There are many situations in which techniques of influence are appropriate. They are particularly useful in matters of child rearing, on which the worker, because of expert knowledge, is able to give the client good advice. Often the client is not yet ready to think things through, or strong cultural differences in expectations of the worker may lead the client to misinterpret the worker's refusal to give direction as a sign of disinterest or incompetence. While the worker does not need to comply with a client's expectations throughout the whole of treatment, it is often important to do so at the beginning.

The very anxious or depressed client is also sometimes in need of direction. It may be appropriate for the worker to provide it in the initial contact or throughout a period of crisis, gradually supplanting it, as the client's self-confidence grows, by methods that rest on understanding. Very dependent people, too, are often not capable of complete self-direction and need at least a measure of guidance from the worker,[13] as may also people whose sense of reality is weak, such as ambulatory schizophrenics or borderline personalities.[14] As long as the worker is philosophically committed to the value of self-direction, reasonably conscious of his or her own reactions to the client's need for dependence, and alert to every possibility of encouraging clients to think for themselves, wise use can be made of these procedures.

## Risks in Advice-Giving

Direct influence is, however, a treatment procedure in which there are several pitfalls. The most obvious is that one may give the wrong advice. Hence, the worker must be reasonably sure of knowing enough about what is best for the client to warrant advice. Especially on important decisions, the worker rarely knows enough to justify influencing another person. For instance, in a decision about whether or not to break up a marriage, a third person is usually not sufficiently aware of the subjective feelings and needs involved to weigh them adequately. This is true even when the objective realities seem, perhaps all too obviously, to point toward the wisdom of separation. As a safeguard against giving the wrong advice or preempting the client's decision-making abilities, the worker is best advised to use reflective discussion to try to help individuals arrive at awareness of both subjective and objective factors in their situations and to enable them to reach wise solutions for themselves. Only then may there be reason for the worker's reinforcing the client's decision by expressing agreement, but even this amount of influence is best used sparingly.

A second safeguard is to be quite sure that the need for advice rests in the client and not in the worker. It is so tempting to tell people what to do; one feels so good to be called upon for professional advice! All the negative connotations of the word "authority" can be removed simply by putting "professional" in front of it, thereby transforming "authoritativeness" into "strength the client can lean on." That there is such a thing as professional expertise is not to be denied, and under certain circumstances it can be put to very good use.[15] However, the need to see oneself as an authority is not sufficient reason for invoking that role.

A third safeguard is to induce the client, whenever possible, to think things through for himself. Clients sometimes seduce the worker into thinking advice is necessary when it is not. Some people like to be told what to do because passivity or dependence interfere with their ability to think things out for themselves and later, if things go wrong, they can always blame someone else. Anxious people, people with little self-confidence, people who want very much to please others often ask for more direction than they really need.

In general, then, one can say that advice about decisions or goals is risky. Advice about *how to reach* a goal the *client* has set is more often appropriate, especially if it is unlikely that the client can think this through without help.

Refusal to give advice, of course, should not be done in an abrupt or withholding way. Sometimes it is necessary to explain—"I'd give you advice if I thought it would help—but really *you* are the only one who can know what you want to do—let's work on it together and see if you can't work through to your decision." Or, with a different client, "It would be arrogant of me and insulting to you for me to assume I know better what is good for you than you do yourself."

Among the clients who typically seek a great deal of advice are obsessive-compulsive people.[16] Because they are usually very ambivalent, having a hard time making up their own minds, they tend to find an initial relief in being told what to do. Moreover, they are also usually dependent and have very strong superegos, so that they are very anxious to please people whom they regard as authorities. Asking for advice, in other words, is one way of playing out an inner wish to be a very good little boy or girl.

Because of the anxiety involved and the fact that the asked-for guidance becomes a gift (in the sustaining sense) that helps to build up a positive relationship, it sometimes is wise, especially in the early stages, to accede to the compulsive client's request. Direct advice, however, should be given tentatively, the worker offering it as something the client might like to try or as something that is often found helpful. Since the negativism of compulsive people sometimes leads them to ask for direction for the unconscious purpose of proving it will not work, this kind of qualifying comment will temper their need to show the advice is poor. If, on the other hand, they are truly trying to please the worker by following the advice, the tentative way in which it is offered will provide them with an anxiety-relieving excuse if they should fail.

## Secondary Directiveness

Just as it has been found that there can be a secondary form of sustainment as a by-product of the use of other procedures, so direct influence is sometimes a secondary feature of other worker communications. This has not been systematically studied in the way Boatman examined sustainment. However, it seems obvious that in varying degrees workers word their communications even in reflective discussion, in ways that suggest a course of action the worker thinks the client should take. For example, suppose a worker asks a woman, who has said she wants to improve her relationship with her husband, whether she thinks she will achieve her purpose by so consistently attacking or belittling him. In this instance, by implication, the worker is advising the client to change behavior toward her husband in order to achieve her goal of a better marriage relationship.

If one believes in the importance of self-direction, one needs to be very careful in reflective work about exerting a kind of secondary direct influence, by phrasing comments in a manner that leads toward a certain answer. As already noted, it is especially important to avoid guiding clients toward *decisions* the worker favors. In other matters, one may sometimes want to lead a client to understand himself or herself or others in a particular way or, as in the above example, to help a person recognize how a particular mode of behavior may be self-defeating. But we need to be aware of the extent to which we are being directive, and clear about our purposes for being so.

A close relationship exists between sustaining techniques and direct influence. Procedures of direct influence, except for active intervention, are effective only in proportion to the client's trust in the worker. The client will come to the worker with certain preconceptions growing out of past experience with, or knowledge of, other social workers. Also, certain expectations are inherent in the worker's position —that is, they are *ascribed* to anyone functioning in this particular role. Immediately upon contact, the worker has to begin to *achieve* the reputation of a person to be trusted by virtue of his or her own ways of acting with the client. The client's trust in the worker will be made up mainly of two components—respect for the worker's competence and belief in the worker's good will.[17] The latter is built up largely through sustaining processes.

Both direct influence and sustainment draw upon the client's dependence on the worker, a fact that must be kept in mind both in using these techniques and subsequently in helping the client regain or strengthen the ability to be self-reliant.

## EXPLORATION–DESCRIPTION–VENTILATION

The third major division of the typology includes two related but different concepts: exploration–description and ventilation. To *describe* or explain is simply to give the facts as one sees them. To *ventilate* is to bring out feelings associated with the facts. Exploration–description is a part of psychosocial study—an effort to secure from clients descriptions of themselves and their situations and the interactions that are part of their dilemmas. It occurs not only in the beginning interviews when the initial picture is emerging, but also in each subsequent interview, as the most recent events are gone over and bring to mind other connected events. It usually happens, however, that these factual descriptions are not neutral or emotionless. Clients frequently experience and sometimes express strong feelings on reviewing the facts as they see them. The distinction between experiencing and expressing feeling is an important one, and it is the chief reason that exploration–description and ventilation are placed together. Clients often experience feelings, even strongly, without showing them. Less strong feelings, especially, are often not overtly expressed. The worker, therefore, needs to be alert throughout the exploration–description process for feelings that would have been expected but may not have been revealed, responding in a way that will bring relief if these feelings do exist.

These procedures are also interlocked with those of reflection. In the latter, one often helps a client to become aware of feelings that have been suppressed. This is often followed by a great deal of ventilation concerning the events and feelings involved. This release or discharge of emotion is an important way of reducing the intensity of feelings.

Ventilation of suppressed feelings is altogether different from "abreaction," the analytic term for the reliving in the treatment hours of life experiences—chiefly from the early years—that have been repressed and therefore are deeply unconscious. The question of casework and the unconscious will be discussed in Chapter 13.

## Anger and Hatred

Feelings of anger and hatred are especially likely to lose some of their intensity if they can be given adequate verbal expression. This is particularly true for clients who have difficulty accepting negative or aggressive emotion. Very frequently, ventilation makes it possible later to move to reflective discussion of the circumstances and provocations under which anger is felt. Eventually, the client may be able to reach greater understanding of other people involved in the problem, faulty communication, ways of preventing anger-arousing situations, and so on. It is often important that such ventilation be accompanied by the sustaining process of acceptance.

## Grief Reactions

The importance of enabling people to mourn has long been recognized in casework. Some individuals, either for cultural reasons or because they place an especially high value on being stoical or "strong," are embarrassed to show their grief. Ventilation plays an important role in bringing these feelings of grief to expression in a sympathetic atmosphere. With a person who is depressed following the loss of a loved one —whether through death or separation of any other kind—it can be of special value to feel that here is a place where it is all right to cry and where the grief is understood.[18]

Similarly, expression of feeling can give relief to a person who has experienced a permanent crippling illness or injury or disfiguring surgery, or who is facing death or the diagnosis of a fatal illness. Relatives, friends, and sometimes medical personnel may praise patients for their courage in maintaining a calm exterior when the person's greatest need is really to "let go."

As is true in the use of any treatment procedure, timing is important. When helping a client to bring out grief reactions, one must be ever sensitive to defenses holding back the discharge of feeling, and wait until the client is sufficiently comfortable to express his feelings.

Not infrequently, where we would expect grief, the underlying emotion is a different one—anger or fear. Often, guilt or shame are also felt—for example, by a client who has lost a breast due to surgery for cancer or one who has had a colostomy. For the terminally ill, there are often periods of denial or, occasionally, absolute refusal to believe that death is imminent. Such denial of the fact, of course, temporarily precludes the expression of feelings associated with it. In all of these instances, one does not get ventilation until after there has been a process of bringing the deeper emotions to awareness. Thus, a form of reflection will need to precede and make possible the actual ventilation of emotion.

Here, again, the worker must respect defenses and proceed with gentleness. Certainly, feelings about impending death should be approached when the client shows some sign of wanting to talk about them, not just when the worker thinks it would be good for the person to do so. In the case of Mrs. Stasio, to be presented in Chapter 19, denial was unusually mild and ventilation could be an ongoing emphasis in treatment.

## Guilt Feelings

In the ventilation of guilt feelings, the interplay between ventilation and sustainment is particularly close.[19] Alleviation of feelings of guilt requires more than mere expression, although expression may be an important first step. It is the worker's attitude toward the guilt that is of primary importance. If the guilt is an appropriate response to events in the client's life, the worker's continued acceptance of the person after the guilt has been verbalized is of great value in reducing the intensity of these feelings. An accepting gesture is sometimes enough. Expressing sympathy with the feeling of guilt sometimes helps: "Yes, it is hard to find you have been wrong." "We all do things sometimes that we later wish we hadn't." "Yes, I know, it's awfully hard to face it." Guilt feelings are also often inappropriate: one may blame oneself too much, for too long, or for no reason. All too often, guilt that is derived from a harsh, punitive superego can be immobilizing and destructive to self-esteem. Ventilation should usually be followed by either sustainment or reflective discussion of these overreactions—or both—in an effort to help the client assess these feelings more realistically.

This is not to say that it is always helpful to relieve guilt. Guilt is sometimes a healthy and realistic reaction. Critical self-evaluation that helps individuals reflect on the disparity between their behavior and the ways they want to act or feel they should act, or the kind of persons they wish to be, can lead to productive change. Particularly for some clients with personality disorders, the development of greater concern for the consequences of their actions on others is a sign of growth. This may be accompanied by mild feelings of guilt when an interim stage has been reached, in which actions are still primarily at a self-gratifying stage but regret is beginning to be felt for harm to others.

Even when the problem is not real lack of concern for others, people often do not realize the extent to which they may be hurting others. When they become aware of the impact they do have—say, on husband, wife, or child—they may experience guilt over what they are doing. When this is so, it should be accepted as such. It can reinforce the building of sound ego controls. It can mark the growth of understanding of others and concern for them. It can be an incentive to acts of restitution that heal torn relationships as well as restore feelings of self-worth.

## Anxiety

Feelings of anxiety may be acute and primarily related to a particular event or situational stress, including that of coming to a professional for help. On the other hand, some clients experience chronic or repeated states of anxiety and have little knowledge of their causes. In both instances, such feelings can often be relieved in some measure during the exploratory phase. As the client relates the facts that precipitated the distress, or describes various aspects of present or past life, there is generally also a discharge of some of the emotion associated with these. The fact that the worker is not anxious can help the client find a way of dealing with the underlying issues contributing to the anxiety once it is expressed. Here, again, ventilation is followed by sustainment or reflection or both. Often, the worker's realistic confidence that the client has the strength to bear the anxiety, and can find ways of reducing it, is an important contributing factor to the client's being able to do so.

Sometimes anxiety is not directly expressed, but the worker can be alert to its signs. For example, a client may become restless or "block" when certain material is discussed, or may perspire or tremble. Under these circumstances, sometimes a sustaining word from the worker (e.g., "You seem to be having difficulty talking about this") can help the client ventilate the discomfort enough to allow further exploration of the trouble. Of course, there are times when anxiety is so keen that it is necessary for the worker to postpone exploration of a particular topic until the client can approach it without such apprehension.

## Contraindications

Although a certain amount of emotional release is of value in all cases, there are some circumstances under which it should be held in check. Occasionally, so much anxiety, anger, or other emotion is ventilated that it seems to be "feeding on itself." Talking does not bring the client relief and a reduction of feeling, but instead deeper engrossment in it. If this seems to be occurring, the expression of emotion is not helpful, and the worker should not encourage it to continue, but should turn the client's attention either to less emotionally laden content or to the question of what can be done to modify the situation or the feelings about which the client has been talking. The worker may even say quite directly that it does not seem to help to go over these matters, and that it might be better to try not to dwell on them so constantly.

Moreover, sometimes the expression of one emotion serves to keep another hidden. For example, a client may defend against feelings of anger by excessively venting reactions of grief. Similarly, we often find that intense anger masks "softer" feelings such as sadness, fear, tenderness. Thus, when we put value on the "open" expression of feeling, it is important to be sure that the expression is of the basic emotion and not just of its "cover." A worker who is alert to this will listen for clues to the underlying feeling, and turn from ventilation to reflective discussion to promote the client's awareness of the tendency to use this form of protection against exposing a particular emotion, and of the reasons for feeling this is necessary.

Occasionally, especially with the psychotic or near-psychotic person, ventilation may lead to the production of increasingly bizarre material, or it may become a stimulus to irrational actions. Accurate diagnostic assessment of the presence of psychotic trends alerts a worker to this possibility and to the fact that it may be more helpful to explore areas that will strengthen realistic thinking, rather than to encourage ventilation that may evoke material that in less seriously disturbed people would remain unconscious. This is not to say that all ventilation by disturbed people should be discouraged. For example, such clients can feel—sometimes very justifiably—that they are not taken seriously by others who have labeled them "crazy." In such situations, it can be extremely important for the worker to elicit and acknowledge feelings of hurt or anger about this, as was the case with Mrs. Barry (see chapter 19).

Occasionally, a worker may observe that the client is deriving marked gratification from talking freely about himself or herself and seems to be making no effort to use the interviews to move toward any improvement either internally or in the situation. Sometimes this represents excessive self-pity and an effort to enlist the worker's sympathy. At other times, the client's complaints seem to be only an excuse for not doing anything for himself or herself and a way of putting all the blame for the troubles on others, or the talking may provide sexual or masochistic satisfaction. Gratification of any of these kinds is of no value in helping clients to better their plights and should not be continued once it becomes clear that this is the prevailing mood. Sometimes, too, clients who seek gratification in these ways are people who cannot be helped by casework. Care should be taken, however, to move away from this type of communication in a constructive rather than a destructive way. Often the reason for discouraging it can be explained directly to the client, thus leading into a discussion of this aspect of the resistance. But to do so successfully, the worker must be free of the hostile countertransference reactions that are so easily aroused by clients who make use of ventilation primarily for self-gratification.

## Ventilation in Joint Interviews

As in sustainment, there is a difference in the extent to which ventilation of certain types can be used in joint and individual interviews. Ehrenkranz,[20] contrary to expectation, in a study comparing 58 joint interviews with 68 interviews with individuals, found "conspicuously" less ventilation in the joint interviews. She suggests that this may have been due to the workers' tendency to accentuate the positive when clients with marital problems were willing to have joint interviews. Hollis had a similar finding in comparing 20 joint interviews with 20 single-person interviews, reporting that this was especially true in ventilation of feelings about others.[21] There was probably some restraint in expressing hostile feelings in the presence of the other person. Actually, the expression of hostility in a joint interview can be a powerful therapeutic tool, and it is sometimes encouraged. This is particularly true if one partner has been unable to express such feelings to the other and is able to bring out the true feelings with the support of the worker. This expression can lead to more honest communication and prevent the bottling up of feelings that then either explode when the pressure becomes too great or find an outlet in devious and sometimes more harmful ways. Such expression can also have a profound influence on a partner who has been unwittingly hurtful because of lack of awareness of the spouse's feelings.

The extent to which such ventilation should be encouraged or discouraged in joint interviews depends upon its effect on both partners. Every effort should be made to discontinue it if it creates too much anxiety in either partner or leads to ever increasing hostility and counterhostility instead of greater understanding or the emergence of positive feelings. This need for caution is no doubt another cause of the finding that there is quantitatively less ventilation in joint than in individual interviews. It is also the authors' impression that if there were a measure of *intensity* of ventilation, in most cases it would be found to be much higher in joint interviews. When ventilation of hostility appears not to be helpful, this should be discussed with the clients. Sometimes it is best at such times to turn to individual interviews until a less destructive stage of the relationship has been reached. But, once again, the anger may in fact be a defense against risking "softer" feelings of disappointment, loneliness, and the longing for affection. Frequently, when these are elicited in joint interviews the destructive, hostile attacks subside.

### NOTES

1.  For interesting discussions of this see Clare Britton, "Casework Techniques in Child Care Services," *Social Casework,* 36 (January 1955), 3–13; Jerome Frank, "The Role of Hope in Psychotherapy," *International Journal of Psychiatry,* 5 (May 1968), 394; and Elizabeth Salomon, "Humanistic Values and Social Casework," *Social Casework,* 48 (January 1967), 26–32. See Chapter 12 for further references.

2.  The importance of this concept has been emphasized in many articles beginning in the thirties. See especially Annette Garrett, *Interviewing: Its Principles and Methods* (New York: Family Service Association of America, 1942), pp. 22–24; Gordon Hamilton, "Basic Concepts in Social Casework," *The Family,* 18 (December 1937), 263–268; and Charlotte Towle, "Factors in Treatment," *Proceedings of the National Conference of Social Work, 1936* (Chicago: University of Chicago Press, 1936), pp. 179–191. See Chapter 12 for additional references.

3.  See Alice W. Rue, "The Casework Approach to Protective Work," *The Family,* 18 (December 1937), 277–282; and Dale Hardman, "The Matter of Trust," *Crime and Delinquency,* 15 (April 1969), 203–218. See also Note 13, Chapter 8.

4.  For illustrations and discussions of these sustaining techniques see, for example, L. P. Laing, "The Use of Reassurance in Psychotherapy," *Smith College Studies in Social Work,* 22 (February 1952), 75–90; Grace K. Nicholls, "Treatment of a Disturbed Mother–Child Relationship: A Case Presentation," in Howard J. Parad, ed., *Ego Psychology and Dynamic*

*Casework* (New York: Family Service Association of America, 1958), pp. 117–125; and Hank Walzer, "Casework Treatment of the Depressed Parent," in Francis J. Turner, ed., *Differential Diagnosis and Treatment in Social Work*, rev. ed. (New York: Free Press, 1976), pp. 302–312.

5.  For an early discussion of work with "the hard to reach," see especially Alice Overton, "Serving Families Who Don't Want Help," *Social Casework*, 34 (July 1953), 304–309. See also Walter Haas, "Reaching Out—A Dynamic Concept in Casework," *Social Work*, 4 (July 1959), 41–45, and *Casework Notebook* (St. Paul, Minn.: Family Centered Project Greater St. Paul, Community Chests and Councils, 1957); and Charles King, "Family Therapy with the Deprived Family," *Social Casework*, 48 (April 1967), 203–208. For examples of situations in which "feeding" (symbolic and concrete) is used to demonstrate worker interest see, for example, Blanca N. Rosenberg, "Planned Short-term Treatment in Developmental Crises," *Social Casework*, 56 (April 1975), 202–204; and James D. Troester and Joel A. Darby, "The Role of the Mini-Meal in Therapeutic Play Groups," *Social Casework*, 57 (February 1976), 97–103. Florence Lieberman also gives an interesting illustration of this type of work in her discussion of work with emotionally deprived parents in *Social Work with Children* (New York: Human Services Press, 1979), pp. 264–268.

6.  Louise S. Bandler, "Casework—A Process of Socialization," in Eleanor Pavenstedt, ed., *The Drifters* (Boston: Little, Brown, 1967), pp. 255–293. See also Lorraine Pokart Levy, "Services to Parents of Children in a Psychiatric Hospital," *Social Casework*, 58 (April 1977), 204–213.

7.  Louise Boatman, "Caseworkers' Judgments of Clients' Hope: Some Correlates Among Client–Situation Characteristics and Among Workers' Communication Patterns" (doctoral dissertation, Columbia University School of Social Work, 1974).

8.  Shirley M. Ehrenkranz, "A Study of Joint Interviewing in the Treatment of Marital Problems," *Social Casework*, 48 (October 1967), 500.

9.  For an interesting study of one of these procedures, see Ruth T. Koehler, "The Use of Advice in Casework," *Smith College Studies in Social Work*, 23 (February 1953), 151–165.

10.  Inger P. Davis, "Advice-giving in Parent Counselling," *Social Casework*, 56 (June 1975), 343–347. See also Levy, "Services to Parents," and Lieberman, *Social Work with Children*, pp. 268–270.

11.  William Reid and Barbara Shapiro, "Client Reactions to Advice," *Social Service Review*, 43 (June 1969), 165–173. For further support of this view, see also findings by Patricia L. Ewalt and Janice Katz, in "An Examination of Advice Giving as a Therapeutic Intervention," *Smith College Studies in Social Work*, 47 (November 1976), 3–19.

A study by John E. Mayer and Noel Timms, *The Client Speaks: Working Class Impressions of Casework* (New York: Atherton, 1970), p. 93, suggested that satisfied clients received more guidance than less satisfied clients. A questionnaire devised by Marcia K. Goin et al. reported on in "Therapy Congruent with Class-Linked Expectations," *Archives of General Psychiatry*, 13 (August 1965), 133–137, was given to 250 applicants —mostly of lower socioeconomic status—seeking help at an outpatient psychiatric center; interestingly, only 34 percent indicated they wanted advice, in contrast to 52 percent who wanted to solve their problems by talking about feelings and past life. Of those seeking advice, one group received it while another did not, but no apparent differences in improvement rates were found. On the other hand, Geismer and his associates, after examining treatment outcomes, report: "The relatively more successful worker was found to have been supportive rather than directive ... and to have elicited greater client participation in treatment." See Ludwig L. Geismer et al., *Early Supports for Family Life: A Social Work Experiment* (Metuchen, N.J.: Scarecrow Press, 1972). Clearly, further study of the question of directiveness in general is needed.

12.   As suggested by Emanuel Klein in "The Reluctance to Go to School," in Ruth S. Eissler et al., eds., *The Psychoanalytic Study of the Child,* vol. 1 (New York: International Universities Press, 1945), pp. 263–279. See also Edwin Thomas, "Selected Sociobehavioral Techniques and Principles: An Approach to Interpersonal Helping," *Social Work,* 13 (January 1968), 12–26; and *The Sociobehavioral Approach and Application to Social Work* (New York: Council on Social Work Education, 1967). There is considerable evidence that conditioning, essentially a form of direct influence, can be effective in removing phobic symptoms. However, as Lieberman (*Social Work with Children,* pp. 173–176) points out, crisis intervention to remove school phobia is important, but the underlying anxiety and other symptoms are likely to persist or increase without additional treatment. For further readings on school phobia, see Elisabeth Lassers et al., "Steps in the Return to School of Children with School Phobia," *American Journal of Psychiatry,* 130 (March 1973), 265–268, reprinted in Francis J. Turner, ed., *Differential Diagnosis in Social Work,* 2nd ed. (New York: Free Press, 1976), pp. 658–665; Esther Marine, "School Refusal: Review of the Literature," *Social Service Review,* 42 (December 1968), 464–478; and "School Refusal: Who Should Intervene? (diagnostic and treatment categories)," *Journal of School Psychology* (1969), 63–70.

13.   For illustrations and discussion, see Katherine Baldwin, "Crisis-Focused Casework in a Child Guidance Clinic," *Social Casework,* 49 (January 1968) 28–34; Ethel Panter, "Ego-Building Procedures That Foster Social Functioning," *Social Casework,* 48 (March 1967), 139–145; Eva Y. Deykin et al., "Treatment of Depressed Women," in Turner, *Differential Diagnosis,* pp. 288–301; Irving Kaufman, "Understanding the Dynamics of Parents with Character Disorders," in *Casework Papers, 1960* (New York: Family Service Association of America, 1960); Frances Scherz, "Treatment of Acting-out Character Disorders in a Marital Problem," in *Casework Papers, 1956* (New York: Family Service Association of America, 1956); Irving Weisman, "Offender Status, Role Behavior, and Treatment Considerations," *Social Casework,* 48 (July 1967), 422–425; and Sheldon Zimberg, "Principles of Alcoholism Psychotherapy," in Zimberg, et al., eds., *Practical Approaches to Alcoholism Psychotherapy* (New York: Plenum Press, 1978), pp. 3–18.

14.   See, for example, Nathan W. Ackerman, *Treating the Troubled Family* (New York: Basic Books, 1966), especially pp. 237–288; and Margaret M.

Heyman, "Some Methods in Direct Casework Treatment of the Schizophrenic," *Journal of Psychiatric Social Work,* 19 (Summer 1949), 18–24.

15. Some general considerations involved in the use of authority of all degrees are well presented by Eliot Studt. See her articles: "An Outline for Study of Social Authority Factors in Casework," *Social Casework,* 35 (June 1954), 231–238, and "Worker–Client Authority Relationships in Social Work," *Social Work,* 4 (January 1959), 18–28. See also Robert Foren and Bailey Royston, *Authority in Social Casework* (New York: Pergamon Press, 1968); Hardman, "Matter of Trust," pp. 203–218; and Samuel Mencher, "The Concept of Authority and Social Casework," *Casework Papers, 1960* (New York: Family Service Association of America, 1960), pp. 126–138.

16. This is discussed by Sid Hirsohn in his "Casework with the Compulsive Mother," *Social Casework,* 32 (June 1951), 254–261. See also Catherine Bittermann, "Marital Adjustment Patterns of Clients with Compulsive Character Disorders: Implications for Treatment," *Social Casework,* 47 (November 1966), 575–582; and James F. Suess, "Short-Term Psychotherapy with the Compulsive Personality and the Obsessive-Compulsive Neurotic," *American Journal of Psychiatry,* 129 (1972), 270–275, reprinted in Turner, *Differential Diagnosis,* pp. 280–287.

17. This question was studied in the 1950s by Norman A. Polansky and his associates. See Norman A. Polansky and Jacob Kounin, "Clients' Reactions to Initial Interviews: A Field Study," *Human Relations,* 9 (1956), 237–264; and Jacob Kounin et al., "Experimental Studies of Clients' Reactions to Initial Interviews," *Human Relations,* 9 (1956), 265–293. See also Chapter 12, note 2 for additional, more recent, references.

18. See Elizabeth Kubler-Ross, *On Death and Dying* (New York: Macmillan, 1969), especially Chapter 9 on "The Patient's Family." Dory Krongelb Beatrice, in "Divorce: Problems, Goals, and Growth Facilitation," *Social Casework,* 60 (March 1979), 157–165, discusses the importance of "grief work" for divorcing people. In an excellent article by Lois I. Greenberg, "Therapeutic Grief Work with Children," *Social Casework,* 56 (July 1975), 396–403, case examples are given that demonstrate various ways in which children are helped to ventilate grief reactions to parental deaths.

19. See Gary D. Anderson, "Enhancing Listening Skills for Work with Abusing Parents," *Social Casework,* 60 (December 1979), 602–608. See also Fred K. Briard, "Counseling Parents of Children with Learning Disabilities," *Social Casework,* 57 (November 1976), 581–585, for an excellent discussion of the need to help parents of learning-disabled children express guilt so they can respond constructively to their youngsters' needs.

20. See Ehrenkranz, "Study of Joint Interviewing."

21. Florence Hollis, *A Typology of Casework Treatment* (New York: Family Service Association of America, 1968), p. 33.

# CHAPTER 6

# Reflective Discussion of the Person–Situation Configuration

As is evident from the preceding chapters, psychosocial casework places great emphasis on drawing clients into reflective consideration of their situations and of their functioning within them. In Chapter 4 we suggested the usefulness of three major divisions in work of this kind: person–situation reflection, in which consideration is given to the nature of the client's situation, his or her responses to it, and the interaction of situation and responses; pattern-dynamic reflection, in which response *patterns* or tendencies are considered; and developmental reflection, in which attention is centered on *developmental* factors in these patterns. The first category, the subject of this chapter, is a form of treatment universally used in casework. In the psychosocial approach, the worker characteristically tries to help the client arrive at some form of increased understanding, no matter how much reflective discussion may need to be buttressed by sustaining, directive, or ventilating work.[1] Because of the tendency for a number of years to think in dichotomous terms of either "supportive" casework or "clarification" or "insight development," the type of reflective discussion that leads to an understanding that is neither clarification nor insight was lost sight of and not given the thorough study or accreditation it deserves. And yet this treatment type comprises a rich store of useful procedures fundamental to casework practice.

The procedures used in person–situation reflection are comments, questions, explanations and paraverbal communications that promote the client's reflecting primarily upon current and recent events. Person–situation reflection is distinguished from developmental reflection by the fact that the latter is concerned with early life experiences, those that occur during the period when the individual would normally be living with parents, the years of growth to adulthood. Pertinent material located in time between the beginning of adulthood and the present is also considered as part of person–situation reflection.

As indicated earlier, it is possible to break this category into six

132

subdivisions: the clients' consideration (1) of others, of the situation, or of their physical health; (2) of their own actions in terms of outcome, effects on self and others, or alternatives; (3) of the *nature* of their acts, thoughts, and feelings; (4) of the external provocations or stimuli or the immediate inner reasons for reactions and responses; (5) of their own acts, feelings, and thoughts from an evaluative stance; and (6) of their reactions to the worker and the treatment process.

## OTHER PEOPLE, HEALTH, SITUATION

The first of these subdivisions has to do with the client's thinking about the situation, a form of reflection that might be called "extrareflection." Here we are dealing partly with perception and partly with a question of knowledge. So often people see only a distorted or one-sided picture of the reality before them, either because they see or hear what they anticipate or because their feelings lead them to ignore or blot out important aspects of a situation. The father who is convinced that his son is stupid like his own older brother may remember or stress only those subjects or activities in which his son has failed, but may without noticing it reveal to the worker areas in which the son's learning has been unimpeded. The worker's first approach would usually be to call the father's attention to events that show the other side of the boy's capacities. In this sort of situation, workers often err by rushing into a discussion of the distortion itself—in this case, the displacement from brother to son—instead of seeing whether, when the client's attention is called to the reality picture, he or she is able by this procedure alone to modify earlier misconceptions. By testing the client's capacity to do this, one can measure the force of the need to distort.

There is a rule of parsimony in treatment as well as in science. If a person is able, with a little help, to perceive more realistically, it is not necessary to pursue the whys and wherefores of a previous failure to do so. If, on the other hand, the distortion does not yield to a look at the facts, the diagnostic information and material that this preliminary effort has provided can later be used to draw the client's attention to the discrepancy itself, between reality and his or her view of it. A perceptive client will often accept the cue and go on to talk about the matters that complicate feelings toward a child. Another will need more prompting from the worker in order for treatment to move on from person–situation reflection to pattern-dynamic or developmental reflection.

A person's lack of understanding of a situation may be due not so much to distortion of the facts or blindness to them as to actual lack of knowledge about normal reactions. Parents, unaware of the universal turmoil of adolescence, the need to assert independence that so often shows itself in negativism, the seeking for peer approval—whether in clothes, hair, language, or dating behavior—mistake normal and healthy reactions for alienation and revolt. In so doing, they may drive their children toward the very associations they fear. We do not mean to imply that casework (any more than any other profession) holds the magic key to the turmoil of youth. Much of the turmoil has to do with grave problems of our total society for which we all bear responsibility. But nothing is to be gained by the parent's misconstruing normal development as complete loss of a child and overreacting in a way that drives the child away at the very moment when communication most needs to be kept open. More understanding can lead to more patience, which in turn furthers the chance of greater exchange of ideas between generations. This implies neither supine parental abnegation of adult thinking about wise and unwise activities nor evasion of parental guidance when reality demands it and the ability to influence the child effectively exists. But it does mean that the parent can be helped to see his child more realistically and in better perspective, thereby coming to understand more fully what the son or daughter is experiencing and to what inner needs and outer pressures he or she is responding. The parent then is certainly in a better position to help rather than hurt the child. Harmful responses can also be due to commonly held prejudices and fears. A mother, for instance, may accept a child's report of being threatened by a child of another background—class, race, religion, or ethnicity—without inquiring for details of what actually happened to see whether the child might have misinterpreted or exaggerated the event or might have provoked the incident. The caseworker, first demonstrating appreciation of the mother's concern, can go on to ask about the details of what happened. This not only clarifies the reality for the mother, but indirectly demonstrates the way in which the mother could have handled the situation. For the mother too needs first to comfort her son but then to help him to see whether his report of what happened was entirely accurate. If it was, then thought needs to be given to next steps—the second form of person–situation activity. What can the mother help the child to do? What can the mother herself do? If the report is not accurate, the mother can help her child not only because she enables him to see this particular episode more realistically but because this constitutes a step in the process of strengthening his ego's ability to assess reality.

Lack of imagination about another person's feelings or behavior or failure to identify with the feelings of another may also generate hostility between people. The husband intent on his own successful legal career fails to see that his wife is frustrated by a dead-end job that does not call on any of her college training. Nor does it occur to him that since she is really inexperienced in keeping house, and tired after eight hours at the office, she needs some household help in caring for their home and child, even though they have bought expensive modern equipment. One man in such a situation had concluded that his wife was stupid because he did not realize the extent to which her feelings of frustration and anger were interfering with her functioning. He was not incapable of understanding his wife's reactions when he was helped to do so—that is, to perceive her more accurately and fully—but without help, he was becoming constantly more irritated and more scornful of her capacities—the very thing that drove her to distraction.

The very process of understanding another person more fully sets in motion a change in behavior. As we saw earlier, we do not respond to the actual situation, but to our perception of it. Thus, when a distorted perception is corrected, the response often corrects itself.

Joint and family interviews offer excellent opportunities for increased understanding of one person by another. People often reveal aspects of themselves in the relative safety of the treatment situation that they have not had the courage to show in the hostile or anxiety-ridden home situation. A worker can draw out a client's thoughts and feelings for the specific purpose of enabling another family member who is listening to understand the one who is speaking.

The process of understanding the external world takes place not only in relation to people but also in respect to life events. Clients sometimes need help in understanding a budget, a business or work situation, medical recommendations, or the implications of their own or someone else's physical condition.[2] The more fully they can comprehend these things, the more appropriately will they handle them. Reflective consideration is a more tedious process than the giving of advice, but it increases the client's competence in a way that advisory processes do not.

Several choices of technique are open to the worker in helping clients to reflect upon their understanding of people and situations. Some workers like to explain things to their clients in a more or less didactic way; others are skillful in leading people to think things through for themselves. Some workers might immediately explain the universality of sibling jealousy to a mother who does not understand the irritability of her three-year-old after the birth of a new baby. In the psychosocial approach, we believe it is usually more effective to ask the mother if she has herself thought of any explanation for the older child's peevishness. If she has not, there is still the possibility of inquiring whether she thinks the arrival of the new baby might be making Jane feel left out. Psychosocial theory holds that the more one can get clients to think for themselves, the more conviction they will have about the answers they find. Furthermore, their dependency on the worker will not be so greatly increased, and at the same time they will be helped to develop an ego skill that they can apply to other situations.

One form of reflective consideration of the situation is currently receiving more thought: that of telling the client about ways in which changes can be brought in the situation through either legal or social action. For example, as lawyers have become more interested in the problems of poverty and social injustice, more resources have become available for clients seeking legal help to meet some of their external problems, but they often do not know of these possibilities. Straight information by the worker can increase the client's awareness of the resources within reach. Similarly, there are today many organizations and neighborhood groups in which families can participate in effective group action to bring about improvement in adverse social conditions. It is just as important for workers to be well informed about these resources as about those of health, education, employment, and recreation.

## DECISIONS, CONSEQUENCES, AND ALTERNATIVES

The second type of reflection concerning the person–situation gestalt lies between extrareflection and intrareflection and partakes of both. It involves decisions and activities of the client and their effects in interaction with the situation and the people with whom the client lives or associates. Over and over again, workers strive to help clients think about the effects of their own actions on others, or about their consequences for themselves.[3] An action may be a matter of practical decision, such as advantages and disadvantages of moving into a housing project, the advisability of changing from one job to another, or the wisdom of training for a particular vocation. Or it may be a decision about a medical problem, such as whether or not to undergo recommended surgery.[4] Often, it involves a complicated interpersonal decision, such as whether or not to separate from husband or wife, to adopt a child, or to place a child for adoption. In any of these instances, the client tries imaginatively to foresee what personal consequences a plan or decision may have and how it may affect other people whose lives are involved in the decision. The worker contributes to the reflective discussion by bringing the client's attention to aspects of the situation that may have been overlooked.

At other times, it is not a direct decision but an understanding of the effects of the client's own behavior on someone else that is involved in the reflection. A mother may not realize that when she hits her fourteen-year-old son in front of his friends, she is compelling him to defy her in order to maintain the respect of his peers. A husband may not see that when he nags his wife about her figure, he is only increasing her hunger for forbidden sweets.[5] A child may not realize that when he is a poor sport in losing games, his friends go to play with someone else.

Here as elsewhere, psychosocial workers hold that the best procedure for the worker is not to "explain" the relationship between behavior and consequences, but to lead the clients to see the sequence themselves: "What did Mike do when you hit him in front of the other fellows?" "Does your wife eat less when you needle her about her weight?" "What happened just before Johnny left you to play with Bud?" Many times clients will draw the correct conclusions, once the effects of the behavior are brought to their attention. If more help is needed, the worker may go on with, "Do you suppose that ... ?" or "Have you noticed that . . .?" or "Often boys of this age . . ." When a full explanation is really needed, the worker should give it, but not until an effort has been made to see whether the client can arrive at conclusions independently, so that he or she will at least gain experience in thinking in terms of consequences in general as well as some understanding of the particular matter under consideration.

Discussion of decisions and future action is often linked with situational understanding. Greater knowledge of another person or of resources at one's command is naturally followed by consideration of what to do in the light of this knowledge. "How can I talk with Ted about this?" "What should I say to Jean?" The worker could respond with advice, but again it is usually more helpful to encourage clients to think the answer out for themselves, since this will increase their capacity to respond to future situations without help. Similarly, when the use of a resource is at issue, clients should be led step by step to consider the advantages and disadvantages rather than being advised to take one course or another.

A more subtle sort of misunderstanding about consequences is that of fearing reactions that in fact need not occur. A husband or wife may underestimate a spouse's ability to accept difference. A man may think that his wife will be angry if he takes a night to play poker with his friends when in actuality she might be glad for an evening alone— or vice versa. Fear that differences in life style, tastes, pastimes will necessarily bring withdrawal of love is common and sometimes these do in fact become a separating factor. But this is not a necessary consequence if thought is given to the effects of one person's behavior on another. Often, it is not the difference itself but the way in which the difference is asserted that makes the trouble. Close examination of this type of interaction is a very important type of reflection about consequences.

The worker can ask for details of the circumstances surrounding what appears to be a difference of this sort. "How did it come up?" "How did you put it?" "What did John really say or do?" "Have you talked it over?" "She doesn't sound so upset to me—are you sure . . .?" And so on. In this sort of situation, there is a close interweaving of thinking about consequences and trying to understand other persons and their needs.

## INWARDLY DIRECTED AWARENESS

The third subdivision of this type of treatment, which parallels the procedure of helping the client look outward with greater perceptive accuracy, has to do with increasing the client's awareness of the nature of his or her own responses, thoughts, and feelings. These processes, which are forms of intrareflection, sometimes involve awareness of so-called hidden feelings or reactions. There are many degrees of "hiddenness." A client may be perfectly aware of reactions but may be afraid to speak of them because of shame or fears of ridicule or criticism. This may be the case, for example, with a mother who is fully aware of her anger toward one of her children but is ashamed to admit it, or with a woman who hesitates to tell the worker about a recent abortion. Or the client may have refrained from talking about feelings because of a lack of recognition of their significance or importance: a man may know he is ashamed of having had a mental breakdown, but may never speak of it to the worker because he does not realize the way in which this shame is related to his employment failures. Or the client may be truly unaware of feelings because they are not part of conscious thought: a mother may not even be aware, for example, of the strong feelings of hostility she is harboring toward her child. We are talking here not of *early* memories but of reactions to current life. The uncovering of hidden *early* memories is part of the process of developmental reflection rather than of the current person–situation gestalt.

When a worker can "read" a client's thoughts, it is a great temptation to do so out loud. There are occasions when this is necessary— either because the client is quite unable to bring these thoughts into the open but will be relieved if the worker does so, or because there is therapeutic justification for bringing them out even though this may produce discomfort. Far more often, skill lies in finding ways of enabling clients to bring out the hidden material themselves. Where full awareness is present, the client generally does this without any specific prompting, on becoming more secure with the worker in response to a sustaining approach. If, however, it is obvious to the worker that the client is struggling with the question of whether to speak of something or not, the worker may want to handle this hesitation directly by commenting that it is hard to speak freely but, that perhaps as the client becomes more comfortable, he or she will be able to do so. Or the worker may say, "I know it is hard to talk sometimes, but I can only help you with the things you can bring yourself to talk about." Or, "Can you tell me what it is that makes it so hard for you to talk about this?" Or,

"I have a feeling that you may be afraid I will criticize you. Is there anything I've said that makes you feel this way?" Or, "I'm not here to criticize you but to help you." Sustaining comments are particularly useful in putting the client more at ease.

At other times, when the worker is fairly sure of what a client is withholding, it may be possible to make comments that refer tangentially to the anticipated content, thus inviting the client to talk about it but still not facing him or her with it directly. One can, for instance, give reassurance of acceptance in advance of the client's communication: "It isn't always possible, you know, to feel love for a difficult child." Or, "Sometimes mothers, even though they try not to, do dislike a child." Or, "Sometimes a person is so unhappy about a pregnancy that they feel they have to do something about it." Often one can call the client's attention to discrepancies between fact and feeling, or overemphasis, or inconsistencies, as these may point toward important feelings. Sometimes this can be done merely by repeating the revealing statement in a questioning tone.

On the less frequent occasions when it is actually advisable to put the matter into words for the client, this can be done tentatively, making it possible for the client to maintain defenses if needed and also safeguarding the person from agreeing too readily to a possibly incorrect interpretation if the worker is not certain of the client's thinking. Occasionally, a direct, unqualified interpretation is helpful, but for this the worker should be very sure of the ground on which the comment is based.[6] As in the simpler process of spontaneous ventilation, when feelings are brought to expression, the worker has several choices as to the next step. It may be helpful to turn to sustaining procedures, trying immediately to allay the client's anxiety or guilt; one may seek to involve the client in further understanding of the dynamics or of developmental aspects of his or her reactions; at other times, it may be more advisable to concentrate on the immediate consequences of these reactions in the client's current life.

Closely related to the process of helping a person to become aware of feelings and thoughts is the process of encouraging the individual to recognize and consider inappropriate, unusual, or problem activities or reactions. The worker calls the client's attention to the fact that she has several times called Mary "Janet," or comments on the oddity that the client continuously works overtime without extra compensation for a boss he says he hates, despite the fact that he could easily get another job. This very important procedure is often neglected by inexperienced workers who lack the patience to wait for clients to do their own thinking. Again, the psychosocial position is that the more clients can think for themselves the better. When the client's attention is called to irrational or unproductive behavior, if the individual is capable of so doing he or she is very likely to go on to consideration of either the consequences of the behavior or the reasons for it. The worker who omits this step and rushes on to an explanation or interpretation deprives the client of the chance to seek this out for himself. Furthermore, the risk of an inaccurate or inadequate explanation is always greater when trust is put in one's own insight instead of the client's.

## RESPONSES TO SITUATIONAL PROVOCATIONS AND STIMULI

A fourth form of reflection consists of the effort to understand some of the reasons for reactions—that is, the external provocations and internal thought processes that contribute to a reaction. A husband who is opposed to his wife's working looks at the possibility that he feels unloved because for him her "homecaring" symbolized love. Or he considers the possibility that her working seems to him to belittle his own place in the family. This type of causation lies in interactions with others, reasons for doing something that lie either in "the outer" or in a person's own feeling about "the outer." The worker might comment: "You have talked about how upset you were to lose the baby. Do you think this made you irritable with Ben?" Or, simply, "You seem tense today. What has happened?"

## SELF-EVALUATION

Still another type of reflection, the fifth, has to do with self-evaluation. This may be in the superego sense of right or wrong or in the sense of thinking about the self-image, principles, values, preferences that have value implications. A worker may comment, "Don't you think you are really expecting too much of yourself?" Or, "Which means more to you, success in this competitive job or a closer relationship with Betty?"

Another facet of this process comes into play when the worker helps a client to use external realities to correct a distorted self-image. A boy who is excessively fearful of a school test is reminded of his successes in previous tests. A woman is helped to evaluate whether her image of herself as weak and helpless is justified by the facts. A girl who says she has no one to invite to a party when she has told the worker of many friends is asked to think over the many people she actually knows. This type of reflection is closely related to reflection that develops a better understanding of external realities; indeed, the two processes often occur in rapid succession. But consideration of external reality here is the means by which clients are helped to become aware of misperceptions about themselves; it is not for the purpose of understanding another person. It is essentially *in*wardly, not *out*wardly, directed reflection.

## REACTIONS TO THE WORKER AND TO TREATMENT

Psychosocial casework stresses the importance in person–situation reflection of a sixth form of reflection. This concerns the client's reactions to the worker, to treatment, or to agency rules and requirements. Just as the client may misperceive other aspects of the situation, so he or she may distort or fail to understand casework and the caseworker. Here, too, previous life experiences may lead the client to imagine hostility where it does not exist, to anticipate criticism, to fear domination, or to expect inappropriate gratification of dependency wishes. Or the client may simply lack knowledge of the nature of the casework "situation."

The probability of this type of reaction can be greatly lessened if there is adequate discussion—preferably in the first interview—of the purpose and nature of the contact—what the client wants, how the worker will try to help, the fact that these two people will be working together in an effort to lessen or resolve the dilemma—bringing out the mutuality of the effort.

There is a tendency to think that there is something mysterious about the casework relationship, something that makes it fragile and untouchable except by the very expert. In fact, it is no more complicated than—but just as complicated as—any other relationship. In the type of reflective discussion considered here, attitudes and responses to the caseworker are handled in the same way as other attitudes and responses. Where distortions or misunderstandings exist, the clinical social worker tries to straighten them out by demonstrating the realities of his or her behavior toward the client and the actual nature of treatment.[7] If a dependent client accuses the worker of disinterest because the worker is unwilling to prolong the interview, the worker may explain that time has to be scheduled, that it is not a matter of lack of interest, and that they can go on with the same discussion in their next interview. If, on the other hand, this represents a repeated attempt to control the worker, it is well to suggest that it seems to have become a problem, and that it is one that the client and the worker should look at in the next interview.

Understanding by the client of reactions to the worker can be a very fruitful source of understanding of similar reactions in other parts of his or her life. If the client thinks the worker is angry, it is well to find out what this conclusion is based on. If a remark has been misinterpreted, the worker can indicate what was really meant and reassure the client that there is no anger. (This assumes that the worker is truly not angry. When, as occasionally happens, one *is* angry, it is usually best to admit it and either explain why, or, when appropriate, apologize, or do both.) If the client expects advice and is disappointed at not getting it, a simple explanation of why the worker doesn't think it will help may clear the air. Clients do not need long and theoretical explanations of treatment processes, but when they ask for information or when misunderstandings arise, it is not only appropriate but essential to discuss the nature of casework in order for it to become a constructive participatory process. Participation in treatment is a role to which clients may be unaccustomed and it may need to be explicitly defined.

If a client is angry at being kept waiting, this annoyance should be aired or at least acknowledged. If clients are dissatisfied with treatment and think it is a waste of time to come for interviews, the dissatisfaction should be brought into the open so that the reasons for it can be discussed and misunderstandings straightened out. If they fantasize that the worker is interested in a personal relationship with them, this, too, must be brought into open expression.

Differences in background—education, nationality, color, religion, or minority status of any kind—may create a barrier to the development of a relationship of trust. This may be because of previous experience, prejudice, reluctance to turn to a representative of another race or ethnic group for help, or lack of knowledge on the worker's part that has led to misunderstanding or to actions that have unintentionally offended the client. The worker's first concern, of course, is to avoid such tension by being sufficiently sensitive to the likelihood of its occurrence as to guard against behavior that will either precipitate or aggravate it. This requires both knowledge of how a person of a different background may react and sensitivity to beginning reactions indicating that offense has been given or is anticipated. If hostility exists or offense occurs—or is thought to exist or to have occurred—it is best to try to bring it into the open so that it can be discussed. More frequently than not, honest discussion combined with sincere good will at least alleviates the tension. Obviously, it is important not to assume that hostility exists where it does not and not to assume it is due to race, ethnic, or class differences when in reality it has a quite different source.

When clients come to an agency because someone else insists—a school principal, marital partner, or concerned person in the community—the worker can anticipate hostility and resistance. Although sustaining techniques are important, as noted earlier, reflective procedures cannot be dispensed with. Clients must know why the worker is there and for what initial purpose. They must know that they will not be pushed around or manipulated. They must know that resentment is both understood and respected, and that the worker asks primarily for a chance to demonstrate good will and potential helpfulness. The worker need not say this in so many words, but in one way or another the substance of these communications must get across to the client, along with an opportunity to express anger and fears about the intrusion.

It is sometimes held that caseworkers should not bring the client's thoughts about them to the surface, except in intensive psychological treatment. Experience has repeatedly shown the value of frank discussion of client's reactions to workers in the most matter-of-fact practical work. Psychosocial casework holds that all casework depends in part upon establishing and maintaining a sound relationship between client and worker. Obstacles to such a relationship can occur in any form of treatment and can best be removed by recognition and discussion. We discussed earlier the sustaining steps that must often be taken to convince the hard-to-reach or involuntary client of the worker's good will. It is equally important in such cases to bring the client's distrust into the open so that misconceptions can be explored and, when possible, corrected. Hard-to-reach clients have often had very bad experiences with other social workers or with people whom they mistakenly thought to be social workers, or their neighbors or friends have had such experiences. It is natural that they should expect and fear similar treatment from the current worker. Realistic discussion can be a first step in opening up the possibility of a more constructive casework relationship.

It has taken a good many pages to describe the treatment processes involved in reflective discussion of the person–situation configuration. This is not inappropriate, however, for, as we have seen, the type of understanding examined here is a central part of psychosocial casework treatment with all types of clients and problems.[8] In a great many cases, more extensive understanding is either unnecessary or inadvisable. Frequently, however, a certain amount of dynamic and developmental understanding is embedded in what is primarily person–situation understanding. Sometimes the worker sees an opportunity to deepen the client's understanding at crucial points. Interviews sometimes flow back and forth between the two types of understanding with person–situation reflection forming the base to which from time to time dynamic or developmental understanding is added. In situations in which dynamic and developmental reflection is a *major* part of treatment, preliminary discussion of current realities can provide important diagnostic information and serve as a base from which to proceed to thought about dynamic or developmental factors.

### NOTES

1.  Although the same term is not always used, the importance of "reflective discussion" has been referred to in the literature over the years. See, for example, Rosemary Reynolds and Else Siegle, "A Study of Casework with

Sado-Masochistic Marriage Partners," *Social Casework*, 40 (December 1959), 545–551, for discussion of the use of reflective or "logical" discussion along with other techniques. Sidney Berkowitz also implies the use of such techniques in his article "Some Specific Techniques of Psychosocial Diagnosis and Treatment in Family Casework," *Social Casework*, 36 (November 1955), 399–406, though it is not directly spelled out. Gordon Hamilton, in the revised edition of *Theory and Practice of Social Casework* (New York: Columbia University Press, 1951), p. 250, uses the term "counseling" to designate many of the techniques referred to in this chapter. William Reid and Ann Shyne refer to similar procedures in their terms "logical discussion," "identifying specific reactions," and "confrontation"; see *Brief and Extended Casework* (New York: Columbia University Press, 1969), pp. 70–72.

2.  For an excellent discussion of the use of this procedure with schizophrenics, see Margaret M. Heyman, "Some Methods in Direct Casework Treatment of the Schizophrenic," *Journal of Psychiatric Social Work*, 19 (Summer 1949), 18–24. See also Esther S. Marcus, "Ego Breakdown in Schizophrenia: Some Implications for Casework Treatment," in Francis J. Turner, ed., *Differential Diagnosis and Treatment in Social Work*, 2nd ed. (New York: Free Press, 1976), pp. 322–340, for examples of the use of this as well as other reflective procedures with schizophrenics. For use with parents faced with problems concerning their children, see Katherine Baldwin, "Crisis-Focused Casework in a Child Guidance Clinic," *Social Casework*, 49 (January 1968), 28–34; Audrey T. McCullum, "Mothers' Preparation for Their Children's Hospitalization," *Social Casework*, 48 (July 1967), 407–415; and Ann Murphy et al., "Group Work with Parents of Children with Down's Syndrome," *Social Casework*, 53 (February 1972), 114–119. Donna M. Oradei and Nancy S. Waite, in "Admissions Conferences for Families of Stroke Patients," *Social Casework*, 56 (January 1975), 21–26, discuss a hospital program designed, in part, to provide families with information about the medical condition of the patients. Louise Bandler also gives many illustrations of this form of reflective discussion from her work with extremely deprived families in her chapter, "Casework—A Process of Socialization: Gains, Limitations, Conclusions," in Eleanor Pavenstedt, ed., *The Drifters: Children of Disorganized Lower-Class Families* (Boston: Little, Brown, 1967).

3.  For illustrations and further discussion, see Margaret Ball, "Issues of Violence in Family Casework," *Social Casework*, 58 (January 1977), 3–12; Laura Farber, "Casework Treatment of Ambulatory Schizophrenics," *Social Casework*, 39 (January 1958), 9–17; Marcus "Ego Breakdown"; and Frances H. Scherz, "Treatment of Acting-out Character Disorders in a Marital Problem," *Casework Papers, 1956* (New York: Family Service Association of America, 1956). Of value also is Reeva Lesoff's article, "What to Say When . . .," *Clinical Social Work Journal*, 5 (Spring 1977), 66–76, which discusses the writer's own interesting approach to helping parents recognize and reflect on the effects of their attitudes and actions on their children's behavior.

4.  An excellent example of this is found in Barbara Bender, "Management

of Acute Hospitalization Anxiety," *Social Casework* (January 1976), 19–26. Here the person–situation technique is combined with ventilation and developmental reflection, but the emphasis is on fuller understanding of the surgery.

5. Miriam Jolesch refers to this type of work in joint interviews with marital partners in her article "Casework Treatment of Young Married Couples," *Social Casework*, 43 (May 1962), 245–251. See also Sally A. Holmes et al., in "Working with the Parent in Child-Abuse Cases," *Social Casework*, 56 (January 1975), 3–12, who discuss and illustrate approaches to helping abusive parents become aware of the developmental needs of their children, and the effects of placing unrealistic expectations upon them.

6. A very interesting illustration of the use of this procedure is found in Pauline L. Scanlon, "Social Work with the Mentally Retarded Client," *Social Casework*, 59 (March 1978), 161–166.

7. See Sonya L. Rhodes, "The Personality of the Worker: An Unexplored Dimension in Treatment," *Social Casework*, 60 (May 1979), 259–264, for further discussion of the point. Good illustrations of this can be found especially in articles on work with schizophrenics, with the "hard-to-reach," and with other clients who have high resistance to accepting help. See Margene M. Shea, "Establishing Initial Relationships with Schizophrenic Patients," *Social Casework*, 37 (January 1956), 25–29; H. Aronson and B. Overall, "Treatment Expectations of Patients in Two Social Classes," *Social Work*, 11 (January 1966), 35–41; Celia Benny et al., "Clinical Complexities in Work Adjustment of Deprived Youth," *Social Casework*, 50 (June 1969), 330–336; Dale E. Hardman, "The Matter of Trust," *Crime and Delinquency*, 15 (April 1969), 203–218; I. E. Molyneux, "A Study of Resistance in the Casework Relationship, " *The Social Worker*, 34 (November 1966), 217–223; Thomas J. Powell, "Negative Expectations of Treatment: Some Ideas About the Source and Management of Two Types," *Clinical Social Work Journal*, 1 (Fall 1973), 177–186. See Chapter 12 for additional references.

8. Additional illustrations can be found in Janet Bintzler, "Diagnosis and Treatment of Borderline Personality Organization," *Clinical Social Work Journal*, 6 (Summer 1978), 100–107; Samuel P. Chiancola, "The Process of Separation and Divorce: A New Approach," *Social Casework*, 59 (October 1978), 494–499; Salvador Minuchin and Braulio Montalvo, "Techniques for Working with Disorganized Low Socio-Economic Families," *American Journal of Orthopsychiatry*, 37 (October 1967), 880–887; Jeanette Oppenheimer, "Use of Crisis Intervention in Casework with the Cancer Patient and His Family," *Social Work*, 12 (April 1967), 44–52; Ethel Panter, "Ego-Building Procedures That Foster Social Functioning," *Social Casework*, 48 (March 1967), 139–145; Veon Smith and Dean Hepworth, "Marriage Counseling with One Partner: Rationale and Clinical Implications," *Social Casework*, 48 (June 1967), 352–359; Philip W. Walker, "Premarital Counseling for the Developmentally Disabled," *Social Casework*, 58 (October 1977), 475–479; and Edna Wasser, "Family Casework Focus on the Older Person," *Social Casework*, 47 (July 1966), 423–431.

# Chapter 7

# Reflective Consideration of Pattern-Dynamic and Developmental Factors

The two remaining forms of reflective communication are those that seek to promote dynamic and developmental understanding. Intrapsychic forces of which a person is not fully aware may so strongly influence behavior that it is not possible to perceive and act differently in response to person–situation reflection alone. It is sometimes helpful to turn such a person's attention briefly to the underlying dynamics of his or her personality or to early life experiences that are still unfavorably influencing current adjustment. Often, but not always, both types of understanding can be developed.

We are using here the word "understanding" rather than the term "insight" because the latter is used in psychoanalysis primarily to refer to understanding the workings of the *un*conscious.[1] Readers will recall that the terms "dynamic" and "developmental reflection" and the understanding to which these can lead refer in psychosocial theory primarily to *pre*conscious rather than *un*conscious material. Some *pre*conscious material, however, is not accessible merely by shifting attention to it (see pp. 324–326 for further discussion). It has long been recognized that certain technical procedures can be and are employed by casework for the purpose of keeping the work for the most part on conscious and preconscious rather than unconscious verbalizations. Interviews are usually held with client and worker able to look directly at each other, they are spaced farther apart than in analysis proper— most often a week between interviews, though sometimes the client is seen several times a week—we use a permissive, eductive type of interviewing, distinctly not the same as free association; explanations are held to conscious and near conscious material with little use of symbolic content.

Readers will recall the discussion in Chapter 2 about the question of the balance of forces within and between the various parts of the personality. Psychosocial theory supported by practice experience maintains that dynamic and developmental reflection, even though

146

they do not lead to insight into the unconscious, can in many instances bring enough modification in the balance between functional and dysfunctional aspects of the personality system to strengthen the individual's ability to cope with the problems for which he or she seeks a clinical social worker's assistance.

## REFLECTION CONCERNING DYNAMIC FACTORS

When we consider dynamic factors with the client, we are simply extending the process of intrareflection, using procedures—comments, questions, occasionally explanations—the content and timing of which is designed to help the individual to pursue further some of the intrapsychic reasons for his or her feelings, attitudes, and ways of acting, to understand the influence of one personality characteristic upon another —in other words, the way in which thoughts and emotions work. Here we go beyond the understanding of single interactions or even a series of interactions, as was done in the person–situation gestalt, to consideration of the intrapsychic *pattern* or tendency that contributes to the interaction. Often, the client is aware—sometimes clearly and sometimes vaguely—of unrealistic or inappropriate behavior. The client may delve into the question of "why" without any prompting from the caseworker. At other times, the worker takes the first step by calling the inappropriateness or inconsistency to the client's attention: "Have you noticed that you don't have trouble in being firm with Paula but seem to be so afraid to be firm with Ed?"—to a mother who does not realize that her difficulty in disciplining her son springs from her desperate fear of losing his love. At this point, the worker is moving beyond one interpersonal event to raise a question about a series of such events, a pattern. Presumably, individual instances of difficulty in showing appropriate firmness had been considered before, but without enabling this mother to act more appropriately. The worker then suggests to the client that this may be part of a general tendency. Recognition of the pattern can turn the client's attention to the question of why. The answer may lie in displacement from husband to son, in underlying hostility to her son, in greater desire for this child's love, in specific early life events—to name a few of the possibilities—or in some combination of these.

Similarly, in another situation the worker says, "I wonder how it is that you can be so understanding of the children and yet seem unable to try to understand your husband"—to a woman who is ordinarily very perceptive of other people's feelings, but does not want to lessen the conflict with her husband because she fears the sex relationships he would want to resume if they were on good terms. Or, "What do you suppose makes you constantly insult people you say you want to be friends with?"—to a man who defends himself against his fear of rejection by first antagonizing others. Often, the worker has already sensed what the underlying tendency is. Whenever possible, however, the worker encourages the client to seek the answer for himself rather than interpreting it for him.

Sometimes the client does not recognize problem behavior; in other words, it is "ego-syntonic," acceptable to the ego, and must become "ego-alien," unacceptable to the ego, if there is to be motivation to try to understand and modify it. A mother who continually got into tempestuous fights at the table with her son saw her reactions only in terms of his slow and sloppy eating habits, which she felt made such scenes inevitable. After a substantial period of patient listening, reflective discussion, and suggestions, the worker responded to the heated description of a stormy session with the comment, "You are like two children battling each other, aren't you?" Obviously, the remark carried a value judgment, for adults do not consider it a compliment to be told that they are behaving childishly. It carried force with this client because a strong relationship had been established between her and her worker, which made her value the worker's opinion. The fact that the worker rarely took a position of this sort gave it added significance. Sometimes the client, in response to such a stimulus, begins to think about reasons for his or her reactions; at other times, further comment is needed: "There seems to be something between you and George that we need to understand—what thoughts come to you about it?" In this situation, the client went on first to the realization that she prolonged the scenes at the table for the pleasure she derived from hitting her son, and later to the discovery that she had identified her son with her husband and was taking out on him anger she did not dare to express directly to her husband.

Clients will seek understanding of thoughts or actions only when some dissatisfaction is felt with them, when they are recognized as unprofitable or in some way inappropriate or ego-alien. Until this attitude exists, dynamic interpretations will fall on deaf ears. When it does exist or has been brought into being, the client will often be able to arrive at understanding with relatively little use of interpretation by the worker.

Almost any aspect of the personality that is either conscious or near-conscious may come under scrutiny in this type of procedure. Occasionally, unconscious matters may come through, but in general basic casework is not designed to uncover unconscious material.

## Ego Defenses

A very common area in which understanding is sought is that of the ego defenses, such as avoidance, defensive hostility, and the various mechanisms of turning against the self—projection, intellectualization, rationalization, suppression, inhibition, and isolation. "Have you ever noticed that sometimes people get angry when they are scared? I wonder if you weren't pretty edgy about having that talk with your brother-in-law, and in a way hit out at him before he had a chance to hit you." "Have you noticed how often you go off into this kind of theoretical discussion when I'm trying to get you to think about your own feelings toward Mary?" "You know, it's good that you try to learn so much about children, but sometimes I wonder if it isn't a way of avoiding letting yourself realize what strong feelings you have when Johnny acts this way." "Do you think your wife was really mad, or were you so angry yourself that you kind of expected she would be? What did she actually say at the beginning?" "Do you think that you are feeling depressed because you are really so mad at Fred but feel you can't let it out? Sometimes, you know, you can turn those angry feelings against yourself and then you feel depressed."

Initially, defense mechanisms often have to be explained to clients because they may not be familiar with the way they work and cannot be expected to arrive at this kind of understanding entirely on their own. Subsequently, however, clients are frequently able to spot their own use of a particular defense. One of the goals of this type of treatment is to enable them to do this for themselves.

The greatest care is necessary in work with defenses, however, for they are self-protective mechanisms used by the personality to ward off anxiety. They should not be abruptly "broken through," but "worked through" when evaluation indicates that the individual is able to bear the anxiety involved. For the most part, interpretations should be made tentatively, and certainly in an atmosphere of acceptance, which often needs to be put into words.[2]

## Superego

Important as defense mechanisms are, they are by no means the only part of the personality under scrutiny in the process of dynamic understanding. Often, certain superego characteristics need to be thought about, especially the oversensitivity of the severe conscience. A client who is too hard on herself may be helped by knowing that she is suffering from self-criticism rather than from the too-high requirements of others. The person who feels deeply hurt by the discovery of imperfections in himself may be helped by recognizing that the demand for perfection is a function of his own personality. "Have you noticed how upset you get whenever anyone makes the slightest criticism of your work?" "You hold very high standards for yourself, don't you?" "I think you are harder on yourself than anyone else would be."[3]

One of the hazards of helping a person to become aware of superego severity is that the worker may appear to the client to be too lax in standards. It is extremely important to avoid this impression; and great care must be taken not to seem to be sponsoring antisocial behavior. If the client does, nevertheless, react in this way, the reaction must be brought into the open and discussed. "I have a feeling that you are worried that I may be too easygoing. Let's talk about it." It is important to clarify this question, making it clear that the worker is not opposed to standards as such but to unrealistic or harmful severity of conscience. When the client's feelings about this are brought out in the open and discussed, not only is the worker's position clarified, but this may lead to a reflective discussion that reveals that it is the client's pattern to judge others in a similar manner.

A client who specifically illustrates this point is the mother of a child who had been sent to the agency for treatment because of school failures inconsistent with his intelligence. She was a very religious woman who set extremely high standards for herself and who initially found treatment difficult because the need to recognize that she might be contributing to her son's troubles shattered her faith in herself as a good mother. Every attempt at developing her understanding, no matter how carefully worded, was taken as a criticism from which she cringed. One of her underlying problems was her effort to suppress and inhibit all hostile impulses, and she felt extreme guilt over her failures to do so. When the worker tried to reduce her self-condemnation, she thought the worker was trying to undermine her faith and principles.

One day she brought a Bible to the interview, and seemed quite agitated. When the worker asked her gently if she had brought the Bible for a special reason, she opened it to the famous letter of Paul to the Corinthians on love, reading particularly the verse, "When I was a child, I spoke as a child, I felt as a child, I thought as a child; now that I am a man I have put away childish things," and she cried as she finished it. The worker said it was a beautiful letter and asked if she had ever thought of why it was written. Did she think perhaps Paul might have observed that many people brought into adulthood feelings and thoughts from childhood? Perhaps he wished to counsel men to put away these feelings and behave like adults. No one could quarrel with the ideals of love, charity, and understanding. Religion and psychiatry have the same goals; the only question is how to achieve them.

As the client still seemed confused, the worker put her thoughts in terms of gardening, a known interest of this client. "If you had a garden and weeds were choking out the good plants, you could cut off the tops of the weeds and the garden would look good, but the roots would still be there. Wouldn't it be better to pull out the roots? It would be harder but the results would be better. The same thing is true for human emotions. Many of us try to hide our difficulties and stamp them down, but this takes energy that could be used for better things. It seems worthwhile to try to uproot the difficulties. The only method I know for uprooting them is to understand and face things that are painful and intolerable. I'm not arguing against the goals of religion, but sometimes I question the way it goes about attaining them." The client was silent for several minutes, and then said she was greatly relieved and that she had had no idea the caseworker had such deep understanding of her feelings.

A similar difficulty can occur under almost opposite circumstances. The client whose control of impulses is tenuous may have great anxiety about a possible breakthrough of hostile or sexual impulses if these desires are allowed to reach awareness. With such clients, it is extremely important for the worker to make clear the distinction between recognizing a desire or wish and carrying it out, and to make explicit the position that one is not trying to encourage the client to act out impulses, but to recognize them so that they can be controlled more effectively. If this type of approach is to be used, however, knowledge of the client must indicate that the ego is in fact able to control such impulses once they are recognized. When a danger of breakthrough does exist, obviously, it is better not to disturb the defenses against it. Careful diagnostic assessment, while always important, is essential to work in which greater understanding of one's own emotional patterns is involved.

## Ego Functioning

Understanding can also be gained of various ego functions when they contribute to personal problems. It can be helpful for some individuals to become aware of excessively strong needs of the personality that, showing themselves in such traits as great dependence or a high degree of narcissism, can cause trouble for the individual. Persisting distortions in perception and unrealistic ideas about one's own tendencies and capacities are also among the many ego areas in which help can be given. In the following case, for instance, part of the difficulty lay in the client's unrealistic fear of being unable to control impulses.

A retired man in his late sixties was extremely angry at his wife for pressuring him to relocate with her to another part of the country, a move he did not want to make. She had taken several trips to explore retirement homes, and he was becoming extremely anxious and frustrated by her persistence. At the same time, he had not been able to state his position on the matter firmly, nor did he initiate a discussion with her of possible alternatives or compromises. He felt victimized and defeated. The day his wife was to fly home from one of her trips, he called his caseworker in a severely frightened state. He confided that he had momentarily wished that the plane would crash. The worker, whom he trusted, was able to help him reduce his fear by pointing out that it often happens that when people feel angry and frustrated they have violent wishes and thoughts. Knowing the man as well as she did, the caseworker was able to reassure him that his impulse to see his wife dead in no way meant that he would therefore act on his wish in any way. The breakthrough of deeply hostile feelings led this very controlled and passive man to believe that he would either become ungovernably violent ("I feel like a murderer," he said) or else that he would break down emotionally. Once these suppressed feelings came to the surface, he was finally able to talk with his wife about his wishes for retirement. From this experience, he was able to reflect on his lifelong pattern of suppressing his own desires for fear he would lose the love of people close to him. Furthermore, he began to recognize how his pent-up anger was based on his feelings of helplessness in the face of his wife's tendency to dominate him.

An important step in the process of dynamic understanding is the client's bringing reason and judgment to bear upon the personality characteristic and its functioning that has been brought to his or her attention. It was not enough for the religious mother to see that she was trying to handle her anger by suppressing it; she had to be able to think about what she was doing, to bring her own judgment to bear upon it. She had to become convinced that her way of handling her feelings was not helping her son before she was ready to try to give it up.

The client's reactions to the worker are also a fruitful source of dynamic understanding. As defense mechanisms or personality characteristics such as fear of criticism or excessive dependence come into play in the client–worker relationship, they can be used to enable the client to see the inner workings of his or her personality in action. The client can then use this understanding to recognize similar dynamics operating in other life experiences.

Pattern-dynamic reflection is usually built upon previous consideration of the current person–situation configuration. A few comments about the dynamics involved may enable the client to understand personality patterns more fully. This in turn may lessen the strength of some of the deterrents to realistic and appropriate perception and response. Discussion usually returns soon to the person–situation realm, where progress can be made in relating better to other people. Even in those cases where pattern-dynamic reflection is a major component in treatment, discussion never rests long in that realm exclusively. It is always accompanied by sustaining measures, and may at times be supplemented by procedures of direct influence. Exploration, description, and ventilation, of course, remain an essential ongoing process. Dynamic understanding is frequently achieved without going into the development of the personality characteristic under discussion.

## Personality Disorders

In earlier years, caseworkers—particularly those engaged in intensive or long-term treatment—worked mostly with clients handicapped by neurotic symptoms or conflicts. More recently, large numbers of people in the caseloads of clinical social workers are diagnosed as having personality disorders. For some time, it was generally believed that people in this group—in contrast to neurotic clients—were not capable of pattern-dynamic and developmental reflection. It was thought that their behavior was "ego-syntonic"—that is, acceptable to the ego—and the presence of underlying anxiety and pain was not recognized. Hence, it was believed that only person–situation reflection would be useful—helping such clients to see the ways in which they were really hurting or depriving themselves. However, clinical experience has since indicated that many such clients can be greatly helped by greater self-understanding, and that they are capable of achieving this. Mrs. Zimmer in Chapter 3 is a clear example of this type of work.

Better understanding of the varieties of character disorders and of their varying dynamics reveals great underlying discomfort, pain, and anxiety. The socially dysfunctional behavior is often only superficially ego-syntonic. The client's motivation for reflecting depends upon the degree to which his or her behavior can become "ego-alien" (i.e., unacceptable to his ego). If the client has the capacity for establishing a working relationship, and ego functions, especially reality testing and impulse control, are strong enough or can be strengthened sufficiently to work in these ways, tremendous benefit can come from intrareflection about personality dynamics or early life experiences. Since the difficulties in which people suffering from personality disorders find themselves tend to result from rigidly repetitive emotional, attitudinal, and behavorial patterns, understanding of these can be an important step toward change. Generally speaking, the more severe the character problem, the more sustainment is necessary before turning to reflective procedures; furthermore, during the course of exploring and understanding the intrapsychic bases for their troubles, these clients may need particular support to help them through the anxiety or depression that may accompany growing self-awareness. However, when given sufficient support as discomfort increases, these clients' motivation for treatment and change may increase dramatically.

## DEVELOPMENTAL UNDERSTANDING

Encouragement of reflection upon developmental material is usually undertaken in an episodic way in psychosocial casework, certain themes being explored as it becomes apparent that factors in the client's development are blocking improvement in current social adjustment. The procedure is used to help the client become aware of the way in which certain present personality characteristics have been shaped by earlier life experiences, and sometimes to modify reactions to these experiences. It is sometimes necessary because certain dysfunctional characteristics cannot be overcome except by understanding of the experiences that contributed to their formation. The term "contributed" is used advisedly because casework never reaches all the determinants of a given phase of behavior. The ability to reach early causative factors is a relative matter, in any case. Analytic theory readily acknowledges that, in addition to constitutional factors, early preverbal experiences that cannot be reached even by analysis are potent in preparing an initial "personality set" that profoundly influences the way later infantile and childhood experiences are received by the individual.[4] In Chapter 2, we pointed out that the factor of later reinforcement of earlier experiences is extremely important in personality development. Harmful infantile experiences are sometimes overcome by health-inducing later ones, but often, unfortunately, events serve to confirm and reinforce the child's misconceptions or distorted generalizations. Again, the concept of a balance of forces in the personality comes into play. Psychosocial casework theory holds that understanding of these later reinforcements can lessen the strength of damaging tendencies in the personality and may enable healthier components to take the ascendancy in controlling and directing personality functioning. The purpose of encouraging the client to reflect upon early life experiences is to bring about such a change in the personality system. In general, casework does not attempt to reach infantile experiences, but later childhood and adolescent events, which can be considered genetic only in the sense that they are contributory developmental experiences.

## Reflection Versus Description–Ventilation

The worker cannot assume that every time clients talk about past life they are engaging in the process of developing understanding of it. Most of the time this is not the case. Often, the client is simply describing past experiences rather than reflecting upon them. At other times the client's talk about the past is for the purpose of catharsis. At such times a person may get considerable relief from telling the worker about painful life events and from expressing anger or grief about them. Again, the client very often brings in the past to justify present feelings, attitudes, or behavior. The individual is not then really trying to gain understanding but instead trying to explain to the worker why this or that reaction or feeling was appropriate or at least that he or she should not be blamed for so reacting; in other words, the past is used as a defense of a present position. This type of defense is sometimes of great importance to the client, for it serves as protection against overly severe self-criticism. When this is so, care needs to be taken to assure that it is not thoughtlessly or prematurely stripped away. Other clients talk about the past to evade thinking about the present. And, finally, clients sometimes have the impression that the past is what the worker is interested in, and talk about it in order to please the worker.

## Movement into Developmental Reflection

There are other times, however, when the client can be helped greatly in understanding unhealthy and unprofitable ways of acting by coming to understand some of their historical sources. Some clients quickly and spontaneously seek this kind of understanding. Others need help from the caseworker before they are ready and able to do so. Apparent readiness needs to be carefully distinguished from real readiness. The current sophistication about Freudian ideas and other personality theories makes intellectualization about childhood events a particularly popular form of defense.

Sound movement into consideration of developmental factors follows much the same pattern as that just described for moving into the dynamics of psychological functioning. The client's attention is drawn to inappropriate or inconsistent behavior. Sometimes the client makes the choice of seeking further understanding, reacting in one way or the other to the worker's pointing up of the problem. At other times the worker takes the lead in steering thinking toward his or her earlier life. "Have you had feelings like this before?" "Does this make you think at all of similar things that have happened to you?" Or, more specifically, to a mother who is very upset by her son's barely average school report:

"How was it for you in school?" Or to a man who is unduly upset in mentioning his brother's childhood failure in school: "You haven't told me much about your brother—what was he like?"[5] In these illustrations, the worker first explores the past and gives opportunities for ventilation about it in areas that would be expected to be related to the client's present feelings or actions. The client may then spontaneously move into developmental understanding by seeing connections, or the worker may promote thinking about this by suggesting them. "Yes, that must have been awfully hard to take—are there times when Mary seems to be doing the same thing?" Or, "Did you notice that you used exactly those same words in telling me about Jim?"

Often, in previous general exploration of the client's earlier life, or as the client has talked about his or her childhood for other reasons, the worker will have obtained clues to areas in the client's life that may be of significance in understanding a particular reaction. These clues should certainly be used in guiding the client's associations. A woman who was unreasonably resentful of what seemed to her neglect by her husband had earlier mentioned to the worker that her father had paid very little attention to her as a child. When she complained at length about her husband's neglect of her, the worker responded by asking her more about her father. The client, simply by thinking of the two parallel situations in juxtaposition, saw the similarity and asked if she could be carrying some of her feeling toward her father over to her husband.

But sometimes the worker must make the connection. A mother was unreasonably angry with her adolescent daughter for borrowing her costume jewelry. The worker was already aware of this woman's deep hostility to her mother and suspected that it was being displaced onto her daughter. She also knew that as an adolescent and later, the client had been required to carry too much of the financial burden of the home, so that she had been deprived of many things she wanted. The worker ventured the comment, "I wonder if Joan's taking your things that way doesn't arouse the same feelings you had as a girl when your mother didn't let you get pretty things for yourself." This touched off an outburst of feeling about the client's deprived adolescence, followed by the realization that she had been taking out on her daughter the stored-up feelings of her own childhood.

Sometimes a client is fully aware of pertinent early experiences and little or no anxiety is involved in recalling them; the problem is simply to enable the individual to recognize the influence of past on present. At other times, the early feelings or experiences are to a degree hidden from view, for reasons that directly parallel the reasons for hiding current feelings and reactions. There may be fear of criticism of things that are perfectly well remembered, or an event may not be regarded as significant or pertinent to the interview, or memories may have been suppressed or repressed because of their painfulness.

There are times when the recollection of an event and recognition of its influence in current life may not be enough. Rather, the past event itself may need to be thought about and reevaluated so that the feelings about it are modified. If a woman who is very resentful that her father did not provide adequately for his family can be helped to realize that his failure was due to a combination of illness and widespread national unemployment rather than to weakness of character or unwillingness to carry his family responsibilities, the amount of hostility she displaces upon her husband, a hard-working, conscientious individual who does not earn as much as she would like him to, may be substantially reduced. A woman who had felt that her parents discriminated against her by not letting her go to college was helped to recognize that she herself as a girl had not shown any interest in college. Thus, she saw that her parents might not have been discriminating against her but were perhaps unaware of her interest in further education. This recognition, in turn, not only led to a reduction of the client's hostility toward her parents and enabled her to have better current relationships with them, it also substantially reduced her feeling, which had carried over into all her adult relationships, that she was not loved and was somehow unworthy of love.

Before moving into this reevaluation process, it is often necessary to allow considerable ventilation of initial hostile feelings, partly because of the relief the client obtains from such an outpouring and from the worker's continued acceptance despite feelings about which the client may feel quite guilty, but also because there probably will not be readiness to reconsider earlier relationships until there has been an opportunity for catharsis. If the worker attempts the reevaluation process prematurely, the client is apt to resent it, thinking that the worker is unsympathetic, critical, or siding with the person toward whom the client is hostile.

Obviously, reevaluation is useful only when the client has really misconstrued the earlier situation. Many times the early reality has in fact been extremely painful or even traumatic. Under such circumstances, ventilation, plus sympathetic acceptance by the worker and realization of the way in which early events are unnecessarily influencing current life, is appropriate.

## Relationship with Worker

The relationship with the worker can also often be used as a source of developmental understanding. When the client is clearly reacting to the worker in terms of attitudes carried over from early life, the worker should, if consideration of these factors is deemed appropriate, help the person to recognize what he or she is doing. "Do you think that you fear criticism from me as you did from your father?" "Do you see what you are doing? You are trying to get me to urge you to study just as your mother used to do. Then you will be angry at me for 'nagging', just as you used to be angry at your mother." Interpretations like these would be appropriate only after a client has achieved some measure of under-standing of feelings toward parents. Sometimes such transference inter-pretations are necessary to straighten out the relationship with the worker so that treatment can proceed. They are also of great value in helping the client to become aware of similar transferred reactions in other parts of current life. Because the worker is observing the client's reaction directly in a controlled situation, he or she is in an excellent position to make an accurate, convincing interpretation.[6] This is, of course, similar to the way in which transference reactions are some-times handled in psychoanalysis. The difference lies in the type of relationship that the two approaches develop. In psychosocial case-work, although in general we emphasize the reality relationship rather than the transference, a certain degree of transference nevertheless occurs. Our procedures are designed, however, to prevent *regression* in the transference. In other words, we do not seek to enable the client to go back to a reliving of infantile and very early childhood attitudes, needs, and reactions in the treatment relationship.

Again, the more the client can do independently, the better. If the client sees connections without help or questions the accuracy of his or her understanding of earlier events, fine. Otherwise, the more the worker can limit communications to starting the client on an appropri-ate train of thought by a question, suggestion, or tentative comment, the better. Interpretations, when they are necessary, should be made tentatively, unless the worker is absolutely sure of their accuracy. Here, as in every other form of understanding, the worker should endeavor to minimize the client's dependence, encouraging the ability to think for himself.[7] Periods of work on developmental patterns occur in many cases that are mainly focused on the person–situation configuration. Dynamic and developmental procedures often serve to push forward the process of person–situation understanding where such under-standing is temporarily blocked by intrapsychic influences. And as with reflection upon dynamic factors, episodes of thinking about develop-mental factors are followed in treatment by a return to the person–situation configuration as soon as the new understanding has cleared the way for better perception and handling of current affairs. Sustaining comments often help to provide the client with the necessary confi-dence in the worker's good will and competence. When anxiety mounts as a result of some of the memories, feelings, and connections that are uncovered, sustaining communications can help to carry the client through a difficult period of work.

The procedures discussed in this and the preceding chapter are closely related. The intrareflective procedures of the person–situation configuration can be skillfully used only when the worker has substantial psychological knowledge and understanding. A 1969 study reported by Mullen[8] and also by Reid and Shyne[9] found that some workers avoided using either pattern-dynamic or developmental reflection even when it would have been appropriate to do so. This would seem to represent a lack in either their training or in their capacity for this kind of work. From the psychosocial point of view, any caseworker engaged in treatment of disturbances in interpersonal relationships stands very much in need of the total repertory of casework procedures.

In order to promote consideration of dynamic or developmental matters as a major part of treatment, the worker must, in addition to being skilled in all the other casework processes, be thoroughly familiar with the workings of the personality—of unconscious as well as of conscious factors—and with the way in which the personality develops and early life events find continued expression in the adult personality. Workers must be particularly sensitive to the nuances of the clients' feelings, have considerable security when dealing with anxiety, and be aware of and able to control the flow of their own reactions. They must also be free of the need to probe into a client's life to secure vicarious satisfaction either of their own curiosity, of an appetite for power, or for other narcissistic gratifications.

### NOTES

1. Greta Bibring, "Psychiatry and Social Work," *Journal of Social Casework,* 28 (June 1947), 203–211.
2. Annette Garrett, in her article "The Worker–Client Relationship," in Howard J. Parad, ed., *Ego Psychology and Dynamic Casework* (New York: Family Service Association of America, 1958), pp. 53–54, 59–60, discusses this point in her section on transference and interpretation. See also Emanuel F. Hammer, "Interpretive Technique: a Primer," in Hammer, ed., *Use of Interpretation in Treatment: Technique and Art* (New York: Grune and Stratton, 1968), pp. 31–42; and Rudolph M. Lowenstein, "The Problem of Interpretation," *Psychoanalytic Quarterly,* 20 (January 1951), 1–14. Excellent illustrations and discussion of the need for some clients to defend against pervasive anxiety and depression through denial can be found in Alice H. Collins and James R. MacKey, "Delinquents Who Use the Primary Defense of Denial," in Francis J. Turner, ed., *Differential Diagnosis and Treatment in Social Work,* 2nd ed. (New York: Free Press, 1976), pp. 64–75.

Florence Lieberman, *Social Work with Children* (New York: Human Services Press, 1979), p. 282, also deals with the importance of respecting defenses in the context of work with children.

3. See Lillian Kaplan and Jean B. Livermore, "Treatment of Two Patients with Punishing Super-Egos," *Journal of Social Casework,* 29 (October 1948), 310–316. For an interesting point of view and discussion of the superego, shame, and guilt, and implications for treatment, see Helen Block Lewis, *Shame and Guilt in Neurosis* (New York: International Universities Press, 1971).

4. For elaboration of this point, see Gertrude and Rubin Blanck, *Ego Psychology: Theory and Practice* (New York: Columbia University Press, 1974); and Phyllis Greenacre, ed., *Affective Disorders: A Psychoanalytic Contribution to Their Study* (New York: International Universities Press, 1953). For further readings on developmental psychology and personality disorders, see Chapter 3, note 3.

5. For illustrations, see Lucille N. Austin, "Diagnosis and Treatment of the Client with Anxiety Hysteria," in Parad, *Ego Psychology and Dynamic Casework;* and Hank Walzer, "Casework Treatment of the Depressed Parent," in Turner, *Differential Diagnosis,* pp. 302–312. For an interesting approach to leading clients to developmental reflection in joint interviews, see Arlene S. Fontane, "Using Family of Origin Material in Short-Term Marriage Counseling," *Social Casework,* 60 (November 1979), 529–537.

6. See Andrew Watson, "Reality Testing and Transference in Psychotherapy," *Smith College Studies in Social Work,* 36 (June 1966), 191–209. Kenneth E. Reid, in "Nonrational Dynamics of Client–Worker Interaction," *Social Casework,* 58 (December 1977), 600–606, deals very well with the nuances of the worker's own attitudes in transference situations.

7. For very useful discussions of the timing, methods, and purposes of interpretations, see Blanck and Blanck, *Ego Psychology: Theory and Practice,* especially pp. 314–337; and Ralph Ormsby, "Interpretations in Casework Therapy," *Journal of Social Casework,* 29 (April 1948), 135–141. Also of interest are several papers in Hammer, *Use of Interpretation,* and Jules Masserman, ed., *Depressions: Theories and Therapies* (New York: Grune & Stratton, 1970).

8. See Edward J. Mullen, "Differences in Worker Style in Casework," *Social Casework,* 50 (June 1969), 347–353.

9. William J. Reid and Ann W. Shyne, *Brief and Extended Casework* (New York: Columbia University Press, 1969), pp. 82–93.

# Chapter 8

# Environmental Work: Part One

## PSYCHOSOCIAL THERAPY AND THE ENVIRONMENT

Psychosocial casework is, as we have said many times, concerned with the improvement of social functioning, interpersonal relationships, and life situations. Sometimes personalities or families are truly "pathological," "dysfunctional," or "inadequate." At other times, these same assessments can be applied to aspects of the world around the client. In addition to relatives and friends, these environments include other people, physical surroundings, cultural attitudes, organizations or institutions, even communities and large social systems. When one or more of these are unhealthy or substandard (an ill spouse, poor housing, discrimination, a tight job market, etc.), the client is, of course, directly affected. Problems may also be created by dysfunctional transactions *among* various systems in a client's milieu (take, for example, the stress for a child whose foster parents, natural parents, and child welfare worker are in conflict or are pulling in different directions). And, certainly, many client difficulties are the consequence of dysfunctional interactions *between* the client and one or more aspects of the environment (employer, fellow employees, in-laws, teachers, for example).

Psychosocial therapy, as the term implies, does not mean that every person–situation imbalance or disturbance requires that individuals must make changes from within. It is often the *situation*—or environment—that must be treated, modified, changed. Since causation is complex, a vast number of problems encountered by clinical social workers do not rest primarily upon the diagnosis of the personality system; rather, they require an analysis of the person–situation disequilibrium. For instance, "deviance" of some sort may be an expected response to a closed or inadequate opportunity structure; myriad kinds of "pathology" may be the outcome of mystifying or double-binding communications; "acting out" may be the only apparent alternative to resignation and hopelessness in the face of noxious social conditions.[1] As the psychosocial framework has incorporated a systems perspective, caseworkers following this approach have become increasingly sophisticated in their conceptualizations of the client–situation interplay, and this in turn has contributed to more precise assessments of what is wrong or what is needed in a given situation.

Nevertheless, sometimes it can be very difficult indeed to differentiate between an individual's inner life and the world outside, particularly those aspects of the environment that impinge directly on the person's situation. In practice, we often find that modifications of a client's external situation can result in emotional or behavioral changes, just as emotional growth can often give the individual the strength required to fully utilize or make changes in the environment. The caseworker may concentrate, therefore, on that system or those systems that seem most accessible to change—not necessarily the most dysfunctional ones. Sometimes a client is helped to find personal alternatives to an unjust external condition; at other times, emotional disturbance may best be treated by altering the environment. For example, it may be more efficient and caring to help a man, victimized by unemployment, to retrain or relocate than it would be to wait until pressure can bring about changes in the unhealthy economic situation. On the other hand, a person with a severe or chronic personality disorder may respond better to a supportive milieu than to therapy aimed directly at his intrapsychic disturbance. Paradoxically, then, the caseworker's focus for intervention may be the healthiest aspect of the person–situation configuration, when this is the one most amenable to influence. The psychosocial approach to problems in or with the environment, therefore, requires an understanding of the people involved, the impinging environments, and the interactions among these in order to evaluate which of them are likely to be modifiable.

Some social workers think it is reactionary and/or futile to attempt to assist individuals in the face of societal evils and ills that can so profoundly grind them down. As the writers see it, however, one need not support or be satisfied with the *status quo* of a grossly imperfect social system in order to attempt to help people improve the quality of their lives *now*—before more basic changes become possible.

In this connection, it is important to remind ourselves of what casework can and cannot do. Some professional modesty is called for. While as *social workers,* individually and through professional organizations, our heritage compels us to advocate social change, to participate in movements and vigorously support legislation that challenges oppressive aspects of our social structure—our goals for change can far exceed our power. Yet we know what we, as *caseworkers, can* do. When working with victims of social injustice: We can be supportive. We can share with clients our distress with conditions and not (as we have sometimes been accused) try to "adjust" them to intolerable situations. We can develop techniques that are responsive to the needs of people living under miserable circumstances. We can assist people in their efforts to "negotiate the system." We can offer concrete help in changing or in opening up opportunities in the client's environment. We can promote policies and approaches in agencies and institutions where we have influence, and thereby try to make service delivery more human and relevant. We can participate in reflecting on ways in which clients themselves, or in concert with others, can induce environmental changes. We can help to locate or create services or social networks for people who need or want them. Increasingly, social workers are providing resources *before* serious problems develop, by offering educational, therapeutic, facilitative services in clinics, schools, day care centers, to populations "at risk," and so on—thereby helping to contribute to the *prevention* of future life problems or personality disturbances.[2] In this chapter and in the one that follows, we will be discussing some of the casework principles and skills required for such environmental work.

But the treatment we offer cannot "cure" the extraordinary problems that a large group of our clients face today. We readily acknowledge that casework does not and cannot eradicate poverty, unemployment, discrimination, or the dehumanizing effects of a society that can place low priority on improving the quality of the lives of citizens increasingly beleaguered by the effects of urban conditions, political corruption, and impersonal bureaucracies. But casework should not be discredited because it does not do everything we wish it could.[3]

Sometimes students and caseworkers make the mistake of assuming that environmental work is needed only by the poor and the disadvantaged. The fact is that this kind of casework is of great importance to many clients—to children, the elderly, and the physically and mentally ill or disabled, and to many other individuals and families facing either "expectable" or extraordinary crises. Although those in poverty are particularly pressed by practical problems, people from all income groups benefit from environmental intervention to help them through difficulties or to improve their lives. Just as many poor or poorly educated clients with emotional problems have the capacity and motivation for introspection, so some well-to-do clients seek only "concrete" services. The tendency to assume that social action and environmental work are only relevant to the poor and that psychotherapy is useful only to the financially comfortable sells both groups short.[4]

Some people tend to believe that environmental work can be routinely delegated to paraprofessionals, or even to untrained volunteers. In some instances, such staff can be extremely helpful.[5] They can become experts on resources, on clients' rights, on eligibility procedures. They can be forceful advocates. By demonstration, they can teach the client to become more effective in the use of resources. But extensive in-service training added to natural aptitude is necessary, if they are to become skillful in differential communication in environmental work. Furthermore, in our opinion, environmental work should be assigned to untrained workers only selectively, with the clinical social worker carrying responsibility not only for the general direction and coordination of the work, but also for making collateral contacts when a high degree of differential interviewing skill is needed. It should not be assumed that environmental work is simple and does not involve a knowledge of people and casework procedures similar to that required for direct work with clients. We have seen many a failure directly caused by this type of oversimplification.

The complexity of environmental work was highlighted by one study that examined the use of concrete environmental modification by caseworkers employed in the family and children's services of one of the largest public welfare agencies in the Midwest. Even in such an agency—where one would expect that the need for concrete services might be high—concrete environmental intervention, compared to other intervention techniques, was found to be employed infrequently. The researchers suspected that its relatively low use, and its greater use by MSW than non–MSW caseworkers, might be accounted for by the intricacy of the interventive technique required to bring about environmental modification.[6]

## Environmental Change by Client or by Worker?

The general casework value of enabling the client to increase in competence has a direct bearing on the decision of how to deal with problems that either involve environmental etiology or in general depend upon the use of environmental resources for their solution. We are always confronted by the question of whether to intervene on the client's behalf or to encourage the client to attempt to tackle the milieu problem alone. By and large, the more one can do for oneself, the greater the increase in one's competence and in one's self-respect. But if this is to be the outcome, the change that is required must be one that the client is likely to be able to bring about. Some milieu—or environmental—factors are more responsive to the worker than to the client. Not infrequently the worker, because of status and role, has more "clout" and can influence the environment in a way that the client cannot. At other times, knowledge or skill in human relations may enable the worker to effect changes beyond the client's capacity to achieve by his or her own efforts.[7] For instance, while a patient could talk to a doctor about a medical problem, the worker's knowledge of both doctor and patient may lead the worker to think that the client would not get the information needed for future planning if he or she asked for it initially.

The decision of when and when not to intervene in the environment rests upon the knowledge gained in the worker's assessment of both the modifiability of milieu facts and the client's capacity to handle them. In Chapter 9, we will discuss more fully how assessment of the client relates to environmental work.

Often, worker and client *together* may see a collateral person (i.e., a person in the client's environment who affects or can be enlisted to affect the situation) to explore opportunities or resources, or work toward desired changes in the client's milieu. Such joint efforts have two advantages. First, the worker's knowledge and influence may contribute to a more successful result; and, second, the client has an opportunity to raise questions, express reactions, and perhaps learn through demonstration how to handle certain situations. But we would add a note of caution here: there are times when a worker's presence can be a liability rather than an asset—for example, if it seems to the worker or to the client that a collateral would interpret the worker's involvement as intrusive or as a sign that the client is too weak or incapable to take care of his or her own affairs. Such interpretations, in some instances, might result in less willingness on the collateral's part to take an interest in the client than if the client made the contact independently.

In any event, in the view of the writers, whenever possible, clients should become *active* participants in bringing about the changes they seek. Even when caseworkers become advocates or "social brokers" for their clients and attempt to alleviate abhorrent environmental conditions or help them to "negotiate the system," the best results come when the worker carries out these functions *with* and not simply *for* individuals and families. Self-esteem and autonomy are better nurtured thereby. Treatment that reinforces the client's growth and competence will render the person better able to act on his or her own behalf when, inevitably, future difficulties arise.

In previous chapters, we have considered forms of communication between worker and client. More often than not, this direct work with the client is accompanied by intervention in environmental systems of which the client is a part. In the preceding chapter, we saw that reflective discussion of dynamic and developmental factors is interwoven with all the other forms of client–worker communication. Cases vary: in some there is no work of this type, in others it occurs in a scattering of interviews, in still others it plays a major role. Similarly, some clients do not need environmental help, either because their problems do not involve the type of situational matters in which the worker can intervene directly or because the clients are able to act on their own behalf. At the other extreme are cases in which a major part of the work consists of bringing about environmental changes through communications between worker and collateral, through joint efforts with the client to modify some aspect of the milieu, or through the location of needed services and resources. Again, the concept of a blend is useful. Environmental work is intertwined with other procedures. It also involves subtleties and complexities that must be understood if it is to be carried on with skill.[8]

As outlined in Chapter 4, milieu work can be viewed in at least three ways: (1) in terms of the types of *communication* between worker and collateral; (2) in terms of the type of *resource* involved; and (3) in terms of the *role* or function that the worker is carrying. In this chapter, we will discuss types of communication and types of resources. In Chapter 9 we will examine worker roles, and present two case examples of environmental work.

## TYPES OF COMMUNICATION

It is important to emphasize that the first four sets of communication procedures (sustainment, direct influence, exploration–description–ventilation, and person–situation reflection) are just as germane to environmental work as they are to direct work with the client. There is an unfortunate tendency to think of work directed toward the individual's environment as "manipulation" and therefore rather different in nature from actual contacts with the client. The contrary is true. As we have said, the skills needed for bringing about changes in the environment on the client's behalf are in many respects identical to those employed in direct work with the client.

Discussions with collaterals have many purposes. A worker may want to learn more about a client or about services or opportunities possibly available to the client. The worker may attempt to change or expand the collateral's understanding of the client and the circumstances—so that the collateral's attitude or actions will be tempered, or resources will be provided, or conditions over which the collateral has control will be modified and improved. But collaterals are often not free agents. They may be part of a system—school, business, court, police—with policies and regulations. Relatives of a client may have heavy pressures of their own and therefore be reluctant to participate in a discussion or take steps to help. Therefore, many influences in addition to the client's needs may enter into a collateral's decisions.

As with the client, the worker has to assess—often very quickly, sometimes during a telephone conversation—the collateral's attitudes and feelings toward the client, the degree of interest, and the willingness to get involved in the client's concerns or situation. In an interview, the worker has to be attuned to the collateral's subtle responses, including the facial expression and other nonverbal behavior, to evaluate accurately the person's receptivity.

In work with collaterals, obviously contact has to be established, and *sustaining* procedures beyond common courtesy are often of great value. The client is not the only person who may be afraid of being blamed: so may the teacher, the public welfare worker, the nurse, the landlord, and, of course, the relative. They can be angry. They can be anxious. They have needs too. Their way of handling their feelings may be defensive hostility that leads them to attack either the worker or the client. Often, they too will respond better if the worker shows an understanding of the problem they are up against and has not come to criticize, if the worker is interested in their point of view and is willing to listen to the headaches the client has caused them. They, too, sometimes need encouragement concerning efforts they have already made to deal with the situation.

Procedures of *direct influence* have an important place in environmental work, particularly when the worker is trying to modify the way in which another person is acting toward the client. Reinforcement and suggestion play a large role in such activity, with advice sometimes of value, and insistence or even coercion occasionally necessary. The administrator of a nursing home, pressured by a long waiting list, may have to be strongly encouraged to admit an elderly client in urgent need of immediate care. A busy public welfare worker may have to be urged to cut through red tape quickly to give aid to a family burned out of its home by fire. Landlords who cannot be persuaded by other means may have to be told that violations in their buildings will be reported to the appropriate government agency unless immediate repairs are made.

*Ventilation* is sometimes useful when the person being interviewed has a great deal of emotion about the client, or about the situation in which the person and the client are involved. The landlord resolved to report to the police a young boy who has broken a window may need to express a good deal of feeling about this and other aggravations experienced with the child-client before being ready to consider a less punitive course of action. So, too, may the nurse or the teacher who has had to put up with an "acting-out" child or the landlord who sees the money that should have been received as rent going for what seems to be "frivolous" purchases.

Sometimes collaterals vent feelings and express attitudes that are offensive to the caseworker. A landlord may complain that a building is being destroyed because the tenants are of a particular color or ethnic background. A teacher may be prejudiced—incensed by actions of a black student that would be tolerated from a white one. Even a public welfare worker may make denigrating remarks about "those people" on his or her caseload. In such instances, it requires particular discipline and skill to listen, to continue to be supportive, to respond uncritically, and at the same time to avoid seeming to agree with the point of view being expressed or arguing for one's own view when this will do no good. It is obviously important not to alienate the very person from whom one is seeking help on behalf of a client; in many cases, direct confrontation could make matters worse rather than better. And often, once anger is expressed, the collateral may then be better prepared to listen to what the worker wants to say or ask. When this does not happen, certainly a more aggressive approach may be necessary. But such a decision should be made only by worker and client together, and only after full consideration has been given to the risks and possible repercussions involved. This point will be discussed more fully in Chapter 9 where worker roles are examined.

It goes without saying that when a worker attempts to persuade a collateral to adopt or change an attitude toward a client, careful diagnostic evaluation of all pertinent aspects of the client–situation system is necessary. In every instance, the caseworker must have confidence that the client will benefit from the changes being promoted; in order to know this, the worker must know the client. If, for example, a caseworker helps to reinstate a student suspended for truanting without understanding what this behavior means, or if a worker helps a man whose job performance has been erratic to locate a job he will not hold, does not want, or for which he is not qualified, the probability is great that the result will be frustration for the client and collateral alike. Past failures experienced by the client will only be reinforced by the caseworker's interventions based on faulty or inadequate assessment.

As in direct work, experience has shown that procedures for *reflective discussion* are of great value with collaterals wherever they can be used, particularly in the process of helping one person to understand another. Often, such understanding is brought about simply by telling the person about some aspects of the client and his or her life. At times the worker may enter into the reflective process with the interviewee in much the same way as with a client, although the scope of the contact is more limited, indeed frequently to a single interview. Often, worker and collateral—sometimes with the participation of the client, too—are actually thinking together to arrive at a solution in which the interviewee is involved. Of course, care must be taken to estimate the ability as well as the willingness of the collateral person to listen or engage in reflective discussion.

The worker is less likely in such contacts to use reflective procedures that involve thinking about consequences to the *self*, although this, too, can occasionally take place. Sometimes, for example, collaterals will discover that the changes being sought will benefit them as well as the client. This kind of reflection may be extremely useful when the vested interests of the collaterals have made them resistant to understanding or being responsive to client needs.

> In one situation, Tom, a teenage boy—employed after school in a restaurant to supplement his family's modest income—was fired for stealing food. "That's not my problem," the employer told the caseworker who had explained the difficult conditions under which the boy and his widowed mother lived. The worker realized that efforts to expand the employer's view by giving information about the boy's background angered rather than appeased him; it was apparent that he needed to vent his feelings about Tom's actions. Therefore, the worker listened with understanding, making no attempts to deflect the anger. Then, only after the employer became calmer, Tom—who was present at the meeting—and the worker offered the idea that Tom could pay off his debt if he were allowed to work it off. Since Tom had been a good employee, the discussion of this suggestion led the employer to recognize the advantage to himself of giving the boy another chance.

In this example, it became clear that the employer was unwilling to be responsive to Tom's needs. Therefore, the worker used procedures of sustainment, encouraged ventilation, and only then made a direct suggestion. These procedures were followed by reflection in which the employer realized that his self-interest could be served by rehiring his youthful employee. The fact that Tom, who genuinely regretted what he had done, participated in the discussion—and offered a solution as well as apologies—may have supported the employer's confidence that the boy would not steal from him again. This case also illustrates that the *extent* of the communication procedures differs, but the greater part of the *range* is common to work with collaterals and clients alike.

Reflective procedures may also be necessary to straighten out the relationship between the caseworker and the collateral. The worker's intent or attitudes may need to be clarified before effective work can proceed. Sometimes a simple explanation will suffice. In other instances, the worker may try to elicit a collateral's negative reactions about the worker and the purpose of the interview, so that misinterpretations can be cleared up. Naturally, the details of achieving this kind of understanding depend on the context in which they are being applied, the need for such discussion, and the willingness of the collateral to engage in it. But, whether or not the interviewee's reactions are brought out into the open, the worker must be ever sensitive to them and skillful in finding tactful ways of conveying his or her own true attitudes and role. This is true whether the collateral is an employer, teacher, or landlord, or a member of the client's family.

> Mrs. Davis, who was being seen in individual treatment by a clinical social worker, complained that her mother—who cared for Mrs. Davis' children during the day—was undermining Mrs. Davis' authority with the youngsters, with the result that they were becoming unmanageable. The grandmother disapproved of case-work treatment, yet reluctantly agreed to come to a joint interview with her daughter. It was necessary for the worker to be accepting of the grandmother's view of her as an "interferer" and to realize that this woman was expecting to be criticized. Through a supportive manner and by telling her that her help was needed to better understand the children's problems, the worker conveyed her respect for the grandmother and the purpose for the meeting. Only then, and after giving a good deal of credit for her conscientious care of the children, was the worker able to discuss with her the apparent effects the conflicts between the adults were having on the youngsters.

In summary, then, all that has been said about sustaining work, directive procedures, ventilation, and reflective discussion of the person–situation gestalt applies to work with people in the client's milieu as well as to contacts with the client—to indirect as well as direct treatment. On the other hand, it is extremely unlikely that collaterals will become involved in extensive intrapsychic reflection, especially dynamic or developmental aspects of their own reactions. When people in the client's milieu are sufficiently involved in the client's affairs to be willing to engage in the process of gaining self-understanding, the situation is one of interpersonal adjustment in which they, too, become clients. This can occur when a client's family becomes engaged in ongoing family treatment.

## TYPES OF RESOURCES

Moving from types of communication to variations in the type of resource or collateral that the worker is using or attempting to use on behalf of clients, we arrive at a new set of considerations. In Chapter 4, five types of resources were distinguished: (1) the worker's own social agency; (2) the non–social work organization in which the worker is on staff or a member of its social work department; (3) the social agency where the worker is not employed; (4) the non–social work organization that (a) has social workers on staff but where the worker is not employed, or (b) does not employ social workers at all; (5) individuals in (a) an instrumental relationship with the client, or (b) an expressive relationship with the client.

## Worker's Own Social Agency

The first type is the social agency in which the caseworker is employed. These are organizations that are under the leadership or direction of social workers. Here the worker has a twofold responsibility; first, to use these services appropriately and skillfully, whatever they may be, and second, to share responsibility for constant improvement in these resources. In a family service agency, for example, program changes and the addition of new agency services must often be approved by a lay board or by funding agencies. Becoming skilled at effectively presenting proposals to these bodies may be as important an aspect of the caseworker's function as is the skillful delivery of existing services.

For child welfare agencies, public and private, the foster home is an agency resource used on behalf of the client. No resource is more complicated and no resource requires more careful, thorough diagnostic assessment of the total child–parent–situation gestalt than that required in child placement. Certainly, the first four types of casework communication are continuously used in work with foster parents. As in work with other resource people, the expertise of the foster parent must be respected. Even the new foster parent usually has skill in child rearing, though he or she may be ignorant of the special complexities of caring for a *foster* child. The successful experienced foster parent has much to teach the caseworker new to the child placement field, just as the successful experienced teacher knows far more about the child as a learner in the classroom than the school social worker does.

There is a cooperative quality in work with other experts that calls for delicate sensitivity to considerations of status if a good working relationship is to be achieved. The fact that the foster parent receives money from the agency is an important component in the total picture. Worker and foster parent are both parts of the same agency system, both subject to agency policies; they are allies in caring for the child, but they have different places in the agency structure. The worker carries an authority that the foster parent does not have in that the worker's opinion carries great weight not only in the decision about the removal of particular children from the home but also in the decision of whether to use, or to continue using, the home at all. All that the worker says and does, then, has special meaning for the foster parent because it occurs within this context. A feeling that suggestions must be taken may lead to resentment and pretense. It is especially important that an atmosphere be created in which the foster parent is free both to express opinions different from the worker's and to ventilate feelings about the children in his or her care. Since the foster mother especially has not only the family income at stake but also her self-esteem, which may rest in large part upon her confidence in herself as a good mother, sustainment can be of vital importance.

Sometimes, it is true, work with foster parents moves close to the client–worker pattern found in parent–child adjustment problems in the natural family. Even then, however, the foster parent's status as an agency resource, and hence as a collateral, is still in existence. When the worker loses sight of this role, complications ensue. A particular type of complication can occur around visits between foster children and their own parents. Recent research suggests that visits by natural parents are of critical importance to the overall adjustment of foster children.[9] Yet there are many problems in working out such visits, not the least of which are the reactions of some foster parents who feel threatened by the children's feelings toward their natural parents. Skilled casework is required to handle these delicate issues, to help foster parents if they have feelings of competition and resentment toward the children's parents, but always without minimizing the role the foster parents are playing in the lives of the children for whom they are caring, and their importance to the agency system. Similarly, often foster parents need sensitive understanding of the heartache they feel when a child—to whom they have become attached—has to be given up to another home or to be reunited with natural parents.

The child welfare agency is a particularly good example of the type of social agency in which the worker has a major responsibility for influencing agency policy. The worker is in a key position to observe the effects of policy on both clients and foster or adoptive parents, and should be thinking in terms of policy formulation as well as in terms of work with clients and substitute parents. Agencies can and sometimes do provide effective channels for passing on the worker's observations and ideas so that policy can be a fluid instrument with wide room for change and experimentation rather than a set of relatively fixed administrative rulings. Experimentation with new ideas is essential if service is to be pertinent and effective.

The public welfare agencies—which provide financial assistance and social services—are difficult to classify as to type of resource. Historically, they have been social agencies and as frustrated as its position often was, social work leadership unquestionably gave some measure of protection to public assistance clients, offering them services and representing their welfare as no other profession or interested group did. In recent years, however, there have been significant changes in the ways in which income assistance programs are being administered. Some categories of recipients have been transferred from state and local welfare programs to a federal income assistance program administered by the Social Security Administration, which provides no casework services. At the time this book is being written, even with those income maintenance programs handled by public welfare departments, the trend has been, and continues to be, one in which these have been separated out from other public welfare services. More often than not, financial aid is dispensed on a standardized, impersonal basis with little direct connection with casework services that in the past, in the best agencies, were to a degree available when needed.

At present, some public agencies rendering various social services (child welfare and family services, preventive and protective services for children, protective and custodial services for adults who because of age or disability are unable to handle their affairs, homemaker services, etc.) have at least a small proportion of BSWs and MSWs on staff, particularly as supervisors. But many others have very few or no trained workers. Hence, although these agencies are technically social agencies, they are often staffed with workers not fully equipped with the knowledge, skills, or professional values required to render such difficult and demanding services adequately. Furthermore, increasingly, control of programs is in the hands of administrators with no social work background, and basic policy is controlled to a high degree by law.

The trained caseworker employed by public welfare agencies (or, for that matter, other, especially large, bureaucratic, social service organizations) is often in the difficult position of being the representative of an agency but in disagreement with many of its policies. Sometimes workers can influence program or policy. Certainly, they have responsibility for doing everything possible to improve services and to use the resources available. Actually, in some agencies there is a degree of leeway in administrative policy and an opportunity for constructive change in response to pressure at the caseworker and supervisory level.[10]

But in many other agencies, where undesirable policies prevail that are destructive to individuals or families in some way, the workers face many complications in bringing the agency's resources to their clients. It is difficult enough when a policy that is necessary and fair creates hardship. Then the path is fairly clear—allow or even encourage the anger to be expressed, genuinely appreciate the hardship for the client, sometimes explain why the policy is necessary, and help the client to make the best possible adaptation to it. Under these circumstances, there is no basic conflict about carrying out the policy. But when the policy is either unfair, unwise, or unnecessary, it is even more important for the client to express anger and to know that the worker recognizes the hardship and genuinely regrets it.

Four alternative courses are open to workers. One is to express to clients personal disagreement with policy, and perhaps to tell of efforts that are being made to change it. At the same time workers may help clients to decide whether alternatives are available and, if they are not and if no legitimate way around it can be found, help them either to comply with agency policy or, if possible, to register their protests effectively.

The second course is for the workers to decide that they can no longer carry out policy with which they are in basic disagreement, and leave the agency. There are situations in which this action is justified, but it is not a truly satisfactory solution. If all workers who disagree with a bad policy leave the agency, no one is left to fight for better ones. Workers who leave are all too easily replaced by workers without any social work education, who may not find it so difficult to carry out destructive agency policies. This is not to say that every worker needs to feel duty-bound to work forever under impossible conditions. Eventually, one may feel that one has fought long enough, and that someone else should take up the cudgels.

The third course is that taken by workers who stand strongly for better policy and stay within the system to work for it. In favorable situations, they are able to bring about improvements in policy and its administration. Sometimes they have the power, especially at the supervisory and higher administrative levels, through flexibility and intelligent application of policy, to modify its impact on the client considerably. (See the case of Mrs. Stone in Chapter 9 for an example of this kind of creative practice.) They may be able to give some protection to clients; at the very least, they can help keep things from getting worse. Workers in public welfare services who choose either the second or third courses can also work through channels external to the agency to bring about better legislation that can improve the whole system. The effort to bring such change has gone as far as court action by social work employees (sometimes joined by client activist groups) to challenge the legality of extreme policies.

The fourth course is the most precarious one—that of staying in the agency but circumventing its policies. It usually carries no particular danger to the workers, for if they lose their jobs they can generally find others and loss of the job is the worst that is likely to happen unless workers engage in criminal misconduct. But this course of action does introduce all sorts of complications into the client–worker relationship. Usually, it involves dishonesty in intrastaff relationships—often at several levels. And, aside from these hazards, the sidestepping of unjust policies can have the effect of postponing concerted efforts—on the part of staff and clients alike—to work toward changing them.

Many people from all walks of life want and can use casework services. Individuals and families in poverty and those receiving income assistance often need the kind of help casework can give to deal with the many pressures in their lives.[11] They must have the same opportunity to receive first-rate services from professionally trained workers, from agencies with a social work orientation, as have those who can pay for them. Certainly, many of these services have to be operated under public auspices or, at least in part, to be publicly financed. As welfare policies change and keep changing, we believe it is incumbent on us all —whether we work in public departments of social services or not—to press for making sure these are available, readily accessible, and of high quality.

## Non–Social Work Organization Where Worker Is Employed

The second type of resource is the organization with caseworkers on staff or with a department that employs them, but that is primarily controlled by another profession—for example, a hospital, school, or court. Included in this type would also be large government organizations (such as many of the public welfare agencies just described), some public mental health departments, and others where social workers are employed. In agencies of this type, caseworkers offer the client a resource with which they are associated but which is not their primary responsibility. Other things being equal, the workers are in a less advantageous position than the predominant profession to bring change in the major agency service.

Nevertheless, in some such organizations social workers are hired (sometimes on a consultant basis) to share their expertise on human social behavior with school personnel, lawyers, medical professionals, public housing officials, and the like. In some school systems, for example, social workers run seminars for teachers and administrative personnel on such matters as family structure and dynamics, cultural influences on personality, and group dynamics. There are also hospitals with comparable programs run by social workers that have considerable influence on the services rendered by these facilities. In every case, the social workers are part of the service, and therefore must do everything possible from their own observations of its effect on clients to contribute toward changes that will improve this service. Social workers in such settings must have thorough knowledge of the system within which they are working, its lines of responsibility, and its power structure. The workers must understand the "culture" of the other profession or professions with which they are dealing. They must have infinite tact, a high degree of self-confidence and confidence in their profession, and the courage and zest to pursue aims in spite of exasperating discouragements.[12] Usually, progress in this situation is cumulative. Once the competence and value of the department have been established and recognized, the head of the service is more likely to be listened to and, under the best circumstances, an attitude of mutual respect will permeate interrelationships.

In one hospital, the director of social service learned from an audit of drug overdose patients that a number of these patients had not been referred for casework attention. Therefore, she consulted with the nurses and discussed the importance of automatic notification of the social work department of all such cases at the time of admission. The nurses had not understood that casework services might be helpful to the families involved, and had not made the referrals because the patients were frequently unconscious at the time of their arrival! Similarly, this same director persuaded the hospital administration to institute changes in the admitting procedures so that certain items of information could be elicited (such as whether or not a patient lives alone); by reviewing the screening data on every patient, the social work department could reach out to those who might be in need of casework services.

Systems theory observations concerning the importance of the *point of maximum reverberation** are fully confirmed in the role played by key persons in the medical and nursing hierarchy. It is extremely important that pressure for change be exercised only after sound diagnostic assessment of the system has been made. Usually, the most effective way for change to take place is for the department head to give courageous leadership to the staff, following through in pressing for needed changes. At the same time, the staff needs to understand the complex forces within which change takes place in a large multiprofessional organization; sometimes an administrator cannot share with staff all that is going on, including all the efforts made, matters of timing, and all the sad, frustrating reasons for lack of progress. It is practically impossible to keep this sort of information confidential once it is shared, yet to divulge it may completely defeat the objectives in which all are

*According to systems theory, change applied to part of a system will reverberate in a differential way throughout the system. A point of maximum reverberation is the point at which change will have the greatest effect on the total system.

interested. Change in a "host agency" calls for team play of the highest order, and nothing is more important in team play than mutual respect and trust.

Changes within the social work department itself have much in common with changes in the more autonomous social agency of the child welfare or family service type. Money is a factor in all agencies. Just as family agencies must often seek the approval of a lay board or a funding agency, so a department of an organization with a different primary function must secure approval of whatever intraagency authority it is responsible to.

When we turn from the worker–agency to the worker–client relationship in this second type of resource, we find that the worker is seen by the client not only as a caseworker but also as representing the major functions of the hospital, school, or court. Therefore, client reactions to these services, including their weaknesses, must be handled. The probation worker, for example, must try to find the common meeting ground between the function of the court and the aspirations of the client. The worker must be responsive to the client's often angry feelings about the policies of the agency that the worker represents. (In this respect, if the worker disagrees with important policies, the same considerations hold as discussed earlier concerning the worker in the social agency.)

> A family court probation worker, assigned to explore a case in which the parents were vying for the custody of their two children, received an anonymous telephone call alleging that the nine-year-old retarded daughter was frequently left in full charge of her six-year-old brother while the mother worked. When the worker contacted the mother, she was outraged that someone had complained about her and that she was being investigated on the basis of such flimsy evidence; she vented her anger at the worker. The worker listened, understood the embarrassment the woman felt about his visit, and explained that although he had to follow up on the complaint, he had not come to blame her but to determine whether there was any way he could be of help. As it turned out, the complaint was considerably exaggerated; an adult relative, temporarily in the hospital, usually cared for the children and recently the mother had taken off from work when she could not locate another babysitter. By using the approach he did, the worker was able to convey his wish to be helpful rather than punitive. In fact, the mother welcomed his suggestion that the children be placed in an after-school day care program until the relative was well enough to look after them again.

Certainly, investigations of complaints received by courts (and protective agencies) may result in client reactions ranging from unyielding

resistance to physical violence against the workers. Yet, in the experience of the writers, many involuntary clients *can* accept and do utilize
casework services once it is established that the worker respects the
client's wishes and goals.[13] (In the case of Mrs. Stone, described in
Chapter 9, the mother accused of beating one of her children was able
to accept a referral from the protective services worker to the family
services division.)

In addition to whatever practical or therapeutic services one may
offer the client, it is also one of the important functions of a worker in
an agency primarily under the auspices of another profession to facilitate the way in which the agency is being used as a resource by the
client. The worker often interprets the agency services to the client,
and develops methods for inviting client feedback. Caseworkers in
hospitals, for example, may arrange group meetings of patients or of
patients' relatives to give them an opportunity not only to share their
feelings about illness, but also to express their reactions to the hospital
services. Similarly, parent groups in day care centers are often organized to encourage parents to raise questions, to offer suggestions, and
to get clarification about the operations of the program their children
are attending.

The caseworker also helps the other professionals to understand
the needs of the client better. Because the worker sees the client from
a different vantage point and within a different professional frame of
reference from the doctor, teacher, or judge, he or she can contribute
greatly to the quality of the other service. At times the worker may
need to act as mediator between the service and the client and sometimes even as active advocate on the client's behalf. Doctors may be
reluctant to give adequate attention to certain patients because of their
critical or hostile attitudes or their failure to understand or follow medical advice. The medical social worker can try to remedy this situation.
A teacher may take a disliking to a child. By acquainting her with the
facts of the child's background, the social worker in the school system
may be able to modify the teacher's reactions. Here again thorough
understanding of the organization as a system and of the ways of working, patterns of thought, and values of the other profession is essential
if either mediation or active advocacy is to be successful.

## Social Agency Where Worker Is Not Employed

The third type of resource is the social agency resource that employs social workers but where the worker who is helping the client is
not a staff member. This type includes not only casework agencies but
also community centers where there are opportunities for group expe-

riences, hobby development, recreation, and social action through groups. Organizations such as homemaker services, day care centers, and employment counseling services also fall in this category when they are administered by social workers.

The worker who has had a sound social work education is familiar with what social agencies in most fields do. Entering a new community, the worker will usually want to become familiar as quickly as possible with a wide range of agencies. Caseworkers who have been in the community longer will be knowledgeable about such resources. It can be very valuable to meet with colleagues from other agencies over lunch, and to plan exchange visits so workers can get to know one another's facilities firsthand.

Agencies often keep resource files. Common objectives, a common professional language and body of knowledge, and a common value system facilitate the use of such resources. But no profession is completely homogeneous. Within a range, values, objectives, language, and even knowledge differ. Idiosyncrasies and different points of view exist within as well as among professions. Here, too, one must be sensitive to the reaction of the other worker within the other agency and use communication skills. Social workers are people too. They can feel threatened or competitive; they also have their off days, days when they are under pressure or upset about work or personal affairs and not operating in good style.

A further factor in work with another social agency is, of course, the policies and resources of that agency. Some of these are fixed, others are flexible. In milieu work, it is often necessary for the caseworker to push toward the maximum extension of that flexibility. In so doing, if the worker has correctly assessed the client's need and interpreted it skillfully, a best ally should be a colleague in the other agency. Sometimes, too, the worker in the other agency is more familiar with other similar resources than is the first worker, and therefore able to suggest alternatives when his or her own agency is unable to meet the need. There are times also when this worker's greater experience with the type of problem experienced by the client leads rightly to a different assessment of the client's need. Under these circumstances, conferences between workers are usually the best means for arriving at reassessment. It is extremely useful to develop friendly colleague relationships with workers in other agencies to facilitate this type of cooperative work.

## Non–Social Work Agency Where Worker Is Not Employed

The fourth type of resource refers to the agency or organization not administered by social workers that either (1) has a social work department or social workers on staff, but where the worker helping the client is not a member, or (2) does not employ social workers at all.

When working with non–social work agencies that employ social workers, many of the considerations discussed in connection with social agencies, the third type of resource, can be applied. One difference, of course, is that workers in these non–social work agencies may be constrained by the profession or bureaucracy that administers them. We described this kind of problem in the discussion of the second type of resource—the non–social work agency where the worker is employed. Therefore, for example, if one is attempting to get certain services for a hospitalized client, the medical social worker may have to get clearance from the administrator or the doctors in order to see that they are provided. But again, the more one has established friendly working relationships with social workers in these settings, the more likely it is that efforts on a client's behalf will be given maximum consideration.

Various forms of group living for adults have become widespread. Halfway houses, under many different names and various auspices, offer protection to patients released from hospitals for the mentally ill, to rehabilitated drug addicts, and others. It is now well known that many mentally retarded adults can learn to function in the community when living in protected settings. Recreational and educational programs, including day care, are now offered to the above groups and for elderly people living in the general community. Usually these resources are not administered by social workers, although they may be employed there. Some of these facilities are part of large state departments, and therefore they are often subject to the many restraints and regulations associated with large bureaucracies.

The type of organization that does not employ social workers at all can include, among many others, legal aid organizations, public health and housing agencies, and tutoring and vocational or employment services, as well as schools, hospitals, and group and nursing homes that do not have social workers on staff.

The greater the worker's knowledge about the other organization or profession and the resources of the particular institution, the more likely he or she is to be able to help clients to make appropriate use of it. Much exploratory work may need to be done before the proper help can be secured. Not only will clients' time be wasted if they are sent to inappropriate places, but some clients may also be discouraged from trying further. It may be ego-debilitating for some people. It may also reduce confidence in the worker's interest and competence, and it may have a negative effect on simultaneous direct work with clients. Both phone work and footwork may be necessary to prepare the way for a client's own first contact. Ingenuity in locating appropriate resources and skill in interesting other organizations in a client are particularly valuable in milieu work using resources not connected with social work.

> A busy child welfare worker referred a woman client, with a marginal income, to the legal aid society to obtain advice about a custody suit that had been initiated by the client's divorced husband. After waiting weeks for an appointment, the client was then informed that she was not eligible on the basis of her income, as modest as it was. The worker then sought assistance from the bar association, which advised that there was a panel of low-fee attorneys who could assist the woman. Precious time and frustration could have been saved had the worker explored the available resources prior to making the referral.

## Individual Collaterals

We have already seen in the section on types of communication a number of illustrations of contacts with *individuals* on the client's behalf. The fifth and last type of resource involves two categories of individuals: those in an *instrumental* (or *"task-oriented"*) relationship with the client, and those in an *expressive* (or *"feeling-oriented"*) relationship with the person the worker is trying to help.

*INSTRUMENTAL COLLATERALS.* This subdivision includes, among others, employers or landlords. With these task-oriented individuals, the worker may be seeking such opportunities as jobs or better housing for the client, or may be intervening on behalf of the client in a misunderstanding or clash that is creating hardship for the client. In each of these cases, the worker deals not with another profession or some type of service organization but with people who have their own interests at stake. They tend to be either indifferent to the client or hostile. In preparation for meeting with such collaterals, it is essential that the worker be sure of facts or else be aware of the possibility that he or she does not have all the facts. Overidentification with the client is a frequent cause of failure in this type of contact. There is no sense in persuading an employer to make special plans to hire a client by giving a false picture of the client's abilities or readiness for work. It will only end in embitterment on both sides. When liabilities are acknowledged and sympathetically interpreted, the collateral makes a decision realistically in the light of attitudes about the liabilities, willingness to take a risk, and assessment of how much damage may be done to the business if the liabilities cannot be overcome or contained. If the situation is such that the worker cannot be frank, it is better for the client to find his or her own job.

Similarly, when trying to modify the attitudes or actions of an instrumental collateral, the worker has to listen with an open mind to the collateral's side of the story. For example, a client may complain that the landlord has not painted his or her apartment. On speaking with the landlord, however, the worker may be told that the tenant-client has been neglectful or destructive of the property and for that reason the landlord feels justified to refuse to paint. The worker must then judge whether to press for greater understanding of the client's point of view, or perhaps to drain off some of the irritation and then work with the client to arrive at some mutual amelioration of the total situation.

*EXPRESSIVE COLLATERALS.*    This subdivision includes those individuals who have an expressive, or feeling-oriented, relationship with the client. With these individuals the situation is quite different than that connected with instrumental collaterals, since an expressive relationship implies some investment in the client's welfare. This is true even when anger exists and the worker is intervening in the hope of improving their interaction. In such relationships, anger itself is a sign of caring —of involvement. With caring, a new component enters. The relative or even friend may feel that he or she knows the client better than the worker does—and indeed this may be true. Those collaterals who feel they have a stake in the situation may want the worker to change the client rather than to respond positively themselves to the worker's need for their help or to the worker's efforts to modify the collateral's relationships with the client. Some collaterals may even be opposed to the worker's efforts. As we shall discuss further in the chapters on family therapy, family members can be threatened by any change in the balance of the family system. They may, therefore, oppose change even though theoretically such change would benefit them as well as the client.

In work with these collaterals, we reach ground that is very close to work with the client. Sometimes, in fact, it turns into direct work in which the collateral becomes a second client, either through individual interviews or by a shift to family or joint interviewing. Short of this, however, relatives and friends can become powerful allies in treatment. Sometimes it is sufficient to let them know they are needed. At other times, work must be done to help them understand ways in which they can assist the client. Simply helping relatives and friends to see their importance to the client and the ways in which they can help often motivates them to offer opportunities and psychological support. They may need assurance that a little involvement in the client's troubles will not result in their being left with greater responsibility than they are either obligated to assume or want to assume. This is particularly true when the client is elderly or disabled or when help with child care is required. Needless to say, the question of whether to intervene directly with friends or relatives or to help the individual to approach them is a delicate one calling for careful assessment and discussion with the client.

FAMILY SESSIONS ON BEHALF OF INDIVIDUAL TREATMENT. As the family therapy chapters will describe, often the problems of an individual are the impetus for exploratory family therapy. When a family is in treatment, each family member is in some way committed to the therapy. On the other hand, when an individual is in treatment and family members are invited for sessions, they are viewed as part of the individual's environment and related to as expressive collaterals. Besides providing the client with psychological support or practical help, the presence of family members in sessions can provide a powerful tool for freeing the client of internalized distortions that are interfering with functioning.

A twenty-two-year-old secretary, Sally, living with her divorced mother, sought treatment at a family agency during a crisis in her relationship with her fiancé with whom she was constantly arguing. She described her feelings toward her mother as "indifferent" or "mildly friendly." She was estranged from her father and had been angry with him since his separation from the family ten years earlier. A few weeks after she began treatment, her mother announced that she planned to remarry; after hearing this Sally became seriously depressed and had suicidal thoughts. Although reluctant at first, she accepted the caseworker's suggestion to bring her mother to a session with her. In the course of a total of three meetings, mother and daughter shared some old pains and achieved an intimacy and openness they had not enjoyed in many years. Sally recognized that her mother truly cared about her and she allowed herself to care in return. Later on in treatment, a joint meeting was arranged with Sally and her father who made a special trip from another state to attend the session. Her father was able to clarify his reasons for leaving the family and reassured Sally that these had nothing to do with her. To Sally's amazement, he said he was very much interested in rebuilding his relationship with her. Sally's early parental introjects (her internalizations of an indifferent mother and a remote, punishing father) clearly had distorted her view of the current situation. As it turned out, she was able to share feelings and develop relationships with her parents that she never believed would be possible. Furthermore, she realized, she had been displacing and projecting some of these distortions onto her fiancé, and these had contributed heavily to the hostilities that had developed between them. During the latter part of the therapy, Sally's fiancé joined Sally for premarital counseling; in joint sessions, some of these issues became better understood by both.

Had the caseworker confined the treatment to individual meetings, Sally's myth about the hopelessness of deepening her relationships with her parents would have taken longer for her and the worker to recognize—either by talking about her parents or through the transference with the worker. Since her distortions had a direct bearing on her difficulties with her fiancé, this relationship (which originally motivated her to seek help) might have deteriorated to the point that it could not have been saved, had she not resolved the longstanding problems with her mother and father. And, of course, the direct participation of her fiancé further facilitated the treatment.

NETWORK THERAPY.   Sometimes the worker and client invite other people to help to accomplish psychological objectives identical in nature with those sought in direct treatment. Relatives, friends, teachers, and doctors are sometimes in a far better position than the social worker to give sustaining help to a client. Often they do so spontaneously, but the caseworker can also motivate them to take this type of responsibility. Particularly with extremely anxious or depressed people, it is sometimes most helpful to enlist the interest of friends or relatives who like the client and have warm natures, a good deal of common sense, and capacity for equanimity. It is surprising how often such people can be found if the worker is alert to the possibility and not so tied to a desk that he or she never makes contact with them.

In recent years, there has been considerable interest in the idea of social or natural "network" intervention.[14] Simply stated, "network therapy" involves mobilizing relatives, friends, neighbors, and other feeling-oriented collaterals to provide a stable support group to a client in crisis and as a prevention against future difficulties. Some therapists have been known to organize "networks" of thirty or forty people; almost always a smaller group is sufficient.

Mrs. Antonini, a recently widowed fifty-eight-year-old housewife, whose children were grown and married, sought help at a community mental health clinic for depression. Her symptoms were so severe that it was feared that she could become suicidal and might have to be hospitalized, an idea Mrs. Antonini opposed. The clinical social worker was able to encourage her to join with her in calling a meeting of her children and a neighbor. Several of her in-laws, with whom there had been some friction over differences they had about decisions Mrs. Antonini had made about her husband's burial, were also invited. In a two-and-a-half-hour session, the worker introduced the problem of her client's depression and isolation and then turned to the assembled group for ideas about what could be done and how this "network" might be able to help. Mrs. Antonini's daughter, who took the most initiative during the meeting, suggested that a schedule could be worked out whereby family members and friends would alternate in being available for telephone or personal visits. Everyone agreed to this plan. Once the details of how each person in the "network" could be reached were worked out, it was decided that Mrs. Antonini would take the initiative for making the contacts when she needed or wanted them. It should be added that during this meeting the tensions with the in-laws were, in large part, relieved.

Slowly but surely, with the "network" as a consistent resource of support for Mrs. Antonini, combined with casework sessions and the location of some babysitting jobs, this client's depression lifted. Long after treatment ended, her "network" was available to her and, as it turned out, she was also able to provide support to other members when they faced difficulties in their own lives.

Similarly, in one family therapy case of a teenage boy—an only child in angry rebellion against his elderly parents—the therapist invited one of the boy's peers, a cousin, and a teacher to join a few sessions. The presence of "network" members was supportive to the entire family and helped to lend perspective to the boy and his parents, whose relationship had become so seriously polarized.

Although a relatively new term, so-called "artificial networks" (in contrast to natural ones of relatives, friends, and others whom the client already knows) with mutual aid functions have long been utilized by Alcoholics Anonymous, weight-losers groups, and so on. More recently, various kinds of groups—organized formally and informally—provide support and a feeling of relatedness to single parents, homosexuals, members of a particular ethnic group, and so on. When family and friends are not available, artificial networks may have to be created. Many social agencies and organizations provide groups for widows, for parents of disabled, retarded, or ill children, or for relatives of terminally ill patients. Indeed, group therapy itself can provide—among other things—a network of peer supports.

We conclude this chapter by emphasizing the obvious: the clinical social worker is usually not the person who can *directly* provide the client with the major supports needed. Even when the worker–client relationship is a sustained and very important one, every client needs much more than that. If inadvertently a worker, out of enthusiasm to help or through posessiveness, in any manner implies he or she can meet most of a client's needs, this fosters an unhealthy dependency and holds out a promise that cannot possibly be delivered. Beyond that, as in the case of Sally, in many instances reassurance from family members is far more meaningful and bolstering to self-esteem than ongoing support from the most caring worker. All people require a sense of belonging and importance, and efforts to activate supportive people in the environment—for clients who do not have enough of them—can be among a caseworker's most helpful and rewarding functions.

Furthermore, it should also go without saying that the worker is often not in the best position to exercise direct influence in a client's life in ways the latter wants or needs it. Very often a friend or relative, "big brother," doctor, clergyman, lawyer, guidance counselor, or teacher carries more influence with the client, is better qualified to advise or aid in a particular area, and can be enlisted in the client's interest. A visiting nurse or homemaker can take on educational and supportive functions in their realms of expertise that the worker cannot. We do our clients a disservice if we neglect to provide easy access not only to essential agency services, but to the many opportunities for nourishment and growth that can become available when we search hard enough to find them.

In this chapter, we have discussed two of the three ways in which environmental work can be viewed: in terms of the types of communications between workers and collaterals, and in terms of the types of resources involved. In Chapter 9 we will examine the types of roles or functions of the worker in milieu work.

## NOTES

1. See, for example, Richard A. Cloward, "Illegitimate Means, Anomie and Deviant Behavior," *American Sociological Review,* 24 (April 1959), 164–176; Gregory Bateson, Don D. Jackson, Jay Haley, and John H. Weakland, "Toward a Theory of Schizophrenia," *Behavioral Science,* 1 (October 1956), 252–264; Ronald D. Laing, "Mystification, Confusion, and Conflict," in Ivan Boszormenyi-Nagy and James L. Framo, eds., *Intensive Family Therapy* (New York: Harper & Row, 1965), 343–363; and Sophie Freud Loewenstein, "Inner and Outer Space in Social Casework," *Social Casework,* 60 (January 1979,) 19–29.
2. See Martin Bloom, "Social Prevention: An Ecological Approach," in Carel

B. Germain, ed., *Social Work Practice* (New York: Columbia University Press, 1979), pp. 326–345; Carol Meyer, ed., *Preventive Intervention* (Washington, D.C.: National Association of Social Workers, 1975); and Lydia Rapaport, "The Concept of Prevention in Social Work," *Social Work*, 6 (January 1961), 19–28.

3. There have always been some social workers who have disparaged the casework approach, believing it puts the burden for change on the individual rather than on the society that deprives and oppresses. It is beyond the scope of this book to address this issue at length, but the reader may be interested in comments made on this subject by one social worker still well known for her years of dedication to advancing fundamental social changes. Writing during the depression of the 1930s, Bertha Reynolds responded to those who believed that casework should be put aside until "a just and healthy social order is achieved," by asking, "is there not a place also for the development of personality, individual by individual?" If, she went on, casework can free men "from crippling accumulations of fear and hate so that they may have energy to use what intelligence they possess; if it educates in the best sense of the word for the use of freedom of choice and for healthier social relationships, it becomes not a luxury but a necessity in a time of social change. For, after all, do we not know, when we are most thoughtful about it, that we are held back from a better social order not by the absence of some lucky change to set in motion the wheels of normal living, but rather because we are not ready, as a people, to think freely and maturely? If social case work itself can grow up to a maturity which will create the conditions of more abundant and responsible life in the individuals with whom it enters into relationship, then indeed it has a place in the cooperative commonwealth which is our only hope for the future." Bertha Capen Reynolds, "A Study of Responsibility in Social Case Work," *Smith College Studies in Social Work*, 5 (September 1934), 126–127.

4. See, for example, Henry Wasserman, "Some Thoughts About Teaching Social Casework Today," *Smith College Studies in Social Work*, 43 (February 1973), 124–125, who comments that the general or ecological systems approach seems to appeal to students working in black or Chicano communities, and that the psychological orientation is often seen as useful primarily in work with middle-class "neurotics." In our view such an unfortunate dichotomy, when put in practice, also sells graduate education short!

5. See Norman Epstein and Anne Shainline, "Paraprofessional Parent-Aides and Disadvantaged Families," *Social Casework*, 55 (April 1974), 230–236; Charles Grosser, "Local Residents as Mediators Between Middle-Class Professional Workers and Lower-Class Clients," *Social Services Review*, 40 (March 1966), 56–63; David A. Hardcastle, "The Indigenous Nonprofessional in the Social Service Bureaucracy: A Critical Examination," *Social Work*, 16 (April 1971), 56–63; Harold M. Kase, "Purposeful Use of Indigenous Paraprofessionals," *Social Work*, 17 (March 1972), 109–110; Philip Kramer, "The Indigenous Worker: Hometowner, Striver, or Activist," *Social Work*, 17 (January 1972), 43–49; B. D. Rigby, ed., *Short-Term Training for Social Development: The Preparation of Front-Line Workers and*

*Trainers* (New York: International Association of Schools of Social Work, 1978); and Francine Sobey, *The Non-Professional Revolution in Mental Health* (New York: Columbia University Press, 1970).

6.  Richard M. Grinnell, Jr., and Nancy S. Kyte, "Environmental Modification: A Study," *Social Work*, 20 (July 1975), 313–318.

7.  Bernard Neugebore, "Opportunity Centered Social Services," *Social Work*, 15 (April 1970), 47–52, provides sound examples.

8.  The following discuss various aspects of work on the situational component of the person–situation gestalt: Alice Q. Ayers, "Neighborhood Services: People Caring for People," *Social Casework*, 54 (April 1973), 192–215; Louise Bandler, "Casework—A Process of Socialization: Gains, Limitations, Conclusions," in Eleanor Pavenstedt, ed., *The Drifters: Children of Disorganized Lower-Class Families* (Boston: Little, Brown, 1967), pp. 255–296; Raymond Mark Berger, "An Advocate Model for Intervention with Homosexuals," *Social Work*, 22 (July 1977), 280–283; Bruce B. Bennett et al., "Police and Social Workers in a Community Outreach Program," *Social Casework*, 57 (January 1976), 41–49; J. Donald Cameron and Esther Talavera, "An Advocacy Program for Spanish-Speaking People," *Social Casework*, 57 (July 1976), 427–431; Berta Fantl, "Preventive Intervention," *Social Work*, 7 (July 1962), 41–47; Charles E. Farris, "American Indian Social Worker Advocates," *Social Casework*, 57 (October 1976), 494–503; Marion G. Foster and William A. Pearman, "Social Work, Patient Rights, and Patient Representatives," *Social Casework*, 59 (February 1978), 89–100; Henry Freeman et al., "Can a Family Agency Be Relevant to the Inner Urban Scene?", *Social Casework*, 51 (January 1970), 12–21; Alex Gitterman, "Social Work in the Public School System," *Social Casework*, 58 (February 1976), 111–118; Grace Hardgrove, "An Interagency Service Network to Meet Needs of Rape Victims," *Social Casework*, 57 (April 1976), 245–253; Evelyn A. Lance, "Intensive Work with a Deprived Family," *Social Casework*, 50 (December 1969), 454–460; Judith A. Lee and Carol R. Swenson, "Theory in Action: A Community Social Service Agency," *Social Casework*, 59 (June 1978), 359–370; Mildred D. Mailick, "A Situational Perspecitve in Casework Theory," *Social Casework*, 58 (July 1977), 401–411; Bernard Neugebore, "Opportunity Centered Social Services," *Social Work*, 15 (April 1970), 47–52; Ben A. Orcutt, "Casework Intervention and the Problems of the Poor," *Social Casework*, 54 (February 1973), 85–95; Arthur Pierson, "Social Work Techniques with the Poor," *Social Casework*, 51 (October 1970), 481–485; Howard E. Prunty et al., "Confronting Racism in Inner-City Schools," *Social Work*, 22 (May 1977), 190–194; Lydia Rapoport, "Social Casework: An Appraisal and an Affirmation," *Smith College Studies in Social Work*, 39 (June 1969), 213–235; Max Siporin, "Social Treatment: A New-Old Helping Method," *Social Work*, 15 (July 1970), 13–25; and James C. Stewart, Jr., et al., "The Poor and the Motivation Fallacy," *Social Work*, 17 (November 1972), 34–37.

9.  David Fanshel and Eugene B. Shinn, *Children in Foster Care: A Longitudinal Investigation* (New York: Columbia University Press, 1978), especially pp. 486–490. See also Joan Laird, "Child Welfare," in Germain, *Social Work Practice*, pp. 174–209, for an intelligent and compassionate

discussion of the importance of preserving ties between foster children and their biological families. Of interest also is Mary Ann Jones, Renee Neuman, and Ann W. Shyne, *A Second Chance for Families* (New York: Child Welfare League of America, 1976)., a research report of a demonstration project in foster care designed to reduce or shorten placements away from home.

10.  The following articles deal with the role of caseworkers in the public welfare agency: Daniel Knight, "New Directions for Public Welfare Caseworkers," *Public Welfare*, 27 (1969), 92–94; Irving Piliavin and Alan E. Gross, "The Effects of Services and Income Maintenance on AFDC Recipients," *Social Service Review*, 59 (September 1977), 389–406; Russell Smith, "In Defense of Public Welfare," *Social Work*, 11 (October 1966), 90–97; Jane K. Thompson and Donald P. Riley, "Use of Professionals in Public Welfare," *Social Work*, 11 (January 1966), 22–27; Thomas H. Walz and Harry J. Macy, "The MSW and the MPA: Confrontation of Two Professions in Public Welfare," *Journal of Sociology and Social Welfare*, 5 (January 1978), 100–117; Harry Wasserman, "The Moral Posture of the Social Worker in a Public Agency," *Public Welfare*, 25 (1967), 38–44; and Elizabeth Wickenden, "A Perspective on Social Services," *Social Service Review*, 50 (December 1976), 570–585.

11.  The contention that casework is ineffective with the poor is contradicted by the findings of Doris Fahs Beck and Mary Ann Jones, *Progress on Family Problems* (New York: Family Service Association of America, 1973). In this nationwide study of clients' and counselors' views on family agency services, based on 3,596 cases from 266 agencies, the researchers report that "the socioeconomic status of clients proved to be a relatively minor factor in outcomes," adding that the "minimum differentials in outcomes were achieved in spite of the greater handicaps faced by lower status clients—more problems, more difficult problems, less adequate environmental supports, and less knowledge of when and where to go for help" (p. 116). As they point out, some earlier research in casework and psychiatry had led to the opposite view: that the casework approach is not effective with such clients. "Perhaps," write Beck and Jones, "the explanation [for their own findings] lies in the improved awareness of and accommodation to the needs and problems of the disadvantaged that are inherent in the current multiservice approach of many agencies and in their increasing use of planned, short-term, crisis-focused service." (p. 116) For a discussion of the background and research that led to the opinion that casework does not help the poor, see Ludwig L. Geismer et al., *Early Supports for Family Life: A Social Work Experiment* (Metuchen, N.J.: Scarecrow Press, 1972), especially pp. 72–77 and p. 108. It is interesting to note that Geismer's study of a broad range of social services also does not support the view that casework is less successful with lower status clients than with upper status clients.

12.  For readings on some of the problems faced by social workers in various organizational settings, and suggestions about how changes may be brought about, see George Brager and Stephen Holloway, *Changing Human Service Organizations* (New York: The Free Press, 1978); William

Brennan and Shanti Khinduka, "Role Discrepancies and Professional Socialization: The case of the Juvenile Probation Officer," *Social Work,* 15 (April 1970), 87–94; Wilbur A. Finch, Jr., "Social Workers Versus Bureaucracy," *Social Work,* 21 (September 1976), 370–374; Emanuel Hallowitz, "Innovations in Hospital Social Work," *Social Work,* 17 (July 1972), 89–97; Katherine and Marvin Olsen, "Role Expectations and Perceptions for Social Workers in Medical Settings," *Social Work,* 12 (July 1967), 70–78; Rino J. Patti and Herman Resnick, "Changing the Agency from Within," *Social Work,* 17 (July 1972), 48–51; Rino J. Patti, "Limitations and Prospects of Internal Advocacy," *Social Casework,* 55 (November 1974), 537–545; Herman Resnick, "Effecting Internal Change in Human Service Organizations," *Social Casework,* 58 (November 1977), 546–553; Gerald M. Shattuck and John M. Martin, "New Professional Work Roles and Their Integration into a Social Agency Structure," *Social Work,* 14 (July 1969), 13–20; and Harold H. Weissman, *Overcoming Mismanagement in the Human Services* (San Francisco: Jossey-Bass, 1973).

13. See especially the excellent article by Norman Ostbloom and Sedahlia Jasper Crase, "A Model for Conceptualizing Child Abuse Causation and Intervention," *Social Casework,* 61 (March 1980), 164–172. Using case examples, the writers discuss the importance of support, a meaningful worker–client relationship, and respect for client autonomy and decision making in work with abusing parents. See also David Ehline and Peggy O'Dea Tigue, "Alcoholism: Early Identification and Intervention in the Social Service Agency," *Child Welfare,* 56 (November 1977), 584–592; Gale Goldberg, "Breaking the Communication Barrier: The Initial Interview with an Abusing Parent," *Child Welfare,* 54 (April 1975), 274–282; C. Henry Kempe and Ray E. Helfer, eds., *Helping the Battered Child and His Family* (Philadelphia: Lippincott, 1972); Genevieve B. Oxley, "Involuntary Clients' Responses to a Treatment Experience," *Social Casework,* 58 (December 1977), 607–614; and Frederick Roth, "A Practice Regimen for Diagnosis and Treatment of Child Abuse," *Child Welfare,* 54 (April 1975), 268–273.

One of the authors (Woods) worked for seven years in a child protective agency's law enforcement division—located in a large metropolitan area—investigating complaints of serious child abuse. During part of this time, she specialized in working with parents of "battered children." In the course of interviewing many hundreds of such involuntary clients (from 1956–1963), *not once* was she or any other member of staff physically attacked—a worry that, unfortunately, has deterred some workers from entering the field. Of course, in the present climate, assaults do occur on occasion, but, in general, when workers are skilled and meet their clients with respect, such incidents are certainly rare. And, more to the point, a large proportion of the clients of the protective agency *voluntarily* returned, requesting services and referrals, in spite of the fact that originally casework services had been imposed upon them.

14. See Carolyn L. Attneave, "Social Networks as the Unit of Intervention," in Philip J. Guerin, Jr., ed., *Family Therapy* (New York: Gardner Press, 1976), pp. 220–232; Alice H. Collins and Diane L. Pancoast, *Natural Help-*

*ing Networks: A Strategy for Prevention* (Washington D.C.: National Association of Social Workers, 1976); Anne O. Freed, "The Family Agency and the Kinship System of the Elderly," *Social Casework,* 56 (December 1975), 579–586; Uri Rueveni, *Networking Families in Crisis* (New York: Human Services Press, 1979); Ross V. Speck and Carolyn L. Attneave, "Social Network Intervention," in Clifford J. Sager and Helen Singer Kaplan, eds., *Progress in Group and Family Therapy* (New York: Brunner/Mazel, 1972), pp. 416–439; and Carol Swenson, "Social Networks, Mutual Aid, and the Life Model Practice," in Germain, *Social Work Practice,* pp. 213–238.

# CHAPTER 9

# ENVIRONMENTAL WORK: PART TWO

In the previous chapters, we described two of the three ways in which environmental work can be viewed. In this chapter, we will examine the third perspective—the types of roles or functions of the worker.[1] This will be followed by a discussion of environmental work and the assessment of the individual. We will conclude with two detailed case illustrations of milieu work.

Before proceeding, however, it is important to accentuate two key aspects of the worker's function, whatever particular role or roles are assumed. The first of these is *confidentiality.* When the caseworker shares specific information about a particular client with an agency or collateral, it is essential that permission to release such information is obtained. Often, this should be secured in writing (particularly when dealing with resources outside of the family). Not only are problems regarding the legal liability of the worker or of the employing agency thereby minimized, but obtaining consent also conveys respect for the client's ethical right to privacy and right to take charge of his or her own affairs.

Second, as already indicated in Chapter 8, it is always best—and usually possible—for the *client to take responsibility* for making decisions about environmental interventions. If the worker's help in directly intervening is necessary—as it frequently is—it is often feasible for the client to be present during conferences with agencies and collaterals. Not only does the client's participation promote growth and competence, but it can allay suspicion about what others are saying about the client and planning for him or her.

## TYPES OF ROLES

The aspect of environmental work that remains to be discussed is that of variations related to the role of the worker: (1) provider, (2) locater, or (3) creator of a resource, (4) interpreter, (5) mediator, and (6) aggressive intervener. Obviously, a worker often carries more than one role simultaneously when working with the client on various aspects of the milieu. The role may shift rapidly and conflict between roles can exist. Each role has its own characteristics.

One is a *provider* of a resource when one gives the resource through the agency in which one works. Many of the intricacies of this role have been discussed in the section of the previous chapter on the worker's own social agency. Sometimes the worker's role as resource provider involves efforts to expand agency services. A caseworker in a mental health clinic, for example, may decide to organize a group for the relatives of recently discharged mental hospital patients, or may plan a multiple family group for these patients and their families.

From the point of view of role, the worker represents the resource and the client reacts as thought the worker were directly responsible for both the positive and negative features of the service given or withheld. A client may feel very appreciative of the caseworker who describes the agency's homemaker service that can be enlisted in the care of an elderly relative. On the other hand, a client may blame the caseworker or make accusations of discrimination if it is found that her income is too high to enroll her child in the agency's day care center funded by the federal government to serve children of impoverished families. In the first case, there may be positive effects on concomitant direct work with the client; in the second, direct work may be impeded by the client's anger. Thorough knowledge of agency policies, flexibility in their application, readiness to help clients decide whether they want the resource or want to qualify for it are all part of the administration of a resource. So also is working with clients' resentment and resistance when these occur. Direct and indirect work are here closely intertwined.

The role of *locater* of a resource is an extremely important one. Success in it depends not only on thorough knowledge of the local community, but also on imaginative assessment of the client's need. The worker must display ingenuity in finding the resource in unexpected places and skill in interesting particular individuals in making special provisions for the client's special needs. Assessing certain needs and locating some resources—such as the appropriate public welfare office or the state employment service—may be simple enough. But sometimes clients' needs are less routine: genetic counseling may be helpful to a newly married couple where one spouse has a family history of genetic problems; a clinic specializing in the treatment of headaches may be able to diagnose and bring relief to a suffering client; a teacher of braille may be helpful to a man who has recently lost his eyesight. Patience and much phone work and some footwork may be required to locate the resources that can be most helpful to the client. Especially in large urban areas, where there are so many agencies and services of all types, the caseworker may need to consult directories of social agencies and health facilities, or else seek guidance from organizations that specialize in information and referral services.

Just beyond the locater role comes that of *creator* of a resource. The same qualities and activities are involved in this as in the more difficult aspects of the locater role. If, for example, the resources mentioned in the above paragraph cannot be located in or near the client's community, the worker—often with the help of a supervisor or department head—may attempt to influence a hospital to create specialty clinics for genetic counseling or for headache treatment; the worker may encourage a local school for blind children to offer classes for adults. Volunteers can often be interested in providing or arranging for various kinds of services when organized resources are not available or when those available do not offer quite what the client needs. Churches can sometimes be involved in such activity, as can "service-oriented" clubs of various types. For example, such organizations are frequently willing to sponsor Alcoholics Anonymous groups where there are none, children's camps, activities for single parents, special interest groups, and so on. The wider the worker's network of associations in the community, the more likely he or she is to be able to become a resource creator.

In the role of *interpreter*, the worker is helping someone else to understand or behave differently toward the client. The accuracy and completeness of the worker's own understanding of the client is the obvious base line. As has been noted in the discussion of communication procedures with collaterals, it is essential also to be attuned to the attitudes and feelings of the person to whom one is trying to explain the client. Much of the time this is no simple fact-giving process, but an interactional one in which information and opinions are exchanged and feelings often come into play. Thus, the worker is often oriented to previously unknown aspects of the client's functioning that may be pertinent to direct work with the client.

Again, the worker must be absolutely sure that the client is willing to have the contact made and for information to be shared. The information given should be only that which is pertinent to the objective of the interview. Particular care must be taken not to divulge inadvertently information that might create difficulty for the client. The nature of interpretive communications is strongly influenced by the type of collateral to whom information is being given. Other things being equal, the worker can share more freely with a fellow social worker or with a member of another helping profession. Beyond this, special care must be taken to be guided not only by the collateral's personality and attitude toward the client, but also by knowledge of the role played in the client's life and of ways in which self-interest or other responsibilities may be involved. Occasionally, despite the greatest care, misuse is made of information. In one situation, which illustrates the need for extreme caution, a clinical social worker had seen a husband and wife for marital counseling. Several weeks after they terminated the couple separated. Family court had become involved and requested information about the agency contact. The worker obtained a written release from the wife and sent a summary of the treatment of the couple to the court, including some personal information about the husband, who later sued the agency and the worker for revealing confidential matters without consent. Sometimes, too, a client may think information has been misused even when it has not. The worker should be alert to the possibility of this in interviews with the client, and should bring into the open any feelings on the client's part that the contact has misfired. Of course, as noted earlier, one way of minimizing suspicion is, when practical, for the client to be a participant in the conference with the collateral.

The next two roles to be discussed are those of *mediator* and *aggressive intervener*. They share some common features, since mediation and aggressive intervention are two aspects of case advocacy. Both go further than interpretation. Both assume some strain or conflict in the relationship between client and collateral. They differ, however, in method. Mediation relies on the force of greater understanding of the client and of his or her needs and rights by the collateral. Aggressive intervention calls for the use of some type of force.[2] Mediation involves both direct and indirect casework. In this type of work with the collateral, all that has been said about the role of interpreter holds for that of mediator—some of it with even greater force. Since this role usually applies when there has already been tension between a client and another individual or representative of an institution, there is often anger or at best irritation or annoyance. When an institution or agency of some sort is involved, there is usually defensiveness about a decision already made or an action already taken. The possibility of client distortion or simply of misunderstanding or misinterpretation is high. The worker must be ready to listen to the other side and be able to withhold judgment. One must try to understand the collateral's point of view and sometimes must modify one's own. Mediation is a two-way street, and the interview with the collateral may lead the worker to expand a view of the client; the worker may feel that the client will have to make changes in behavior or viewpoint if improvement in the interpersonal situation is to occur. It is the worker's responsibility to share such impressions with the client who, if in agreement and possessing the motivation, may then decide to try to alter his or her approach. Once worker and client are both convinced that their position is sufficiently persuasive, the right moment and the right words then need to be found to induce the collateral to reconsider actions or attitudes toward the client.

A sixteen-year-old boy, David, had been periodically suspended from school for cutting classes and for his surly attitude toward teachers. David disliked the academic program and wanted to be transferred to a special vocational program to train in automobile mechanics, for which he had a special gift. The school authorities, however, who were clearly angry, were unwilling to refer him to this program, which would cost the school district money, because they assumed from his behavior that he would be a poor risk. After learning this, the worker was able to help David recognize that his attitude contributed to the school's unyielding position. Subsequently, a conference at the school was arranged by the worker. David participated and, with the worker's support, was able to speak for himself; he explained his unhappiness with his present program and apologized for his behavior. The worker's expression of confidence in David's seriousness about vocational training was instrumental in tipping the balance, and the transfer was approved. Months of direct work, in which the worker encouraged David's strengths, preceded mediation with the school. Had the worker intervened prematurely, before David was willing to share in the responsibility for the problem, the work undoubtedly would have backfired.

In terms of communication procedures, mediation requires ventilation and person–situation reflection, with timing and tact of the utmost importance.

In another situation, a landlord refused to rent an apartment to Mrs. Watson, who was receiving public assistance, stating that he had had bad luck with "welfare tenants." The worker from the welfare department, who knew this woman well, met with the landlord and assured him that Mrs. Watson's past record as a tenant was beyond reproach; the worker's willingness to vouch for Mrs. Watson persuaded him to rent to her after all. The worker's tact and appreciation of the landlord's concern for his property were crucial; had she discouraged him from revealing his strong feelings, or argued with him about the injustice of stereotyping, the chances are that she would have alienated him and thereby unwittingly participated in preventing Mrs. Watson from getting the apartment she very much wanted.

The recent growth in the problem of destructive activities, especially by youths in their teens and young adults, has greatly complicated the question of intervention on the client's behalf. On the one hand, fear and hysteria lead to unjustified punitiveness, to hasty accusations founded on little evidence, and to exaggerated fears concerning what in other times would be considered a "normal" degree of "acting up." On the other hand, some of the forms that youth aggression now takes are often truly dangerous, and individuals have a right to protect themselves and others in legitimate ways. The social worker is not a lawyer for the client and does not have the legally recognized responsibility to plead the client's case, right or wrong. The social worker is just as deeply concerned about the client's rights and well-being as the lawyer, but the worker's orientation and responsibility are to the whole as well as to the part—to some degree to "the other" as well as to the client. Therefore, the decision about intervention calls for careful evaluations of long–run as well as short–run effects. In the role of mediator, the worker's *over–* or *under–* protection of the client can be unrealistic and lead to further aggressive activities that help neither client nor others. In any event, direct work with some clients may be needed to help them recognize their effects on others, as in the case of David, cited earlier.

There are times when it is clear that a client's rights are being ignored, denied, or abrogated and mediation has not been successful in attaining a correction of the injustice. Here the worker must turn to the second type of advocacy—aggressive intervention. The worker may argue forcefully for the client, often going beyond the collateral to a supervisor or a higher executive, and enlisting the efforts of upper administrative levels of the agency. The worker may use other community resources—individual or organizational—to bring pressure to bear in the client's favor.

The staff of a family service agency had obtained repeated evidence that a large company in the city was refusing (sometimes blatantly, sometimes more covertly) to hire qualified black workers except on the janitorial staff. For the agency members who wanted to protest, the situation was complicated by the fact that one of the lay board members of the agency held a management position with the company. For this reason, the board member was protective toward the firm and was also concerned—as were other board members—that the agency would alienate the company if it took a direct stand against it. Staff members, determined to take some kind of action, met with the board and persuasively argued that the local Commission on Human Rights should become involved. This public agency could assist several clients who had been discriminated against without revealing the agency's interest in the situation. A lengthy investigation by the Commission resulted in an order to the company, backed up with the threat of penalty, to cease discriminating; as a result, the personnel practices of the firm were changed.

Furthermore, groups of lawyers and various activist organizations, particularly interested in protecting the rights of clients who are in poverty or subject to discrimination, have provided new and valuable resources upon which to call for case advocacy that go beyond what the social worker can do alone.

When the worker moves from persuasion to a form of pressure or exercise of power, new considerations come into focus. The use of power inevitably arouses hostility and resistance. If the worker uses it and loses, the client may be worse off than before because of the counterhostility that has been generated.

For instance, in the above example, had the agency itself taken direct aggressive action against the company that was discriminating against blacks, not only would it have lost an important board member but, of greater significance, the action might have antagonized this powerful firm enough to attempt to use its influence with the United Way—the funding body on which the agency heavily depended—to retaliate against the agency. If the agency's finances had thereby been jeopardized, the loss to many clients benefiting from its services would have been immeasurable. On the other hand, referral of the matter to a public agency with greater expertise and the authority to investigate eventually brought about the long overdue changes without any repercussions to the clients and without exposing the agency to attack.

Aggressive intervention is obviously a form of advocacy to be turned to only after other methods, including mediation, have failed, when one is quite sure that injustice is being done, and when the aggressive effort has some possibility of succeeding. When there is danger of backfire, clients should know this and decide themselves whether they want to take this risk, with the worker helping to weigh the pros and cons realistically. The means that are taken will also affect the worker's total relationship with the clients and other objectives the worker may have with them, so these effects must also be taken into consideration.

Professional goals and ethics are also involved in the way in which aggressive intervention is carried on. The worker is still operating as a caseworker, and means that are in conflict with professional ethics are not justified by the ends they serve.[3] A caseworker should not, for example, wittingly misrepresent the facts, let alone lie under oath, or advocate blindly violent conduct against adversaries of the client, no matter how unjust their actions might be.

The interpreter and mediator roles stress the social worker's art of reconciliation, of bringing opposing interests into a cooperative relationship built on greater understanding. These are powerful tools. Aggressive intervention, on the other hand, is an approach of confrontation. It relies on force rather than on reconciliation. It, too, is powerful, but it is a two-edged sword that should be used with caution and with an effort to anticipate unintended consequences.

When the worker is employed by an agency, the total system becomes pertinent to decisions about what means to use. Often, a higher level within the worker's own agency can bring pressure more effectively than the worker, possibly even succeeding through mediation so that aggressive intervention is not needed at all.

A distinction is commonly made between *case advocacy* and the more general *social action* or *social advocacy.* The former refers to the worker's efforts to remedy an immediate concrete injustice to which the individual client is being subjected. The latter refers to a more general attempt to bring about changes in policies or practices that adversely affect a whole group of clients or others in the community. In practice, the line between case advocacy and social action advocacy is sometimes blurred, as in the case of company discrimination described earlier. This is also true in the "store front" type of local community operation, which is set up in part to give individual service and in part to promote community activity in social improvement projects. While the same *agency* may operate on both levels, complications may arise when clients who need individual help beyond brief contacts are assigned to a worker who is at the same time involved directly with the client in general social action.

It often happens that when clients gain self-confidence, some freedom from their own pressing concerns, and greater knowledge of the effect of community conditions, they join groups in the general community through which they can participate in social action. If clients show interest in this, one frequently can help locate appropriate groups to join just as one helps the clients locate other resources. We believe it is unwise to use the casework treatment relationship to *enlist* clients in causes, no matter how good those causes may be. To do so is similar in principle to steering clients into one's own church or political party and carries all the same hazards of clients feeling impelled to please their workers upon whom they are dependent for social and psychological help. The caseworker's role differs in this respect from that of the group worker or community organizer, whose recognized role is often this very activity and is sometimes an acknowledged reason for contact with group members.

With so much injustice and, often, widespread indifference to the needs and rights of others prevailing today, the need for social action and advocacy is great. Poverty, inadequate income assistance grants, discrimination, poor housing, unemployment, and inferior educational facilities are conditions that have denied millions of citizens access to opportunities that many others take for granted. For some—particularly for many of the elderly, sick, and disabled—there are often no individual solutions. There must be massive reform to even touch upon the inhuman, day-in-day-out realities of people trapped or neglected because of societal deficiencies.

Certainly, as we have said before, social work as a whole—let alone casework—cannot eradicate massive social problems. On the other hand, the caseworker does have avenues through which to participate in bringing about more modest but nevertheless significant social changes. Often, the agency of which the worker is a staff member is already engaged in social action within its area of competence and effectiveness. It may, then, be part of one's regular work to participate in this action. The movement from case to cause is essential. By collecting information about injustice as it appears in individual cases, the worker can supply the data that can initiate the social advocacy, giving evidence through which change can be accomplished.[4] Agencies carry a definite responsibility for providing ways in which such information can be used. If the agency is not active in areas in which it could be effective the worker, as a staff member, can try to influence it to develop a social action program. The worker also has a personal political life, professional associations, and opportunities for common action with groups of colleagues.[5] Socially minded lawyers and social workers have also found recently that they have similar objectives, and they have worked collaboratively with great effectiveness. In fact, some social workers particularly interested in championing human rights have sought additional training in law. For psychosocial caseworkers, we see participation in social advocacy of one type or another as a clear professional responsibility.

## ENVIRONMENTAL WORK AND THE ASSESSMENT OF THE INDIVIDUAL

Pervasive institutional changes come slowly. But there are times when, even within the framework of oppressive conditions, individuals *can* make changes to improve their lives rather than wait until their needs are met by hard-won social changes. In a particular situation, a worker and client may clearly see that the client's problems are induced by outer forces. But if the larger environment is not immediately modifiable, it may still be possible to find some avenue of relief. This is where *the caseworker's ability to assess the individual becomes crucial.* For example, a lonely elderly woman living on meager income assistance benefits may be healthy enough and emotionally suited to be employed as a foster grandmother for neglected children; a man who is demoralized because he can no longer find employment in his own craft may be versatile enough to train for another, more employable trade; an intelligent black student getting a second-rate education in an inferior segregated school system may have the courage and drive required to seek a transfer to a nearby all-white school that better suits his educational potential. The worker must be able to evaluate each situation separately and determine whether a particular client has the capacity or motivation to at least partially circumvent the unhealthy social conditions which led to the difficulties.[6] What is important is that we not assume that *all* victims of a limited opportunity structure are totally trapped. Even though it would be our wish to help everyone so afflicted, there are some who can be helped—up to a point—in spite of the large odds stacked against them.

Skillful environmental treatment of all kinds calls for knowing the person whom the change is designed to benefit. In virtually every case, the worker's assessment of the individual, of what one can and cannot do for oneself, and of what changes the client wants and needs is as important as the assessment of the modifiability of the environment. In Chapter 8 we noted some of the factors involved in considering whether it should be the worker, the client, or both who directly intervene—by contacting collaterals, exploring resources, or protesting injustices. As we pointed out, often the worker's knowledge and influence can expedite environmental change. This can be true even when the client is extremely competent and well motivated. But a very large part of the time, it is possible and preferable for the client to be the one to bring about environmental changes. When this is so, direct work to this end is often helpful. In addition to other procedures, this may involve reflection in which the client goes over various ways that might be used to bring about the desired improvements. Some clients may need help to learn how to make their needs known to the public welfare worker, to know what their rights are, how to pursue them effectively, and how to enlist the help of others in the community—persons or organizations —in their own behalf. The same is true for other external "instrumental" problems—difficult landlords, problems with the school system, health systems, and so on. Community resources for effective citizen and consumer action now provide many opportunities for clients to help themselves, but they often need to know about these resources, their purposes and methods, and how to use them. In these and many other ways, the caseworker can help clients to take action themselves —and more effectively master their own situations.

The decision of who should intervene directly in the client's milieu is almost always a joint decision arrived at through discussions between worker and client. (Only in instances of protective work, when a client's safety is involved or the well-being of a child is seriously jeopardized, and mutual agreement cannot be reached, is the worker sometimes forced to take unilateral action.) In coming to a decision with the client, the worker's assessment and the client's attitudes both play important roles. Factors within clients may make them unable or reluctant to act on behalf of themselves. For example, depression or great anxiety—the very state of mind that the client has sought help to alleviate—may make it impossible to reach out for the comfort and support of relatives or friends, and this may have to be done for that person.

In the assessment, the worker attempts to get a broad impression of the client's personality, evaluating the client's capacity *in relation to the particular task at hand.* Is the client intellectually able to deal with the situation? Can the client verbalize adequately? Does he or she have the necessary language ability, or is an interpreter needed? Are perception, judgment, control, and self-directive capacity sufficiently good that, with help in understanding the situation at hand, the client will be able to handle it without help? Is the client immediately ready to do this, or are feelings so deeply involved in the situation that there is need for ventilation as a prelude to clear thinking? When the pressure of underlying emotion is so great that it interferes with wise action or even consideration of action, ventilation may be required. When anxiety is high, or the self-image low, or the defense of turning against the self is crippling the client's self-confidence or causing him or her to behave in self-damaging ways, a large measure of sustaining procedures may need to precede and accompany reflective discussion of the situation and ways in which it can be changed.

Note that personality is not being assessed in the abstract here, but in relation to the task or situation that the individual faces. A person may be capable of rational consideration of one type of dilemma, but not of another; amenable to advice about matters on which the case-worker is regarded as an expert, but not amenable about others; overwhelmed by anxiety under some circumstances, cool and collected in others that to an outsider might seem just as threatening.

An important factor can enter into a worker's decision to "do for" clients at certain points rather than to try to encourage them to handle environmental matters themselves. This is the question of what effect the use of one mode of treatment or another in dealing with a particular aspect of a problem will have on treatment as a whole. For instance, it has been demonstrated that in order to convince "hard-to-reach" or involuntary clients that the worker is really well disposed toward them and interested in helping rather than reforming them for someone else's benefit, it may be necessary to do practical things from which the clients can derive benefit or pleasure.[7] In such cases a worker might welcome the opportunity to bring about environmental changes the clients want, whether or not they might eventually learn how to effect the changes themselves. Learning to do for themselves can come later. In the early stages of treatment, attention given to measures that will build a therapeutically useful relationship may take top priority.

Occasionally, too, the matter of timing enters into the decision. For the benefit of a child, it may be important for a teacher to be seen immediately. Though it might seem better for the child's mother to make the contact, it may take some weeks before she can bring herself to do so. Under these circumstances, if the mother is willing for the worker to visit the teacher, this would be the advisable course to follow. Whichever is done, of course, the question of who should see a collateral is discussed with the client so that a mutual decision about the approach can be made.

Environmental work, then, depends not only on an assessment of the modifiability of environmental factors, discussed earlier, but on the client's and worker's view of the client's ability to bring about the necessary changes. Although the general direction is one in which the client is helped to achieve as much competence and independence as possible, intervening factors just discussed strongly influence the decision of whether the worker or the client takes a particular action in the environment.

> A young, unmarried woman with two small children lived in an apartment which had many violations, several of which were detrimental to health and even dangerous for the children. The woman's impulse control, her welfare worker knew, was poorly developed and her reality testing—especially under stress—could become distorted. Furthermore, the woman had already had screaming encounters with the landlord who was known to be hostile and indifferent to the needs of his tenants. On the basis of her assessment of the woman's ego functioning, and of her powerlessness in the face of this particular landlord, the caseworker agreed to intervene herself and—by threatening to report him to the city housing department—to force the landlord to make the urgently needed repairs. Had the worker insisted that the woman deal with the landlord herself, she might well have ended up hitting him and being taken to court by him. Needless to say, the repairs in the apartment—so necessary to the health of this family —might never have been accomplished.
>
> In a contrasting situation, a depressed woman who had recently lost her job, recognized that she was probably eligible for

unemployment insurance benefits, but she felt unable to mobilize herself to go to the appropriate agency to apply for them. The caseworker considered accompanying her to the state insurance office. However, his assessment of her was that of a competent woman with no serious ego deficiencies for whom "doing for" in this way would only reinforce her seemingly "helpless ego." Instead, he chose to encourage and support her capacity for autonomous functioning, in spite of her depression which, in large part, was precipitated by her sense of helplessness upon losing her job.

The utility of environmental work is sometimes denigrated because it is too often seen vaguely as "only ego supportive," without further analysis of what part of the ego it is supporting or how the intrapsychic balance of the individual can be affected. In Chapter 2, we referred to the balance of forces in the personality system and pointed out that a small amount of change sometimes can tip the balance and result in considerable relief of distress or improvement of an individual's social functioning. For example, in the above illustration of the young woman for whom the caseworker intervened with the landlord, the caring evidenced by initiating the action could satisfy some of the client's longings for someone to minister to her needs; the worker further hoped that the support would quiet some of the woman's angry feelings. Less pressured by inner (id) drives, it was possible that some of her adaptive (ego) functions could be freed, strengthened, and mobilized. These, in turn, could help her to begin to gain better mastery over other aspects of her life. On the other hand, had the worker accompanied the depressed woman to apply for unemployment benefits, he might have unwittingly reinforced her depression by supporting her feelings of helplessness. It should be recognized, however, that although this woman actually was able to make the trip alone, many depressed clients could not have done so without being accompanied. Sometimes one must "test" a situation by observing a client's response when encouraged to act without help.

In another case, a man earning a marginal living became depressed and self-depreciating. His caseworker helped him to locate a better paying job and—with very little direct treatment —his mood lifted and his attitudes and relationships improved. His self-critical, punishing superego was less active and replaced by greater self-approval; his adaptive ego functions were no longer inhibited and immobilized. He was thereby freed to enjoy life more fully. In this situation, the worker correctly assumed that as this client's superego became less harsh there would be a shift in the balance of other aspects of his personality.

Here, again, the assessment of this client's personality structure, his abilities, and his motivation was essential to successful environmental treatment.

## TWO CASE EXAMPLES OF ENVIRONMENTAL TREATMENT

Viewing milieu work from the three vantage points discussed in these chapters—communication procedures, type of resource or collateral, and role of the worker—brings out the complexity of this type of work and highlights the breadth of skill necessary for successful environmental work. It is a part of the total treatment process in most cases, and in some it plays a decisive role. A worker who fails to apply basic understanding and skills to work in the environment is seriously handicapped in efforts to help clients with intra- or interpersonal problems. The case examples presented in this section illustrate situations in which a complex blend of environmental procedures and activities were crucial to the success of the casework treatment.

The two cases also demonstrate the usefulness of milieu work to people of widely varying circumstances, class, educational, and ethnic backgrounds. The first family to be presented lived in a middle class, suburban community; the parents and grandparents were college educated and trained for professions; they were white, of English–Scotch origins; their religious affiliation was Episcopalian. The second family was black, originally from the rural South, and had moved to a northern urban ghetto neighborhood; none of the adults had completed high school; the family was receiving public assistance; by tradition, the family members were Baptists. Yet both families had multiple problems. In this connection, we caution against the lumping together of "multiproblem," "hard-to-reach," and poverty families.[8] These terms do not connote diagnostic entities; valid generalizations cannot be made on the basis of these labels about family structure, individual personalities, or sociological characteristics. Many multiproblem families are not poor, many poor are not hard to reach, and many well-to-do families resist change.

## A Three-Generation Family: Environmental Intervention

A forty-four-year-old widower—living with his ailing mother of seventy-seven and his fourteen-year-old daughter—applied for help at a community mental health agency. He had been referred by a guidance counselor at the high school because his daughter Ellen was failing her major subjects, was truanting, and associating with a disruptive group of classmates. She had been suspended several times and the counselor's efforts to guide her had failed. Very early in the initial interview, Mr. West also discussed other problems: He himself had been depressed since the death of his wife three years before. He was concerned about his pattern of periodic heavy drinking. Employed as an inspector for a government agency where he had worked for twenty years, his job was not in jeopardy because he could take sick leave when his drinking became incapacitating. Every few months he would sign himself into the hospital to "dry out" and then function well until he started drinking again. A further concern was his mother's rapidly failing health. When his wife died, Mr. West decided to move with Ellen and his son John (at the time of intake living away from home with a friend) into his mother's comfortable home in order to provide supervision and companionship for the children. Since then, however, the elder Mrs. West had become almost blind and hard of hearing, and she had developed a serious heart condition; her arthritis had become so severe that sometimes she could not come downstairs without help. She seemed dispirited and hopeless, Mr. West told the worker. For the most part, Ellen fended for herself, and she and her grandmother were more irritating than helpful to one another.

Home visits by the worker and several meetings with all three family members resulted in a group decision to search for a live-in homemaker. Although there were several reasons for arriving at this plan, the need seemed all the more pressing because Mr. West's work required him to be out many evenings, which left Ellen and his infirm mother alone. The family income was limited, but as they talked it over with the worker, they realized that by cutting down on certain expenses they could afford a modest wage.

Fortunately, as it turned out, also on the worker's caseload was Mrs. Wilson, a seventy-two-year-old retired domestic and food caterer who had recently become depressed after the death of her sister with whom she had lived for many years. She had considered doing day work, but believed this too grueling for her at her age. Yet she was lonely and disliked being idle. When it occurred to the worker that this client also might be helped by taking a job with the West family, she assessed the entire situation carefully. It was important that she consider any aspects that might cause the arrangement to fail. Mrs. Wilson was a capable, dependable person who was interested in other people. At various times she had been active on church service committees and she had taken care of her ill sister at home for many months before the latter died. She had a sense of humor and seemed to get along with young people, as evidenced by the fact that two teenage great-nieces visited her often. And she had homemaking skills; she had earned her living in related areas for most of her life. There were no apparent reasons why the West family would not find Mrs. Wilson a very pleasant and suitable housekeeper. The worker's major concern was that Mrs. Wilson, who tended at times to be overaccommodating to others, might feel obliged to take the job even if she did not really want to—either to please the worker or because she would consider it a duty to help people in trouble. Therefore, without any pressure, the worker fully explained the West family situation to her, adding that she might not be interested since the family had many problems. The worker urged Mrs. Wilson not to consider it unless she thought it would be of benefit to her. She assured her that the Wests could find a solution if she was not interested. The worker watched closely for any signs that might betray a negative reaction to the idea. But Mrs. Wilson seemed genuinely enthusiastic and said she wanted to meet the Wests. When introduced, she liked them all immediately. Afterwards, Ellen—at that time not given to expressing positive feelings about anything—exclaimed: "What a lady!" Mr. West and his mother concurred. Mrs. Wilson agreed to the wage offered since, because of her age, her Social Security benefits would not be jeopardized.

Within a short period of time, this motherly, very competent woman was able to bring both warmth and organization to the West home. The family was eating regular meals together instead of haphazardly grabbing snacks as they had; Mrs. Wilson was able to enlist Ellen's help with many household tasks too difficult for both older women. Ellen told the worker that she enjoyed coming home from school to the aroma of Mrs. Wilson's cakes and cookies baking in the oven.

The adults, too, seemed heartened to have a home life again. When Mrs. Wilson went home for two days each week, both Ellen and her grandmother were impatient for her return. Mrs. Wilson herself reported that she had gained a "new lease on life" now that she felt needed and her days had a sense of purpose. John, who had moved out of the home a year before, after an angry argument with his father, returned to live in the household. A few family group meetings—which often included Mrs. Wilson—were held with the caseworker, in which the discussions ranged from practical housekeeping matters, to difficulties that arose among them, to sharing of some intense feelings of grief over the loss of the younger Mrs. West, which had deeply affected all the family members.

The caseworker arranged for a public health nurse to visit Mr. West's mother twice weekly to give her baths and nursing care. Ellen stopped truanting and, slowly, her academic work improved. The caseworker and Ellen met with the high school guidance counselor to make changes Ellen wanted in her course program. Learning that Ellen had an interest in the theater (her mother had been an actress), the caseworker located a drama class at the YWCA that the girl enjoyed and where she made friends. By the time Mrs. Wilson had been in the home for a year, no significant school problems remained for Ellen; Mrs. West, in spite of her infirmities, was more cheerful and comfortable; and the sullen, irritable relationships that had characterized the Wests' family life were replaced by greater affection and cooperation among them. Mr. West, however, continued his pattern of excessive, periodic drinking. In between bouts with alcohol—which were a little less frequent but just as intense—he felt better than he had. The family physician, to whom Mr. West turned for hospitalization when his drinking became incapacitating, warned him of the damage he was doing to his body. The caseworker explored his willingness to join Alcoholics Anonymous, but Mr. West staunchly refused. He disliked the organization's religious emphasis and, even more to the point, he could not bear the humiliation of sharing his private "weakness" with strangers.

Mr. West, who, after the first few months, was the only family member who still had regular weekly treatment sessions, began to realize that the onset of a period of drinking usually followed a disappointment in a relationship with a woman. For many reasons he had repeatedly failed in his attempts to find a loving, sexual companion, and after each letdown he would become depressed and take "one drink," which would start the cycle all over again. A case that had begun with the need for considerable environmental intervention, now became one in which direct treatment of Mr. West was the primary focus. At the time this case summary is being written, Mr. West is still in individual treatment, exploring the emotional aspects of his drinking and the problems that interfere with his developing a satisfying love relationship.

As this family's case illustrates, environmental intervention requires skilled and intricate work, coupled with sensitive understanding of individual and family dynamics. The worker employed four of the six communication procedures (sustainment, direct influence, exploration–description–ventilation, and person–situation reflection) with collaterals, including Mrs. Wilson. These were combined with direct, therapeutic service to the West family members—individually and as a family group. Roles shifted—at times the worker was a resource provider, locater, referrer, and creator; at other times she was an interpreter. An unusual aspect of this case was that while Mrs. Wilson served as a resource for the family, the Wests were an equally important resource for Mrs. Wilson—who no longer required individual treatment after she began to work again. In addition to relieving some of the acute distress for all involved, treatment in this case certainly served a preventive function. There was substantial evidence that, as the quality of life improved for the clients, feelings of well-being, relatedness, and self-esteem were nurtured. Without intervention, it is likely that these would have continued declining for each individual, as they had prior to referral to the caseworker.

## A Family in Crisis: Casework in Public Welfare

Mrs. Stone, a thirty-year-old woman receiving AFDC assistance for herself and five children—ranging in age from fourteen to two years—was reported by a neighbor to the child protective services of the public welfare department. It was alleged that she was severely beating one of the children with a belt. Although the worker investigating the case determined that the report was unfounded, because of the many problems the family was facing, he referred Mrs. Stone to the family services division of the welfare agency. The oldest child, Doreen, was staying out late at night, was truanting from school, and did not help around the house. Of even greater concern to the worker were his observations of Brian, age nine, who appeared withdrawn and depressed; the worker heard this child talk only when he muttered to himself. And, most pressing of all, the protective worker learned that the family was to be evicted because the landlord intended to use their apartment for a member of his own family—his right, according to city law.

In the heavily populated, metropolitan area in which Mrs. Stone lived, the welfare department's income maintenance functions were separated from other services, two of which were the child protective service that had investigated the complaint against Mrs. Stone, and the family services division, to which she was referred when it was ascertained that she had so many pressing problems. Many of the supervisors in the specialized services were MSWs; only a few of the caseworkers had master's degrees. As is often the case, the commissioner of welfare did not have a social work background, but was trained in public administration.

The family services worker made a home visit and found Mrs. Stone to be an attractive, intelligent woman who seemed depressed, almost listless. When the worker told Mrs. Stone she knew of the impending eviction and wanted to help, Mrs. Stone hardly responded. She had asked the landlord for time but he was adamant; the city marshal would put the Stones out if they did not move within the next month. Mrs. Stone agreed to allow the worker to speak with the landlord, although neither she nor the worker felt hopeful about influencing him. Mrs. Stone said she felt sure nobody would want to rent to a "welfare family" with five children. Knowing of the acute housing shortage and widespread discrimination in the city, the worker agreed that finding another apartment would be very difficult indeed.

On this first visit, three of the five children were in school. The youngest, Michael, age two, an apparently placid baby, seemed well cared for and healthy. Brian, age nine, was lying in the bedroom staring (vacantly, the worker thought) at the ceiling with his thumb in his mouth. When the worker asked whether Brian was ill, she learned that he was not but that his teacher said he was not learning, even though he was smart. He was not to return to school until he was tested. Describing Brian as a good boy, "quiet and very deep," Mrs. Stone said she did not understand why the teacher was having trouble with him. She was more worried about her oldest child, Doreen, who had a "loud mouth," did not mind, and was always in trouble. As much as she yelled at Doreen, nothing helped.

Most of Mrs. Stone's relatives lived in the South, where she had come from six years ago. She had one brother, Robert, age twenty-one, who lived in another part of the city and attended a government training program for carpentry. She and Robert were close. Mrs. Stone married when she was fifteen and Mr. Stone, the father of the four oldest children, had left the household permanently three years before, after several previous separations. He was a heavy drinker, a sometimes violent man who did not keep in touch with the children or send money to the family. On the other hand, Michael's father visited often and voluntarily contributed to his child's support.

The worker later telephoned the landlord, who maintained he had been more than patient because Mrs. Stone was a "nice woman." But with so many children, he could hardly call her an ideal tenant. Although not totally unsympathetic to the difficulty the family would have finding other housing, he planned to give the apartment to his son and nothing would change his mind. The worker then called Mr. Beck of the Legal Aid Society who said that perhaps action could be stalled but, eventually, the landlord would be allowed to evict. The lawyer agreed to meet with with Mrs. Stone.

The next home visit was scheduled when all of the children would be at home. When the worker arrived, Doreen was just leaving after a screaming exchange with her mother. Quietly, but angrily, Mrs. Stone said, "Sometimes I could kill her." Raymond, age twelve, and Cynthia, age six, were playing good-humoredly. Pointing to Raymond, Mrs. Stone said bitterly, "That's the one I was accused of beating." The worker said she could understand how upsetting it was to have been investigated. Mrs. Stone did not know who to be maddest at, the person who had lied about her or the man who came to the house to "snoop." As she listened, the worker realized that it might take time for this client to trust her too.

Mr. Beck, the lawyer, was able to get a forty-five-day extension from the court to give the family time to find housing. Mrs. Stone spoke to her minister who headed the Housing Action Council, a grassroots group that worked for tenants' rights, but he was unable to find a suitable apartment. Those that were available were in deplorable condition. The worker met with the welfare housing consultant who had little to offer but his pessimism. After exerting considerable pressure on the welfare commissioner's office, the supervisor got "broker's approval," which meant that Mrs. Stone was authorized to pay a realtor fee to locate an apartment.

Appearing unexpectedly at the welfare office late one afternoon, Mrs. Stone, close to tears, told the worker that the psychologist from the Board of Education thought Brian should go into the hospital. The more she talked, the angrier she got. She asked if anything could be done. The worker, who had immediately sensed that Brian was emotionally disturbed, realized that Mrs. Stone was still determined to believe her child was not in trouble. While the mother was there the worker telephoned the psychologist who told her that Brian's intelligence was above average, but that he was severely emotionally damaged; the boy was hallucinating and his fantasies were filled with violence. He had witnessed his father brutally attacking his mother when he was six. The psychiatrist, who had also seen Brian, was strongly recommending hospitalization for observation; even long-term inpatient treatment might be necessary.

Mrs. Stone was furious, insisting, "He's *not* crazy." The supervisor, whom the worker had asked to sit in, pointed out that if, after observation, it was believed that Brian was not in danger of hurting himself or anyone else, by law he could not be kept in the hospital without Mrs. Stone's consent. Noting that the mother was listening now and not arguing, the supervisor added that since the psychologist seemed worried about Brian it might be best to have him checked and settle the matter one way or the other. When Mrs. Stone asked whether she had a choice, the supervisor admitted that she was not sure but told Mrs. Stone she could ask.

Reluctantly, Mrs. Stone allowed Brian to be admitted to the children's psychiatric unit of the city hospital. After three weeks, the doctor told her that the boy was definitely not suited for a regular classroom, or even for a class for the emotionally disturbed within the school system. He was not likely, however, to be destructive to himself or others. Angrily, Mrs. Stone retorted that she could have told him that. Later, after talking with the hospital psychiatrist, the worker, at the suggestion of her supervisor, told Mrs. Stone about a new special day school program for psychotic children, administered by the state hospital. Although the psychiatrist had recommended further hospitalization he, too, was aware of how strongly Mrs. Stone opposed this. Also, Brian wanted to go home. The referral to the day school was made and, fortunately, Brian was accepted almost immediately.

Two days before the stay of eviction had expired, Mrs.Stone had not yet found an apartment. She pleaded with the worker to help. The supervisor had a good working relationship with the city marshal and was able to persuade him to delay the final action, but only for a few days. The following afternoon, Mrs. Stone, who had been following every lead, located a large, attractive apartment in a two-family brownstone. The rent, however, was sixty dollars over the amount allowed by the Welfare Department's regulations, and efforts by the supervisor to secure an "exception" from the commissioner's office met with failure. From Mr. Beck, Mrs. Stone learned that she had a right to a fair hearing from the state to determine whether the rent guidelines could be exceeded, and a petition was filed for a state review. The lawyer also filed for another stay of eviction. Mrs. Stone was aware, however, that these processes would take time, and that the particular apartment she had found surely would be rented before the decisions were handed down.

The next morning Mrs. Stone and her brother Robert, whom the worker had not met before, were waiting at the welfare office when the worker arrived. Robert, it turned out, had agreed to move with his sister to the new apartment if they could get approval for having his contribution cover the excess rent. After a series of calls to the commissioner's office, the worker was able to get this plan accepted. Robert said he was looking forward to living with his sister and helping to fix up the new apartment. Mrs. Stone learned that the landlord was slow to make repairs, and the worker offered information about a tenant education class given by the state university on home maintenance.

The worker praised Mrs. Stone, as she had throughout their work together, for taking the initiative, in spite of her understandable discouragement about the problems she faced. She had fought hard to hurdle what seemed to be almost impossible obstacles, and her work had paid off: now she had an apartment that she liked and Brian was adjusting very well to the day school. Before leaving, Mrs. Stone asked if the worker would stop in and see her when she got settled. To herself, the worker wondered whether now that some of the crises were over, Mrs. Stone would want to work on her still contentious relationship with Doreen.

The complexity of environmental treatment is well demonstrated by this case. In spite of the many factors mitigating against effective work (not the least of which was the fact that the worker was simultaneously carrying a hundred families on her caseload, some with comparable emergencies), the worker and her supervisor were in contact with over a dozen collaterals and agencies up to the point that this part of the summary of the Stone case ends. They were able to establish an excellent, mutually respectful relationship with the lawyer—one that would facilitate work for other clients in the future. This was particularly important because Mr. Beck had had less cooperative contacts with some members of the Welfare Department staff previously. As in the West case, four communication procedures (sustainment, exploration–ventilation, direct advice,and person–situation reflection) were used in direct and indirect work. Patience, tact, persistence, and optimism were all qualities the worker had—and needed to have—to gain Mrs. Stone's trust and to succeed as she did—with client and collaterals. On the other hand, cynicism, indifference, "burn-out," and prejudice —characteristics often (sometimes unjustifiably) attributed to public welfare workers—might well have led to the demoralization of the Stone family. Clearly, Mrs. Stone became more hopeful and active when she had others who gave support and shared in her efforts. The worker and her supervisor functioned in a broad range of roles in their endeavor to provide and locate resources, and to interpret, mediate, and intervene in this family's environment. Together, they sought to bring about changes within the agency as well. Even when stymied by restrictive policies and laws, they, along with Mrs. Stone, found workable alternatives.

Given the commitment of worker and supervisor, this case illustrates that effective casework *is* possible in a public welfare agency, even in a dense urban area. Such commitment is most likely, we believe, where there is strong social work involvement. In this case, the supervisor had an MSW and years of experience and the caseworker had had one year of advanced training. We would add, that, while similar work might have been possible in a private agency, the workers there probably would not have had the same access to or influence with public officials within and outside of the welfare system; it is unlikely that they would have been able to bring about the modifications of rules and policies so important to the work with Mrs. Stone. On the other hand, of course, when caseloads are large, as they were in this agency, it follows that some clients will not get the services they need. When asked about caseload management, the supervisor interviewed about this case frankly admitted that often those clients and situations most accessible to change receive the most attention. There are many other clients whose emotional, physical, and situational difficulties are so recalcitrant and of such long standing, that only small caseloads and, more likely, major social changes could begin to remedy them.

In conclusion, it is sometimes difficult to assess where the effects of environmental pressures leave off and emotional relationship problems begin. As in the West case, once the critical issues facing the Stones were handled, the worker and family then could address other areas, including the angry relationship between Doreen and her mother; the need for special help for six-year-old Cynthia who, it developed, had a learning disability; and the location of a day care program for Michael so that Mrs. Stone—who had long wanted a high school diploma—could attend a course to prepare for the equivalency examination. By remaining active with the family for six months after the family moved into the new apartment, the worker was then able to help with these and other matters. As the supervisor of this case pointed out: "When a family can't find a decent place to live, it hardly has the stamina to attend to much else, no matter how important."

## NOTES

1. Lest we forget! The social worker's role in reducing environmental pressures has been recognized for many years. Wrote Mary Richmond: "Social casework may be defined as the art of doing different things for and with different people by *cooperating* with them to achieve at one and the same time their own and society's betterment." See Mary Richmond, *The Long View* (New York: Russell Sage Foundation, 1930), p. 174; Florence Hollis, "Environmental (Indirect) Treatment as Determined by Client's Needs," in *Differential Approach in Casework Treatment* (New York: Family Welfare Association of America, 1936); and Florence Hollis, *Social Case Work in Practice: Six Case Studies* (New York: Family Welfare Association of America, 1939), especially pp. 295–298.

2. A controversial subject! For varying viewpoints and approaches to advocacy, social action, and aggressive intervention, see George A. Brager, "Advocacy and Political Behavior," *Social Work,* 13 (April 1968), 5–15; Richard A. Cloward and Frances Fox Piven, "Notes Toward a Radical Social Work," in Roy Bailey and Mike Brake, eds., *Radical Social Work* (New York: Pantheon Books, 1975), pp. vii–xlviii; Irvin Epstein, "Social Workers and Social Action: Attitudes Toward Social Action Strategies," *Social Work,* 13 (April 1968), 101–108; David Hunter, "Social Action to Influence Institutional Change," *Social Casework,* 51 (April 1970), 225–231; S. K. Khinduka and Bernard J. Coughlin, "A Conceptualization of Social Action," *Social Service Review,* 49 (March 1975), 1–14; Mary J. McCormick, "Social Advocacy: A New Dimension in Social Work," *Social Casework,* 51 (January 1970), 3–11; Robert H. MacRae, "Social Work and Social Action," *Social Service Review,* 40 (March 1966), 1–7; William Schwartz, "Private Troubles and Public Issues: One Social Work Job or Two?", in National Conference of Social Welfare, *Social Welfare Forum* (New York: Columbia University Press, 1969), pp. 22–43; Harry Specht, "Disruptive Tactics," *Social Work,* 14 (April 1969), 5–15; Harry Specht, "The Deprofessionalization of Social Work," *Social Work,* 17 (March 1972), 3–15; Daniel Thurz, "The Arsenal of Social Action Strategies: Options for Social Workers," *Social Work,* 16 (January 1971), 27–34; Harold Weissman, "The Middle Road to Distributive Justice," *Social Work,* 17 (March 1972), 86–93; and David Wineman and Adrienne James, "The

Advocacy Challenge to Schools of Social Work," *Social Work,* 14 (April 1969), 23–32.

3. Gordon Hamilton discusses this in "The Role of Social Casework in Social Policy," *Social Casework,* 33 (October 1952), 315–324. See also Charles S. Levy, "Advocacy and the Injustice of Justice," *Social Service Review,* 48 (March 1974), 39–50; and Neil Gilbert and Harry Specht, "Advocacy and Professional Ethics," *Social Work,* 21 (July 1976), 288–293.

4. Alvin S. Schorr, "Editorial Page," *Social Work,* 11 (July 1966), 2; Robert Sunley, "Family Advocacy from Case to Cause," *Social Casework,* 51 (June 1970), 347–357; Charlotte Towle, "Social Work: Cause and Function," in Helen H. Perlman, ed., *Helping: Charlotte Towle on Social Work and Social Casework* (Chicago: University of Chicago Press, 1969), pp. 277–299.

5. National Association of Social Workers, *Ad hoc* Committee on Advocacy, "Champion of Social Victims," *Social Work,* 14 (April 1969), 16–22.

6. On the need to understand the individual client, Bertha Reynolds wrote that "since human beings need all sorts of things—ranging from food and shelter to recreation, education, friendship—and since attitudes play a part in their getting or not getting all of these, there can be no such a thing as social case work that does not take account of attitudes." She added: "But I am equally sure that no case work can succeed in isolating a person's attitudes and treating them apart from the conditions of his life in which they find expression." Bertha Capen Reynolds, "A Study of Responsibility in Social Case Work," *Smith College Studies in Social Work,* 5 (September 1934), 12.

7. See especially Henry Freeman et al., "Can a Family Agency Be Relevant to the Inner Urban Scene?", *Social Casework,* 51 (January 1970), 12–21; Eleanor Pavenstedt, ed., *The Drifters: Children of Disorganized Lower-Class Families* (Boston: Little, Brown, 1967); Arthur Pierson, "Social Work Techniques with the Poor," *Social Casework,* 51 (October 1970), 481–485.

8. Florence Hollis, "Casework and Social Class," *Social Casework,* 46 (October 1965), 463–471.

# Chapter 10

# Family Therapy and Psychosocial Casework: A Theoretical Synthesis

One of the distressing paradoxes of modern life is that at the same time that the support of the family structure is needed the most, the turbulence of the larger social system is endangering it. As American society has become more impersonal and bureaucratized, it has rendered people in ever greater need of the shelter and solace of family life. Concurrently, rapid social changes and widespread shifts in traditional values have had a disturbing effect on the quality of family relationships, often depriving the individual members of essential built-in supports.

Indeed, the family is being challenged from within as well as from without. Families have given up some of their former functions: socialization of the very young and the nursing care of the old and ailing, for example, are shared with the broader community. Women are more independent economically than ever before. Many customary family patterns have died out and unfamiliar lifestyles have sprung up. Often, families splinter and disperse. Although the trend is leveling off, the divorce rate doubled from 1967 to 1977.[1] Many children are now living in single-parent homes. When the family has been weakened or fractured, it may be unable to fulfill its ideal—if never fully realized—function as a haven of love and acceptance. With greater frequency than ever, we hear people denying any commitment to their families. There are even some who question whether the American family as an institution will survive the forces that threaten to undermine it.

In our view, however, it is inevitable that some form of family life will endure. No adequate substitute has been found for the nurturance and socialization of the young. Family relationships cannot be compared to any other social connections in the depth and intensity of their effect upon individual members. Indeed, "the family is the cell to which people revert in times of social disorganization."[2] In spite of the many changes it has undergone, and the diversity of life styles it now encompasses, the modern family is still seen by many of its members of all ages as the primary place for comfort and refuge from the larger, unpredictable world.

The burgeoning of the family therapy movement has been, in part, a response to the growing need to counteract the disruption of the traditional family network in this age of unsettling change.[3] It is beyond the limits of these chapters to present an overview of the literature or to review in detail the often disparate points of view that have flooded the family therapy field. Nevertheless, our intent is to provide a synthesis of some of the basic concepts and to demonstrate that these relatively recent developments in family treatment have broadened casework theory and now provide us with additional procedures for assessment and intervention. The psychosocial approach, with its commitment to understanding families and interpersonal relationships, is uniquely equipped not only to assimilate the principles but to contribute to their synthesis.

## FAMILY GROUP TREATMENT AND THE SOCIAL CASEWORK TRADITION

The family outlook is woven into the fabric of the social work tradition. From the earliest days of the profession, social workers have recognized the importance of family life to the healthy development and functioning of its individual members. The report of the first White House Conference on Child Welfare in 1909 defined home life as "the highest and finest product of civilization," and urged that homes should not be broken up for reasons of poverty alone.[4]

In her groundbreaking work of 1917, *Social Diagnosis,* Mary Richmond was remarkably cognizant of the need to study the individual in interaction with the environment. Recognizing what we, today, may take for granted, the pioneering Miss Richmond pointed out that the individual must also be regarded in the context of the family group:

> Family caseworkers welcome the opportunity to see at the very beginning of intercourse several of the members of the family assembled in their own home environment, acting and reacting upon one another, each taking a share in the development of the client's story, each revealing in ways other than words social facts of real significance.[5]

In less quaint language, perhaps, current family therapists, including those interested in home visits and nonverbal communication, share her approach to understanding the family.

Over sixty years later, Miss Richmond's advice can serve to remind us that "the man should be seen," and that other relatives (now referred to as the "extended family") must not be overlooked. How modern her ideas seem to us as we read: "The need of keeping the family in mind extends beyond the period of diagnosis, of course." Without a family view, "we would find that the good results of individual treatment crumble away." Miss Richmond had a prophetic grasp of the "drift of family life," as she called it, that heralded casework's understanding of the complexities of family interrelationships.[6]

Social casework continued to emphasize the interdependence of people and their environments. Nevertheless, following World War I, the field began to take a serious interest in psychology, which strongly influenced the profession in the 1920s. In spite of keen concern with the problems of the "real world" during the depression years of the 1930s, Freudian ideas were also taking hold and by 1940 social work was inundated by psychoanalytic thinking. During these periods, social workers temporarily abandoned some of their interest in the broader social issues. Never, however, did these shifts to more intense fascination with the inner emotional life of the individual client totally obscure the significance of family history and interaction. Caseworkers, vital contributors to the mental hygiene and child guidance movements of the 1920s and 1930s, realized that the behavioral and emotional problems of children as well as the mental disorders of adults were profoundly influenced by family relationships. However reasonable—or even agreeably received—the worker's advice to a client's relatives was not enough. Family members needed treatment, too, if the problems of the individual (or, nowadays, the "index client" or "identified patient") were to be resolved.

By the late 1930s, caseworkers in family welfare (now family service) agencies were also working "above the poverty line," ministering to the emotional and interpersonal disturbances of family life as well as to the financial and environmental aspects. Although frequently the individual was of major interest, family casework objectives of almost a half century ago were broadened to include: "remedial and preventive treatment of social and emotional difficulties that produce maladjustment in the family"; "intrafamily harmony"; and the development of "the capacities of all family members to the fullest."[7] In short, neither environmental assistance to the family, on the one hand, nor treatment of the individual out of his milieu, on the other, were deemed sufficiently helpful. Many caseworkers recognized that the family as a whole required attention.

Gordon Hamilton, in her classic introductory text on psychosocial casework, built on the earlier casework approach to the family as the "unit of work." Today's family therapists would have little quarrel with her view:

Using "group process" in family life does several things: it locates and clarifies the problem through discussion; it permits expression of opinions; it dissipates anxiety for each child, because the situation is shared with the other, as well as with with the worker; and this participation releases ability to move toward action. Work with families inevitably includes children, adults, adolescents, young married couples, and the aged; none of these can be treated as isolated problems, because of the nature of social relationships themselves.

She added that "there are considerations of family balance and behavior as a group as well as from the point of view of each individual member." In the ordinary course of the child's development, she said, "first through identification and then through increasing the psychological 'distance' between the self and the persons around him . . . [he] moves healthily out of the 'undifferentiated unity' . . . of the parent–child relationship."[8]

Hamilton's concepts preceded the family therapy movement, yet they had much in common with ideas that followed. Jackson's work on "family homeostasis," Bowen's notion of the "undifferentiated family ego mass," and the concept of "individuation," are elaborations and refinements of these rudimentary formulations of Hamilton. Mudd, Josselyn, and Hollis, too, were among those who took early steps to develop a family-centered approach to family and marital problems.[9]

Modern-day family treatment, like casework, rests on a blend of knowledge, theory, and "practice wisdom" from various disciplines and sciences—with input from psychoanalytic, communication, and systems theories, ego psychology, and several of the social sciences. Diverse schools of thought abound, however, with much controversy stirring within family therapy circles. The student (and, indeed, the practitioner, supervisor, or teacher) is faced with a staggering array of material about family dynamics and treatment procedures, as would be expected in a new field. One bibliography lists some two thousand articles and books published on family therapy between 1950 and 1970.[10] The deluge confounds us less, however, as soon as we recognize that many of the new concepts and techniques can be embraced comfortably by the psychosocial framework. If, in the past, casework's family orientation was in some ways underdeveloped, the seeds were there. The ever growing family therapy movement adds impetus to the creative integration of the wealth of theory, specialized techniques, and research that flow from practice.

Social work professionals, although not always sufficiently credited with their contributions to the movement, can be proud of their place in the rapid growth of family treatment over the past quarter century. They have not simply received and assimilated theory and procedures;

they have been in the forefront of their development. A most renowned trailblazer, Nathan Ackerman, accredited much of his early work in family treatment to his association with a social work family agency, Jewish Family Service.[11] Virginia Satir, Frances Scherz, Arthur Leader, Sanford Sherman, and Harry Aponte are among many others with social work backgrounds who have made substantial contributions to family treatment.[12] Many graduate schools of social work have developed curricula and research in family studies and treatment practices. By 1970, social workers constituted 40 percent of the practitioners (the largest professional group) treating families.[13] Some social workers view casework and family therapy as separate practices. We, on the other hand, see no need to choose between them. Later in this chapter we will discuss more fully how, in our view, the psychosocial framework can theoretically accommodate the principles of family treatment.

## CHANGE, STRESS, AND FAMILY ADAPTATION

Without exception, families are repeatedly required to adapt to stress and change. Over time, roles must be modified, positions shifted, and patterns of behavior adjusted. As the familiar means of meeting needs become outmoded, new ways must be discovered. There are no "problem-free" families. Pressures may result from:

1. *A new developmental phase of an individual member of the nuclear or extended family.* When a child reaches adolescence, or a young adult leaves the family home for good, or a daughter challenges her parents' mores and chooses not to marry, or an elderly grandparent can no longer function independently, the family is required to adapt to new roles and rules and new patterns of interaction. Having a baby, however joyful, can create a crisis for a marriage. Each such change is often accompanied by a sense of loss, and a period of mourning and temporary regression on the part of at least one family member.

2. *Illness, injury, or impairment of a family member.* When one person gets sick or has an accident, or when a mentally or physically defective child is born to a family, the special needs of the situation call for reassignment of family roles and functions. Whether the outcome is recovery, institutionalization, or death, adaptations and readaptions will be required.

3. *External stress on an individual member.* A crisis on the father's job, a change in a child's school, the death of a close friend of the mother's, or an act of discrimination encountered by any member, all reverberate upon the family system.

4. *External stress on the entire family.* When the family home burns down, when urban renewal forces relocation, when the bread-

winner loses his or her job, or when the economic situation compels a family to apply for public assistance, the whole family is directly affected, and mechanisms for coping must be activated. The addition to the household of a foster child, a new stepparent, or an elderly relative requires adjustments in the system to enlarge the family boundaries.[14]

Families facing transitions and stresses such as these are almost inevitably faced with conflict and pain. They fear change, yet they need to change. Feelings of bereavement can be profound when familiar relationships and patterns have to be modified. A period of disorganization and confusion may follow. For some families, the outcome is resolution and growth. Others, however, become chronically regressed, chaotic, or symptomatic. When, as caseworkers, we meet with a family, we require a framework for analyzing and assessing the relationships, interactions, and patterns that operate within its structure. Specifically, we must be able to evaluate whether the overall family style is essentially functional or dysfunctional. Usually, when a family comes for treatment, one or more of its members feels the pressure of a problem. We must be able to determine whether the difficulty relates to a transient phase of stress, a transition to which the family must painfully accommodate, or whether the family process in and of itself is too dysfunctional or resourceless to regain its balance. Some key concepts from family theory can assist us in our efforts to explore the family's structure and functioning. Combined with our knowledge of the individual personality, and of the interaction of the individual with the larger social environment, these concepts—which describe the internal workings of families—provide us with a clearer picture of the degree of health or disability in a particular family situation. From this understanding, we can proceed to fashion techniques of intervention.

Before presenting these concepts, let us be reminded of the diverse family roles and relationship patterns that exist in our society. In family therapy, as in all other methods of casework, we must be keenly sensitive to variations in style that are either culturally determined or idiosyncratic to a particular family group. However atypical, these modes of family relations may be functional and adaptive. For example, the extended "urban matriarchal" family, which can include grandmother, mother, and children, may operate well and even creatively if roles are well defined. The sharing and cooperation that can occur in poor families with this structure, or in communal living arrangements that have sprung up in recent years, sometimes allow for a good balance of mutuality and independence. Single parents—mothers or fathers—can successfully provide a home for children. Male–female roles based on individual preference rather than on traditional expectations can be adaptive. Homosexual couples—who must develop special role definitions—sometimes do raise children, and need not be diagnosed as dysfunctional on the grounds of life style alone. The quality of interactions and the nature of the family relationships are far more significant as indicators of family functioning than are the facts of the family's composition or role designations as such. How, more specifically, do we determine where a family falls on the functional–dysfunctional continuum? The following summary of some central concepts of family therapy provide us with useful criteria.

## BASIC CONCEPTS OF FAMILY THERAPY

The early family research of the 1950s, which led to some of the central principles guiding the development of the family therapy movement, focused primarily on the study of schizophrenia.[15] Often stymied by the resistance of the schizophrenic process to therapeutic intervention, researchers and practitioners of various disciplines were spurred on to study the schizophrenic within the family environment. As the family therapy movement took hold, it became clear that many of the original concepts could be applied more broadly to families with various symptomatic members, or even to "normal" families. A review of casework and other journals reveals that increasingly clinicians have used the family approach with alcoholics, delinquents, the psychosomatically or terminally ill, and the aged, and with a broad range of marital and parent–child conflicts.

The purpose of this chapter and the one that follows is twofold. First, we will introduce and organize some of the central concepts that have emerged from the family therapy field. We hope the reader's appetite will be whetted sufficiently to study the literature further. Second, we intend to demonstrate the relevance of family therapy to the psychosocial orientation. In some social work and family therapy circles, there is resistance to relating concepts derived from the psychoanalytic study of the individual with those that describe the properties of the family as a unit. In our view, however, a theoretical synthesis of the two can be attained. We shall return to a fuller discussion of this later; it is enough, for the moment, to note that these chapters aim to bridge transactional and systems concepts with intrapsychic theory.

The concepts we have chosen to include here are those that we in practice have found useful in our work. In some instances, the language of family theory is so abstruse that it can seem hard to apply to the real people who visit our offices. In our presentation, however, we have attempted to connect the concepts as closely as possible to the human beings they attempt to describe. Needless to say, family theory has wide gaps, and the principles vary in their levels of abstraction and inclusiveness. Refinements and corrections will derive from ongoing research and clinical experience. Theories about intrapsychic phenomena and even small group concepts have had a longer history of validation. The reader will note further that concepts from various "schools" of family therapy often overlap and can be interrelated—in some instances, a similar idea is expressed by different terms. The constructs that follow, nevertheless, provide a beginning language for a field barely past infancy with which to understand family life and functioning.

## Differentiation and Boundaries

Central to family theory are two assumptions around which many of its principles can be organized.[16] First, it is believed that each human being strives for a sense of relatedness and closeness in associations with others. Needless to say, relationships may come and go over a lifetime, but the individual's need for sharing with others is ongoing. Second, and equally important, it is postulated that every person seeks a sense of personal identity—a self-definition—that has consistency and cohesion over time, in spite of emotional ups and downs or external pressures. Each new developmental phase, of course, will alter some aspects of an individual's self-definition. On the basis of these assumptions, we can see that difficulties arise when the pursuit of interpersonal relationships drives a person to negate a sense of self or, conversely, when an individual is so determined to maintain a sense of identity that the need to share his or her life intimately with others is forfeited.

The student of family literature will repeatedly come across a group of more or less analogous terms such as "differentiation," "individuation," and "autonomy." Equally prevalent are an assortment of words that express the opposite idea, including "fusion," "undifferentiation," "symbiosis," and "enmeshment." Generally speaking, these terms (many of which can be found as well in the writings of psychoanalysts and ego psychologists) refer to the degree to which individuals and subsystems within the family accept—or do not accept—themselves and each other as distinct, self-defined, and self-directing. According to our assumptions, growth occurs when individuals accept themselves, their thoughts, feelings, and qualities as uniquely theirs, and separate or differentiated from those of others; at the same time, they recognize the need for close relationships. The functional family, then, provides its members and subgroupings (such as the marital pair or the sibling subsystem) with definite yet flexible boundaries and functions. In other words, one person or subsystem can operate independently, and yet share intimately with other members.

The dysfunctional family, by contrast, whose members define

themselves primarily in relation to others, is often threatened by divergent or independent points of view or expectations. Often in families we see clinically, differences among members are resisted or denied. A father, for example, who has made his living in the construction trade, may see his son's interest in becoming a musician as a challenge to the value of his own way of life and may, therefore, react with fear or anger. Sometimes family members explain their own feelings, actions, or sense of personal worth on the basis of the behavior of others. "If it weren't for you, I'd be happy" is a sentiment frequently expressed in family meetings. A wife may measure her self-esteem by the degree or type of affection she receives from her husband. By the same token, in troubled families, change and spontaneity are often resisted for fear that these will result in the deterioration of the family relationships, without which the members fear they cannot survive.

Bowen suggests a basis on which to assess the level of an individual's self-differentiation.[17] According to his theory, people can be placed on a continuum according to their ability to distinguish their subjective feeling processes from their objective thinking processes. The higher the level of differentiation, the more the individual—even under stress—can distinguish between emotions and intellect. One can be intimate with others without fear of fusion and loss of self-differentiation. Decisions can be based on reason. Close relationships are formed on the basis of choice rather than compulsion. The person's definition of "self" is not severely shaken by the disapproval of others, nor must there be constant approval to feel adequate. Complete differentiation or emotional maturity, in Bowen's terms, describes a degree of functioning that none of us actually achieves.

The poorly differentiated individual, on the other hand—especially when stressed or anxious—often cannot distinguish feeling from fact. The intellect is so flooded by emotion that decisions are based on what will temporarily reduce anxiety rather than on judgments or beliefs. In more familiar psychoanalytic terms, ego functioning (especially judgment and impulse control) is impaired, or overriden in the face of powerful instinctual drives. These individuals depend on the feelings and opinions of others to define them, and often cannot distinguish their own emotions from those of the people close to them. Relationships are marked by extreme dependency on others.

Notions about differentiation are sometimes misunderstood. When we speak of independent, self-defined individuals, we do not imply that they operate exclusively in their own orbits or that they are necessarily self-absorbed, self-centered, or "selfish" in their relationships. To the contrary, as people accept the need for intimacy they can also be very responsive to the feelings and attitudes of others. Without sacrificing one's personal identity—one's values, one's goals, one's emotional life —one can also be altruistic. In fact, in our experience, those who can maintain a sense of themselves as uniquely special, separate, and self-directing people, are better able to be giving and loving to those close to them than individuals who cannot. The person who relies on others for self-definition, who operates out of fear and extreme dependency, eventually harbors resentment toward those on whom he so thoroughly relies.

Returning now to Bowen, marriages, he believes, usually occur between two people of similar levels of self-differentiation. The lower the level of differentiation of family members, the greater the fusion or blending (or symbiotic dependency) with one another. For example, one spouse may appear to function more independently than the other. Close examination, however, reveals that the "strength" of one partner may be contingent on the "weakness" of the other. In clinical practice, we frequently observe the rapid decline of the "strong" family member when the "fragile" or "sick" one (e.g., spouse or adult child) separates or dies. The incompetence of one is required for the stability of the other. Bowen's concept of the "undifferentiated family ego mass"* describes the quality of fusion or "emotional oneness" that these kinds of family relationships evidence. Members of an undifferentiated family ego mass, particularly when under pressure, can become deeply involved in the feelings, thoughts, and fantasies of one another. Often the phase of extreme "we-ness," which can be overwhelmingly intense, is followed by a period of distance and even hostile rejection. We frequently see in practice marital pairs, or families with adolescents, going through such cycles of profound dependence and angry repulsion.

For many years, social workers have been aware of the phenomenon of "complementarity" in marriages and in the interactional behavioral patterns of entire families. This concept, along with the concepts of dependence and symbiosis, long familiar to psychosocial workers, is closely related to some aspects of Bowen's theory.[18]

*Boundaries* are the means by which individuals, subsystems, and generations protect their differentiation and maintain a sense of identity. As Minuchin[19] conceives them, boundaries at one pole are very rigid and the individuals and subgroups within the family are quite uninvolved and disengaged from the others. At the other pole are those families with diffuse or loose inner boundaries; the family members and subsystems are enmeshed or fused with one another. Most families fall within a wide range between these extremes and have clear yet pene-

---

*Although Bowen no longer uses this phrase to describe a family's emotional fusion, it appears so frequently in family literature that we have chosen to include it.

trable boundaries that permit close relationships among their members. At various stages of a family's development, disengagement and enmeshment can coexist. For example, it is common to find a tendency toward enmeshment and diffusion of boundaries between a mother and her small children, while the father is more disengaged. Greater disengagement may occur, and clearer boundaries may be drawn, as adolescents prepare to separate from their families of origin. When related to developmental phases, these concepts of Minuchin's do not in themselves represent functional or dysfunctional family styles.

Families that consistently operate at one pole or the other, however, can be dysfunctional. Thus, a family system with rigid inner boundaries can accept a wide range of individual differences, but the disengagement can be so marked that support from the family group is called forth only when the system is severely stressed. Otherwise, family members operate independently, with minimum help from the others and little sense of belonging.

> The professional parents of an eleven-year-old boy, both deeply immersed in their respective careers, were unaware that their youngster was being bullied and forced to hand over his carfare to older boys each day, until a sensitive janitor alerted the school social worker. The boy, trained to be self-reliant, had been walking home from school and suffering the humiliation of his plight without feeling free to seek his parents' guidance and comfort.

In the extremely enmeshed, fused, or overly dependent family, on the other hand, the most minor event occurring to one member immediately creates a stir of activity among others. Boundaries are so diffuse that privacy is minimal, and the feelings of one person seem indistinguishable from those of another. The tasks of one member may be absorbed by others, often arresting the development of the individual's sense of competence and autonomy.

> A seventeen-year-old girl with recurrent headaches, for which no physical basis could be detected, was referred for treatment by her physician. In family sessions it was revealed that her mother, who had always thought of her daughter as "delicate," did a major portion of the girl's homework, recommended which friends she should or should not choose, and bought much of her clothing without consulting her about her preferences. The mother told the worker that she knew Alice's feelings "better than Alice does." The father complained that his wife always put Alice's needs above his.

Caseworkers frequently meet families, such as this one, in which one parent is in an "undifferentiated alliance," or a symbiotically dependent relationship, with one or more children. In these situations the marital relationship is often distant or hostile, and the child frequently becomes symptomatic. Similarly, when a parent has remained fused or excessively involved with his or her parents, the marital boundaries are sacrificed to hostile–dependent relationships with families of origin. Reverberations upon the entire system are inevitable.

A couple and their sixteen-year-old son (the youngest of four children and the only one living at home) were in family treatment because the boy, although extremely bright, was failing in school and was isolated from his peers. The mother's mother lived in an "in-law" apartment in the family home. Shortly before the boy's symptoms were exacerbated, his usually sullen and remote father, in a rage, pushed the grandmother against a wall, bruising her. Although the mother and grandmother argued frequently, it was clear that the mother kept trying to win her mother's rarely expressed approval. They spent many hours together during the day. Even after the father came home, the mother visited the grandmother for part of every evening. The boy "could do no wrong" in his grandmother's eyes, and she often allowed him privileges denied by one or both parents.

In this situation, the individual, marital, and generational boundaries were repeatedly violated. The grandmother, who had little other life of her own, was excessively involved with her daughter and her daughter's marriage; she also intruded on the parenting of the boy. Rather than confronting his wife directly for being more closely connected to her mother than to him, the father attacked the mother-in-law. At other times, he displaced his rage and became critical of his son. The wife was more deeply invested in her relationship with her mother than with her husband, or, for that matter, her son. The goals of family treatment were to help the marital pair to achieve a warmer, less hostile relationship; to assist the grandmother in developing some social group contacts that would bring her satisfaction and reduce her need to intrude on the life (or boundaries) of her daugher's family; and to support the boy in developing peer friendships as well as closer relationships with his older siblings, who could guide him in his efforts to differentiate from this complexly enmeshed family system. Family therapy progressed accordingly, and the boy became less burdened by the family pathology. Eventually, he was able to establish more comfortable relationships with every member of his family. His schoolwork improved and his friendships increased. When treatment terminated, every family member felt benefited by it.

## The Family Is a System

Family members can be viewed as interacting, interdependent parts of an organic whole. Some concepts from systems theory have been described elsewhere in this book (see especially Chapter 2). The family unit, like an intricately coordinated clock, is greater than the sum of its parts—because of the interactions and interrelationships within it. Without the interdependence, there is no family system, simply a cluster of individuals. Intrapsychic events alone cannot account for the movement and flow of the family system that develops its own patterns of behavior and affective expression, its unique rules and role expectations.

It follows that family dysfunction is not simply the sum total of the disturbances of individual members, but also the product of the family as an entity. The "identified patient" or "index client" (i.e., the individual who seeks treatment or is "chosen" by the family as the troubled member) is often a family symptom through whom the family expresses its difficulties as a system.[20] When a family comes for treatment, the therapist's focus may not be on individual pathologies as such (even though these would be included in the overall assessment), but on the family system or interactions that produce symptomatic members—frequently in shifts, with individuals taking turns. Often we find that when a problem child improves, the marital strains of the parents are exposed. When change occurs in one part of the system, all parts are affected in some way. When one person is in pain, it can be assumed that the others are too. Family processes are regulated and reinforced by corrective "feedback mechanisms" that work within the family's internal structure to maintain its stability.

> In one family treatment case, the presence of an adult son in the home was the key to maintaining the balance of his parents' marriage; both parents were closer to him than they were to each other. Marital dissatisfactions remained hidden since the parents were united by their overinvolvement in their son's life. Moves the young man made toward independence were met with his parents' efforts to discourage him (feedback mechanisms) in order to maintain the status quo (or equilibrium) of the marital relationship.

*FAMILY HOMEOSTASIS.* This familiar term refers to the capacity of the family's internal environment to maintain a constancy or equilibrium—healthy or dysfunctional—by a continuous interplay of dynamic forces that restores it to its familiar state following disturbances in its balance. Such family equilibrium does not imply a static condition, but a balance of its dynamic components comparable to the interacting factors that keep a bicycle balanced while in motion. The source of disturbance can be internal or external. In the above case, the son's attempt to separate from his family represented an internal disturbance that was followed by his parents' attempts to return the family system to its former steady state. Frequently, a change in the system is most possible when the homeostatic balance is upset. The notion that a family in crisis can be most accessible to growth-producing change derives from this principle. The entry of the family therapist on the scene can disturb the balance, and many family therapists recommend deliberately inducing an upset to make way for a new and healthier homeostasis. Developed by Bateson, Jackson, and others as a family concept, Ackerman elaborated on the idea by describing the homeostasis of the personality, of the family, and of the larger environment, and the interdependence of the three.[21]

## Family Roles

A concept important to family theory, as Spiegel defines it, a role is "a goal directed pattern or sequence of acts tailored by the cultural process for the transactions a person may carry out in a social group or situation." Furthermore, "no role exists in isolation but is always patterned to gear in with the complementary or reciprocal role of a role partner."[22] Particular roles are defined in part by the cultural or subcultural values held by a family; thus, the larger society defines certain aspects of the husband–wife roles, or the mother–child roles. Within the family, however, roles are additionally designated according to the family's particular needs or values. Sometimes an individual's role lasts the lifetime of the family: "the brain," "the black sheep," "the baby," and "the clown" are among many we see again and again. Over time, roles can be interchanged. Although all families designate roles, some are assigned to cloak a dysfunctional family balance.

A husband and wife came to treatment for severe marital problems. The husband was a heavy drinker at whom the wife self-righteously raged. After a brief period of treatment, the husband stopped drinking altogether, and the wife—to her own amazement—became depressed. Her low self-esteem and her deep-seated expectations of disappointment were masked by her husband's willingness to accept the "alcoholic" role. As long as she could rant about his behavior, she could maintain the illusion of superiority that protected her from facing her feelings of worthlessness and despair.

This case illustrates the reciprocal nature of roles. In no way do we mean to imply that the man's drinking problem was "caused" by his wife's behavior. In fact, in a somewhat similar situation, over the course of treatment a wife stopped nagging her husband about his drinking; shortly afterward, the husband was fired from his job for stealing equipment. In treatment he began to recognize his stake in finding another way to provoke his wife to "scold" him. The point is that just as a change in one part of the system requires a shift in the other, so if one person changes or drops a role, the role partner, too, will have to modify his or her actions.

SCAPEGOATING. In family therapy, the term "scapegoat" is frequently used to describe the individual—often the "identified patient" —who reflects the family pathology by becoming symptomatic. Hostility or unresolved disappointments between parents, for example, can be displaced onto a child who then "acts out." Frequently, clinicians view the "identified patient" as the scapegoated "victim" because his or her problems mask the problems among other family members. In reality, however, there is no single victim. Thus, the incorrigible child whose role is to obscure the marital tensions in the family may be "victimized" by carrying the burden of the parents' problems, but the rest of the family ultimately become the victim of the child's behavior. In this sense, *every* member is scapegoated by the hidden, often unconscious, issues that plague the family as a whole.

Although never fully accepting the view that the family is a system, Ackerman commented on the clinical situation in which one part of a family seems to "draw the breath of life at the expense of the other." Disturbed families, he hypothesized, threatened by differences among their members, create alliances that battle for dominance. A member or faction attacks, and the victim (scapegoat) finds family allies with whom to counterattack. Another member or faction, at times even the scapegoat, takes on the role of "healer." Thus the roles are fulfilled by particular members and, with the passage of time, by other members. Each is selected for his respective role by unconscious emotional processes within the family.[23]

*TRIANGLES.* As we mentioned earlier, an idea stressed by many family therapists is that the human being simultaneously strives for close relationships and for a sense of personal identity. The balance between the two, of course, can be difficult to maintain. When, as we have already illustrated, a close relationship between two people becomes tense (out of a fear of overdependency or as a result of any unresolved conflicts), the pair may involve a third person on whom the anxieties are displaced. A mother, for example, disappointed by her emotionally distant husband, may try to fill her unmet needs in her relationship with her young son. The father, equally dissatisfied, may vent his feelings by criticizing the boy. By "triangulating" or pulling in the child in this way, the tension between the parents is displaced and reduced, the balance of the relationship is resumed, and the issues between them remain obscured. Triangulation can also describe the process when two people pull in a family pet, the television set, or an external event to evade the problems between them and to stabilize the relationship. Numerous triangles exist simultaneously in a family, but, over time, the emotional forces within it can reside mostly in one triangle. When this happens, the triangulated or "triadic" one—such as the boy in the above example —takes on a role not unlike that of the scapegoat.

Minuchin has identified three sets of conditions that produce dysfunctional triadic structures: (1) When each parent demands that the child side with him or her against the other parent. (2) When marital stresses are expressed through the child and the illusion of parental harmony is thereby maintained; unconsciously, the parents may reinforce any deviant or "sick" behavior of the child and then unite to protect the youngster. (3) When one parent establishes a coalition with a child against the other parent.[24]

> A nine-year-old boy was in treatment for encopresis (soiling), which was interfering with peer relationships and creating general embarrassment for him. Meetings with the family, including a fifteen-year-old daughter, mother, and father, further revealed that the girl was a severe nailbiter and underachieved in school. Seating positions of the first sessions were the same. The boy sat close to and interacted mostly with his mother; the girl assumed a similar position vis-a-vis her father. The parents, although polite to one another, sat as far apart as the office chairs allowed. When they spoke together they talked almost exclusively about their concern for the children. After four meetings, the worker was convinced that there were some charged issues between the parents and arranged a session without the children. With considerable difficulty—and much support from the worker—they disclosed that the father, a diabetic, and the mother, a rather timid

woman, had not had sexual relations for three years. They had never shared with each other their feelings about this, nor had they made any attempts to adapt their sexual practices to accommodate the father's potency problem—a common symptom of diabetes. As their relationship became more distant, each turned to a child for emotional support to bolster waning self-esteem. The children, unable to bear the strain of demands they could not meet, became symptomatic.

In this family, both children were "triangulated" (or, one might say, scapegoated) by the marital pair. And, as we frequently find, the children became the "passport" for the parents' marital treatment. The symptoms of both children subsided after more than a year of marital treatment. The daughter's symptoms cleared up more quickly than the son's, perhaps because the father had many outside interests that he had pursued more avidly following the deterioration of his marital relationship; he was not totally dependent on his daughter to fulfill his emotional needs. The mother–son dyad, on the other hand, was the most intense connection in the mother's life, and greater differentiation for her and her son took time to achieve.

It is probably clear to the reader that various writers on family therapy may approach the same or similar points of view but often by using different language. For example, triangulation is one form of scapegoating in which a third person is blamed, alienated, or "chosen" to be symptomatic in order to obfuscate the conflict or stress between two people. In psychological terms, both of these concepts involve the ego defense of displacement and sometimes of denial—that is, the strain between family members is denied and then displaced onto another.

*PSEUDOMUTUALITY.* All family relationships and roles are by nature, in some form, complementary; compromises are required to achieve compatibility and smooth functioning. When there is *genuine* mutuality in a family, divergent interests, opinions, and feelings are tolerated; flexible role behavior can add stimulation and vitality to family life. Pseudomutuality, on the other hand, refers to the family's compulsive absorption with "fitting together" that, as Wynne describes it, creates "the illusion of a well integrated state even when that state is not supported by the emotional structures of the members."[25] Threatened by differences among its members, the family promotes the myth of harmony. To maintain it, the individual members must lock themselves into rigid roles and relinquish their personal identities. They must suppress or deny differences that they fear may destroy the family relationship. If sufficiently persistent, the resulting inhibition of self-expression can create severe personality disturbances in family members.

Neighbors complained to the police about an eighteen-year-old young man exposing himself in the courtyard of the housing project where he lived with his parents and three younger siblings. Placed on probation, he was referred to a mental health clinic for treatment. He related superficially to his young male worker, but contended he had no problems. Referred for family therapy, the parents insisted they had a "perfect family," and that the boy was framed by jealous neighbors whose testimony had convicted him. Both parents were cordial and, on the surface, cooperative. It was not until some relatives of the mother came from the West Indies to live in the household that the family became intolerably stressed. At this point, family tensions surfaced and hidden grievances between the parents were uncovered. Work with the family could then begin.

In this situation, the parents had been unwilling to recognize the serious implications of their son's behavior. They feared that giving up the illusion that all was well with him—or, for that matter, with the marriage—would threaten the family structure. After the family was engaged in treatment, it became evident that the denial of all differences and problems among the members had placed such a strain on the young man's internal psychological system that he became symptomatic. The younger children, too, were manifesting stressed reactions to the family mandate to conform—to think, feel, and behave in a prescribed manner. Wynne sees no real victims in pseudomutuality since all members of the family participate. In this case, the young man, as well as his parents, maintained that family life was ideal, despite the high price he paid as an individual; he, too, promoted the myth of harmony. Had external forces not stressed the family beyond endurance, family meetings—a contingency of the young man's probation—might have gone on as meaningless exercises. In all likelihood, without therapy, even more disturbing personality problems would have developed in this family.

*FAMILY MYTHS AND SECRETS.*   Myths serve the function for families that defenses serve for individuals.[26] To protect itself against conflict or ambivalent feelings and to maintain its balance, the family—or individuals within it—paint a picture of a situation or of relationships that, when explored, prove to be distorted or untrue. The myth may be shared by the family as a whole, or it may be promoted by one or more of its members. Role designations that misrepresent particular family members as "weak" or "bad" are myths. Myths may be perpetuated to avoid or to deny painful feelings of self-blame, as they often are in families that exclusively attribute their miseries or misfortunes to one family member. For example, the alcoholic in a family may be assigned the role of "culprit" to exonerate others of responsibility for family problems. Families may protect themselves against intrusions or judgment of the outside world with myths, such as with the myth of pseudomutuality described above. Myths and secrets may go hand in hand to cloak "unspeakable" events of the past, or a family tragedy.

> A nine-year-old girl with an incessant and obsessive fear of snakes was referred for family therapy after a period of unsuccessful individual treatment. The parents appeared to enjoy a loving relationship with each other and with their only child, Deborah. Yet the family climate seemed unexplainably strained. Only after several sessions, in response to a random question, did the worker learn that the mother suffered from a heart condition, a fact the parents had not shared with Deborah. The worker sensed that the mother's illness was more serious than the parents were acknowledging and hypothesized that the child had picked up the tension about it—as the worker had. Not understanding its meaning, Deborah, the worker suspected, had displaced her feelings of dread onto snakes. After some careful and sensitive work in family therapy, the child (and the worker) learned that both parents feared the mother's illness could prove fatal. With the support of the worker, the relationships among the three became more open and intimate. As the underground anxieties surfaced, the family members could share their feelings of heartbreak and affection. Deborah's fear of snakes all but disappeared. It was fortunate for the child that her symptoms were alarming enough to prompt her parents to seek outside help, because the mother died less than a year after treatment terminated. Had the family denial persisted, Deborah would have been left with guilt, lack of resolution about the loss of her mother, and—if she learned the truth—bitterness toward her parents for having promoted the myth that all was well in a household in which her mother was dying.

In this family, the parents consciously perpetuated the "all-is-well" myth to "protect" Deborah. (The notion that children cannot tolerate tragedy is in large measure itself a myth.) The parents had been less aware of their *own* need to maintain the myth in order to obscure from themselves their feelings of terror and sadness.

## Communication Concepts

Jackson, Haley, and Satir, among others, turned to communication theory to conceptualize the workings of the family system. Summarizing her view, Satir wrote:

A person who communicates in a functional way can:
  a.  Firmly state his case
  b.  yet at the same time clarify and qualify what he says,
  c.  as well as ask for feedback
  d.  and be receptive to feedback when he gets it.[27]

Work with family groups necessarily involves interventions by the therapist to focus and clarify the messages exchanged among members. Beyond this, the distortions and unexplored assumptions that generally pervade the communication process of disturbed families become the grist for treatment. The myths and misapprehensions on which the family operates must be exposed and dispelled. In family therapy, members can learn to inquire about the thoughts and feelings of others, and to share their own. Any tendency on the part of family members to act on untested suppositions often can be revealed more quickly in family therapy than in individual treatment. The child who believes his behavior caused his parents' divorce, and the woman who erroneously assumes her daughter-in-law hates her, have opportunities to correct their distortions in family group meetings.

Principles of communication set forth by Jackson and his colleagues have become important in family assessment and treatment:

Relationships and interactions depend not only on *what* is communicated, but on *how* the message is sent. Thus, the *quality* of the communication can reveal more about the relationship than the *content.* For example, the manner in which we ask someone to pass the salt (i.e., our tone of voice, inflection, physical gestures, and so on) can define a peer or a superior–inferior kind of relationship. The content is similar, but the message about the relationship can be very different. A metacommunication (defined as a communication about a communication) serves to qualify the literal content of a message by means of a second verbal or nonverbal statement.

In a family session a usually passive and agreeable husband turned to his wife and said with feeling: "You make me angry." Immediately following this statement he smiled, adding, "I was only kidding." His second message, the metacommunication—it was later revealed—masked his fear of his wife's retaliatory anger.

In Jackson's view, verbal communications reveal less about relationships than nonverbal messages. The latter, however, can be more ambiguous: tears, smiles, and frowns have many meanings. Furthermore, he points out, it is impossible *not* to communicate. Silence and withdrawal are strong messages. If a family comes for treatment and the teenage son sits silently, or the daughter sits outside the family circle, these are nonetheless communications for the therapist to decipher.

Often, then, in trying to appraise the relationships of the family system, the therapist can learn more from the feeling tone and body language that accompany the intercommunications than from the message content itself. No message is simple. The family therapist looks for an accompanying, often abstract, message that confirms or denies the first.[28]

THE DOUBLE BIND. "Toward a Theory of Schizophrenia," a classic article written by Bateson, Jackson, and others, describes the double bind as "a situation in which no matter what a person does, he cannot win."[29] The essential ingredients of this particular kind of communication situation are:

1.  Two or more persons, one designated as "victim."
2.  Repeated experience or a continuing condition.
3.  A primary negative injunction such as : "Do this or I will punish you."
4.  A secondary injunction conflicting with the first at a more abstract level, enforced by punishments, threats to survival, or the promise of a reward.
5.  A situation in which the victim can neither leave the field nor comment on the discrepant messages.

The child whose mother accuses him of not loving her enough is in a "no-win" situation when he tries to kiss her and she anxiously recoils, as though to say "go away." If this condition is repeated, it is double binding. The boy needs his mother, so he cannot leave. If he comments on the contradiction, he will be scolded. Obedience to one message results in disobedience to the other.

The double bind can be perpetrated by one or more individuals:

A father constantly complained that he wanted his twenty-one-year-old, unemployed son to get a job and "become a man." In words, the mother agreed, but whenever the young man found work, she told him it was either dangerous or "beneath" him. In a family session he told his mother he thought she was babying him. Both parents then called him "stupid."

In this case, if the son remained idle, his father belittled him. If he found a job, his mother disapproved. If he complained about the bind, his parents joined together to insult him. Unfortunately, this young man participated in the double-binding situation by defining himself as too weak to make a move without his parents' approval.

In a follow-up article, written in 1962, the same writers modified one aspect of this important theoretical contribution: "The most useful way to phrase double bind description is not in terms of a binder and a victim but in terms of people caught up in an ongoing system which produces conflicting definitions of the relationship and consequent subjective distress."[30] As illustrated in the above example, the participation of the "victim" is as essential to the perpetuation of the bind as are the parts played by the "binders." This modification is an important one for family therapists to remember when they find themselves feeling partisan to the "underdog" who, unless he or she is a very small child, has taken on the role and may (to the therapist's surprise) fight to protect it.

*MYSTIFICATION.* R. D. Laing coined this term to describe an indirect means of handling differences or conflict. When A's perceptions contradict B's, for example, A may insist to B: "It's just your imagination," or "You must have dreamt it." Or, another example of mystification given by Laing: A child is playing noisily in the evening and his mother is tired. She could make a direct statement, such as: "I am tired and I want you to go to bed." Or, a mystifying statement would be: "You are tired and should go to bed." Mystification becomes a serious matter when

> one person appears to have the *right* to determine the experience of another, or complementarily, when one person is under an *obligation* to the other(s) to experience, or not to experience, himself, them, his world or any aspect of it, in a particular way.[31]

Thus, the not necessarily tired boy in the above example may or may not be confused about his own feeling state, but he may feel obliged at some level to disclaim his subjective experience. In mystification, Laing says, some kind of conflict is present, but evaded. (Perhaps in the above example, the mother was in conflict about wanting to be a "good mother," yet feeling too tired to tolerate her son's din. In order not to face her inner conflict, she projected her tired feelings onto the boy. In this way, she could send him to bed yet avoid doubts about her "good mothering.") The double bind is necessarily mystifying, but mystification need not be truly double binding, if the one being mystified does not disclaim his or her own experience. While the victim of the double bind cannot leave or comment on the bind, the person being mystified may protest or be aware that mystification need not affect one's inner experience. Laing's concept can be useful to clinicians when identifying family process.

A seven-year-old, very bright boy was behaving disruptively in school, and the teacher referred the mother to a family agency to arrange individual treatment for the child. In the first interview with mother and son, the worker noted that when the boy complained that his teacher never punished an equally mischievous student, the mother dismissed him with "the teacher wouldn't play favorites." At another point, the boy told his mother *with a smile* that he was frightened when she yelled at him, to which the mother responded, "You couldn't be or you would behave." The worker pointed out to the mother that she was denying the boy's experience, to which only he could attest. In this case (unlike many others), the mother, a hard-working and caring single parent, got the point immediately. She was able to acknowledge that the boy's school problem had been "one more pressure," and that she was probably trying to ignore it by insisting to her son that he saw and felt things differently than he did.

After a total of four joint sessions, the school reported significant improvement in this boy's behavior, and the mother commented that it was easier to listen to her son than to struggle with him. When the mystification was eliminated, the boy's symptoms did not return. Incidentally, it can be assumed that the boy protected himself by smiling; in the event that his mother had persisted in her "right" to define his experience, he was prepared to oblige by disavowing what he felt with a smile. We might add that the mother continued for some brief individual treatment, consisting mainly of emotional and environmental support. The worker offered encouragement and resource suggestions to help her broaden her social life. As she became more personally fulfilled, she was better able truly to "hear" her son. Had the worker decided on play therapy for the boy, the mystification might never have been revealed. By the same token, had the school symptoms been less vexing, this mother might have unwittingly participated in the creation of a deeper personality disturbance in her son.

## THE PSYCHOSOCIAL FRAMEWORK AND FAMILY THERAPY

Is family therapy casework? Can the psychosocial framework comfortably accommodate principles and methods from the family therapy field? There are some who would insist that one must take sides and declare oneself as either a caseworker or as a family therapist. Among casework advocates of the either/or position are those who contend that family problems are fundamentally the function of the psychosocial difficulties of each individual member. From this point of view, improved family functioning depends on the resolution of individual problems.

On the other hand, there are some family therapists who claim that assessment or diagnosis of the individual family members is irrelevant for therapy purposes. From this standpoint, change for the family and the individuals in it requires therapeutic approaches aimed at the family structure—the transactions, behavior, and communication patterns of the dysfunctional family system. The individual's inner life, personality structure and dynamics, and even past history are downplayed or disregarded.[32]

In our view, the dichotomy is unfortunate. Certainly, a particular caseworker may feel better equipped by training or temperament—or may simply prefer—to concentrate on one treatment method over another. As individual practitioners we may be partial to particular kinds of clients, problems, or settings, and our propensities may lead us to choose among modalities as well. To confine ourselves theoretically to one point of view to the exclusion of another, however, is quite a different matter. We need not close out new information and approaches that can expand our knowledge base and enhance our effectiveness as caseworkers. Conversely, as we welcome new ideas, let us not assume that we must scrap traditional knowledge and methods of proven value.

The rationale for the incorporation of family therapy concepts by casework or clinical social work requires a review of some of the central features of our psychosocial framework.

*THE PERSON-IN-HIS-SITUATION.* Social work treatment—by tradition and by definition—has never exclusively addressed either the inner life of the individual, on the one hand, or the social-environmental situation, on the other. In fact, despite variations in emphasis during different historical stages or in particular settings, social work thinking has always stressed person–situation interaction and the interdependence of the person and the context. "The-person-in-his-situation" concept, as we pointed out in Chapter 2, has three components: (1) the person—including personality system, emotional life, and biological characteristics; (2) the situation or environment, including other people; and (3) the nature of the interactions between the two. Whatever the particular theoretical orientation, consistent attention to all three components has distinguished social work from the other helping professions.[33]

Of particular importance to casework's integration of family therapy principles is the interactional component. Human beings are influenced by their environments and, in turn, affect the people and circumstances around them. Often, the most salient feature of a person's environment is the family. The transactions and the quality of the interdependence between the individual and the family are of prime importance to casework diagnosis and treatment. Systems theory reminds us that "encounter between an organism and the environment *leave both changed;*"[34] in fact, our clinical practice has always been based on this awareness. Although we can think of the person, the situation, and the interaction between them as discrete matters, casework recognizes how each affects the others. Internal and external phenomena are intertwined. When changes occur in a family system, the behavior and inner lives of individual members shift. Conversely, individual changes reverberate upon the family as a whole. The actions of one individual are both cause and effect of the actions of others. In contrast to the single-cause, linear approach to understanding human behavior, the psychosocial orientation is one that assesses the multidimensional, reciprocal influences of the personality, the family, and the larger social system—as each acts on and reacts to the others.

Psychiatry and Freudian theory have deepened our view of individual dynamics. The social sciences have advanced our understanding of the human environment. More recently, the ideas that have emerged from the family therapy movement equip us with means for studying the transactions of individuals in the family environment; new information about the properties of the family as a system has become available. The family concepts described in this chapter fill some real gaps in casework theory; the place for including them is provided by the psychosocial framework.

*THE PERSONALITY SYSTEM.*   Freud, whose ideas have been basic to the psychosocial approach, broke new ground with his proposition that personality is shaped by social as well as biological forces. Neurosis, he asserted, is an outgrowth of the individual's family experience and inborn drives. The intrapsychic Oedipal conflict, for example, is grounded in early parental relationships. In his well known case of "Little Hans," Freud worked with the father, not with the boy himself. The successful treatment of the boy's horse phobia was achieved through interventions in the family system. Unfortunately, as psychoanalytic theory was passed down, some followers not only failed to expand on the interactional aspects of personality, but narrowed the theory to minimize the social side of Freud's thinking, which—although not fully developed—was there all along.[35]

Concepts derived from the study of personality—*internalization* and *introjection*—point us to some of the significant theoretical links between intrapsychic and family systems phenomena. As we know, the child's superego internalizes or introjects the commands, prohibitions, and ideals of the parents or other authority figures, with the result that the youngster learns to conform to their demands and values even in their absence. Yet our understanding of a particular client requires an additional, interactional perspective. Take, for example, a man who feels hostile toward his mother, oppressed by demands he believes she makes on him. Often we discover that he is reacting to his early mother introject, which bears little resemblance to his mother of today; the demands—if she ever made them—are no longer hers but his own. Yet his negative attitude toward her may provoke angry or defensive responses from her that, in turn, tend to reinforce his internalized representation of her. To see the total picture, then, we must understand the client's inner life, the interdependence of the past and the present, and the circular nature of the mother–son interactions. Joint or family sessions may be the most efficient approach with which to expose and correct internalized distortions as they are played out in interpersonal relationships.

Similarly, our understanding of the notion of *externalization* (sometimes referred to as *projection*) helps to bridge theories of individual dynamics and family relationships. Externalization refers to the act of attributing inner, subjective phenomena—including wishes, fears, conflicts, and thoughts—to the external world. We can see how such internal matters or aspects of one's self, once externalized, become part of an interactional process, particularly when they involve other people. For example, a client may tell us he is unhappily married but that he will not leave his wife for fear she will break down emotionally when, in fact, he is externalizing his hidden concern about his own stability. Or, a wife who says she wants to plan a vacation because her husband needs it may have difficulty giving herself permission for a holiday. Unacceptable, dissociated inner experiences—in these examples fears and wishes—once externalized are no longer discrete internal events. They affect and are affected by the interpersonal arena.

Taking this process one step further, Wynne describes the *trading of dissociations*. This concept refers to the complementary and interlocking externalizations of intrapsychic dissociations. To illustrate: a man, unaware of a particular quality in himself, sees it located in the personality of his wife, and believes his problem can be relieved only by changes in her. Similarly, the wife locates her own unacceptable qualities or ideas in her husband and sees her difficulties as a function of his personality. The fixed view that the man has of his wife is unconsciously exchanged for the fixed view she holds of him. The purpose of the reciprocal and shared trading of dissociations is twofold: first, both individuals protect themselves from experiencing their dreaded feelings; yet, second, each is able to "retain these qualities within his purview, at a fixed distance from his ego." A teenage daughter may perceive her mother's punitively moralistic qualities, while dissociating those same features in her own personality; the mother, unaware of dreaded sexual impulses within herself, becomes keenly attuned to those of her daughter. Each sees the need for change in the other, since each perceives aspects of the other that are outside of the awareness of that person. It is easy to see how complicated and futile the relationship between this mother and daughter could become. As Wynne explains: "The trading of dissociations means that each person deals most focally with that in the other which the other cannot acknowledge. Thus, there can be no 'meeting,' no confirmation, no mutuality, no shared validation of feelings or experience."[36] This process can be extended to involve every family member in a network of traded perceptions. The individuals involved, as Wynne points out, might be diagnosed as ego-syntonic character disorders who may not be motivated for individual treatment. Often, these same people become engaged in family therapy because they recognize the need for other family members to get help. In family sessions, intrapsychic, dissociated aspects of individuals that they have located in the personalities of others can be identified.

Individual and family thinking merge again when we examine the writings and research findings of Bowlby, Spitz, Mahler, and others from the psychoanalytic tradition on *separation* and *individuation*.[37] Family theorists too—as discussed earlier in this chapter—have been keenly interested in these matters. There is general agreement that the development of a relatively autonomous, self-reliant personality depends heavily on two conditions of the individual's childhood: (1) consistent parental availability, responsiveness, and support; and (2) parental encouragement of the child's independence and self-direction appropriately timed to the child's age. Absence of either of these conditions can contribute to lasting separation anxieties in the youngster. A mother (and/or a father, grandmother, or other key person to whom the child is attached), sensing her child's emerging independence, may be threatened by separation feelings and withdraw more completely and abruptly than the child—who still requires steady reassurance and support—can bear. Or, on the other hand, the mother's anxiety may lead her to cling to the child; she may do this by overprotecting or "parentifying" the child (i.e., treating him or her as a parental substitute). In any case, the mother's separation and abandonment fears are transmitted to the child. Unwittingly, parents may pass on to their children the unfulfilled longings, or wishes to retaliate, that grow out of their own childhood experiences.

Thus, the adult who in early life was abandoned—literally or emotionally—may cling to a person or even a memory out of fear of feeling alone again. Or the individual may set up interpersonal situations in which the experience of abandonment is painfully repeated over and over again. Similarly, the adult who was steadily discouraged from

functioning independently may hold on desperately to others to maintain a sense of belonging. In family treatment, we frequently see families in which the members—sometimes alternately—cling to or
abandon their parents, their spouses, or their children. Such overdependency and estrangement among family members can often be
traced to earlier separation–individuation disturbances. The longings,
fears, and anger derived from old parent–child experiences are transferred to current family relationships. It is Leader's hunch that "in the
majority of families seeking help, the intergenerational theme of abandonment flows deep like an underground stream."[38] Family myths,
roles, and interactions are patterned to guard against conscious and
unconscious separation fears. As we have already illustrated, often family members deny inevitable differences of opinions, thoughts, or feelings among them—for fear that these will lead to separation or
estrangement. In these situations, each individual is deeply enmeshed
in the larger family process. Symptoms and troubled feelings—although
in part a function of the dynamics of the personality—cannot be ap-
praised fully in isolation from this outer reality.

In summary, the selected illustrations included in this section support our view that the psychosocial framework can accommodate family concepts. Caseworkers can improve their treatment skills when they
are equipped with specific information about the nature of the complex
interplay of forces that prevail in a family system. "How," asked Ackerman shortly before his death, "can we choose between the family and
the person? The person is a subsystem within the family, just as the
family is a subsystem within the community and culture."[39] We agree
with Minuchin that "changes in a family structure contribute to
changes in the behavior and the inner psychic process of the members
of that system."[40] Repeatedly, in our clinical practice, we see how the
moods and behavior of individuals change as their families change.
However, with Ackerman, we would caution against a mechanistic
approach to systems that tends to deny the force and integrity of the
individual personality. Each family member has a private inner world,
unique natural endowments, character structure, and personal identity
that endure over time. The special qualities of the individual reverberate upon the family system as well. The greatest possible sophistication about the dynamics of the personality system and the family
system, and the nature of the reciprocal influences between them is
required to understand the problems individuals and families bring to
treatment.

In the chapter that follows we will demonstrate how, as we broaden
our knowledge base, we increase our choices of treatment methods,
strategies, and goals.

## NOTES

1.  *New York Times,* November 27, 1977, p. 74. This article also cites statistics
    on the increased number of single-parent families, and of mothers of
    young children working outside of the home.
2.  Kingsley Davis, "The Changing Family in Industrial Society," in Robert C.
    Jackson and Jean Morton, eds., *Family Health Care: Health Promotion and
    Illness Care* (Berkeley: University of California Press, 1976), pp. 1–16. See
    also George Peter Murdock, "The Universality of the Nuclear Family,"
    and Talcott Parsons, "The Stability of the American Family System," in
    Norman W. Bell and Ezra F. Vogel, eds., *A Modern Introduction to the
    Family,* rev. ed. (New York: Free Press, 1968), pp. 37–47, 97–101. A
    discussion of the vital functions that families perform can also be found in
    Shirley L. Zimmerman, "Reassessing the Effect of Public Policy on Family
    Functioning," *Social Casework,* 59 (October 1978), 451–457. An excellent
    compilation of articles that examine recent shifts in family patterns and
    relationships can be located in Arlene S. Skolnick and Jerome H. Skolnick,
    eds., *Family in Transition,* 2nd ed. (Boston: Little, Brown, 1977). (On the
    other hand, the notion that the family in any form has outlived its purposes
    is argued by David G. Cooper, *The Death of the Family* [New York:
    Pantheon Books, 1970].)
3.  See, for example, Sanford N. Sherman, "Intergenerational Discontinuity
    and Therapy of the Family," *Social Casework,* 48 (April 1967), 216–221;
    Nathan W. Ackerman, "Family Healing in a Troubled World," *Social Case-
    work,* 52 (April 1971), 200–205; Sanford N. Sherman, "Family Therapy,"
    in Francis J. Turner, ed., *Social Work Treatment* 2nd ed. (New York: Free
    Press, 1979), pp. 449–477; and Nathan W. Ackerman, *Treating the Trou-
    bled Family* (New York: Basic Books, 1966).
4.  Quoted in Frank J. Bruno, *Trends in Social Work: 1874–1956* (New York:
    Columbia University Press, 1957), p. 177.
5.  Mary E. Richmond, *Social Diagnosis* (New York: Russell Sage Foundation,
    1917), p. 137.
6.  Ibid., pp. 134–159.
7.  Greater detail on the history of the shifts in social work emphases can be
    found in Helen Leland Witmer, *Social Work* (New York: Rinehart, 1942),
    especially chapters 8 and 17; Arthur E. Fink, *The Field of Social Work*
    (New York: Holt, 1942), especially Chapter 4; and Kathleen Woodroofe,
    *From Charity to Social Work in England and the United States* (Toronto:
    University of Toronto Press, 1962), especially Chapter 6.
8.  Gordon Hamilton, *Theory and Practice of Social Case Work,* 2nd ed. (New
    York: Columbia University Press, 1951), pp. 95–97.
9.  Emily Mudd, *The Practice of Marriage Counselling* (New York: Associa-
    tion Press, 1951); Irene Josselyn, "The Family as a Psychological Unit,"
    *Social Casework,* 34 (October 1953), 336–342; and Florence Hollis,
    *Women in Marital Conflict* (New York: Family Service Association of
    America, 1949).
10. Ira D. Glick and Jay Haley, *Family Therapy and Research: An Annotated
    Bibliography* (New York: Grune & Stratton, 1971).

11. Nathan W. Ackerman, *The Psychodynamics of Family Life* (New York: Basic Books, 1958), p. xi. This volume is one of the classics in the field of family therapy.

12. Among the many books and articles on family treatment written by these social workers are Virginia Satir, *Conjoint Family Therapy*, rev. ed. (Palo Alto, Calif: Science and Behavior Books, 1967); Frances Scherz, "Theory and Practice in Family Therapy," in Robert W. Roberts and Robert H. Nee, eds., *Theories of Social Casework* (Chicago: University of Chicago Press, 1970), pp. 219–264; Arthur L. Leader, "Current and Future Issues in Family Therapy," *Social Service Review*, 43 (January 1969), 1–11; Sherman, "Family Therapy" and Harry J. Aponte, "Underorganization in the Poor Family," in Philip J. Guerin, ed., *Family Therapy* (New York: Gardner Press, 1976), pp. 432–448.

13. Group for the Advancement of Psychiatry, *The Field of Family Therapy*, vol. 78 (New York: GAP, March 1970), p. 536.

14. A still very useful volume, Howard, J. Parad, ed., *Crisis Intervention* (New York: Family Service Association of America, 1965), contains some excellent articles that describe the impact of various crises and stressful events on family life; of particular relevance to this section are those articles in Part 2, "Common Maturational and Situational Crises," pp. 73–190. The ways in which family and individual developmental tasks necessarily run parallel is discussed more fully in Scherz, "Theory and Practice in Family Therapy," pp. 229–231. See also, Trevor R. Hadley et al., "The Relationship Between Family Developmental Crisis and the Appearance of Symptoms in a Family Member," *Family Process*, 13 (June 1974), 207–214; in a study reported on in this article, a positive and significant relationship was found between the onset of symptoms in family members and two types of family crisis: the addition of a family member and the loss of a family member.

15. There were exceptions: Ackerman, *Psychodynamics of Family Life*, and John E. Bell, *Family Group Therapy*, Public Health Monograph No. 64 (Washington, D.C.: U.S. Government Printing Office, 1961). Ackerman and Bell were among some of the early pioneers who became interested in the study of the family environments of nonpsychotic clients.

For an orientation to the rationale and historical development of family therapy see the following: Gerald H. Zuk and David Rubinstein, "A Review of Concepts in the Study and Treatment of Families of Schizophrenics," in Ivan Boszormenyi-Nagy and James L. Framo, eds., *Intensive Family Therapy* (New York: Harper & Row, 1965), pp. 1–25, and Philip J. Guerin, "Family Therapy: The First Twenty-Five Years," in Guerin, *Family Therapy*, pp. 2–22.

A number of studies about pathological family interaction in families with a schizophrenic member appeared in the 1940s and 1950s. In these studies, emphasis was on dynamic relationships. Unsuccessful efforts were made to relate specific abnormal traits in parents to their children's abnormal traits or specific type of family to type of symptoms. Finally, the central object of attention became the pathological family system. Don D. Jackson and Virginia Satir, "A Review of Psychiatric Developments in

Family Diagnosis and Therapy," in Nathan W. Ackerman, Frances L. Beatman, and Sanford N. Sherman, eds., *Exploring the Base for Family Therapy* (New York: Family Service Association of America, 1961), pp. 29–49; Elizabeth H. Couch, *Joint and Family Interviews in the Treatment of Marital Problems* (New York: Family Service Association of America, 1969); Christian C. Beels and A. S. Ferber, "Family Therapy: A View," *Family Process,* 8 (1969), 280–318; Nathan W. Ackerman, "Family Psychotherapy Today," *Family Process,* 9 (1970), 123–126; and David H. Olson, "Marital and Family Therapy: Integrative Review and Critique," *Journal of Marriage and the Family,* 32 (1970), 501–538.

16. See Lyman C. Wynne et al., "Pseudomutuality in the Family Relations of Schizophrenics," in Bell and Vogel, *Modern Introduction to the Family,* pp. 628–649; and Thomas Fogarty, "Marital Crisis," in Guerin, *Family Therapy* pp. 325–334.

17. See Murray Bowen, "The Use of Family Theory in Clinical Practice," in Jay Haley, ed., *Changing Families: A Family Therapy Reader* (New York: Grune & Stratton, 1971), pp. 159–192; and Murray Bowen, "Theory in the Practice of Psychotherapy," in Guerin, *Family Therapy* pp. 42–90.

18. See Nathan W. Ackerman, "The Diagnosis of Neurotic Marital Interaction," *Social Casework,* 35 (April 1954), 139–147; Hollis, *Women in Marital Conflict,* pp. 90, 97, 209; Carol Meyer, "Complementarity and Marital Conflict: The Development of a Concept and Its Application to the Casework Method" (doctoral dissertation, Columbia University School of Social Work, 1957); and Bela Mittlemann, "Analysis of Reciprocal Neurotic Patterns in Family Relationships," in Victor W. Eisenstein, ed., *Neurotic Interaction in Marriage* (New York: Basic Books, 1956), pp. 81–100.

See also two excellent articles on intergenerational dependency and separation anxiety: Gerda L. Schulman, "Treatment of Intergenerational Pathology," *Social Casework,* 54 (October 1973), 462–472; and Arthur L. Leader, "Intergenerational Separation Anxiety in Family Therapy," *Social Casework,* 59 (March 1978), 138–144.

Sometimes an unequal yet complementary relationship is so necessary to the functioning of the individuals involved that it can be dangerous to disturb the balance, even though it clearly involves a pathological adaptation; see Frank S. Pittman, III, and Kalman Flomenhaft, "Treating the Doll's House Marriage," *Family Process,* 9 (June 1970), 143–155.

19. Salvador Minuchin, *Families and Family Therapy* (Cambridge, Mass.: Harvard University Press, 1974), pp. 51–56.

20. See James L. Framo, "Rationale and Techniques of Intensive Family Therapy," in Ivan Boszormenyi-Nagy and James L. Framo, eds., *Intensive Family Therapy* (New York: Harper & Row, 1965), p. 149. Framo's thorough chapter is a very useful and readable discussion of many of the theoretical and technical aspects of family treatment, and is highly recommended to the student of family therapy, as is the entire volume.

21. Don D. Jackson, "The Question of Family Homeostasis," in Don D. Jackson, ed., *Communication, Family, and Marriage: Human Communication,* vol. 1 (Palo Alto, Calif. Science and Behavior Books, 1968), pp. 1–11; Don D. Jackson, "Family Interaction, Family Homeostasis and Some Implications for Conjoint Family Psychotherapy," in Don D. Jackson, ed.,

*Therapy, Communication, and Change: Human Communication,* Vol. 2, pp. 185–203; and Ackerman, *Psychodynamics of Family Life,* pp. 68–79.

22. John P. Spiegel, "The Resolution of Role Conflict Within the Family," in Bell and Vogel, *Modern Introduction to the Family,* p. 393.
23. Nathan W. Ackerman, "Prejudice and Scapegoating in the Family," in Gerald H. Zuk and Ivan Boszormenyi-Nagy, eds., *Family Therapy and Disturbed Families,* pp. 48–57. See also the excellent paper by Ezra F. Vogel and Norman W. Bell, "The Emotionally Disturbed Child as the Family Scapegoat," in Bell and Vogel, *Modern Introduction to the Family,* pp. 412–427.
24. Minuchin, *Families and Family Therapy,* p. 102. See also, Murray Bowen's discussion of triangles, in Guerin, *Family Therapy,* pp. 75–78; and Thomas Fogarty, "Systems Concepts and the Dimensions of Self," in Guerin, *Family Therapy,* pp. 147–148.
25. Lyman C. Wynne et al., "Pseudomutuality in the Family Relations of Schizophrenics," in Bell and Vogel, *Modern Introduction to the Family,* p. 628.
26. Antonio J. Ferreira, "Family Myth and Homeostasis," *Archives of General Psychiatry,* 9 (July–December 1963), 457–463. See also Helm Stierlin, "Group Fantasies and Family Myths," *Family Process,* 12 (June 1973), 111–125.
27. Satir, *Conjoint Family Therapy,* p. 70.
28. See the very important volume on communication by Paul Watzlawick, Janet Beaven, and Don Jackson, *Pragmatics of Human Communication* (New York: Norton, 1967). The reader who wishes to study body movement and communication will be interested in a collection of essays by Ray L. Birdwhistell, *Kinesics and Context* (Philadelphia: University of Pennsylvania Press, 1970). See also two articles by Albert E. Scheflen: "The Significance of Posture in Communications," *Psychiatry,* 27 (1964), 316–331; and "Human Communication: Behavioral Programs and Their Integration in Interaction," *Behavioral Science,* 13 (1968), 44–55.
29. Gregory Bateson, Don D. Jackson, Jay Haley, and John H. Weakland, "Toward a Theory of Schizophrenia," *Behavioral Science,* 1 (October 1956), 251–264, reprinted in Jackson, *Communication, Family, and Marriage,* pp. 31–53.
30. Gregory Bateson et al., "A Note on the Double Bind—1962," *Family Process,* 2 (March 1963), 154–161, reprinted in Jackson *Communication, Family, and Marriage,* p. 58.
31. Ronald D. Laing, "Mystification, Confusion, and Conflict," in Boszormenyi-Nagy and Framo, *Intensive Family Therapy,* p. 346. See also, R. D. Laing and A. Esterson, *Sanity, Madness and the Family,* 2nd ed. (New York: Basic Books, 1971); this book includes clinical studies of the families of schizophrenic patients and identifies mystification as an important aspect of the families' communications.
32. See, in particular, Jay Haley, *Problem-Solving Therapy* (San Francisco: Jossey-Bass, 1976). Salvador Minuchin, although to a lesser extent, also minimizes the importance of diagnosis of the individual.
33. In addition to other references on the history and practice of social work already cited in this book, see Bernice K. Simon, "Social Casework Theory:

An Overview," in Roberts and Nee, *Theories of Social Casework,* especially p. 375; in spite of many variations in orientation among casework theoreticians, the person-in-situation concept is widely recognized by most points of view.

34. Gordon Hearn, "General Systems Theory and Social Work," in Turner, *Social Work Treatment,* p. 364.

35. Sigmund Freud, "Analysis of Phobia in a Five-year-old Boy," in James Strachey, ed., *The Complete Works of Sigmund Freud,* vol. 10 (London: Hogarth, 1964), pp. 5–148. See also Ackerman, *Psychodynamics of Family Life,* pp. 26–51, for an interesting approach to the integration of psychoanalytic concepts and the influences of the family environment.

36. Lyman C. Wynne, "Some Indications and Contraindications for Exploratory Family Therapy," in Boszormenyi-Nagy and Framo, *Intensive Family Therapy,* pp. 297–300.

    For particularly helpful and scholarly discussions of the concepts of projection and externalization, see Jack Novick and Kerry Kelly, "Projection and Externalization," in Ruth S. Eissler et al., eds., *The Psychoanalytic Study of the Child,* vol. 25 (New York: International Universities Press, 1970), pp. 69–95; and W. M. Brodey, "Some Family Operations and Schizophrenia," *Archives of General Psychiatry,* 1 (1959), 379–402.

37. See John Bowlby, "Grief and Mourning in Infancy and Early Childhood," in Ruth S. Eissler et al., eds., *The Psychoanalytic Study of the Child,* vol. 15 (New York: International Universities Press, 1961); René A. Spitz, *The First Year of Life* (New York: International Universities Press 1965); Margaret S. Mohler, Fred Pine, and Anni Bergman, *The Psychological Birth of the Human Infant* (New York: Basic Books, 1975); Gertrude and Rubin Blanck, *Ego Psychology: Theory and Practice* (New York: Columbia University Press, 1974), pp. 40–60; and Shirley S. Taylor and Norma Siegel, "Treating the Separation–Individuation Conflict," *Social Casework,* 59 (June 1978), 337–344.

38. Leader, "Intergenerational Separation Anxiety," p. 141.

39. Nathan W. Ackerman, "The Growing Edge of Family Therapy," in Clifford J. Sagar and Helen Singer Kaplan, eds. *Progress in Group and Family Therapy* (New York: Brunner/Mazel, 1972), p. 451.

40. Minuchin, *Families and Family Therapy,* p. 9.

# CHAPTER 11

# THE CLINICAL PRACTICE of FAMILY THERAPY

From the point of view expressed in the preceding chapter, it follows that we cannot fully understand individuals without knowledge of the families to which they belong. Conversely, as we build a conceptual system with which to evaluate a family's dynamics, the total picture requires a grasp of the characteristics of the individual members. In some case situations, the understanding of the biological and psychological qualities of the individual(s) is the most important guide to treatment; in others, the properties and transactions of the family system are of greatest consequence. In still other cases, of course, we must be particularly attuned to how individuals and families are influenced by and interact with the larger community and social system. We need not choose among these levels of conceptualization. Rather, as we collect the mass of information that clients bring, we must try to organize the germane data from as many perspectives as possible. After weighing the influence of diverse levels on each other and on the problem at hand, we are then in a position to select treatment methods and procedures.

To demonstrate the thinking that goes into arranging our data, and deciding whether or not to engage the whole family in treatment, we introduce the Russo case. This family will serve to illustrate how the theoretical framework presented in these two family chapters can be applied in practice.

## AN INTAKE REQUEST: THE RUSSO FAMILY

Mrs. Russo telephoned the mental health clinic in her area, seeking an appointment for her husband whom she described as depressed and withdrawn. He had not asked her to call and, in fact, she had not told him she was doing so. She believed she could persuade him to keep the appointment, however. Since Mrs. Russo was making the application, the worker recommended that she come in with her husband. From the telephone conversation the worker learned that this couple, in their late forties, had two daughters: Linda, age twenty-two (who moved with her husband from her parents' apartment building to Canada three months before Mrs. Russo's call to the clinic), and Angela, age seventeen (a senior in high school). At the time of intake, Angela was vacationing with her maternal grandmother—a widow—who lived next door and to whom Angela had always been close.

During an extended interview with Mr. and Mrs. Russo, the worker found Mr. Russo to be quite severely depressed, self-blaming, and indecisive, yet still able to function on his job. Mrs. Russo came across as a very managerial and perfectionistic woman. She talked at length, often on her husband's behalf. On the basis of this first contact, the worker ordered and weighed the information she had gathered from four vantage points:

1. About his *biochemical* situation, she learned that during a previous depression Mr. Russo had responded favorably to mood-elevating drugs. To help relieve his symptoms, one treatment option would be to refer him to a psychiatrist who could evaluate him for medication.

2. On the *intrapsychic* level, the worker hypothesized that Mr. Russo's depression was rooted in early deprivation. His mother had died when he was three, after which he spent several years in a series of foster homes and institutions. His current depression developed shortly after his daughter Linda, with whom he had always had a warm relationship, moved to Canada. He regressed into a partial withdrawal and experienced a pervasive sense of emptiness and hopelessness. His negative feelings about himself tormented him, overwhelming his inner life. The worker surmised that the feelings of loss experienced in his young years had been reactivated. Based on her knowledge about early deprivation and depression, she tentatively concluded that Mr. Russo's tendency toward self-depreciation and low self-esteem were exacerbated when Linda left. Without Linda's kindness and interest in him, he felt abandoned and alone once again. Yet, unable to accept his anger at her, he turned it against himself.[1] The worker considered the option of individual treatment in which sustainment, some direct advice, and reflection could take place in the context of a "corrective relationship."

3. Various aspects of Mr. Russo's *family relational* situation were revealed. Although Mrs. Russo was genuinely concerned about her husband, her tolerance for his morose dependency was strained and her anger poorly masked. The younger daughter, Angela, who was close to her mother, often ridiculed and demeaned her father. Fairly openly, the mother defended Angela's contempt for Mr. Russo, blaming it on his apathetic and self-pitying manner. From her knowledge of family systems, the worker hypothesized that the mother–daughter collusion provided the mother with external support and gratification (and probably gave the daughter some of the same), while the father had become the outsider, particularly now that the older daughter had moved away.

Mr. Russo participated in the collusion and promoted his "odd man out" status by being so self-depreciating. Paradoxically, his pathetic demeanor also brought out the motherly side of Mrs. Russo, who was taking more and more responsibility for many areas of her husband's life. Thus, although the price both paid was high, she protected him from feeling totally alone. Family sessions, the worker considered, might foster a more mutually rewarding relationship between Mr. and Mrs. Russo, thus reducing Mr. Russo's depression and providing greater gratification for Mrs. Russo. In turn, this might assuage her anger and reduce her need to ally herself with Angela. Involving Angela in treatment, the worker suspected, could be preventive by helping her to separate from her mother enough to begin to establish her own life and plan for her college years. Without Angela's participation, furthermore, she might work against any progress made by her parents if her role in the family process continued.

4. The larger *socioeconomic* system had also influenced Mr. Russo's situation. In fact, Mr. Russo blamed his depression mostly on a recent shift in his job. As a receiving clerk, Mr. Russo had been in charge of two other men and had successfully organized his small department. His boss had often commended him for his reliability, his willingness to work overtime, and his pleasing manner. Two months before the intake meeting, the company for which he worked was taken over by a large concern. Although given a promotion in terms of job title and salary, he no longer supervised other men and he had little contact with his old boss. Because of automation, his job no longer challenged his organizational talents and his work was duller and more routine. The impersonal climate of the new company provided little positive support for Mr. Russo. The worker speculated that referral to an employment service for vocational testing and placement in a smaller, more intimate establishment might better utilize his capabilities and fulfill his strong need for praise from others.

On the basis of the above facts about the past and the present reported by Mr. and Mrs. Russo, and her observation of the couple's behavior and interactions, the worker evaluated the Russo case on these four conceptual levels. No single hypothesis or conclusion reached at any one level could be considered more intrinsically "true" or "right" than any other. In fact, as the worker studied the Russo case from each perspective, the overall assessment became richer and more complete. The question of choice came up only as she considered which treatment approach could most effectively relieve Mr. Russo's depression. It was clear that she could address more than one level at the same time. For example, she could arrange an evaluation for medication and then set up individual or family sessions. Or, in addition to other treatment approaches, she could refer him to an employment service. Of particular interest to us in this chapter are the criteria that helped the worker determine whether she should see Mr. Russo in individual treatment (with, perhaps, occasional family or couple meetings), or whether she should arrange to see the family as a unit.

## INDICATIONS FOR CONSIDERING FAMILY TREATMENT

Although we will resume our account of the Russo family later on in this chapter, we pause now to consider the conditions under which a worker might decide on family therapy as the treatment of choice. There are differences among practitioners and writers on the question of indications (and contraindications) for family therapy. Unfortunately, there are no rigorous studies on the effectiveness of family therapy methods, nor is there a body of research that has examined the outcomes of family treatment as contrasted to those of individual treatment.[2] Consequently, a typology of criteria for choosing the family therapy approach must rest on empirical evidence and clinical experience. The list that follows represents a blend of selected recommendations made by several authors in the field[3], combined with our own views, on the conditions under which family therapy might be considered the treatment of choice:

1. When the family as a group—whether in crisis or handicapped by longstanding problems—*requests* family treatment and defines its difficulties as involving all family members. As family therapy has become better known, more such requests are initiated by families.

2. When the presenting problem immediately suggests a family relationship difficulty—or, of course, more than one. Examples would include marital or parent–child conflicts, problems with extended family members, and strife among siblings.

3. When children's disturbances or symptomatology are the impetus for seeking treatment. Exploration usually reveals that the child's symptoms are, at least in part, an expression of other difficulties in the family system. Also, as Sherman says: "The child's boundaries are so fluid and interlaced with the little world outside himself—primarily his family—that, in important respects, we cannot be sure what is inside him and what is outside him."[4]

4. When adolescents or poorly differentiated adults—particularly but not exclusively those living in their parents' home—either cling to or defensively disown their families. In these situations, boundaries are either diffuse or rigid and impenetrable. In either case, such individuals have been unable to separate effectively. Whether a person is submissively tied or rebelliously acting out, usually similar problems can be

found in other family members. Individuation of the identified patient or index client may be discouraged by the family situation. Furthermore, we agree with Mitchell: "The clinical evidence is overwhelming that the human being does not separate from what he needs but has never had, until he finds it or its equivalent."[5] As we pointed out earlier, individuation is most successfully achieved when the family group supports the young person's (or immature adult's) growth and autonomy. Contrary to the view of some emerging adults (and, on occasion, their caseworkers), geographical distance from their family of origin does not in and of itself foster differentiation. A change in the pattern of relationships—which allows closeness and independence alike—often does.

5. When family communication appears impaired. When it is extremely distant, restrained, vague, or bizarre, or when messages are contradictory, double-binding, or mystifying. Such faulty communication patterns may be addressed most incisively in the context of the family group. Also, bewildering symptoms can sometimes be understood when viewed as a reaction to the family communication style.

6. When the index client believes that his or her distress or behavior are the function of the personality or personalities of *other* family members. Consistent externalization or "trading of dissociations" (see pages 241–242) can respond to intervention aimed at the interpersonal aspects of these processes. Since individuals who project in these ways are often not very amenable to intrareflection, family treatment may be preferred.

7. Similarly, when family members can express their feelings of distress but see them entirely as reactions to the symptoms or behavior of the index client. In these situations, the burden for the well-being of the entire family is unrealistically placed on the shoulders of the scapegoated one. Interventions that promote the sharing of responsibility for the difficulties call for the participation of the entire family in treatment.

8. When there is evidence of consistent violation of generational boundaries. For example, when parents "parentify" children, they deprive them of needed nurturing and delegate authority to them that they cannot manage. When dysfunctional intergenerational coalitions become a way of life for the family, as when two family members team up against a third (mother and son against father, grandmother and grandchild against mother, and so on).

9. When it appears that one or some family members' perceptions of other members, or of family values and ideals, are seriously distorted. Or when myths and secrets appear to be the family style. These can be exposed and corrected in the family context.

10. When intrafamily relationships are affectively inpoverished,

chaotic, or hostile. The participation of all family members in the here-and-now may be the most effective way to help them to learn alternative styles.

11. When an individual is receiving inadequate physical or emotional support from the family and is therefore poorly cared for or lonely. This condition applies to many elderly or ill clients who are estranged from or neglected by family members, as well as to some psychiatrically ill or retarded individuals living at home, in halfway houses, or institutions. In some instances, it may not be possible or advisable—because of his or her condition—for the index client to be present at family sessions. Other members, however, often have conflicts and unresolved feelings about the client or among themselves that can be clarified in family group meetings and that may result in more support for the neglected member. Sometimes the family as a unit becomes the client and engages in treatment. In any event, the potential for improving the presenting situation can be explored by calling together the relatives.

12. When the index client is either unmotivated for or has been unsuccessful in utilizing individual treatment.

13. Similarly, when individual treatment for any family member is recommended but the member is resistant. He or she may need—at least temporarily—the support of being seen with the family. In our experience, for example, there are a significant number of men who are more amenable to family or couple treatment than to individual therapy.

14. When the worker has not been able to decide on a treatment approach. To begin with family meetings reduces the probability that the worker will become strongly identified with the index client and thus unable to maintain the "involved impartiality" so important to family (or any other) therapy, should that become the treatment of choice. By the same token, the family may be less likely to believe the worker's impartiality if the worker has had a longer relationship with one member than with the others. Individual meetings can always be arranged later. This is not to say that individual treatment cannot comfortably evolve into family therapy as well as vice versa. (In some situations, a phase of individual therapy—or concurrent individual treatment—may be necessary for one member. A severely scapegoated one, for example, may need extra support to relinquish this role.)

Even when one or more of the above conditions point to the selection of family therapy, there may be other factors that interfere. First, the worker may not feel comfortable or competent enough to treat the family as a group. In this instance, if family treatment is indicated, the worker would be best advised to refer the family to another therapist or to invite a more experienced colleague to act as cotherapist.

Second, a small percentage of families cannot be persuaded to enter treatment as a group. Or, some family members may adamantly refuse to be involved, with the result that family meetings are incomplete. In these cases, the worker will have to work either with the index client alone or with part of the family. The worker need not, however, abandon the family orientation or efforts to understand the family system. The worker should be alert to changes in the index client that may have repercussions on the family. (Sometimes, of course, changes made by the motivated member can result in positive changes in others in the family.) Third, in some cases there are geographical obstacles. Many young adult clients, for example, live many miles away from their parents; even when family treatment would be helpful, it may be impossible to arrange. Also, residential treatment centers, training schools, and state hospitals and state institutions for the retarded are often located at considerable distances from the family homes. Family treatment may be limited thereby, although not necessarily ruled out.[6]

Sometimes, after a series of family meetings, the worker may decide to move into individual treatment with one or more of the family members. This may occur when there seems to be motivation to explore personal issues. However, in making the shift, it is important for the worker to utilize all of the available knowledge about the workings of the particular family system. The worker must consider whether the family's dysfunctional equilibrium will be reactivated thereby and militate against changes the individual is working toward.

> A worker permitted a resistant family to discontinue weekly sessions in order to give support to a twenty-three-year-old daughter, who wanted to work on her relationships with men. But, the young woman's problems were so intertwined with those of her parents that, as soon as she made moves to individuate and live an adult life, her mother and father began to interfere by infantilizing her—as had been their lifelong pattern—thus drawing her back into a dependent role. The daughter allowed and unconsciously encouraged this out of years of familiarity with the pattern. Progress achieved earlier was reversed until the worker resumed family meetings.

In families such as this, one member's effort to grow up can seem like an abandonment threat to the others, and tendencies toward enmeshment are intensified. In this case, the worker had been "inducted" into the family system (i.e., drawn in on the side of the family's defensive resistance to change) in the hope that the young woman's efforts to individuate might be better served. It became clear, however, that the family process was so powerful that the daughter was unable to make changes from within herself when she was so pressured by the family from without. After a year of family work, including some marital treatment of the parents, the daughter was then able to make progress in individual treatment.

## CONTRAINDICATIONS FOR FAMILY THERAPY

Under what conditions would we recommend against family group meetings? With Sherman, we agree that family therapy may "take" even under circumstances that seem to contraindicate it.[7] Nevertheless, we present a list of those situations that call for the exercise of particular caution as a worker considers the family therapy approach:

1. When a family member is in the throes of a psychotic break. Usually, it is best to wait until there is some stabilization of the most acute symptoms.

2. When a family member or family members are grossly deceitful, psychopathic, or paranoiac, and family work is thereby rendered virtually impossible.

3. When the family process or some of the members are so destructive that the intensely negative interactions have a snowball effect.

4. When a family member has a severe psychosomatic illness. There have been some reports from clinicians that in these cases family therapy occasionally sets off dangerous somatic reactions. In such situations, before embarking on family (or individual) treatment, medical or psychiatric consultation is advisable.

5. When a relationship (e.g., marital or parent and adult child) appears to be "pathological" yet stable, and efforts aimed at change are likely to result in the emotional deterioration of one or more family members. Consultation or psychiatric advice may be required to identify such situations and to determine—on the basis of diagnostic appraisal—whether there are family members who are psychologically so delicately balanced that they cannot tolerate family meetings, or who might decompensate over a course of intensive family therapy.

6. When an individual's defensiveness or anxiety would be so intensified by family group meetings that he or she would be too uncomfortable to benefit from them. Of course, to a degree, many clients will become apprehensive when family therapy is suggested. But, just as a worker treating an individual must be careful not to press hard for material that will stimulate immobilizing discomfort, so the family therapist must be able to assess differentially a particular client's level of anxiety about family group meetings before strongly encouraging them. The work with Jed Cooper, to be presented in Chapter 19, illustrates this type of situation, in which family therapy was contrain-

dicated despite the fact that this client's difficulties were intimately intertwined with his relationships with his parents.

7. When family relationships are "dead" and family members cannot mobilize the energy to work on them. However, even divorcing or divorced couples sometimes work together effectively to separate, to sort out for each spouse the issues that led to the breakdown of the marriage, or to work out problems relating to the children.

8. When a client is strongly motivated for and prefers individual therapy, and is able to make progress in treatment without suffering setbacks caused by counterpressures from the family. Individuals who have established living arrangements and lives separate from their families—including many single young adults—often fall into this category. Frequently, one member of a family may have personal issues or particular problems to resolve that do not require the ongoing participation of the others. The large bulk of some clinical caseloads is comprised of such individuals. Nevertheless, occasional or intermittent joint and family meetings may be arranged to facilitate a particular piece of work with an individual client. Sometimes, as we have mentioned, family sessions may lead to a course of individual treatment for one or more members who are motivated to continue. When the entire family is in treatment, each individual is an equal participant in the therapy. When an individual is in treatment, and the family is invited for sessions, the worker still observes the family system, but the family members are viewed as part of the individual's environment; they are related to as collaterals—unless, of course, they are engaged subsequently in ongoing family treatment. (See Chapter 9 for a discussion of the use of family sessions in the service of individual treatment.)

In our experience, the feasibility of family therapy is often best tested during exploratory sessions. Sometimes the most unwieldy, disorganized, or uncommunicative families respond surprisingly well. In very difficult situations it may be wise to involve a cotherapist. Not only can two heads be better than one, but the dangers of being hopelessly "inducted" by the family pathology may be averted. The "blind spot" of one therapist may turn out to be readily discerned by the other. If they work well together, cotherapists can supplement each other as they address the multifarious and perplexing issues that can spring up in family meetings.

Finally, we share Wynne's view that it is easy to exaggerate the possible dangers of embarking on a program of family treatment: "The likelihood of bringing about drastic or precipitous changes unintentionally is extremely low."[8] As in individual treatment, worrisome symptoms that reflect longstanding dysfunctions may emerge in the course of family therapy. In these instances, it is usually best not to terminate family sessions abruptly. Rather, the worker may have to work harder to devise a treatment strategy that will confront the dysfunctional system. As Wynne goes on to say, helping families to make real and enduring changes is a formidable task. We are less likely to contribute to unwanted change than we are to discover that the family system is so intransigent that it is difficult to foster any change at all!

## ADVANTAGES OF FAMILY THERAPY

In cases where conditions favor treating the family as a unit, we have found this approach to have distinct advantages over individual treatment:

1. Observing the family as a group affords the worker a deeper and more complete understanding of the complex situations of the individual members. Direct observation is worth a thousand descriptive words. Reports from a client—no matter how conscientiously rendered—are necessarily limited to material that is conscious. Much of the behavior and interpersonal transactions—verbal and nonverbal—that penetrate a dysfunctional system may be distorted by or be beyond the awareness of the family members. Of course, experience and diagnostic skills help the worker to make intelligent inferences about a family situation, even when only one family member is seen. But by sitting with the family as a whole, the worker can learn firsthand about the interlocking "fits," the quality of individual and subsystem boundaries, and the repetitive patterns that perpetuate the difficulties. Data obtained in individual therapy rely heavily on conjectures; in family sessions, many more facts can be witnessed in the here-and-now.

2. Distortions, projections, myths, and family secrets that are burdening individual members can be exposed and challenged. When timed appropriately, the worker can raise questions sensitively, such as: "Have you any idea what makes your son think you prefer his sister?"; "Do you always act as though your feelings don't matter?"; "When you tell Johnnie that you are going to call the policeman to take him away do you really mean you would want him to go away for good? Johnnie seems to think you do"; "Were you angry when you said that—as your husband assumes—or is that the way you act when you are frightened?"; "Were you trying to protect your daughter by not telling her how sick your husband really is?"

3. On the same order, once identified, dysfunctional sequences can be addressed or interrupted *when they occur*. Bringing attention to them *in vivo* may have far more impact than talking about them in individual sessions where they can become intellectualized rather than experienced on the spot. For example, in a family meeting, a worker might inquire of a passive father: "Have you noticed that you often let

others in the family answer questions for you?" Or, with a light touch, the family therapist might ask an angry adolescent girl: "What do you think would happen if you told your mother again how you feel about your early curfew, but this time without insulting her?"

4. Family sessions can provide the opportunity to shift the focus to the marital relationship when the problems of the children or adolescents appear to be a reflection of problems between the parents. Similarly, since parent–child relationships can be heavily influenced by relational patterns that were established between the parents and *their* parents, family sessions provide an arena for exploring how introjects and intergenerational issues manifest themselves in the present family system. For example, the worker might ask a mother: "Do you notice that the things you hated most in your relationship with your mother are occurring here between you and Susan?"

5. In family meetings, family members can make new and real connections with each other and thereby gain the freedom to separate effectively. As discussed earlier, threats and fears of abandonment can stand in the way of family members accepting differences among them, or of allowing each other autonomy. In enmeshed families, since the issues of one member are so complexly intertwined with those of the others, it is often difficult to sort out the problems in individual treatment.

6. Family sessions provide the climate, with the support of the worker, for family members to learn about and empathize with one another as each shares experiences, feelings, and past history. So often in family therapy we hear: "I never knew you felt that way." Or: "Gee, Dad, you never told me you played minor league baseball." The fears about sharing vulnerable feelings or the belief that no one really cares can be dissolved as families learn to talk together.

7. Family meetings can circumvent the problems that arise when family members are suspicious or frightened about what the index client is doing or talking about in one-to-one therapy. Often unconsciously, those who are not in treatment may worry about changes in the family balance, and therefore interfere with or sabotage the efforts of those who are.

8. The way in which therapists use their personalities is important in every kind of treatment, but there is an added dimension to the impact they can have in family therapy. Workers not only encourage family exchanges by generating a climate of acceptance and trust, but their tenderness, ability to laugh at themselves and willingness to take chances in relationships with the family provide a model that can lead the members to risk new ways of relating to each other. In many families that we see clinically, despair and low self-esteem run rampant; this special kind of "corrective" experience provided by the worker can

promote greater intimacy and a sense of belonging among family members, as well as an opportunity for the healing of old wounds.

## THE INITIAL INTERVIEW: THE RUSSO FAMILY

Returning now to the Russo family, once the worker had organized the data from her first interview with Mr. and Mrs. Russo, as outlined earlier, she considered treatment approaches. She referred Mr. Russo to the clinic's consulting psychiatrist who prescribed a mild dosage of a mood elevating drug.[9] She decided it would be premature to refer him to an employment service until she had more information about his overall job situation, his interest in making the change, and the opportunities that might be available to him.

The important choice the worker had to make was whether to treat the entire Russo family. As she reviewed the conditions for considering family treatment, the following indications (see pages 252–254) seemed relevant:

Although the family was not requesting treatment for the entire group, Mrs. Russo had made the application and willingly participated in the interview with her husband. (Indication 1.)

Marital difficulties were not the impetus for treatment, but the strains between the couple were immediately apparent. Mrs. Russo's anger and Mr. Russo's depression seemed partially linked with the marital interaction. The parents did not complain specifically about Angela, but difficulties in her relationship with her father were reported. (Indication 2.)

The worker suspected that the mother and daughter were clinging to one another, to the detriment of the marriage. It also seemed possible that Angela would have difficulty separating. (Indication 4.)

Communication patterns were not yet fully understood by the worker, but she did note considerable restraint and indirectness. Mr. Russo did not reveal his feelings about his marriage or about Angela's attitudes toward him; instead, he retreated into silence or self-blame. Mrs. Russo spoke on behalf of her husband and daughter but expressed little about her own feelings. (Indication 5.)

Mrs. Russo believed her husband's behavior and depression were the only family problems to which she and Angela were reacting. Relief of his symptoms, she assumed, would resolve any discomfort the others were experiencing. (Indication 7.)

The worker sensed that Mrs. Russo and Angela frequently teamed up against Mr. Russo. She further speculated that Mrs. Russo's mother might be part of the coalition that cast Mr. Russo into the role of outsider. (Indication 8.)

Mr. Russo's motivation for individual treatment seemed minimal. Not given to introspection or reflection about his situation or dynamics, it seemed probable that he would be more amenable to group meetings. Should he (or any other family member) seek individual treatment in the future, there would be greater clarity about the family situation and all of the family members would have experienced the treatment situation. (Indications 12, 13, and 14.)

There were, then, several conditions that led the worker to favor the family therapy approach. She could think of no contraindications, but any which might exist would be revealed in exploratory family sessions. A week after the intake interview, Angela had returned from her trip and accompanied her parents to the initial family meeting. An abbreviated excerpted summary of the first session (in sufficient detail for the reader to see the complex process) follows:

After the worker and Angela were introduced, there were friendly exchanges between the worker and each family member individually. The worker then briefly brought Angela up to date on the previous meeting with Mr. and Mrs. Russo. Angela said she saw no reason for her being present since the problem was her father's "bad mood." The worker said that in her experience, when one person in the family is unhappy, the entire household is often affected. Mrs. Russo agreed: "We all seem to be getting on each other's nerves lately." She added that she was particularly concerned about how her husband's depression was causing Angela to be "cranky." "Sometimes," she commented, "Angela stays with her grandmother to get away." The worker asked Mrs. Russo whether she was finding the going rough herself, to which she replied, "Not really." She said she would feel better when her husband and Angela got along better. The worker said she thought one purpose of family meetings would be to help everyone in the family to understand one another better, adding that perhaps ways of improving relationships among all of them could be found to make the family a happier place. Angela said she thought her father was acting like a baby and just feeling sorry for himself.

Up to this point, Mr. Russo said almost nothing. Turning to him, the worker said she wanted everyone's opinion about the problem. He answered that he thought the medication was helping him a little and he hoped soon he would be "out of the dumps." He complained about his job change. Angela snapped at her father, saying, "You're stupid." She said the house was like a morgue lately, especially since her sister Linda—who used to visit frequently—had moved to Canada. She added that her father thought Linda was an "angel" and he was happy when *she* was there. Mrs. Russo smiled, apparently in appreciation of Angela's angry remarks. The worker asked the father how he accounted for Angela's sarcasm about him. Before he could answer, Angela blurted out, "You don't have to live with him!" Mrs. Russo began to make a comment supporting Angela. The worker interrupted by indicating that she wanted to hear from Mr. Russo, whose eyes had become watery. Angela sneered. The worker said to Mr. Russo that it looked like he was hurt by Angela's remarks. "I suppose I'm not much of a father to her," he replied. "That makes you sad, I imagine," the worker said. "Of course it does," murmured Mr. Russo. "She's my baby girl," he added almost inaudibly.

Then the worker addressed Angela: "Did you know it mattered to your father how you and he get on?" A little subdued, Angela replied, "He doesn't care." The worker asked Mr. Russo if he ever let Angela know how disappointed he was about the way they get along. He said he supposed he hadn't, but volunteered nothing further. Mrs. Russo began to explain Angela, saying that when Angela was young she "adored" her father, and she only turned on him this way when he started acting like a "zombie." Gently, the worker interrupted what she sensed would be a long defense of Angela, adding that she thought it would help more if each person spoke for himself or herself. The worker asked Angela what she thought. Angela said her mother was right. "Your mother understands you pretty well?" the worker offered. "She's the only one who does," Angela said, noting that she and her sister never got along because Linda was her father's "pet." "That must be hard to take," the worker said. Angela shrugged.

The worker then said to Mr. Russo that she gathered he had never gotten around to telling Angela how much she meant to him, and that perhaps it would be helpful if he did something about that. Mrs. Russo started to interject something when the worker said she thought that Dad and Angela had some things to straighten out with each other, reminding Mrs. Russo that she herself had said that their poor relationship bothered her. The worker added that there was no way she, Mrs. Russo, could do their work for them. Mrs. Russo, a little uncomfortably silent now, glared at Mr. Russo. Angela laughed nervously. The worker turned to Mr. Russo who said, tearfully, "I love both my daughters. One is miles away and the other one hates me." Angela said nothing but did not seem to be sneering; for just a moment, she looked more softly at her father. Mrs. Russo started to say that "Angela doesn't hate him but . . ." Good-humoredly, the worker cut in and reminded Mrs. Russo that it would be good if Angela spoke for herself. There followed some tentative but friendlier exchanges between Angela and her father. Shortly thereafter, characteristically, Mr. Russo withdrew in silence and Angela scoffed. Observing this interaction, the worker commented that she had some ideas about what often might happen between them: On the one hand, she pointed out, Mr. Russo seemed shy about telling Angela how much he cared about her, without putting himself down. On the other hand, Angela made it harder to find out her father's true feelings for her by sniping at him so regularly. Both mildly acknowledged the worker's remarks but said no more. The worker said she thought they could both learn to make their relationship a better one, but that it might take a little practice and willingness on the part of both to stick their necks out.

Deciding to reinvolve Mrs. Russo in the interaction—on her own behalf rather than as a commentator—the worker told her she got the impression that she felt burdened sometimes by having to fix up the relationship between her husband and daughter, and by looking after Mr. Russo when he was depressed. "What," the worker asked, "do you want for yourself from the family?" Mrs. Russo replied that her children had been her life—real joys to her. She said she was glad that Linda was happily married, but she missed her and wished she hadn't gone so far away. The worker commented that Angela was growing up too, and recalled that college plans were in the offing. With feeling, Mrs. Russo said she hoped Angela would find a school nearby so she could live at home. "What would it be like if Angela moved away too?" the worker asked. Mrs. Russo became thoughtful and quiet, finally saying that she did not know what she would do. "Life would seem empty," she said. The worker spoke briefly about how difficult it is to make changes when one has been so devoted to one's children. Mrs. Russo cried. Now including Mr. Russo, the worker said to them both that when children grow up and go away, the parents often have to find each other again and this can be quite a challenge. In a positive but not imposing or directive way, the worker asked if they thought they would like to work on that. It seemed, she continued, that some of the pleasures of family life had gotten lost in the shuffle with all of the recent problems they had been facing. Mr. Russo nodded. Mrs. Russo said she thought everything would feel a lot better if Mr. Russo got over his blues. Maybe, the worker said in a low-key tone, we can find some connection between the two. Mrs. Russo indicated she understood and did not argue.

The worker suggested that the family meet together for six sessions (even though she suspected their work together might take longer), and then reevaluate the situation. Mrs. Russo asked

if she could call if Mr. Russo seemed very depressed. The worker
told her that she certainly wanted to be available to them between
sessions if absolutely necessary, but it would be preferable if they
could bring the issues that concerned them into the family meetings. She further suggested that if Mr. Russo was depressed, he
should be the one to call. In a matter-of-fact way, she added that
she thought it would work best if any contacts made between
sessions were shared at the next meeting so everyone could keep
informed. Angela said she didn't want to come to every meeting
because she had "better things to do." After giving Angela an
opportunity to express her uneasiness about family sessions, the
worker said she thought everyone's help would be needed—at
least for the first six meetings. She added that she was impressed
with the willingness and interest all of them had shown in talking
about the family situation. It was a good sign, she told them. She
thought they were the kind of people who would be able to work
out some of their problems with each other. "He'll never change,"
Angela quipped, pointing to her father. "Don't be rude," the
mother admonished. Mr. Russo seemed to brighten at this apparent show of support from his wife.

To the group, the worker said that she was pleased that the
family had asked questions about the meetings and that she
wanted them to share their feelings about the therapy as it went
along. Sometimes, the worker said, she might make a comment
that they would find irritating. When this happened, she would
like them to tell her about it. After arranging their meeting schedule, the worker added in passing that at some point they might
want to invite Mrs. Russo's mother to join them since she was so
close to the family. The worker shook hands with all three as they
left.

## THE INITIAL INTERVIEW: GUIDELINES AND "GROUND RULES"

It is crucial for the family therapist to establish a tone and point of view
that will help to engage the family in treatment. It is part of the "practice wisdom" of family work that the therapist as a matter of course
moves back and forth between accommodating to the family style and
taking positive leadership. As in any treatment situation, the worker
must try not to "crash" family defenses by pressing for understanding
or changes for which the family is not yet ready. Timing is of the utmost
importance. In family therapy particularly, so much material is witnessed by the worker in such rapid-fire fashion that sometimes the

temptation to interpret or intervene precipitously is difficult to resist. The discipline of the worker is thereby strenuously tested as the family drama unfolds and reveals itself by way of the many-leveled verbal and nonverbal interactions that occur in the treatment session. The worker refrains from overzealous interventions, yet at the same time sets the stage for the therapy by defining its focus and by conveying leadership and expertise early in the relationship with the family.

In the initial Russo family interview described above, the worker carefully followed the cues of mood and the messages of the moment. She respected "where they were." For example, by accepting rather than interpreting Mr. Russo's statement that he had not been "much of a father" to Angela, she recognized his sadness and gave him room to express it. Had the worker made a comment such as "Your wife and daughter seem to gang up on you often," or if she had asked him why he thought he hadn't been a better father, the emotion of the event— which led to a fleeting but touching moment between Mr. Russo and Angela—might have been lost. Similarly, only gently, toward the end of the hour, did the worker touch on the marital problem that was so glaringly evident all along. The point we make is that the art and empathy necessary to do family treatment has much in common with that needed for individual therapy, but the family process by its very nature calls for special care. If the worker prematurely or heavy-handedly reacts to the profound emotional charge and the large amount of dynamic material revealed by the family interactions—especially during the early stages of therapy—the family may defensively try to regain its equilibrium by closing ranks and even bolting from treatment.

On the other hand, the worker for the Russo family did not succumb to the pitfalls of the opposite extreme and allow the family to control the therapy. In the course of the hour, she was able to weave into the process—usually explicitly, sometimes implicitly—a number of "ground rules." She thereby methodically paved the way for a working alliance with the family. Family therapy that lacks direction, focus, or structure can, at best, flounder and become chaotic. At worst, it can be so disenchanting to the family members that they terminate treatment.

As we suggest the ground rules itemized below, we cannot caution the beginning family therapist enough about the importance of offering them to a family—as the worker for the Russos did—in a matter-of-fact yet easygoing and caring way that is in harmony with the process of the meeting. These can be effectively introduced *only* when they are relevant to the evolving interactions. At no time should they be delivered as a series of pronouncements. As the reader studies the following ground rules, it may be clarifying to refer to the Russo interview and to take cognizance of when and under what circumstances the worker used them to guide the treatment.

1. Telephone or interview contacts with one or more family members and the worker prior to the beginning of family therapy should be mentioned at least briefly to the entire group.*

2. The notion that unhappiness or pain in one family member usually involves everyone close to this member should be made explicit.

3. The purposes of family meetings should be defined as: (a) an effort to help everyone in the family to understand one another better; and (b) an attempt to search for ways to improve family relationships so that family life can be more satisfying for all. Even when the initial problem appears to be the symptom of one member, how this affects and is affected by other relationships should be explored with the family.

4. It should be made clear that if contacts between the worker and individual family members occur outside the regular meeting sessions, these should be shared or at least referred to at the next meeting.*

5. In words and actions, the worker must demonstrate an "involved impartiality." It should be made clear that the worker takes no one's side and is equally interested in each member. Family therapists must show that they are not concerned with "blame" or "fault," but with working together toward resolution of the difficulties. By giving support to each family member, and by directing reflective or interpretive remarks to all members on a more or less equal basis, or to the family as a whole, a worker may quell concerns about partiality or about who will be "blamed."

6. Directly or indirectly, family members must be encouraged to speak for themselves rather than for others. "Mind reading" should be discouraged. Family members should be asked to put their assumptions in the form of questions to each other.

7. After a period when family members tend to talk directly to the worker, it is usually best to urge them to talk to one another. Occasionally, family members talk or fight tenaciously with one another, in which case the worker may reverse the general rule and engage each member in interaction.

8. When realistic, the family's willingness to work on problems should be supported and optimism about possible improvement should be conveyed.

9. When a relative (or housekeeper, close family friend, etc.) appears to be important to the family situation, the worker should prepare the family for possibly including that person at future meetings on an as-needed basis.

*See discussion of privacy and confidentiality, pages 272–273.

10. Feedback from the family about the therapy and about the worker should be encouraged. This keeps the worker informed, demonstrates to the family ways of relating openly, and encourages the family to take a share of the responsibility for how the treatment progresses.

11. To reduce resistance to family meetings, it is often important to establish a limited time structure that is definite, yet flexible enough to change later if necessary. A plan for evaluation—after a period of family therapy—in which the family and the worker share reactions, should be announced at the onset of treatment.

## TREATMENT PROCEDURES AND TECHNIQUES IN FAMILY THERAPY

The Hollis typology of treatment procedures (see chapters 5 through 9 in this book) can be adapted to study worker and client communications in joint and family treatment.[10] Certainly, multiperson interviews are far more complex and the classification system requires additional dimensions with which to analyze the interactional process. It is our hope, nevertheless, that the dynamics of marital and family interviews will become an important subject for researchers. Among the many issues that could be studied are: Which treatment procedures and combinations of procedures prove most effective in family (or marital) therapy? How does family therapy compare with individual treatment as a means of resolving the problems people bring to treatment? Under what conditions and for what types of problems is one modality more effective than the other? Do family therapists use the procedures they say they do? The more answers we have to these and other questions, the more effective our practice can become and the better able we will be to teach others how we work.

By reviewing the earlier chapters, the reader will see that all of Hollis' six major categories of worker and client communications can be applied to the analysis of a family session. For example, the first four casework procedures can be located in the initial interview with the Russo family. The worker employed *sustainment* procedures throughout the course of the meeting. She used this procedure when she said to Angela, "That must be hard to take." When she praised the family as a whole for its interest and willingness to talk about the family situation, she used sustaining techniques. In addition to the numerous verbal samples of sustainment there were, of course, the many unrecorded nods, smiles, and gestures that conveyed her interest, her wish to help, and her understanding. Procedures of *direct influence* were important to this first meeting as the worker conveyed the "ground rules" about the treatment process. When she suggested that

Mrs. Russo step back so that Mr. Russo and Angela could work on their own relationship, the worker was giving direction to all three family members. These procedures are perhaps more commonly employed in family sessions than in individual sessions, as Ehrenkranz discovered in her sample of joint marital interviews.[11]

*Exploration, description,* and *ventilation* are evident in many worker and family communications in the Russo session. As Angela described the change in her father since Linda moved away, she also ventilated some bitterness about her sister being an "angel" in her father's eyes. When the worker explored Mr. Russo's relationship with Angela, she opened the door for him to ventilate some of his sadness about it. The worker also paved the way for ventilation about the treatment process. *Person–situation reflection* was encouraged by the worker at several points, and occasionally was volunteered by family members. Examples of this category include Mr. Russo saying about Angela, "I suppose I'm not much of a father to her"; the worker asking Mr. Russo how he accounted for Angela's sarcasm about him; and Mrs. Russo reflecting, in response to the worker's question, about how empty life would seem after both daughters left home.

In the initial meeting, neither *pattern-dynamic* nor *developmental reflections* were encouraged by the worker, nor were they volunteered by the Russo family members. These procedures were sparingly employed by the worker in subsequent sessions in much the same way they would have been in individual interviews. The difference is that the other family members were privy to the process. For instance, with the worker's help, in one very moving interview, Mr. Russo was able to reflect on how the early death of his mother, and frequent changes of foster homes as a boy, contributed to the sadness he felt when his daughter Linda moved. His recognition of this was touching to the rest of the family (including his mother-in-law, who was present). This was one of the events of the therapy that helped to reduce the hostility of the others toward him and that brought the Russo family closer together. The fact that these procedures can be used in family treatment may be encouraging to those who are concerned that family therapy is not as "deep" as one-to-one treatment. Finally, *environmental* work was considered by the worker in connection with Mr. Russo's job situation; in some family therapy cases it can be as important an intervention as it is in any casework treatment.

Particularly exciting—although technically complicated for researchers—is the potential for classifying the diverse meanings of the same communications to each family member. For example, as the worker explored Mr. Russo's positive feelings toward Angela in the initial interview, his ventilation of sadness about their relationship appeared to be sustaining for Angela. Similarly, when the worker spoke to Mrs. Russo in a sustaining way about the burden she carried by having to "fix up" the relationship between Mr. Russo and Angela, and by looking after Mr. Russo when he was depressed, this very same communication suggested a directive (which the worker had already given more explicitly) to Mr. Russo and Angela: that they would have to take more responsibility for their own relationship and problems. These examples only begin to touch on the many ways the Hollis classification could be employed to examine the multilevel dynamic events that occur in family therapy.

In this connection, it is interesting to note that when Ehrenkranz studied joint marital interviews in 1967, she discovered that in her particular sample—most of which came from one agency—the workers rather consistently failed to use procedures that in the literature were considered important to joint interviewing. Specifically, they employed few techniques that would lead to on-the-spot clarification of the marital interactions; definition of the treatment focus; or reflective consideration of either the treatment process or the relationship with the worker. She also concluded that workers were tempted to make interpretations to the marital pair too quickly, and that the clients were either unable to respond, or reacted with hostility. We can speculate that the findings of a more broadly based and up-to-date study might be different. At the time of the Ehrenkranz research, caseworkers (and others in the helping professions) were, as a group, less advanced than they are now in conjoint interviewing procedures. Perhaps because of their lack of experience, they were overwhelmed by the intensity and complexity of the marital interactions. Only further research, however, will reveal just what we do in marital and family treatment, and whether we actually do what we say we do.

It is important to mention at this point that there are some family therapists who declare that they discourage procedures that would lead to the following: the expression (ventilation) of emotion; the development of self-awareness or the understanding of inner dynamics (reflection), which they believe is unlikely to foster change and therefore is irrelevant to treatment; and the exploration of past history, since they believe that the past is manifested in the present family relationships.[12] It is our hunch that if the family interviews of these writer-practitioners were scrutinized in a research study, we would find that they address these issues much more frequently than they advocate doing. When we see them in action—in live interviews or on video tapes—we sense that the psychoanalytic influence or training that is part of the backgrounds of many of the leading family therapists has become second nature to their treatment repertoire, in spite of the protestations of some. How interesting it would be to apply the Hollis typology to the work of those who claim their successes depend exclusively on interventions that address the structure, communication patterns, and behavior sequences of the family.

Along similar lines, some of these same family therapists believe it is unnecessary—or even detrimental to treatment—to make interpretations or to share with the families what they think about what they see. Certainly, as we demonstrated in our discussion of the Russo family interview, interpretations, observations, and interventions of all kinds should be measured and carefully timed. The therapist selects first for intervention those aspects of the family interaction that seem most accessible. As we pointed out earlier, in the first session with the Russos the worker chose to work very little with the marital relationship since the energy in the family could be directed most comfortably to the conflict between father and daughter and the mother's go-between role in it. Defenses against other explorations were respected for the time being. However, for both ethical *and* practical reasons, we strongly disagree with the point of view that admonishes against even well timed interpretations and the sharing of observations and opinions by the therapist.

Our reason for taking this position is threefold: First, we believe that client family members have the right to know what the worker thinks and, on principle, should be privy to as much information as they can understand or tolerate. Second, we believe that when the therapist consistently withholds impressions, the treatment relationship degenerates into an "expert–idiot" format in which the family is at the mercy of manipulations by the worker—which the worker never explains. Interpretations or opinions openly shared, on the other hand, give the family the opportunity to accept, reject, or modify them. Indeed, sometimes the therapist can be operating under a misapprehension that the family can correct. We advocate a treatment environment with as much equality as possible, in the sense that worker and family members —all fallible people—are sitting together, sharing thoughts and feelings and searching for solutions to the dilemmas and aches in the family's life. Family therapists are, of course, experts, trained to understand family processes; they have developed methods and techniques, based on theory and experience, about how people change. Family members, however, are equally important experts on their own experience, on what their hopes and goals are, on what choices and changes they want to make, and on how they feel their therapy is progressing. A climate that promotes such mutual sharing between worker and family is one that encourages the family members to take responsibility for their lives and for their work in therapy. If they are kept in the dark about the worker's maneuvers, their passivity and dependence is encouraged and their initiative is discouraged. Third, in our view and experience, when people can understand and give meaning to their feelings and behavior they are in a far better position to use their intelligence to find their own solutions and to work toward change than they are when they submissively follow the leadership of the family therapist.

In response to some critics of family treatment, we want to emphasize that—as far as we know—there are few family therapists who believe that *excessive* ventilation of negative or destructive feelings and so-called "total frankness" support the purposes of family meetings. Briar and Miller are among those who are legitimately concerned about the danger of "free-for-all" communications that they fear are encouraged in family therapy. They caution us:

> Examination of common experience provides ready examples of situations in which clear and unambiguous communication exacerbated rather than reduced conflict, as in instances where clarity and precision of communication served to expose differences between the interactants of which they were previously unaware. . . . In political and diplomatic negotiations deliberate vagueness and ambiguity in some communications are useful because they serve to minimize conflict, without either denying or ignoring it. . . . it remains to be demonstrated whether the sort of unrelenting, absolute and, if necessary, brutal honesty in family interviews advocated by some clinicians who emphasize communication is (1) an effective tool for problem-solving, and (2) a viable norm for family interaction.[13]

We share certain aspects of this point of view. As indicated earlier, if negative interactions are too intense or destructive, and family members seem unwilling or unable to work together in a more positive fashion, it may be best to arrange individual interviews—at least temporarily—until a less vituperative climate can be promoted. In some families, however, the worker need not be too thin-skinned about insults and anger flying about in family meetings and can understand that in many instances these abuses are everyday occurrences. (In such families, the members are often more frightened by their own and each other's tender feelings than they are by the violence of affect to which they are so tragically accustomed.) If we keep in mind that beneath the bitter attacks and expressions of hostility there is often pain, disappointment, and sadness, the worker can encourage the expression of *these feelings,* which are frequently more "honest" than the anger that masks them.

Furthermore, the family therapist must develop a style with which to respond to ongoing abusiveness among family members. In the Russo family, for example, in essence the worker relabeled Angela's anger at her father as disappointment. Pittman, when confronted with a family of blaming attackers, remarked paradoxically in his low-key manner: "It seems kind of unpleasant to me, but I wouldn't want to change some-

thing y'all enjoy so much."[14] Any intervention or technique, consonant
with worker style, that fosters reflection about the behavior that reinforces the problems the family wants to resolve can help us to avoid the
trap Briar and Miller warn against.

"Brutal honesty" of other kinds—as in the case of the husband who
enthusiastically describes his secretary's bust measurements to his jealous wife—must be explored to determine the underlying meaning of
the communication. More specifically, in this situation the worker
would try to find out why the man wants to hurt his wife in this manner.
Although it is not totally clear what kinds of "differences" Briar and
Miller refer to, it is our opinion that the revealing of disparate thoughts
and feelings among family members can be helpful and, when handled
skillfully by the family therapist, can actually reduce hostility. The purpose of family therapy is not to discourage differences, but to help
family members to recognize that these need not be feared, and that
relationships need not be lost because of them. In fact, when such fears
are quelled, family members often find that diverse feelings, interests,
and points of view are stimulating and enrich their relationships.

"Honest communication" also does not imply that the privacy of
family members should be violated. Certainly, married couples share
intimacies that need not be the property of their children or their
parents. Adolescents, as they grow toward independence, are well
known for their wish to conceal certain facets of their lives. In this
connection, we refer the reader to the ground rules for family therapy
suggested earlier in this chapter. We made the point that contacts
between family members and the worker between family sessions
should be shared with the entire group. This does not mean every
aspect of the content need be revealed. For example, during one phase
of treatment, Mr. and Mrs. Russo were seen in joint sessions, without
Angela and the grandmother, to explore their marriage and sexual
relationship. The *fact* that they met was revealed, but the couple and
the worker indicated to the others that they were working on issues that
were private to the marital relationship. Confidentiality was respected
and marital boundaries were supported. On the other hand, when Mrs.
Russo telephoned to report on her husband's depression, this information was part of the work of the whole family—and particularly of Mr.
Russo. If the worker had concealed it, inadvertently she would have
been inducted into a collusion with Mrs. Russo, thus reinforcing the
latter's managerial tendencies and Mr. Russo's passivity. In short, outside of sessions, communications from a family member to the worker
about *other* family members are discouraged and usually revealed.
Under most circumstances, information that is personal to a family
member or members is treated confidentially. Only under special conditions—such as the pregnancy of a twelve-year-old daughter, or when
there is a danger that a family member will attempt suicide—is confi-

dentiality breached. In *every* instance, however, before revealing personal information, the worker should seek the consent of the individual and explain why it must be disclosed.

In summary, procedures and techniques used in family therapy have much in common with those employed in individual treatment. There *are* differences, however, many of which we have mentioned. The therapist is often more active, and the multilevel interactions offer more choices of interventions. Some procedures—such as direct advice —are used more, and perhaps others are used less. And, of utmost importance, the worker's understanding of the family system strongly influences the interventions chosen.

## ON THE QUESTION OF DIAGNOSIS

Several attempts have been made to conceptualize family diagnosis by developing classification of family types or typologies of family dysfunction.[15] So far these attempts are divergent in their orientations. Some are grounded in the diagnostic assessments of the intrapsychic or social functioning of individuals, and thereby fail to describe overall family functioning. Other attempts at classification are so general (or else they are so limited) that they omit many of the variables of family interactions and fail to grasp the complexities of family dynamics. In addition to a typology of family dysfunction, Ackerman and others have urged the development of a model or set of normative standards that would capture the characteristics of the healthy family, against which other families could be measured.[16] Certainly, the achievement of such classifications and standards would enhance the theory on which family practice is based. Unfortunately, in spite of brave efforts to build a scheme of family diagnosis, no single, satisfactory system has emerged.

As in other modalities, the purpose of diagnosis is to guide treatment. There are some family therapists who claim that diagnosis is irrelevant to family work. Satir is quoted as saying that categorizing families does not help in therapy, adding, "Family diagnosis does not have the practical value of physical, medical diagnosis where specific diagnosis requires a specific treatment."[17] Indeed, a comprehensive diagnostic scheme has thus far eluded us, but *if* the complexities and multiple dimensions of family process could be classified by designating clusters of factors often found together, it would aid us in our selection of treatment procedures. Research would be required to determine which procedures would be most effective in the treatment of particular types of family dysfunction. In spite of widespread concern about diagnosing or labeling, as caseworkers we are always making generalizations, based on the facts before us, in order to determine the nature of clients' problems and strengths. It is true that no two families are precisely alike, but the more grounds we have on which to organize and classify data—without stereotyping or in any way denying the uniqueness of each family situation—the more effective our treatment will become.

Even without a satisfactory scheme for family diagnosis, we are not at sea if we recall our casework framework. As outlined in Chapter 16, the psychosocial approach to diagnosis is one that scans the whole field and builds up a body of facts and assumptions about the multiple aspects of the person–situation gestalt, including the transactional aspects. Choices about therapeutic interventions derive from the worker's assessment of those features of the situation that must be modified to relieve the problem at hand and those aspects that can be strengthened to improve family functioning. In the Russo family, for example, we saw that the worker decided to treat the family as a group rather than Mr. Russo individually, on the basis of her observations of the characteristics of the individuals and of the family's interactions. She chose to intervene in those areas she assumed would be most modifiable.

The family therapy concepts included in the previous chapter may contribute to a systematic typology of family types or family dysfunction. These concepts contain many of the components necessary for the development of a diagnostic system. At this point, they provide us with tools—in addition to those we use to assess personality dynamics—with which to describe and evaluate interpersonal patterns and family relationships. Although unordered in terms of their levels of importance or degree of abstraction, they provide a basis for assessing the strengths and troubled areas of a family's functioning.

Some sample questions, among many—derived from family concepts—that a worker might consider when assessing a family are: Is the index client's symptom a reflection of difficulties in either the larger family or the marital relationship? How well differentiated are family members? Are individual and subsystem boundaries distinct, on the one hand, yet permeable, on the other? Are boundaries either overly rigid or dysfunctionally diffuse in various parts of the family system? What are the roles and role relationships? Are they appropriate to ages and generations? Is a child being "parentified"? Is the mother being infantilized as she clings to a managerial grandmother? Who gets scapegoated? Are family members taking turns as the symptomatic or scapegoated one? Who gets triangulated, and how? Is communication clear, or is it confused, amorphous, mystifying, or double-binding? What nonverbal communications can be deciphered? What metacommunications qualify the verbal statements?

Further areas the worker may explore are: The significance of introjects and projections of family members as they are played out in the interpersonal arena of the family. Can "trading of dissociations" be identified? Are the family supports consistent enough to promote growth in individual members? Do family members cling to each other? Are they estranged? How strong are resistances to change? What kinds of defenses does the family use to maintain a dysfunctional balance? Are there myths and secrets? How are family rules enforced? What is the emotional climate of the family? Are expressions of anger taboo? Are feelings of tenderness, sadness, and disappointment discouraged? Does the family tolerate differences of ideas and feelings among family members?

These and other diagnostic questions start to flow as the worker sits with a family in therapy. Understanding of individual dynamics and the workings of the larger social system are supplemented if the worker is grounded in family theory. Diagnosis and treatment go hand in hand. The more the worker knows about a family, the clearer it will be which problems must be addressed. When attempting to effect changes in the family system, the worker will learn more about the areas of accessibility and vulnerability, which, in turn, will influence further treatment strategies and techniques.

## TRANSFERENCE AND COUNTERTRANSFERENCE IN FAMILY THERAPY

Much of the discussion in Chapter 12 about unrealistic reactions of the individual client and the worker toward one another applies to family work as well. But there are some real differences. In some instances, transference and countertransference reactions may be more diluted in family therapy than in individual treatment, where the emotional forces are totally concentrated on the one-to-one relationship. More often, however, the complexity of the family process intensifies—for both worker and family—the tendency to subjectify reactions. Patterns and defenses within any family group have been functioning for a long time, and the family has an established set of (often unrealistic) attitudes and responses with which to face any threat—including the intrusion of a family therapist! These reactions from the family can keenly affect the worker's perspective.

In any therapy situation, the person who applies for help to some degree feels vulnerable. Old childhood feelings, derived from relationships with parents, authority figures, and siblings—or feelings associated with later relationships—can be reactivated as clients acknowledge to a professional that they cannot solve their problems by themselves. Fear of blame and disapproval, as well as hopes, warm feelings, awe, and longings for approval are among the many "portable" reactions that people bring into treatment from other parts of their lives. In family group therapy, such transferences can become contagious and travel from one family member to another. Or they can be a function of the system as a whole, as may happen when, in a defensive effort to protect the homeostatic balance, family members band together to block the worker by assigning him or her a distorted negative role.

> In a family of rigid, critical parents (who both had disapproving parents themselves) and two adolescent sons, the family treated the worker with suspicion. As a group, family members falsely accused him of making judgmental statements about them all to the high school guidance counselor who had referred them for treatment. They joined together and displaced their negative experiences with their respective parents onto the worker. Only after many weeks, as greater trust was established, was the family able to risk exposure to the worker without the fear of his disapproval.

In other cases, deprived or dependent families may attribute to the worker the role of family "savior"—a role impossible for anyone to fill.

To further complicate the picture, a family's unrealistic attitudes and responses may be divisive in the therapy situation. For example, the father who experienced himself as the "black sheep" of his original family may assume that his wife will get better attention than he will from the therapist (as perhaps his sister did from his mother). If the wife in this situation brings from *her* past a seductive or manipulative manner with which to curry favor from parental or authority figures, the husband's fears may be reinforced. When family members have divergent responses to the therapist, rivalrous feelings can be aroused within the family group. Of course, if there are cotherapists, the family may assign one the role of "good parent" while the other is seen as the "bad" one. As unsettling as some family reactions may be, the worker who encourages open discussion and begins to challenge or interpret some of the distortions, can use them to help family members learn more about themselves, each other, and the repetitive patterns that hamper the growth of the entire family.

Similarly, the family caseworker may displace early or unrealistic feelings or attitudes onto the family being treated. In fact, as important as it is for a worker interested in family work to master the theory and techniques of family therapy, it is equally essential that one be constantly alert to countertransference and countertherapeutic reactions. In individual treatment, when listening to descriptions of the family situation, the therapist can more often maintain an objectivity that may be elusive in the face of powerful family forces operating *in vivo*.

As we indicated earlier, when we speak of "induction" in family therapy, we usually mean that the worker is inadvertently pulled into the family system—on the side of its defenses and resistance.

> A mother who was diabetic, arthritic, and had suffered a "nervous breakdown" many years earlier, was seen by the father and by the children as fragile. In frequent telephone conversations with the worker, the father expressed concern that family therapy would be detrimental to his wife's health. The worker allowed his own clinical judgment about the mother's very evident strengths to be discounted, and was persuaded to treat her with "kid gloves" as the family did. Only after it was clear that therapy was at a standstill did the worker begin to challenge the family myth about the mother that, it turned out, was promoted by the father to shield himself from facing worries about his own emotional well-being. Had the worker allowed his induction to continue, the family resistance would have won out and treatment would have failed.

Such family forces at work can place extraordinary stresses on the most mature worker and thereby sap his or her effectiveness. It takes a secure therapist indeed to feel comfortable in a family that pressures him as this one did. It is even harder, perhaps, to maintain one's perspective when faced with a family that closes ranks and isolates the worker as the worker begins to touch on patterns and interlocking defenses that have taken years to develop. Similarly, it can be difficult for the therapist to hold on to hope when meeting with a family immobilized by apathy or rigidity. In some instances, the therapist may be prompted to work too hard, too fast, or to attack the family.

There are other pitfalls to be avoided. The worker may overidentify with a family member or subgroup or fail to empathize with others. The problem is compounded in a family that attempts to involve the worker in collusions or alignments with one member or subgroup against others within the family. Angry, competitive, or protective feelings may be stirred in the worker. For example, a particular worker may feel hostile toward the parents of an abused or scapegoated child, and may want to prove she is a better "mother." Or another worker may be tempted to take the part of a "henpecked" husband against a controlling wife—if he loses sight of the hand-in-glove aspects of their relationship, which can be equally painful to both partners. Young workers may find it easy to identify with rebellious adolescents. Older workers, facing the trials of raising their own teenage children, may tend to feel partial to the beleaguered parents. A worker who has (or had) either an angry or overly dependent relationship with either of his or her parents (or with a sibling, grandparent, etc.), may transfer feelings about that person to the relationship with the corresponding member of the client family. Finally, more often than we would wish, family therapists are tempted to repair the marriages of clients in ways that they have never been able to influence their own parent's relationships —or, for that matter, their own marriages. Countertransference problems, then, can be provoked by patterns of family interaction as well as by the characteristics of an individual family member.

The goal for workers who choose to treat families is to maintain "involved impartiality." Without involvement, there can be no working relationship. Without impartiality, the worker will be hopelessly inducted into the family system. If the worker consistently takes sides, sooner or later some or all of the family members are likely to refuse to continue in therapy. To be free to work for the benefit of the family, one must be as secure as possible about oneself and one's competence, and must be ever alert to one's "Achilles heel" or unresolved feelings about one's own family relationships. If the worker suspects that countertransference attitudes or responses are impeding progress with a family, supervision or consultation can be effective ways of regaining lost perspective. In many agencies, family therapists have made good use of one-way mirrors, videotape, "live supervision," and cotherapists as aids against slipping into unrealistic, countertherapeutic reactions. In attempting to help troubled families change, the worker is well advised to heed Whitaker's counsel that the therapist "must be available to each person of the family, yet belong to none; he must belong to himself."[18]

## POSTSCRIPT: THE RUSSO FAMILY

Family therapy for the Russos lasted ten months. In six of the thirty-six sessions, Mr. and Mrs. Russo met together—without any other family members—to work on their marital and sexual relationship. Of the remaining thirty sessions, Angela attended all except the last two, which were scheduled after she left for college, several hundred miles away. Linda, on a trip home, came to one session, eager to settle some misunderstandings that had developed between her and her mother.

The maternal grandmother attended three sessions. A deeply religious woman of middle-class, northern Italian background, Mrs. Russo's mother had been critical of Mr. Russo's occupational status and lack of interest in the church since the day she met him. Class and educational differences between Mr. and Mrs. Russo, influenced by Mrs. Russo's mother's attitude about these, played a role in the family conflicts. Mrs. Russo had attended college briefly, and Linda and Angela both aspired to professional careers that placed Mr. Russo, a high school dropout, in an inferior position in the eyes of his family and himself.

On the other hand, the worker's knowledge of cultural factors played only a small part in her work with this family. Both Mr. and Mrs. Russo were third-generation Italian Catholics and yet—even with the differences in their class backgrounds—as a family they were part of an upwardly mobile, lower-middle-class, heterogeneous community. In a minor way, the family members—particularly Mrs. Russo's mother—had a traditional reluctance to bringing their "dirty linen" to a stranger; she believed that if help was needed, the family should speak with a priest. Yet, as frequently occurs with Italian families, every member of the Russo family was able to be quite expressive emotionally in therapy sessions. Mr. Russo was able to cry and to speak of tender and sentimental feelings; at the same time, he berated himself for being less than a "man" as he compared himself unfavorably to his father—a domineering, occasionally violent man. The girls both attended parochial grammar schools, but went on to public high schools, which they preferred; only the grandmother had been disappointed by their choice. Although both parents were reluctant to see their daughters leave home, they did not—as some Italian parents do—resist these moves on the basis of concern about sexual behavior or vulnerability away from the family.

On balance, Angela probably benefited most from family treatment. Without guilt or fear, she was able to follow through on her wish to leave the household and prepare for her own life and career. Mrs. Russo became less intrusive in the relationship between Angela and Mr. Russo and, over the months of treatment, father and daughter enjoyed a warmer relationship than they had for years. During several sessions in the middle phase of therapy, Angela fought hard with her mother, as adolescent girls often do (but as Angela previously had not done), for the "right" to make her own decisions, large and small. Although reluctantly, Mrs. Russo was able to give her daughter some credit for being almost adult. In the last session before she left for college, Angela gave genuine thanks to her parents for their support and shared loving feelings with them both. Family therapy was clearly preventive for Angela who, without it, might have given in to her mother's dependence on her and remained at home. Or else she might have left defiantly for college, burdened with many unresolved feelings about her decision.

At the end of treatment, Mr. Russo was less depressed and was no longer taking medication. Periodically, he slipped back into "the dumps," but these episodes were less intense and of shorter duration than they had been. Without self-blame, he was able to announce to his family—including his mother-in-law—that he felt neither capable nor secure enough to face the "jungle" of the job market and seek employment with more prestige or personal reward. He had made peace, he said, with his current employment situation. The confidence with which he made this choice enhanced his self-respect and, in turn, resulted in far less criticism from his wife, his daughter, and even his mother-in-law. Involving Mrs. Russo's mother in the therapy exposed and diminished her contribution to the family alignment against Mr. Russo. A few weeks before termination, his mother-in-law broke her leg and Mr. Russo willingly gave her practical help he had never offered before.

Mrs. Russo—whose motivation was essential to the therapy—made more gains than she expected, since she had assumed that her husband would have to make all of the changes. Of course, she did benefit from his progress and the greater family harmony achieved through treatment. But by being less intrusive and managerial—not an easy job for her—she also won appreciation from both her daughters and a new kind of closeness with them that was no longer primarily based on mutual dependency. Furthermore, it turned out. Mrs. Russo had many cultural and intellectual interests that her husband did not share. As she became less critical in general, she was able to stop complaining to Mr. Russo about his "narrow mind." Instead, she found friends to join her in activities she could enjoy apart from her husband.

The couple's sexual relationship, which had never been satisfactory, improved only slightly, if at all. However, the resentment they both felt about it was reduced, and neither was motivated to explore the matter further at the time of termination. On the whole, Mr. and Mrs. Russo were able to listen to each other better and to accept their differences more comfortably. Each made personal choices without resorting to self-blame or recriminations. They no longer clung to their daughters' love out of despair over their marriage. All family members expressed positive feelings about the treatment experience and wanted to make sure they could return should the need arise.

Would individual therapy for Mr. Russo have worked well? Medication and supportive casework might have relieved his depression. His improved self-esteem might have resulted in positive repercussions throughout the family. From the point of view of the worker, however, Mr. Russo could not have bucked the collusion of the other family members. Without the participation of them all, the worker believes, he would have retreated again into depression and self-blame. It also seems probable that Angela would not have made the gains she did without the support of family sessions.

Some families continue to grow and change after treatment ends. Others return during crises or setbacks, or to achieve further goals. In some cases, individual members continue in treatment after family meetings are terminated. Many families change more remarkably than the Russo family did. Others make far fewer gains. In families with limited intellectual and emotional resources, or with patterns of longstanding dependency and poor differentiation, change may be minimal. It is the task of the family therapist to travel with the family toward mutually agreed upon goals, and to identify the point at which progress ceases. As in any casework treatment, in the final analysis, the worker cannot expect more change for clients than they wish for themselves.[19]

## NOTES

1. See Otto Fenichel, *The Psychoanalytic Theory of Neurosis* (New York: Norton, 1945), pp. 387–406, 488–492, where he discusses depression and orality.

2. See Jack Santa-Barbara et al., "The McMaster Family Therapy Outcome Study: An Overview of Methods and Results," *International Journal of Family Therapy,* 1 (Winter 1979), 304–323, for a report of one exploratory study of brief family therapy with a large sample size that showed positive outcome results for over three-fourths of the families treated. Their review of other studies leads them to conclude that empirical studies are not only few in number, but in most cases inadequate on methodological grounds. See also two reviews of the research: Alan S. Gurman and David P. Kniskern, "Research on Marital and Family Therapy: Progress, Perspective, and Prospect," in Sol L. Garfield and Allen E. Bergin, eds., *Handbook of Psycho-Therapy and Behavior Change* (New York: Wiley, 1978); and Richard A. Wells and Alan E. Dezen, "The Results of Family Therapy Revisited: The Nonbehavioral Methods," *Family Process,* 17 (September 1978),251–274. These reviewers discuss some of the problems to researchers in the field, one of the important ones deriving from the diversity of treatment methods and approaches in family work. Nevertheless, some optimism is expressed about the effectiveness of marital and family therapy, and about the future of research.

3. See Lyman C. Wynne, "Some Indications and Contraindications for Exploratory Family Therapy," in Ivan Boszormenyi-Nagy and James L. Framo, eds., *Intensive Family Therapy* (New York: Basic Books, 1965); Nathan W. Ackerman, *Treating the Troubled Family* (New York: Basic Books, 1966), pp. 111–112; Daniel Offer and Evert VanderStoep, "Indications and Contraindications for Family Therapy," in Max Sugar, ed., *The Adolescent in Group and Family Therapy* (New York: Brunner/Mazel, 1975), pp. 145–160; and Frances H. Scherz, "Family Treatment Concepts," *Social Casework,* 47 (April 1966), 234–240.

4. Sanford N. Sherman, "Family Treatment: An Approach to Children's Problems," *Social Casework,* 47 (June 1966), 369. See also one of Nathan W. Ackerman's early discussions of the importance of viewing children's difficulties in the context of family and social experiences: "Psychiatric Disorders in Children—Diagnosis and Etiology in Our Time," In Paul H. Hoch and Joseph Zubin, eds., *The Diagnostic Process in Child Psychiatry* (New York: Grune & Stratton, 1953), pp. 205–230.

5.  Celia Mitchell, "The Therapeutic Field in the Treatment of Families in Conflict: Recurrent Themes in Literature and Clinical Practice," In Bernard Reiss, ed., *New Directions in Mental Health* (New York: Grune & Stratton, 1968), p. 75.
6.  See, in particular, Salvador Minuchin et al., *Families of the Slums* (New York: Basic Books, 1967), which describes treatment of families of boys referred to a private residential treatment center (Wiltwyck School for Boys), most of whom lived a considerable distance from the institution.
7.  Sanford N. Sherman, "Family Therapy," in Francis J. Turner, ed., *Social Work Treatment,* 2nd ed. (New York: Free Press, 1979), pp. 471–472.
8.  Wynne, "Some Indications and Contraindications," p. 321.
9.  See the study by Myrna M. Weissman and Eugene S. Paykel, *The Depressed Woman* (Chicago: University of Chicago Press, 1974), in which all of the 150 moderately depressed women studied responded favorably (i.e., experienced some reduction of symptoms) to a period of four to six weeks of drug therapy; social adjustment (not affected by medication) was enhanced by those who received weekly psychotherapy in addition to drugs.
10. An exploratory study of joint marital treatment in which the Hollis typology was used is reported by Shirley M. Ehrenkranz in her doctoral dissertation, "A Study of the Techniques and Procedures Used in Joint Interviewing in the Treatment of Martial Problems" (Columbia University School of Social Work, 1967). Two articles summarizing this excellent beginning effort to use the Hollis classification to examine conjoint treatment were published: "A Study of Joint Interviewing in the Treatment of Marital Problems," *Social Casework,* 48 (October–November 1967), pp. 498–503, 570–574. See also Florence Hollis, "Continuance and Discontinuance in Marital Counselling and Some Observations on Joint Interviews," *Social Casework,* 49 (March 1968), 167–174. The findings reported by Ehrenkranz and Hollis, however, were based on small samples and, as they indicated, further refinements of the typology would be required to study the many dimensions and complex interactions found in multiperson interviews.
11. Ehrenkranz, "A Study of Joint Interviewing," pp. 499–500.
12. See, for example, Jay Haley, *Problem-Solving Therapy* (San Francisco: Jossey-Bass, 1976), pp. 118, 164–165, 174, 206; and Salvador Minuchin, *Families and Family Therapy* (Cambridge, Mass.: Harvard University Press, 1974), p. 14.
13. Scott Briar and Henry Miller, *Problems and Issues in Social Casework* (New York: Columbia University Press, 1971), pp. 191–192.
14. Frank S. Pittman, III. "The Family That Hides Together," in Peggy Papp, ed., *Family Therapy: Full Length Case Studies* (New York: Gardner Press, 1977), p. 2.
15. For discussions of some of the attempts to develop classifications or nosologies of family disorders, see Scherz, "Family Treatment Concepts," pp. 234–240; Nathan W. Ackerman, Frances L. Beatman, and Sanford N. Sherman, *Expanding Theory and Practice in Family Therapy* (New York: Family Service Association of America, 1967); Nathan W. Ackerman, *The Psychodynamics of Family Life* (New York: Basic Books, 1958), pp. 329–

330; Group for the Advancement of Psychiatry, "The Field of Family Therapy," 78 (New York: GAP, March 1970); Eleanor S. Wertheim, "Family Unit Therapy and the Science and Typology of Family Systems," *Family Process*, 12 (December 1973), 361–376; Eleanor S. Wertheim, "The Science and Typology of Family Systems II," *Family Process*, 14 (September 1975), 285–309; and George S. Greenberg, "The Family Interactional Perspective: A Study and Examination of the Work of Don D. Jackson," *Family Process*, 16 (December 1977), 385–412.

16.   Nathan W. Ackerman, "The Growing Edge of Family Therapy," in Clifford J. Sagar and Helen Singer Kaplan, eds., *Progress in Group and Family Therapy* (New York: Brunner/Mazel, 1972), p. 454. See also Thomas F. Fogarty, "Systems Concepts and the Dimensions of Self," in Phillip J. Guerin, ed., *Family Therapy* (New York: Gardner Press, 1976), pp. 149–150.

17.   Quoted in Vincent D. Foley, *An Introduction to Family Therapy* (New York: Grune & Stratton, 1974), p. 145.

18.   Carl A. Whitaker et al., "Countertransference in the Family Treatment of Schizophrenia," in Boszormenyi-Nagy and Framo, *Intensive Family Therapy*, p. 335. See also James L. Framo, "Rationale and Techniques of Intensive Family Therapy," in Boszormenyi-Nagy and Framo, *Intensive Family Therapy*, pp. 194–198; and Helm Stierlin, "Countertransference in Family Therapy with Adolescents," in Sugar, *Adolescent in Group and Family Therapy*, pp. 161–177.

19.   In addition to references cited in this chapter and in Chapter 10, readers may find the following readings relevant to the further study of the practice of family therapy:

Harry J. Aponte, "Diagnosis in Family Therapy," in Carel B. Germain, ed., *Social Work Practice: People and Environments* (New York: Columbia University Press, 1979), pp. 107–149; Donald Bloch, ed., *Techniques of Family Psychotherapy: A Primer* (New York: Grune & Stratton, 1973); Ivan Boszormenyi-Nagy and Geraldine M. Spark, *Invisible Loyalties* (New York: Harper & Row, 1973); L. Ann Hartman, "The Extended Family as a Resource for Change: An Ecological Approach to Family-Centered Practice," in Germain, *Social Work Practice*, pp. 239–266; Curtis Janzen, "Family Treatment for Alcoholism: A Review," *Social Work*, 23 (March 1978), 135–142; Arthur L. Leader, "Family Therapy for Divorced Fathers and Others Out of the Home," *Social Casework*, 54 (January 1973), 13–19; Arthur L. Leader, "The Notion of Responsibility in Family Therapy," *Social Casework*, 60 (March 1979), 131–137; Diane I. Levande, "Family Theory as a Necessary Component of Family Therapy," *Social Casework*, 57 (May 1976), 291–295; Salvador Minuchin, Bernice L. Rosman, and Lester Baker, *Psychosomatic Families: Anorexia Nervosa in Context* (Cambridge, Mass.: Harvard University Press, 1978); Ben A. Orcutt, "Family Treatment of Poverty Level Families," *Social Casework*, 58 (February 1977), 92–100; Gerda L. Schulman and Elsa Leichter, "The Prevention of Family Breakup," *Social Casework*, 49 (March 1968), 143–150; and Helm Stierlin, "The Dynamics of Owning and Disowning: Psychoanalytic and Family Perspectives," *Family Process*, 15 (September 1976), 277–288.

# Chapter 12

# The Client–Worker Relationship

Basic to psychosocial casework treatment, and one of its most powerful tools, is the relationship between worker and client. Experience has demonstrated that successful treatment depends heavily on the quality of this relationship. The Beck and Jones follow-up study of over 3,500 cases from family agencies (in which, however, the theoretical approaches to treatment were not specified) found a very strong, highly significant association to exist between good worker–client relationships and positive treatment outcomes. Those relationships rated by clients and workers as "unsatisfactory" resulted in far less change in treatment than those rated "very satisfactory"; consistent and substantial increases in client gains were found as ratings of the relationship moved along the scale from negative to positive extremes. No other client or service characteristic analyzed in this study was found to be as important to good outcome as the worker–client relationship.[1]

Research and above all observation of practice have identified many of the components or underpinnings of the positive therapeutic relationship. Some of these will be discussed in detail over the course of this chapter. Broadly speaking, therapist characteristics of nonpossessive warmth and concern, genuineness, empathy, and nonjudgmental acceptance have been found by some studies—and are known by many clinicians—to appreciably enhance therapeutic interaction. The worker's optimism, objectivity, professional competence, and capacity to communicate these to the client play an important part in the quality of the treatment relationship.[2] Particularly in intensive therapy, but to some degree in every case, the worker's self-awareness can be crucial to effective casework. The client, too, participates in establishing a favorable relationship: he or she must be able to muster the hope and courage necessary to engage in treatment—and, with the worker's help, the client must develop motivation for change; beyond that, the person must be able to achieve some measure of trust in the worker's desire to help and ability to do so. Furthermore, whether the treatment is centered around individual, interpersonal, or environmental problems—or some combination of these—and whether the contact is brief or long term, an effective relationship requires that the worker and client work together to arrive at some mutual agreement on the purpose of treatment and the objectives they jointly seek.

Four particularly significant aspects of the treatment relationship will be examined in this chapter. We will be viewing it as (1) a means of communication between client and worker, (2) a set of attitudes, (3) a set of responses, expressed in behavior, and (4) a mutual effort. We will then consider the part these elements play in the dynamics of treatment. Since attitudes and responses are basic ingredients in verbal and nonverbal communication and in mutuality, we will begin by discussing these two aspects first.

## REALISTIC ATTITUDES AND RESPONSES

What attitudes and responses exist between worker and client? We customarily think of them as being of two kinds: realistic and unrealistic.[3] Unrealistic attitudes and responses include transference and countertransference.

### Client Reactions

Realistic attitudes, appropriate to the situation, will differ among clients in accordance with variations in the significance the treatment situation has for them. It is common knowledge among clinicians that when people come for help with interpersonal problems, they almost always experience some anxiety. This is partly so because they usually have some awareness that their problems lie to some degree within themselves. Even when an individual has defended against recognizing this, it is still present underneath and a realistic cause of anxiety. Characteristically, people also experience discomfort about entering into relationships in which they expect to be dependent. Clients applying for casework service often express this uneasiness directly: "I wanted to solve it myself" or "I was ashamed to ask for help." Experience has shown us that, to the client, coming for help can signify weakness, despite the fact that the recognition of the need for help and the decision to come for it require strength. To admit that one has been unable to solve difficulties without outside assistance can evoke childlike feelings, feelings of failure. It can be a blow to self-esteem. By seeking casework services, clients often feel they are acknowledging that another person is wiser or stronger. Taking the first step in allowing oneself to came under the influence of another unknown or little known person can be very frightening indeed.

Such feelings are widespread, but the intensity with which they are experienced will vary. Anxiety will be greater, for instance, when clients are consulting the worker about matters of vital interest than when the consultation is about peripheral matters; it will also vary with the degree to which clients consciously or unconsciously believe themselves to be at fault, and with the intrinsic nature of the matters about which they must talk.

Many other types of client reaction can be realistic responses to varying circumstances. If the client has been either overtly or subtly pressed to apply for treatment, there may be anger as well as anxiety. Clients may take referral for treatment as criticism of their abilities or as a reflection on their emotional balance. The involuntary client, on whom casework services have been imposed by an authoritative agency or court action, can be extremely resentful at being compelled to accept help.

The desire to use casework treatment to bring about change, particularly internal change, will vary greatly depending not only upon whether or not the client has come for help voluntarily, but also on the nature of the changes that the client may anticipate, the degree of satisfaction the person has in present ways, and the fixity of the ways of behaving that may have to be given up.

What the client knows about the agency or casework will also affect initial attitudes. If the client has heard favorable reports about the agency or an individual worker, a sympathetic, skillful reception will be anticipated. A previous bad experience or negative reports by others may lead the client to expect the worker to be critical or hostile or condescending. Community, ethnic, and class attitudes toward casework or toward a particular agency may affect one's feeling as to whether coming for help is respectable or degrading, and will condition one's expectation of what treatment itself will be like. Some clients who have not previously experienced casework help may tend to expect advice and a somewhat authoritative approach, whereas others with some knowledge of modern dynamic psychology may anticipate a more sympathetic and thought-provoking approach. The latter group, however, may have even more doubts concerning the competence of the caseworker than the more naïve clients, particularly if they are sophisticated about psychoanalysis or psychiatric treatment and have come to casework because they cannot afford any other kind of help or are not yet ready to commit themselves to it.

It is sometimes assumed that the economically disadvantaged or the poorly educated client—particularly the black, Chicano, or Puerto Rican—will be less interested in casework treatment than the middle-class college graduate, black or white. This is by no means always the case. Furthermore, even when it is so, to label a particular client "resistant" or "unmotivated" may deny certain realities of American life. A client who has experienced prejudice, social oppression, and deprivation of many kinds understandably may approach the middle-class caseworker, the often "white agency," and the treatment process with apprehension. The client may fear that the actual differences between them—in terms of money, power, education, and life experience—are so great that there can be no meeting ground, no understanding by the worker of the client's situation. Trust itself is difficult enough to achieve, but it is all the more difficult to bridge the gap between people from vastly different backgrounds, particularly in the context of a society in which racism and class biases prevail. It is therefore not unusual for some clients to view their caseworkers with fear, suspicion, or anger. Of course, although it is useful to anticipate a particular reaction, one has to be careful not to stereotype. But when distrust *is* evident, it may take a good deal of painstaking work to convince the client that the worker's intent is not to intrude, or to depreciate group pride or aspirations, but to assist. Shortly, we will discuss the worker's responsibility for promoting a climate of mutual respect and understanding, but the point here is that from the client's point of view these are all realistic responses, in the sense that they are either appropriate reactions to the actual situation, or else to reality as it is seen by the client's group.[4]

Similarly, as soon as a client meets a clinical social worker, the latter's physical appearance and manner set new reactions in motion. A young worker may find an older adult distrustful of his or her skill, particularly if this is not counterbalanced by obvious superiority in education. On the other hand, this worker may be more trusted than an older worker by an adolescent, who may expect greater understanding from peers and near peers than from seniors. Although class differences, including general education, may increase the confidence of a blue-collar worker in the professional ability of the caseworker, they may also make him fearful of being misunderstood and misjudged and may increase feelings of anxiety and resentment concerning a situation in which he feels inferior and dependent. In some instances, the less educated client may feel (sometimes realistically) that life experiences have been better teachers than the young worker's books. At another extreme, the professional or upper-class client may believe that the worker is not as "intellectual" or "cultivated," and this client may therefore be doubtful about the caseworker's ability to help.

Sex differences also arouse different realistic reactions. A man may find it initially difficult to turn to a woman for professional help, the extent of this attitude varying with people of different backgrounds. A particularly pretty, handsome, or vital worker may arouse feelings of sexual attraction, even though there is no seductiveness in his or her actual manner. A client may be skeptical about bringing marital or parent–child problems to an unmarried caseworker with no children.

The appearance of the worker's office and experiences in the waiting room will add to the client's reactions. And all these responses can take place independently of what the worker actually *does!*

What the worker says and the way he or she acts when saying it are obviously the next set of reality factors affecting the client's realistic responses. Before jumping to the conclusion that a client is displaying either transference reactions or subjectively conditioned resistance, it is very important for the worker to make certain that he or she is not actually saying or doing something that is giving the client a realistic basis for certain responses. Workers *are* sometimes hostile, or at least critical or disinterested. Some workers, out of their own needs, act in a superior, overly impersonal way. Some enjoy a subtle type of domination that puts the client in an unnecessarily dependent or inferior position. Some reveal their desire to be loved or at least admired and appreciated. Some are unconsciously seductive. Some are late for appointments, forgetful about doing things they have promised, and so on. Even the best of caseworkers will exhibit occasional "untherapeutic" reactions, by which we mean attitudes or responses that are not helpful or healing. Caseworkers too are affected by mood changes, health, events in work or private life quite outside the particular treatment situation, and other factors. Who of us at some time—on a hot day or when short of sleep or under the influence of an antihistamine—has not yawned in a way that could not be entirely concealed from the client? It is also true that some caseworkers do stereotype or react anxiously to clients of particular racial or cultural backgrounds. They may be biased against certain groups, or they may view some clients only as victims of oppression and thereby fail to see them also as people with unique experiences and personalities. There are also workers who have fixed attitudes toward clients of a particular sex, age, or physical condition, or toward those who have certain intellectual or emotional disabilities. As we shall discuss more fully later on in this chapter, the development of self-awareness about countertherapeutic reactions can be among the most challenging tasks for the clinical social worker to achieve. But when these do occur and clients react to them, they are responding realistically.

## Worker Reactions

This brings us to the realistic aspects of the *worker's* part in the treatment relationship. The well trained, self-aware worker's responses are not the natural reactions of one person on the street to another. The worker entering the field begins with such natural responses, of course, but they are subject to other influences that are the product of purpose and training. The worker's perception of the client is not that of the average person; attitudinal response to the perception is different, and overt behavior is different. A person who is trained as a psychosocial therapist does not see a client's behavior as an isolated event. This worker has become attuned to the reasons for client responses, the kinds of life histories that lie behind different response tendencies, the defenses people use to cope with anxiety. The psychosocial therapist reacts not simply to the client's overt behavior but to a complex of stimuli that includes possible reasons for the behavior and the knowledge that, even if they are not apparent, reasons do exist, whether in life experience or in constitution. The stimulus, then, is different for the clinical worker than for the lay person. The perception—or, better, apperception—includes many elements that are the part of the worker's experience and education. To the well trained clinician, the cue "anger" under some circumstances may read "defensive hostility" or "anxiety"; the cue "defensive" may sometimes read "overly severe superego" and may express the client's fear of criticism. If the client's response is thus read, the worker's response is automatically different from what it would otherwise be.

Diagnostic thinking about the client helps the worker to understand and respond realistically to the meaning of the client's defenses. For example, an obsessive-compulsive client may be fending off strong, frightening instinctual urges by intellectualization; a hysterical client may relate seductively to a worker; a dependent, emotionally deprived client may bring anger or unrealistic expectations—derived from past ungratifying relationships—to the caseworker; an ambulatory schizophrenic man may talk evasively out of fear of exposing deeper thoughts and feelings that humiliate him or that he fears will repel the worker. Similarly, the homosexual client may underplay strong feelings about sexual preference for fear the worker will look down on or try to change him or her. Dislike of clients' qualities or behavior can be more easily overcome when they are understood as reactions to pain or fear. In some social work graduate schools and field placement agencies, students are helped through role playing to get as close as possible to the inner feelings of the client. Putting oneself in the shoes of another, so to speak, can help to generate one's empathic responses.

Workers' reactions are further modified by the fact that in their training and experience they have been exposed to observation of a great deal of human suffering. They have lived with clients through disappointment, sorrow, physical suffering, death, crippling frustration; they have been closely associated with the torture of mental illness; they have read and listened to life history after life history in which the distortions of the adult personality could be traced step by step to misfortunes, deprivations, mistreatment, mishandling, and misunderstandings in childhood. Unless they have remained untouched by these experiences, they cannot but respond with more spontaneous understanding and acceptance than would have been the case if they had not become caseworkers. Herein lies one of the answers to the question often put to therapists: "How can you be so unspontaneous? Don't you get worn out controlling, or concealing, your natural reaction?" The point is that the worker's natural, spontaneous reaction itself is different from that of the untrained person because both perception and judgment have been modified by training and experience. Of course, no worker ever reaches the perfection of understanding and acceptance just implied, but that fact does not modify our conviction that successful psychosocial caseworkers must always strive in that direction.

Although genuine responses of the caseworker to the client usually do have a predominantly positive flavor of sympathizing, accepting, liking, and wanting to help, worker responses that are not therapeutically useful, even though they may be realistic, nevertheless occur in varying degree. There may be irritation at the client who is hostile and attacking, or who is resistive and thwarts the worker's therapeutic intent (or aspirations). Workers may feel threatened by a client's anger or negative feelings toward them; they may be overly concerned about whether their clients like them. Despite training, there may be residues of dislike of or insensitivity to clients whose behavior runs counter to the customs or mores of the worker's own class or ethnic group.[5] There may be particular resentment of the client who mistreats another person, child or adult. An especially attractive client may arouse erotic reactions. Very commonly, there is realistic anxiety about ability to help: the client may be confronted by almost insoluble problems, and may sometimes be so seriously disturbed that the problem is beyond the worker's skill. Threats of suicide especially arouse the worker's anxiety. Occasionally, a psychotic or near-psychotic person arouses realistic fear of bodily harm.

Even when workers fail to achieve understanding and acceptance and instead feel hostility, aversion, or some other antitherapeutic emotion, they usually try to keep from translating it into speech or action. This is for two reasons: because the worker knows it will hurt the client and does not want to do this, and because the purpose in being with the client is a therapeutic one and to show feelings impulsively will defeat that purpose. The fact that workers have been trained to become aware of their reactions makes it easier to control their expression than would otherwise be the case.

One sometimes hears the opinion that the worker should never refrain from spontaneous expression of reactions on the grounds that to refrain introduces insincerity into the relationship. In our view, this is at best a misleading half-truth. We are certainly in agreement with the need for genuineness, frankness, and simplicity in the relationship, but to refrain from showing an emotion is not insincerity. Whether the feeling is one of anger, boredom, sexual attraction, or intense like or dislike, the seasoned psychosocial worker makes every effort to guide the expression of personal feelings according to their value to the therapeutic work. As we will soon point out, spontaneous or direct articulations of a worker's emotions—whether positive or negative—*can* sometimes benefit the client when they have a bearing on mutual goals. When this is so, they may be freely expressed. But, as we see it, they are neither justified nor necessary when based on the worker's own need to be "open" or "natural." Objectivity and reserve about the expression of feelings do not preclude warmth and genuineness. The creative yet controlled "use of self" requires that the worker keep a constant and conscious balance between head and heart, distance and closeness. It is true that the therapeutic relationship can be intensely personal—indeed, it can be uniquely intimate—as the client lays bare inner feelings and dilemmas. But it is for this reason, above all, that it is critically important to take every precaution to protect clients from emotional reactions of the worker that are not truly in their behalf.

A man came resistantly with his wife to a second appointment with a clinical social worker to discusss his wife's wish to begin marital counseling. When he entered the interviewing room he protested loudly about the lingering fumes from the cigar smoked by the client who had preceded him. Impulsively, he emptied the ashtray that contained the butt into the wastebasket. A few minutes after the interview began, smoke started to rise from the basket and the worker had to douse the smoldering contents before proceeding. She felt angry in the face of this man's apparently controlling behavior and the inconvenience it had caused her. At the same time, she recognized that his actions derived from his fear and anger at being "dragged" by his wife into treatment (as well as his real dislike of cigar smoke); she knew that he expected to be blamed for the marital problems. Rather than sharing her immediate emotional response to the incident, the worker was able to connect with her empathy for this man's anxiety. Once she had given herself time to put her anger into perspective, with a light touch she simply said: "Sometimes the smoke has to clear before we can get down to work."

There are special circumstances, however, in which it is highly therapeutic to allow clients to become aware of negative (or positive) reactions as part of the process of helping them to understand the effects they sometimes have on other people. Worker feedback can stimulate reflection about habitual patterns of behavior and about the meaning or recurrent feelings or thoughts. But the timing of this type of intervention is important; it must be diagnostically sound and geared to the client's readiness, not to the worker's need for spontaneity.

Mrs. Glass, diagnosed as a borderline personality, periodically accused her worker of not being interested in her; she bitterly attacked the worker for not always being instantly available by telephone. These complaints did not annoy the worker since she saw them as an expression of the client's rage, rooted in early parental deprivation. However, during one phase of treatment Mrs. Glass began to stall at the end of each session; sometimes she would cling to the worker, begging to be hugged. This behavior became increasingly irritating to the worker, who often had another client waiting; she was angered by Mrs. Glass' seeming lack of consideration. But whether the worker became firm or appealed to the client's reason, the latter persisted in trying to prolong the hour. After several weeks of this, the worker finally opened a session by sharing her feeling with Mrs. Glass. She told her that she had begun to resent being delayed; she pointed out that she was always prompt for Mrs. Glass' sessions and that she wanted to give the same courtesy to her other clients. When these reactions were shared with Mrs. Glass, with whom the worker had a solid relationship, the client was then able to work on her intense and ever present feeling of "never getting enough"; discussions that followed gave the worker an opportunity to help Mrs. Glass see how she was alienating other people by so persistently concentrating on what was lacking in a relationship rather than on the benefits available to her.

In another situation, a charming and attractive man, whose wife had recently deserted him, had a gift for recounting amusing stories to his worker that the latter found she thoroughly enjoyed. She gave the client credit for his intelligence and humor; she found herself tempted to sit back and be entertained. However, sensing that his behavior was defensive, she shared with the client the difficulty she was having directing their discussions to the problems that had brought him into treatment; she found herself easily diverted by his wit, she told him. When these reactions were brought to the client's attention, he was able to recognize that he was avoiding painful material by being entertaining. He also realized that he had a longstanding pattern of attempting to curry favor from others by being the center of attention and by making them laugh. As it turned out, reflection on these issues was far more pertinent to the therapy than the worker's ongoing appreciation of this client's talents for showmanship.

Inevitably, a worker—however experienced or self-aware—will on occasion inadvertently or impulsively disclose countertherapeutic reactions to a client. Whether these are based realistically on the client's behavior or are caused by something within the worker, they may be expressed in a way that is not in the client's best interests. Even so, when this happens such reactions can often be turned to therapeutic use. For example, if a client senses anger and asks about it the worker should not deny it (this would be insincerity) but handle the situation realistically, depending on whether the response was appropriate to the client's actions or an overreaction on the worker's part; the worker's honesty can help to strengthen the client's trust. By the same token, when it becomes clear that the worker and the client are interacting in a counterproductive pattern of any sort, usually the question is not whether to bring this up but how and when to do so. By taking responsibility for his or her part in the problem, the worker realistically acknowledges being "human," and capable of making mistakes. The worker is demonstrating that even though people and relationships are complex, open exchanges about difficulties that arise can often lead to resolution and growth. For many clients, fearful of sharing feelings or of being blamed, the worker–client relationship can serve as a model for handling problems that arise with other people in their lives.

In summary, then, despite the worker's efforts to prevent negative responses from affecting the work with the client, they sometimes do show themselves in one form or another and, when they do, usually they can be dealt with openly; above all, they become part of the reality to which the client is reacting and must be taken into account before the worker judges that the client's responses are due to transference.

## UNREALISTIC ATTITUDES AND RESPONSES: TRANSFERENCE AND COUNTERTRANSFERENCE

A client's unrealistic reactions spring from two sources so closely related that it is often impossible to separate them. When we speak of *transference* reactions, we usually mean that the client displaces onto the worker feelings or attitudes originally experienced in early childhood toward a family member—most often but not necessarily the father or mother—and responds to the worker as if he or she were this person. A similar phenomenon can occur with displacement from later important associates. These are clear and specific transference reactions. Less specific is the client's bringing into treatment any distorted way of relating to people that has become a part of his or her personality, whether or not the client identifies the worker in a direct way with early family figures. All these unrealistic reactions can be positive or negative (in the sense of warm or hostile), and they may represent id, ego, or superego aspects of the personality.

Generally speaking, transference is an unconscious or preconscious process. At the same time, however, the client may be well aware that the reaction to the therapist is inappropriately intense; the client may sense feeling unduly angry with, fearful of, or adoring of the therapist. As we have seen, it is usually therapeutic to encourage the client to express openly real feelings toward the worker. Similarly (as we shall explain more fully later in this chapter), discussion of the client's negative or positive displaced feelings can play an important role in the treatment process. There are times when they can complicate and even obstruct it; they can interfere with client–worker communication. They can bewilder worker and client alike. On the other hand, when they are brought out into the open, they often provide the client with one of the richest sources of dynamic and developmental understanding, and therefore can be among the most useful components of the treatment relationship.

The worker is also sometimes unrealistic in reactions to the client.[6] Workers, too, may identify clients with early or later figures in their lives, or may bring into the treatment relationships distorted ways of relating to people that are part of their own personalities. Although a very important part of a worker's training consists in developing awareness of these tendencies in order to keep them at a minimum, they are never completely overcome and may therefore be part of the reality to which the client is reacting. The term *countertransference* is rather broadly used to cover not only these unrealistic reactions of the worker but also realistic responses, such as those discussed earlier, that are countertherapeutic.

Sometimes beginning students have even greater difficulty becoming aware of countertransference of displaced feelings than they have mastering casework theory and skills. Yet irrational reactions can seriously interfere with the therapeutic relationship and the treatment process; when activated, the worker's responsiveness and understanding can be impaired. Personal therapy (which we, the writers, would encourage every clinical social worker to consider seriously) can be of great value in increasing understanding of one's own reactions, prejudices, and relationship patterns. It may definitely increase the worker's ability to be ever sensitive to inner feelings and attitudes catalyzed by clients. As one reflects on the work one does, one must continually ask oneself questions such as: What are my responses to the character or behavior of this particular client? What kinds of clients trigger intense reactions within me? Are these reactions realistic or derived from other life experiences or personality qualities of my own? If realistic, in what way (and when) can I therapeutically share these with the client? If unrealistic (in which case we rarely choose to burden the client with them), to whom or what in my own life am I reacting? For example, do I feel overly protective toward this woman because of my early experiences with a chronically ill sister? Does this man annoy me because he is in some ways like my husband with whom I am having problems? Or is his managerial manner reminiscent of my father? Does this client's resistance threaten my sense of competence? Am I trying to elicit praise or gratitude from my clients to serve my own needs? Given the fact that I am a member of a society that fosters racist attitudes and class and ethnic biases, am I feeling superior (or inferior) to this client? On the other hand, is my compassion for the "underdog" so keen that I fail to understand truly the uniqueness of the particular victim of injustice to whom I am relating?

## PROBLEMS OF COMMUNICATION BETWEEN CLIENT AND WORKER

It follows that the nature of the feelings and attitudes (realistic and unrealistic) that exist between worker and client profoundly affects communication between them. If the parent of a schizophrenic child is trying to describe the child's unreachableness to a worker who has negative countertransference attitudes to mothers and blames them for all their children's difficulties, the worker may fail to understand the mother's communication, interpret it as rejection of the child, and fail to be alerted to this and other danger signals that point to the child's serious illness.[7] Compounding the problem, the mother may sense the worker's reaction (even if it has not been made explicit) and screen her communications in order to please the worker or evade her criticism.

If the client, on the other hand, has identified the worker with an insincere, manipulating mother, he or she may construe the worker's efforts to communicate acceptance and encouragement as flattery with an ulterior motive. This type of misinterpretation can sometimes be overcome by repeated demonstration of the worker's sincerity and lack of desire to manipulate, but the process can ordinarily be greatly accelerated by bringing the client's distrust out into the open. Then it can at least be recognized as a factor in the relationship and reacted to by the worker, and perhaps be understood by the client in dynamic or developmental terms.

Another source of distortion in communication is the assignment of different meanings to symbols. All communication, verbal and nonverbal, makes use of symbols, but if the two people trying to communicate do not assign the same meaning to the symbols, the communication will obviously be distorted. The most blatant example of such distortion is the misunderstanding that can easily occur when the client has only a partial understanding of English. More subtle are differences in choice of words, which may be dependent upon class, education, ethnic background, age, region, and other variables. Not only do workers need to understand the full significance of their clients' words, but they must also be able to express their own ideas in words that will accurately communicate their meanings to the client. This does not require, however, that workers adopt their clients' vernacular: to do so introduces into the relationship an element of falseness that is antitherapeutic. The client whose background differs greatly from the worker's does not expect the worker to be like him or her, and might not come for help if this were the case. But there is a middle ground in which, at key points, words can be introduced that particularly express the worker's meaning in the client's language. With most people, simple nontechnical language is the most likely to be clearly understood.[8]

Not only words but actions or nonverbal communications are symbolic of feelings and attitudes. Facial expression, tone of voice, inflection, posture, gestures all convey meaning.[9] When the worker and client are of different backgrounds, nonverbal messages sent and received require particular attention, as is true for the verbal exchanges between them. But even when people are of similar cultures, class, and education, nonverbal communications can be easily misunderstood. Often, workers will take it for granted that by their actions they have conveyed a particular feeling or attitude when they have not; or they may assume they understand the significance of a client's gesture or facial expression without exploring it further. Accurate communication requires that the worker be alert to any tendency to rely on suppositions about nonverbal messages; the fact is that they often need verbal clarification because they can be so open to divergent interpretations.

Clear communication of every kind is difficult to achieve.[10] Clarifying and qualifying statements we make, and checking out the meaning of messages received, require an understanding of the complexity of communication and of the many subtle ways in which communication can fail. The same word or phrase has different meanings for different people or in different contexts. A client may use the word "we" and mean himself, himself and his wife, his entire family, his social or cultural group. Similarly, people often say "you" when they mean "I" (e.g., "You get angry when your kids act up in public"). The phrase "Take it easy" can imply: "Don't be so hard on me," "Take good care of yourself," or "I'll see you again." Furthermore, the subjective connotation of a particular word varies. Even simple but charged words such as "mothering," "discipline," and "responsibility" call upon the worker to make sure when these expressions are used that their full meanings are mutually understood. Also, many messages—particularly those that attempt to describe inner emotional experiences—are next to impossible to convey thoroughly with words. Even when clients say they are "heartbroken," "pained," or "in love," or use other words of equal intensity, the depth or particular quality of the feeling is not fully transmitted. Similarly, if the worker says "I understand," the client can only begin to know the level on which the worker means this: Does the worker understand the facts or feelings? Is the worker recognizing the truth in what the client says? Is he or she expressing empathy and caring? Sometimes when words are accompanied by nonverbal expressions, the communication becomes clearer. For example, a sympathetic nod, or a facial expression signifying that the worker feels "with" a client's pain may help to clarify what is meant by "I understand." Of course, the possibility of misinterpretation must still be considered.

In everyday life, as well as in treatment sessions, people tend to fill in unknowns about what another person is saying with assumptions. Sometimes these assumptions can be very accurate. On the other hand, one of the primary failures in communication derives from incomplete messages: A sends only a partial message and B, rather than asking A to elaborate, inaccurately completes it and acts upon it. For example, a worker may end a session with "Shall we meet again at this time next week?" The client may assume that the worker is not really asking for an opinion, but that the worker wants another meeting. Or a client may say something like, "I always enjoy sex with my husband," and the worker may assume that the client enjoys orgasm. Unless the worker attempts to get further clarification, it may be much later before he or she learns that the client enjoys closeness and affection with her husband, and gets pleasure from pleasing him, but that she is also disappointed that she has never achieved sexual climax.

It is incumbent upon the worker to attempt continually to get feedback from the client about his or her understanding of the worker's message, such as "What are your thoughts about getting together next week?" By the same token, when the client makes an imcomplete statement, such as "I always enjoy sex," the worker can ask, "What do you find particularly satisfying about your sexual life?" By seeking clarification and feedback, the worker is more likely to elicit mixed feelings, disappointments, and other concerns. Along the same lines, when the worker has a hunch about a client's reaction, it is best to check it out: "You sound as though you were hurt by your husband's remarks. Am I right?" To this, the client can respond with, "Yes, that's right," or she can correct the worker's impression by saying, "No, it's not that I feel hurt, rather I feel inferior, like a child, when he speaks to me in that way."

To complicate the matter, unclear or incomplete communications are sometimes intended to evade certain issues. The worker who simply said, "Shall we meet again at this time next week?" may have hoped to avoid hearing that the client did not want to return. And the client who did not elaborate on her concerns about never achieving orgasm may have been embarrassed to bring it up, or she may have felt that exploring the problem would be too painful to face. This does not mean that the worker should insist that clients discuss issues before they are ready to do so. It does mean that if the communication gets precise enough, the worker can then be alerted to areas that may require further exploration in the future.

Problems in communication derive not only from misunderstood, incomplete, or evasive messages. People can also send ambiguous and contradictory messages: when a worker suggests an appointment change *he* wants, but implies it would be better for the client; when he shows anger or boredom but denies it; or when he articulates warm interest in a client but keeps the client waiting for an appointment without explanation. When the client says, "I really love my wife" and stiffens or frowns, or when he says, "I am angry at my wife" and smiles, he is sending two opposing messages simultaneously. It is the worker's responsibility to enhance worker–client communication by persistently attempting to clarify conflicting communications. "The therapist," writes Satir, "must see himself as a model of communication . . . he must take care to be aware of his own prejudices and unconscious assumptions so as not to fall into the trap he warns others about, that of suiting reality to himself. In addition the way he interprets and structures the action of therapy from the start is the first step in introducing . . . new techniques of communication."[11]

Compton and Galaway[12] identify six worker barriers to effective communication with clients. As they point out, these barriers will seriously affect the validity and reliability of information received from clients, on which treatment plans and goals are based. Barriers are created: (1) When the worker *anticipates* what the client will say. This occurs when one is so sure (or wants to be so sure) of what the client means that one fails to listen to the actual communication; the worker may be threatened by what the client is really saying, or fear having to change a point of view if the full meaning of what the client says is grasped. (2) When the worker *assumes* to know the meaning of an unclear client message, and acts on the assumption rather than checking out the client's actual intent. (3) When the worker *stereotypes* a member of a group—for example, the delinquent, the white Protestant, or the schizophrenic, and thereby fails to perceive an individual above and beyond (or atypical of) the category to which he or she belongs. Communication is impeded, therefore, because the worker will tend to erect barriers (1) and (2) above, and to anticipate or make assumptions about the client's message. (4) When the worker *fails to make the purpose of an interview (or treatment) explicit.* The effect can be that the worker and client have divergent or even conflicting views of the objectives of their work together. Obviously, worker–client communication will become problematical since each will operate on separate assumptions about their joint purpose. (5) When the worker *prematurely expects or urges the client to make particular changes.* The impatient worker may fail to elicit or hear important data on which to base a sound judgment about treatment decisions; the worker may have insufficient information or may disregard communications from the client that clarify what changes the client can and wants to make. Furthermore, the worker's effort to urge or advise change, particularly in the early stages of treatment, can create barriers to trust and therefore to communication. (Along the same lines, we would add, if one attempts to arrive at a diagnosis too soon—before the necessary facts are in—one may tend to listen only to material that supports the premature conclusion.) (6) When the worker is *inattentive.* If the worker's mind wanders (or if excessively fatigued, restless, preoccupied, or given to daydreaming) it is impossible truly to listen and respond to the client.

## MUTUAL AGREEMENT: CLIENT PARTICIPATION AND MOTIVATION

In recent years the trend in the client–worker relationship is one in which the worker tends to be more relaxed than formerly, with the result that the climate between the two is freer, less formal and distant. Among clinical social workers, there are differences in emphasis in the extent to which they follow this trend. There are also variations to be considered on the basis of diagnostic assessment, as we will point out later in this chapter. Nevertheless, generally the worker attempts to promote an environment of equality in which he or she and the client work together to search for answers to the problems at hand. Worker and client are both experts in their own right; they both share responsibility for how the treatment progresses. The worker is trained to assess people's difficulties and strengths, to understand "the-person-in-his-situation," and to use that knowledge and those treatment procedures that can help people make changes, function more effectively, and enjoy life more comfortably or fully. It is only our clients, however, who can know how dissatisfied they are, what their dreams and ambitions are made of, what changes in their situations or emotional reactions they are looking for, and whether they find treatment helpful.

There has been some controversy among clinical practitioners about the question of mutuality between worker and client. We have already discussed our views on this issue as it relates to worker spontaneity; we have stressed the importance, as we see it, of limiting worker openness to those instances when it is relevant to the treatment. However, disagreeements also exist when it comes to defining the differential roles of worker and client in formulating treatment procedures and goals.

The idea of planning treatment and treatment goals raises serious value questions in the minds of some caseworkers.[13] If you truly believe in the importance of self-determination for a client, they say, how can you talk about *planning* treatment for this person? Isn't this something that is up to the client alone? Some solve the dilemma by seeing agencies as offering certain types of services that the client chooses either to use or to reject. In our view, this does not really solve the problem, but only circumvents it, for it is the agencies that make the choices, deciding both what services to offer and what constitutes eligibility for them. A client is not given a foster home for a child just because he or she wants one, nor are clients allowed to choose the type of foster home their children are placed in, any more than they can decide to be given financial assistance. A client is not likely to know whether the superego needs strengthening or liberalizing (although the client may be aware of being too perfectionistic or self-critical and not know what to do about it). It is usually the worker and not the client who is best equipped to know whether a mother should be helped to see her children's needs more clearly or should work on the question of why, if she does see them clearly, she cannot put this understanding into constructive action.

The truth that lies at the opposite extreme, however, is that it is not only inadvisable but almost impossible to impose treatment or goals upon a client. Except in certain aspects of protective work, when a worker may be doing something against the client's will—taking a seriously psychotic woman to a hospital, placing a child who is being badly mistreated, reporting a delinquent's parole violations to the court—the use of treatment and goal-setting always involves the exercise of choice by the client. Under almost all circumstances (including in public welfare agencies), the client does or should have every right to reject casework service as a whole or any particular goal of treatment a worker may espouse.

In actual fact, the client can and often does negate the worker's efforts. The worker can offer wholehearted reassurance, but it will not become reassurance to the client who is unwilling to accept it—to believe in it. The worker can suggest and advise, but it is the client who chooses whether or not to follow the advice. The worker may feel sure that it would be best for a client to end a marriage, to spend money more carefully, to change jobs, to deal with a drinking or weight problem, but only the client can decide, from his or her point of view, whether these plans are best, and whether he or she wants to work toward them. Workers can try to stimulate clients to think about their situations or themselves; only the clients can *do* it. Interpretations are futile unless clients are willing to consider their validity. During the course of treatment, methods often have to be changed from one approach to another simply because a client is unwilling to make use of the kind of help the worker has first offered, or shows that he or she wants (or can better use) something the worker has not yet offered. Similarly, goals are frequently modified or revised as treatment progresses, as worker and client reach an understanding about what the client wants and what will help.

Determining the direction and goals of treatment, then, is almost never the exclusive function of either the worker or the client. Rather, it is a mutual affair in which the worker is responsible for what is *offered* and for explaining why it is being offered, but the client exercises control over what is *accepted*. Thus, except for certain techniques used in protective work, no treatment can be successful if the client lacks *motivation* to use it. The client must have some discomfort with life as it is and have some hope that change is possible. Sometimes motivation exists spontaneously. At other times, the creation of motivation is an early task of treatment.

Not only must client and worker participate in the treatment process, but caseworkers are more keenly aware than ever of the importance of making sure that there is *explicit* mutual agreement between them when it comes to the nature of treatment and its goals.[14] Client motivation and successful treatment can depend heavily on whether the expectations, methods, and objectives of the treatment process are mutually arrived at, whether they are shared and understood. Clinical observations and research indicate that, without such a common difinition, or where there is a clash of perspectives between worker and client, the worker's therapeutic efforts often fail.[15] Disappointments, frustrations, unfocused treatment, and early terminations are among the dangers inherent when there are "hidden" or "double" agendas, or when divergent assumptions are made by worker and client. Throughout treatment, expectations and goals must be openly communicated by the worker and regularly elicited from the client as, together, they formulate and reformulate or expand them. As clients learn new ways of exploring themselves and their situations, the worker accepts the value of clients' ideas about what they want. The "therapeutic alliance" develops as a result of a deepening understanding on the part of both as they arrive at a shared approach to their work together.

Mutuality is as complex as it is necessary. For example, parents may apply for help for their seven-year-old son's behavior problem in school. The immediate goal for the parents is the improvement of the boy's conduct. However, during the exploratory phase, the worker may get the impression that the boy is acting out some of the marital strains between the parents. Although initially the worker and parents mutually agree on the latter's goals, if it seems clear that change for the boy is unlikely unless the parents address the marital difficulties, it is the worker's responsibility to share these views with the clients at an appropriate time. After doing so, it is still the parents' choice, first, *whether* and, second, *how* they want to resolve the marital conflict. Often, the worker has to assume leadership in advancing goals or new options, but it is still the client's prerogative to accept or reject these or to offer alternative proposals.

There are also times when the worker, for ethical or other reasons, cannot agree upon goals advanced by the client. An extreme example is that of the woman who asked a worker to tell her young son that he could be arrested if he continued to wet his bed, on the belief that this would frighten him and "teach him a lesson." The worker could not agree to participate in this plan, but it was the worker's responsibility to explain why she could not, and then to suggest that they reflect on the situation further in order to arrive at an alternative on which both could agree.

It should be clear, then, that in no way do we imply that mutual agreement means that the worker's role is a passive one; in no sense is the worker abdicating authority—to the contrary, defining it. By explicitly stating that it is the client's task to learn to make choices and decide on what life plans are suitable, the worker is freed to offer expert help in the pursuit of mutually understood goals. This function is manifold: The worker can provide information the client does not have. The worker can give feedback about distortions or contradictions in the client's outlook or behavior (such as by asking a man to consider whether he thinks he will get the response he wants from his wife by berating her). The worker can lend active guidance to the client in the selection of treatment aims. He or she can recommend procedures within treatment sessions (such as suggesting that a marital couple discuss a problem with each other, or that they make "I" statements rather than "you" observations). The worker can share ideas about means that experience teaches have been effective in solving problems or bringing issues into focus. The worker can explain—in terms the client can understand—that self-direction and a developing sense of mastery over one's life can be crucial to resolving person–situation difficulties; in this way, the worker urges the client to take responsibility for participating actively in seeking solutions, and in giving the worker feedback about the treatment. Workers who are secure in their skills can distinguish which areas of expertise are theirs, and which must be the client's, and take responsibility for holding both to their jobs.

It is not only ethical and important to client motivation to view the worker–client relationship as a collaborative partnership, but implicit in the above is the further point that mutuality provides an opportunity for the client to strengthen ego functions such as reality testing, judgment, competence, and autonomy. The treatment process itself can be an arena in which clients develop powers, locate resources—from within and without—and gain experience in effectively taking charge of their lives. (Even the "involuntary" clients—such as those seen by protective or probation workers—will be most successfully engaged and motivated if the worker makes it crystal clear that their needs, concerns, visions, and goals are the stuff on which successful treatment depends.) With clients who expect to be given advice about what to do or how to live, the worker must take a particularly active role in helping them to begin to think and function independently.

> Miss Clay, a timid, forty-four-year-old single woman who lived with her domineering mother, came to a clinical social worker because she had begun to cry frequently and uncontrollably. Her job as a swithboard operator was jeopardized because of her tearfulness. Her mother, her older brother, and her boss, she complained, tried to manage her every move; they often ridiculed her and treated her as though she were incompetent. She resented them but was afraid to take independent stands of her own. In the early phase of therapy, she continually asked the worker questions such as: "Do you think I should move?", "Would it help if I changed jobs?", and "Should I learn to drive a car?" The worker warmly but clearly told her that she was not going to direct her in making these choices since she had too many people running her life already. She would, however, talk over various aspects of the options she was considering. At first, the worker had to keep reminding Miss Clay that their purpose together was to help her reach her own solutions. As time went on, however, this client not only began making decisions for herself, but she was able to recognize the important part she played in encouraging others to treat her like a child.

Perhaps a mention of the "contract" would be helpful here. When this term is used to describe the explicit, conscious agreement between worker and client concerning the nature and aims of treatment, we endorse the concept. Too often, however, the contract is viewed as a formal, rigid or binding (sometimes written) agreement. In our opinion, particularly when problems are complicated, neither the client nor the worker can easily arrive at what treatment will entail, how their perceptions of the situation may change, or what new issues or goals may arise as treatment progresses. In fact, at the beginning of treatment, the contract may simply be a mutual recognition of the fact that it may take time to determine the length and objectives of therapy. In the case cited above, the worker and client agreed that only as they worked together would it become clear what steps Miss Clay would want to take to feel better about herself. On the other hand, there are times when a worker may offer a suggestion such as: "Why don't we meet together for six sessions and then, together, evaluate where to go from there?" This kind of approach or proposed contract can be reassuring to resistant clients who fear they will be snared into an interminable treatment process; in other situations, it may mean that the worker believes the problem can be resolved quickly. We, the writers, see little need for the written contract (except, perhaps, around such concrete matters as fees). As long as there is open communication between worker and client, and an understanding that client participation is highly valued and essential, too much literal dependence on a contract can be distracting and can seriously hamper the flexibility necessary to effective treatment.

## THE CLIENT–WORKER RELATIONSHIP IN THE DYNAMICS OF TREATMENT

Thus far, we have been considering the elements that go into the relationship between client and worker. What part do these elements play in treatment?

We must first distinguish between the basic therapeutic relationship and special uses to which elements in the relationship can be put. On the worker's part, no matter what the form of treatment, the attitude must be a positive one, with concern for the client's well-being, liking, respect, and acceptance of the client as an individual, and a wish for that person to be happier, or at least more comfortable and better able to handle situations. For themselves, workers need to have confidence in their skills and in the possibility of their effectiveness in aiding clients. A study by Ripple, Alexander, and Polemis[16] found an attitude of positive encouragement on the part of the worker the primary factor in both continuance of treatment and outcome. The initial work with those clients who continued in treatment was characterized "by warmly positive affect, efforts to relieve discomfort, assurance that the situation could at least be improved, and a plan to begin work on the problem." On the other hand, "a bland, seemingly uninvolved eliciting and appraisal of the client's situation, in which the worker appeared neutral in affect" was strongly associated with discontinuance and with an unfavorable outcome in those clients who did continue despite the worker's lack of encouragement.

Along similar lines, the research of Truax and Carkhuff found that positive outcomes in psychotherapy were associated with the quality of the patient–therapist relationship; three characteristics of the therapist were found to be strongly associated with patient improvement: accurate empathy, nonpossessive warmth, and genuineness. Although some other researchers did not obtain the same results, our experience strongly supports the importance of these "core conditions."[17] Frank has stressed the importance of the therapist's ability to convey hope and confidence to patients.[18] Of course, the worker's positive personality qualities and attitudes are not enough; knowledge of theory, technical competence, and experience can play an equally important part in treatment outcomes. Nevertheless, the more free the worker is of countertherapeutic communications of any sort, the more likely it is that the client will sense that it is safe to trust the worker and engage in treatment.

The client will need to have enough capacity to perceive the worker in these terms to keep coming for treatment, not only "bringing the body," but participating in the process. This means that no matter how great are the transference and other unrealistic components of one's attitude toward the worker, the client must be able at least part of the time to percieve the worker as a person to be trusted. Sometimes, in the early weeks of treatment, the client is kept coming only by external forces or by feelings of distrusting desperation. The first task of treatment, then, is to find a way of communicating cues to the real nature of the worker's attitudes so that the client will gain confidence in the worker as a therapist, counselor, or simply "helper." With many clients there are periods in treatment when the realistic view of the worker is obscured by unrealistic reactions, but these clients are carried over such periods by previous positive perception, of which some parts of themselves remain aware.

The worker's good will and warmth toward the client are demonstrated in large part by sustaining procedures. Variations, in the use of these techniques with different clients should not depend upon the extent of the worker's actual positive feelings toward the clients, but they should reflect the worker's assessment or diagnostic understanding of a particular client. Some clients consistently need to have the basic therapeutic attitude demonstrated to them more clearly than other clients do. A client seeking concrete services may need information primarily and require only a minimum of support; on the other hand, when a particular client is passing through a period of anxiety, he or she especially needs to be aware of the worker's good will. When the client has strong transference feelings toward the worker, sustaining procedures will usually promote the positive side of the transference and will take on added significance to the client, who will feel as if reassurance or love is being received from someone who was important in early life. Borderline and ambulatory schizophrenic clients—although often able to benefit from reflective procedures—nevertheless sometimes need more support than neurotic clients do, particularly in the early phase of treatment. Consistent emphasis on sustaining procedures, however, tends to create a dependent type of parent–child relationship in both its realistic and its transference components.[19]

Techniques of direct influence depend for effectiveness in considerable part upon the client's confidence in the worker as an expert or, particularly in persuasion and active intervention, as a person of authority. Workers using these techniques must also have this self-image if clients are to take them seriously. One of the troubles young workers encounter in the field of child welfare, where they may have to advise foster mothers who are many years their senior and experienced with children while they themselves may have had mainly book learning, is that they quite rightly lack confidence in the extent of their competence and inadvertently communicate this fact to the foster mothers. As we explain in Chapter 14, there is evidence that directive procedures are more often used to help the client learn how to utilize interviews and the therapeutic relationship than they are to give the client advice about personal decisions. Often, an emphasis on directive techniques is combined with stress on sustaining procedures. In combination, these techniques encourage and gratify a positive, dependent relationship of either the real or transference type.

Exploration and ventilation often require support and acceptance that go beyond simple sustaining procedures. The worker's empathy, or ability to feel *as if* he or she were the client, to experience deeply the client's feelings (without, as Rogers and others caution, ever "losing the 'as if' condition")[20] can be highly therapeutic. When, for example, a client is grieving the death of a loved one, or is filled with anxiety, the worker's profound understanding of the pain or desperation involved can in and of itself bring relief.

In considering the person–situation type of reflective discussion, we turn to the possibility of modifying the relationship by bringing the relationship into discussion. In the types of treatment just considered, the worker's attitude is really *demonstrated*. Even though this takes place through words, it is not in itself discussed. But now the client's reactions to the worker are brought into the open and the client is invited to test them against what the worker presents as the reality of the situation between them. In the process, the worker becomes better informed about the client's reactions and if they are unrealistic or inappropriate has an opportunity to judge whether they are due to misunderstandings or distortions on the client's part. In either case, as discussed earlier, the worker has an opportunity to straighten the matter out and to establish a therapeutically positive relationship through which the clients can learn a great deal about themselves, their reactions, and their ways of relating to others.

The nature of the worker's activities in helping clients think about person–situation configurations often conveys to clients a picture of what the worker is like—at least, it shows what the worker is *not* like.[21] The fact that the worker refrains from excessive advice or from condemnation, and encourages clients to think for themselves may establish the worker as different from parents who have had a destructive controlling influence on the clients. This may encourage strong positive feelings toward the worker based on the reality of the relationship. Sometimes this reflective discussion is buttressed by a demonstration of sustaining attitudes and by a mild form of direct influence that encourages pleasurable, psychologically healthy activities discouraged in the past by restrictive or hostile parents. This particular combination of procedures is sometimes known as a "corrective relationship" and is referred to by Austin as "experiential" treatment. Usually the client has at first regarded the worker as a parent substitute, anticipating, because of transference reactions, that the worker will respond to verbalizations and behavior as the client's parent would have done. When the worker reacts differently, the effect of the early parental situation is in a measure corrected.[22] The client, responding to the worker as to a parent, is now accepted as he or she was not by the true parent and given, so to speak, a liberal emotional education instead of the restrictive one originally experienced. While the second experience does not efface the first, it can do much to counteract it.

This corrective relationship treatment, we want to emphasize, is to be distinguished from the type of corrective emotional experience in which the therapist plays a "role" artificially constructed to meet what are judged to be the corrective needs of their patients. It is rather the presentation of a consistently therapeutic attitude toward clients in which the worker is realistic in enlightened terms, represents adult reactions (in the sense of both privileges and responsibilities), and is continuously accepting of clients and their needs.

Not infrequently in present-day clinical practice, character or personality disorders are seen more commonly than neuroses. In certain of these disorders, clients' difficulties may spring not so much from oversevere as from inconsistent or overindulgent parents. These clients, who in their early years have been deprived óf reliable nurturance or well timed encouragement of independent functioning, are likely to manifest "acting out" or other types of character disturbance. When the problem is one of "acting out," the corrective feature in the relationship may be that the worker comes to represent a pattern of more realistic, in the sense of stronger, ego controls than the individual has previously experienced. Sometimes the main therapeutic task is helping clients to find ways to refrain from behavior that constantly causes them trouble and defeats their own purposes. In these corrective relationships, it is most important that clients see the therapist as someone who does not stand for an overly restrictive life and is not disapproving, but who is interested in helping the clients learn not to defeat their own ends by activities that inevitably boomerang. As discussed on page 303, it was necessary for Miss Clay to experience a relationship in which her thoughts, feelings, and capacity for making her own decisions—in short, her independence—were valued rather than denigrated. For clients with borderline personality disorders, the corrective aspects of the relationship may involve the worker demonstrating—often over and over again—consistent caring, optimism, and patience, and the ability to handle hostility without either retaliating or withdrawing. The work with Mrs. Zimmer, discussed in Chaper 3, illustrates this kind of relationship.

An important facet of the corrective relationship is the effect it can have on the client's self-image. We know that children often see themselves as their parents see them. When clients themselves have unrealistically dismal pictures of themselves and the worker holds a more optimistic view, the worker can convey this attitude to the clients in many ways. In the context of a transference, the experiencing of such an attitude in the worker can powerfully affect the client's self-image. It can be even further strengthened if through developmental reflection the clients can become aware of the sources of some of their self-devaluations and can come to understand the dynamics of how certain experiences have given them unrealistic pictures of themselves.

Sometimes, as the chapters on family therapy and environmental work explain, corrective work can be facilitated by bringing the client's parents into treatment sessions. When it is possible for a client to get realistic reactions, acceptance, and support from parents rather than indirectly through the positive transference relationship with the worker, the therapeutic work may be accelerated. One small sign of parental caring and encouragement can be as effective as many sessions with a supportive worker. This is not always possible, however, until the parents themselves have a corrective experience.

The factor of the client's self-image is affected in a special way by the worker's "therapeutic optimism." This, in turn, is related to the worker's professional security and optimism. While one can never know in advance the actual outcome of a phase of treatment, the worker does foresee the possiblility that as a result of treatment the client will be more comfortable or more effective, or both; if there were not some hope of this, there would be no justification for continuing the contact. Such therapeutic optimism can be perceived by most clients and holds the meaning that someone believes in their possibilities, sees them as better than they see themselves. Even in the absence of the type of transference and life experience upon which corrective relationship treatment is based, the worker's optimism affects the client's self-image and is an important therapeutic element in treatment.

Another fairly universal factor in successful treatment springs from the client's tendency to identify with a worker with whom there is a positive relationship. Clients often say, in describing a difficult current happening in their lives, "I tried to think, 'What would———(the worker) do about that?' and then I said———." And what they then say is often close to what the worker has said to them under similar circumstances. This phenomenon is sometimes described as the worker's "lending the strength of the ego" to the client. It is an imitative sort of learning—similar to a child's learning from imitation of the parent with whom he or she identifies—that can be incorporated in a lasting way into the client's personality. Such learning depends upon the existence of positive reality feelings toward the worker, feelings often reinforced by a positive transference.

This type of identification is sometimes accelerated by assigning a worker who is of the same sex, a similar age, and sometimes the same race or ethnic background as the client. In this case, however, the worker has to guard against the possibility of overidentifying with the client and overusing the transference. Paraprofessional workers can sometimes be particularly useful as "role models," but careful supervision by a clinical social worker is especially important here because of both the possibility of overidentification and the tendency of some untrained or insufficiently trained workers to attempt to impose their own values and goals on the client.

Diagnosis affects the nature of transference. For example, an obsessive-compulsive man may be so eager to be a "perfect" client and please the worker that he takes on a deferential attitude. At the same time, his unconscious need to control may influence him to resist the strong positive involvement in the therapeutic relationship necessary for change to occur. Bringing these transference reactions out in discussions can be central to helping him to reflect on his ambivalence toward treatment and on the conflict between his strong need to win favor and his anxiety about intimacy. When the difficulty is a borderline disorder, the client may suddenly vacillate between seeing the worker as "all good" (i.e., the loving, perfect parent) and "all bad" (i.e., depriving and uncaring). The client may alternately cling to and distrust the worker. The quality of the transference not only helps in formulating the diagnosis, but it becomes a useful tool in treatment. With Mrs. Zimmer, the transference and subsequent reflection on the extreme reversals in the ways she experienced the worker were basic to her progress in integrating her "good" and "bad" feelings about herself and others.

From this discussion, it becomes clear that clinical social workers frequently use the treatment situation to help their clients increase dynamic or developmental reflection and self-understanding. However, the therapist–client relationship, particularly in its transference aspects, is markedly different in casework and in psychoanalysis. Unconscious relationship components, as such, are not brought into consciousness, although—as in the example cited above—their derivatives often are. For example, Mrs. Zimmer was unaware of the sources of her feelings or of their displacement from those sources onto the worker; she was keenly aware, however, of the vacillations of affect in all of her relationships, including the treatment relationship, and was thereby able to work productively toward consolidating the extremes within her.

Since clinical social workers do not use free association under ordinary circumstances, the client is under no compulsion to verbalize all thoughts about the worker as in psychoanalysis. And, perhaps most important of all, the general way of conducting casework treatment does not encourage extensive regression in the transference. To put it more concretely, the casework client does not become as deeply immersed as the analysand in the unconscious fantasy that the worker is a parent. Although the client may react to a certain extent as though this were so, the cathexis of the idea is not nearly so strong as it would be in analysis. Likewise, since the client is not encouraged to regress— to feel and, within the treatment hour, to behave as a young child or even an infant—the client in a relationship with a worker reexperiences the phenomena of early childhood in only a very fragmentary way. The client is more apt to reexperience the reflections of these earliest reactions as they appeared later in childhood and adolescent relationships with parents. As Annette Garrett put it in her excellent paper on the transference in casework, the caseworker does not encourage the transference neurosis.[23]

Some caseworkers, fearful of going too deeply into the transference, have taken the position that transference reactions should not be interpreted for purposes of aiding the client's self-understanding, but discussed only as necessary for the maintenance, or restoration, of a positive relationship. Such a position arises, perhaps, from lack of clarity about the various elements in the transference as it appears in clinical social work, particularly about the fact that there are ego-dystonic pre-conscious elements in the transference, just as there are in all other phenomena; irrational components affected by childhood experiences and even those originally based in infancy and very early life are often reflected to some degree in the client–worker relationship. There is in reality no more "danger" in touching these elements as they appear in the transference than there is in commenting on them in other communications.

Among the procedures used in reflective consideration of pattern-dynamic and developmental content, then, are those that help the client to understand dynamically some of the transference and other unrealistic responses to the worker and the way in which these responses repeat earlier reactions to parents and other closely related people.[24] The client can then put this self-understanding to use in recognizing similar reactions as they occur in current life situations outside of treatment. The client is then in a position to correct distortions and to respond to people more realistically. We deprive the client of a potent source of help in the struggle toward realistic living if we neglect to use the vivid "here-and-now" experiences that occur between client and caseworker.[25]

## A Further Word on Client–Worker Mutuality

The tendency in recent years to move toward greater informality and mutuality in the treatment relationship is regarded by the writers as a sound one. It is appropriately responsive to the current and widespread distaste for anything that approaches authoritarianism. It should be evident, of course, that we do not favor a climate so casual that the client assumes the worker is encouraging a social relationship, in which case very obvious and realistic difficulties can ensue; the limits should always be made clear. But, as we have said, we do endorse a caring, professional relationship that avoids aloofness and that fosters as much equality as possible—a working alliance in which the client participates actively in the treatment process and in the selection of treatment objectives.

Certain very real questions arise, however, concerning the degree of informality and expressed warmth that is useful under different circumstances. This is particularly so when self-understanding is an aspect of treatment and in certain types of corrective relationships. For the most part, there is agreement among psychosocial workers that neither a cold, intellectual approach, on the one hand, nor a "hail fellow well met" stance, on the other, is appropriate. But some tend to favor a fairly formal relationship, especially for those clients who have difficulty becoming aware of negative feelings. These practitioners point out that a worker can be so "relaxed" or "kind" that the client is thereby inhibited from expressing even those negatives of which he or she is keenly conscious. Similarly, they maintain, the client can see the informal worker as such a "real person" that transference fantasies or irrational feelings may not get a chance to come to the fore. The less giving, restrained relationship can help to intensify these, making it more possible for the client to become aware of them while attempting to develop self-understanding.

Other caseworkers lean toward a more relaxed relationship, out of concern for those clients who require strong support and an easygoing manner to feel safe enough to share their feelings and fantasies. They point out that in some cases, when the worker is too formal, clients can be inhibited from sharing personal reactions for fear they will be criticized or misunderstood. Clients have been known to terminate treatment prematurely because they felt "put on the spot" by a worker's reserve.

Actually, these differences may not be as great as they seem on the surface. A middle ground between the two positions can be found, even though a worker's emphasis may be influenced to some degree by his or her natural personality style. But, in our view, the approach should depend primarily on diagnostic assessment. For example, particularly in the first months, Mrs. Zimmer required a great deal of sustainment and open encouragement in order to trust the worker enough to engage in long-term treatment. A remote stance would probably have been so anxiety producing that she would have discontinued therapy. Furthermore, she had no difficulty in becoming aware of strongly negative reactions to the worker, even in the face of the worker's warmly outgoing approach. In fact, an important aspect of the therapy involved helping Mrs. Zimmer to contrast her angry accusations about the worker's lack of interest with the worker's actual attitudes and behavior. Since this worker had been consistent in actively helping, in demonstrating that she cared, willing to be available by telephone in times of stress, and so on, it was possible to confront Mrs. Zimmer with her distorted reactions. A more withholding approach might well have confirmed her skewed view that the worker was indifferent or hostile to her. On the other hand, there are many clients who feel so guilty about angry, competitive, or "unkind" feelings of any sort toward the worker that they have particular difficulty expressing these in a climate of relaxed friendliness; they feel more "justified" in sharing them when the therapeutic relationship is less giving than it was in Mrs. Zimmer's case. Certainly, research in this area would be useful to refine our knowledge and help us to distinguish the conditions under which one or the other emphasis is most effective. But lacking that, as we see it, the choice should depend more on the client's personality and circumstances than on the worker's need for reserve or for camaraderie.

The question also arises as to whether it is accurate to say that a "corrective" relationship—in which the worker is in some measure seen as a "good parent"—is truly "mutual" or "equal." For example, Mr. Kennedy (again, see Chaper 3) turned to the worker for nurturance or "mothering" before be could mobilize himself to begin to take constructive action. The temporary positive transference relationship—in which he was indeed dependent, and in that sense unequal to the worker—gave him the support he needed in order to arrive at his own decisions. On the other hand, certainly mutuality was evidenced by the fact that at no time did the worker use the relationship to attempt to induce Mr. Kennedy to resolve his predicament in a particular way; the success of the treatment depended on the fact that he made his own choices and carved out his own directions. The objectives of treatment —to reduce his depression and to find satisfactory solutions to his situation—were mutually understood and agreed upon. In some instances, then, equality per se may be temporarily limited because of the client's need for dependence. The client may need to lean heavily on a worker, sometimes in an almost childlike manner. Yet even when this is so, the overall goal of any treatment is to help the client become as self-reliant and autonomous as possible. As we see it, mutuality—in the sense that worker and client come to a shared agreement about the course and purposes of treatment—must be carefully preserved in every therapeutic relationship.

## NOTES

1. Dorthy Fahs Beck and Mary Ann Jones, *Progress on Family Problems* (New York: Family Service Association of America, 1973), pp. 128–129.
2. For clinical discussions and reports of research findings from several disciplines on some of the ingredients believed to be important to a successful therapeutic relationship, see Fred E. Fiedler, "The Concept of the Ideal Therapeutic Relationship," *Journal of Consulting Psychology,* 14 (August 1950), 239–245; Jerome D. Frank, "The Dynamics of the Psychotherapeutic Relationship," *Psychiatry,* 22 (February 1959), 17–39; Jerome D. Frank, "The Role of Hope in Psychotherapy," *International Journal of Psychiatry,* 5 (May 1968), 383–395; Thomas Keefe, "Empathy: The Critical Skill," *Social Work,* 21 (January 1976), 10–14; Alan Keith-Lucas, *The Giving and Taking of Help* (Chapel Hill: University of North Carolina Press, 1971), especially pp. 47–65; Carl Rogers, "The Therapeutic Relationship: Recent Theory and Research," in Floyd Matson and Ashley Montagu, eds., *The Human Dialogue* (New York: Free Press, 1967), pp. 246–259; Angelo Smaldino, "The Importance of Hope in the Casework

Relationship," *Social Casework,* 56 (July 1975), 328–333; Charles B. Traux and Robert R. Carkhuff, *Toward Effective Counseling and Psychotherapy: Training and Practice* (Chicago: Aldine, 1967), especially pp. 176–189; and Charles B. Traux and Kevin Mitchell, "Research on Certain Therapist Interpersonal Skills in Relation to Process and Outcome," in Allen E. Bergin and Sol L. Garfield, eds., *Handbook of Psychotherapy and Behavior Change: An Empirical Analysis* (New York: Wiley, 1971), pp. 299–344.

See also note 17 to this chapter for discussion related to research on worker characteristics of accurate empathy, genuineness, and nonpossessive warmth.

3.  Annete Garrett points out the importance of this distinction in her paper "The Worker–Client Relationship," in Howard J. Parad, ed., *Ego Psychology in Dynamic Casework* (New York: Family Service Association of America, 1958), pp. 53–54, 59–60.

4.  Variation among groups, especially among different classes in their attitudes toward and expectations of treatment agencies, has been a subject of interest in recent years and is often touched on in articles on work with poverty groups, blue-collar workers, and ethnic minorities. For the most part, these articles are speculative and impressionistic rather than definitive, but they do serve to alert us to attitudes that may exist. See H. Aronson and Betty Overall, "Treatment Expectations of Patients in Two Social Classes," *Social Work,* 11 (January 1966), 35–41; John A. Brown, "Clinical Social Work with Chicanos: Some Unwarranted Assumptions," *Clinical Social Work Journal,* 4 (Winter 1979), 256–265; Leopold Caligor and Miltiades Zaphiropoulos, "Blue-Collar Psychotherapy: Stereotype and Myth," in Earl G. Witenberg, ed., *Interpersonal Explorations in Psychoanalysis* (New York: Basic Books, 1973), pp. 218–234; Alejandro Garcia, "The Chicano and Social Work," *Social Casework,* 52 (May 1971), 274–278; Sonia Badillo Ghali, "Culture Sensitivity and the Puerto Rican Client," *Social Casework,* 58 (October 1977), 459–468; Robert Gould, "Dr. Strangeclass: Or How I Stopped Worrying About Theory and Began Treating the Blue-Collar Worker," *American Journal of Orthopsychiatry,* 37 (January 1967), 78–86; Man Keung Ho, "Social Work with Asian Americans," *Social Casework,* 57 (March 1976), 195–201; Gordon N. Keller, "Bicultural Social Work and Anthropology," *Social Casework,* 53 (October 1972), 455–465; Faustina Ramirez Knoll; "Casework Services for Mexican Americans," *Social Casework,* 52 (May 1971), 279–284; Frederick C. Redlich, August B. Hollingshead, and Elizabeth Bellis, "Social Class Differences in Attitudes Toward Psychiatry," *American Journal of Orthopsychiatry,* 25 (January 1955), 60–70; Elizabeth Herman McKamy, "Social Work with the Wealthy," *Social Casework,* 57 (April 1976), 254–258; Olive Petro and Betty French, "The Black Client's View of Himself," *Social Casework,* 53 (October 1972), 466–474; and John Spiegel, "Some Cultural Aspects of Transference and Counter-Transference," in Jules Masserman, ed., *Individual and Familial Dynamics* (New York: Grune & Stratton, 1959), pp. 160–182.

It is most encouraging that recent research studies (which confirm our own practice experience) indicate that patients or clients of low socioeconomic status do not seem to be as negative or as unsophisticated about or as unable to use psychotherapy as reports and observational findings in the 1950s suggested they were. For an excellent discussion and analysis, see Raymond P. Lorion, "Research on Psychotherapy and Behavior Change with the Disadvantaged: Past, Present, and Future Directions," in Sol L. Garfield and Allen E. Gergin, eds., *Handbook of Psychotherapy and Behavior Change: An Empirical Analysis,* 2nd ed. (New York: Wiley, 1978), pp. 903–938. In the same volume, see also Sol L. Garfield, "Research on Client Variables in Psychotherapy," pp. 191–232, whose review of the research indicates that while lower-status clients tend to terminate treatment more quickly than upper-status clients do, no firm relationship between social class and outcome has been demonstrated. Both writers urge further research and improved methods to better guide us in practice with the disadvantaged.

5. There are many warnings against this in the literature, going back at least to the twenties if not earlier. Mary Richmond dealt with it briefly in *Social Diagnosis* (New York: Russell Sage Foundation, 1917), pp. 97–98. To what extent recognition of this type of bias has modified it in graduate social workers is not known. The writers are not aware of rigorous studies in which such bias in graduate caseworkers has been established as a significantly repetitive factor, though it is often hypothesized. The study by August B. Hollingshead and Frederick C. Redlich, *Social Class and Mental Illness* (New York: Wiley, 1958), indicated that the psychiatrists involved in the study not infrequently responded to their patients in terms of their subjective reactions to the patient's social class. There are other, more recent, research reports that also suggest that clients of low socioeconomic status are less likely than those in the middle or upper classes to be accepted or referred for psychotherapy, and are more likely to be referred for inpatient treatment, to less experienced therapists, or to nonintensive therapy. See Garfield, especially pp. 192–195. This may or may not be true to any degree in casework practice.

Scott M. Briar's carefully designed doctoral study, which was reported in his article "Use of Theory in Studying Effects of Client Social Class on Students' Judgments," *Social Work,* 6 (July 1961), 91–97, indicates that the judgments of social work students were influenced by knowledge of the client's class, but Briar did not find a consistent inverse relationship (as had been hypothesized) between the student's own responses versus his or her predictions of client's responses, and the distance in social class background between worker and client. He did find a slight tendency for students to assume greater similarity between themselves and the client when middle- rather than lower-class status was attributed to the client. The study did not attempt to evaluate whether the judgments themselves were or were not justified in view of the client's ascribed class status. It is possible that the great emphasis in casework training over the past thirty years on acceptance of differences and on self-determination for the client has acted as a safeguard against at least the grosser forms of class bias entering the treatment process.

Nevertheless, social workers and others continue to be alert to the dangers of racism, sexism, class, and other culturally influenced biases on the part of therapists; certainly, the need for awareness of the subtle and blatant adverse influences of such worker attitudes on the helping relationship cannot be overemphasized. Jeanette Alexander, in "Alternate Life Styles: Relationship Between New Realities and Practice," *Clinical Social Work Journal*, 4 (Winter 1976), 289–301, warns against resistance to accepting changing life styles; Caree Rozen Brown and Marilyn Levitt Hellinger, in "Therapists' Attitudes Toward Women," *Social Work*, 20 (July 1975), 266–270, found that many of the therapists in their study, particularly males, held "traditional" attitudes about women; Shirley Cooper, in "A Look at the Effect of Racism on Clinical Work," *Social Casework*, 54 (February 1973), 76–84, suggests that when therapists are influenced either by "color blindness," "ethnocentricity," or "white guilt," they may fail to individualize their clients; Esther Fibush and BeAlva Turnquest, in "A Black and White Approach to the Problem of Racism," *Social Casework*, 51 (October 1970), 459–466, describe an approach to the effects of racism on clients and workers; Alex Gitterman and Alice Schaeffer, in an excellent article, "The White Professional and the Black Client," *Social Casework*, 53 (May 1972), 280–291, optimistically discuss methods for overcoming barriers to the white–black helping relationship; James W. Grimm and James D. Orten, in "Student Attitudes Toward the Poor," *Social Work*, 18 (January 1973), 94–100, found in their interesting study that first-year graduate social work students held varying attitudes toward the poor associated with differences in background and experience; Charles Grosser's "Local Residents as Mediators Between Middle-Class Professional Workers and Lower-Class Clients," *Social Service Review*, 40 (March 1966), 56–63, deals with the question of bias in indigenous workers; David Hallowitz, in "Counseling and Treatment of the Poor Black Family," *Social Casework*, 56 (October 1975), 451–459, discusses the importance of the therapist being aware of and dealing with his own prejudices and with the distrust and hostility that the black client may feel; Kenneth C. Hallum's "Social Class and Psychotherapy: A Sociolinguistic Approach," *Clinical Social Work Journal*, 6 (Fall 1978), 188–201, challenges some of the traditional psychotherapeutic approaches to work with "lower-status" clients; Man Keung Ho and Eunice McDowell, in "The Black Worker–White Client Relationship," *Clinical Social Work Journal*, 1 (Fall 1973), 161–167, discuss the need for the black worker to understand his or her own cross-racial feelings; Alfred Kadushin's excellent review of several studies, "The Racial Factor in the Interview," *Social Work*, 17 (May 1972), 88–98, concludes that, despite difficulties, white workers can and do work effectively with nonwhite clients and that certain advantages may accrue from racially mixed worker–client relationships; Thomas Keefe, in "The Economic Context of Empathy," *Social Work*, 23 (November 1978), 460–465, discusses empathy as an important factor in work with clients beset by harsh economic realities; Helen A. Mendes, in "Countertransferences and Counter-Culture Clients," *Social Casework*, 58 (March 1977), 159–163, discusses the problems of therapist bias against alternative life styles; Salvador Minuchin and Braulio Montalvo, in "Techniques for

Working with Disorganized Low Socio-Economic Families," *American Journal of Orthopsychiatry*, 37 (October 1967), 880–887, deal with the special approaches necessary for working with some poor families; Emelicia Mizio's "White Worker–Minority Client," *Social Work*, 17 (May 1972), 82–86, discusses the need for social workers to subject themselves to critical self-examination of their racial attitudes; Barbara Shannon, in "Implications of White Racism for Social Work Practice," *Social Casework*, 51 (May 1970), 270–276, warns against hidden antagonism due to racism; Benj. L. Stempler, in "Effects of Aversive Racism on White Social Work Students," *Social Casework*, 56 (October 1975), 460–467, argues for the need to reeducate social work students against insidious racist attitudes; Evelyn Stiles et al., in "Hear It Like It Is," *Social Casework*, 53 (May 1972), 292–299, offer case material in which the value of sensitive discussions of racial matters is illustrated.

The reader is also referred to George P. Banks, "The Effects of Race on One-to-One Helping Interviews," *Social Science Review*, 45 (June 1971), 137–146; Julia Bloch, "The White Worker and the Negro Client in Psychotherapy," *Social Work*, 13 (April 1968), 36–42; Crawford E. Burns, "White Staff, Black Children: Is There a Problem?", *Child Welfare*, 50 (February 1971), 90–96; Roger R. Miller, "Student Research Perspectives on Race in Casework Practice," *Smith College Studies in Social Work*, 41 (November 1970), 10–23; and Clemmont Vontross, "Cultural Barriers in Counseling Relationships," *Journal of Counseling Psychology*, 18 (January 1971), 7–13. These articles, among many others, make strong statements about the issues associated with interracial or intergroup helping relationships.

For a review of research on the implications for outcome of the therapist's race, class, and sex, and the relevance of matching patients and therapists according to these, see Morris B. Parloff et al. "Research on Therapist Variables in Relation to Process and Outcome," in Garfield and Bergen, *Psychotherapy and Behavior Change*, 2nd ed., pp. 233–282. No firm conclusions are drawn about the effects of matching to outcome, but the research does suggest that the therapist's attitudes and biases toward patients of different background or gender may be more important to the treatment process than race, class, or sex variables themselves.

6.  See, for example, Rubin Blanck, "Countertransference in Treatment of the Borderline Patient," *Clinical Social Work Journal*, 1 (Summer 1973), 110–117; Dean Briggs, "The Trainee and the Borderline Client: Countertransference Pitfalls," *Clinical Social Work Journal*, 7 (Summer 1979), 133–145; Mary L. Gottesfeld and Florence Lieberman, "The Pathological Therapist," *Social Casework*, 60 (July 1979), 387–393: Florence Lieberman and Mary L. Gottesfeld, "The Repulsive Client," *Clinical Social Work Journal*, 1 (Spring 1973), 22–31, in which the authors discuss therapeutic approaches to clients who are demanding, "schizophrenogenic," helpless, and hopeless; John Maltsberger and Dan Buie, "Countertransference Hate in the Treatment of Suicidal Patients," *Archives of General Psychiatry*, 30 (May 1974), 625–633; Kenneth E. Reid, "Nonrational Dynamics of Client–Worker Interaction," *Social Casework*, 58 (December 1977), 600–606;

Sonya L. Rhodes, "The Personality of the Worker: An Unexplored Dimension in Treatment," *Social Casework*, 60 (May 1979), 259–264, who distinguishes countertransference reactions from worker personality traits; Mary C. Schwartz, "Helping the Worker with Countertransference," *Social Work*, 23 (May 1978), 204–209; and Donald W. Winnicott, "Hate in Countertransference," *International Journal of Psychoanalysis*, 30 (part 2, 1949), 69–74.

7.  For a discussion of this in work with foster parents, see Robert Nadel, "Interviewing Style and Foster Parents' Verbal Accessibility," *Child Welfare*, 46 (April 1967), 207–213.

8.  Camille Jeffers is quite specific about this. See her *Living Poor* (Ann Arbor, Mich.: Ann Arbor Publishers, 1967), p. 122. See also John D. Cormican, "Linguistic Issues in Interviewing," *Social Casework*, 59 (March 1978), 145–151; Sheldon R. Gelman, "Esoterica: A Zero Sum Game in the Helping Professions," *Social Casework*, 61 (January 1980), 48–53; and Nancy A. Mavogenes et al., "But Can the Client Understand It?", *Social Work*, 22 (March 1977), 110–112.

9.  See note 28 in Chapter 10.

10. For a clear and helpful summary of some of the difficulties involved in achieving functional communication, see Virginia Satir, *Conjoint Family Therapy*, rev. ed. (Palo Alto, Calif.: Science and Behavior Books, 1967), especially pp. 63–90. See also Brett Seabury, "Communication Problems in Social Work Practice," *Social Work*, 25 (January 1980), 40–44; and Paul Watzlawick, *The Language of Change: Elements of Therapeutic Communication* (New York: Basic Books, 1978). See also note 26, Chapter 2.

11. Satir, *Conjoint Family Therapy*, p. 97.

12. Beulah Roberts Compton and Burt Galaway, *Social Work Processes* (Homewood, Ill.: Dorsey Press, 1975), pp. 196–198.

13. See Kenneth Pray, "A Restatement of the Generic Principles of Social Casework Practice," *Journal of Social Casework*, 28 (October 1947), 283–290, for a statement of this point of view.

14. See Werner Gottlieb and Joe H. Stanley, "Mutual Goals and Goal-Setting in Casework," *Social Casework*, 48 (October 1967), 471–477; and Anthony N. Maluccio and Wilma D. Marlow, "The Case for the Contract," *Social Work*, 19 (January 1974), 28–36.

15. See Anthony N. Maluccio, *Learning from Clients: Interpersonal Helping as Viewed by Clients and Social Workers* (New York: Free Press, 1979); John E. Mayer and Noel Timms, "Clash in Perspective Between Worker and Client," *Social Casework*, 50 (January 1969), 32–40; and Phyllis R. Silverman, "A Reexamination of the Intake Procedure," *Social Casework*, 51 (December 1970), 625–634.

16. Lilian Ripple, Ernestina Alexander, and Bernice Polemis, *Motivation, Capacity and Opportunity*, Social Service Monographs (Chicago: University of Chicago Press, 1964).

17. Truax and Carkhuff, *Effective Counseling and Psychotherapy*, pp. 176–189, and Truax and Mitchell, "Therapist Interpersonal Skills." These studies and others suggested that therapists who are accurately empathic,

genuine, and nonpossessively warm, regardless of training, modality used, or theoretical approach, are effective with a wide range of problems and client populations, in a variety of treatment settings. Parloff et al., "Research on Therapist Variables," pp. 242–252, raise important questions about the evidence, and are particularly interested in the question of whether these three "core conditions" are the *"necessary and sufficient"* conditions for *all* successful therapy. They point to some findings that demonstrate patient improvement occurred without one or more of these conditions, and sometimes to a greater degree than when they were present. Clearly, as is true of every aspect of psychotherapy research, further work is needed to ascertain under what special conditions improvement occurs. However, our clinical experience and that of many of our colleagues persuades us of the therapeutic *and* humanistic value of these worker characteristics, although certainly they are explicitly expressed in varying degrees depending on the needs of the client, the treatment situation, and the personality of the worker. Furthermore, as indicated in this chapter, we do not believe (nor have we ever believed) that these worker characteristics are *sufficient* conditions for successful treatment; competence of the worker and client motivation and perception of worker qualities and attitudes are among many other factors that must be considered.

18. Frank, "The Role of Hope in Psychotherapy."
19. For an illustration see Leopold Bellak, "Psychiatric Aspects of Tuberculosis," *Social Casework,* 31 (May 1950), 183–189.
20. Carl Rogers, "Client-Centered Therapy," in C. H. Patterson, ed., *Theories of Counseling and Psychotherapy* (New York: Harper & Row, 1966), p. 409.
21. John Spiegel puts this in the language of role theory in "The Social Roles of Doctor and Patient in Psychoanalysis and Psychotherapy," *Psychiatry,* 17 (November 1954), 369–376.
22. For discussion of this see Lucille N. Austin, "Trends in Differential Treatment in Social Casework," *Journal of Social Casework,* 29 (June 1948), 203–211; and Otilda Krug, "The Dynamic Use of the Ego Functions in Casework Practice," *Social Casework,* 36 (December 1955), 443–450.
23. Garrett, "Worker–Client Relationship," pp. 56–58.
24. For discussion and illustrations, see Gerald Appel, "Some Aspects of Transference and Counter-Transference in Marital Counseling," *Social Casework,* 47 (May 1966), 307–312; Rubin Blanck, "The Case for Individual Treatment," *Social Casework,* 47 (February 1965), 70–74; and Andrew Watson, "Reality Testing and Transference in Psychotherapy," *Smith College Studies in Social Work,* 36 (June 1966), 191–209.
25. Additional special aspects of the casework relationship are discussed in the following: Pauline Cohen and Merton Krause, *Casework with Wives of Alcoholics* (New York: Family Service Association of America, 1971), p. 48; Pauline Lide, "Dynamic Mental Representation: An Analysis of the Empathic Process," *Social Casework,* 47 (March 1966), 146–151; Pauline Lide, "An Experimental Study of Empathic Functioning," *Social Service Re-*

*view,* 41 (March 1967), 23–30; I. E. Molyneux, "A Study of Resistance in the Casework Relationship," *Social Worker,* 34 (November 1966), 217–223; and Allyn Zanger, "A Study of Factors Related to Clinical Empathy," *Smith College Studies in Social Work,* 38 (February 1968), 116–131.

For further readings relevant to the therapeutic relationship, the reader is referred to the following: Felix Biestek, *The Casework Relationship* (Chicago: Loyola University Press, 1957); Compton and Galaway, *Social Work Processes,* pp. 138–191; Alfred Kadushin, *The Social Work Interview* (New York: Columbia University Press, 1972); Alice Overton, "Establishing the Relationship," *Crime and Delinquency,* 11 (July 1965), 229–238; and Helen Harris Perlman, *Relationship: The Heart of Helping People* (Chicago: University of Chicago Press, 1979).

# Chapter 13

# Casework and the Unconscious

We have referred several times to the question of how much casework deals with unconscious material. The question has many aspects. The point of view that will be developed in this chapter holds that at the present time psychosocial casework *proper* deals directly with various types of preconscious material but does not ordinarily attempt to bring unconscious material to consciousness. As noted earlier, many clinical social workers have secured additional training that prepares them for exploring the unconscious and dealing with repressed material brought into consciousness. Occasionally, agencies offer this kind of training to staff members; more often, at present, it is secured either in a psychoanalytically oriented training institute or through arrangements for training with a private therapist. In some training centers, caseworkers who are themselves graduates of such courses are, along with psychiatrists and psychologists, teaching members of the staff. With the current interest in expanding clinical training in doctoral programs in schools of social work, it is possible that in the future some social work schools will arrange for joint programs with psychoanalytic institutes, but at present the individual caseworker is responsible for securing additional preparation for work that depends upon direct eliciting of unconscious material. As far as the writers know, this type of treatment is not at present part of the curriculum of any school of social work.

This does not, however, mean that the unconscious is of no importance in the education of social workers. On the contrary, we believe that clinical social workers need a high degree of understanding of the unconscious: what is meant by the word "unconscious," what kind of mental content is kept unconscious, how and why it is kept unconscious, the nature of primary process thinking, the effect of unconscious content on the current functioning of the individual, the ways in which unconscious content can emerge into the conscious mind. Such knowledge is essential both for diagnostic understanding and for treatment of problems of interpersonal adjustment.[1]

Furthermore, it is not in diagnosis alone that the worker touches the unconscious. Psychosocial theory holds that despite the fact that the caseworker does not in general try to *elicit* unconscious material, it is

321

involved indirectly in any form of casework treatment of psychological problems—whether the worker recognizes it or not. The client's reaction to the worker, for instance, is influenced by unconscious as well as by conscious factors. Even though these unconscious transference reactions are not brought into consciousness, they influence the client's perception of the worker and in turn are affected by the worker's behavior. Sustaining procedures often speak more to the unconscious than to the conscious. The client may not be able to tell you how he or she has come to trust the worker, but somehow something within the person has said, "This one I can trust"—or "This one I cannot trust." The unconscious often reveals itself by tone of voice or gesture, signs to which the worker must be attuned, for often we must recognize fear, hostility, and distrust before clients themselves come to know the meaning of their own feelings; or perhaps we must sense greatly feared positive feelings toward us that clients may cover by outward hostility.

A very interesting instance of the worker's using her knowledge of the influence of unconscious factors without bringing them into the open occurred in the case of a woman with a very high degree of repressed infantile hostility. Unconsciously, she still wanted to destroy anyone who thwarted her, but she was very much afraid of this primitive desire. She had covered it up with a cringing, whining, self-abasing personality and strongly overidentified with suffering in other people. Although her destructive impulses were well under control, her fear of hurting others was so strong that she constantly felt responsible for other people's suffering and overly responsible for the ills that befell her children. She had had an extremely traumatic childhood in which, during wartime, she had witnessed the destruction of members of her family, including a younger brother, at a time when infantile death wishes can be expected to be strong. The underlying problem in this client's case was thought to be too severe to respond to casework directed toward developmental understanding. But an effort was made to give her some relief from the constant guilt aroused by her unconscious wishes and her unconscious belief in their magical power.

The work was strongly sustaining, in the hope that a consistently giving and accepting relationship with the worker over a long period of time would to some degree counteract the effects of the client's early life, at least during a period in which her daughter could be given help to withstand her mother's negative influence on her growth. The sustaining process was combined with some directive work, particularly concerned with her relationship with her daughter, as much reflective consideration of the person-situation configuration as she was capable of, and a great deal of catharsis about both past and present. The client had a quick mind and a good sense of humor on which the worker capitalized. One day, the client was commiserating at length about the men who had been wounded and imprisoned in wars overseas. Her whole demeanor, as she spoke, implied that she felt responsible for their suffering. The worker, with a twinkle in her eye, said dryly that of course she would need to feel especially bad about this because she took such a direct part in those wars. The spontaneous response, "No, I did *not*," was followed by a slight rueful smile of recognition and a lightening of the whole tone of the interview. Subsequently, the phrase, "Like in the war, I suppose," could be counted on to interrupt similar self-castigating episodes. Later, in talks about her daughter, the client's childhood jealousy of her brother—much of which was preconscious—and consequent guilt over her harmful wishes toward him—were discussed in terms of the mistake children make of thinking that their wishes will actually cause harm to happen. In none of these interviews was the client's own repressed hostility brought to the fore; that is, the *sup*pressed hostility pushed into the *pre*conscious was explored, but no attempt was made to bring to consciousness the underlying more deadly aggression that had been *re*pressed and kept in the unconscious. Nevertheless, the worker had spoken, as it were, to the unconscious, and a shift seemed to occur in the client's unconscious belief that her own deadly wishes would cause her daughter to commit suicide.

This case, parenthetically, was a remarkable illustration of the way in which the unconscious can create its own environment. The client's daughter had somehow become aware of her mother's underlying fear and sensed that to threaten suicide was the most successful way both to hurt her mother and to express her own great hostility toward her. The mother's unconscious behavior, by eliciting the daughter's threats, had created a situation that raised the possibility that she would once again feel responsible for the death of a child.

The technique of speaking to the unconscious is often used in work with adolescents or young adults of the same sex as the worker, where identification with the worker is encouraged in order to strengthen femininity or masculinity—in effect, to say to the client's unconscious, "You don't need to be afraid of growing up. It is good to want to be a sexually mature adult," and thus to counteract fears engendered in the unconscious by unloving or restrictive parents.[2]

When the client is psychotic or near psychotic, ideation that would be unconscious in other people may not be repressed or may readily rise to the surface so that the worker cannot avoid responding to it. Occasionally, one can use such material in increasing the client's self-understanding or in modifying perceptions. But in any case one does not encourage this breaking through, but rather if possible helps the client concentrate on reality insofar as he or she is capable of so doing.

## UNCONSCIOUS OR PRECONSCIOUS?

This question of whether the caseworker takes responsibility for bring-ing *un*conscious material to consciousness is still somewhat controver-sial and in need of clarification. It has implications both for the education of caseworkers and for professional responsibility. In discuss-ing it, we are referring to work with adults, not to work with children. It is difficult enough to distinguish between unconscious and precon-scious material in adults; with children, the line between the two is almost impossible to draw.[3]

Much of the confusion on the issue stems from the fact that there are different formulations about the unconscious and the preconscious in psychoanalysis itself. In early theory, the boundaries between the different levels of consciousness were thought to be relatively fixed. Present theory sees a more fluid situation, with the degree of accessibil-ity to consciousness more in the nature of a continuum than of several fixed homogeneous levels. Nevertheless, in general, it can be said that some memories, feelings, and attitudes on the continuum can best be described as unconscious and others as preconscious, and that there are major differences between the kinds of material typical of these two locations on the continuum.

Before going into these differences, it may be well to recall the kind of content that casework does reach. We have indicated that much clinical social work is concerned with thoughts that enter consciousness easily when the client's attention is turned to them. But we have also referred repeatedly to clients' discussion of "hidden" feelings, vague and obscure thoughts and memories, of which they had not been aware. We have further noted that clients can become aware of defenses of which they were not previously conscious and that they can recall childhood experiences that they seemed to have forgotten. Certainly, they often become aware of feelings and thoughts, especially ego-alien feelings and thoughts that not only had never before been put into words but had never been consciously experienced.

This area of hidden thoughts is neither freely accessible nor stub-bornly inaccessible. In psychoanalytic theory, it used to constitute a no-man's land sometimes assigned to the unconscious and sometimes to the preconscious. So perhaps it is small wonder that caseworkers too were confused. Freud himself was not consistent on the subject. Often, he wrote as if he were restricting the preconscious to content that needs only "attention cathexis" to become conscious, that is, to thoughts that the individual can bring into consciousness merely by turning attention to them—thoughts that are completely accessible. All else seemed to be considered part of the unconscious, held from consciousness by "coun-ter-cathexis," or by the "censor," which would not allow material that would be offensive to the other parts of the personality to emerge. Even as early as his 1915 article on the unconscious,[4] however, Freud was not entirely satisfied with this simple division of the sheep from the goats. "Study of the derivatives of the unconscious," he said, "will altogether disappoint our expectations of a schematically clear division of the one mental system from the other."[5] And, further, "A very great part of the preconscious material originates in the unconscious, has the characteristics of the unconcscious and is subject to a censorship before it can pass into consciousness. Another part of the preconscious can become conscious without any censorship."[6] The existence of a "second censorship, located between the systems preconscious and conscious, is proved beyond question."[7] Freud is indicating that there are two kinds of barriers to the emergence of ideas into full consciousness—one seems to be a very strong barrier or "censorship," the other a weaker one. The mental content held from consciousness by the weaker barrier seems to be the very kind of content that emerges in response to casework techniques.

The terms "first censorship" and "second censorship" were used by Freud to describe the forces that either push material out of consciousness or prevent its becoming conscious. The term "counter-cathexis" is also used to describe this process. More commonly today, we use the terms repression and suppression. *Repression* is an unconscious process by which thoughts are pushed out of consciousness and kept there. *Suppression* describes a more conscious process of turning the mind away from anxiety arousing concepts. These thoughts are not strongly kept out of consciousness but neither are they readily accessible. Both are considered useful ways in which the ego protects itself from anxiety. Like any other useful defense, these can be used to excess.

Unfortunately, until the 1950s little attention was paid in analytic literature to this notion of preconscious content that is not readily accessible. The tendency was to consider such material as part of the *un*conscious, some of it at least being referred to as "derivative" unconscious material. This obscured the fact that certain characteristics of mental content such as "the primary process" are in fact not restricted to deeply hidden material, but are also found in this not readily accessible "preconscious" ideation. The primary process is characterized by mobility of the psychic energies, dominance of the pleasure principle and striving toward gratification discharge, absence of a time sense, use of displacement and condensation* in thinking, nonrecognition of contradictions, and so on. The secondary process is characterized by less mobility of the psychic energies, dominance of the reality principle and

---

*Condensation:* the representation of two or more ideas, memories, or impulses by one word or image.

the capacity for delayed discharge, a sense of time, recognition of contradictions, and the preeminence of other logical modes of thought.

Analytic writings continued for many years to distinguish between
*unconscious* and *conscious* primarily in the early terms of accessibility.
The assumption was widely accepted that unconscious material could
generally be reached only by free association, hypnosis, or the use of
drugs that suspend the operation of the repressing forces. It also continued to be assumed that the qualities of being ruled by the primary
process and of being inaccessible usually occurred together. Perhaps
because their techniques have given them access to both preconscious
and unconscious material, analysts were not greatly interested in distinguishing between them. It was not until the 1950s that their literature
clarified such matters as whether a given piece of content emerged in
response to free association or independently of it or, more importantly,
whether preconscious thought might sometimes be characterized by
the qualities of primary thinking found in unconscious material.

## NEW UNDERSTANDING

Change in this position came with the development of "ego psychology," which has in so many other ways enriched our understanding
of the casework process. In the 1950s, with the growth of concern about
the nature of the ego—especially in the work of such psychoanalytic
theorists as Hartmann, Kris, R. Lowenstein, and Rapaport—interest
turned to the preconscious. Kris[8] commented on three problems that
arise concerning the accessibility of preconscious material:

> First, not all preconscious processes reach consciousness with equal ease.
> Some can only be recaptured with considerable effort. What differences
> exist between the former and the latter?
>
> Second, preconscious mental processes are extremely different from
> each other both in content and in the kind of thought processes used; they
> cover continua reaching from purposeful reflection to fantasy, and from
> logical formulation to dreamlike imagery. How can these differences be
> accounted for?
>
> Third, when preconscious material emerges into consciousness the
> reaction varies greatly. The process may not be noticed—the usual reac-
> tion if the preconscious process is readily available to consciousness. But
> emergence into consciousness can be accompanied by strong emotional
> reactions. How may we account for these reactions?

Kris then proceeded to say that there appeared to be mobile energy discharges in such preconscious activities as daydreaming, that

such dreams play the same role of wish fulfillment as night dreams, that they may be ruled by the pleasure principle and that they utilize non-logical thought processes in much the same way as the unconscious. He went on to point out that a good deal of creative thinking goes on without conscious awareness during the "elaboration phase," and when it emerges into consciousness may even appear to the individual as something that comes from without—inspiration. He drew attention also to "preconscious lapses" of memory—temporary withdrawals from consciousness of content that can later be recovered without special techniques.

Kris finally suggested that three conditions may exist for eliminating "the countercathexis between preconscious and consciousness": full cathexis of neutral energy, or attention; ego syntonicity in the intersystemic sense, or freedom from conflict between id and superego; and ego syntonicity in the intrasystemic sense, or harmony among the various ego functions.[9]

Rapaport, drawing upon the work of a number of other writers, went even further, suggesting hierarchical series in which the various qualities of the primary and secondary processes exist in varying degrees. "Different degrees of difficulty are encountered in making various daydreams conscious, in holding on to them once they are conscious; this indicates that a countercathectic energy-distribution controls the transition from preconscious to conscious processes."[10] Again, "It is likely we deal here not with only two but with a whole hierarchy of such controlling energy-distributions. At any rate, it seems that consciousness is not an all-or-none proposition; rather there exists a continuous series of its forms."[11]

These writings provide a most useful theoretical explanation for the empirical findings of casework about the emergence of hidden material. In basic casework we do not use free association, hypnosis, or drugs, but we do repeatedly have clients talk about matters of which they have not previously been aware and of which presumably they could not have become conscious without the intervention of the caseworker. Is it not possible that in psychosocial casework we promote the emergence of the less accessible part of the preconscious by meeting the three conditions laid down by Kris? Sometimes the worker merely increases the availability of this content by drawing the client's attention to it. At other times we increase its ego syntonicity through an accepting attitude and "eductive" interviewing methods, either reducing the conflict between the id and the superego by guilt-reducing comments, or else lessening the intraego conflict. For instance, we may explain that contrary emotions, such as love and hate, can exist side by side without the logical necessity for assuming that the presence of the one indicates that the other is not genuine.

Subsequently, Hollis described the basis for the emergence of hidden material in casework as follows:

> The term "unconscious" refers to memories, thoughts, and fantasies which, upon entering consciousness, were so anxiety-creating that they were automatically repressed, and material of a similar or even greater anxiety-producing potential which was never even allowed to reach consciousness. These consist of memories, thoughts, and fantasies representing infantile destructive and sexual impulses and wishes, material concerning matters strongly prohibited or invoking punishment by parents especially in preschool years, later traumatic events, and derivatives so closely related to these matters that to recall them would involve danger of a breakthrough of the associated material. If casework deals with unconscious material at all it is only in a minor way with these derivatives.
>
> The term "preconscious" covers a wide range of memories, thoughts, and fantasies. It includes, first, material that differs in no way from conscious material except that it is not at the moment the subject of attention. Second, it applies to material that has relatively little cathexis, either because it originated very long ago or was not very important to the person. Third, it refers to suppressed material—that is, ideas that were so anxiety-arousing that by more or less conscious choice or effort they were pushed out of consciousness. Fourth, it refers to material that has never been fully conscious but would arouse anxiety comparable to that of suppressed ideas if it entered consciousness. There is a vast amount of content in these last two types of preconscious material and it is primarily this content, I believe, that casework deals with in ... developing self-awareness.[12]

The anxiety referred to is created by the intersystemic and intrasystemic conflicts noted by Kris. Casework experience, in other words, is consistent with the formulations of Kris and Rapaport, and greatly illuminated by them.

## LEVELS OF CONSCIOUSNESS IN CASEWORK TREATMENT

There was a period in the forties when many of us believed that casework in "insight development" had as its aim bringing certain types of true unconscious material to consciousness. For the most part, we were probably confusing "unconscious" with "preconscious," as later defined by the "ego psychologists" of the 1950s.

The Family Service Association of America committee study of classification (referred to in Chapter 4) attempted to locate illustrations of cases of such "insight development" in a wide range of family service agencies but reported finding none. Frequent reading by the authors and others of material from psychiatric and family agencies in which such cases might be expected to be found has confirmed the impression that very few cases in casework agencies uncover unconscious material in the strict sense of that term. In those few that do, there is almost always the special condition that the worker is either operating directly under psychoanalytic supervision and consulting regularly and frequently on the case, with help from the analyst on details of treatment, or that the worker has secured special training in analytic therapy beyond casework training. Occasionally, a psychiatric agency offers direct psychoanalytic supervision to caseworkers. Some caseworkers have secured training as psychoanalytic therapists and are competent in that role. A few caseworkers have gone on to become fully trained psychoanalysts.

It should be recognized, however, that basic casework training has not in itself prepared social workers to do either psychoanalytic therapy or psychoanalysis proper, although it may have given them an excellent base from which to proceed with further preparation.[13] Certainly, a basic requirement for work with the unconscious would be a successful personal analysis or a successful extended period of analytic psychotherapy. A personal analysis is not a requirement of casework training, but many caseworkers have of their own choice undertaken it. Occasionally, caseworkers mistakenly believe that a personal analysis in itself qualifies them to elicit and work with unconscious content.

Psychoanalysis proper is a therapeutic procedure designed to rid the patient of neurotic symptoms and character disturbances that are causing malfunctioning. It often achieves these goals, and with it a much-to-be-cherished maturing of the personality, but such success does not mean that the particular features essential for deeply probing therapeutic work have necessarily been achieved. Furthermore, intensive study of the unconscious and of therapeutic procedures and close supervision by an analyst during a training period are minimum additional requirements of preparation for becoming a psychoanalyst.

Certainly even a moderately successful personal analysis, or substantial period of analytic psychotherapy, is of professional value to the caseworker. It lessens hostilities and personality distortions that may interfere with realistic perception of clients and freedom to relate to their needs in a therapeutic way. It deepens the worker's understanding of the workings of the personality and of the unconscious. Yet, despite the fact that it adds to the therapeutic capabilities of anyone who undertakes it, the basic aptitude for therapeutic work varies so greatly that some workers who have not undergone analysis are more skillful than others who have had its benefits. The ideal is aptitude plus personal therapy.

If the central focus of casework is conscious material and the various levels of preconscious material, by what means does the worker avoid going into deeper layers of the mind than he or she is prepared for? This usually becomes a real issue only in those types of treatment that involve pattern-dynamic or developmental content, although occasionally it arises in other forms of intrareflection. A first consideration in using these processes is a diagnostic one: How strong are the forces of repression and suppression in this person? If, as in psychosis, the repressing forces are weak and material that would normally be unconscious is already breaking through, the worker must be extremely careful not to set in motion a process that will accelerate the breakthrough. He can help the psychotic or near-psychotic client to understand matters of which he is already aware; such understanding can sometimes be very helpful in combination with constant effort to strengthen the client's relationship to reality and to bring about greater control of id impulses. But in work with the psychotic, the caseworker should not become involved in the pursuit of hidden material, for such pursuit may lead to a breakthrough of unconscious matter with which the worker is not equipped to deal.[14] On the other hand, when such material is already in consciousness and the client refers to it, a worker can sometimes use it to therapeutic advantage.

Except with psychotic or near-psychotic individuals, a worker does not need to be afraid of breaking into the unconscious as long as casework techniques are adhered to. Except where the ego is seriously impaired, the forces of repression provide a strong barrier to the unconscious. As noted briefly in Chapter 7, basic casework customarily uses a number of procedures that tend to avoid overcoming repression. Once-or-twice-a-week interviews discourage too great intensity and regression in the transference and keep the client's investment in introspection at a lower level than would more frequent interviews. Seating arrangements by which client and worker can each look directly at the other maximizes the reality elements in the relationship, rather than promoting regressive transference reactions.

Dreams are sometimes thought of solely as manifestations of the unconscious. In actuality, they may have content drawn from either of both unconscious and conscious. Fears about everyday events often appear in dreams—fear of an examination, fears about an illness, fears about moving one's residence, and all sorts of anxiety-arousing current happenings. Although workers often understand some of the unconscious significance of dreams and symbols, psychosocial caseworkers usually interpret them in ways that refer to conscious and preconscious material rather than using them as means to draw unconscious memories to the surface. Even if the reporting of dreams is not actively encouraged, clients not infrequently do bring them in and it is sometimes useful to discuss material of a preconscious nature as well as their *manifest* content.

An illustration of how dream content may be used without interpreting its unconscious significance to the client occurs in the following: A client dreamed that a man fell by her window, and that she then saw him smashed dead on the ground, with arms and legs cut off. The dead man got up and kissed her with "a kiss of death." The dream occurred during a period when the client was extremely angry at a man with whom she was living but who would not marry her. The dream so upset her that she had to go to sleep with one of her children because of an impulse to throw herself out of the window. Much of the meaning of the dream was clear. The client wished that her lover would die, and in both the symbolism of the dream and afterward in reality, she wanted to kill herself as punishment for her wish. She was all the more frightened by the dream and by her own subsequent impulse because she came from a culture in which dreams were taken very seriously and thought to portend the future. It was important to lessen both her continuing anxiety and the magical quality with which she invested dreams. During the discussion of this dream the worker spoke of dreams as childlike wishes, and of the very good reasons the client had for feeling a great deal of anger toward her friend. She spoke of how such wishes are quite different from any plan or intention of action in reality. She explained how in dreams our minds operate like children's in thinking that a wish can actually take effect: hence, the client's need to punish herself. She was able to relate this discussion to earlier talks about the wishes of the client's small children, pointing out the natural-ness of their sometimes wishing that certain people were dead, and then reacting with fear of punishment The worker did not pursue the latent meaning of the dream by asking for associations or by comment-ing on the symbolic significance of the man's passing her window and the missing arms and legs.

The use of "eductive" interviewing is perhaps the most important factor distinguishing casework methods from those designed to elicit unconscious mental content. This distinction is not always as clearly understood as it might be, but the difficulty is in part a semantic one. Some caseworkers maintain that they do use free association because they encourage their clients to speak as freely as possible. Actually, by this they usually mean that they are giving their clients "permission" and encouragement to talk about whatever is troubling them. They are not making it a *condition* of treatment that the client tell them every-thing that comes to mind. But it is precisely this condition that distin-guishes free association. In free association, the patient is really not free to select what he or she says; the patient is *bound* by the obligation to share all thoughts. All patients at one time or another violate this rule, but when they do the content is brought all the more forcefully to their attention, and they often return to it again and again until it has to be blurted out. Until it is, they know they are violating the fundamental analytic rule and feel guilt and embarrassment that only make more trouble for them.

The casework client, filled with hostility toward the worker, is under no obligation to say out loud the thought that may occur— *You look like an overdressed monkey!* The analytic patient is. The client does not feel forced to speak of matters of which he or she is deeply ashamed, nor is the client required to produce seemingly irrelevant or nonsensical thoughts. The analytic patient must. Encouragement to speak freely and the obligation to say whatever comes to mind are different things indeed. This voluntary selection of communications tends not only to exclude from the casework interview the very leads that are nearest to the unconscious, but equally important, it also removes one of the dynamics that produces the transference so important in analytic work. The patient who is under obligation to speak and does not do so often feels like a disobedient child. If the patient speaks unwillingly, he or she still feels like a child who has been forced to do something unpleasant or to confess a fault or misdoing to a parent. This feeling promotes the regressive transference that helps the patient to relive with the analyst early childhood and infantile years and provokes the repressed memories of fantasies and experiences that have contributed to the illness. Psychosocial casework does not seek to establish this type of transference.

## CASEWORK AND OTHER PROFESSIONS PRACTICING PSYCHOTHERAPY

This discussion leads naturally to the question of the relationship between casework and other professions practicing psychotherapy. Clearly, there are fundamental differences between psychoanalysis and psychosocial casework, despite the fact that casework draws upon psychoanalytic personality theory and has many principles in common with psychoanalysis.

Similarly, casework also differs from those forms of treatment generally known as psychoanalytic *therapy* or psychoanalytic psychotherapy,[15] which although they do not attempt as complete an analysis of the unconscious as is characteristic of psychoanalysis proper, do explore unconscious material to varying degrees. The range of treatment among these therapies is great. Some are close to full analysis while others, insofar as the extensiveness of their work in the unconscious is concerned, are close to casework. This group of therapies embraces many different points of view. It includes the work of Freudian-trained analysts with patients for whom full analytic exploration of the unconscious is either unnecessary or inadvisable; some of the treatment carried on by schools of thought such as Horney's, in which it is believed that it is unnecessary to go into infantile fantasy life as fully as Freudians do; and the work of therapists who are Freudian-oriented and have undergone some discipline in work with the unconscious but have not secured full analytic training.

The general term "psychotherapy" is very broadly used by both psychiatrists and psychologists. In common parlance, it can refer to almost any type of psychological treatment. It is important also to understand that psychiatry and psychoanalysis are by no means identical professions. Psychiatry diagnoses and treats various forms of mental disturbance according to the disciplines of a variety of schools of thought. Relatively speaking, only a very small number of psychiatrists have completed psychoanalytic training. American psychiatry was slower than casework to study and accept the Freudian point of view, and currently many psychiatrists use Freudian ideas only superficially, if at all. When conducted by such psychiatrists, treatment referred to as psychotherapy not only does not involve work with the unconscious but often is not even based upon understanding of the unconscious. On the other hand, there is a large group of psychiatrists who, like caseworkers, have found psychoanalytic theory extremely useful and have studied and used it in various ways in their treatment, but who also, like most caseworkers, have not had specific training in the direct handling of unconscious material. Some of the work of this group is very close to casework in its general boundaries, although often it does not include much if any work with the environment and sometimes it does not give what we would consider sufficient weight to the social component or to the needs of other members of the patient's family. There is also considerable variation among psychiatrists in the emphasis they place on directive versus nondirective techniques.

Among clinical psychologists—those psychologists most likely to be practicing psychotherapy—similar variations exist. Some have assimilated Freudian concepts in a fashion parallel to some of their psychiatric and casework colleagues. A very few, mostly Europeans, are fully trained as analysts. A large group has tended toward eclecticism, with Freudian concepts contributing in varying degrees to the blend. Other psychologists follow a variety of other approaches, Rogerian methods, gestalt psychology, existential therapy, transactional analysis, behavior modification, and so on.

The term "psychotherapy" obviously can also apply to casework when psychosocial methods are brought to bear upon psychological problems—as is usually the case when the overt problem is one of interpersonal adjustment.[16] The authors' personal preference is for the term "psychosocial therapy" or "psychosocial casework" for this type of work, because this gives recognition to the social component of the clinical social workers' methodology.

Obviously psychiatry, clinical psychology, and casework are not identical professions, although in many respects they overlap and cross-fertilization is constantly occurring. In addition to being a psychotherapist, the psychiatrist is a physician skilled in the use of drugs and other physical therapies, with special training in differential diagnosis and with knowledge of somatic and neurological disorders outside the caseworker's area of training. The psychologist often has studied certain aspects of the human mind (such as intelligence and sensory perception), methods of testing qualities of the mind and personality, learning theory, comparative theory, and often research methodology more intensively than the caseworker. The clinical social worker, on the other hand, has greater knowledge of family life, of social conditions, of community resources, and of many of the concrete realities of life, and often has a greater awareness of class, racial, and ethnic factors. We also have thorough knowledge of social agency services. It is in their common knowledge of personality and psychotherapeutic techniques that the three disciplines overlap. Each has learned from the other. Their relationships are best expressed as collaborative, not hierarchical. The caseworker should be oriented to variations in treatment and function in the related professions, both for the purposes of collaborative work and for referrals. When one is considering whether to refer a client from a caseworker to a psychiatrist or psychologist for "psychotherapy," one needs to be informed both about the nature of the client's needs and about the kind of treatment that will be available. If referral is for the purpose of enabling the client to make use of deeper treatment than the caseworker can offer, one must make sure that the psychiatrist or psychologist to whom the referral is being made is actually offering this type of treatment. Obviously, such treatment cannot be provided in a clinic offering fifteen-minute appointments once a month.

This is not to say that one would not make referrals to a psychiatrist or clinic that does not offer some form of psychoanalytic therapy. Particularly in psychoses, psychosomatic illnesses, and some severe neuroses, a careful decision must be made as to whether treatment under medical rather than nonmedical auspices may not be more advisable. Some patients get more security from a medical doctor. For others, physical and psychological care must be so closely coordinated that simultaneous treatment under separate auspices is not advisable. For others, the risk of further breakdown may be so great that accessibility of hospital care is important and only treatment under medical supervision is advisable. And psychiatric care will enable still others to take advantage of the possibilities offered by modern psychopharmacology.

Variations in psychiatric training are also important in choosing agency consultants and instructors for schools of social work. The caseworker who identifies with the point of view of this book needs considerable knowledge of Freudian theory, especially ego psychology, and draws to some extent upon Freudian treatment principles. The more thoroughly the consultant or instructor is trained in this point of view, the more helpful he or she is likely to be. This is, of course, not to suggest that such schools would not offer courses in comparative personality theory, or that other theories would not be drawn upon where appropriate. The writers do take the position, however, that there should be concentrated study of whatever point of view a school believes offers the greatest therapeutic potential. When education is for practice, it is more useful for the student to know one point of view thoroughly than to have only a smattering of many divergent approaches.

The emphasis in this and other chapters on psychoanalytic theory has led some social workers to the erroneous view that the psychosocial approach is almost a "branch" of psychoanalysis. This is far from the truth. The diagnostic-differential approach, from which our present practice is derived, did not—as is sometimes held—take over Freudian theory and practice in its entirety, lock, stock, and barrel. We referred in Chapter 1 to the fact that psychoanalysis was only one of many components of that point of view. It was blended with other components and applied in a highly modified form. Particularly in the area of treatment, there was great selectivity in both goals and procedures. Casework has developed its own blends of treatment, resting in part on its own special knowledge, values, responsibilities, and place in society. It is responsible for deciding for itself what bodies of psychological knowledge and theory will best enable it to fulfill its purposes. Clinical social workers and consulting or teaching analysts must work out together what content from psychoanalytic psychology will be of value for students and workers. In the end, casework must be responsible for itself.

## NOTES

1. An excellent discussion of the worker's need to understand the unconscious is found in Ner Littner's "The Impact of the Client's Unconscious on the Caseworker's Reactions," in Howard J. Parad, ed., *Ego Psychology and Dynamic Casework* (New York: Family Service Association of America, 1958), pp. 73–82.
2. An illustration of this procedure with adults can be found in Yonata Feldman, "A Casework Approach Toward Understanding Parents of Emotionally Disturbed Children," *Social Work*, 3 (July 1958), 23–29. See also Albert Bryt, "Dropout of Adolescents from Psychotherapy," in Gerald Caplan and Serge Labovici, eds., *Adolescence: Psychosocial Perspectives* (New York: Basic Books, 1969), pp. 293–303, in which two treatment cases of adolescent boys are described. Therapy for one failed, apparently because the therapist tended to take what his patient said at face value; on

the other hand, the therapist of the second (seemingly more resistant) boy managed to engage and help the youngster by responding through actions rather than words to nonverbal cues. The writer discusses these examples to illustrate problems of verbal communication, particularly between middle-class therapists and patients from lower socioeconomic classes; but a careful reading also suggests to us that the successful therapist "spoke to the unconscious" of his patient, while the one who failed did not.

3. Jeanette Regensburg and Selma Fraiberg deal with this question in the pamphlet *Direct Casework with Children* (New York: Family Service Association of America, 1957). Fraiberg discusses specifically some differences between work with adults and with children, recommending substantial additional training for caseworkers doing psychotherapy with children. See also Berta Bornstein, "On Latency," in Ruth S. Eissler et al., eds., *The Psychoanalytic Study of the Child,* vol. 6 (New York: International Universities Press, 1951), pp. 279–285, for a discussion of the semitransparency of the defense of repression in young children, especially in early latency, age five and one half to eight.

4. Sigmund Freud, "The Unconscious" (1915), in *Collected Papers,* vol. 4 (London: Hogarth Press, 1949), pp. 98–136.

5. Ibid., p. 122.

6. Ibid., p. 124.

7. Ibid., p. 125.

8. Ernst Kris, "On Preconscious Mental Processes," *Psychoanalytic Quarterly,* 19 (1950), 542.

9. Ibid., p. 556.

10. David Rapaport, *Organization and Pathology of Thought* (New York: Columbia University Press, 1951), p. 718.

11. Ibid., p. 719.

12. Florence Hollis, "Personality Diagnosis in Casework," in Parad, *Ego Psychology and Dynamic Casework,* pp. 85–86.

13. For a similar point of view, see Lucille N. Austin, "Qualifications for Psychotherapists, Social Caseworkers," *American Journal of Orthopsychiatry,* 26 (1956), 47–57.

14. See Paul Federn, "Principles of Psychotherapy in Latent Schizophrenia," *American Journal of Orthopsychiatry,* 1 (April 1947), 129–144, and "Psychoanalysis of Psychoses," *Psychiatric Quarterly,* 17 (1941), 3–19, 246–257, 470–487.

15. See also Austin, "Qualifications for Psychotherapists."

16. A usage followed by Nathan W. Ackerman in "The Training of Caseworkers in Psychotherapy," *American Journal of Orthopsychiatry,* 19 (January 1949), 14–24, and many others. For discussions going back more than thirty years, of the place of casework in psychotherapy, see Annette Garrett, "Historical Survey of the Evolution of Casework," *Journal of Social Casework,* 30 (June 1949), 219–229, and Gordon Hamilton, "Psychoanalytically Oriented Casework and Its Relation to Psychotherapy,' *American Journal of Orthopsychiatry,* 19 (April 1949), 209–223.

# Chapter 14

# Studying and Working with the Typology

It is not uncommon for clinical social workers to have an antipathy toward research. We say we are interested in *people,* not in abstractions and generalizations. But the time has come when research—highly sophisticated research—is necessary not only for further progress in improving our methods, but also for the very survival of our branch of social work. In Chapter 1 we referred to a number of evaluative research studies that have been interpreted to indicate that casework in general is ineffective, and we discussed some of the fallacies that exist in much of this research. One of the misfortunes of recent years has been the separation of research from practice. Only as skilled practitioners invest at least part of their time in research will we have sophisticated clinical studies.

The purpose of this chapter is to describe some clinical research that is not evaluative, but seeks to throw light on the actual nature of the psychosocial form of treatment as practiced by clinical social workers. What do we really do? What processes do we use? Not until this is definitively clarified can we begin to study with precision such important questions as: What procedures are most useful in helping in one kind of problem or another? With one type of personality or another? One socioeconomic group or another? Does a given procedure affect the client in the way we expect it to? What part does the client take in this process? We say this is a mutual undertaking. To what extent is it, and under what circumstances? To answer such questions convincingly, we need to make detailed analyses of what actually takes place in interviews, and we need research tools with which to do this.

It was in an effort to develop such a tool and to answer the initial question of what procedures the psychosocial caseworker uses that the research which is the subject of this chapter was undertaken.[1] The studies were made possible by a five-year grant from the National Institute of Mental Health.* The first objective was to develop a typology

*Grant No. MH-00513, National Institute of Mental Health, U.S. Department of Health, Education and Welfare.

or classification of casework processes that would describe all the procedures the worker uses in communicating with clients. In Chapter 4
(pages 95–97), we described the early case studies, beginning in 1958,
from which Hollis arrived at a classification that could be tested and
experimented with in a larger, more rigorous study. In these studies,
the researcher had set up the best classification she could devise on the
basis of theory then current, and tried to use it to sort out the interview
content in a preliminary series of cases. When it was found that certain
activities of the worker did not fit this classification, corrections were
made in the typology to achieve a better "fit." This occurred over and
over again until the classification began to accommodate the data.
Meanwhile, a logical organization began to emerge that made it possible to set up clear, mutually exclusive categories.

Concurrently with these studies, the classification was used in
teaching, and thus exposed to the thinking and criticism of students in
both master's and doctoral programs. As was noted earlier, students
were also helpful in using the classification at its various stages in both
master's theses and doctoral dissertations. Several of the most important features of the typology emerged from class discussion and student
suggestions. One of these was the realization that the treatment process
cannot be fully represented by classifying worker communications
alone, since to varying degrees the client is self-propelling—that is,
treats himself. To catch the full dynamics of what is going on, one must
include what the client is doing as well as the worker's activity. Interestingly enough, we were unable to find at that time any other classification for content analysis in any of the therapeutic fields that had
attempted this type of study of client activity. It was found that most
of the treatment categories developed for workers in our study could
refer to client communications as well as to those of the worker. By
including client communications in any study, one is giving full recognition to the fact that to a large degree treatment is something the client
either does—or fails to do—for himself or herself. In the reflective
categories, these codings also serve to indicate to what extent the worker's intent of stimulating the client to reflection is followed by actual
reflection by the client. A second major idea first suggested in class
discussion was that work in the environment on the client's behalf
basically involves many of the same forms of communication as those
used in direct work with the client.

## TESTING THE TYPOLOGY'S USEABILITY

The next step taken by Hollis in the continuing study was to use the
classification on new material to see to what degree independent coders

could agree in classifying interview content. This was first undertaken by two groups of Smith College and New York School students in the studies referred to in Chapter 4. These studies located ambiguities in the typology and led to changes in several items. It was following this that the NIMH grant was obtained and larger studies undertaken with the help of doctoral students. Fortunately a number of students with good backgrounds in casework practice were studying for their doctorates when this project was in its early stages and it was possible to enlist their interest. Francis Turner and Yetta Appel were the principal coders in the early stages and contributed a great deal to the clarification and application of the typology. Appel searched the literature and organized it into comparative charts. Turner also used the typology in his dissertation and later in other studies. Shirley Ehrenkranz, in her dissertation, was the first to experiment with the typology in joint interviews. Others who worked with me from time to time included Trudy Bradley, Shirley Hellenbrand, Edward Mullen, Ben Avis Orcutt, William Reid, and Fil Verdiani. Many of these associates are now well known in education, research, and practice.

A total of 123 interviews from 63 cases were used in these subsequent studies. The cases were carried by workers in six family service agencies in Cleveland, Cincinnati, Detroit, New York, and Philadelphia. The following criteria were set up:

1. The case be one in which at the end of the first interview the problem to be worked on was marital adjustment.
2. The case be new to the agency.
3. The case be the first of the above type assigned to the worker in the natural course of work, either after a given date or after completion of five interviews in a case previously assigned for study.
4. Participants be master's degree caseworkers.
5. The recording meet certain criteria discussed by the project director with the workers who volunteered to participate. Workers were asked to do very detailed "process recording," particularly indicating the interplay between client and worker in a way that would make clear which one initiated topics. Interviews were to be recorded not later than the second day after the interview was held. A minimum length was set at three single-space pages of typing.

Obviously, this was not verbatim reproduction, but a detailed description of what transpired with considerable paraphrasing. Although studies using both tape recording and process recording indicate that some skewing of material occurs in process recording,[2] on the whole there is great similarity in the findings derived from these two kinds of recordings. Excerpts from three of the interviews reproduced in figures 1, 2, and 3 (pages 342, 344, and 346) illustrate the kind of detail secured. See pages 352–354 for comments on some further differences found between tapes and process recording.*

This material was initially used to develop operational definitions for each category of the classifications, and to clear up ambiguities in the typology. Where necessary, modifications were made in the definitions and new categories were developed. Procedures were also worked out for coding in a way that would make it possible to handle the material quantitatively. This is not necessary for ordinary on-the-job use of the classification, but it is essential if it is to be used in research comparing groups of cases. For the purposes of the studies, it was decided to do line-by-line content analysis determining the proper coding by using the clause having its subject and predicate on the coded line.†

The next step was a reliability study. A report of this is in the Appendix. The typology had by then reached the point that it appeared to accommodate over 95 percent of all casework communications between client and worker, and could be used with reasonable reliability to make these communications accessible to quantitative research. The reliability study was followed first by a profile of the first five interviews, then by a study of continuers and discontinuers, and finally by studies of cases in which joint interviewing of married couples was the treatment mode.

## The Coding

Three examples taken from interviews coded in the study show how case material was analyzed with this tool. See figures 1, 2, and 3 and their accompanying codings in charts 1, 2, and 3. The capital letters in the chart correspond to the major divisions of the classification discussed on pages 98–101 in Chapter 4. The numerals correspond to the subdivisions of current person-situation reflective comments discussed on pages 100–101. In these examples, the units coded were clauses.

---

*Four students, Marianne Buchenhorner, Robert Howell, Minna Koenigsberg, and Helen Sloss, made an exploratory study of this question in their master's thesis, "The Use of Content Analysis to Compare Three Types of Casework Recording" (Columbia University School of Social Work, 1966). The principal difference found was a smaller proportion of sustaining communication on the tapes than in the process recordings.
† For use in formal research, a Manual for Coding giving further details concerning units for either process or tape recordings can be secured from Hollis.

Each line was coded according to the clause having its subject and predicate on that line. When there were two such clauses, two codings were given. When there was no such communication, the line was placed in the "U" column.

The symbols used in the chart are as follows:

X = Client communication
O = Worker communication
A = Sustainment
B = Direct influence
C = Exploration–description–ventilation
D = Person–situation reflection
E = Pattern–dynamic reflection
F = Developmental reflection
U = Unclassified

Subdivisions of D are as follows:

1. Concerning others or any aspect of the outside world or of the client's physical health
2. Concerning the effect or outcome of the client's own behavior
3. Concerning the nature of the client's own behavior
4. Concerning the provocation or current causation of his or her behavior
5. Concerning evaluative aspects of his or her behavior
6. Concerning treatment and the client–worker relationship

The coded chart makes it easy to follow the flow of an interview. Did a worker's reflective comment induce a period of reflection on the client's part or did the client respond briefly and return to explanations and ventilation? To what extent does the client initiate reflective comments without needing stimulation by the worker? The charts give the answers. Note how clearly the contrast between the three interview samples shows up. Both client and worker in the first case stick almost entirely to exploration–description–ventilation. In the second sample, communications are almost entirely in person–situation reflection, with the worker taking an active part in stimulating this and also offering sustainment. In the third interview, the worker's comment initiates the switch from the client's exploration–description–ventilation to reflection, but thereafter the worker is considerably less active than in the second excerpt.

15  but her husband would want to go home every other weekend. He would
16  leave her with his mother and then he would go out for the entire
17  weekend. Sometimes she would visit her mother on Sunday. If
18  they went there he would behave but if he stayed with his parents,
19  he didn't. With some anger in her voice she told me they
20  had bought furniture three times since they are here. Each time
21  he would want to go back home to live and actually they moved
22  back three times. However, when they went down there they wouldn't
23  have anything. In fact, she said there were times when they
24  didn't have enough to eat. I wondered how he always managed to
25  get jobs. She said one time he worked in a filling station;
26  another time he helped a man build a garage. I wondered what
27  he does up here and she said he works for the D. plant, and they
28  have taken him back each time that he returned. I said he must
29  be a good worker if they did this and she said he is and that is
30  the reason he has always gotten his job back. She said they
31  could have bought a home in the time they have been here if he
32  would only have stayed and acted like people should act. Now
33  he wants another baby. He told her when he came back last weekend
34  if she had another baby that would be all he wants. Their
35  youngest child is seven.
36      I asked how Mr. Z. was with the children. She said he is real
37  good with them. Makes over them and does like any normal father.
38  She feels the marital problem is hard on the children. The one
39  girl has dropped in her grades in school and while she isn't
40  certain it is because of the trouble at home, Mrs. Z feels
41  there must be some connection. The older girl can cry but the

Figure 1.
Record No. 18: Excerpt from a First Interview

|    | A | B | C  | D | E | F | 1 | 2 | 3 | 4 | 5 | 6 | U |    |
|----|---|---|----|---|---|---|---|---|---|---|---|---|---|----|
| 15 |   |   | X  |   |   |   |   |   |   |   |   |   |   | 15 |
| 16 |   |   | X  |   |   |   |   |   |   |   |   |   |   | 16 |
| 17 |   |   | X  |   |   |   |   |   |   |   |   |   |   | 17 |
| 18 |   |   | X  |   |   |   |   |   |   |   |   |   |   | 18 |
| 19 |   |   | X  |   |   |   |   |   |   |   |   |   |   | 19 |
| 20 |   |   | X  |   |   |   |   |   |   |   |   |   |   | 20 |
| 21 |   |   | X  |   |   |   |   |   |   |   |   |   |   | 21 |
| 22 |   |   | X  |   |   |   |   |   |   |   |   |   |   | 22 |
| 23 |   |   | X  |   |   |   |   |   |   |   |   |   |   | 23 |
| 24 |   |   |    | O |   |   | O |   |   |   |   |   |   | 24 |
| 25 |   |   | X  |   |   |   |   |   |   |   |   |   |   | 25 |
| 26 |   |   | X  |   |   |   |   |   |   |   |   |   |   | 26 |
| 27 |   |   | OX |   |   |   |   |   |   |   |   |   |   | 27 |
| 28 |   |   | X  |   |   |   |   |   |   |   |   |   |   | 28 |
| 29 |   |   |    | O |   |   | O |   |   |   |   |   |   | 29 |
| 30 |   |   |    | X |   |   | X |   |   |   |   |   |   | 30 |
| 31 |   |   | X  |   |   |   |   |   |   |   |   |   |   | 31 |
| 32 |   |   | X  |   |   |   |   |   |   |   |   |   |   | 32 |
| 33 |   |   | X  |   |   |   |   |   |   |   |   |   |   | 33 |
| 34 |   |   | X  |   |   |   |   |   |   |   |   |   |   | 34 |
| 35 |   |   | X  |   |   |   |   |   |   |   |   |   |   | 35 |
| 36 |   |   | O  |   |   |   |   |   |   |   |   |   |   | 36 |
| 37 |   |   | X  |   |   |   |   |   |   |   |   |   |   | 37 |
| 38 |   |   | X  |   |   |   |   |   |   |   |   |   |   | 38 |
| 39 |   |   | X  |   |   |   |   |   |   |   |   |   |   | 39 |
| 40 |   |   | X  |   |   |   |   |   |   |   |   |   |   | 40 |
| 41 |   |   | X  |   |   |   |   |   |   |   |   |   |   | 41 |

Chart 1.

13  man should. I asked if she thought it was possible to force him
14  to marry her if he really did not want to, that many men do not
15  and of course many women do not care to marry either regardless
16  of pregnancy, by her own statements earlier his relatives tried
17  to influence him against marrying her, but he did anyway, and
18  from my impression of Mr. R. from the one interview, he did not
19  indicate any regrets about marrying her and does seem to care about
20  her. She answered that it is true, his uncles tried to persuade
21  him against marriage, but he could not have gotten away with it
22  anyway, because she was the "apple of my daddy's eye" and
23  her daddy made Mr. R. marry her, and Mr. R. knew her daddy would
24  not take any foolishness from him. Breaking down completely she
25  continued that she loved her daddy so much, and he her, and yet
26  she disgraced him and her mother, she disgraced her whole family,
27  when they had so much confidence in her and such high hopes for
28  her. They were shocked when she got pregnant and it was weeks
29  before they even spoke to her, and they forgave her but they have
30  not forgotten. I said it was rather cruel of them to stop speaking
31  to her for getting pregnant, but more importantly, since she
32  feels there is something to forgive she has not forgiven herself,
33  when everyone else has, and I thought perhaps her feeling against
34  herself for getting pregnant before marriage is causing her much
35  too much grief and other emotional problems, which is causing
36  herself and her whole family trouble. She continued crying, saying
37  "I know it is, I know it is, but I can't help it," to which I said
38  that we would continue to talk more about it and perhaps after
39  she will be able to feel differently about it. Eventually she
40  calmed down and meekly asked, "Do you really think I will?" to
41  which I said I thought she would if she really wanted to.

Figure 2.
Record No. 27: Excerpt from a Third Interview

| | A | B | C | D | E | F | 1 | 2 | 3 | 4 | 5 | 6 | U | |
|----|---|---|---|---|---|---|---|---|---|---|---|---|---|----|
| 13 | | | | O | | | O | | | | | | | 13 |
| 14 | | | | O | | | O | | | | | | | 14 |
| 15 | | | | O | | | O | | | | | | | 15 |
| 16 | | | | O | | | O | | | | | | | 16 |
| 17 | | | | O | | | O | | | | | | | 17 |
| 18 | | | | O | | | O | | | | | | | 18 |
| 19 | | | | O | | | O | | | | | | | 19 |
| 20 | | | | X | | | X | | | | | | | 20 |
| 21 | | | | X | | | X | | | | | | | 21 |
| 22 | | | | X | | | X | | | | | | | 22 |
| 23 | | | | X | | | X | | | | | | | 23 |
| 24 | | | | X | | | X | | | | | | | 24 |
| 25 | | | | X | | | X | | X | | | | | 25 |
| 26 | | | | X | | | | | | | X | | | 26 |
| 27 | | | | X | | | | | | | X | | | 27 |
| 28 | | | X | | | | | | | | | | | 28 |
| 29 | | | X | | | | | | | | | | | 29 |
| 30 | O | | | | | | | | | | | | | 30 |
| 31 | O | | | | | | | | | | | | | 31 |
| 32 | | | | O | | | | | | | O | | | 32 |
| 33 | | | | O | | | | | | | O | | | 33 |
| 34 | | | | | O | | | | | | | | | 34 |
| 35 | | | | | O | | | | | | | | | 35 |
| 36 | | | | O | | | | O | | | | | | 36 |
| 37 | | | | X | X | | | | X | | | | | 37 |
| 38 | | O | | | | | | | | | | | | 38 |
| 39 | O | | | | | | | | | | | | | 39 |
| 40 | | | | X | | | | | X | | | | | 40 |
| 41 | O | | | | | | | | | | | | | 41 |

Chart 2.

1 I learned at this point that for five years during the marriage,
2 at the time when Mrs. Y. became involved with the other man, she had
3 worked as a doctor's assistant. Since then, she has on occasion done
4 fill in work for a doctor who has provided all kinds of free medical
5 services. This doctor recently called saying that one of his employees
6 was leaving, and asking if Mrs. Y. would work on Saturdays temporarily.
7 Her husband opposes this on the grounds that she should stay home
8 with the children. Mrs. Y. could not see this—he is at home on
9 Saturdays, can watch the children. Besides, they have their own
10 activities. She didn't see that it would hurt anyone for her to work
11 one day a week. I said perhaps her husband wants her to stay home
12 with him. She became a little thoughtful, saying that this might be
13 true, but when they are home together on Saturdays, he is out in the
14 barn working, she is running errands, etc., it is not that they are
15 sitting there kissing and holding hands.
16   At this, Mrs. Y. began to tell me that she is a very affectionate
17 person. But she can't show affection overtly to her children. This
18 sometimes bothers her—though she likes to cuddle "the baby in the
19 family." She guessed she felt this way about her oldest daughter
20 when she was born, but when the 2nd came along 2 years later she was
21 so overwhelmed with responsibility that she stopped being so affec-
22 tionate. She commented that neither of her parents had been people
23 who were affectionate with children. Maybe this explains the need she
24 has for affection. She commented here that her husband is not so af-
25 fectionate as she wished he was. When I asked about this, she said in
26 some ways they are very affectionate with each other, they always kiss
27 hello and goodby, she waves to him from the door, etc. Their friends
28 have commented on this. However, something is missing. I asked her
29 to think about what this was. She guessed she felt her husband's af-
30 fection was routine. She goes to him, hugs him, just on impulse,
31 but he never does this with her. I said this seemed to puzzle her,
32 and she believed it did. Went on to say that her husband doesn't like
33 her relationship with the children, her not being affectionate with
34 them. I said earlier she seemed to be connecting this with the fact
35 that her parents had not been affectionate with her. It might be
36 that because she hadn't received affection, it was hard to give it.
37 She couldn't understand this, though, because she can give it to her
38 husband. Maybe this seemed so important to him because his mother
39 was very affectionate with him. Even now, she kisses him when she
40 sees him. He has always been her favorite child. Perhaps he expects
41 that she be the same way with her children. She commented, as she

Figure 3.
Record No. 34: Excerpt from a Second Interview

| | A | B | C | D | E | F | 1 | 2 | 3 | 4 | 5 | 6 | U | |
|---|---|---|---|---|---|---|---|---|---|---|---|---|---|---|
| 1 | | | | | | | | | | | | | X | 1 |
| 2 | | | X | | | | | | | | | | | 2 |
| 3 | | | X | | | | | | | | | | | 3 |
| 4 | | | X | | | | | | | | | | | 4 |
| 5 | | | X | | | | | | | | | | | 5 |
| 6 | | | X | | | | | | | | | | | 6 |
| 7 | | | X | | | | | | | | | | | 7 |
| 8 | | | X | | | | | | | | | | | 8 |
| 9 | | | X | | | | | | | | | | | 9 |
| 10 | | | X | | | | | | | | | | | 10 |
| 11 | | | | O | | | O | | | | | | | 11 |
| 12 | | | | X | | | X | | | | | | | 12 |
| 13 | | | | X | | | X | | | | | | | 13 |
| 14 | | | | X | | | X | | | | | | | 14 |
| 15 | | | | | | | | | | | | | X | 15 |
| 16 | | | | X | | | | | X | | | | | 16 |
| 17 | | | | X | | | | | X | | | | | 17 |
| 18 | | | | X | | | | | X | | | | | 18 |
| 19 | | | | X | | | | | X | | | | | 19 |
| 20 | | | | X | | | | | | X | | | | 20 |
| 21 | | | | X | | | | | | X | | | | 21 |
| 22 | | | | | | X | | | | | | | | 22 |
| 23 | | | | | | X | | | | | | | | 23 |
| 24 | | | | X | | | | | X | | | | | 24 |
| 25 | | | | O | | | | | O | | | | | 25 |
| 26 | | | | X | | | | | X | | | | | 26 |
| 27 | | | | X | | | | | X | | | | | 27 |
| 28 | | | | X | | | | | X | | | | | 28 |
| 29 | | | | OX | | | | | OX | | | | | 29 |
| 30 | | | | X | | | | | X | | | | | 30 |
| 31 | | | | XO | | | XO | | | | | | | 31 |
| 32 | | | X | X | | | X | | | | | | | 32 |
| 33 | | | X | | | | | | | | | | | 33 |
| 34 | | | | | O | | | | | | | | | 34 |
| 35 | | | | | O | | | | | | | | | 35 |
| 36 | | | | | O | | | | | | | | | 36 |
| 37 | | | | | X | | | | | | | | | 37 |
| 38 | | | | X | | | X | | | | | | | 38 |
| 39 | | | | X | | | X | | | | | | | 39 |
| 40 | | | | X | | | X | | | | | | | 40 |
| 41 | | | | X | | | X | | | | | | | 41 |
| Total: | | | | | | | | | | | | | | |
| X | 0 | 0 | 11 | 21 | 0 | 3 | 9 | 0 | 10 | 2 | 0 | 0 | 2 | X |
| O | 0 | 0 | 0 | 4 | 0 | 3 | 2 | 0 | 2 | 0 | 0 | 0 | 0 | O |
| T | 0 | 0 | 11 | 25 | 0 | 6 | 11 | 0 | 12 | 2 | 0 | 0 | 2 | T |
| | A | B | C | D | E | F | 1 | 2 | 3 | 4 | 5 | 6 | U | |

Chart 3.

## Informal Use of Typology

When using the typology informally for study of one's own work or analysis of a single case, one can simply indicate the categories in pencil by code letter in the margins of the record. This can give a quick picture of the type of intervention the worker is using and the nature of the client's participation in the treatment process. One can quickly spot, for instance, whether client or worker is entirely involved in description and ventilation or engaged in reflection. Having made this objective observation, the worker is then prompted to consider its significance: Has one perhaps not been sufficiently active in stimulating the client to reflection? On the other hand, perhaps at that particular stage it is necessary and important for a great deal of ventilation to take place.

It is possible to observe whether sustaining comments seem to have enabled a client to talk more freely or think more actively, or if they have instead merely induced complacency or passivity. Or whether there has been an absence of sustainment where it could have been helpful. Similarly, many different questions concerning the nature of the worker's activities and the client's responses can be observed.

Analysis of a series of interviews of one's own with a number of clients enables a worker to spot personal idiosyncrasies. Do I tend toward activity or toward passivity? Am I too reassuring? How directive am I? In reflective communications, do I tend to stimulate the client to think or tend to give explanations or interpretations? To what extent are my procedures varied in accordance with the needs of different clients?

Employed in this way, the typology can be a most useful tool for analyzing general tendencies in one's own work, and also in examining individual cases to determine exactly what both client and worker are doing. If one's main interest lies in self-study or in comparing the treatment style of one worker with another, or even one group of workers with another, it may be sufficient to analyze worker comments alone. This is far less time-consuming since, the study found, in psychosocial work the client usually talks at least three times as much as the worker.

## Study of Distribution of Procedures

The first study in which the classification was used in hypothesis testing attempted to answer such questions as "What are caseworkers really doing? What procedures do we use? Where do we put our emphasis?" The researcher's thinking at that time—1960—was expressed in a series of hypotheses. It was predicted that communications (of both client and worker) would appear in the following order of frequency: first, exploration–description–ventilation; second, person–situation reflection; third, sustainment; fourth, developmental reflection; fifth and sixth, either pattern-dynamic reflection or direct influence. It was also predicted, seventh, that person-situation reflection would reach a maximum in the third interview and, eighth, remain steady from then on and that, ninth, pattern-dynamic reflection would be rare in the first and second interviews but more frequent in the third, fourth, and fifth. It was predicted, tenth, that early life reflection would be similar to pattern-dynamic reflection, though somewhat more frequent, and eleventh, that direct influence would be rare throughout.

For this study, the first five interviews of fifteen individual interview cases of marriage counseling were used. Seventy-five interviews were coded by two independent judges. When there was disagreement between judges, the material was reviewed by a third judge—the principal researcher—who entered a final rating in each instance. These codings then became the basis for establishing a "profile" of the distribution of communications.

Table 1 and Chart 4 show the results of this analysis. Table 1 gives the average percentage of all communications (i.e., client plus worker) in which each major type of procedure occurred in each of the five successive interviews. Chart 4 pictures this in graphic form for A, B, C, and D (E and F communications were so few they could not be charted).

One is at once struck by the extent to which client talk outweighs worker talk—three to five times as much—although the amount that the worker contributes increases as the interviews progress. This shift can be attributed to two major factors. First, the client's need for unburdening and the worker's need to learn as much as possible about the situation combine to put the emphasis on ventilation–description–

### Table 1.
Major Category Communications Expressed as Percentages
of Total Communications (15 Cases)

| CATEGORY | CLIENT COMMUNICATIONS | | | | | WORKER COMMUNICATIONS | | | | |
|---|---|---|---|---|---|---|---|---|---|---|
| | Interview | | | | | Interview | | | | |
| | 1 | 2 | 3 | 4 | 5 | 1 | 2 | 3 | 4 | 5 |
| A* | — | — | — | — | — | 02.0 | 01.7 | 01.5 | 01.6 | 01.6 |
| B* | — | — | — | — | — | 00.6 | 00.8 | 00.7 | 01.3 | 00.7 |
| C | 78.3 | 62.4 | 60.8 | 60.8 | 56.4 | 08.4 | 07.0 | 06.9 | 06.0 | 06.7 |
| D | 05.7 | 14.4 | 17.3 | 17.1 | 18.7 | 04.8 | 10.8 | 11.7 | 12.1 | 14.6 |
| E | — | 00.4 | 00.3 | 00.2 | 00.1 | — | 00.2 | 00.5 | 00.5 | 00.6 |
| F | 00.1 | 01.8 | 00.2 | 00.2 | 00.2 | 00.1 | 00.5 | 00.1 | 00.2 | 00.3 |
| Total | 84.1 | 79.0 | 78.6 | 78.3 | 75.4 | 15.9 | 21.0 | 21.4 | 21.7 | 24.5 |

*Not applicable to client communications.

Chart 4.
Client and Worker Communications by Major Category:
Percentage of Total Interviews (15 Cases)

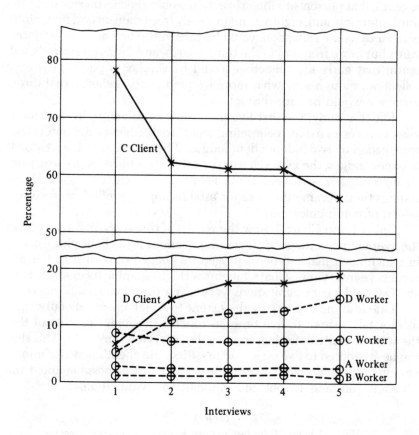

exploration on the first interview. Usually, a brief inquiry from the
worker suffices to touch off a fairly lengthy response from the client.
Second, the worker's increased understanding of the situation, the
client's desire for more definitive responses, and often the client's growing readiness for understanding lead to greater activity on the worker's
part in subsequent interviews. Note that the proportion of both client
and worker communications falling in reflective categories triples between the first and fifth interviews. Equally apparent is the important
part played continuously by the client's descriptive communications
and ventilation. A small part of this material relates to the client's early
life, but predominantly it has to do with current and recent events.

Current person–situation reflection is clearly the second most important treatment process. Sustainment, although quantitatively small, is remarkably steady throughout the five interviews. Direct influence, pattern-dynamic reflection, and developmental reflection are all rare, with pattern-dynamic reflection, contrary to prediction, slightly more frequent than developmental reflection except in the second interview, where exploration of the past occasionally seems to lead to reflection about it. The fact that direct influence, contrary to prediction, is somewhat more frequent than developmental or pattern-dynamic reflection is accounted for by the number of comments made by the worker concerning how to use the interviews themselves. That is, they pertain to the treatment process itself rather than to advice about the client's decisions or actions in outside life. Further analysis indicated that an average of only 0.3 percent of the total content was of the latter type over the five interviews. Both client and worker person–situation reflection take their main jump in the second interview and increase slowly thereafter. The amount of developmental and pattern-dynamic reflection is so small that changes from one interview to another cannot be considered sufficient to indicate trends. Of the original hypotheses, then, the first, second, and third were fully supported by the study; the seventh and ninth were partially supported. Direct influence was somewhat more frequent than predicted; developmental reflection and pattern-dynamic reflection were both of low frequency, as predicted. Contrary to expectation, however, pattern-dynamic reflection was slightly more frequent than developmental.

What about variations between individual cases within these groups? Do they tend to be very much alike, or is there considerable variation in the work done with different families and individuals even when they seek help for the same problem? Uniformity is not the rule. On the contrary, there is great variation. Analysis revealed that over the first five interviews, total person–situation reflection varied from an average of 9 percent per interview in one case to 48 percent per interview in another. Over the third, fourth, and fifth interviews, one-third of the cases had less than 20 percent of their content in this category, one-third had between 20 and 39 percent, and one-third had 40 percent or over. Pattern-dynamic reflection varied from one case in which it did not appear in any interview to four cases in which it was touched on in three of the five interviews, although it never reached more than 4.2 percent of any one interview. Developmental reflection was absent in almost half the cases. Its maximum in a single interview was 9.4 percent.

This diversity is as we should expect it to be, for many factors influence the development of treatment—the nature of the problems the client is dealing with, the qualities and abilities of the client, the worker's preferences and skills, the time available, and other variables.

## COMPARISON OF DATA FROM SEVERAL STUDIES

It is of value to compare these findings with those of three other researchers who have conducted similar studies. Mullen,[2] who used the Hollis instrument in a study of 87 taped interviews of marital and parent–child problems, included in his report a table combining four profiles: his own findings, the Hollis findings, the findings of a study of 121 taped interviews of marital and parent–child problems by Reid, and of one by Pinkus consisting of 111 taped interviews from psychiatric clinics and family agencies. The last two studies used the Reid-Shyne reformulation of the Community Service Society classification[3] (see Table 2). Mullen was thoroughly familiar with both classifications and was able to work out approximate equivalents between the two typologies.

In Table 2 worker communications only are used, and the percentages represent proportions of total worker communications rather than, as in the previous tables, percentages of the total of worker plus client communications.* Note that in all four studies more than 80 percent of the worker's part in the interview is devoted to exploration–description–ventilation and person–situation reflection. Pattern-dynamic reflection (which Mullen terms "personality reflection") is 5 percent or less, developmental (which Mullen terms "early life reflection") does not exceed 2 percent, direct influence is never more than 5.2 percent, and sustainment does not exceed 8.1 percent. As noted above, direct influence in the sense of advice or suggestions about matters outside the treatment situation itself is very small.

It is probable that more sustainment actually occurs in interviews than these studies reveal. Sustaining communications are very often of a nonverbal or paraverbal nature. Tape recordings do not reveal nonverbal communications at all, and the coding unit used did not provide for paraverbal phenomena from the tapes. Use of the typology on interviews recorded on videotape would probably reveal a far larger component of sustainment than has been noted in the studies so far reported. In the process recording, such communications were coded if they were

---

*For instance, total directive communications, which in the Hollis study constituted approximately .8 percent of all worker plus client communications, are 3.6 percent of worker communications.

Table 2.
A Comparison of Four Process Studies

| Treatment Procedure[a] | PROPORTION OF WORKER COMMUNICATION | | | |
| | Mullen[b] | Hollis[c] | Reid–CCS[d] | Pinkus[e] |
| --- | --- | --- | --- | --- |
| Sustainment (A) | .027 | .081 | .043 | .050 |
| Direct Influence (B) | .052 | .036 | .040 | .015 |
| Exploration–Description–Ventilation (C) | .368 | .398 | .463 | .508 |
| Person–Situation Reflection (D) | .459 | .457 | .354 | .313 |
| Personality Reflection (E) | .005 | .013 | .014 | .050 |
| Early Life Reflection (F) | .014 | .015 | .020 | .016 |
| Other[f] | .073 | — | .066 | .048 |
| Total | .998 | 1.000 | 1.000 | 1.000 |

Source: Edward J. Mullen, "Casework Communication," *Social Casework*, 49 (November 1968), 551.

[a] Two classifications were used in these four studies, the Hollis and the Reid–CSS typologies. The figures are, therefore, approximations.

[b] Marital and parent–child problems. Hollis system. Continued-service client interviews one through fourteen. N = 87 taped interviews, 35 clients, 6 workers. See Edward J. Mullen, "Casework Treatment Procedures as a Function of Client Diagnostic Variables. A Study of Their Relationship in the Casework Interview" (doctoral dissertation, Columbia University School of Social Work, 1968), p. 119.

[c] Marital problems. Hollis system. Client interviews one through five. N = 75 process (written) interviews, 15 clients, 11 workers. See Florence Hollis, "A Profile of Early Interviews in Marital Counseling," *Social Casework*, 49 (January 1968), 39. (The figures are the means of the five groups of interviews reported by Hollis.)

[d] Marital and parent–child problems. Reid–CSS system. Short-term and continued-service client interviews one through five. N = 121 taped interviews, 30 cases, 7 workers. See William J. Reid, "Characteristics of Casework Intervention," *Welfare in Review*, 5 (October 1967), 13–14.

[e] Psychiatric and family problems. Reid–CSS system. Primarily beyond client interview fifteen. N = 111 taped interviews, 59 workers. See Helen Pinkus, "Casework Techniques Related to Selected Characteristics of Clients and Workers" (doctoral dissertation, Columbia University School of Social Work, 1968), p. 176.

[f] Technical and inaudible.

described in the recording. This may account for the higher figure in the Hollis study. It is doubtful, however, if more than a very small proportion of the nonverbal and paraverbal sustaining communications were actually recorded even in the process material.

Note that in the relative proportion of C and D material, Mullen and Hollis find more D while Reid and Pinkus both find more C material. It is very likely that this is due to differences in the coding units used in the two systems. The units used by Reid and Pinkus did not give weighting to the length of a communication, whereas the Hollis system did. Since C-type comments by the worker tend to be shorter than D-type comments, which often include explanations and interpretations, this technical difference might explain the lighter weighting given C and the heavier weighting given D by the Hollis system.

These then are the central tendencies, the picture one gets by averaging the work done over many cases. Exploration–description–ventilation and person–situation reflection are clearly the central procedures, with the other four in a peripheral role.

Two important features of these studies must be kept in mind. (1) The first three studies used by Mullen in Table 2 consisted of cases in which *only* interpersonal adjustment problems were the focus of attention. The fourth study included was heavily weighted with such problems. In work with severely disorganized families, for instance, we should probably find more use of directive techniques and perhaps also more sustainment. Even so, the core treatment procedures would probably still be exploration–description–ventilation and person–situation reflection. Other types of problems might produce somewhat different profiles. Further studies are needed to test these assumptions. (2) None of these studies included an analysis of environmental treatment. Undoubtedly, some direct work with factors in the environment was going on in many of these cases, even though the type of dysfunction involved called mainly for direct work with the individual. In other types of cases, in which the problem lies more in the social system than in interpersonal relationships, environmental work might assume major proportions.

A further word about pattern-dynamic and developmental reflection. The extremely small number of communications in these categories might lead one to think that forms of treatment leading to understanding in these areas are of little importance. This is not true. It used to be supposed that there were only a few cases in which this type of understanding was sought, and that in those cases a considerable portion of time was spent in talking directly about the dynamics of behavior and its development. It is now apparent that bits of such reflection are, not infrequently, embedded in a much larger matrix of understanding of current life events and responses, and that moments of such insight are followed by further person–situation content, which benefits from the insight gained. Such moments of insight are found in a wide range of cases. In a few cases, pattern-dynamic and developmental reflection become an extensive part of treatment.

Self-understanding is, of course, much broader than pattern-dynamic and developmental understanding. Readers will recall that the last four divisions of current person–situation understanding look at inward aspects of functioning. The second division looks both inwardly to what a person has done and outwardly to its effects or potential effects on others. So it can be said to be half inwardly directed and half outwardly. The first subdivision of person-situation reflection looks outward. By adding these communications to the outward-looking half of the second subdivision of person-situation reflection, one can arrive at an index of extrareflection. In contrast, by adding the inward facing D communications to E and F communications, one can secure an index of intrareflection. Examination of interviews 3, 4, and 5 of the profile study reveals that reflective comments are about evenly divided between intra- and extrareflection despite the very small amount of pattern-dynamic or developmental reflection.

## A PROFILE OF THE CASEWORK PROCESS

Research inevitably deals in such abstractions that one tends to lose sight of the meaning and significance of the findings. What do these studies tell us about the nature of worker–client communications in psychosocial casework involving individual work with clients? Are they harmonious with the position set forth in earlier chapters?

The picture we get in these studies of clients having principally interpersonal relationship problems is of a reality-based treatment in which the individual is helped to learn about himself or herself primarily by learning to understand what is going on in the interactions—the transactions—of current life. On the one hand, it is a process of trying to understand other people with whom one has meaningful relationships, elements in one's practical life situation, sometimes one's physical condition and medical care. On the other hand, and intertwined with this, a person attempts to become more aware of reactions to specific people and, in specific circumstances, more aware of what touches off certain kinds of reactions. Sometimes one evaluates reactions; sometimes one looks at them in terms of their actual or possible consequences. In order to engage in these reflective processes, the client is encouraged to talk at length, descriptively, and often with emotion about the self, about associates, and about the situation, to a worker who listens with attention, understanding, and acceptance. The worker helps to focus the exploration–description–ventilation process on pertinent content, and through sustaining expressions encourages the formation of the relationship of trust necessary for one person to use another's help. Directive techniques are used sparingly. Understanding of intrapsychic patterns and their development is by no means unimportant, although procedures dealing with them are used much less frequently than person–situation reflection. Procedures of pattern-dynamic and developmental reflection are used in highly varying degree. In many cases they do not appear at all, in others occasionally, and in some with fair regularity over a period of treatment. They usually rely for much of their impact on substantial prior and subsequent work on understanding the current person–situation gestalt. The picture is distinctly one of a blend of procedures, with the admixture of those procedures leading to intrapsychic understanding following the pattern of a continuum.

## FURTHER STUDIES

This typology has now been used as a research instrument in a number of other studies, as can be seen from the following partial list.

Boatman, Louise. "Caseworkers' Judgments of Clients' Hope."[4]
Chamberlain, Edna. "Testing with a Treatment Typology."[5]
Davis, Inger P. "Use of Influence Techniques in Casework with Parents."[6]
Ehrenkranz, Shirley M. "A Study of the Techniques and Procedures Used in Joint Interviewing in the Treatment of Marital Problems."[7]
Hollis, Florence. "Continuance and Discontinuance in Marital Counseling and Some Observations on Joint Interviews."[8]
Montgomery, Mitzie I. R. "Feedback Systems, Interaction Analysis, and Counseling Models in Professional Programmes."[9]
Mullen, Edward J. "Casework Treatment Procedures as a Function of Client Diagnostic Variables."[10]
Orcutt, Ben Avis. "Process Analysis in the First Phase of Treatment"— a part of a larger study, *Casework with Wives of Alcoholics.*[11]
Turner, Francis J. "Ethnic Differences and Client Performance."[12] "Social Work Treatment and Value Differences."[13]

   In most of these studies, groups of cases were compared in order to determine the extent to which procedures used in treatment vary in association with other variables. Each of the ten studies produced important findings. Some of these findings support aspects of currently accepted theory. Some throw other aspects into question. Others that are primarily descriptive have brought previously unnoted or at least undemonstrated tendencies to light. One study (Montgomery) used the typology successfully in analyzing three different treatment approaches using interviews conducted by Fritz Perls, Carl Rogers, and Virginia Satir.

## Sustainment and Countersustainment

The study by Boatman is of special interest here because it deals with an important aspect of sustainment. As we began using the typology, it became apparent that workers varied a great deal in the ways in which they chose and expressed communications designed primarily for other than direct sustainment. One has the impression that some workers seem to maintain a sustaining "atmosphere" while others do not. Others even seem to come close to a "counter-sustaining" climate. Boatman studied this phenomenon as part of a doctoral dissertation investigating correlates of various factors with caseworkers' judgment of client hopefulness.

She examined the possibility that sustainment is given not only by the directly sustaining communications coded A but also *in*directly by the supportive quality of some communications whose primary dynamic is either reflection, exploration–ventilation, or direct influence. Indirectly sustaining communications were designated as those B, C, D, E, and F communications expressing "encouragement, approval, agreement, reassurance or identification of the worker with the client's ideas, attitudes, feelings or behavior." In contrast, B, C, D, E, and F communications expressing "discouragement, disapproval, disagreement, stimulation of anxiety, or identification of the worker with attitudes, ideas, feelings or behavior contrary to those of the client were considered to be 'counter-sustaining'. "

For instance:

> Indirect sustainment: To a wife who overreacts to her husband's anger and fears that he no longer loves her—"Do you think Ted may express anger pretty easily? You told me his family is much more spontaneous than yours. Lots of people can be angry and love very much at the same time, you know."
>
> Or—To a client with excessively high self-expectations: "Why are you so hard on yourself?"
>
> Counter-sustainment: A client who has told her worker she has a hard time getting to work on time, complains that her boss is "so irritable" in the mornings. Worker asks if she thinks her late arrivals might have anything to do with it.

Boatman found that almost 8 percent of the "non-A" communications in her study were indirectly sustaining. This was more than two and a half times as much sustainment as was given in her sample by direct sustaining (A) comments. She also found that over 5 percent of the coded communications were *counter*-sustaining. The study went on to examine the extent to which workers differ from each other in their general supportiveness. Mullen had already shown that workers vary a great deal in the extent to which they use different procedures. Direct sustainment, however, he found to be an exception to this tendency. In contrast, Boatman's findings show that if one includes *in*direct sustainment, there is indeed very great variation among workers. The extremes ran from one worker whose interviews showed sustainment and countersustainment in almost equal degrees to another whose sustainment/countersustainment ratio was eight to one.

Obviously, this is an area needing much further study. One could, for instance, examine relationships between total sustainment/countersustainment and client progress in either problem solving or general functioning, by combining a measurement of progress such as that developed by Dorothy Beck of the Family Service Association of America,[14] with measurements of sustainment/countersustainment. With the Beck technique, one could easily locate a small group of workers with high outcomes and another with low outcomes; analysis of each group over even a small sample of interviews might reveal highly significant differences in approach. A similar phenomenon exists in the measurement of directiveness. Undoubtedly, workers differ in the extent to which their reflective comments contain directive elements. This has not yet been studied but would be a very useful area of exploration.

## NEED FOR FURTHER RESEARCH

Much interesting research lies ahead for skilled practitioners who are intellectually curious, accurately discriminating, very patient, and seriously interested in helping strengthen the scientific foundation of clinical social work practice.

The typology itself needs further development. Work needs to be done on the unit to be coded. The small units used, although good from the point of view of precision, are expensive to use because the coding becomes very time-consuming. If a way can be found to code larger units reliably, the usefulness of the typology will be increased. It should be noted, however, that it is not necessary to use the entire typology in every study. If one is interested in directiveness, for example, it could well be that only the B worker comments needed coding. Once located, each such unit could be studied for appropriateness, effect, differences between workers, and so on. It is also quite possible to add new categories, especially subcategories of the major six, when these are needed to study special questions. For instance, one might want to subdivide the C category by a time factor in order to see how much emphasis is placed on past history. Or one might look into the *content* of worker interpretations by devising suitable sub-categories to the three reflective divisions.

The value of the typology in environmental or milieu treatment has not as yet been examined at all, and of course this should be done.

As for substantive studies, the questions that need examination are myriad. To name a few: Are certain "worker styles" associated with higher effectiveness of treatment with certain types of problems or certain types of personality? What are the components of these styles? What are the emphases within them? How do such factors as socioeconomic class or education relate to treatment procedures? In another type of study, one could take a series of person–situation reflection episodes or a series of pattern-dynamic or developmental episodes to examine what evidence there is that these did or did not affect the client's subsequent responses.

Caseworkers have long and inconclusively debated, on the basis of observed data, many issues that would lend themselves to more rigorous study. To move ahead in such studies, we must state our hypotheses in accurate terms based on the realities of casework practice, we must define our objectives far more precisely than heretofore, and we must continue to develop research instruments specifically designed for the examination and measurement of the phenomena to which they are to be applied.

### NOTES

1. Readers interested in the full report of the research should turn to Florence Hollis, *A Typology of Casework Treatment* (New York: Family Service Association of America, 1968).
2. Edward J. Mullen, "Casework Communication," *Social Casework,* 49 (November 1968), 546–551.
3. This classification is described in William J. Reid and Ann Shyne, *Brief and Extended Casework* (New York: Columbia University Press, 1969), pp. 70–72.
4. Louise Boatman, "Caseworkers' Judgments of Clients' Hope: Some Correlates Among Client–Situation Characteristics and Among Workers' Communication Patterns" (doctoral dissertation, Columbia University School of Social Work, 1974).
5. Edna Chamberlain, "Testing with a Treatment Typology," *Australian Journal of Social Work,* 22 (December 1969), 3–8.
6. Inger P. Davis, "Use of Influence Techniques in Casework with Parents" (doctoral dissertation, University of Chicago, March 1969). See also her article "Advice-Giving in Parent Counseling," *Social Casework,* (June 1975), 343–347.
7. Shirley Ehrenkranz, "A Study of the Techniques and Procedures Used in Joint Interviewing in the Treatment of Marital Problems" (doctoral dissertation, Columbia University School of Social Work, 1967). Two articles based on the dissertation were published," A Study of Joint Interviewing in the Treatment of Marital Problems," *Social Casework,* 48 (October and November 1967), 498–502, 570–574.

8. Florence Hollis, "Continuance and Discontinuance in Marital Counseling and Some Observations on Joint Interviews," in Hollis, *Typology of Casework Treatment*, pp. 27–34.

9. Mitzie I. R. Montgomery, "Feedback Systems, Interaction Analysis and Counseling Models in Professional Programs" (doctoral dissertation, University of Edinburgh, 1973).

10. Edward J. Mullen, "Casework Treatment Procedures as a Function of Client Diagnostic Variables" (doctoral dissertation, Columbia University School of Social Work, 1968). Three articles based on the dissertation were published: "Casework Communication," *Social Casework*, 49 (November 1968), 546–551; "The Relation Between Diagnosis and Treatment in Casework," *Social Casework*, 50 (April 1969), 218–226; "Difference in Worker Style in Casework," *Social Casework*, 50 (June 1969), 347–353.

11. Ben Avis Orcutt, "Process Analysis in the First Phase of Treatment," in Pauline Cohen and Merton Krause, eds., *Casework with Wives of Alcoholics* (New York: Family Service Association of America, 1971), pp. 147–164.

12. Francis Turner, "Social Work Treatment and Value Differences" (doctoral dissertation, Columbia University School of Social Work, 1963). An article was based on the dissertation: "A Comparison of Procedures in the Treatment of Clients with Two Different Value Orientations," *Social Casework*, 45 (May 1964), 273–277.

13. Francis Turner, "Ethnic Difference and Client Performance," *Social Service Review*, 44 (March 1970), 1–10.

14. Dorothy Fahs Beck and Mary Ann Jones, *Progress on Family Problems* (New York: Family Service Association of America, 1973).

# PART THREE

# Diagnostic Understanding and the Treatment Process

# Chapter 15

# The Psychosocial Study and Initial Interviews

Thus far we have considered the frame of reference concerning the nature of the individual and his or her situation, upon which psychosocial casework treatment rests, discussing the various means by which the worker endeavors to enable the client to bring improvement in his or her life. We must now turn to the more specific question of how treatment is related to a particular individual confronted by the need to cope with practical and interpersonal problems.

Strong emphasis is placed in psychosocial casework on the importance of trying to understand clearly what the client's problem or dilemma is, and what contributes to it as the basis upon which treatment can be individualized. This understanding rests first upon an accurate and adequate factual base that is obtained primarily, though not by any means entirely, in early interviews; it is called the psychosocial study.

Both client and worker contribute to defining the course treatment will take. It depends first on the nature of the client's difficulty, what he or she sees as the problem, and the kind of help that is sought by each person. In many instances, as the contact moves on, clients develop a different understanding of their troubles and become ready for a kind of help for which they did not at first have any motivation. The worker's contribution to the course treatment takes depends upon knowledge of the nature of the individual who is seeking treatment, of the current situation, of interactions within the person–situation system, and of the variety of factors that are contributing or have contributed to the client's predicament. This seeking of understanding is actually a continuous process, although it is emphasized especially in early interviews. It goes hand in hand with the helping or treatment process itself. At the very beginning, it provides the basis upon which choices are made by client and worker about the duration and nature of treatment.

The way in which the client handles his or her part in such choices, in turn, becomes an important part of the social study. Indeed, the first interview, in which social study begins and important decisions about treatment are made, is of central importance.

## INITIAL DECISIONS

In a first interview, two of the many questions to be answered are (1) is this the right place for the client to be helped? and (2) for how long shall we decide to work together? We usually begin with the first of these—"Can I help you?" or "Can you tell me what the difficulty is?" Later in the interview, perhaps—"Are there other troubles?" "Are there other things you are worrying about?" or even "I get the impression there are other things that may be worrying you." At some later point, one often asks, "How do you think we can help you?" or "Did you have something special in mind that you hoped we could do?"

Sometimes the problem is not one with which the worker or the agency can help, and this has to be explained. Usually, there is some other resource about which one can tell the client. When this is so, it has been demonstrated that "referral" is far more effective than simple "steering."[1] In referral, the worker does not stop with giving information about another resource but, if, the client consents, contacts the other agency, sometimes arranging an appointment, but in any case preparing the way for an easy reception. One must be certain here that the client *wants* this assistance and that our efforts to expedite matters are not seen by the client as either rejection by the worker or railroading him or her into an undesired contact. Sometimes there are questions to be answered about the other resource, and sometimes feelings need to be worked through about whether or not to pursue help at still another place.

### Deciding on Length of Treatment

If it appears that the client has "come to the right place," sometime during that first interview—usually toward the end—a preliminary estimate is made of how long the work will take. (Types of brief service will be discussed further on pages 401 and 438–440.) Sometimes, in the initial interview, client and worker both believe that the client has received all the help needed or available. "Thank you, that's what I needed to know"—from a client who was seeking homemaking services to help with the care of an elderly relative and was given information about resources. "I guess if that's the way it is, I'd better not try to find a job."—from a mother who has learned that there are no local day care facilities for her year-old baby while she works. "I see, I hadn't thought of it that way, I think I can handle it better now"—from a man seeking ideas about how to handle a discussion with his teenage son about marihuana. If the worker does not agree when the client believes the single interview is all that is needed, it is possible to indicate that things seem complicated and that it would be better to go a little more slowly: "Would you be willing to come back to talk further about it?" or "I'm not sure you are entirely clear about that. I could give you another appointment" or "Are you sure about that? Maybe it would be a good idea to talk it over a little more."

Sometimes the agreement at this point is only for another interview so that client and worker can understand the dilemma better before deciding whether or not to continue. At other times a definite commitment can be made for a longer period. The worker usually suggests the time span. It may be, "I think we will need two or three more interviews to think this through" or "I suggest that we plan on weekly interviews for two months"—or three months, as the case may be—or something like, "It takes time to work these things through, it's been a long while that all this has been building up, as you just told me. I think we had better plan to meet weekly for three months and then decide whether you want to go further."

The suggestion of an initial definite time span can be especially helpful with many resistant clients. With others, we may want to say, "It's hard to know yet how long we may want to meet. Let's decide that as we go along and know more about what is involved." There is some evidence that many men tend to prefer a commitment to planned short-term service and that women may be comfortable with open-ended service.[2]

The decision is always a mutual one. The client may refuse, or may suggest a different time period. The worker may either accept the client's decision or pursue the matter further as seems appropriate. Clarifying the time arrangements and arriving at agreement about these as well as about time of appointment and, where appropriate, fees, are part of what is sometimes called "the contract."

## Locating the Problem

A second area for which mutual understanding is needed is that of ascertaining "the problem to be worked on." Sometimes this is quite simply and directly the problem the client brings. It may be concrete —housing, complications in receiving public assistance benefits, planning for day care for children, and so on. Or it may be both practical and psychological—job difficulties, a child's school problem, a marital problem. Experience leads us to think, however, that one can never be sure of this without asking the client whether there are other troubles, or exploring factors that may be contributing to the presenting problem that may also require consideration. For instance, it may develop that the housing problem is acute because neighbors object to unruly children and a host of other contributing problems. The housing problem is still real and perhaps the most urgent part of the problem to be dealt with, but this problem is likely to repeat itself if this remains the sole focus of attention. Or it may be a very elderly person having to move from a fourth-floor walkup. The question then may arise, Is moving to another apartment the best solution? This may require much broader discussion than the housing question alone. Or the client may appear depressed. This needs to be commented on and, if the client is willing, talked about in terms of how long, what precipitated the feelings, and how deep the feelings of depression are (e.g., "How else does it affect you—how is your appetite? Are you sleeping a lot? What do you do with your time? Do you see friends, relatives? What medicines are you taking?"). Not a barrage of questions, of course, but such areas as these should be covered as they appear relevant.

With a child's school problems, in addition to getting specific details of the problem and prior school history, one would certainly inquire about the child's behavior with other children and in the home. One would ask, too, how other children in the home are getting along and about relations between the parents. The latter can easily be explored if one begins with the question of how the other parent responds to the child or the problem. In other words, in psychosocial work we explore outwardly from the problem to areas that one theoretically expects will be related to it. For the child with a school problem this will probably include health, evidence of intellectual ability, signs of learning problems, previous school history, sibling relationships, and so on. Other leads may come from the content of the interview itself. Sometimes there are indications of illness of a family member, work problems, addictions, parental conflict, cultural conflict, and so on.

When the actual problem seems broader than or different from the presenting one, this needs to be commented on in a way that will bring possible complications to the client's attention and ascertain whether the person is willing for these to be a part of the casework process along with the presenting problem. Sometimes one can be quite specific about this, but at other times a more general "These things all seem related, don't they?" or "You do seem troubled about a lot of things, don't you think we need to look at them and try to sort them out" is sufficient. The important thing is that these possible additions to the client's original request for help be brought to his or her attention and that the worker find out whether the client is willing to participate in consideration of them.

In some casework approaches, this defining of the problem is a very specific process ending in a contract that is occasionally put into writing, which specifies just what facet of the problem or behavior will be modified. In the psychosocial approach, initially, while the problem or some aspects of it may be well defined, attention is broader, focusing on other potentially relevant parts of the gestalt, and the process is kept more open for greater understanding as it unfolds to both client and worker. Nevertheless, the client should become aware of what the area of work will be, insofar as it can be foreseen, and should either explicitly or tacitly agree to it.

Sometimes the problem of coming to a common understanding of the dimensions of a difficulty is so complicated that several interviews are needed to help the client arrive at a decision as to whether he or she wants to continue and whether along broad or narrow lines. When the worker thinks it will be impossible to give help if discussion is limited to the restricted area of the presenting problem this must be explained when the time is ripe for it. This might be the case, for example, if it appeared that a child's behavior problem was so directly related to a serious conflict between parents that it would be impossible to help the child without also working on the parents' conflict.

## Who Is to Be Seen?

There is also the question of whether to proceed with the applicant alone or to suggest seeing others in the family. If the latter seems to be advisable, a brief explanation of the advantages of seeing more than one person in a family relationship can be made. If there is resistance to this suggestion, reasons for the client's feelings can be discussed. Sometimes it is best to plan individual interviews, sometimes joint treatment of two or more people, at other times the whole family may become involved. As was discussed elsewhere, one can move back and forth from one mode to another as each seems called for. In the first interview, one merely decides upon the immediate future. Diagnostic understanding in many family problems can be greatly facilitated by multiple-person or family interviews, for then one has an opportunity to observe directly the interplay, or transactions, among family members.

## Observation and Deduction

While all this is going on, the worker is observing closely the ways in which the client handles the interview and the way in which he or she relates to the worker. Is the client direct and open, relating naturally to the worker and explaining the situation in a fairly clear way? Or does the person appear anxious and fearful? confused? withdrawn? hostile? overly friendly? Are some of the ego defense mechanisms apparent? Is affect appropriate to the material the client is discussing? Does he or she seem depressed? Is there reason to suspect any form of neurological illness? Such things are learned from observation and deduction within the interview as the client explains the problem and talks about the present situation, related past events, and his or her own efforts to deal with the relationships and the situation. It is particularly useful to get a full picture of what the client has already tried to do about the trouble —what has worked, and what has failed. This tells us a great deal about the client's ego capacities, ability to "cope," and ways of doing so.

## GAINS IN FIRST INTERVIEW

Progress can usually be made in the first interview, not only in defining the problem but also in securing information that will lead to understanding of the interlocking factors that may be contributing to it. This not only helps the worker, but also turns the client's mind toward factors that he or she may later want to think about more fully.

Where the problem concerns feelings, the client typically experiences relief in the first interview simply by talking about himself or herself and situation to a worker who is constantly attentive, appreciates the person's feelings, is accepting, and offers help. On the other hand, sometimes when the client is part of the problem, it is difficult for him or her to come to even a beginning realization of this fact. Such difficulties can be recognized by the worker and talked about together.

Treatment thus begins immediately. The worker's way of greeting the client and opening the interview conveys respect, interest, and a desire to help. If the interview is unhurried, with the time protected so that it will not be interrupted, the client benefits by feeling the full and undivided attention of the worker. Surroundings, insofar as possible, should be attractive and professional in style for this conveys respect for the client. Ideally, a client will leave the first interview feeling some relief from pressure, some hope that here is someone who is competent to help, and, at best, take the first steps toward an understanding and alleviation of the problem.

## EXPLORATORY PERIOD

After the first interview, social study, diagnostic understanding, and treatment continue to go hand in hand. Each interview adds its increment as new aspects of the person and the person–situation gestalt emerge. The worker is dealing with a living, changing process. Feelings change, new events constantly occur, people reveal themselves more fully as trust grows. One needs to continue to be sensitive to nuances of the client's feelings and responses and to the significance of new information throughout the contact, although the main outlines of a psychosocial study are arrived at early in the contact. The length of time this takes and the amount of information secured is proportionate to the time span agreed on for treatment. All of these are directly related to the complexity of the problem and the extent to which client and worker try to deal with these complexities. Obviously, if it is decided that a very brief contact is appropriate, one sticks close to the "problem to be solved" in seeking information. In more extended treatment, the original social study, leading to a fairly good understanding of the client's needs and the main treatment themes, is usually completed within the first five or six interviews. During this early exploratory period, the client himself also gains further understanding of the trouble, benefits from the ventilation that occurs, and experiences support from the worker. Often, considerable progress can be made in working on and resolving practical problems. Intrareflection is usually also encouraged, but with some cautiousness and tentativeness until the dimensions of the problem are clarified. The client's responses to all forms of reflective communications are among the most important sources of diagnostic understanding. The better the client is able to think clearly about himself or herself and the situation, the more likely it is that he or she will be able to make the necessary changes.[3]

## THE FACT-GATHERING PROCESS

It is extremely important to be clear about the difference between psychosocial study, a process of gathering facts, and diagnostic understanding. They do go on at the same time, but this does not mean that they are the same thing. Psychosocial study is a process of observation and orderly arrangement of the facts observed about a client and his or her situation. Diagnostic understanding, on the other hand, represents *the thinking* of the worker *about* the facts—the inferences drawn from them. It will be strongly influenced by the frame of reference used for guidance in understanding the meaning of the facts. Mary Richmond once quoted an apt statement from Dr. Richard Cabot: "In social study you open your eyes and look, in diagnosis you close them and think."[4] If these diverse processes are not kept separate in the worker's mind, there is great danger of skewing the facts to fit the theory, asking questions in such a way that answers fitting a priori assumptions are apt to emerge. As we have indicated, during the study process the worker will indeed be reaching for diagnostic understanding in his or her own mind. Preliminary formulations help in knowing what areas need further exploration. Nevertheless, it is essential to guard against "contamination" of one by the other, making a clear distinction between facts and opinions.

How does the worker know what lines of inquiry to follow in a psychosocial study, and how does one go about it? People come to a caseworker with a specific problem. "My child is irritable, mopes, and pays no attention to what I say." Or, "Since my husband died a year ago everything has gone wrong. Now the rent is going up. I don't want to be a burden to any of the children." Or, "We just can't understand each other any more—every time I open my mouth she takes the other side." Always there is an interpersonal or a person–situation gestalt involved. Or, to put it another way, certain systems are involved—the husband–wife system, the family system, the parent–child system, health, school, work. A set of interacting forces is at work, and what goes on in one system, may be affecting what happens in another. The worker listens to the client receptively but not passively. Knowledge of factors that often contribute to different kinds of dilemmas immediately suggests the various systems that may be pertinent. In a marital problem, for instance, the worker is concerned first with the interactions between the partners. Then the worker needs understanding of the major features of the two personalities. Children may also be part of the picture. Since marital problems are so often complicated by interactions with relatives, the worker is alert to references to members of the extended family, either currently or earlier in life, and uses these to inquire about major relationships. Factors in the husband's or wife's employment system are often of significance. Friendships may be important.

A parent–child problem would involve some of these same systems plus additional ones, especially at school. In the case of the older person facing a decision about living arrangements, not only are immediate family relationships important, but also the families of the children (if living with them is at issue), friends and neighbors, the housing situation, the client's health, and resources for alternative living arrangements. Each type of problem that emerges in early interviews suggests to the worker avenues that may need to be explored.

The fact-gathering process receives its impetus and direction from two sources: the client's desire to tell about the difficulties and the worker's desire to understand what they are, how they came about, and what capacities exist for dealing with them. Psychosocial casework uses a fluid form of interviewing that combines these two sets of interests. By encouraging the client to follow trends of thought related to the problem as they come naturally to his or her mind and by leading the client to develop them further, the worker gains access with relative ease to the elaboration of significant matters. At the same time, the worker often must fill the inevitable gaps in this type of exploration by directing the interview along lines that the client does not spontaneously introduce. The worker can do so easily when such matters are "adjacent" to subjects the client is discussing or flow logically from them, or he or she can explore them when the client has temporarily exhausted spontaneous productions and is ready to follow the therapist's lead. "You have never told me much about your father." "Set me straight on your schooling—where were you when you finished?" "You haven't said much about your work—what do you do and how do you like it?" The caseworker needs to take a fairly active part in the gathering of information, for, as we have seen, it is not possible in casework to depend on free association to lead to significant material. Clients cannot be expected to know completely what information is needed, nor can they always free themselves, without help, from reluctance to discuss painful material that may be highly relevant to an understanding of their troubles.

In areas in which a problem appears, it is important to inquire not only about the details of the problem but also about the client's participation in the difficulty. It is not enough for the client to say, "My wife is a spendthrift"; the worker needs to follow up with specific questions. "In what way?" "Can you tell me something that has happened recently?" By getting detailed accounts of what happens in the client's household when there is a conflict about money, the worker can evaluate to what extent overspending is actually occurring, what sorts of situations either within the wife or in the interaction between husband and wife touch it off, what purpose it may serve in the marital relationship, the part the husband's response to the overspending may play in its repetition, and so on. The event or circumstances that precipitated the client's decision to come for help are usually of considerable significance, although it may be a minor event in itself.

The best way to secure a clear picture of interaction is not to ask direct questions, but rather to encourage the client—or, if it is a joint or family interview, the clients—to describe things in detail. This tends to bring a good deal of ventilation and enables the client to relive the situation with details of what each partner said and did. This style of interviewing does not interrupt the natural flow of the client's thoughts, yet allows the worker to observe the nature of the interplay.

If initial evidence indicates that there is little or no basis for an accusation made by a husband, for instance, the worker looks for the circumstances under which the client believes it to be true, what within the client or in the marital interaction might have touched it off, and what purpose his unrealistic reaction serves. Again, an important aspect of these explorations is their revelation of how the client tries to cope with whatever difficulty he is experiencing, knowledge that is especially useful in throwing light on the question of ego functioning.

Throughout the interview, the worker is also observing carefully the client's reactions in response to the treatment situation itself. How much does he demand of the worker and what is the nature of these demands? How sensitive is he to criticism? What defenses are being used? How accurately is he aware of the worker's reactions? To what extent and under what circumstances is he warm, hostile, remote toward the worker? These observations throw light particularly on the nature of the client's demands of others, and of his life situation, and on ego and superego functioning.

## Physical and Emotional Illness

An important area of the social study that should not be neglected is the client's physical health. In fact, some writers refer to a "biopsychosocial" study. The psychosocial worker is alert not only to what the client says about his or her health, but also to other signs that might point in the direction of illness. Appearance, of course, tells a good deal. Other indications of illness that the client may not fully appreciate appear in references to poor appetite, tiredness, or trouble sleeping, as well as to mild symptomatology such as pain, swelling, rashes, indigestion, dizziness, and so on. It is known that certain physical conditions have characteristic effects on personality functioning, and alertness to them will often help account for the client's reactions. Quite aside from these constant effects, any illness is also likely to play a significant part in interpersonal difficulties. It frequently causes pain or anxiety;[5] it often increases narcissistic attitudes and provokes regression to greater dependence; it can be used as an escape from unpleasant responsibilities; it can change the self-image and distort relationships in family life, between husband and wife and between siblings. The worker is also alert to the effect of bodily changes associated with different periods of life—the uneven growth rate and the genital as well as secondary sexual growth changes of adolescence, reactions to the climacteric, and to the physical changes of old age. Unusual physical features or disabilities also have direct bearing on social and inner functioning.

When personal adjustment problems are involved, it is also well to inquire about the use of drugs that have psychological effects. Legal drugs of this type are still frequently prescribed by physicians, and supplies can sometimes be secured for self-dosage. They often contribute to troublesome moods. "Are you under a doctor's care? What has he prescribed?" Or, "Has your doctor given you anything to quiet your nerves?" Or, "To help you sleep?" Or, "To pep you up?" To the person who is not seeing a doctor—"Do you sometimes need to take something to keep your nerves quiet?" One need not inquire routinely about such drugs as deliriants, hallucinating agents, and the opiates. But it is most important to be alert to the possibility of their use, especially with younger clients, and to ask about them if there is some likelihood that they are being used. Familiarity with physical changes and behavioral indicators associated with drug addiction is essential. The timing and way in which these inquiries are made are, of course, of crucial importance.[6]

The worker needs also to be alert for indications of mental or emotional illness or symptomatology. Clients often refer to these tangentially, or even describe them without realizing their significance. Periods of "nervousness," "tiredness," "depression," or extreme boredom should be inquired about. References to periods of hospitalization or long absences from work may mean mental illness or alcoholism as well as physical illness. If reference is made to loss of memory or to periods of "blanking out," further questions about this should be asked. Data that might point toward depersonalization should be followed up. Flight of ideas and substitution of associative thinking for logical thought should be noted if they occur. Affect can be observed. Compulsions usually reveal themselves or are mentioned by the client.

## Early History

So far we have been considering mainly data from the present or recent past. To what extent does the psychosocial caseworker go into earlier history? Certainly, the worker wants to learn the client's thoughts about when the present difficulty began. This may be in the recent past, some years earlier, or, in some instances, in early life. Sometimes, however, the client does not see childhood and adolescence as pertinent to the problem unless the worker in some way makes a connection. Exploration of early life, of course, is made only when the worker has specific reason to believe that this will throw light on the problem. Such exploration tends to be thematic rather than wide ranging, pursuing certain relationships or certain time periods that seem to have relevance.

Unexplained gaps in a history are sometimes due to a period of trouble—mental or emotional illness, difficulty with the law, or periods of mental conflict and pain. One needs to be alert to the sequence of events, especially important happenings that preceded or coincided with periods of symptomatology or poor functioning. For instance, a child's regression may have followed the severe illness or death of a parent, especially if the child was kept in the dark about it and never helped to work through the grief. Changes in employment may bring a change in family patterns and perceptions and contribute to marked changes in family behavior and relationships. The same careful regard for details must attend the exploration of the client's past that accompanies the exploration of current events. It is not enough for the client to say, "My mother always preferred my older brother." The worker seeks out the details, asking, "In what way?" "What makes you think so?" "Could you tell me more about that?"

Thus, the study starts with what the client sees as the problem and its antecedents, as well as what he or she has tried to do about it and has thought about how it can be resolved. If appropriate, the study can then move on to look for present and sometimes past factors that may be contributing to the current dilemma.

Throughout this exploration, one must be attuned to the anxieties of the client. One does not push through defenses. If a client is reluctant to talk about something that seems important, it is possible to comment on this reluctance. Perhaps the client can tell you why. Perhaps he or she cannot do so or continues to resist. One can say, "Perhaps later on you will be able to talk about this. I think it will help you if you can bring yourself to it." Or, "It will help us to understand what is happening better." If the worker thinks the reluctance to talk may be due to distrust or to the worker's attitudes, this too can be explored. "I know it's hard to talk about some things. You don't know me very well yet. Perhaps later you will trust me to understand."

We see, then, that although psychosocial workers do not follow a set pattern for social study interviews, they do have in mind definite ideas concerning the type of information they want to obtain about the client and his or her situation. A great deal of ineffectual drifting and failure to formulate suitable treatment approaches results when the caseworker is too passive in seeking specific information, especially in early interviews.

## Additional Sources of Information

In recent years, there has been a growing emphasis upon the importance of not limiting social study to office interviews with the client only. It is now widely accepted that in cases of marital difficulty, for example, there are great advantages in seeing both spouses—either individually or in joint interviews—for their value in social study at least and, whenever possible, for treatment also. Some therapists refuse treatment altogether unless such interviews can be arranged. Others (with whom the writers agree) would certainly favor interviewing all persons involved in a major way in a problem, but would not insist on it if the client is strongly opposed or if the others concerned are unwilling to participate. Just as we would not push past defenses, we would explore the client's reluctance to having joint or family meetings rather than insist that the client or others participate in them. However, if this type of interview is handled as a routine expectation rather than as a major issue, the client usually accepts it as a natural procedure, unless there are special reasons for the interview to be regarded with concern. If there are such reasons, it is important to understand them, for they often can contribute information that is of great diagnostic significance. Such interviews may include husband and wife, parent and child, or a whole family together. As was noted in the chapters on family therapy, observing the interaction between people can throw a great deal of light on the complementarity, or lack of it, of their behavior, on discrepancies between their individual perceptions and the realities of how they act and how others respond and act, as these appear to a trained outsider.[7]

Another possible important source of understanding is the visit to the client's home.[8] Clients may be sensitive about this because in some settings it has become a form of "snooping" for information that may be purposely withheld. With this in mind when a home visit would be important, the client must be given an honest explanation of how such a visit will add to the worker's understanding and ability to help. Such a plan would be pursued only if and when the client is clearly willing for the worker to come. The home visit makes possible important observations about family functioning, the family's pride in its home, and many personality characteristics of its occupants. Firsthand witnessing of a client's interaction with children in the natural setting of the home provides especially significant diagnostic data. When certain types of situational problems are of importance, or with the "hard-to-reach" family, home visits are essential. In other cases, it is well to grasp any natural opportunity that arises for an interview in the home as a means of widening the scope of the social study. It is not, however, essential or even advisable in all types of cases.

In addition to interviews with the client and the immediate family, it is also sometimes useful to consult, with the client's knowledge and on a very selective basis, other people who may be in a posistion to add to the worker's understanding of the client. When a child is involved, it may be particularly useful to talk with the teacher or nursery school leader. Often, a contact with a doctor yields valuable medical information. Occasionally a clergyman, employer, relative, or friend can add to the understanding of a particular aspect of the client's problem. As discussed in the chapters on environmental work, it is always important in seeing collaterals to gauge the potential effect of the interview on the client and his or her relationship to the worker. Only under exceptional circumstances, principally of a protective nature, is it wise to seek information at the expense of arousing antitherapeutic reactions in the client. This is not to say that contacts with other people should never be made if the client is anxious about them. Anxiety frequently occurs, at least to a mild degree, but discussion with the client beforehand gives an opportunity for helping the client with the anxiety before and after the interview with the collateral. As was suggested earlier, under some circumstances, one can lessen such anxiety by suggesting that the client participate in discussions with collaterals if he or she wishes to do so.

Obviously, reports of medical or psychiatric diagnosis or treatment, of psychological tests, and of treatment in other social agencies may be pertinent to the social study. These and other types of written material should be secured selectively during the social study period as well as later in the contact.

As the caseworker learns about the client and his or her life, the worker begins to form opinions about the nature of the client's difficulty. Often, in trying to formulate diagnostic thinking, the worker recognizes gaps in a psychosocial study, areas of information about which further inquiry must be made in order to arrive at a clearer picture of the client and the situation. This is good and necessary. The worker must guard against allowing speculation to substitute for facts. The best way to obtain a clear and accurate picture is to enable the client to have sufficient confidence in the worker so that he or she can speak fully and frankly.[9]

## NOTES

1. See Leonard S. Kogan, "The Short-Term Case in a Family Agency," *Social Casework*, 38 (June 1957), 296–302. Also, in their broad study of family agency services, Dorothy Fahs Beck and Mary Ann Jones report: "Advance contact by the counselor with the resource to which a client is referred was found to increase significantly the proportion of clients who follow through on a referral." See *Progress on Family Problems* (New York: Family Service Association of America, 1973), pp. 6, 67.

2. See Brenda Wattie, "Evaluating Short-Term Casework in a Family Agency," *Social Casework*, 55 (December 1973). For references to planned short-term treatment, crisis treatment, and the "contract," see Chapter 18, notes 6, 7, 8, 9, 10.

3. For a valuable approach to initial interviews from the point of view of communication, see Judith C. Nelsen's chapter on the subject in her book, *Communication Theory and Social Work* (Chicago: University of Chicago Press, 1980), pp. 43–65. See also Wayne D. Duehn and Nazneed Mayadas, "Starting Where the Client Is: An Empirical Investigation," *Social Casework*, 60 (February 1979), 67–74, for an interesting study and discussion of the importance of empathically "hearing" the client's concerns and priorities in intake interviews.

4. Mary Richmond, *Social Diagnosis* (New York: Russell Sage Foundation, 1917), p. 347.

5. For an interesting discussion of this, see Mark Zborowski, "Cultural Components in Response to Pain," *Journal of Social Issues,* 8 (1952), 16–30. For other readings relevant to this subject, see Norman Decker, "Anxiety in the General Hospital," in William E. Fann et al., eds., *Phenomenology and Treatment of Anxiety* (New York: Spectrum, 1979), pp. 287–298; Ursula Granite, "Foundations for Social Work on Open-Heart Surgery Service," *Social Casework,* 59 (February 1978), 101–105; and Alice Ullmann, "Teaching Medical Students to Understand Stress in Illness," *Social Casework,* 57 (November 1976), 568–574.

6. See Julius Rubin, "Drug Addiction," Chapter 22, in George Wiedeman, *Personality Development and Deviation* (New York: International Universities Press, 1975).

7. See notes to chapters 10 and 11. A recent article examining family-oriented interviewing and treatment in social work suggests that caseworkers' lack of knowledge and training for family work has limited its use by them. On the basis of a survey designed to determine family, caseworker, and agency needs, specific training objectives are recommended to help caseworkers learn to understand family interaction and communication and become skilled at intervening. See Linda M. Anderson et al., "Training in Family Treatment: Needs and Objectives," *Social Casework,* 60 (June 1979), 323–329. Without adequate training, of course, the caseworker can be confounded by the vast amount of data derived from family interviews and thus be unable to use it meaningfully for social study purposes.

8. Recently, the value of the home visit for observation, diagnosis, treatment, and research has been increasingly recognized, having fallen into disrepute for some years previously. For readings that discuss and illustrate its use for a wide variety of client populations and problems, see Marjorie Behrens and Nathan Ackerman, "The Home Visit as an Aid in Family Diagnosis and Therapy," *Social Casework,* 37 (January 1956), 11–19; Rachel A. Levine, "Treatment in the Home," *Social Work,* 9 (January 1964), 19–28; Sharon K. Moynihan, "Home Visits for Family Treatment," *Social Casework,* 55 (December 1974), 612–617; David Kantor and William Lehr, *Inside the Family* (San Francisco: Jossey-Bass, 1975); Jules Henry, *Pathways to Madness* (New York: Random House, 1971); and Frances H. Scherz, "Family Interaction: Some Problems and Implications for Casework," in Howard J. Parad and Roger R. Miller, eds., *Ego-Oriented Casework: Problems and Perspectives* (New York: Family Service Association of America, 1963), especially pp. 139–141.

9. For historical background as well as their relevance to this chapter, the reader is referred to chapters 3, 4, and 5 in Richmond, *Social Diagnosis* and chapters 6, 7, and 8 in Gordon Hamilton, *Theory and Practice of Social Casework,* 2nd ed. (New York: Columbia University Press, 1951).

# Chapter 16

# Assessment and Diagnostic Understanding

Understanding is central to psychosocial treatment. Much understanding is intuitive. One immediately senses anxiety, anger, grief. Common knowledge of causative factors brings immediate explanations to mind. But common knowledge is notoriously unreliable.[1] It constitutes only a first step in the process of understanding, providing hypotheses to be checked against reality. Through the psychosocial study, the worker seeks to come as close as possible to securing an accurate picture of the client's inner and outer situation. In assessment and diagnosis, the worker attempts to *understand* that picture in order to answer the question, "How can this person be helped?"

The term "diagnosis" has been under a shadow in recent years because it has come to symbolize for some social workers what they term the "medical model" of casework. These workers claim that those who use the word "diagnosis" are placing all the responsibility for difficulty on the client rather than on the situation and are furthermore concentrating on the person's weaknesses—the "illness," the "pathology"—rather than on his or her strengths and abilities. This would be true if one sought diagnostic understanding of the client and his or her weaknesses alone. It is *not* true if one seeks also to understand situational components, to assess both strengths and weaknesses and to understand the interactions or transactions that constantly recur between the various components of the system or gestalt of which the client is a part. Without wasting time arguing about semantics, let it be said that the point of view of this book is that either the client or the situation or both may be making a major contribution to the problem, that it is in their interaction and interrelationships that many explanations can be found, and that the recognition of strengths is of paramount importance to diagnostic assessment.

## CLIENT–WORKER PARTICIPATION

Client and worker in psychosocial casework both participate in developing diagnostic understanding. Once the value of trying to understand the reasons for feelings and behavior is established—or better still, experienced—clients themselves will often seek explanations and contributing factors. The worker also suggests lines of thought and often tests hypotheses by asking for the client's reactions to them. "From what you say it seems as though Steve's bed wetting began shortly after Jane broke her leg—I expect you had to concentrate a lot on Jane for awhile.—Do you think there's a connection?" Or, "It sounds as if you were really furious at your mother for staying so long. Was it easier to take it out on Ann?" Or, "Have you asked Bill if he would put the kids to bed or do you just wait for him to offer?"

In each of these illustrations, the worker's thinking was ahead of the client's. This is not always the case. Many clients spontaneously seek explanations of behavior and express their own thinking to which the worker in turn reacts. These explanations sometimes show considerable insight; at other times, they are rationalizations and intellectualizations to which the worker may listen in silence or respond with indications of doubt—"Perhaps, but I think there is more to it than that." Or, "Are you really satisfied with that yourself?" Or, "You know, you've read a lot of psychology and sometimes knowledge of that kind can get in the way of real understanding. It's your feelings that are important. Try just to let them come and not bother so much about reasons and explanations."

Ordinarily, the worker can be expected to understand more quickly and more fully than the client. This is so for several reasons. (1) People are often blind to what they are doing and reveal by behavior many things of which they are not aware. (2) Although every situation is unique and different in detail from all others it is also true that, in general, human beings have a great deal in common, react in similiar ways, develop in similar ways, and are exposed to similar life events. Working over and over again with clients caught in successive dilemmas, not identical but nevertheless similar, enables the clinical social worker to understand the new client's problem more quickly and more fully than would be possible without prior experience. (3) Knowledge has been accumulated by social work, psychiatry, and the social sciences that can illuminate human problems and that is part of the clinical social worker's education. This consists of knowledge of the dynamics of behavior and of human development, knowledge of family functioning and of the social environment, and knowledge of the various ways in which interacting factors in both past and present can create problems of either pressure and deprivation or of dysfunctioning.

## THE ASSESSMENT PROCESS

How, then, does the process of diagnostic assessment proceed? The total process of assessment consists of trying to understand (1) what is the trouble? (2) what seems to be contributing to the trouble? and (3) what can be changed and modified? In each of these questions, strengths as well as weaknesses in both person and situation are important considerations.

Diagnostic assessment takes place in two different ways. First, as the worker listens in each interview to what the client is saying, he or she constantly tries to answer the three questions just posed, for what he or she does in the immediate interview will be determined by this understanding. Second, periodically during the total contact, the worker needs to look back over all that is known about the person–situation gestalt in order to answer these questions more fully in the light of this total knowledge. When treatment is expected to continue beyond a few interviews, the first of these more extensive assessments should occur no later than the fourth to sixth contact when the initial social study will have been completed. This should provide sufficient information to arrive at a working basis for the major outlines of ongoing treatment, subject to modification by later diagnostic reassessment. This first diagnostic thinking is taken as a set of working probabilities to be constantly rechecked, extended, and modified, as additional information emerges during ongoing treatment and as the client's feelings, attitudes, and circumstances change.

In order to understand what the trouble is, the worker begins by a sort of scanning of the whole "field"—all the facts brought out in the psychosocial study. Assessment of the individual and the situation here go hand in hand. One must understand the pressures a person is under before one can have any opinion about the adequacy or inadequacy of his or her functioning. In the end, we are concerned with the interaction between the person and the situation, but in order to comprehend this interaction we must see the separate elements clearly.

## The Situation

In evaluating the situational component, one can use the concept of "an average expectable environment" where the term "average expectable" signifies "within the range of normally healthy experience."[2] It is where the actual experiences vary to a substantial degree from these expectable ones, expecially where they vary in the negative direction, that worker and client both look for external "press"—factors that contribute to the client's problem. By this standard, an income below the poverty line would constitute an external pressure; so would being subject to race prejudice; so would substandard housing, poor schooling, inadequate medical care, poor health, lack of employment opportunity, extremely stressful or unpleasant working conditions, and so on.

On the positive side, one looks for the availability of better schools, the practical possibility of moving to a better neighborhood, the strengths of a skillful teacher, the young adult in family or friendship network who might help a disturbed adolescent, the relative or friend on whom a depressed adult or a disabled older person might depend, the availability of work, of retraining, of an understanding employer, and so on. If the family has church connections, is this a resource? Within the family, one also looks for strengths—who are the giving people? Who can take leadership in resolving problems? Where are the strengths of the family?

In personal relationships, an "average expectable environment" assumes reasonably satisfying family relationships and opportunities for friendships. This does not mean that these relationships are necessarily conflict-free or completely satisfying, any more than, in the area of income, "average" is equated with great wealth. There is room within the norm in human relationships for considerable tension. These expectations vary, of course, according to ethnic, class, race, and other variables, and must be viewed from the standpoint of both general expectations and those of the client. An extremely authoritative husband may be "expectable" in Turkish culture, but he may be experienced as a distinct "pressure" by a woman brought up in this country or even by a Turkish woman if she has lived here long enough to partially take on more equalitarian ideas. The client's own view of these factors is of paramount importance. To what extent does he or she experience these as stress factors?

If a parent is concerned about a child, whom the parent sees as a problem, the worker can assess the quality of the parents' functioning only in the light of the realities of the child's behavior, by which the parents are confronted. What is this son or daughter like to live with at the moment? Has the child withdrawn into himself or herself so that he or she is hard to reach? Is the child provocative in a hostile way, giving ample cause for parental anger? Is the child's behavior publicly embarrassing to the parents? If the child is ill, how much of a strain does caring for him or her cause? Does this deprive the parents of sleep? Is the mother constantly running up and down stairs, or involved in all sorts of special cookery?

Obviously, in any sort of interpersonal problem, the worker must get as accurate a picture as possible of the pressures, or "presses," to which the client is responding. Moreover, it is the exception rather than the rule to find the pressure in one spot alone; usually, there are other people in either the immediate or wider family who are also contributing to the client's difficulty. Family functioning is of paramount importance. Otto Pollak[3] rightly called our attention to the pressures brought by grandparents, aunts, and uncles, and by other more distant relatives of either of the parents, on the problems of children. Not infrequently, these pressures occur in marital problems also.

Even when they are not presented by the client as a major problem, employment, housing, and neighborhood conditions are possible sources of pressure in parent–child and husband–wife conflict. Certainly, the realities of the school environment are of great significance for children. Social institutions such as the courts and police have causative as well as remedial impact in problems of nonconformity.

A dimension of assessment that seems to lie midway between the external and internal factors is the individual's physical condition. In assessing the extent of health factors as pressure components, the worker takes account not only of any diagnosed medical condition, but also of all the information secured in the social study about the person's physical condition. Specific illnesses have known specific effects on personality. Slowness or precociousness in physical maturation can contribute in a major way to interpersonal and intrapersonal difficulties. Especially with older people, physical limitations are of paramount importance. Poor hearing and poor eyesight severely limit pleasure in social contacts and in interests such as TV watching, reading, sewing, and many hobbies. Sheer weakness and lack of endurance can interfere with the client's seeking medical and other services that require street travel or long periods of waiting. Some older people are malnourished to the point of severe incapacity simply because they no longer have the strength to cook or to go to the store. The latter is true both in poor or dangerous neighborhoods, where older people are often found in the cheaper fourth- , fifth- , and sixth-floor walk-up apartments and in more affluent areas where stores are several blocks away.

It is particularly important to weigh the degree of *functional* disability in any of the more permanent handicaps. A heart specialist, for instance, usually classifies patients according to their capacity for normal life. Varying degrees of legal blindness carry differing functional capacities. There seems to be wide divergence between the amount of brain damage that exists and the extent to which functioning is impaired. Functional disability may well lessen as the client's hope and confidence increase.

## The Personality System

In assessment of the personality system, it is again helpful to use the concept of "average expectations." Flexible norms exist within every cultural group that set up in a general way expectations of how an individual with a "healthy" personality will act. These expectations create a theoretical frame of reference against which one can view the functioning of any individual. It is important to keep in mind the fact that this is *theoretical*. It does not imply a *stereotype* of expectations of how a "healthy individual" will function. Wilson Bentley, who spent a lifetime studying snow crystals, took over 6,000 photomicrographic pictures of snow flakes. Out of these 6,000 pictures, he was unable to discover any two that were identical. John Stewart Collis[4] in his discussion of Bentley's research writes: "The variety is inexhaustible, but very often (though it would be rash to say always) the foundation of a hexagonal shape is adhered to, so that each is a little star with six rays crossing at an angle of sixty degrees. Then if the crystal looks like a composition of ferns it will have six outpointing leaves; if like a windmill, it will have six sails; if like a sundial, it will have six corners; if like an assembly of swords, it will have six blades; if like a star-fish, it will have six ribs; if a fir tree, it will have six stems likewise set in perfect symmetrical precision." People are a bit more complicated than snow flakes, but they too have both infinite individuality and patterns in common!

Personality is so complicated that one has to view its functioning in a systematic way in order to understand and to assess its strengths and weaknesses. Here psychoanalytic personality theory can be useful. It can provide a picture of the "patterns"—the basic structures of humans —from which individual variations grow. Just as one scans the field of the client's milieu, the various systems of the person–situation gestalt, so one can assess the data of the social study that concerns the person. To do so quickly and carefully, the worker is helped by keeping in mind general knowledge of the major aspects of personality functioning. These include the three major divisions of drive functioning, ego functioning, and superego functioning. Again, it must be stressed that the breadth of personality assessment needed depends upon the nature of the problem and the sort of assistance or treatment that can be offered.

*DRIVES.* We referred earlier to two major types of drive—libidinal and aggressive. Despite the risk of repetitiousness, we will list some of the factors to look for again because it is so important to keep them in mind. Essentially, the worker will want to evaluate to what extent a person is capable of mature love, friendship, consideration of others, and trust in others. To what extent is an individual handicapped by an unusual degree of narcissism, or an unusual amount of dependence? Is the person relatively free of residuals of infantile stages of development or does greediness or overtalkativeness point toward excessive orality? Do too many residuals of the habit training period show in such traits as stinginess, compulsive orderliness, or overcleanliness? Is there overconcentration on qualities normal to the phallic period of the child's development, when the child is preoccupied with the wonders of sexuality but has not yet integrated this with the tenderness and constancy of mature love? Is the person relatively consistent in his or her feelings, or is there an unusual amount of ambivalence? Are there unresolved hostilities or overly intense positive attachments to parents? Is the person able to love someone of the opposite sex, or is he or she attracted primarily to his or her own sex? What about aggression? Is the individual able to stand up for himself or herself and to pursue goals with vigor? Is the person able to be angry appropriately and to a realistic degree? Or is aggression characterized by destructiveness, a desire to hurt, and hatred and hostility that are too easily aroused?

The term "oedipal problem" is often used to describe an overly strong attachment to a parent, as if this were a total diagnosis. When properly used, this term denotes a type of drive assessment describing the degree of psychosexual maturation. An error to be avoided is that of mistaking a primitive oral attachment to the mother for an oedipal disturbance. Even if the observation of an overly strong oedipal tie is correct, it will not be of much value if the worker regards it as a total answer to the problem and is satisfied to stop diagnostic thinking at that point. It is only as the assessment is later used in the dynamic diagnosis that it takes on real meaning. Then one looks at such questions as how the oedipal tie affects relationships to others. Obviously, the extent to which such questions as these can be answered depends upon the facts secured in the social study, and this in turn would have been guided by the kind of problem with which the client was seeking help.

THE EGO.   As noted earlier, particular attention has been given in recent years to *ego qualities*. From the data of the social study, the worker needs to assess many of these qualities. One of the most important of these is perception.

Is the individual capable of seeing things as they are, or is there some constant distortion of reality? Is the person able to test perceptions and plans for action against reality before coming to conclusions about them? How sound is the person's judgment? Does the individual appear to be intellectually average? dull? exceptionally keen? To what extent is his or her thinking still dominated by primary thought processes? Is the self-image fairly accurate or does he or she overestimate or underestimate actual abilities? Does the person have adequate self-respect, a sense of self-worth? To what extent is the individual clear about his or her own identity? What major identifications does he or she have? Is there anything unusual about fantasies? Is impulse control adequate? How able is the person to act, to cope, to get things done? Is the person usually able to take charge of his or her own behavior? Are affects appropriate, and is the person able to express them adequately? Is the individual capable of establishing satisfying relationships with others? How anxious is the person, and how does he or she handle this anxiety?

What defenses are there against anxiety? Are these in the main helpful, or are they dysfunctional in terms of the life situation? Are they adequate, or is the anxiety breaking through? Are they distorting relationships? Impoverishing the emotional life? In general, what is the level of competence?

One must be especially careful in assessing intelligence, for it is easy to confuse the results of educational level or cultural background with basic intelligence. Recent years have demonstrated only too well the shortcomings of most intelligence tests. Furthermore, functional intelligence can be lowered by depression, anxiety, distraction, and other emotional features. If assessing intelligence appears to be a problem, a more definitive assessment can be made by a well trained psychologist.

One sometimes hears the term "ego strength" used as if the ego were some kind of composite force that could be measured as a unit. Rather, it is a series of functions and qualities of many different dimensions. Perception is accurate or inaccurate, judgment is sound or unsound, self-image is appropriate or inappropriate. One may be highly competent or relatively incompetent; function more or less autonomously; one may have good or poor capacity for object relationships. Only controls may be strong or weak. One may say about the ego as a whole that it functions well or poorly, but this description is not useful as a delineation of *which* aspects of the ego function well and which poorly, and when poorly, in what way.

As with the drives, the extent to which the worker needs to assess ego qualities varies with the predicament about which the client is seeking or willing to accept help. Their assessment is arrived at by deductions from the picture the client gives of the problem, the situation, and himself or herself, and from the direct observation of the client and his or her functioning in interviews.

*THE SUPEREGO.* Superego qualities are also important. When a person feels guilt, is it appropriate and commensurate with its cause? Is the person overly critical or overly self-punishing for what would usually be thought of as minor shortcomings? Are there lacunae—spots where standards would be expected but are absent? Is there general weakness in self-standards? Is the ego ideal commensurate with background and life roles? How stable is it? Are there indications of inconsistencies, such as those characteristic of narcissistic and borderline personalities?

In evaluating the client's *superego* functioning, the worker considers both the general structure of the superego—its relative strength or weakness in the personality—and the *quality* of its demands, that is, the level of its demands and the consistency of the standards it supports. Particularly in this aspect of the personality, assessment is made in the light of ethnic background, class, education, regional differences, and variations in age. Aspirations are an important part of the ego ideal, a component of the superego. Clients sometimes have multiple reference groups from which the ego ideal is derived: they are exposed to the general culture, which upholds one set of aspirations, and to family and peer cultures, which may be quite different. Is there conflict among these demands?

*VARIABLE EXPECTATIONS.*   Forming an opinion about whether or not a person's functioning is within the "average expectable" range or varies from it sufficiently to be problematic is not an easy task. As indicated in Chapter 2 in the discussion of role expectations, there is no single model of appropriate responses. What is adequate or normal or appropriate or realistic or healthy (or whatever term is chosen) is influenced by many variables[5]—sex, age, class, ethnic background, religion, educational level, geographic location, social role. Normal aggression for a person of one background is overaggressiveness for one of another. People of different backgrounds normally emphasize different defenses and have different norms for sexual expression and for the expression of aggression. Even the level of psychosexual maturity expected of men and women may vary in different cultures.[6] Certainly, concepts of appropriate male and female ways of acting are very differently defined in different parts of the world.

It is especially difficult today to evaluate such traits as aggressiveness in women. Women over the years have had to conceal or subdue anger and aggressiveness. Many normally assertive women have had to seek their ends by devious behavior, often manipulating male associates into accomplishing their ends, keeping themselves in the background. As women become more natural and straightforward, they are sometimes labeled "aggressive females." The clinical social worker has to be able to distinguish new healthy feminine aggressiveness from that of the woman who really hates men, and consciously or unconsciously wants to belittle and hurt them.

The general atmosphere within which an individual is reacting and particular antecedent events are also significant to personality assessment. In periods of turmoil, such as when students or blacks are enraged by events such as unpopular wars, assassinations, police brutality, unbearable neighborhood conditions, and the like, it would be a grave error to think that the passions unleashed indicated abnormal character traits in the participants. Campus and community rioting, it is true, provides a heyday for overly aggressive individuals with poor impulse control, but many normally well controlled individuals also find themselves enraged beyond their endurance, or may even have become convinced that aggressive action is essential. As can be seen, assessment of personality factors is far from a simple process. It requires not only knowledge of the general nature of personality, but also finely tuned judgments about the weight to be given to many kinds of social and situational realities brought together in the social study.

*DISENTANGLING INTERACTIONS.* How does one go about assessing complicated personality characteristics? It is a process of applying clinical judgment to knowledge of the ways in which the client interacts with others, including the caseworker, and handles his or her own affairs. Again, let us emphasize that it is impossible to evaluate components of the personality properly, except as they are seen in the context of the individual's situation. One must take into account the whole gestalt. For instance, one cannot judge whether a reaction of anger or anxiety is normal or excessive unless one knows the realities behind it. It is one thing to be plagued by the fear of losing a job in normal times when one's performance is adequate, and quite another when there is a recession or one's performance is marginal. It is one thing for a client to accuse his wife of belittling him when in actuality she does constantly criticize and devalue him, and quite another for him to distort her remarks, projecting on to them his own devaluated self-image. Feelings of depression may be part of a particular physical illness syndrome, a reaction to the loss of a valued friend, or, in the absence of any such provocations in reality, evidence of emotional or mental illness.

This disentangling of the reverberating interactions between external realities and the individual is a most complicated task. It is simplest when it has been possible in the social study to observe the externals directly, or for the worker to bring his or her own general knowledge to bear on the situation. For instance, the worker often knows what a given neighborhood is like, or how a particular doctor reacts to patients, or the eligibility procedures in the local public assistance agency. General knowledge of this type, however, has to be used with caution. Sometimes the doctor, public assistance worker, or school principal has not acted in a specific instance in the way prior knowledge would lead one to expect. Direct observation is more certain. Here lies the great advantage of the worker's having direct contact during the social study with the principals in any interpersonal problem, and of the home visit, and of joint and family interviews from which so much can be learned. But even insights thus gained are not infallible, and can sometimes give the worker a false sense of certainty.[7] Things that have been "seen with my own eyes" and "heard with my own ears" carry great weight, but they are also subject to misinterpretation by the worker because of countertransference and other subjective judgments.

Another method of disentangling the objective from the subjective is to evaluate the circumstantial detail that the client uses to support opinions and reactions. Does the situation described bring the worker to the same conclusion? Insofar as the worker's own perceptions and judgments are realistic, he or she can then evaluate the client's reactions. One reason for emphasizing the importance of self-awareness in worker training is to reduce biases, or at least bring them near enough to consciousness to alert one to possible sources of error in judgment.[8]

Repetitiveness provides another useful clue in assessing behavior, for if an individual has a tendency to over- or underreact or to distort, it will not occur in a single instance only but will show itself again and again. If the same type of seemingly unrealistic response arises several times, and particularly if in each instance it occurs in reaction to different people, the chance is very great that a dysfunctional personality factor is involved. This illustrates the special value of knowing the client's past history when the nature of the problem requires particularly careful assessment of the personality. Since psychosocial workers believe that much of the personality structure is shaped in early life, it is expected that repetitive patterns will often show themselves clearly in the life history. Specific symptoms of neurotic or psychotic disorders in the client's past are, of course, of great significance.

The assessment process provides a workable knowledge of the client's strengths and weaknesses and of the pressures, gratifications, and potentials of the situation, based on a study of his or her current life, pertinent aspects of the past life, and behavior in the casework interviews. Strengths and weaknesses are not viewed independently, but are seen in relationship to each other.

## DYNAMIC UNDERSTANDING

The discussion of the diagnostic process now moves from delineating *what* the realities of the client–situation gestalt are to *why* the problems and/or dysfunctions in this gestalt exist. In dynamic understanding, we look at the data of the social study to see which of the observed features seem to be contributing to the client's difficulties, and particularly at the ways in which these components interact to bring about the present degree of discomfort. Worker and client together seek to understand the dynamics of the client's dilemma in terms both of current interactions and of the effect of prior events—recent or remote—on current functioning. As in the assessment of personality factors, we try again to learn to what extent and in what way the causative factors of the client's problem lie within the situation that confronts him or her, to what extent and in what way they are the product of unusual needs within the clients or of poor functioning within ego or superego, and to see how these many factors interact with each other to produce current dilemmas.

In this process, a systems theory approach is again useful. For the problem does not lie simply in a given weakness in the personality or in a specific lack or condition in the milieu, but in the way that various weaknesses or idiosyncrasies in the total system interplay and affect each other. Since, as we have seen, every factor in a system affects every other factor in that system, the worker scans the field again, looking now for interactions.

Suppose that we have noted that Johnnie is retarded in school despite normal intelligence, and we know that he and his teacher are in constant conflict. Is the teacher critical of Johnnie because he is impudent, or because he is overgraded, or because his mother criticized her, or because Johnnie comes from a black, Hispanic, Chicano, or Indian neighborhood, has poor clothing, or because he is big for his age and looks as though he ought to behave in a more grown-up way than he does? Or is she critical because the principal is pressing her about the reading-grade average of her class, or because she is embroiled in faculty disagreements about the wisdom of a strike and is irritable with all her students. Only by talking with her can we get hints of what the cause of the strain between her and Johnnie may be. And only as we come to understand this will we know what steps might or might not be helpful.

Pete sees himself as a delinquent and begins acting like one. What does the social study tell us about his neighborhood, his housing, the lack of decent recreation facilities, his teacher's attitude, the curriculum offered by the school? If he has been taken into court for truancy, has he come to think of himself as a delinquent because of this? Does the picture of his family give reason to believe his problem can be traced to his family situation?

When it has been observed that a client's affect is characterized by high anxiety, we seek to understand possible contributing factors—current provocations, historical factors, and interrelationships within the personality itself. Could it be fear of the superego or fear of external reality? Or a mixture of these? Does it seem to be a recent development or a long-term pattern? If the latter, are there developmental factors that might account for it? Could health be a factor? What in the situation may be provoking anxiety? What effect does it have on the client's functioning? What responses does it seem to provoke from others toward the client?

## Systems Theory and Complementarity

In problems of interpersonal adjustment, such as marital or parent–child problems, one person is in a sense the other person's situation, and vice versa. The term "complementarity" is sometimes used to describe these characteristic patterns.[9] As we noted earlier, the action of one person upon another takes effect only in the form in which it is perceived by the other. The first person may have used a complaining tone because of tiredness, but if the other perceives the tone as anger, he or she will react to it as such. The response, in turn, may be silence, or martyrlike murmurings, or explosive retaliation, depending upon the other's personality, earlier experiences of the day that have set a mood, his or her perception of the first person, his or her notion of the requirement of the role in which he or she is functioning, and a variety of other things. The first speaker's next response is subject to similarly complicated influences.

If one studies a series of such transactions, one finds that similar patterns in interaction can characterize the behavior of whole families. Without question, the dynamic diagnosis in cases of interpersonal conflict must include comprehension of the interaction between the main participants in the conflict. Such comprehension involves understanding of the way in which one person's behavior sets off or provokes certain responses in the other, the extent to which this is consciously or unconsciously purposeful, and the extent to which unrecognized complementary needs are being met in the process. In marriage conflict, certainly, the worker will make serious treatment errors if not aware of the factor of complementarity in such combinations as "father–daughter marriages," "mother–son marriages," marriages in which new patterns of masculine–feminine division of responsibilities are being tried, sado-masochistic marriages, certain marriages of alcoholics, and so on. Often, the worker may find that serious trouble has emerged in a family where a previously existing complementarity has been disturbed.[10] In such cases, serious consideration should be given to the possibility of restoring the previous balance in the family. Marriage is not infrequently the means by which two individuals who each have rather serious handicaps in functioning are enabled through complementarity to function at a reasonably high level of personal satisfaction and social effectiveness.

Not infrequently today, complementarity is disturbed by the new definitions of women's values and roles. Here, return to the previous complementarity is often not possible. Rather, a new one must be found with compensating gratifications for the husband and/or the development of understanding and acceptance by the husband of his wife's needs, and also appreciation by the wife of how her new needs are complicating life for her husband. If this is not possible, either separation ensues or the marriage continues under great strain.

## Communication Factors

The important part played by communication in any social or interpersonal system was noted in earlier chapters. One needs to look carefully at this factor. Are certain ego defenses interfering with either full expression of attitudes, desires, and reactions? Are they interfering in reception of these by another? Is nonverbal behavior contradicting words? Are either words or gestures being misinterpreted because of variations of meaning related to sociocultural factors?

## Use of the Past

It was also noted earlier that previous life history sometimes reveals repetitive patterns. These can be immensely valuable in helping the worker to understand causation in the developmental sense of how the person came to be the way he or she is. Knowledge of early family relationships is particularly helpful in understanding the level of psychosexual development, parental attachments, sexual identification, superego development, and the basis for the anxieties against which the ego is defending itself. Early family history can also give greater understanding of many qualities of the ego. Sharp discrepancies in the way an individual functions at different times in life provide excellent clues to the ways in which situational factors affect the person.

Some schools of thought now found in clinical social work deny the value of the past, seeing talk of such things as escape from the realities of the present. They believe that reference to the past is an example of "linear causation," which has been "displaced" by the modern "transactional model." If one selected a single, or even several, factors from the past and said, "This is the total cause" one would indeed be falling into the fallacy of narrow linear causation. For many, many years caseworkers have thought rather in terms of *multiple* causation, recognizing the circular effect of interacting contributing factors. Systems theory embraces this way of thinking by emphasizing transactional behavior, with emphasis on the interplay of one factor on another. Psychosocial workers hold that transactions of the past are incorporated in the present personality, and thereby influence the nature of the current systems components, thus living on to modify the present. Often, by acquiring a different understanding of such past experiences or a different attitude toward them, people come to interact differently in the present and thereby help both themselves and others who are part of the same family or other social system.

## Precipitating Factors

The event, or events, that finally brought about the request for assistance and those that seem to have precipitated the emergence of the problem itself are especially revealing. They are often keys to the dynamics of the dilemma. Frequently, the client will talk about these spontaneously. At other times one can ask, "What happened that you decided to come in just now?" Or, "Can you put your finger on just when you first became aware of this?" Or, "Did anything special happen at that time?" Sometimes the client has no awareness of the precipitating event but the worker can deduce it by looking for the dynamics of things that occurred either at the same time or in close succession. "You told me last week that Mary went to work in January. . . . I imagine that complicated life for you quite a bit. . . . I'll bet it was hard not to get mad even though you agreed to it. . . . Am I right in remembering that you told me your headaches began just about then?"

The dynamic part of the diagnosis, then, represents the caseworker's effort to understand the nature of the interaction of the multiple factors contributing to the client's difficulty. It seeks to discover *why* the situation is as it is. It tries to establish interrelationships among the various factors that combine to create the client's discomfort or poor social functioning. It seeks to comprehend the interaction of internal and external factors, the past sources of the present difficulty insofar as these lie in the past, and the internal dynamics within the personality or among the environmental forces. The assessment process and the dynamic diagnosis go hand in hand, each contributing to the clarification of the other, as greater understanding of the client and his or her situation develops. Together, the assessment and the dynamic diagnosis should define as clearly as possible the key features that treatment must attempt to modify, and locate the assets in both person and situation that can facilitate change.

## CLASSIFICATION

A third step in diagnosis is classification or categorization—recognizing that a characteristic or set of characteristics belongs to a known grouping about which generalized knowledge exists. Three types of classification or categorization have so far been found by psychosocial workers to have value for treatment—health, problem, and clinical diagnosis.

# Health

The *medical classification*—or diagnosis—often has implications for personal and social consequences, which are guideposts to casework treatment. For instance, a childhood diabetic may need help with feelings that he or she is defective, and with resentment at the deprivation of foods or activities that friends can enjoy. An adolescent athlete whose knee is injured may consequently lose status as "star" of the high school team or have to give up a dream of making the major leagues. Following a diagnosis of heart dysfunction, a successful businessman may have to limit his activities and find less strenuous interests and outlets. A person with multiple sclerosis is confronted with the certainty that physical functioning will become increasingly impaired over time, and this fact will have implications not only for the person but also for the family. Knowledge of the implications of various physical disorders and handicaps, and the adjustments they may require, immediately provides the worker with information about treatment steps once the medical diagnosis has been made.

# Problem

A second type of classification refers to problems—terms such as marital conflict, parent–child problem, unwanted pregnancy, delinquency, drug addiction, alcoholism, unemployment, old age, premature baby, preoperative syndrome, disablement, dying patient, and so on. These are essentially descriptive categories. They tell something about the difficulty and can become the focal point for assembling data about the disorder. They also suggest major dimensions of the treatment steps that will need to be taken.

Unwanted pregnancy, for instance, immediately suggests that prenatal care may be needed. Arrangements for confinement may have to be made. The worker will need to explore the mother's feelings toward the child and toward the child's father. If it is an intact family—with or without formal marriage—the mother and the father together may need to be helped to come to a decision about whether to go through with the pregnancy and about plans for the child.

If the parents are not living together, they, or sometimes the client alone, may want to come to decisions about their relationship. The single-parent solution may be considered in terms both of its possibility, and of the problems that would be involved for this particular parent. If the parents are making a home together, they may want to talk about the possibility of marriage. The reasons for the child's not being wanted will need to be explored. Sometimes problems interfering with acceptance of the child can be worked through. If not, the client may want to consider the pros and cons of abortion. If the pregnancy is not interrupted but the child continues to be unwanted, alternative plans have to be made for the child's custody and care. Sometimes parental families are involved. One does not necessarily deal with each of these dimensions in every case of unwanted pregnancy, but each of them needs to be in the worker's mind as possible matters for consideration.

Similarly, a tentative outline of treatment dimensions can be made in relation to any problem category, though it may not be so complicated as the one just given. Obviously, a given client or family may have several different types of problems, each with its own treatment requirements.[11]

## Clinical Diagnosis

Third, the *clinical* classification—or clinical diagnosis—is a combination of terms derived from psychoanalysis and psychiatry and used to designate certain major personality configurations. The worker does not always have a sufficiently extensive contact with a client to make a clinical classification with any degree of certainty. In many situations, especially in brief treatment, if there is no indication of psychosis, further delineation of the clinical diagnosis is not needed in order to help the client with the particular problem that has brought him or her to the worker. But especially when difficulties in the personality itself are the object of treatment, such a diagnosis is very useful in bringing clarity to the treatment process.

For a number of reasons, clinical classification is more complicated than problem classification. The client usually tells the worker what the problem is, but the clinical classification must be deduced from the facts and observations of the social study and assessment. It depends in part upon the recognition of symptoms that are generally recognized as characteristic of known neurotic or psychotic disorders, such as phobias, compulsions, hallucinations, depression, and many others. ("Acting out" is not technically a symptom, but such behavior without neurotic or psychotic symptoms is often a sign of some type of personality disorder.) The clinical diagnosis is an attempt to define or classify—or put in a category—the predominant way in which the personality as a whole functions, when there is indication of substantial dysfunctioning. Notice that it is the *functioning* that is categorized, *not the person.*

Whenever possible, clinical diagnosis is more than a descriptive classification. Increasingly, it is based not only on behavior but also on systematized understanding of the underlying structure or nature of the difficulty. This is best seen in the designations for different neuroses and the major distinctions between neurosis, psychosis, and personality or character disorders. Predominantly, each of these categories rests upon common etiological and dynamic features, and thus can be particularly useful in guiding treatment. Personality disorders are not as well defined and understood as neuroses and psychoses, but there has been much study of such disorders in recent years.

Contrary to a currently popular assumption, casework has not borrowed psychiatric terminology in wholesale fashion but uses only those terms that apply to conditions with which caseworkers are recurrently familiar and concerning which they have access to diagnostically discriminating data. The worker first attempts to arrive at the broadest discriminations. Is this client probably psychotic, or does he or she fall somewhere in the neurotic group, or does there seem to be a personality disorder of some type? Or is this individual within the broad normal range? If the person does not fit clearly into any one of these classifications, between which major categories does the difficulty seem to lie?

PSYCHOSIS. The caseworker's competence to diagnose psychosis is sometimes questioned on the grounds that such a diagnosis is a medical question. Perhaps it would be more accurate to say that the clinical social worker must be able to recognize psychotic *symptomatology*. If the social worker did not arrive at the opinion that such symptoms of psychosis exist, how else would he or she know enough to refer the client to a psychiatrist for a medical diagnosis or to consult the psychiatrist for confirmation of the opinion? Should every client in every casework agency be seen routinely by a psychiatrist to determine whether he or she is psychotic? Of course not, but if in the worker's opinion psychosis may be involved, psychiatric consultation may be advisable and the possibility of the client's being helped by medication should be considered.

The extent to which clinical workers are familiar with psychoses depends on the setting in which they practice. Obviously, in a psychiatric hospital or outpatient facility, workers will be familiar with many types of mental disorders. All practitioners, however, should recognize the major symptoms of the various types of schizophrenia and manic-depressive psychoses. Where an organic factor is involved, the caseworker has very little diagnostic competence, but here too the worker should have sufficient knowledge of symptomatology to recognize signs that should be reported to the medical consultant.

The worker is not making a medical diagnosis simply by using the same terms as the psychiatrist. An opinion about the nature of a mental disturbance becomes a medical diagnosis only when it is expressed by a physician. Furthermore, such a diagnosis is designed for use in medical treatment. When the caseworker recognizes psychosis, it is a casework opinion designed for casework treatment. When a diagnosis is being transmitted from one agency to another it is essential, if there is any possibility of confusion as to whether a diagnosis is medical or casework, that the professional source of the opinion be made clear.

PSYCHONEUROSES AND PERSONALITY DISORDERS.   When psychosis is not indicated, but the cause of the problem seems to lie sufficiently within the client to indicate some type of personality disturbance, the next distinction to be made is most frequently between some type of personality disorder and psychoneurosis. Neurosis and neurotic symptoms are basically responses to intrapsychic conflicts, stress between ego, id, and superego. This stress can be augmented by life events. In neurosis, the individual in childhood has reached a fairly high level of psychosexual development in dealing with oedipal problems, although his or her personality may have regressed from this level under late pressures.[12]

In certain types of personality disorder, in which identity problems and difficulties in organization of the self are evident, this level of development has never been fully reached. The roots of such difficulties lie in the very early formation of the ego—the failure to achieve ego synthesis. Anxiety in neurosis results from conflict between differentiated parts of the personality. In severe personality disorders, such as borderline and narcissistic personalities, it may result from the ego's effort to avoid regression to a very early stage of development characterized by strong feelings of helplessness—to stave off ego disorganization.

In most cases in which long-term treatment of interpersonal maladjustment is undertaken, it is possible for the experienced caseworker to make finer distinctions among the neuroses, such as those among hysteria, obsessive-compulsive neurosis, and neurotic depression. There is less standarized nomenclature for the various personality or character disorders. The terms hysterical personality, dependent, obsessive-compulsive, paranoid, antisocial, masochistic, "as-if," cyclothymic or affective, passive aggressive, borderline, and narcissistic are all in use. There is much variation among different psychiatric writers. Some of these personality disorders are close in character structure to neurosis, others are close to psychosis. The hysterical personality, for instance, is similiar to the hysterical neurosis. Clinical social workers dealing with intrapsychic and interpersonal problems need to be familiar with the literature discussing these disorders and the behavior associated with these terms.[13] Often, features of several categories appear together, and it is very hard to know what one is dealing with. Today, as we have noted earlier, the clinical worker is far more apt to be meeting personality disorders, than psychoneurotic disturbances. It is important, therefore, to study work that is being done in the psychiatric field, in psychoanalysis, and by clinical psychologists, as well as by our own colleagues. Clinical terms represent a cluster of focal points on several different continua. When individuals show features of more than one disorder, all possibilities should be kept in mind with indication of where the greater emphasis lies.

When intensive work on interpersonal problems is being undertaken with individuals suffering from any type of severe clinical disturbance, there is value in psychiatric consultation. The more severe the dysfunction appears to be, the more important such consultation is. Any sort of physical illness also calls for medical evaluation, even when in the worker's judgment the illness appears to be of psychological origin. Psychological problems in clients with serious psychosomatic disorders should be treated under medical auspices, or, if the work is of a supportive nature, in close coordination with medical treatment. If depression is present to any significant degree, psychiatric consultation is often helpful, partly because the border between neurotic and psychotic depression is sometimes hard to distinguish, partly because medication may be indicated, and partly in order to have a medical opinion as to whether the severity of the depression or the possibility of suicide makes medical supervision or even hospitalization advisable. When deviations such as sadism, masochism, voyeurism, and drug addiction come to the caseworker, they also may call for psychiatric consultation.

One has to add that the helpfulness of psychiatric consultation depends upon the quality of psychiatry available. There is much variation in the training and experience of psychiatrists and in the hospital conditions under which they practice. Consequently, the advantages of consultation vary. If a patient interview is required, these advantages have to be weighed against the disadvantage of procedures that the client will be put through and the attitudes that may be faced in the medical disgnostic process. Communities and settings vary enormously in the quality of psychiatric consultation available.

Homosexuality is no longer considered to be a psychiatric illness by the American Psychiatric Association. Some people with a homosexual mode of life do, however, have problems and come for help just as heterosexual people do. So also do individuals whose orientation is bisexual. The kind of assistance that is given depends upon the client's description of his or her problem and desires. Some people want help in turning toward a heterosexual adjustment, some are not dissatisfied with homosexuality itself but suffer guilt and anxiety because of social or personal disapproval. Others want to improve their relationships with their partners. Others may have trouble in coping with the various personal or practical problems that people must deal with irrespective of their sexual orientation. In all such instances, diagnostic understanding would rely upon the problem classification and the dynamic diagnosis.

## Value of Clinical Diagnosis

From time to time the value of the clinical diagnosis is questioned, for there is a tendency to feel that the dynamic diagnosis is sufficient. But the clinical diagnosis has the additional value of designating a cluster of factors characteristically found together. For instance, the term "obsessive-compulsive neurosis," when correctly used, immediately conveys certain information about a client. It signifies that the individual has reached the oedipal stage of development in relationship to parents but has not resolved the conflicts of this period and has regressed in a substantial degree to ways of behaving characteristic of the anal or habit training period of development. As we have noted in other chapters, it indicates that the person has a severe superego to which he or she may be overly submissive on the surface but which he or she is unconsciously fighting. The individual tends to be very sensitive to criticism and to have strong dependency needs, although they may be covered over; the person sometimes very much wants to please the worker and other parent figures, but at other times is either negative to suggestions or subtly sabotages them. The individual is often perfectionistic, usually ambivalent, often confused in masculine–feminine identifications. He or she is apt to make heavy use of such defenses as intellectualization, rationalization, isolation, and reaction formation. The person usually has had a strict upbringing by a parent or parents who gave love but imposed rigid training in habits and behavior. The individual may be strict in bringing up his or her children, or ambivalent in training them, or strict on the surface but unconsciously promote vicarious acting out. Of course, not all these characteristics will be true of every obsessive-compulsive person, but the presence of a few of them in the absence of contrary evidence will alert the worker to the probable diagnosis and to avenues to explore that will either confirm the diagnosis or contraindicate it.

As it takes firm shape, the clinical diagnosis becomes a sort of index to many things about the individual that have not yet become clear from what has been observed or said. It often enables the worker to anticipate reactions to contemplated treatment steps and to guide them accordingly. Such foreknowledge can also help greatly in the control of antitherapeutic countertransference reactions. The obsessive-compulsive's intellectualism, for example, can arouse feelings of frustration and dislike in the worker. If, however, the worker can recognize this trait as a defense against the anxiety created by an oversevere conscience, knowing that the client feels in part like a child afraid of a harsh mother or father, the dislike may well be displaced by the desire to help. In borderline personality conditions, the worker will not be surprised by extreme oscillations of feelings about the self and others, and feelings toward the worker. Splitting of others into the "good" and the "bad" often occurs. The use of projection and denial will be expected and understood as familiar components of the disturbance.

In other words, if one knows enough about characteristics of a person to designate a clinical diagnosis, one immediately has the key to a great deal of other knowledge that will be useful in the process of helping the individual. In the psychoneuroses proper, specific symptoms such as phobias, hysterical paralyses, obsessions, compulsive rituals, and evidences of depression, distinctively related to different categories, quickly alert the worker to the possible diagnosis. Symptoms alone, however, do not establish a clinical diagnosis. There are always several possible explanations of any symptom. It is only when a specific form of behavior can be shown to be part of a larger configuration characteristic of the disorder in question that any certainty can be felt about the diagnosis.

One weakness of the dynamic diagnosis taken by itself is that it tends to see a little bit of this and a little bit of that in an individual without reaching a definite delineation. It is when one tries to say whether the difficulty is primarily a personality disorder or a neurosis, whether a borderline personality disorder, schizophrenia, or severe hysteria, and so on, that incompleteness in the psychoscial study or lack of clear-cut evaluation of the facts becomes apparent. This assumes, of course, that the clinical diagnosis itself is not a glib designation based on superficial impressions.[14]

## Misuse of Clinical Diagnosis

There are indeed several dangers involved in the use of diagnostic categories. One is that of stereotyping, assuming that all people in the same category are exactly alike. As noted earlier, each person has many individual qualities that make him or her unlike anyone else, despite the fact that in the rough outlines of a personality disturbance an individual may have much in common with others suffering from the same disorder. Another danger is careless categorization, assuming a person belongs in a given group because of superficial qualities or overlooking other qualities that point in another direction. Again, it is essential to be clear that we are not diagnosing *people*, but *characteristics* of people and their situations that interfere with their coping and contentment.

Diagnosis is admittedly a subjective process, despite the fact that it is an effort to increase the objectivity with which one views the client and his or her treatment needs. As a subjective process that often deals with impressionistic data, it is open to influence by suggestion. One form of suggestion that is prevalent is the currently popular diagnosis. Just as appendicitis was widely overdiagnosed in a recent period of medical history, and before that tonsillectomies were far too widely performed, so in psychiatry schizophrenia has sometimes been too easily assumed to exist, and, especially today, borderline personality disorder may too often seem the appropriate designation.

Another danger is that of premature diagnosis. When definitive material is not available to make a clinical diagnosis, it is far better to admit that we have not been able to establish a clinical diagnosis than to affix a label superficially. The rate of agreement among diagnosticians in psychiatry and psychology is not high. The same is undoubtedly true of clinical social workers. But the fact that no profession has yet developed a high degree of accuracy is no argument against an effort to improve diagnostic skill. It *is* an argument against snap judgments and against *overreliance* on the clinical diagnosis. The greatest safety lies in building our understanding on many sources of information—the assessment, the dynamic diagnosis, the problem classification, health, and the clinical classification—using all the knowledge that each of these can locate for us.

Some diagnoses—particularly schizophrenia and borderline personality—can seem so discouraging that there is danger that they may in effect relegate the person to very superficial treatment or even to no treatment at all. Obviously, this should not happen. A clinical diagnosis is never a pejorative. The diagnosis tells the worker something about what will help and what will not help, but it certainly should not be used as an excuse for not *trying* to help. Realization of the great variation among individuals having the same clinical diagnosis precludes such stereotyping of treatment. Furthermore, the whole person–situation gestalt concept puts the clinical diagnosis in perspective as only one of several aspects of the total diagnotic assessment. The reader will recall the work described in Chapter 3 with Mrs. Zimmer whose clinical diagnosis was borderline personality disorder. In Chapter 19, work with a client, Mrs. Barry, who was suffering from paranoid schizophrenia, will be presented. Paranoid schizophrenia is often considered an especially discouraging diagnosis. Yet Mrs. Barry came to understand and overcome her reluctance to continue medication. Subsequently she was able to live in the community, avoiding rehospitalization. In such cases knowledge of the clinical diagnosis makes a substantial difference in treatment, but the assessment of the client's individuality and strengths are equally important.

# THE TIME FACTOR

Naturally, the degree to which one can arrive at an understanding of a person-in-his-situation varies with the fullness of the social study on which it depends. Even in the short contact of one to four interviews, one must understand enough of the interplay of inner and outer dynamics to enhance the client's ability to cope with the main problem (often the presenting one) in a way that either resolves it or diminishes its severity. Presses in the situation and resources that can be modified or used within the limits of the time available are assessed. On the stress side of the assessment, in such short contacts one can get an impression of certain features of the client's ego—perceptive ability, coping powers, degree of anxiety, and ways of handling it. One sometimes also observes major defenses such as projection, turning against the self, reaction formation, rationalization, and intellectualization. Aspects of the superego may show themselves if it is unusually severe, or lax, or inconsistent. We may also observe impulsiveness or rigidity of control. But it will be difficult to assess the degree to which any of these characteristics exist.

Turning to the dynamic diagnosis, one certainly has to understand something of the dynamics of both inner and outer forces and of the interplay between them in all clinical social work whether the contact is brief or extensive. Without this, very little help can be given, whether treatment is long or short. Crisis treatment in particular, where former conflicts and problems may be brought to the surface by the present trauma, calls for quick recognition of the dynamic elements by the worker.[15]

A clinical diagnosis, on the other hand, can rarely be arrived at in the first interview, and will be established only very tentatively if at all in the entire brief contact. So little time is available in which help can be given that treatment occupies the center of the stage very quickly. Because the factual basis is therefore inevitably restricted, it is difficult and sometimes risky even to try to establish a clinical diagnosis. As noted elsewhere, one can often recognize the possibility of psychosis. If neurotic symptoms are severe they may also be evident in a single interview, but it is most unlikely that one can get more than very preliminary indications of neurosis unless the evidence is blatant. The same holds true for personality disorders.

In general, one can say that diagnostic understanding in very brief treatment will be limited to components of the person–situation gestalt that are close to the matters to be dealt with and close to the immediate treatment process.

Diagnostic assessment, then, involves a many-faceted but orderly understanding of the client–situation configuration. In preparing for treatment planning, all that is known—strengths as well as weaknesses —is reviewed and evaluated for the purpose of learning how best to help.

As the contact progresses, the fund of knowledge grows and the worker repeatedly refers to it in making the decisions that either modify or implement plans made at the outset of treatment. The more orderly the ongoing diagnostic process in which assessment is made and dynamic understanding grows, the more wisely will the worker decide what treatment to offer the client.

### NOTES

1.  Intuition is defined by Webster as "the act or process of coming to direct knowledge or certainty without reasoning or inferring; immediate cognizance or conviction without rational thought; revelation by insight or innate knowledge." The subject is rarely discussed in the literature on psychotherapy; in fact, a search led us to only one reference that cautions against reliance upon it: Robert Cancro, "An Overview of the Schizophrenic Syndrome," in Cancro et al., eds., *Strategic Intervention in Schizophrenia* (New York: Behavioral, 1974), p. 6. He writes: "We must be wary of the intuitive diagnosis in which we sense the presence of the thought disorder but cannot illustrate it with the patient's verbal productions." This admonition applies equally to the assessment of any client quality or condition; we must be able to back up our intuitive understanding with facts, knowledge, and reason. On the other hand, for discussions of empathy as a component in understanding, see Thomas Keefe, "Empathy: The Critical Skill," *Social Work*, 21 (January 1976), 10–14; and note 25, Chapter 12.

2.  Heinz Hartmann, *Ego Psychology and the Problem of Adaptation* (New York: International Universities Press, 1958), p. 23.

3.  Otto Pollak, *Social Science and Psychotherapy for Children* (New York: Russell Sage Foundation, 1952).

4.  John Stewart Collins, *The Vision of Glory* (New York: Braziller, 1973). p. 81.

5.  The sources of knowledge concerning these variations are myriad. Many useful references have been included in note 7, Chapter 2; notes 1 and 2, Chapter 3; and notes 4 and 5, Chapter 12. The following are also of value: Urie Bronfenbrenner, "Socialization and Social Class Through Time and Space," in Eleanor E. Maccoby, Theorore M. Newcomb, and Eugene L. Hartley, eds., *Readings in Social Psychology* (New York: Holt, Rinehart & Winston, 1958); Shirley Hellenbrand, "Client Value Orientations: Implications for Diagnosis and Treatment," *Social Casework*, 42 (April 1961), 163–169; Alex Inkeles, "Some Sociological Observations on Culture and

Personality Studies," in Clyde Kluckhohn, Henry Murray, and David Schneider, eds., *Personality in Nature, Society, and Culture* (New York: Knopf, 1959); Elizabeth Meier, "Social and Cultural Factors in Casework Diagnosis," *Social Work,* 41 (July 1959), 15–26; S. M. Miller and Elliot Mishler, "Social Class, Mental Illness, and American Psychiatry: An Expository Review," *Milbank Memorial Fund Quarterly,* 37 (April 1959), 174–199; Charles H. Mindel and Robert W. Habenstein, *Ethnic Families in America* (New York: Elsevior, 1976); Emelicia Mizio, "Commentary," *Social Casework,* 58 (October 1977), 469–474; John G. Red Horse et al., "Family Behavior of Urban American Indians," *Social Casework,* 59 (February 1978), 67–72; and Arlene S. Skolnick and Jerome H. Skolnick, eds., *Family in Transition,* 2nd ed. (Boston: Little, Brown, 1977). See also the first four articles on changing sex roles in *Social Casework,* 57 (February 1976); the special issue on "Ethnicity and Social Work" of *Social Work,* 17 (May 1972); and the entire issue on women of *Social Work,* 21 (November 1976).

6.  See Margaret Mead, *Sex and Temperament in Three Primitive Societies* (New York: Morrow, 1935), and *Male and Female: A Study of the Sexes in a Changing World* (New York: Morrow, 1949).

7.  For an excellent discussion of "evidence," see Mary E. Richmond, *Social Diagnosis* (New York: Russell Sage Foundation, 1917), Chapter 4.

8.  See especially Mary C. Schwartz, "Helping the Worker with Countertransference," *Social Work,* 23 (May 1978), 204–209. For further discussion, see Chapter 12.

9.  In addition to discussions and references on this in chapters 10 and 11, see also some of the valuable writings that over the years have described and provided examples of this phenomenon: Nathan W. Ackerman, "The Diagnosis of Neurotic Marital Interaction," *Social Casework,* 35 (April 1954), 139–147; Florence Hollis, *Women in Marital Conflict* (New York: Family Service Association of America, 1949), pp. 90, 97, 209; Carol Meyer, "Complementarity and Marital Conflict: The Development of a Concept and Its Application to the Casework Method" (doctoral dissertation, Columbia University School of Social Work, 1957); Bela Mittlemann, "Analysis of Reciprocal Neurotic Patterns in Family Relationships," in Victor W. Eisenstein, ed., *Neurotic Interaction in Marriage* (New York: Basic Books, 1956), pp. 81–100; and Otto Pollak, "Systems Theory and the Functions of Marriage," in Gertrude Einstein, ed., *Learning to Apply New Concepts to Casework Practice* (New York: Family Service Association of America, 1968), pp. 75–95.

10.  See, for example, Marjorie Berlatsky, "Some Aspects of the Marital Problems of the Elderly," *Social Casework,* 43 (May 1962), 233–237; Frank S. Pittman, III, and Kalman Flomenhaft, "Treating the Doll's House Marriage," *Family Process,* 9 (June 1970), 143–155; and Sue Vesper, "Casework Aimed at Supporting Marital Role Reversal," *Social Casework,* 43 (June 1962), 303–307.

11.  See, for example, Ursula Granite, "Foundations for Social Work on Open-Heart Surgery Service," *Social Casework,* 59 (February 1978), 101–105; Mary-Lou Kiley, "The Social Worker's Role in a Nursing Home," *Social*

*Casework,* 58 (February 1977), 119–121; and the entire issue of *Social Casework,* 59 (January 1978), devoted to "Dimensions of Alcoholism Treatment." The case of Mrs. Stone, described in detail in Chapter 9, offers an example of a client family with various problems and treatment needs.

12. See John C. Nemiah, "Psychoneurotic Disorders," in Armando M. Nicholi, Jr., ed., *The Harvard Guide to Modern Psychiatry* (Cambridge, Mass.: Harvard University Press, 1978), pp. 173–197; and chapters 15, 16, 17 of George Wiedeman, ed., *Personality Development and Deviation* (New York: International Universities Press, 1975).

13. See Alfred H. Stanton, "Personality Disorders," in Nicholi, *Harvard Guide to Modern Psychiatry,* pp. 283–295; and chapters 18 and 19 in Wiedeman, *Personality Development and Deviation.* Also highly recommended are Gertrude and Rubin Blanck, *Ego Psychology: Theory and Practice* (New York: Columbia University Press, 1974), and the references in note 3, Chapter 3.

14. Although necessarily we have had to be selective, in addition to those already cited we particularly recommend the following writings and compilations of papers relevant to clinical diagnosis and to the understanding of personality development and disturbance: Florence Applebaum, "Loneliness: A Taxonomy and Psychodynamic View," *Clinical Social Work Journal.* 6 (Spring 1978), 13–20; Silvano Arieti, *Interpretation of Schizophrenia,* 2nd ed. (New York: Basic Books, 1974); Leopold Bellak et al., *Ego Functions in Schizophrenics, Neurotics, and Normals* (New York: Wiley, 1973); William E. Fann et al., eds., *Phenomenology and Treatment of Anxiety* (New York: Spectrum, 1979); Sherman C. Feinstein and Peter L. Giovacchini, eds., *Adolescent Psychiatry: Developmental and Clinical Studies* (Chicago: University of Chicago Press, 1978); Peter L. Giovacchini, *Psychoanalysis of Character Disorders* (New York: Aronson, 1975); Edith Jacobson, *Depression: Comparative Studies of Normal, Neurotic, and Psychotic Conditions* (New York: International Universities Press, 1971); Theodore Lidz, *The Person: His Development Throughout the Life Cycle* (New York: Basic Books, 1968); Margaret S. Mahler et al., *The Psychological Birth of the Human Infant: Symbiosis and Individuation* (New York: Basic Books, 1975); Judd Marmor, ed., *Homosexual Behavior* (New York: Basic Books, 1980); Judith Mishne, "Parental Abandonment: A Unique Form of Loss and Narcissistic Injury," *Clinical Social Work Journal,* 7 (Spring 1979), 15–33; Joseph Palumbo, "Theories of Narcissism and the Practice of Clinical Social Work," *Clinical Social Work Journal,* 4 (Fall 1976), 147–161; Leon Salzman, *The Obsessive Personality* (New York: Science House, 1968); and Benjamin B. Wolman, ed., *Clinical Diagnosis of Mental Disorders: A Handbook* (New York: Plenum Press, 1978).

15. For references on crisis treatment see note 6, Chapter 18.

# CHAPTER 17

# UNDERSTANDING AND CHOICE OF TREATMENT OBJECTIVES

We now come to questions associated with treatment planning. This includes the clarifying of the objectives of treatment, various subobjectives or subgoals to be sought as stations on the way to final goals, and the choice of means, in the sense of treatment procedures by which such objectives can be achieved. It is generally agreed by caseworkers that the final word on objectives is said by the client. It is his or her life that is being changed, and for the most part the client is the one who will change it. However, at the outset, the client may or may not be clear about what he or she wants, or be aware of what he or she needs and can do. The worker, on the other hand, on the basis of an understanding of the client–situation gestalt, is responsible for formulating the kind of help that will be offered the client. When the client has become clear about what he or she wants to work on or achieve, the worker in turn can begin formulating the various subobjectives that will constitute steps toward the achievement of the client's objectives. Some are immediately apparent, while others emerge gradually as treatment and further diagnostic understanding develop.

The knowledge made available by the psychosocial study and the diagnostic assessment is used in two ways. First, it provides both client and worker with a basis for major decisions concerning the objectives and general direction of treatment and for details of its early stages. Second, it provides a fund of information on which the worker will continue to draw throughout the whole association with the client. Knowledge attained in the initial stages gives perspective to what comes later and is often drawn on in helping the client to increase his or her understanding. Throughout psychosocial treatment, diagnostic conclusions remain a backdrop against which necessary decisions about details of procedure can be made. In thinking about the best way to help a client in his or her effort to cope with a difficulty, the worker first envisages tentative goals of treatment and then assesses the procedures by which the client can be helped to reach them. Objectives are influenced not only by what types of changes might be desirable, but also by whether or not means for bringing such changes exist, both in the client–situation gestalt and in the casework process. In the present

405

chapter we will consider objectives, moving on in the next to treatment methodology.

## ULTIMATE OR LONG-RANGE OBJECTIVES

The ultimate, mutually accepted objective of treatment is always some type of improvement in the client's personal-social life. This may be in the individual's personal sense of comfort or satisfaction or achievement in life, or in his or her functioning as it affects the people with whom the person is associated. These two types of improvement often go hand in hand, although the client may be primarily concerned with one more than with the other. The interplay between an individual and family or other people in the "person environment" is so close that improvement in an individual's functioning usually makes him or her an easier person to live with—often more relaxed, freer, sometimes more giving in love and friendship, less hostile, more direct and clear in communications. Occasionally, to be sure, there are exceptions, as when a person with low feelings of self-worth who has allowed others to dominate begins to assert needs and give up the "doormat" role.

The long-range goal is, of course, related to the problem that the client is aware of at the beginning of the contact. It may, however, differ from the initial objectives as the client comes to redefine problems and needs. Sometimes the client has a broad awareness of the nature of the problem at the outset of treatment. In the very first interview a mother may say, "I know there must be something wrong with the way I am handling Tommie." She does not know all that lies behind the trouble, but she sees that she herself is involved as well as Tommie and, either explicitly or implicitly, recognizes that the goal of treatment includes modification of herself as well as of the child. Very often, however, in interpersonal problems, the client sees the trouble as lying only in the other person—child, husband, wife. Parents may see the problems of their teenage boy as unrelated to their unhappy marriage when, in fact, he is reacting strongly to his concern that they will divorce.

Sometimes the problem does lie primarily in someone else, but even here interaction is involved and there is need for some change in the person seeking help along with whatever is occurring in other members of the family. Frequently, too, the very location of a problem appears to be in one area of functioning at the outset of treatment but in another after a few interviews. The client may see the problem as difficulty with a child, while the worker, listening to him describe the divergent ways in which he and his wife handle the child, may locate the trouble as being also, or even primarily, in tension between husband and wife. The worker then will need to find ways of helping the client to make this connection so that he too will have the objective of improving the marriage, at least as it contributes to the child's problems.

In some cases where the problem is almost exclusively an external one, the goal is to bring changes in the outer situation, either directly or by helping the client to do this. In others the client may be led to expand this goal to include learning to cope with such situations, so that when similar ones occur in the future he or she will be more able to handle them without outside help.

In the process of dealing with the initial problem, others often emerge, which clients bring to their sessions for discussion, thus broadening the scope of treatment. Workers can *prevent* this by keeping the focus narrow and by settling too easily for brief treatment. In such instances, it is the worker who really decides on limited treatment, by never letting the client know that more help is available and might be beneficial.

Ultimate goals are sometimes quite limited and specific and at other times quite broad. The goal may be to enable an older person to arrange more suitable living arrangements, to work through a patient's reluctance to consent to a necessary operation, to help a mother decide whether or not to send a deaf child to a residential school. On the other hand, as we have seen, it may be to bring about a better marriage adjustment or a better parent–child relationship, or to help a schizophrenic client make a better work and social adjustment, or to enable a person with a personality disorder to function more realistically and with greater personal satisfaction. Occasionally, worker and client simply cannot agree. A case in point is that of a client who asked a worker to arrange for her seven-year-old son to be put in the local jail for a few days to impress him with the consequences of disobedience. Obviously, the worker could not comply. The only possible course was to accept her desire to help her son behave differently but explain that the worker did not think jail would really help and would be glad to help her find other ways of influencing him. If the client had stuck to her original goal, help would have had to have been refused.

## MOTIVATION AND OBJECTIVES

No matter how accurate the worker's thinking about appropriate subgoals may be, the force creating movement toward these objectives is dependent on the client's motivation.[1] This motivation, in turn, is dependent upon a variety of factors. One of these is the client's own degree of discomfort with things as they are. Has the client come in of his or her own volition or has the person been urged or even coerced into seeking help? In the latter instance, much will depend on the therapist's skill in enabling the person to recognize the potential gain that may come from participating in treatment. The client may need to ventilate a good deal of feeling about the situation that precipitated the opening of the contact and the person responsible for his or her coming. More important, the client will need to gain some preliminary understanding of the nature of the treatment situation. Above all, the individual will need to be convinced of the worker's acceptance and interest in understanding and helping—for his or her own sake rather than to please others who are expressing dissatisfaction. And, except in certain protective situations, the client will also need to know that the worker does not intend to impose help or change, but is there as an enabler, and only with the client's consent.[2] It is the absence of such motivation that makes casework with involuntary clients so difficult. In correctional work, where the client often does not have real freedom, workers have had to devise special techniques to deal with or compensate for this block to the acceptance of help.

Motivation is also affected by hope. It is always easier to pursue a goal if one has hope of achieving it. Hope is partly controlled by the dilemma itself, which may be either a stubbornly intransigent one or one that can be remedied with relative ease. Most troubles, however, fall between these extremes. The worker's attitude, both expressed and unexpressed, can then have considerable influence upon the degree of hope felt by the client. It often helps if the worker puts into words a belief that the client can achieve greater comfort or satisfaction through treatment, when the worker is confident that this is so.[3]

## Values

Motivation is closely related to values. Only if the parent believes that a child should do well in school will he become interested in improving the child's school adjustment. Only if the parent believes that a child should be happy and spontaneous will he or she be disturbed by the child's excessive anxiety and inhibitions. Only if a wife believes in an equalitarian marriage will she complain if her husband is dominating. Clearly, class and ethnic factors, as well as more individualized family and personal norms, enter into these values.[4]

The fact that a certain way of functioning is the "mode" for a particular ethnic group or class is not in itself, however, sufficient to assure that it is the most useful way of functioning, either for the client's associates or for himself. We are well aware of the fallacy in a worker's trying to impose on the client his or her own way of doing things. It is equally fallacious to give blind allegiance to cultural pluralism.[5] The worker must steer carefully between these twin errors, neither introducing culturally foreign goals because of personal preference for them nor feeling inhibited from trying to motivate the client to change culturally conditioned ways if there is reason to believe that his or her social functioning and personal well-being or that of other family members will be improved by such change.

Here we can see the value of encouraging reflection. For example, in a family where a teenage son may be angry at his father's "old world" expectations and demands, the worker can help the father see how hard it is for the son to make friends when he is so much more restricted than these peers are, possibly asking the father about his own teenage experiences and the importance of his friendships outside the family, if indeed these have been of value. Along with this, the son can be encouraged to reflect on his father's ideas and how different life in this country is for him. The worker's major task here is to offer options and help both father and son reflect on whether and how they wish to resolve the conflict between them.

In recent years there has been a healthy reemphasis on the long-recognized fact that the worker's personal values, including those of class and ethnic background, often enter into judgments concerning treatment goals, and that attention must be paid to the question of whether these are realistic in the client's terms. Certainly, the worker's *personal* values must not be translated into goals for the client. His or her *professional* norms and values, on the other hand, inevitably and quite appropriately become a factor in what are proposed as treatment objectives. When a mother complains about an adolescent daughter's behavior, the worker compares the mother's description with a general knowledge of the range of adolescent behavior that can be tolerated without bringing harm to the child or her associates, and weighs the relationship of the type of behavior shown by the child in terms of later adult adjustment. The worker's evaluation should include, as well, considerations of class and ethnic background that influence role expectations and constitute part of any evaluation of norms. Under some circumstances, the worker's tentative objective may be to bring about a narrowing of the gap between the initial situation and the worker's professional conception of socially and personally healthy functioning. Such an objective is realizable only if the client also comes to see its value. This type of evaluation leading to client–worker reflection is a constant part of the development of treatment themes and objectives.

## Factors Affecting Motivation

We know that the client often comes to treatment with a good deal of trepidation, and often with underlying resentment at having to take what is in varying degrees a dependent position. This can be true even when the client comes of his or her own volition, with favorable knowledge of the agency and of the nature of treatment. In a culture that values independence as much as ours does, it is not easy to admit that one cannot handle one's own problems. Fear of criticism and fear of the changes to which treatment may lead are often present too. The resulting anxiety and discomfort may decrease motivation.

On the other hand, without some anxiety motivation may lag. For anxiety is often the mobilizing force behind the request for help. The ideal therapeutic situation is one in which the client is anxious enough to want help and to keep coming for it, but not so afraid that fear interferes with the ability to use help.

Motivation is also affected by the client's appreciation of the nature of a problem and its ramifications. Most individuals tend, in one way or another, to minimize or to blind themselves to their difficulties. A husband remembers that he was grouchy last night but does not appreciate the fact that last night was only one of many and that he is slowly becoming disgusted with his marriage, while his wife is becoming withdrawn and despondent. His motivation for treatment may be very low unless in the first few interviews he can come to realize that his marriage is really breaking up and that his wife, despite her defensive appearance of disinterest, is deeply hurt because she still has a great deal of love for him. Not infrequently, when in joint interviews one partner's caring for the other comes to light during the exploratory period, the other will exclaim, "But I didn't know you cared any more —why didn't you tell me?" or "How could I have been so blind!" Following such realizations, motivation may come to life. Their occurrence at any stage of treatment may mark the turning point from resistance to full participation, and may make possible intermediate treatment goals quite different from those thought feasible before.

## INTERMEDIATE OBJECTIVES

The intermediate objectives of treatment are way-stations on the road to the ultimate aim, means by which it is hoped the final objectives will be achieved. For guidelines to these subgoals, the worker relies upon the insights gained in the diagnostic study. The strengths and weaknesses and the dynamics of the person–situation systems have now been at least partially clarified; there is some degree of understanding of the major intermeshing factors that contribute to the problem. Again, the field is studied—this time to see where modification may be possible. What factors seem to be salient in bringing the difficulty about? Which of these factors can be changed? Which are not likely to change, or would do so only with great difficulty? Where are the weaknesses or idiosyncrasies in either the client's personality or in his milieu? What strengths can be brought to bear on the dilemma?

Illustrations of intermediate goals may be useful. We speak of hoping to induce a mother to send her child to camp, or a husband to share his thoughts and feelings more fully with his wife. Or we say that we will endeavor to reduce the severity of the superego, or to strengthen the client's ability to assert needs or to modify a tendency to project. These are "shorthand" descriptions of what may be a lengthy process. The plan to "induce" a mother to send her child to camp was a treatment objective in the situation of a woman who had been widowed over a year before and was still overly dependent on her fourteen-year-old son. As a result, the son was being deprived of normal growth experiences. The mother wanted her son to mature, but found many reasons for its not being possible for him to go to camp when this was suggested by the worker. It took many weeks of work to enable this mother to recognize her fears, to discuss her husband's death and her grief and resentment, to see that her dependence on her son was keeping him from companionship with boys of his own age, and that this was not a good thing for him in the long run. The mother did not let the boy go to camp, but in the following fall for the first time she agreed to his joining a group at a nearby youth center, an important step for both mother and son.

Such intermediate objectives are sought only because they are seen as necessary for the achievement of an ultimate goal of improved personal–social functioning. They are closely related to the procedures of treatment, and are often articulated in combination with them. A worker will say that he "hopes to reduce anxiety by acceptance and reassurance and by getting the sister-in-law who lives nearby to visit daily," or that he "will try to reduce hostility to child by ventilation of mother's anger," or "endeavor to get father to see he is displacing hostility to John from his own brother," or "help mother to see that her failure to control Sidney is increasing his anxiety," or "use corrective relationship to help Mrs. George reduce her tensions about sex," or "try to get Mr. Brown to recognize his underlying hostility to his father," or "confront Mrs. Field with the consequences of her impulsiveness in an effort to get her to control it." None of these objectives is an end in itself, but a way-station on the road to better personal–social functioning. Each is a means to the client's own overall objective. The connection between these intermediate goals and the client's wishes can often be discussed with the client. Such discussion has the double advantage of increasing motivation to participate in this treatment step and to understand the value of similar ways of handling stress and other problems in the future.

## The Problem and Intermediate Objectives

Kaplan and Mason,[6] in their analysis of the help needed by a mother facing the crisis of the premature birth of a child, pointed out that four distinct psychological tasks confront the mother. Beginning with her expression of "anticipatory grief" in preparation for the possible loss of the child, she must also face her feelings about her inability to deliver a normal full-term baby. If the infant survives, he or she may be kept in the hospital for as long as eight to ten weeks. The mother is thus confronted by the task of establishing her relationship with the child long after this would have grown through natural maternal tasks and the child's response to her care. Finally, she has the task of understanding how a premature baby differs from a normal baby in its special needs and growth patterns. The accomplishment of each of these psychological tasks constitutes an intermediate goal of casework treatment.

Similar analyses could be made of many other situations that confront clients. In the previous chapter (pages 393–394), the problem of an unwanted pregnancy was used to illustrate the significance of the problem classification for treatment. The points listed in that case were intermediate goals. Similarly, in the situation of Mrs. Kord, a sixty-five-year-old woman whose husband's mental and physical deterioration following several strokes appeared to require permanent institutional care, a worker could delineate a number of such subgoals: (1) to learn through a medical appraisal whether he was right in believing that institutional care was the best plan; (2) to help Mrs. Kord to realize the need for this step; (3) to prepare Mr. Kord for this change insofar as this was possible; (4) to help Mrs. Kord work through her feelings of guilt over no longer being able to care for her husband; (5) to help Mrs. Kord work out the actual plans for her husband; (6) to deal with close relatives who were concerned about Mr. Kord and unrealistically brought pressure to bear on Mrs. Kord to continue to keep him at home; (7) to help Mrs. Kord work through her guilt over the placement itself and her grief over losing her husband; and (8) to help Mrs. Kord resume former interests and pleasures. The nature of the problem itself, that is, is an important determinant of both long-range and intermediate goals.

## Dynamic Understanding and Intermediate Objectives

Obviously, intermediate goals are related to the worker's view of what factors are contributing to the difficulty—the many factors that, taken together and interacting within a common system or among related systems, comprise the problematic condition. It is not enough, however, simply to locate what appear to be the salient contributing factors.

A second question then arises: Which of these numerous factors lend themselves to modification?

*MODIFIABILITY OF CONTRIBUTING FACTORS.*   Not infrequently, the most important factor in the dynamics of the problem is not the one most likely to yield to treatment. The most directly disturbing element in a family may, for instance, be the presence of a severely retarded son who, for the benefit of the rest of the children as well as the mother, it would seem, had best be removed from the family. Early work, however, may show that it is impossible at this time to enable the mother to agree to place the child, or even that there is no suitable place to send him. The objective might then become improvement in the mother's household management and in her relationships with the rest of her family. It may be possible to find day care facilities for the child to at least remove him from the home a large part of the time. If needed, a visiting homemaker might be used to free the mother's time for the other children. It may be possible for her to improve her perception of their requirements so that she responds more adequately to their needs. Later, work with the other children's problems may lead to intrapsychic shifts that make it possible to return to the question of placement of the retarded child. Perhaps this may no longer seem to be necessary.

Poor housing is often a factor that cannot be improved. A family's low income and crowded conditions in the city may make it impossible to move to a better location. Attention may have to be focused instead on the children's peer relationships and on opportunities to build these up in the local community center, and on health care and income management. Sometimes a marital and parent–child problem arises because of mental disturbance in one parent, which is not so serious as to require hospitalization but does make substantial modification of the marital relationship impossible. Although this major cause of the family's problem cannot be remedied, as an alternative it may be possible for the healthier parent to work on the problems of the children.

Sometimes the unmodifiable contributing factor lies within the personality of the client. An illustration of this occurred in the case of a woman who was overly dependent, with an excessive need to be cared for in a childish fashion, which led her to involve herself in unwise relationships with men who gave the appearance of strength but always turned out to have character defects that eventually caused her unhappiness and suffering. Her dependence was so strong and deep-seated that it was impossible to reduce it very much, but the caseworker was able to help her recognize her pattern and the consequences of her haste to satisfy her needs, and endeavored to strengthen her perception and judgment so that she would be more able to find a more stable person to lean on. Similarly a mother may be overly protective of her daughter because she is thus attempting to control or compensate for unconscious wishes to destroy her, but her guilt and anxiety may be so great that it would be unwise to bring any of her hostility into the open. Even though the underlying cause of the overprotectiveness may not be modifiable by casework methods, other treatment goals may be possible, seeking either to protect the child from the mother or to enable the mother to modify her behavior toward her daughter through helping her to understand her needs better.

Indeed, there is one whole group of contributing factors that can never in themselves be changed—harmful developmental experiences. The individual's *reactions* to these experiences can be modified, but not the experiences themselves. Sometimes the client can reevaluate them in the light of more mature judgment, or can see that he or she has distorted the early picture. This was true, for example, of the woman described in Chapter 7 who blamed her parents for not letting her go to college when, as she later came to see, she had never let them know that college interested her. At other times, however, even the reactions cannot be modified, but some control can be gained over them as the client becomes aware of them and of their effects in his or her current life. Thus, modifiability is related to the assessment of strengths and weaknesses in the client's situation, to the relative strength of the various ego capacities, and sometimes to his or her willingness to engage in extended treatment.

## Systems Considerations

Several concepts concerning the nature of systems bear on the question of ascertaining intermediate goals. Since, as we know, any change in any element in a system has an effect on every other element, it is not necessary to work directly with every aspect of a problem. Improvement in one part may well bring improvement in another. Sometimes, however, improvement in one part of a system can affect another part adversely. For instance, in a situation where the presenting problem is a teenage boy's hostility to his mother, if this is accompanied by jealousy between father and son, encouraging a better mother–son relationship may result in greater father–son tension and greater husband–wife tension also. In such a situation, other approaches may be both possible and preferable. A better husband–wife relationship may need to precede work on the son's problem. Or it may be best, depending on other factors, to work first with the father, helping him with his fear of displacement by his son. Or it may be better to work with the boy himself, helping him to build greater security outside the family. Under most circumstances, the best approach would be to treat the total family problem in family interviews or to combine these with individual interviews.

The question of the order in which different aspects of the problem had best be considered can also be of importance. A pertinent illustration of this is found in the Russo case, described in Chapter 11, where the father–daughter conflict was made an initial focus of family treatment. This was so for two reasons: First, because it was one of the problems the family was most willing to discuss in the early sessions, and, second, because on assessment of the family system, it was predicted that an improved relationship between Mr. Russo and his daughter would diminish the force of the mother–daughter collusion or "gang-up" against the father. As mother and daughter became less dependent on one another, the treatment focus could then shift to the marital relationship.

In choosing which aspect of a dilemma to deal with, workers often make use of another characteristic of systems, the fact that there is usually in each system what is called "a point of maximum reverberation." As was noted earlier, this refers to a salient spot in a system at which change will bring about the greatest amount of modification in other elements. One member of a family may be a "key person." Or in an employment problem the key person may be a shop steward rather than the foreman, or it may be the client's wife or husband. In other words, by looking at the interrelationships within and among systems, the worker can judge where the point of greatest potential effectiveness lies. The same principle holds for factors within the personality, or personality system, of the individual.

## Clinical Diagnosis

As indicated in the previous chapter, the clinical diagnosis is in one sense supplementary to dynamic understanding. It helps to clarify dynamics and increases sensitivity to elements that are likely to exist, even if they are not yet apparent. In this sense, it affects intermediate treatment goals in the same way that dynamic understanding does, with the additional value that it sometimes suggests some goals and provides information about what may or may not be acceptable or helpful to an individual.

For instance, a person suffering from a hysterical neurosis is likely to be ready much sooner to understand and accept goals directed toward the well-being of another than will a person having a personality disorder of the borderline or narcissistic type. A client whose difficulty is a compulsive neurosis may accept such a goal readily enough but if the goal is not immediately achieved, unless care is taken to ward it off there is a risk of greater guilt and reinforcement of the already too punishing superego. When a narcissistic personality disorder is involved, the very early narcissistic injury must be kept in mind and great care taken not to ask for consideration of altruistic objectives until a relationship of trust and acceptance is well established.

With psychosis in general, treatment objectives are usually closely related to developing a stronger and more accurate sense of reality and to coping with concrete problems. In schizophrenia, in particular, one important subgoal is to establish a steady, objective, not-too-close relationship. For we know that in schizophrenia the fear of engulfment by another person is usually strong and great anxiety may be stirred up if the relationship is experienced as too warm or close, much as that is desired by the client. As noted earlier, it is sometimes an objective when psychosis is evident to help the client accept medication and psychiatric care.

## INTERVENING VARIABLES

Thus far we have been discussing treatment goals from a client-centered perspective. A number of other factors must of necessity enter into the emergence of both intermediate and long-range goals.

## Needs of Other Family Members

It is the exception rather than the rule that the worker can be concerned with the welfare of the client alone. The total client–situation system usually includes other members of the client's family, or at least other individuals of significance to the client. The social worker always has an indirect responsibility to these other people. This constitutes another factor intervening between motivation, etiology, and treatment. For the worker must take into consideration the effect on others in the family of changes sought in the individual who for the moment is the focus of attention. This does not mean that the worker sacrifices the interests of one individual to those of another, but that it is the worker's responsibility to bring into the treatment planning in both his or her and the client's mind pertinent interrelationships between the client and other members of the family. Nor is this an intrusion into the integrity of the treatment process, for neither worker nor client can move wisely without giving full consideration to the interactions among family members.[7] Because of the complementarity that exists in family relationships, a change in one part of the equilibrium not only brings changes, as we have noted, in other parts but also results in "feedback," counterreactions that in turn affect the person with whom the change originated.

While treatment, whether in individual, joint, or family interviews, makes substantial use of these interactions, mutual provocations, and misunderstandings among family members, for full effectiveness it must be guided by diagnostic understanding of each individual as well as by knowledge of family interrelationships. Otherwise, it will lack sufficient direction and specificity and may even be seriously misdirected. It is change in the individuals, after all—in perceptions, judgments, understanding, motivation, controls—that enables people to contribute their part to change in any social system of which they are members.

## Peripheral Factors

Before going on to an examination of the choice of treatment procedures in the next chapter, we must consider a few additional variables —somewhat peripheral but nevertheless important—that intervene between treatment and the ideal objective of modifying or removing some of the factors contributing to the client's difficulty.

An obvious one is time. If experience indicates that a certain type of change is likely to require a number of months of work and the client will be available for only a few interviews, it certainly makes no sense to embark upon a line of treatment that will have to be interrupted midway. A decision on this factor will be influenced not only by the special function of the agency—as in Travelers' Aid, where contact is almost always limited to a short time span—but also by circumstances affecting the client. The matter about which the client is coming for help may have to be settled within a few days or a few weeks. Even in long-term treatment, the time factor may unexpectedly become important. After six or nine months of treatment, a client may have to move to another city. Themes may be emerging at this point about which treatment decisions must be made. If they cannot be developed profitably within the time available, they should be circumvented rather than opened up and dealt with inadequately.

Another variable affecting the nature of treatment may be the way in which the agency function is defined. The course of a case in which there are both parent–child and marital problems is apt to be very different, depending upon whether the client applies to a child-oriented clinic or to a family service agency. A woman who is deciding whether to separate from her ill but very difficult husband may be offered very different treatment, depending upon whether she goes to the social service department of the hospital for the mentally ill where her husband is being treated or to a mental hygiene clinic in her own community.

An agency's view of priorities in its function will often translate itself into other variables affecting treatment: offices that do or do not provide privacy or protection from interruption during interviews; caseloads that permit forty-five- to sixty-minute interviews per week for each client who needs the time, or caseloads that are too large to permit interviews of this length or frequency; and so on. Casework that has as its objective a substantial change in individual functioning usually requires uninterrupted and regular interviewing time. Exceptions to this do occur in crisis treatment. Crisis treatment, for instance, of necessity occurs in the midst of interruptions and unplanned interviews. Here the intensity of emotion aroused by the crisis may make concentration possible in spite of distractions, and the immediate availability of interviews may be more important than other considerations.

The availability of dynamically oriented psychiatric consultation is another variable that may influence choice of treatment aim and procedure. Especially in work with types of intrapsychic problems in which considerable anxiety may be stirred up, consultation with an analytically trained consultant can be of great value.

The caseworker's skill is another intervening factor of great importance.[8] Different themes, aims, and procedures require different kinds of skill. It is essential that the worker define treatment objectives that lie within his or her range of competence and, within these limits, treat with skill rather than venture in a clumsy fashion into forms of treatment of which the worker is unsure. This requirement, however, must not be taken to mean that treatment skill is static and cannot be further developed in workers, but that development is achieved by gradual reaching just beyond the border of one's present well established ability —not by luring the client into deep and troubled waters to sink or swim along with the worker.

Ideally, of course, the client's need should be met by whatever form of treatment will bring the greatest relief from discomfort. This means either that the agency function should be sufficiently flexible to adapt to varying needs or that, when possible, transfers should be made to other agencies that offer the required treatment. It also means that within agencies clients should be referred to workers whose skill is adequate to meet their particular needs.

The ultimate objectives of treatment, then, are arrived at jointly by client and worker. The client's motivation as it relates to goals is central to treatment. Intermediate goals are means to the client's ultimate objective, usually formulated by the worker, shared with the client, and acceptable to him or her. Intermediate goals rest on the nature of the problems to be dealt with, on dynamic understanding, and on the clinical diagnosis. They are guided also by the assessment of modifiability, strengths, and weaknesses. Certain intervening variables are also important. The objectives of treatment must be thought of as fluid, modified as changes develop in the client's understanding of his or her needs and in motivation, and as the worker's understanding of the client's needs and capacities grows. The response to treatment itself is a major component in these reformulations. Goals not only enable worker and client to avoid drifting along in a friendly, noneffective way, but also make it possible to avoid blind alleys. Conscious treatment planning serves the purpose of trial action. It compels the therapist to think through the possibilities and consequences of a line of treatment before undertaking it and involving the client in fruitless effort. Well focused and consciously planned therapy is apt to be effective therapy.

## NOTES

1.  The subject of motivation is often discussed under the name of its opposite —that is, resistance, by which we mean any attitude or behavior on the part of the client (of which he or she may be unaware) that interferes with the work of treatment. In many ways, resistance and motivation are two sides of the same coin: to "reduce resistance" is often to "increase motivation." For discussion of resistance in early interviews, see Gordon Hamilton, *Theory and Practice of Social Casework*, 2nd ed. (New York: Columbia University Press, 1951), pp. 52, 56–57, 80, 210. See also Judith C. Nelsen's very good article, "Dealing with Resistance in Social Work Practice," *Social Casework*, 56 (December 1975), 587–592; and Herbert S. Strean, *Clinical Social Work: Theory and Practice* (New York: Free Press, 1978), pp. 61–67, 198–203. For a useful discussion of motivation and related factors, see Helen Harris Perlman, Chapter 12, "The Client's Workability and the Casework Goal," in *Social Casework: A Problem-Solving Process* (Chicago: University of Chicago Press, 1957), pp. 183–203.

2.  In recent years, the term "contract" has come into use to describe the explicit common understanding of conditions and goals of treatment arrived at by client and worker. For the general subject of client and worker goal setting, see Werner Gottlieb and Joe Stanley, "Mutual Goals and Goal Setting in Casework," *Social Casework* 48 (October 1967), 471–481; Sylvia McMillan, "Aspirations of Low-Income Mothers," *Journal of Marriage and the Family*, 29 (May 1967), 282–287; Genevieve Oxley, "The Caseworker's Expectations and Client Motivation," *Social Casework*, 47 (July 1966), 432–437. For further readings on the contract, see note 9, Chapter 18.

3.  Lilian Ripple, Ernestina Alexander, and Bernice Polemis, *Motivation, Capacity and Opportunity*, Social Service Monographs (Chicago: University of Chicago Press, 1964), deal extensively with the foregoing in their study

of the "discomfort–hope" balance in the client's use of treatment. For their conclusions, see pp. 198–206; Jerome Frank also stresses the importance of hope·in "The Role of Hope in Psychotherapy," *International Journal of Psychiatry,* 5 (May 1968), 383–395, as does Angelo Smaldino in "The Importance of Hope in the Casework Relationship," *Social Casework,* 56 (July 1975), 328–333.

4. See, for example, Karen W. Bartz and Elaine S. Levine, "Child Rearing by Black Parents: A Description and Comparison to Anglo and Chicano Parents," *Journal of Marriage and the Family,* 40 (November 1978), 709–719; Melvin L. Kohn, *Class and Conformity: A Study in Values* (Chicago: University of Chicago Press, 1977); Mirra Komarowsky, *Blue-Collar Marriage* (New York: Random House, 1964); Hylan Lewis, *Culture, Class and Poverty* (Washington, D.C.: Cross Tell, 1967); Teresa Donati Marciano, "Middle-Class Incomes, Working-Class Hearts," in Arlene S. Skolnick and Jerome H. Skolnick, eds., *Family in Transition* (Boston: Little, Brown, 1977), pp. 465–476; Charles H. Mindel and Robert W. Habenstein, *Ethnic Families in America* (New York: Elsevior, 1976); and Hyman Rodman, "Lower-Class Family Behavior," in Skolnick and Skolnick, *Family in Transition,* pp. 461–465; for further references, see note 5, Chapter 16.

5. A case example presented by John P. Spiegel, "Conflicting Formal and Informal Roles in Newly Acculturated Families," in Gertrude Einstein, ed., *Learning to Apply New Concepts to Casework Practice* (New York: Family Service Association of America, 1968), pp. 53–61, illustrates this point. On the other hand, in recent years pluralism and increasing acceptance of a wide variety of life styles and family relationship patterns has led sociologists and clinicians to be more cautious than they were about viewing alternative modes and value differences as "pathological"; see Rodman, "Lower-Class Family Behavior." Furthermore, understanding family life of various cultures is a complicated matter indeed. For example, in a persuasive paper, Robert Staples' examination of recent theory and research on the black family leads him to conclude that much of it has been biased and fraught with myths and stereotypes; see his "Towards a Sociology of the Black Family: A Theoretical and Methodological Assessment," *Journal of Marriage and the Family,* 33 (February 1971), 119–135, reprinted in Skolnick and Skolnick, *Family in Transition,* pp. 477–505. See also William Ryan's polemic against *Blaming the Victim,* rev. ed. (New York: Random House, 1976). The interested reader may also want to refer to Ludwig L. Geismer, "Family Disorganization: A Sociological Perspective," *Social Casework,* 59 (November 1978), 545–550, which raises important questions about linking family disorganization with low socioeconomic status.

6. David M. Kaplan and Edward A. Mason, "Maternal Reactions to Premature Birth Viewed as an Acute Emotional Disorder," *American Journal of Orthopsychiatry,* 30 (July 1960), 539–547.

7. In addition to the numerous references on family and marital interaction and treatment cited elsewhere, see Arthur Leader, "The Notion of Responsibility in Family Therapy," *Social Casework,* 60 (March 1979), 131–137, in which he discusses the importance of helping family members to take

responsibility for the effects of their communications and behavior on one another.

8. Mullen's and Reid and Shyne's findings concerning worker differences amply demonstrate variations in worker approach. Edward J. Mullen, "Differences in Worker Style in Casework," *Social Casework*, 50 (June 1969), 347–353; William Reid and Ann Shyne, *Brief and Extended Casework* (New York: Columbia University Press, 1969), pp. 76, 84. Ripple et al., *Motivation, Capacity and Opportunity*, demonstrates the effect of differences in worker warmth and encouragement. Frank, "Role of Hope in Psychotherapy," sees this aspect as one of primary importance. See also notes to Chapter 12, especially 1, 2, and 17.

# Chapter 18

# Understanding and Choice of Treatment Procedures

When we turn to the choice of treatment procedures by which we hope to move toward long-range and intermediate goals, we see that certain overall decisions about procedures are dictated by both objectives and diagnostic understanding. Obviously, if one objective is to bring about environmental improvement, either environmental treatment or extrareflection is certain to be prominent. If there are problems of personal dysfunctioning and both diagnostic thinking and the client's motivation make self-understanding a reasonable objective, intrareflection, including, perhaps, dynamic and developmental reflection, will play a major role. Where the objective is improvement in interpersonal relationships, all aspects of current person–situation reflection will of necessity be in the forefront.

Not only does the broad initial diagnostic thinking guide the details of treatment, but also indispensable to the immediate choice of procedures is continuous sensitive understanding. For instance, after an interview in which a client had ventilated much feeling about her husband's "TV addiction," the worker anticipated that there would be an opportunity to encourage her client's beginning awareness that her intense annoyance at her husband's preoccupation with sports on TV paralleled a childhood reaction to her father's regular Saturday trips to the "Game." However, as soon as the client entered the room the worker noted her harassed expression and the recurrence of an eye twitch. The anticipated plan for the interview had to be laid aside, and instead the worker sought to learn the cause of her client's present distress. Both basic diagnostic thinking and the immediate perception of the client's need and readiness for one of these alternatives enters such decisions, decisions that must be made in a flash.

Each interview, then, is a constantly moving encounter between two people undertaking a common task. The worker's part in that task includes being continuously alert to the client's immediate feelings and attitudes, thinking and reactions. In communication language, this is alertness to feedback—feedback that reveals how the interaction is proceeding and guides the worker's next procedures. Accurate reception of these communications requires not only close attention but, even more important, empathy with the client, a capacity to *feel with* him or her at the same time that one is *thinking* about what type of response will be most helpful.

## ENVIRONMENTAL CHANGE

Many aspects of the relationships between diagnostic understanding and the procedures of treatment have been discussed in the chapters describing these procedures and their uses. Clearly, the location of factors contributing to a client's dilemma is the first indicator of whether environmental treatment is needed. If such factors are located, a second indicator is the assessment of whether or not it is likely that change can be brought in them. If it appears that such change might be possible, the next decision to be made is that of *how* to bring the change about—through direct intervention by the worker or by helping clients to act for themselves.[1] We have often referred to the general preference of the psychosocial worker for enabling clients to do things for themselves whenever possible. So we must turn again to assessment—is the client able or likely to become able to do this. Is the environment likely to respond to the effort? The dynamic diagnosis will also be involved—how important is this pressure in the total gestalt? Is it urgent that change be made faster than the client is likely to be able to bring it about? One further diagnostic consideration—what is the state of the client's motivation and trust in the worker? Is it important for the worker to win the client's confidence by immediately doing something that will better his or her situation?

If direct environmental work is decided upon, the actual steps taken will again depend upon diagnostic thinking about collaterals as well as about the client. In work with people in the client's social environment, some impressions can be formed from what the client has said to the worker but much of one's understanding is arrived at on the spot, as the person consulted responds to the worker's approaches. Since details of environmental work and of the issues involved were discussed in chapters 8 and 9 we do not need to deal further with them here.

## INTERPERSONAL RELATIONSHIPS AND INTERNAL CHANGE

When we turn to problems that primarily concern interpersonal relationships and internal change, we find that the nature of the problem makes it necessary to emphasize procedures designed to promote both outwardly directed and inwardly directed understanding. The Hollis study of marriage counseling cases, for instance, showed that from the second interview onward over 50 percent of the worker's communications were of a reflective type—predominantly, of course, person–situation reflection. The client responds to this by a gradual increase in reflective comments. Occasionally, diagnostic observation shows that a person is so depressed or grief-stricken that treatment at first is very heavily weighted with sustainment, ventilation, and some direct influence. But, characteristically, there is soon some movement into thought about the details of everyday living and an effort to expand the client's awareness of his or her own feelings beyond depression and grief per se to other emotions.

As the worker listens to a client discussing interpersonal problems, the question constantly arises: Which thread of the communications should be picked up? The worker tries to find a way that will enable the client to gain the understanding needed to deal with the dilemma more competently as rapidly as he or she can, but without running the risk of overloading the client with more new ways of looking at things than he or she can comfortably assimilate or is ready to take on. To go too fast may be to lose the client.

## The Anxiety Factor in Early Interviews

The Hollis study, which compared fifteen clients with marital problems who continued in treatment with fifteen who dropped out after the first or second interview, found that the workers had made a markedly greater number of lengthy interpretations and explanations in the initial interviews with those who dropped out than with continuers. Furthermore, it was found that these communications in many instances had a distinct potential for arousing anxiety. In contrast, in early interviews with clients who continued, anxiety-arousing comments had in large part been avoided.[2] This is not to say that reflective techniques —even intrareflection—can never be used in early interviews. If care is taken to assess the anxiety factor, introduction of some person–situation reflection into early interviews induces feedback that is often of great value to diagnostic understanding, and to the mutual clarification of the early objectives of treatment. This also gives the client a sample of what the contact will be like, providing something to take away as an immediate treatment gain.

Mrs. Ford, a young, single mother was referred by a school psychologist to a family service agency because her eight-year-old son was daydreaming and crying in class. Projective tests revealed that he was consumed with rage and with fears that his family would abandon him.

In the first interview, the mother—who had had a very unstable childhood herself—wept and said that she saw history repeating itself. She had lived with a series of men, had moved frequently, and had been hospitalized for a "nervous stomach" three times over the past two years. She was sad, she said, that she had not given better care to her son than her alcoholic parents had given her. Accompanied by expressions of understanding for this woman's deep distress, the worker said that it sounded as though Mrs. Ford was, perhaps, asking for some help in stabilizing her own life as well as that of her son. Mrs. Ford, looking relieved, said, "That's exactly what I want. I've been unhappy with myself for a long time." At the end of the first interview, it was clear that this client wanted to think introspectively about her own life and about her part in her son's problems. Mrs. Ford's availability for reflective thinking was a positive diagnostic sign and an indicator of her motivation for change.

When the sequence in which matters are taken up rests on the worker's choice in following one lead or another, assessment of the anxiety-arousing potential of each choice is highly pertinent. We referred earlier to the fact that when the worker recognizes tension and anger in family relationships, it is usually very important to give the client adequate opportunity for the expression of this hurt and anger. Interpretations concerning how the other person feels or why the other person acts as he or she does are more likely to be accepted if they come later, unless diagnosis shows unusual openness to self-awareness. Little readiness may exist for any appreciation of the way in which the client is hurting the other person or provoking negative reactions such as withdrawal or counter-hostility. Assessment often indicates that not only ventilation of the feelings involved, but also acceptance of the hurt and understanding of the desire to retaliate, may be needed to prepare the way for the client's willingness to understand the other's needs or to consider his or her own contribution to the troubles.

## Personality Factors

Factors within the personality of the client will greatly influence readiness to try to understand another. This is well illustrated by two contrasting marital counseling cases carried by the same worker. In the first case, the worker was very active during early contacts in promoting the wife's reflection concerning her husband. In the second, emphasis was placed instead on the wife's awareness of her own feelings. The reasons for the difference in treatment lay not in the situations, but in the worker's diagnostic understanding of the personalities of the two women. Both women were very afraid of not being loved, both were volatile women of southern European background, both were belittling their husbands and initially putting all the blame for the family unhappiness on their husbands. Both were intelligent and motivated to seek help. The first client, however, had no doubt of her love for her husband and had matured emotionally to the point that she was well related to other people and cared for their welfare as well as for her own. Clinically, one could say that her personality was relatively healthy and mature, or perhaps that her psychological problem lay in the hysterical range. This client immediately responded with understanding to the worker's carefully worded questions about how her husband might feel, why he might be acting as he was, and what effect some of her impulsive hostility might be having on him. So it was possible for client and worker to proceed rapidly with this. The second client, clinically classified as having a narcissistic personality disorder, was a more dependent person, preoccupied with her own anxieties; she clung to her husband but was less giving of love herself. She had less spontaneous interest in her husband's feelings and reasons for them. She wanted and needed to talk about herself and how he had hurt her. Her understanding of the nature of her own feelings and the way in which this affected her feelings toward her husband had to be given precedence over attempts to develop her understanding of him.

The quality of a person's capacity to love others—referred to in Freudian terminology as the ego's capacity for object relationships—is of primary importance in influencing his or her readiness for understanding others and the effects of his or her own ways upon others. An individual greatly retarded in this capacity may lack motivation to look inward for the cause of difficulties. Such a person is not sufficiently attuned to others to appreciate their feelings easily, or to see the ways in which he or she provokes and hurts them. These clients are very unlikely to be able to put to good use treatment that requires much self-examination. There may be introspection, but it is a narcissistic or self-pitying type of introspection. The person often can be reached only to the extent that he or she feels very strongly the worker's interest in helping for his or her own sake. Sometimes an individual with this difficulty can be led to think of the effects of actions on others in the context of his or her own self-interest.

*THOUGHT PROCESSES.* The client's capacity for logical thinking—another ego quality—experience with this type of thinking, and the extent to which secondary rather than primary processes are dominant also strongly influence the extent to which reflective procedures in general can be used and the direction and pace at which the work can proceed. Can the client make only rather simple connections, or is he or she a sophisticated thinker? Can the person be led to reason things through independently, or must the worker explain concretely step by step? Some people know a good deal about psychological mechanisms long before they see the worker. Others are psychologically naive and must have things explained in detail. As we noted earlier, greater intellectual knowledge sometimes leads to a superficial acquiescence or to a facile denial of the importance of an interpretation, even though it may be an accurate one.

The need for a worker to distinguish between a client's sophistication about psychological theory and his or her capacity for reflection that leads to change is illustrated by the following contrasting examples:

One client, a brilliant chemist, often talked at length in treatment sessions about the "cause" of his anger with his wife, which he related to the influence of his "overprotective" and "seductive" mother. In his view, his early experiences resulted in his being wary of women, always fearful that they wanted to control him. Therefore, he would explain, when his wife made affectionate or sexual overtures, he would convert his fright into hostility. To be sure, his appraisal of his difficulties had merit, but he seemed far better motivated to perfect his elaborate analysis of himself and his reactions than he was to make changes.

In contrast, Dick Jones (Chapter 3), who was seen in marital therapy with his wife, had no advanced education and little knowledge about psychological matters. Nevertheless, his capacity for introspection led to productive work in treatment far surpassing that of the chemist. Dick Jones' quickness in understanding the roots of his passivity, the effect of this on his wife, and the dysfunctional pattern of interaction that had developed between them, were important to the marked improvement in the marital relationship that was achieved in brief treatment.

Often, behavior similar to what the worker is trying to help the client to understand is commonplace in children and can first be understood in them. "Look, have you ever noticed how Verne when he's mad at Phil (older brother) starts jumping on Stella (little sister)?" If the client's response shows understanding—"What about that! He sure does, he just takes it out on her"—the client will probably be able to understand the same defense mechanism in her own displacement from husband to son.

For some people, however, this sort of reasoning and the carryover from one situation to another parallel one are impossible. Yet in some of these situations the interpersonal adjustment problem is acute. If the handicap in thought processes is not accompanied by general emotional immaturity, progress can sometimes be made by suggestion and advice. But this is not likely to be effective unless a strong positive relationship has been established, so that the client has confidence in the worker's good will as well as in his good sense.

## Situational and Ethnic Factors

When families are plagued with severe environmental problems, these sometimes dominate the whole gestalt so completely that relationship problems seem of little importance. Casework should then concentrate on these practical problems. Once these are alleviated, perhaps there will be motivation for tackling strain in other parts of the system such as internal family stress.[3] Family members can sometimes make progress toward learning to be mutually supportive in times of stress rather than taking frustrations out on each other. Family interviews are often the best way to move toward such a goal.

Ethnic factors are extremely diverse in their significance for treatment. In some cultures, there is strong aversion to discussing family troubles and complaints with outsiders. In some, men especially regard the need for such help as a disgrace and a sign of weakness. Certainly, language differences of any major proportion are a deterrent to the kind of communication necessary for intrapsychic reflection. In the social study, workers need to be alert to attitudes of personal reticence, distrust between races, a marked difference in experience and values between client and worker, difficulties in casting the worker in a therapeutic role. For these are all obstacles to treatment of any type, and might be particularly obstructive to the pursuit of inward understanding. Obviously, the degree to which these handicaps to treatment can be overcome varies in different cases. They are not necessarily insurmountable.

The choice of procedures within the various types of person–situation reflection obviously depends very strongly upon the kind of problem the client is trying to resolve and the worker's assessment of the factors contributing to the problem. In interpersonal problems, treatment themes usually include both outwardly and inwardly directed reflection concerning the current interactional gestalt.

## Diagnostic Understanding

The specific content of any interpretation is directly dependent on diagnostic understanding. The worker who tries to help an individual see another person more clearly depends upon his or her diagnostic impression of the meaning of the other person's actions. This understanding can be expected to be more accurate than the client's only to the extent that the worker has taken more factors into consideration than has the client, has looked at the matter from the other person's point of view, is not hampered by the distortions of perception that skew things for the client, and makes use of knowledge that the client does not have concerning the functioning of personalities and of interacting systems.

Specifics of what the worker seeks to help the client to become aware of and understand, that is, will depend directly upon the ongoing diagnostic assessment of what factors are contributing to the social dysfunctioning, modified constantly by the assessment of how much understanding the client can assimilate. Only as the worker recognizes dysfunctional responses and sees the factors in personal interactions that touch off such responses can he or she enable the client also to recognize them.

## PATTERN-DYNAMIC AND DEVELOPMENTAL REFLECTION

The decision as to whether or not to lead the client to pattern-dynamic or developmental reflection, or to expand the client's own spontaneous move in this direction, is again guided in psychosocial casework by the various types of diagnostic understanding.

These types of reflection would be encouraged when the difficulty is one for which this type of help is useful and when the client appears to be capable of participating in the process of self-understanding and is willing to do so. Developmental or dynamic understanding can help the client see how and why he or she is reacting in unrealistic or dysfunctional ways, strengthen his or her grasp of the patterns, and contribute to the ability to change them. Here we are talking about *patterns* of intrapsychic behavior, not isolated instances.

## Motivation

Opportunities for developing more than isolated bits of understanding arise primarily when the client is motivated toward the development of considerable self-understanding. Such motivation often occurs when an individual is caught in a crisis or faced by developmental changes within the self or within another member of the family. Instances of the latter would be the birth of a child, especially the first one, a wife's decision to work outside the home, a husband's decision to change to a radically different form of work, the departure of grown children from the home, and so on. These rather sudden changes may overtax the ego defense system or upset a long-time balance of forces. Dynamic or developmental reflection is not always needed, but in many instances it is exceedingly helpful in enabling the client to deal with the new situation.

These procedures can also be particularly useful when an individual is dissatisfied with his or her ways of relating to others or with feelings about the self or when the person feels he or she is not living up to abilities in study or work. They can also be very helpful in many family or other relationship problems when current person–situation reflection is not sufficient to enable the person to change dysfunctional ways of relating to others.

## Widespread Use

Some years ago, when we were first attempting to understand the significance of the clinical diagnosis for choice of treatment procedures, some of us thought that one could generalize to the point of saying that efforts to help the client understand the dynamics of his or her psychological functioning and its development should be limited to individuals who appeared to be only mildly neurotic. This turned out to be simplistic. Actual examination of work that was being done by skillful practitioners showed that these techniques were being used more widely than had been anticipated, and that broad diagnostic classification was only a rough indicator of when they could be helpful. Finer criteria related to the assessment of various aspects of ego and superego functioning, and especially to the ability to deal with anxiety, began to be developed.

The cases discussed in detail in Chapter 3 and to be presented in Chapter 19 demonstrate how clients with a wide range of problems and clinical diagnoses were able to participate in pattern-dynamic and developmental reflection. These reflective procedures, combined with person–situation reflection and the frequent use of sustainment, were to varying degrees components of the long-term treatment of Mrs. Zimmer (Chapter 3), diagnosed as a borderline personality. Dick and Susan Jones (Chapter 3)—both basically sound psychologically—were able to be introspective about their personality patterns and their early life experiences as they worked to resolve their relationship difficulties. Betty Kovacs (Chapter 3), an "acting out" adolescent with a character disturbance and some hysterical symptoms, could be reflective about herself, her patterns of behavior, and her childhood relationships with her parents. Mrs. Barry (Chapter 19), diagnosed as paranoid schizophrenic, astonished the worker with her capacity for making connections between her present situation, her father's alcoholism, and her position as the overlooked "middle child." Mrs. Stasio (Chapter 19), faced with terminal cancer and an awareness of some of her neurotic patterns, used these types of intrareflection a number of times in her treatment experience. Jed Cooper (Chapter 19), whose anxiety had many hysterical features, was able to make helpful connections between his current difficulties and his complicated ties to his parents. Finally, Mr. Russo (Chapter 11), although not characteristically given to introspection, was able to reflect movingly in family sessions on how the early death of his mother and frequent changes of foster homes when he was a boy had contributed to his depression at the time his older daughter moved away from home.

## ANXIETY AND GUILT

Assessment of the degree of anxiety and understanding of the client's way of handling it are very important considerations in the choice of treatment procedures, and especially so in intrareflection. Although we have commented a number of times on the significance of this factor, further points remain to be considered and reemphasized. Anxiety and guilt may logically be discussed together, for guilt is one form of anxiety —in Anna Freud's words,[4] the ego's fear of the superego—and what is said about anxiety in general applies with equal force to guilt. Anna Freud also calls attention to anxiety caused by the ego's fear of the instincts—that is, fear that thoughts, feelings, and actions not approved by ego or superego will break through despite efforts to control them. This form of fear is especially prevalent in psychosis, and in borderline and narcissistic personality disorders.

Sensitivity to the actual existence of anxiety and to the degree to which it is present in the client at any one moment is essential, as is also awareness of the extent to which the client chronically carries anxiety around or is vulnerable to its arousal. What particular things in the client's present or past provoke this anxiousness? How does this anxiety show itself, and how does the client handle it? In particular: Does anxiety impel the client to unwise acting out? Does it result in increased neurotic or somatic symptomatology? What defenses does the client use against it? Is the person immobilized? Will he or she run away from treatment?

## Observation of Anxiety

In order to be alert to the presence of anxiety in the client, one must be aware of the ways in which it expresses itself. Occasionally anxiety is shown physically, by trembling of body or voice, body tenseness, sweating or pallor, nervous gestures or excitement, and so on.[5] Sometimes the client reveals it by posture or gesture, sitting on the edge of the chair or at a distance, wrapping a coat tightly or refusing to take it off. More often, however, it shows itself in increased use of the client's characteristic defense mechanisms. The intellectual may go off into theoretical, often contentious discussions; defensive hostility erupts in the challenge that treatment is not helping, with the implication that the worker is incompetent; rationalization, reaction formation, denial —any of the mechanisms of defense—may be brought into play in their characteristic role of attempting to protect the individual from experiencing anxiety. Avoidance may finally result in the client's skipping interviews altogether. If these signs are spotted early enough, they can alert the worker to the presence of the anxiety, and to the need for this to become part of the discussions between client and worker. Sensitivity to the presence of anxiety needs to be accompanied by awareness of the conditions under which anxiety tends to be high, both for clients in general and for the particular individual with whom one is working.

## The Treatment Process

We have already commented in earlier chapters on the many ways in which anxiety can be aroused by the use of various treatment procedures. A brief review at this point will emphasize the importance of this factor in applying diagnostic understanding to the treatment process. Reflective consideration of intrapsychic content is by no means the only set of treatment procedures by which anxiety is aroused. Merely describing, as part of the application process, life events of which one is ashamed may be a very painful, anxiety-provoking experience. Ventilation that involves the expression of emotions or desires of which the client is afraid may bring fear that talking will be a forerunner of acting. Guilt may very easily be aroused in a sensitive person by discussions that produce awareness for the first time of the harmful effects of his actions on others, or even of needs of his child or wife to which he has been blind. The individual with a very severe superego will feel guilt very keenly whenever matters come up in which he or she appears to be even slightly in the wrong. Even when the worker merely listens, such an individual anticipates criticism, often projecting his or her own self-condemnation onto the worker; the person then may fear loss of love, or the worker's disinterest, and may in self-defense project blame onto others or resort to outright denial or defensive hostility, or even withdraw from treatment.

Even the giving of suggestions and advice, under certain conditions, can arouse anxiety. In a case known to one of the writers, the worker was greatly and rightly concerned about the severity with which an impulsive mother was in the habit of discipling her seven-year-old son. Early in the contact, the worker advised her against this and was gratified at the change in her client's handling of the child and his immediate improvement. Unfortunately, however, she had not made a careful diagnostic study of the mother or thought ahead to possible consequences of her advice. In the first place, the child had never been controlled in any other way. His initial reaction was to be very good, but, as could have been foreseen, he soon began to explore the limits of his new freedom and became increasingly defiant of his now disarmed mother. In addition to being impulsive, the mother had a great deal of compulsiveness in her makeup. A good diagnostician could easily have identified the clinical signs of this and would have known that along with her impulsiveness this mother had a very severe conscience and a great need, like a small child, to win the worker's approval. She tried very hard to be a good mother along the lines the worker suggested. In fact, however, after the initial good news of improvement in the child, she found it very hard to let the worker know that things were not going so well. This also could have been foreseen. Eventually, one day "all hell let loose," and her anger against her son burst forth in a really dangerous way. Then, to justify herself, she had to condemn the child as uncontrollable by any other means, and turned completely away from the worker and her advice.

*SELF-UNDERSTANDING.*   On the whole, the development of understanding of oneself and one's own functioning, whether in discussion of the current person–situation interaction or of personality patterns, tends to arouse more anxiety than do other treatment processes. The reasons for this are several. These are types of self-examination. As the client becomes involved in such treatment, he or she may become more acutely aware than previously of his or her faulty functioning. This realization can cause discomfort and pain, particularly, again, if the client has a severe superego. This may also constitute a narcissistic injury. These discomforts, in turn, characteristically stir up anger at the worker—the bearer of evil tidings—that causes the client still further discomfort.

*PRECONSCIOUS MATERIAL.*   Anxiety can be great, too, when treatment involves the client's bringing to consciousness memories and realizations that have been hidden, or at least that a person has not talked about with others. These matters would not be hidden away if they were not in some way painful. It may be the pain of sorrow and frustration. Or the superego may be affronted, for the client may be defying parental standards in producing particular memories or becoming aware of certain feelings and attitudes. This source of anxiety is similar to that experienced by the patient in analysis, who feels it even more strongly in relation to unconscious, repressed material. In analysis it is recognized as a principal source of resistance, and in casework a similar factor is involved. Painful early experiences have sometimes been of such traumatic proportions that extreme anxiety would be involved in reliving them. In such cases there is usually strong resistance to recalling them, and this should serve as a caution signal to the worker. This situation arose with people who suffered the extremes of persecution in World War II. Some of the things that happened to them could be assimilated only by very exceptional people, and more often could be surmounted only as they could be walled off by suppressions and repressions that it would be unwise to disturb.

On the whole, a past experience that arouses anxiety concerning only the pain of reliving the experience itself is more easily borne than one that arouses guilt. If, for instance, the memory involves actions or even feelings and wishes that the individual thinks are shameful or wrong, fear of his or her own and the worker's disapproval may be very strong. Guilt is frequently associated with childhood hostilities toward parents and others in families where such high value was placed on surface amiability that all anger had to be hidden. It is also associated in many people in our culture with childhood sexuality, with current and past masturbation, and often with sexual deviation. Both individual and cultural values are strong determinants here. For one person, hostile feelings will be taboo; for another, lying; for still another, erotic responsiveness.

OTHER SOURCES.   Even positive feelings in treatment can cause anxiety in some people. Some individuals who have been badly hurt in close relationships fear further suffering if they allow themselves to come too close to others, fearing this as they experience warm feelings toward their worker. Others, as we have seen, fear entrapment or enmeshment.

A further source of anxiety that may be present in any form of treatment having as its goal some degree of change in personality functioning is fear of the change itself. Even though present ways of functioning may cause discomfort, there have usually also been secondary advantages in the faulty functioning. The new understanding may require greater self-control, less expression of hostility, less blame of others, more altruistic and less narcissistic behavior. The client may desire change, but may also feel uneasy about it and reluctant to give up ways that, in some respects, may be comforting and self-gratifying.

This is not to say that intrareflection is universally anxiety arousing. Certain themes, even when they are dynamically or developmentally explored, may be fairly low in their anxiety potential, and therefore can safely be explored even in "fragile" personalities. A case in point is that of a schizophrenic woman who was able to see that her suspicious expectation of hostile attack from a woman in her current life was a displacement from a childhood experience in which she had actually been very badly treated by a harsh grandmother. Discussion of the circumstances not only did not arouse anxiety, but actually allayed it. Talking about the oppressive grandmother was not frightening, because the worker did not attempt to explore whether the client was partly at fault, but accepted the situation as an externally caused and regrettable hardship. Recognition of the possibility of displacement also involved no blame for the client; instead, it gave her a rational explanation for some of her fears, so that she was able to look more realistically at the lack of evidence in the current situation to justify them.

## Anxiety Reduction

Clients sometimes find great relief in talking about painful experiences in the presence of a sympathetic worker who is not overwhelmed by their ventilation. This process may help the ego to assimilate the memories, to be less afraid of them, to be more able to bear the pain involved, and to express the natural emotions of grief and anger associated with the experiences. Such verbal activity is similar to the play activities of children, in which they repeat painful and frightening experiences in an effort to assimilate them. When the happenings that are being aired are also responsible for some current reaction that is causing the individual trouble, he or she may in the very same interview also experience a sense of relief from talking about them. For instance, a person who in reality had very critical parents, with consequent feelings of distrust in his or her own ability, may obtain almost immediate relief from talking about their unjust criticisms. By sensing the worker's confirmation that they were indeed unjust, the client can experience some freeing from the earlier acceptance of the parents' views. The main reason that a person pursues understanding in spite of anxiety is the satisfaction gained from this new understanding—of the self, of fears, and of inhibitions. A load is often lifted, and sometimes genuine excitement is felt as a piece of insight exposes an encumbering defense.

There is much the worker can do in helping the client deal with anxiety. Of primary importance is the worker's basic attitude of support and acceptance, which softens the impact of comments. When this is communicated to the client, he or she can find support in a basic security with the worker; whatever the exigencies of the moment, the client can then hold to a strong underlying conviction that the worker feels positively toward him or her, respects and is endeavoring to help him or her. This conviction is inevitably obscured, from time to time at difficult moments in treatment, by transference elements and by projection of the client's own attitudes. Such distortions can be corrected, however, only if the actual relationship is a positive one, and is fundamentally perceived as such by the client. To achieve this basic relationship and keep it alive, both direct and indirect sustainment are important.

WORKER STYLE.   What might be called the "form" or "style" of worker communications used in promoting reflective thinking also has direct bearing on the client's potential anxiety. Worker comments can vary, as we have seen, from direct interpretation or explanation to completely nonsuggestive questions or comments that merely draw the client's attention to something about which the worker would like the person to think. An illustration of the latter is the repetition of the last phrase or so of something the client has said. In general, the more open-ended a worker comment is, the less likely it is to arouse anxiety, since it can be ignored—if the client is not ready to follow the worker's lead, he or she can easily respond without any recognition of the matters to which the worker is trying to draw attention. More direct comments and questions push the client harder, and interpretations, of course, formulate an opinion with which the client must deal. Other things being equal, the more direct the comment, the greater the possibility of stirring up anxiety.

A skillful worker finds ways of expressing things that support rather than hurt. The worker in effect often "rewards" the client when he or she has gained a piece of understanding. It is natural for the worker to be pleased. Sometimes this is put into words: "You've done a good job of thinking that through." More often facial expression and tone of voice communicate the feeling that the client has taken a step forward. Sometimes interpretations can be softened by humorous wording.

## BALANCING ANXIETY AND MOVEMENT

When this basically secure relationship has been established, a person can often make very good use even of anxiety-provoking comments. It is sometimes necessary to refrain from reassuring and comforting remarks at specific points in order to keep the client at work pursuing understanding of difficulties.

To illustrate: A woman who tends to be overly critical of her husband tells the caseworker about an incident in which this tendency was prominent and half apologizes for her disparaging words. The worker may either make a reassuring remark about her annoyance being understandable, or may comment more directly, if the basic relationship is a good one, "You do have a sharp tongue!" The latter procedure will not be very reassuring. It will increase rather than decrease the client's anxiety and, if the worker has correctly gauged her ego and superego qualities, will serve to motivate her to seek understanding of her overreaction. Great care must be exercised in finding the balance by which to give enough warmth and security to nourish progress and protect the client from excessive anxiety, and at the same time to maintain a level of tension conducive to motivation toward self-understanding.

A worker sensitive to either the likelihood of anxiety or its actual presence can often help the client bring this into the open, often thereby reducing it. "Perhaps it scares you a little to tell me about this." Or, "I guess that was a tough question." Or, during an anxiety-arousing interview, "Let me know if you think we're going too fast." Remarks such as these may not only provide relief, but may also promote feedback from the client as part of his or her responsibility for guiding treatment. If it seems wise to go on, the worker can proceed in a number of ways. Sometimes it is possible to draw the client's attention to defensiveness. At other times, it may be necessary to work first on the personality characteristic that makes the individual respond so strongly—with compulsive clients, for instance, the overly severe superego and perfectionism. At other times it is necessary to have a period of relaxation in treatment, the worker saying directly or in effect, "Perhaps later you will feel more able to talk about this." And at still other times, when the worker has good reason to think that the client is close to talking about certain experiences but is afraid to do so, ways can be found for framing a question or comment that relieves guilt or anxiety before the frightening content is actually expressed.

One often finds that after a difficult piece of self-understanding, the client, in the next interview, stays on superficial, more or less self-congratulatory, material. This relaxation may be necessary. A balance needs to be found between relaxing and sustaining measures, on the one hand, and procedures pressing toward self-understanding, on the other.

When anxiety—or guilt—is either chronically very high, or aroused because of the experiences the client is going through when he or she comes for treatment, a goodly measure of sustaining procedures, especially indirect sustainment, is of particular value. There are times, for instance, when it is well to draw the client out about experiences in which he or she has played an especially helpful role. Or one may refer to good motivation even while pointing out mistakes a person has made.

"You meant to be helpful to Johnnie even though you frightened him by treating him the same way your father treated you." It is important, of course, that such supportive interpretations be realistic.

If the client is unable or unwilling to deal with anxiety, one can refrain from pursuing the anxiety-arousing content. It may be possible later, when the client has gained strength or is more trusting of the worker, to reintroduce it or, on the other hand, worker and client may agree that this particular content may have to remain untouched.

As noted earlier, timing and sequence are important. The worker's continuous diagnostic assessment of the client and sensitivity to current moods and reactions can enable him or her to avoid observations and insights for which the client is not yet ready.

If treatment is kept close to the realities of life, if person–situation reflection is the central focus, the client who develops more understanding usually experiences improvement in interpersonal relationships. The client receives different responses from others in reaction to changes in his or her own ways of handling things. Indeed, in situations where this is lacking, it is very difficult for the client not to become too discouraged to continue. This is one of the reasons for the importance of seeing both individuals involved in problems of interpersonal adjustment.

If the worker is thoroughly attuned to the client by means of sensitive diagnostic assessment of both the underlying personality pattern and the nuances of feelings and reactions while interviews are in process, casework treatment is not basically a painful process. There are, of course, ups and downs from interview to interview. But if efforts to develop understanding of self and others are well paced, clients can experience satisfaction in their greater grasp of their dilemmas and increased ability to cope with them. They can also experience a strengthening of self-esteem, for the relationship in many different ways is a nourishing one.

## LENGTH OF CONTACT

There remains the question of length of time for treatment. For many years it was assumed that a contact continued until the needed help was given, or the client withdrew, or the worker decided there was nothing more to be done. Many clients withdrew after only a few interviews. Others continued for many months, sometimes for several years. The functional school of social work had long advocated the setting of limits for the length of contact at the outset. Proponents felt that the client worked best against such limits. This was part of the Rankian conception of growth through the negative will. Largely because of this theoretical underpinning, other caseworkers objected to what seemed to them an arbitrary setting of limits. Then came World War II, with an increase in applicants, shortage of workers, and long waiting lists of clients needing service. On the basis of expediency, many different devices were tried to bring help more quickly. Among them was briefer service with more limited goals.

At first this was considered only an emergency measure, but workers began to see that it was more possible than they had thought to give a valid service in relatively few interviews. One form of such service was *crisis treatment.*[6] This type of service is appropriate when a person has been thrown off balance by some hazardous life event of a time-limited nature, which touches off within the personality reactions with which he or she is unable to cope. Anxiety is usually very high, so high in fact that it can produce reactions that bring the client to a psychiatric clinic, where much crisis treatment has been carried on. It has been found that in a period when the personality system has lost its equilibrium, it is in a state of flux in which rapid change is possible within a short time. In order to know what help is needed in terms of both objectives and procedures, a rapid diagnosis, well grounded upon theory, must be made. Treatment tends to be quite active. Pertinent interpretations are made quickly. Goals are limited and well defined. A number of interviews may be held within a short time span.

Another type of brief service is *time-limited contacts.*[7] Whereas crisis treatment tends to be self-limiting, since it revolves around a crisis, in time-limited contacts a specific time for ending is set up that may vary from as little as two or three interviews to as much as a three-month period. Various ways in which time can be set were discussed under "Initial Decisions" in Chapter 15. Workers vary in the extent to which they use the device of a set time limit. Reid and Epstein,[8] who have been studying such work for a number of years, have combined with it the use of the techniques of task planning and implementation, which they recommend as a useful approach to a wide range of problems and for the achievement of specific goals.

Most psychosocial workers today do make use of the short contact and also sometimes of the device of time limits where they believe them to be diagnostically indicated, either because the problem appears to be one that can be resolved quickly or because the worker's diagnostic impression is that the client will make better use of short than of longer treatment. It may also be chosen because the client expresses a preference for it or seems resistant to longer contact. The work with Mr. and Mrs. Jones in Chapter 3 illustrates the process of using the device of a contract to arrive at the decision to limit the number of interviews.[9]

Similarly, some workers of the psychosocial orientation are making

use of the technique of task assignment, where diagnostic understanding indicates that this may help the client either to try out or to
implement some of his or her thoughts about how to modify relationships or functioning. Here it would be used as one part of the total
treatment approach and would involve procedures of both direct influence and person–situation reflection.

In the authors' view, we do not yet have adequate or firm knowledge of diagnostic indicators as to when time-limited treatment is preferable and when longer help is needed.[10] In view of this it seems
reasonable, when a limit is set, to keep the option open for reconsidera-
tion in case at a later point further treatment would seem to be useful.
When clients aspire to extensive understanding of themselves and their
relationship with others, in order to bring changes in their ways of living
and in their feelings about themselves, treatment may take a long time.
Psychosocial casework involves at times either contact over a lengthy
period or intermittent contacts of varying intensity over years. The
latter requires *continuity* of understanding and of the treatment process, even though there may be long or short intervals in which contact
is not needed. It is often well to prepare the client for the possibility of
return and, when feasible, for the client to be seen each time by the
same worker. Much work with children, the elderly, the handicapped,
discharged mental patients, adolescent mothers, and so on would seem
to be of this type.

It is important not to overestimate the usefulness of brief treatment, as administrators are sometimes tempted to do, as a way of
solving budgetary problems. There is no way of measuring the value of
personal development in quantitative terms. One can waste money by
giving too little service just as truly as by giving too much if either is
inappropriate. Mrs. Zimmer (Chapter 3) is a case in point: little or
nothing could have been accomplished with her within a three-month
time limit. Cost to the agency is a valid consideration, but not an over-
riding one. The real question is, How can we help the client make the
maximum use of each interview in view of what he or she really wants
and can use.

We have been endeavoring, in this chapter, to delineate ways in
which the casework treatment procedures used to help a client rest
upon the worker's differential understanding of a wide range of characteristics of the client and the personal–social situation.[11] Treatment is
always an individualized blend of the objectives mutually arrived at by
client and worker, the themes or subgoals in the service of these objectives, and the procedures by means of which these themes are developed. The nature of the blend is not a matter of individual worker
artistry or intuition, important though these may be. On the contrary,

choice and emphasis follow definite principles and rest upon a most careful evaluation of the nature of the client's problem, external and internal etiological factors and their modifiability, the client's objectives, motivation, and pertinent aspects of his or her personality. In addition, there must be comprehension of the nature, effects, and demands of the different types of casework procedures and of the criteria by which the worker can match the client's needs and capacities with the particular combination of procedures most likely to be of value in enabling the client to overcome, or at least to lessen, his or her difficulties. As much as possible, the process is shared by the client. Feedback is encouraged and often modifies treatment. It should by now be clear that the process of diagnostic assessment is an ongoing one, with the emphasis in treatment varying in harmony with the changing needs, capacities, and wishes of the client.

## NOTES

1. See good examples of this in Bernard Neugebore, "Opportunity Centered Social Services," *Social Work*, 15 (April 1970), 47–52. Many of the references in note 8, Chapter 8, also address this issue.
2. Florence Hollis, "Continuance and Discontinuance in Marital Counseling and Some Observations on Joint Interviews," *Social Casework*, 49 (March 1968), 167–174.
3. Good discussions of points related .to this can be found in Geoffrey B. Barnes et al., "Team Treatment for Abusive Families," *Social Casework*, 55 (December 1974), 600–611; Henry Freeman et al., "Can a Family Agency Be Relevant to the Inner Urban Scene?", *Social Casework*, 51 (January 1970), 12–21; Eleanor Pavenstedt, ed., *The Drifters: Children of Disorganized Lower-Class Families* (Boston: Little, Brown, 1967); and Arthur Pierson, "Social Work Techniques with the Poor," *Social Casework*, 51 (October 1970), 481–485.
4. Anna Freud, *The Ego and the Mechanisms of Defense* (New York: International Universities Press, 1946), pp. 58–60.
5. Lotte Marcus, "The Effect of Extralinguistic Phenomena on the Judgment of Anxiety" (doctoral dissertation, Columbia University School of Social Work, 1969).
6. A great deal has been written on crisis theory and practice by and for social workers. Special mention is made of an early compilation that is still in wide use and very valuable reading: Howard J. Parad, ed., *Crisis Intervention: Selected Readings* (New York: Family Service Association of America, 1965). For other readings, see also Katherine Baldwin, "Crisis-Focused Casework in a Child Guidance Clinic," *Social Casework*, 49 (January 1968), 28–34; Margaret Ball, "Issues of Violence in Family Casework," *Social Casework*, 58 (January 1977), 3–12; Naomi Golan, "Crisis Theory," in Francis J. Turner, ed., *Social Work Treatment: Interlocking Theoretical*

*Approaches,* 2nd ed. (New York: Free Press, 1979), pp. 499–534; Naomi Golan, *Treatment in Crisis Situations* (New York: Free Press, 1978); David L. Hoffman and Mary L. Remmel, "Uncovering the Precipitant in Crisis Intervention," *Social Casework,* 56 (May 1975), 259–267; Charlotte Kirschner, "The Aging Family in Crisis: A Problem in Living," *Social Casework,* 60 (April 1979), 209–216; Danuta Mostwin, "Social Work Interventions with Families in Crisis of Change," *Social Thought,* 2 (Winter 1976); Jeanette Oppenheimer, "Use of Crisis Intervention in Case Work with the Cancer Patient and His Family," *Social Work,* 12 (April 1967), 44–52; Lydia Rapoport, "Crisis Intervention as a Mode of Brief Treatment," in Robert W. Roberts and Robert H. Nee, eds., *Theories of Social Casework* (Chicago: University of Chicago Press, 1970), pp. 265–311; Larry L. Smith, "A Review of Crisis Intervention Theory," *Social Casework,* 59 (July 1978), 396–405; Larry Smith, "Crisis Intervention in Practice," *Social Casework,* 60 (February 1979), 81–89; and Reva S. Wiseman, "Crisis Theory and the Process of Divorce," *Social Casework,* 56 (April 1975), 205–212.

7.   There is also a wealth of literature on brief treatment and time-limited contacts. See, for example, Norman Epstein, "Techniques of Brief Therapy with Children and Parents," *Social Casework,* 57 (May 1976), 317–324; James Mann, *Time-Limited Psychotherapy* (Cambridge, Mass.: Harvard University Press, 1973); Jennie Sage Norman, "Short-Term Treatment with the Adolescent Client," *Social Casework,* 61 (February 1980), 74–82; Genevieve B. Oxley, "Short-Term Therapy with Student Couples," *Social Casework,* 54 (April 1973), 216–223; Leonard Small, *The Briefer Psychotherapies* (New York: Brunner/Mazel, 1971); and Lewis R. Wolberg, ed., *Short-Term Psychotherapy* (New York: Grune & Stratton, 1965).

8.   William J. Reid and Laura Epstein. *Task-Centered Casework* (New York: Columbia University Press, 1972), and *Task-Centered Practice* (New York: Columbia University Press, 1977).

    See also Marlin J. Blizinsky and William J. Reid, "Problem Focus and Change in a Brief Treatment Model," *Social Work,* 25 (March 1980), 89–93; Elin Cormican, "Task-Centered Model for Work with the Aged," *Social Casework,* 58 (October 1977), 490–494; Anne E. Fortune, "Communication in Task-Centered Treatment," *Social Work,* 24 (September 1979), 390–396; Dean H. Hepworth, "Early Removal of Resistance in Task-Centered Casework," *Social Work,* 24 (July 1979), 317–323; and William J. Reid, "A Test of a Task-Centered Approach," *Social Work,* 20 (January 1975), 3–9.

9.   The contract, referred to several times in earlier chapters, was useful in work with this couple in defining the problem to be addressed, the goals, the treatment modality, and the number of sessions they planned to meet together. In this case, the contract was an explicit, but informal, mutual agreement, with emphasis on its flexibility if further goals emerged or more time was required. For a fuller discussion of the contract approach, see Anthony N. Maluccio and Wilma D. Marlow, "The Case for the Contract," *Social Work,* 19 (January 1974), 28–36; and Sonya L. Rhodes, "Contract Negotiation in the Initial Stage of Casework Service," *Social Service Review,* 51 (March 1977), 125–140. See also Brett Seabury, "The Contract:

Uses, Abuses and Limitations," *Social Work*, 21 (January 1976), 16–21, for a very good discussion of the value of the contract, but also of its shortcomings and possible dangers.

10.   Although brief therapy has been used for a wide range of problems and, seemingly, with every diagnostic group, according to Butcher and Koss there is fairly general agreement that it is best suited for those patients or clients (1) whose behavior problem is of recent onset; (2) whose previous adjustment has been good; (3) who have good ability to relate; and (4) who have high initial motivation. See James N. Butcher and Mary P. Koss, "Research on Brief and Crisis-Oriented Therapies," in Sol L. Garfield and Allen E. Bergin, eds., *Handbook of Psychotherapy and Behavior Change*, 2nd ed., (New York: Wiley, 1978), pp. 725–767.

In their examination of the literature, Butcher and Koss also found that those mentioned as definitely unsuitable for short-term therapy are clients who desire "personality reconstruction," are deeply dependent, chronically "act out," are very self-centered, masochistic, and so on; these clinical opinions are in accordance with our own belief that especially when there have been critical early traumas, serious developmental deficits, or faulty ego formations brief therapy is of little or no value. In their overall analysis of the clinical literature and empirical research, Butcher and Koss conclude: "The effectiveness of time limitation over unlimited therapy for bringing about change has not been clearly shown in research. We believe that there is a lower limit on the amount of time a therapist can spend with a patient and demonstrate any gain at all. . . . However, time limitation has not been studied sufficiently as a variable itself to allow firm conclusions on the relationship of time allocation to therapeutic gain" (p. 759).

11.   As supplements to references already cited in this chapter and the two previous chapters on diagnosis and treatment, the following are relevant. In addition to useful theoretical discussions of casework diagnosis and treatment, many of the readings also provide clinical case illustrations:

Lucille Austin, "Dynamics and Treatment of the Client with Anxiety Hysteria," in Howard J. Parad, ed., *Ego Psychology and Dynamic Casework* (New York: Family Service Association of America, 1958).

Bernard Bandler, "The Concept of Ego-Supportive Psychotherapy," in Howard J. Parad and Roger R. Miller, eds., *Ego-Oriented Casework: Problems and Perspectives* (New York: Family Service Association of America, 1963).

Catherine Bittermann, "Marital Adjustment Patterns of Clients with Compulsive Character Disorders: Implications for Treatment," *Social Casework*, 47 (November 1966), 575–582.

Margaret C. Bonnefil, "The Relationship of Interpersonal Acting-Out to the Process of Decompensation," *Clinical Social Work Journal*, 1 (Spring 1973), 13–21.

Margaret C. Bonnefil, "Therapist, Save My Child: A Family Crisis Case," *Clinical Social Work Journal*, 7 (Spring 1979), 6–14.

Margery Chapman, "Salient Need—A Casework Compass," *Social Casework*, 58 (June 1977), 343–349.

Pauline Cohen and Merton Krause, *Casework with Wives of Alcoholics* (New York: Family Service Association of America, 1971).

Joyce Edward, "The Use of the Dream in the Promotion of Ego Development," *Clinical Social Work Journal*, 6 (Winter 1978), 261–273.

Patricia L. Ewalt, "The Crisis-Treatment Approach in a Child Guidance Clinic," *Social Casework*, 54 (July 1973), 406–411.

Anne O. Freed, "Social Casework: More than a Modality," *Social Casework*, 58 (April 1977), 204–213.

Jennie S. Fuller, "Duo Therapy Case Studies: Process and Techniques," *Social Casework*, 58 (February 1977), 84–91.

Sid Hirsohn, "Casework with the Compulsive Mother," *Social Casework*, 32 (June 1951), 254–261.

Hilliard Levinson, "Communication with an Adolescent in Psychotherapy," *Social Casework*, 54 (October 1973), 480–488.

Lorraine Pokart Levy, "Services to Parents of Children in a Psychiatric Hospital," *Social Casework*, 58 (April 1977), 204–213.

Florence Lieberman, *Social Work with Children* (New York: Human Services Press, 1979).

Sophie Loewenstein, "An Overview of the Concept of Narcissism," *Social Casework*, 58 (March 1977), 136–142.

Herta Mayer and Gerald Schamess, "Long Term Treatment for the Disadvantaged," *Social Casework*, 50 (March 1969), 138–145.

Roger S. Miller, "Disappointment in Therapy," *Clinical Social Work Journal*, 5 (Spring 1977), 17–28.

Danuta Mostwin, "Multidimensional Model of Working with the Family," *Social Casework*, 55 (April 1974), 209–215.

Judith C. Nelsen, "Treatment Issues in Schizophrenia," *Social Casework*, 56 (March 1975), 145–151.

Jeanette Oppenheimer, "Use of Crisis Intervention in Case Work with the Cancer Patient and His Family," *Social Work*, 12 (April 1967), 44–52.

Ben A. Orcutt, "Family Treatment of Poverty Level Families," *Social Casework*, 58 (February 1976), 92–100.

Joseph Palumbo, "Perceptual Deficits and Self-Esteem in Adolescence," *Clinical Social Work Journal*, 7 (Spring 1979), 34–61.

Renee Pellman et al., "The Van: A Mobile Approach to Services for Adolescents," *Social Casework*, 58 (May 1977), 268–273.

Helen Pinkus, "Casework Techniques Related to Selected Characteristics of Clients and Workers" (doctoral dissertation, Columbia University School of Social Work, 1968).

Rosemary Reynolds and Else Siegle, "A Study of Casework with Sado-Masochistic Marriage Partners," *Social Casework*, 40 (December 1959), 545–551.

Blanca N. Rosenberg, "Planned Short-Term Treatment in Developmental Crises," *Social Casework*, 56 (April 1975), 195–204.

S. James Rowland, Jr., "Ego-Directive Psychotherapy in Limited Treatment," *Social Casework*, 56 (November 1975), 543–553.

Pauline I. Scanlon, "Social Work with the Mentally Retarded Client," *Social Casework*, 59 (March 1978), 161–166.

Bertha G. Simos, "Grief Therapy to Facilitate Healthy Restitution," *Social Casework,* 58 (June 1977), 337–342.

Max Siporin, "Social Treatment: A New-Old Helping Method," *Social Work,* 15 (July 1970), 13–25.

Francis J. Turner, ed., *Differential Diagnosis and Treatment in Social Work,* 2nd ed. (New York: Free Press, 1976). This is an excellent source for articles pertinent to the relationship between diagnostic factors and treatment. His prefaces to the first and second editions, pp. xix–xxxi, are recommended.

Hank Walzer, "Casework Treatment of the Depressed Parent," *Social Casework,* 42 (December 1961), 505–512.

Sydney Wasserman, "The Middle-Age Separation Crisis and Ego-Supportive Casework Treatment," *Clinical Social Work Journal,* 1 (Spring 1973), 38–47.

Reva S. Wiseman, "Crisis Theory and the Process of Divorce," *Social Casework,* 56 (April 1975), 205–212.

Monna Zentner, "The Paranoid Client," *Social Casework,* 61 (March 1980), 138–145.

# Chapter 19

# The Psychosocial Approach: Clinical Case Examples

To complete our discussion of casework methods of psychosocial study, diagnosis, and treatment, we have selected three cases in which the relationship between diagnostic thinking and treatment methods and objectives can be demonstrated. These particular cases have been chosen because they illustrate three very different treatment problems. The presenting difficulties, the dynamics of the personalities and situations, and the clinical diagnoses called for considerable variation in emphasis. Nevertheless, almost all of the major types of procedures discussed in earlier chapters were used, at one point or another, in each of the cases.

Although abbreviated, the material is presented in ample detail. The purpose is to provide the reader with as precise an understanding as possible of the actual practice of psychosocial therapy. Specifically, attention will be given to demonstrating: (1) how the clinical social workers arrived at diagnostic assessments; (2) how they worked with the clients to define and move toward mutually agreed upon goals as these evolved over the course of treatment; and (3) how treatment procedures were selected and how, as the needs and capacities of the clients changed, the worker adjusted the blend of these procedures. In each case, it will be seen, differential understanding of the clients and their situations led to individualized clinical judgments. As the fund of knowledge grew and as client trust developed, the worker accordingly made shifts in treatment methods.

## PSYCHOSIS: SHORT-TERM INPATIENT TREATMENT

Louise Barry, a thirty-four-year-old black woman, was involuntarily committed to the inpatient facility of a county psychiatric hospital with the diagnosis of paranoid schizophrenia.[1] It was her fourth such hospitalization in four years. On the day she was admitted she had gone to a medical clinic for treatment of a stomach virus. When the doctor attempted to give her an injection of antibiotics, she began to scream

446

wildly and accuse the doctor of trying to kill her. Since it was feared she might physically attack some member of the clinic staff, she was forcibly restrained and taken to the psychiatric hospital. Once admitted, she began to scream: "All men are trying to kill women" and "People are trying to kill me." Shortly thereafter, she began to sob uncontrollably and repeat over and over: "It's no use. I just want to die."

The caseworker, later assigned to Mrs. Barry, was first brought into the case to speak with Mr. Barry, who had been notified at work of his wife's hospitalization. He arrived within minutes, clearly shaken by the recurrence of her illness. He spoke openly and impressed the worker as being extremely devoted to his wife of eighteen years, genuinely concerned for her welfare.

Mr. Barry said that his wife's present breakdown followed the pattern of the others. Prior to hospitalization, she would suddenly decide to stop taking Thorazine, on which she had been maintained since her first breakdown. The past week, without medication, she had been unable to sleep; she sat at the foot of their bed until late at night, wrapped in blankets, muttering to herself and asking Mr. Barry questions that he interpreted as intended to "trap" him. She would say, for example, "How would you like to go out Friday night with Alice and Joe?" When Mr. Barry agreed "too quickly," she would then accuse him of being sexually interested in Alice. He emphatically denied involvement with Alice or with any other women. Aside from her "mental troubles," and the fact that she was deeply disappointed that they seemed unable to have children, he felt their marriage had been harmonious and satisfying—at least to him. He could not suggest any reasons or precipitating events—other than her refusal to take medication—that would account for her becoming disturbed at this particular time.

Mr. Barry and wife grew up in a small town in the South, but rarely went back to visit. Shortly after they were married (she was sixteen and he was nineteen), they came North to settle in the city in which they now lived. The major reason they moved was that Mr. Barry had wanted to pursue a career as a musician, but his efforts failed. Instead, he found employment as a repairman with the telephone company—the job he still held.

He spoke about his wife with pride, describing her as a very bright woman. She had not finished high school, but now was studying for an equivalency examination. She had also begun taking courses in electronics and television repair. Mr. Barry not only accepted his wife's interests, but he actively encouraged them. Recalling that Mrs. Barry had repeatedly screamed that "all men are trying to kill women," the worker wondered to herself whether Mr. Barry's enthusiasm for her studies had been perceived by his wife as pressure. Apparently, Mr. Barry had also encouraged her to supplement their income by working part time as a waitress.

It was obviously painful to him that his wife became suspicious when she had these breakdowns. She also had blamed him for "locking her up" in the past and for the fact that she had never become pregnant. Actually, neither he nor his wife had consulted any doctors about the latter problem in recent years. Since it was a sensitive subject for Mr. Barry, the worker did not press the matter, or ask how he felt about having no children. She did inquire, however, whether he had ever been involved in outpatient therapy with his wife, and learned that though it had been suggested, he had been reluctant. At this point, he said, he would be willing to "do anything" if it would help.

Later the same day the caseworker introduced herself to Mrs. Barry, suggesting that they might speak together. Mrs. Barry responded angrily: "You don't want to talk to me. *I* don't know. My husband knows." Softly, the worker replied that she was sure that Mrs. Barry knew a lot, especially about how unhappy she was feeling. She said she hoped they would be able to talk about it while she was in the hospital. Mrs. Barry complained that everyone talked with her husband behind her back to get her locked up. Challengingly, she added that people should talk to them together "to find out how things really are." The worker told her that she had seen Mr. Barry, even though she would have preferred to meet with her first, explaining that he had come to the hospital worried and wanting to talk with someone. The worker added that in the future she would let Mrs. Barry know beforehand if she planned to be in touch with him; she, too, hoped the three of them could arrange to talk together. Mrs. Barry said no one in the hospital had offered this before. She was suspicious of her husband's willingness to join in sessions with her. Nevertheless, she listened carefully to the worker's account of the meeting with him.

From her knowledge of schizophrenic episodes, the worker recognized that her first encounter with Mrs. Barry had to be one in which she conveyed clearly and quickly her caring and sincerity. As important as these therapist qualities are for any client, they are crucial for the acutely disorganized, decompensating, frightened person with paranoid ideation. A break in reality such as Mrs. Barry was experiencing is usually accompanied by diffuse suspiciousness. On the other hand, the worker was aware, as she reached out to Mrs. Barry to gain her trust, that she should not press for greater closeness than Mrs. Barry could tolerate.

It is well known among clinicians who work with such patients that they can not only fear encroachment, but often are keenly sensitive to a therapist's mood, indifference, or lack of genuineness. In this case, the worker's attentiveness and words of understanding were also accompanied by facial expressions and gestures to convey to Mrs. Barry that she felt "with" and "for" her in her unhappiness.

On this first day of hospitalization, Mrs. Barry was alternately lucid and incoherent. When the worker gently asked how she had come to the hospital, she muttered that men are trying to kill her and that someone had "wired my head so I can't think right." The worker commented on how frightening it must be to feel that way, saying she imagined it was exhausting always to have to be on guard against getting hurt.

Without suggesting that she believed the delusional statements to be true, the worker related to the emotional affects. Furthermore, knowing that schizophrenic patients—particularly those who are delusional—are apt to respond poorly to probing questions, the worker refrained from making inquiries that could be construed as intrusive and that could exacerbate Mrs. Barry's hostility or withdrawal from reality. Even an effort to seek background information might well have resulted in undoing the worker's efforts to establish a trusting relationship.

Mrs. Barry was unwilling to sign voluntary commitment papers as she had in the past. Without pressure, the worker suggested that she consider this because it worried her and others that Mrs. Barry was saying she wanted to die. But Mrs. Barry insisted that she did not need help. She knew, however, that the doctors might recommend commitment and the worker agreed that this was so because they were concerned for her safety and well-being. Mrs. Barry's desire to talk was a good prognostic sign in the worker's view. Although even the sickest person usually wants human contact, some schizophrenics are so frightened and withdrawn that they cannot or will not communicate. Mrs. Barry, however, was actively attempting to reach out in spite of her suspiciousness. Moreover, the worker felt hopeful because of Mrs. Barry's evident strengths: she had functioned well in various areas of her life over the years; she had mastered new skills; she was able to hold a job.

As it turned out, Mrs. Barry was committed to the hospital for twenty days. The hope was that she would respond well in this period of time as she had to similar hospitalizations in the past. However, the worker and the psychiatrist assigned to Mrs. Barry were in disagreement about some aspects of the treatment. The psychiatrist believed that since this patient was denying the need for help, her prognosis was probably poor. Since she was so "uncooperative," he said, he would not try to work with her until the Thorazine begain to take effect; even then he doubted she would respond to psychotherapy.

The worker knew she faced a delicate situation. First, she and the doctor had significant ideological differences. For example, he saw treatment as a process in which the patient is passive. He was primarily interested in medication and tended to see this as the major, if not the only, treatment procedure of value to schizophrenic patients. Second, of European, aristocratic origin, he seemed unable to understand or relate well to people with divergent cultural or economic backgrounds. He appeared to give up on such patients—especially those who were poor and black. Third, his position at the hospital was in jeopardy; he had recently been demoted, and he handled his insecurity about this by being authoritative with the worker.

Although the worker found the doctor exasperating, she knew it was important not to antagonize him. If she challenged his views, it might limit her helpfulness to Mrs. Barry, since he was in charge of the case. Furthermore, she was truly sympathetic about his tenuous position at the hospital and realized he was reacting defensively. Consequently, the worker stressed their areas of agreement; she told him that she, too, believed medication was of primary importance to Mrs. Barry's treatment. She then added that she wanted to meet with Mrs. Barry and to keep in touch with her husband since she felt they both would benefit from a show of personal interest. She offered to share any information that would be helpful. He said the worker would be wasting her time. but agreed to her plan, adding—with a paternal smile—that he saw it as the worker's need rather than the patient's.

As discussed in the chapters on environmental work, a worker's understanding of the power structure and hierarchy of an agency, and of the particular professionals who staff it, is essential to good service. With this doctor (as with collaterals in general), tact and understanding were of prime importance to the treatment.

During the first week of Mrs. Barry's hospitalization, the caseworker saw her three more times and subsequently at least three times weekly. At first her visits were brief, since Mrs. Barry was often acutely confused. She had many delusions, to which the worker listened carefully, in order to determine what they might be expressing about how Mrs. Barry perceived herself in relationship to other people and to the world around her. This client had several repetitive complaints: she believed her husband was persecuting her because he wanted her to work in the restaurant where all the other waitresses hated her; she thought her money was being stolen at the hospital; she believed people were tampering with her brain; and she thought the nurses were deliberately passing her over by giving medication first to other patients, even when she was at the head of the line. The worker did not employ reflective procedures designed to help Mrs. Barry understand what these recurring themes meant; at this point, any such attempts might have been construed as invasions or demands.

Recognizing that Mrs. Barry truly believed she was singled out for bad treatment at the hands of others, the worker made special efforts to be considerate of her. For example, she tried to see Mrs. Barry afternoons, when she had more uninterrupted time; she also made a point of telling her early in the day the exact time of their meeting; she looked for ways in which she could give her genuine compliments, and greeted her in passing as she made her rounds through the hospital. She also investigated what might be causing misunderstandings—such as Mrs. Barry's feelings of being passed over in the medication line—and learned that the nurses, to whom Mrs. Barry frequently complained, viewed her as a "demanding" patient. On the other hand, the nurses reported that Mrs. Barry would say she wanted to be "invisible" and then seem to hope she would be noticed spontaneously.

The caseworker observed that when she came to the floor, Mrs. Barry would respond cheerfully when waved to, but if the worker was briefly intercepted by another person, Mrs. Barry's smile would fade and she would become absorbed elsewhere and not acknowledge the greeting they just exchanged. In one interview, when Mrs. Barry seemed particularly well related and relaxed, the worker tentatively asked whether at medication time she did something similar by trying to "fade into the woodwork" when another patient broke into line in front of her. Mrs. Barry then revealed, with self-awareness that astonished the worker, that she felt she had never really been noticed—much less preferred—by her parents when she was growing up. Her older brother was her mother's favorite; her very "pretty" and "clever" younger sister, whom Mrs. Barry referred to as "spoiled," was her father's "pet." She, on the other hand, was the "plain" one who had gotten little encouragement or recognition. With feeling, she told the worker that she had developed a habit of pretending not to care whether she was noticed, and to hide her feelings of resentment and sadness. With words and by her attitude, the worker gave recognition to Mrs. Barry for being able to understand herself so well.

The worker sensed that Mrs. Barry had truly begun to trust her. With her client's consent, she shared some of this information with the nurses to help them understand their patient better and feel less antagonistic. She also gave them suggestions about ways Mrs. Barry might be drawn out in patient therapy groups, since she tended to be reticent there and try to make herself "invisible."

The first task of treatment, then, was to attempt to establish a solid relationship. Only when this was achieved, and after Mrs. Barry had become somewhat better organized with the help of Thorazine, was the worker able to help her reflect on some of the issues and feelings she had never before shared in detail with anyone. Feelings of alienation, so pervasive in disturbed clients, can often be alleviated when a warm and personal interest is taken in their private feelings and thoughts. The worker's next treatment objective was to help Mrs. Barry understand the importance of medication—without which it seemed probable that this client would periodically decompensate. In this setting—where patients were hospitalized for a maximum of sixty days—it was important to help her with this quickly.

While eliciting Mrs. Barry's attitudes about medication, the worker looked for comments that might throw light on her refusal to take it prior to admission. Was there a connection between the Thorazine and Mrs. Barry's notion that people were tampering with her brain or "wiring" her head wrong? Similarly, did Mrs. Barry's interest in electronics represent her way of attempting to gain control over her "brain"?

In one meeting, Mrs. Barry protested: "Why do *I* have to take medication and everybody else in the world doesn't?" When asked how she felt about that, she simply answered: "Crazy." The worker said that many other people *did* in fact take medication—for example many diabetics use insulin—because body chemistry is different in everyone and does not always provide what is needed to stay well and feel good. The worker added that she herself also had to take medication regularly. Her approach was designed to help Mrs. Barry consider the reality of the situation; at this point, she did not pursue intrapsychic issues.

As they talked, however, Mrs. Barry admitted that, to her, being on medication not only meant she was "different" and "crazy," but "weak" as well. It made her feel she could not make it on her own, that she needed a "crutch"; and that this was why she had wanted to test herself by trying to get along without it from time to time. She said she had always been "disgusted" by her alcoholic father, whom her mother had belittled for needing drink to "lean on." The worker helped her to examine ways in which she might view her situation differently: In contrast to her father, who was incapacitated when he drank, she—Mrs. Barry—functioned well and felt better when she took Thorazine. The need to make up for a biochemical deficit was quite different from the excessive use of alcohol.

During subsequent meetings, Mrs. Barry indicated she had given thought to these talks about medication. Until now, she had not looked at it in these ways. Probably never before had she linked her perception of herself to her father's "weakness." Since the issue of control is important to most paranoid patients, and was clearly so to Mrs. Barry, the worker pointed out that when she was on medication she was able to control herself so that other people did not think she was sick and put her in the hospital against her will.

As Mrs. Barry became increasingly less confused, it seemed likely that some of her money *had* been stolen at the hospital, as she had suspected. Mr. Barry confirmed his wife's assertion that she always carried a ten-dollar bill pinned on her person. Although the money was not listed among her belongings in the property office, Mrs. Barry was convinced that it was being kept from her there. The worker took Mrs. Barry to the safe—which other staff members had refused to do on the grounds that she was delusional—and they looked for it together. It was not there, but the worker said that it was indeed very possible that her ten dollars could have disappeared in the struggle on the day she was admitted. Together, they "mourned" the loss of the money. The worker said she knew how helpless and out of control one feels when carefully kept possessions disappear. Mrs. Barry spoke about an occasion when she found a wallet belonging to a coworker and how "of course" she returned it, adding that she never did expect people would treat her as well as she treated them. To this, the worker responded that when these things happen, it certainly makes it harder to trust others.

In the session following her trip with the worker to check the safe, there was a marked change in Mrs. Barry. She greeted the worker with the statement that she felt she was "too suspicious"; she could not understand why she did not trust people and had to "see everything with my own eyes" before she could believe it. She had not believed the worker when she said the money was not there. The worker repeated that when people have been hurt or disappointed, it can be difficult to trust. At this, Mrs. Barry began talking about her husband and his early promises that he would give her everything when he became a successful musician. Now, not only were her husband's wages low, but he was a reckless spender. Moreover, in recent years he went out by himself much more often than he had in the early years. She felt lonely and often thought he must be seeing another woman. She believed her husband was sterile. He knew how much she wanted to have children, and she felt that if he truly cared he would have himself checked.

For the most part, the caseworker listened to Mrs. Barry and expressed her understanding of how disappointed she felt. She said she hoped they could arrange a session with her husband so they could talk over some of these matters. On speaking to the psychiatrist in charge of Mrs. Barry's case, however, the worker learned that the doctor disapproved of the idea of conjoint sessions; it was his belief that Mrs. Barry was trying to "control" the treatment and "manipulate" the worker. Tactfully, but with conviction, the worker shared her view that in spite of Mrs. Barry's illness and paranoia, there seemed to be some important reality aspects to the marital relationship that required Mr. Barry's participation. Reluctantly, the psychiatrist agreed to "go along" with the worker, who then scheduled a joint session.

During the third week of hospitalization, in spite of her improvement, Mrs. Barry was still periodically confused. But self-awareness was keener than it had been, and she often commented on how frustrated she became when she had difficulty expressing herself. The worker reassured her that she was sounding clearer than she had and encouraged her to take the time she needed to pull her thoughts together. When less pressured by others, she was often able to be more coherent and relaxed. Mrs. Barry acknowledged this and said she wished her husband would pressure her less about her high school equivalency test.

On the day before Mrs. Barry's twenty-day commitment was to expire, and a few hours before the joint session with her husband was scheduled, the worker found her to be depressed, withdrawn, and uncommunicative. She was unresponsive to the worker's overtures. Returning an hour later, the worker asked Mrs. Barry if she was apprehensive about going home or about the meeting planned with her husband. Mrs. Barry said she wanted to stay in the hospital to make sure she would feel well when she left. Moreover, she wanted to have more than one meeting with her husband; she did not want to go home until certain matters were discussed that she was afraid to bring up alone. She signed voluntary papers to remain another week, adding that this time she would be in the hospital "for myself, not for the court."

During this last week in the hospital, the three individual sessions turned out to be the most productive of all. It was Mrs. Barry who had chosen to extend her hospitalization, and she seemed determined to benefit from it. She was able to reflect further on her decision to stop medication that had resulted in her "going crazy." Aside from viewing Thorazine as a hated "crutch," she had also been extremely fearful that she would not be "smart enough" to pass the high school equivalency examination. Fearing that she would fail and prove to others, particularly her husband, who had such high expectations of her, that she was worthless and had "mixed-up brains," she supposed that she had played it "safe" by getting sick; she knew that if she discontinued Thorazine she would be rehospitalized. Again, she related her fear of failure to having felt like the "plain" and "stupid" middle child. Once she was able to share her understanding and feelings with the worker, she also brought them up in the group therapy sessions where she got further support.

There were two conjoint meetings with Mr. and Mrs. Barry. Mrs. Barry was able to tell her husband that his encouragement about the test felt like pressure to her, and that his enthusiasm about her courses in electronics made her feel that she would disappoint him if she did not do well. She told him it angered her that he wanted her to work at the restaurant she despised. Mr. Barry had a tendency to evade, but he did listen to her complaints and try to understand them. He realized there might be some misunderstandings between them and made efforts to change. Even though he had little insight into his wife's problems or his contribution to them, he agreed to marital therapy, reassuring her that he loved her and did not want her to get sick again.

The worker had the impression that Mr. and Mrs. Barry were in competition with one another, that Mrs. Barry was trying to measure up to her husband, who was skilled in telephone repair, and that there were hidden mixed feelings below his overly determined interest in his wife's achievements. In these joint meetings, however, the focus was limited almost entirely to the problem of pressure. The worker chose not to open up other issues of the marriage, even though many of these seemed problematical, for fear of further upsetting the marital relationship. They had little time to work. Instead, prior to Mrs. Barry's discharge, a referral for marital therapy was arranged that the worker was not too optimistic about. First, Mr. Barry was resistant to it and, second, the choice of resources was limited. In the clinic near the Barrys' home, there was only one therapist—a pastoral counselor—who did marital therapy, and it was the worker's hunch that he might not do well with this particular couple. Fortunately, Mrs. Barry was also interested in joining an outpatient group, in which the worker expected she would do well.

From time to time after she left the hospital, Mrs. Barry telephoned the worker. She said that they had gone only once for marital treatment and then discontinued, feeling they did not need it. She attended group therapy sessions regularly for four months until the group disbanded, following a cut in funding to the clinic. A year and a half after Mrs. Barry's discharge, the worker made a follow-up telephone call to her. She learned that Mrs. Barry felt she was doing well. She had continued to take medication despite the fact that she was suffering side effects (constipation, blurred vision, dryness of the mouth, and so on). She kept her appointments at the medication clinic regularly. She also told the worker that when she left the hospital she had decided not to take the equivalency test. The following year, however—on her own and not because her husband expected it—she went back to study for it, took it, and failed by only a few points. She did not seem discouraged and said she would try again soon. Mrs. Barry also told the worker that if she felt further treatment was necessary she would definitely go for it. She wanted to stay as well as she was.

This case illustrates how diagnosis and treatment go hand in hand, and how even short-term treatment can be effective in laying the ground for more extended therapy when needed. It demonstrates how the often discouraging clinical diagnosis of "paranoid schizophrenia" need not, in and of itself, lead to despair about a client's ability to grow and change, to make more satisfactory adjustments to life. In this case, the worker's primary objective was to help Mrs. Barry recompensate with the help of medication, and resume her previous adjustment.

However, within a short time, further goals of awareness of self-defeating behavior and of improvement of the marital relationship seemed possible.

The worker's assessment evolved and changed as she learned more about her client. Similarly, her treatment approach shifted as Mrs. Barry began to be better related, to trust the worker, and to be ready for self-understanding. In the context of a great deal of support, Mrs. Barry was able to pour out many pent-up feelings and emotionally charged memories. Careful timing made it possible to help her gain understanding about her decision to stop taking medication, without which she might have discontinued it again after her discharge. Contrary to the view of those who believe that the mentally ill cannot benefit from procedures other than those that are supportive or directive, the work with Mrs. Barry demonstrates that she was able to think reflectively on several levels—about herself, her situation, and her patterns of thinking and behaving, and on influential aspects of her childhood experiences.

Effort was also made to improve the quality of service for Mrs. Barry by working closely with the nurses to help them treat their patient with greater understanding. Attuned to the client–situation interplay, the worker identified how certain features of the hospital milieu—such as the staff's refusal to allow Mrs. Barry to examine the safe —tended to exacerbate her delusions. In spite of the pessimistic approach of the psychiatrist in charge, the worker was able to find a way of working with him without alienating him; she was able to persuade him to accept her plan for conjoint meetings—a plan that the worker believed was not only diagnostically sound, but imperative to the success of Mrs. Barry's treatment. As a result, Mr. Barry was no longer viewed simply as a consultant about his wife's illness, but also as an important participant in her environment.

This case also shows how important it is for clients—even those as disturbed as Mrs. Barry was—to take an active part in their own treatment. At several points, the work was guided by directions Mrs. Barry chose: the worker supported Mrs. Barry's wish to include her husband in treatment and helped to arrange it; she accepted Mrs. Barry's request to see for herself if the money was in the hospital safe. And, of utmost importance, Mrs. Barry worked most productively when *she* made the decision to remain in the hospital. In each instance, her autonomy and self-esteem were reinforced.

It is important to note that the handling of this case differed significantly from what it would have been two or three decades ago. Prior to the development of antipsychotic drugs, Mrs. Barry's future surely would have been less hopeful; it is possible that she would have become a chronic schizophrenic, hospitalized for years or for the rest of her life.

Furthermore, deinstitutionalization—a trend greatly accelerated in the last decade—has resulted in shorter periods of inpatient treatment and greater emphasis on outpatient services (which, as this case confirms, are still far from adequately financed or staffed in many areas). Happily, Mrs. Barry's chances for a relatively adequate adjustment—particularly if she returns for treatment when necessary—are far greater than they would have been just a generation ago.

## TERMINAL ILLNESS[2]

Anna Stasio, age forty-four, telephoned a mental health clinic asking for an appointment with a woman therapist as soon as possible, to discuss "serious personal problems." As it happened, the worker assigned to intake on the day she called was a man. He asked her if there was any particular reason why she thought he could not help her. She replied abruptly: "I haven't got time for that." She asserted that under no circumstances would she agree to see a man, adding that she needed someone mature and experienced. In response to her request, an experienced woman worker was assigned.

At the beginning of the first interview—with startling directness— Mrs. Stasio stated that a malignant tumor had been discovered on one of her lymph nodes several months previously. More recently, it was determined that the cancer had spread throughout her system. She was receiving chemotherapy. Although the doctors believed she was now in remission, she was, as she put it, "sitting with a time bomb." She had no idea how long she would live—having been given estimates ranging from six months to two years—but she knew her days were numbered and she wanted to have someone who was "dispassionate" to talk with on a regular basis. Her father was old, her mother had a serious heart condition, and she described her husband as "weak" and "neurotic." None of them were comforting to her, she said, because she felt *she* had to soothe *them* when she talked about her illness. She had insisted on a mature woman because she felt women were "stronger" than men. Furthermore, she did not want to see a social worker who was "wet behind the ears," or unduly frightened by a dying woman. The worker —a senior on staff with many years of experience—was genuinely moved by this woman's courage and determination to get what she needed for whatever time she had left to live. By gesture, tone of voice, and mood, she conveyed this. She agreed it was important for Mrs. Stasio to feel satisfied with the person she was seeing, urging her to tell her if she felt uncomfortable. Operating on Mrs. Stasio's clue that she was a person who tended to feel protective of the feelings of others— even at her own expense—the worker assured her that though she would be pleased to work with her, she would not feel hurt if Mrs. Stasio decided she was not the right therapist. At this, Mrs. Stasio visibly softened; her eyes filled and she said gently: "I liked you from the moment we met."

In taking this straightforward approach, the worker conveyed that she, too, was a strong person who could, in the interest of her client, tolerate a rejection. This was undoubtedly supportive to Mrs. Stasio, who seemed to need someone whom she felt was as fearless as she saw herself to be. As she sat with this remarkable woman, the worker considered how her own emotional resources were being put to the test. Paradoxically, Mrs. Stasio came across as attractive, vital, and colorful —yet she was dying. As the client talked about herself, she did so with a wide range of feeling: at times she was angry and impatient; at times she spoke with tenderness and sadness; in spite of everything, she had a sense of humor. In every instance, her emotions were expressed vividly. The worker realized she would have to prepare herself now to be intimately associated with the many physical and emotional processes associated with terminal illness.

In early interviews with Mrs. Stasio, the worker learned that she came from a middle-class, intellectual family; her mother had been a professional ballet dancer and her father a college professor of literature. Her father was English born, her mother of Italian origin. Both parents were of Protestant background but neither was religious; Mrs. Stasio described herself as an atheist. She was an only child and had always been thought of as "headstrong." In college, she majored in fine arts during which time she married her first husband, an actor with whom she lived for five years. They had an exciting but stormy marriage that ended because they were both too "stubborn" and aggressive. Each fought to overpower the other. When she married again, she chose a man of the opposite extreme; she portrayed Mr. Stasio as insecure, passive, and dull, but very kind—an engineer who had worked at the same government job for twenty years. He was not well paid, but had not had the courage to get his master's degree or to seek more challenging work. They had two children, Roger, age fifteen, and Elizabeth, age thirteen. The marriage had never been a truly happy one for her, but she had resigned herself to it, knowing that her domineering qualities had led her to choose him. For the past few years, she and a woman friend (with whom she had had a brief sexual affair) had operated a small picture-framing business that had been fairly successful and important to the family income. Mrs. Stasio had had two years of intensive psychotherapy when her children were small; it had helped her to understand herself better, and to feel less angry and disappointed about her husband.

In her characteristically definite way, Mrs. Stasio declared she did not want family therapy or joint meetings with her husband. The worker had not yet suggested these but, once again, this client was taking charge of getting the kind of treatment she wanted. She would find her own way of saying goodbye to her family; she did not need help with this. What she did want, she said, was someone whom she could use as a sounding board, to help her think over how to plan the rest of her life. There were also certain aspects of her behavior she wanted to change, particularly toward her husband and her daughter. She did not want to continue to feel guilty, as she did, about the way she took out her anger over her illness on Mr. Stasio. She was falling into the pattern she had been in when she went into therapy the first time; she belittled her husband and raged at him over minor matters. After all, it was not his fault that she had "settled" for a marriage that bored her. When she learned that she would soon die, she realized she would never experience a better relationship—a fantasy that had kept her anger "in tow" in recent years. She worried about the effect of her hostility on the children who would have only their father when she died; she did not want to contaminate their future relationship by her actions toward her husband now.

She felt concern for both children. But Roger, she thought, would handle himself; she described him as an "all-American boy"—a fine student, an athlete, with many friends. Elizabeth, however, who had been born with a cleft palate and had had many operations since infancy, was a withdrawn, immature girl who did not do well in school and had very few friends. Mrs. Stasio said that she tended to overprotect her daughter and did not want to do this now that Elizabeth would have to learn to be self-reliant. The worker pointed out that, if it seemed indicated, the children—or at least Elizabeth—might benefit from individual sessions. Mrs. Stasio opposed this idea as strongly as she resisted family treatment; emphatically, she said that changes in her own behavior would be the most helpful thing that could be done for Elizabeth. Mrs. Stasio's characteristic need to control—undoubtedly reinforced by her illness—necessarily limited treatment options.

Very early in therapy, Mrs. Stasio said that she would like to meet twice weekly, if possible. She had a lot to talk about and very little time. Although it was a general rule at the clinic to make appointments with clients on a once-a-week basis, for two reasons the worker arranged to make an exception. First, she wanted to be responsive to this client's wishes, and, second, Mrs. Stasio did indeed have many issues to talk over. From the worker's knowledge of this kind of cancer (which she later verified with a medical consultant), it very often resulted in rapid decline and early death. For the next five months, except when Mrs. Stasio had to go into the hospital for treatment, they met twice weekly.

After the first month of therapy, Mrs. Stasio came in saying that her

husband also wanted to see the worker, that he was "falling apart." She
still did not want to have meetings with him, but said she had no
objection to his seeing her worker on his own. In fact, she was urging
him to come.

Indeed, Mr. Stasio—although hardly "falling apart"—did want
someone to talk to, with whom he could share his very mixed emotions.
He was frightened and grief-sticken; he both resented and admired his
wife. He also wanted suggestions about ways the children should be
handled during this time. An intelligent man, Mr. Stasio was not usually
introspective, but he needed a great deal of support and an opportunity
to ventilate and to discuss the practical problems he was facing. Occasionally, the worker offered direct advice about the children, but primarily she encouraged him to make his own decisions, helping him to
evaluate various options. During the course of their work together, as
his wife became weaker, Mr. Stasio took on more and more responsibility for the household and child care. He was concerned about money
now that Mrs. Stasio was no longer working, and was having difficulty
with Elizabeth, who was clinging to her mother and seemed irritable
and sarcastic with him. Since he did not want to upset his wife, he
preferred to share these worries with the worker. He, too, opposed
family meetings, wanting to establish close relationships with his children on his own. In his view, to have a "mediator" would detract from
his efforts to strengthen family bonds. For too long he had been in his
wife's "shadow," and now he did not want to "hide behind" the worker.

Some clinicians might take the view that the worker should have
pressed harder for family meetings (or for individual treatment for the
children), particularly since Elizabeth appeared to be having difficulties. The worker believed that some avoidance was operating for both
parents, but decided not to urge them to involve the children. She
thought she could persuade Mr. Stasio to change his mind, but was quite
sure that any attempt to convince his wife could be deeply damaging
to the therapeutic relationship. Furthermore, she believed it was important to respect Mrs. Stasio's method of handling her illness and her
wish to do as much as she could herself. For Mr. Stasio, the decision not
to urge family meetings may well have been one of the factors that
encouraged him to function more independently with his children. It
was he who would have to learn to take charge of the family and, if the
worker conveyed the opinion that he could not do this without her
direct help, she might have fostered his dependency. Under different
circumstances, the worker might have been more forceful in recommending family meetings. As it was, both Mr. and Mrs. Stasio discussed
in detail their relationships with the children, reflecting on how they
could be most helpful to them.

From meeting to meeting, Mr. Stasio would report on his increasingly effective efforts to get closer to the children. He was able to talk with them about the sadness they shared; he found he could enlist their help around the house in ways he never had before. They were showing him more respect than previously and this gratified him; but he regretted that he had waited until his wife was dying to change his "image." Mrs. Stasio was no longer berating him frequently and he attributed this, in part, to the changes he had made. The worker was supportive of his new role, but disagreed with him when he gave her more credit than he gave himself for the changes. She pointed out that he had worked hard, and wondered why now he would want to downplay the importance of his own efforts and only recognize hers.

After three months, it became apparent to the worker that Mrs. Stasio's condition was rapidly deteriorating. Chemotherapy was no longer effective in forestalling the advance of the malignancy. Nevertheless, she remained mentally clear and actively engaged in all aspects of her life. She was grateful to her husband for taking more initiative at home; she spoke with appreciation of his good qualities and now found it comforting to view him as a "friend.' She had neither the energy nor the inclination to belittle him now, and she was glad to achieve one of her major objectives—to behave differently toward him. By expressing her anger in the sessions, rather than directly at him, she had relieved the tension between them. She was also proud of the fact that she had been able to have loving talks about her condition with both children, and had been able to listen to their concerns and questions. In a moving discussion with Elizabeth—which she had "rehearsed" with the worker beforehand—she told her daughter that she had probably "babied" her too much and that she regretted that, particularly now that Elizabeth would have to become increasingly independent. Mrs. Stasio spoke with compassion of her parents, now sick and old, who would have to face the loss of their only child; she gave a good deal of thought to how she could make it easier for them, fully aware that even now she was relating to them in a caretaking way, as had been her lifelong pattern.

Particularly after Mrs. Stasio had achieved the relationships she wanted with her family—or, perhaps, because she knew she was close to death—she began to use her sessions to reflect spontaneously, sometimes in minute detail, on various periods of her life. She talked with regret about never having had a fulfilling marital relationship. Her most satisfying sexual experiences, she confided, had been with women; she was glad now that she had allowed these, although she had felt very guilty about them at the time. Sharing these confidences, she said, had a "cleansing" effect. She joked that even though she was not religious, she seemed to have the need to "confess." Her relationship with her parents—both of whom tended to be passive, indecisive people—interested her. In her view, she had become a "powerhouse" because they were so unassertive and needed her leadership, even when she was very young. If this situation had been a liability for Mrs. Stasio, she saw it now as an asset. From her standpoint, her aggressiveness had served her well. She had been part of life, and had not simply watched from the sidelines as she felt her parents had.

As she spoke of her marriage, she said that her angry domination of her husband had, in some way, represented her effort to "make him over" into the strong man her father never was. As she saw it, she had taken on the role of the "man" in her parents' home, and again in her current family. Her disappointment in her father had led her to choose her first husband, who she viewed as his opposite. Unable to tolerate the power struggles that ensued, she made sure her next husband would be easier to manage! Her occasional homosexual affairs, she assumed, were a response to frustrations with the men in her life.

It had always been Mrs. Stasio's inclination to be introspective; moreover, her two years of psychotherapy several years earlier had contributed to her sophisticated self-understanding. In contrast to many treatment situations in which change in emotional or behavioral patterns is a primary objective, for Mrs. Stasio this phase of treatment (which involved dynamic and developmental reflection) was important to her attempts to come to peace with or "make sense" out of her life. There was no attempt on her part or the worker's to help resolve longstanding conflicts or neurotic issues; reflections on these matters were important only to the degree that Mrs. Stasio was interested in them.

Since Mrs. Stasio could not control her disease, she was determined to manage its effects. She would take charge of her own dying. Unlike many terminally ill patients, at no point did she use the defense of denial against the *fact* of her impending premature death. If there was denial on her part—as the worker believed there was—it was the denial or repression of anxieties and helplessness naturally associated with terminal illness. She handled these through "counterphobic" behavior. In the face of death, she continued to orchestrate—how her therapy would be handled, how her husband would get treatment, and how she would say goodbye to her children. To one session she brought three long typewritten letters—one to her husband and one to each child— to be read after she died. In these she gave instructions about her funeral, and made suggestions about the management of finances, de- tailing ideas for them all to follow in the future. Gently, the worker asked Mrs. Stasio if she thought the letters conveyed her doubts about whether the family would be able to manage without her. After think- ing it over between sessions, Mrs. Stasio returned with a new set of letters—having discarded the first—in which she told each how much she cared, expressing confidence in them all. The only instructions she included were those related to her funeral arrangements.

Diagnostically, Mrs. Stasio was seen as a woman who approached life intensely, even in the face of her debilitated physical condition. She had many well developed ego functions that helped her master difficult situations in health and in illness. She had a clear sense of values and a capacity for self-criticism and change, even in the last months of her life. Her chief defenses—repression and some denial of her fear of imminent death—allowed her to function effectively, not only for her own benefit, but for that of her family. She helped them prepare for the inevitable, and offered them an opportunity to grieve with her while she still lived. Her characteristic mode of handling anxiety, as she often said, had been to "grab life by the tail," and this style served her through these days of illness. As already noted, there were character problems and neurotic patterns that Mrs. Stasio had never resolved, although she was aware of some of them. Her inordinate need to control undoubtedly masked a longstanding fear of dependency; she allowed herself to rely on the worker only after she was absolutely sure that the worker could "take it." Her ambivalence toward men and uncertain sexual identification were evident. The worker's diagnostic understanding was of utmost importance to the treatment. It was essential, for example, for the worker to respect Mrs. Stasio's need for control and to recognize which defenses were necessary to protect her from overwhelming anxiety or despair. By getting to know her client as well as she did, the worker was also able to stay empathically attuned to the great vicissitudes of feeling Mrs. Stasio experienced during this final phase of her life.

Throughout the therapy, sustaining procedures were highly important. The worker used several forms of support. Mrs. Stasio needed the worker's strength, consistent interest, and encouragement. She enjoyed the worker's praise about the changes that led to warmer family relationships. A woman keenly connected to her emotions and experiences, Mrs. Stasio required an intense therapeutic relationship. She originally requested a worker who could be "dispassionate," but evidently she meant someone who did not need to be taken care of; she did not mean (and would not have tolerated!) a therapist who was emotionally unavailable. Following Mrs. Stasio's lead, the worker shared how genuinely privileged she felt to have gotten to know her; they spoke of their time together as a special kind of "journey." Empathically, the worker shared Mrs. Stasio's anger at the arbitrary way illness chooses its victims. She truly understood her client's tears of frustration and sadness: Mrs. Stasio had always wanted to live a long life; she would never see her children become adults; she would miss out on her grandchildren; she would have no "third chance" at a better marriage. The worker avoided offering false reassurances; Mrs. Stasio counted on her to share in the agony of accepting the inevitability of her early death.

With Mr. Stasio, the worker was also supportive. She reinforced his capacity for independent functioning, and helped him to be aware of his strengths, which he generally underestimated. With the worker's encouragement, he was able to take more initiative with his children, particularly when not faced with his wife's extraordinary aggressiveness. As Mrs. Stasio related more softly with him, he, in turn, could be more confident and assertive. It proved important for Mr. Stasio to have someone to whom he could vent his longstanding resentments. He was then free to feel less conflicted in his loving feelings for his wife. He began truly to grieve her and to face his fears about life without her. Like his wife, he never denied the reality of her condition, and this enabled them to share their pain. From his point of view, and Mrs. Stasio's as well, their times together became more tender and meaningful than ever.

In addition to sustaining procedures and those that fostered ventilation, the worker helped Mr. Stasio reflect on the many day-to-day difficulties and decisions that faced him. He became more aware of his pattern of either withdrawing or deferring to others, particularly his wife but at times the worker too. Occasionally, he mentioned his relationship with his domineering mother—to whom he was still close—and recognized some of the roots of his current behavior. But, in general, there was little emphasis on developmental reflection; he had no interest in concentrating on his early life. The most productive work seemed to come from the use of procedures that addressed his present feelings and behavior.

In what turned out to be her last office session, Mrs. Stasio looked very ill; she was failing quickly but, though subdued, remained mentally alert. She said she had talked over all the important matters that concerned her when she first came. She wanted the worker to know how much their meetings had meant. The following day she entered the hospital.

By telephone, a few days later, Mrs. Stasio asked the worker to visit. When she got there, she saw that Mrs. Stasio had many bruises, the result of falls when she tried to get out of bed. She said she did not want the worker to visit her again. She did not want anyone to see her in this weakened condition or to be remembered as a hospital patient. She knew she would die soon. She had said goodbye to her children, her parents, and a few close friends. She only allowed her husband to see her now; he was there many hours each day. She took the worker's hand, held it tightly for a minute, and then turned away. The worker touched Mrs. Stasio's shoulder, said goodbye, and left sadly, realizing that her client's battle for life was ending. She had turned over the controls—to her illness, to the doctors, to death itself.

Two weeks later, Mr. Stasio called to say that his wife had died. At the funeral, for the first time, the worker briefly met the children, who stayed close to their father throughout.

Mr. Stasio returned to therapy for a period of seven months. He expressed his grief and anger; he and the worker shared memories of Mrs. Stasio. The fact that the worker was unashamed of her own sadness helped Mr. Stasio to express his feelings of loss. He said it comforted him to speak with someone who had known his wife so well and who could understand the range of emotions he was experiencing. He was both consoled and frustrated as he reviewed the final weeks of his wife's life when they had become closer than ever before. He used his sessions to discuss issues related to the children who, on the whole, were relating well with each other. And they truly respected him now, too. He talked over practical plans and decided to move to another town, at some distance from the clinic, which would be closer to his mother, who could help with care of the children. Having a woman to lean on was still important to him, he said. Roger was doing well, but Elizabeth seemed unhappy and Mr. Stasio sought information, which the worker gave, about a mental health service in the area where they would be living. He was a lonely man now, but strikingly more confident about his ability to take charge of his family.

The process of dying is as individualized as the process of living. Similarly, the style of one's grief is idiosyncratic. Every adaptation, every expression of outrage and despair about death takes its own form, depending on the personalities of the dying patient and of those who are left behind. In contrast to the Stasios, the gravity of terminal illness is minimized by some patients and their families, who cling to hope for recovery long after the doctors have given up. Sometimes relatives feel they must "protect" patients by giving false reassurance, in order to make their last days as untroubled as possible. In other situations, such avoidance is maintained to shield the family members themselves from anxiety and depression. Some doctors do not believe terminal patients should be given the whole truth about their condition, although this is less frequently so than it was only a few years ago. In every instance, the social worker has to take the lead from the client and family. One cannot recklessly intrude on defenses against death any more than one should push hard against any defense that has been erected to protect an individual from overwhelming emotion; otherwise, the psychological balance of some clients might be seriously endangered. On the other hand, there is increasing evidence that, when possible and diagnostically indicated, the opportunity for dying patients to share grief with those who will survive protects them from feelings of alienation and the sense that they are being dealt with dishonestly. Furthermore, often openness can provide a family with the opportunity to begin to face grief, to reduce potential guilt, and to prepare for adapting to life after the patient has died.

Almost two years after Mr. Stasio terminated treatment, he telephoned the worker asking for a joint session with a divorcee whom he planned to marry. For the most part, he and his family had done well since he last saw the worker. But he wanted help with problems related to tensions occurring between his and his fiancée's adolescent children. The worker met with the couple twice. However, Mr. Stasio's future wife—who appeared to have strong managerial tendencies and definite opinions—took a dark view of psychological help; she had always worked out difficult problems herself, she said. Efforts to explore this woman's adamance were met with unyielding resistance. Reluctantly, with only a token protest, Mr. Stasio acceded to her wishes not to meet again. The worker thought the children might be responding to unspoken struggles between the adults. But, under the circumstances, exploration was not possible. It seemed that once again Mr. Stasio was planning his life with a woman who—in a somewhat different manner from Anna Stasio—was, nevertheless, determined to take charge of situations her way.

In every treatment situation, the clinical social worker has to accept limitations imposed by the client. One can suggest other options, as the worker in this instance did, but the work can go on only to the extent that the client is willing to participate. Although she had been tremendously helpful to Mr. and Mrs. Stasio during the months before the latter died, and to Mr. Stasio for a period thereafter, she saw no way to help forestall problems that might well ensue in this new family unless they were willing to examine the issues. Only time would tell whether the couple—whom the worker was careful not to alienate— would return if, in fact, difficulties did arise.

## ANXIETY HYSTERIA[3]

At the suggestion of his sister, who worked in the mental health field, Jed Cooper, twenty-two, made an appointment with a clinical social worker in private practice. In his first interview, he said he felt tongue-tied. He blushed frequently and shifted uneasily in his chair. When he tried to explain why he had come, he became flustered and inarticulate. In this session, therefore, the worker took a very active, supportive role; she told Jed that it was hard for most people to talk to a strange person about personal matters. She added that she thought it would become easier for him as they went along, saying too, that it can become more difficult if one tries too hard, before one feels more relaxed. Mostly, the worker asked factual questions—to which Jed responded fairly comfortably—postponing, for the time being, those related to his reasons for wanting help.

She learned that Jed was the youngest of four children; his three sisters were married and now only he lived at home with his parents. His father, a retired policeman, was working as a security guard. Recently, his mother had begun working part time as a saleswoman in a department store. His mother was born in Ireland and his father was second-generation Irish; both were Catholic. At his mother's insistence, Jed had attended parochial schools. After graduating from high school, he had held various jobs and, for the past year, was learning carpentry by working as an assistant to a cabinetmaker. He seemed most at ease talking about his work, and smiled for the first time when he answered questions about his job; he said he wanted to become an "A-1" craftsman. Speaking more spontaneously now, Jed said that his employer was "like a father" to him. Rather than inquiring immediately about this, the worker waited a moment, at which point Jed volunteered that he hated his father, who was an alcoholic and has been one for as long as he could remember. Once this was said, Jed's tension obviously mounted again and the worker, while demonstrating that she understood his strong feelings, did not explore the matter further. She simply agreed that it must feel good to have a boss he could really enjoy.

When the session ended, it was still unclear just what had precipitated Jed's request for help. Only in the last few minutes was he able to say that he tended to get "nervous" and his sister thought he should have "someone to talk to." At this point, the worker did not have enough information to assess the nature of Jed's difficulties. She *was* aware that his anxiety was high and that supportive measures designed to reduce it took precedence over getting more information. She considered cultural factors that might have contributed to his uneasiness. Clients with a strong Catholic background are sometimes loath to share personal material with outsiders, particularly those not connected with the Church. As yet, she had no way of knowing whether some particular event had catalyzed Jed's acute state of anxiety and embarrassment. Some early childhood fears may have been activated. The possibility that Jed was severely disturbed could not be ruled out. But, seemingly well oriented, he functioned constructively on his job, and there was no apparent thought disorder. His affect was restricted, but when relaxed, he seemed emotionally responsive. In order to convey her caring and yet elicit Jed's motivation for and participation in treatment, the worker asked if he wanted to meet again. When he nodded, she offered him three alternative dates for the next session, ranging from three to ten days away from the first interview. Jed chose the nearest date and left, firmly shaking the worker's hand and thanking her.

In the second meeting, again Jed was tense and constricted for the first few minutes, but became calmer more quickly than in the initial session. Still blushing frequently, he was able to say fairly fluently that he had become worried when, two weeks before, he had been sitting in the living room with his father watching a ball game and suddenly became extremely "nervous" and dizzy. When he tried to get up, his knees buckled and he fell to the floor. The episode did not last long, but afterward he began to sob uncontrollably. He went to work the next day but could not concentrate. He was so frightened that he spoke with his oldest sister who suggested that he see a doctor, who told him there seemed to be nothing physically wrong. Again, at the suggestion of his sister, he called the worker. He had come, he said, to find out what was wrong with him. When the worker said that the incident must have worried him, Jed asked, "Does it mean I'm crazy?" He did not seem "crazy" to her, she said, but it did sound as though something was frightening him a lot. Jed volunteered that he had had a similar "spell" two years before, again when he was alone with his father. He asked the worker if she had ever heard of anything like this before. He seemed to be asking to be reassured—either that the worker was competent to help him, or that his situation was not unique or hopeless. She answered that indeed she had known of other people who had responded to intense feeling or fear in similar ways, but that it might take a little time to find out why this had happened to him. "Is there a cure?" Jed asked. The worker, knowing that Jed was functioning normally in his daily life, said that the worst of his "attack" seemed to be over, adding that she thought it was possible some of his nervousness may have come from fear that he was "crazy." Jed agreed but added that he tended to be a nervous person, especially when he was at home. The worker could not be totally reassuring, since she still did not understand all of the dimensions of his symptoms, but she did say very positively that usually when people learn about themselves and their feelings they get considerable relief. Jed seemed encouraged.

For many meetings to come, Jed would arrive and say he did not know what he "should" talk about. His thoughts would block until he could find a comfortable subject—often his job, his car, the weather— from which he could then ease into more difficult material. In one session, after about two months of treatment, Jed asked the worker to come out to his car to see a bureau he had built and brought to show her. She was genuinely impressed with his work and freely told him so. Jed evidently needed support and encouragement, not only to reduce his anxiety, but to be reassured that the worker thought of him as a competent, worthwhile man.

Positive—as well as negative—countertransference is important for a worker to recognize. In this case, the worker was aware of very warm feelings for Jed; she saw him as an appealing, sensitive person who sparked in her a "motherly" response—a wish to look after him. It took conscious effort to keep the expression of some of her strongest feelings in check and still provide the sustaining climate he required. Furthermore, since one's subjective reactions to a client can often be helpful in diagnosis, the worker was alerted to the possibility that Jed's manner might elicit overly protective responses from other people in his life, including, perhaps, his mother, about whom he had said very little.

Jed had particular difficulty talking about his feelings toward his parents. Although he discussed his girlfriend Laura, of whom he was very fond, he also shied away from any discussion of their intimate relationship. When Jed became flustered, even by gently placed questions, the worker would make remarks such as, "Perhaps you'll feel more like discussing that at another time," or, "Maybe you can let me know when you feel comfortable enough to tell me something about that." Of these troublesome subjects, Jed was least inhibited about his anger at his father—for being unavailable and critical of him as a child, for being a "whiner," for his excessive drinking and for the fact that he had let Jed's mother "wear the pants." He felt that his father had never liked him. His resentment was conscious and strong. Nevertheless, once he could ventilate it, he said it felt really good; in his family, people rarely shared deep feelings about anything. He said he usually did not confide in anyone, even his girlfriend. Only when he became very frightened by his "attack" had he told his sister about it.

Aided by the worker's consistently calm, accepting supportive approach, Jed slowly but surely took more initiative in starting sessions and in getting into the issues he had been sidestepping. He still needed sustainment, but to a far lesser degree. Having ventilated his anger at his father, he seemed relieved enough to begin to talk about his mother, whom he described as domineering and a "nag," although he knew she loved him. She had always catered to him, more than she did to his sisters and father. As he revealed more, it turned out that even as a small child his mother complained to him about his father, and this always made him feel very uncomfortable; in fact, it still did. His mother often asked him personal questions—about what he was doing and where he was going. She seemed hurt when he went out in the evenings. In the last year, since he had been dating Laura, his mother would ply him with inquiries about her, giving him the impression that she was eager to find something to criticize. Mostly, he evaded her questions, but they annoyed him and made him "nervous." His mother, he complained, went through his bureau drawers, ostensibly searching for laundry. He never said anything to her about it, but made sure he didn't keep anything private there. Jed also said he felt sorry for her because she had had "such a hard life," especially with his father.

By the time Jed had revealed this much—after about three months of therapy—he reported that on the whole he was feeling more relaxed than he had "for years." He was no longer afraid of "going crazy." Periodically, however, he felt guilty or, as he put it, "disloyal." He felt justified complaining about his father; but talking about his mother, he said, made him very uncomfortable. He felt he was hurting her, even though he knew she could not know what he was saying. He had not even told her he was in therapy.

Although initially it was difficult to evaluate the seriousness of Jed's problems, by this point in treatment the worker had formulated a fairly well rounded diagnostic assessment. She viewed him as a man with intelligence, competence, and talents who functioned well in most areas. He had the capacity for good interpersonal relationships. Although shy, he had many friends of long standing. When he spoke of his girlfriend, he did so with tenderness and sensitivity. He related warmly and positively to the worker. He had a clear sense of his own values and ethical standards. On the whole, then, ego and superego functions were well developed. Although in early meetings Jed appeared quite disturbed, in time it seemed certain that his conflicts were centered in the psychosexual area. As the worker saw it, his perception of his mother's intrusiveness and, perhaps, actual seductiveness, influenced Jed to feel guilty and conflicted about his relationship with her. He loved her but feared her impingement on his life. Furthermore, his father's apparent lack of assertiveness and degraded status in the family had deprived Jed of a strong model to admire and emulate. The worker speculated that Jed's unconscious "castration fears" (derived from repressed incestuous wishes and fears of his father's retaliation), as well as his conscious anger at his father, were expressed by anxiety attacks, both of which had occurred in his father's presence. Unresolved oedipal issues were defended against primarily through defenses of inhibition, suppression, and repression. The clinical diagnosis the worker gave to Jed's condition was "anxiety hysteria." Subtle doubts about his masculinity, evidenced by his strong need for confirmation as a "male" (e.g., his wish for praise from the worker and his employer about his carpentry skills), lent further support to this diagnosis. There also appeared to be some unfulfilled needs related to having been ignored or criticized by his father and "babied" by his mother.

In the early months of treatment, the worker concentrated on procedures that were sustaining, or that led to description and ventilation. On the whole, reflective procedures were limited to those related to current, practical matters. (For example, at one point Jed wondered whether he should consider moving out of his parents' home since he was so uncomfortable there. He decided that he was financially not prepared to make the change since he wanted to save money for the time when he would marry. He concluded that instead he would spend as little time at home as possible, which, incidentally, may have contributed to his greater relaxation at this juncture.)

The worker made few interpretations except those that were reassuring. The "corrective" relationship—one that was consistent, accepting, and neither seductive, intrusive, nor possessive—was in contrast to the one he perceived he had with his mother. Although individual situations differ, in this case it was probably helpful that the worker was a woman roughly in his mother's age group, and yet treated him with understanding and as an adult. It was also fortunate that concurrent with therapy he was benefiting from what might be called a corrective relationship with his employer who, apparently unlike Jed's father, truly liked Jed, treated him "like a man," and admired his talents.

Throughout this early period, the worker refrained from encouraging reflection about issues close to Jed's psychosexual conflict, even though she suspected many of these were conscious or preconscious. Her reason for this was that trial questions—about his girlfriend or his parents—that could have tapped greater awareness in these areas were generally evaded by Jed. She knew it would not help to press him to the point that he would become blocked or immobilized by anxiety; nor, of course, did she want to risk the possibility that he would bolt from therapy.

Gradually, after Jed had been in treatment close to six months, he began talking more about the discomfort he felt when he was around his parents. He wanted to understand it, realizing that his anxiety attack was related in some way. He also discussed some of his concerns about his relationship with Laura (heretofore he had only spoken of his pleasant, tender feelings for her), now confiding that he thought he had a "sexual hangup." He blushed when he said this, but did not block or evade. He explained further that he would often spend the day excitedly thinking about Laura but, when they got together for intercourse, as often as not he lost his erection. Laura was very understanding, and he knew she loved him anyway, but he felt deeply humiliated.

Once he felt safe enough to approach these subjects, the worker began to elicit more and more relevant material. He could reflect now on how his anxiety when he was with his father related to unexpressed anger, but Jed could see that this was only a small part of a larger picture. He had known he was angry, and talking about it had brought relief, but he searched for more. He became interested in early memories. He recalled a frequent scene at home when he was young: his father would come from work, still wearing his gun and holster and he, Jed, would run in terror to his bedroom. On his day off, Jed's father would sit in the living room, drinking continuously, and Jed would imagine that as his father became increasingly intoxicated, he might grab for him and beat him. In reality, his father never assaulted him, but the fear remained. Jed recalled recurrent childhood nightmares related to his fear of his father. As he reviewed these early events, he realized that his mother had wanted him as an ally against his father, frequently complaining about what a "bum" the latter was and telling Jed that she hoped he would not grow up to be a "drunk." Evidently, she turned to him to try to make up for her disappointing marriage. The more he talked, the more resentful he became toward her for berating his father, who "didn't have a chance" in the face of her attacks.

Spontaneously, Jed recognized that there was something "sexy" about his mother's intrusiveness and overprotection of him. He remembered being uncomfortable at age five or six when his mother seemed "too eager" to help him with his bath. He once asked if his father could bathe him instead, a request that insulted his mother. Jed was torn between wanting to "wriggle out" from her grip and wanting to please her. From a very young age he guarded his private thoughts and fantasies, knowing that by being secretive he was disappointing her. On the other hand, he helped her with her chores and would run all the way home to show her his good report card. Some of his happiest moments were when she told him he was the "nicest boy in the world." Much of this material was conscious; in fact, Jed said that he sometimes felt his head "swimming" with thoughts about his early years. Some of the memories were preconscious (such as those about his baths), but came to the surface over the course of treatment. An important aspect of this phase of therapy was that Jed was able to see his anger at his parents in another perspective; he knew he resented his father, but he had never dared to feel more than mild annoyance toward his mother.

There were some connections Jed never actually made. For example, it was probable that his intense uneasiness in the presence of his father derived in part from "castration anxiety," generally an unconscious fear that cannot be tapped in neurotic clients except through psychoanalysis. Similarly, incestuous wishes were also repressed. He reflected at some length, however, on the connections between his mother's need to intrude and his anger at his father for not taking charge of the situation and protecting him from her. The more he thought about it, the surer he was that what he had always believed was not true—his father *did* like him. He now saw him as a "coward" in the face of a domineering wife. Jed even remembered occasions when his father had invited him for a day of hunting and his mother would say it was too dangerous and not allow it. Instead of confronting his wife, Jed's father would drop the matter. One of the high points in treatment came when Jed realized with sadness that his father was not anyone to fear at all, but a pathetic man. Thus, although the actual oedipal issues were not uncovered, many of the residues and related matters were, with the result that Jed no longer irrationally feared his father as he had.

It is true that a client sophisticated about psychological matters might be able to express his difficulties by using such terms as "castration anxiety," "mutilation fears," "sexual identity" problems, "incentuous" wishes, and so on—but this does not necessarily mean that unconscious material would be brought to consciousness any more than it was for Jed. In general, clinical social workers concentrate on the derivatives that, in Jed's case, not only greatly reduced his fears but also his anger and guilt. By the time treatment terminated, Jed's greater comfort with himself also led him to feel genuine sympathy for his parents' unhappiness.

After revealing his sexual problem with Laura, there was very little further discussion about this. Intuitively, Jed seemed to know that it was related to (or, as the worker saw it, a displacement from) feeling about his parents. One can only speculate about the actual connections. For example, was his fear of sexual intercourse related to his fear of his father's anger? To anxiety about incest stimulated by his mother's seductiveness? To guilt about betraying his mother? To a fear of losing his sense of privacy? To the fact that a parental model for adult love and intimacy was lacking? Most likely, it was some combination of these. In any event, as he worked through some of his childhood feelings and the ways they related to his present situation, his sexual relationship with Laura markedly improved. He rarely had difficulty now maintaining an erection, and felt more deeply satisfied than ever with their sexual life. By the time the treament (which lasted a little over a year) ended, Jed was planning to share an apartment with Laura whom, he assumed, he would eventually marry. After the final session, Jed asked the worker to come outside to meet Laura, who was waiting for him. As the worker recorded it, "It was hard to tell whether Jed was more proud of himself or of Laura."

To summarize, the complexity of diagnosis, the importance of the treatment relationship, and the selective, carefully timed use of treatment procedures are all well illustrated by this case. As is often true for clients with hysterial symptoms, at first Jed appeared to be more disturbed than he was. As his many strengths—including his capacity to engage in a warm relationship with the worker—became apparent, so did the diagnosis. Even though Jed was basically sound psychologically, the worker recognized he sorely needed a relationship he could trust without fear of being criticized or overwhelmed by the needs of another. She supported his achievements, his many fine personal qualities, and—perhaps, above all—his right to feel "like a man."

The mutual long-range goals, more or less explicitly shared by Jed and the worker, were to enable him to feel less anxious—about himself and about "going crazy." As therapy progressed, he also wanted to improve his sexual functioning. Intermediate goals, primarily determined by the worker, were to provide a climate that would foster positive transference, necessary for the "corrective" experience and for helping him feel safe enough to be reflective. His neurosis, combined with his Catholic school and family training (where emotional expression was discouraged), required an extended period of sustainment. When the diagnostic picture becomes clear, it is sometimes difficult to resist premature interpretations. However, it was fortunate that this worker was sufficiently empathic with the intensity of Jed's anxiety to wait. Once ready, he made good use of reflective procedures and was in large measure freed from burdensome inner pressures. It is important to note again that the successful treatment was undoubtedly expedited by the reassuring, "man-to-man" relationship he had with his employer.

Readers might wonder why family therapy or family group meetings were not considered in this case, since Jed's difficulties were so intertwined with his relationships—past and present—with his parents. The worker was experienced in family therapy, but did not view it as the treatment of choice. As discussed in Chapter 11, family treatment is contraindicated when a client's defenses or anxiety would be so intensified by group meetings that he could not benefit from them. Jed's inhibitions and anxiety were so marked—even when he was not in the presence of his parents—that the worker felt certain his blocking and discomfort would have presented insurmountable problems in family sessions. Only close to the end of therapy—by which time Jed had resolved the major issues that handicapped him—would he have been able to relax enough to express himself meaningfully to his parents. Jed was able to make progress in individual treatment. Only if counterpressures from his family had prevented him from moving forward, or had resulted in setbacks, would family therapy have been indicated. Finally, the fact that Jed was in treatment on his own and taking charge of resolving his difficulties supported his wish to feel adult and self-reliant.

Successful treatment, of course, requires a worker with the personality, intuition, talent, and concern to do the work; it calls for enough personal security and flexibility to accept the pains and defeats as well as the pleasures and achievements of the clients we see. But as important as these worker characteristics are, they are not enough. A broad body of knowledge of people, their situations, and how these interact is required to individualize the particular client who asks for help. Responsible treatment rests on a theoretical framework, tested through practice, combined with a knowledge of the nature and effects of clinical methods and procedures. The cases presented in this chapter are certainly not offered as "proof" either of theories or results, but as demonstrations of the relationship among psychosocial study, diagnostic understanding, and treatment presented in previous chapters. They are among the cases from which the theories developed in this book derive.

## NOTES

1. For an excellent and comprehensive work on schizoprenia, see Silvano Arieti, *Interpretation of Schizophrenia,* 2nd ed. (New York: Basic Books, 1974); the reader may be particularly interested in the discussion of psychotherapy, pp. 525–664, as companion reading to this case presentation. See also Robert Cancro et al., *Strategic Intervention in Schizoprenia* (New York: Behavioral, 1974), for several good papers on treatment.
2. See Elisabeth Kubler-Ross, *On Death and Dying* (New York: Macmillan, 1969); Colin Murray Parkes, *Bereavement: Studies of Grief in Adult Life* (New York: International Universities Press, 1974); Elizabeth R. Prichard et al., eds., *Social Work With the Dying Patient and the Family* (New York: Columbia University Press, 1977); and Avery D. Weisman, *On Dying and Denying: A Psychiatric Study of Terminality* (New York: Behavioral, 1972).
3. See Lucille N. Austin, "Dynamics and Treatment of the Client with Anxiety Hysteria," in Howard J. Parad, ed., *Ego Psychology and Dynamic Casework* (New York: Family Service Association of America, 1958), pp. 137–158. See also Hilde Bruch's paper, which offers helpful information about treatment of anxiety, "The Sullivanian Concept of Anxiety," in William E. Fann, ed., *Phenomenology and Treatment of Anxiety* (New York: Spectrum, 1979), pp. 261–270. In the same volume, see Robert M. Gilliand's "Anxiety: A Psychoanalytic View," pp. 251–260, for a good theoretical discussion of anxiety from the psychoanalytic point of view.

# Chapter 20

# And in Conclusion

As we wrote at the outset, it has been the purpose of this book to describe and analyze the psychosocial approach to casework. It has not been our aim to *prove* that it is the best approach for helping troubled people. We would not waste our time writing about psychosocial casework, however, if we did not believe it to be a very valuable approach. We have observed its effectiveness in our own practice and in that of many colleagues. Its empirical base is well documented in a great many reports of single cases and small groups of cases as well as in larger studies. There is no need to repeat here the discussion of research methodology of Chapter 1, except to reiterate our conviction that further study by practitioners of psychosocial casework methods and their effects is greatly needed. Better techniques are now more available than formerly for small case studies analyzing in detail the effects of various procedures, as well as for overall estimation of the extent to which clients with various types of problems do or do not improve in their functioning and sense of well-being.

## DIVERSE APPROACHES

Students are often dismayed—and also confused—by the varieties of approaches by which they are confronted in the literature, each with its own claims to effectiveness. The rich array of theories or "models" of social work treatment that have emerged in recent years witness the fact that clinical social workers are in touch with other therapeutic fields and with new developments in the social sciences, and are actively engaged in formulating their own ideas. It shows that many practitioners are alert and do not routinely follow accepted methodology without knowledge of new findings and theories. Indeed, each new theory throws additional light on some aspect of the helping process.[1]

From time to time, one hears complaints that there is no "one" comprehensive theory of social work or even of clinical social work. Heaven forbid that we should ever arrive at that state of stagnation! We do need a larger base of agreement in social work about many issues, but a "grand theory" accepted by all practitioners is hardly a realistic goal.

Undoubtedly, each approach now in use can be helpful in certain ways with certain kinds of troubles. Some are mutually compatible, others are not. In combining techniques from one point of view with those of another, one has to examine carefully this factor of compatibility. It has been possible, for instance, during the past decade or two for psychosocial workers to draw upon crisis treatment, family treatment, problem solving, and short-term treatment extensively. Task-centered treatment is currently being experimented with by a number of practitioners. Problem solving and psychosocial casework overlap considerably. There may be differences of opinion about how widely the techniques developed in these approaches should be used and concerning which is more effective, but there is no basic conflict of principle involved in their use.

The two chapters on family treatment demonstrate very well the way in which practice principles developed by others can be integrated into psychosocial practice. These chapters also show how one sometimes translates concepts from one theory into the language of another. But such translating is not always possible. Family treatment is also a good example of this latter fact, because there are several different approaches to family therapy that differ very greatly from each other and in their compatibility with psychosocial practice. Some give little weight to the nature of individuals in the family and address themselves almost entirely to group interaction or family structure. Furthermore, the techniques used by some family practitioners seem to psychosocial workers to be manipulative, or at least more directive than we would think advisable.

It is also true that there are large areas of overlap in practice between workers who follow different approaches. For instance, in specific situations in which the psychosocial worker would not regard exploration of past events as essential, differences in theory about the nature of the effect of the past on the present might not lead to differences in treatment. These areas of overlapping practice may account in part for the observation that differences in practice among workers are not as great as the differences in the theories they supposedly follow.

However, there are also distinct differences between some theories that make them truly incompatible. In order to make informed choices about the use of diverse approaches, one needs to be clear about these incompatibilities. Theories vary in so many ways. They differ greatly, for instance, in the emphasis they put upon the client–worker relationship—its nature, and the extent to which it is used in treatment. Some theories refer often to such concepts as acceptance, caring, sympathy, empathy, respect. Others, even when not necessarily opposing such ideas, seem to give them very low priority in treatment. The concept of self-determination is also widely accepted, but there are great variations in the degree to which this quality is emphasized or adhered to in practice.

Obviously too, current approaches are based on differing understanding of personality development and dynamics. Some personality theories have many common elements; others are far apart on such matters as the influence of past experiences on present behavior, and the question of whether or not important ongoing mental activities exist of which a person is not conscious or not fully conscious, but that nevertheless influence his or her current ways of functioning. Ego psychology, with its knowledge of defenses, is not included in some theories. There are also great variations in concepts about the ways in which people can best be helped to change—through relationships, through purely cognitive measures, through educational techniques, through achieving the implementation of mutually agreed upon tasks, through conditioning, through the expression of feeling, through developing understanding of the self and of others, and so on. All theories use some, but by no means all, of these procedures to promote change. The emphasis placed upon each, however, varies greatly. Some procedures and principles, stressed by one school of thought, are incompatible with those used by another. They cannot be combined because they would work at cross-purposes.

Theories differ also in their definitions of the "problem to be worked on." This aspect of practice ranges from those who would deal only with the presenting problem to those who feel that in many cases there should be some exploration at the outset for the possible existence of other related problems with which casework could be helpful. Some would limit work to the "interface" of interacting systems, while others would see a much more inclusive gestalt as needing attention in order to help at the interface.

One thing that one needs to beware of in reading about several points of view is that writers may have insufficient or inaccurate knowledge of the viewpoints of others. There are still authors, for instance, who write as if psychosocial casework were tied to a narrow linear type of causation that relies largely—or even primarily—on past events. Some seem not to be aware of the relationship between psychosocial concepts of causation and systems theory. Some apparently think psychosocial casework is merely a pale version of psychoanalysis. Some think little or no attention is given to the environment. The reader can judge for himself or herself the accuracy of such statements.

As we see it, psychosocial casework constitutes a broad and expanding set of concepts and theories concerning the nature of the person–situation gestalt and its dynamics and concerning ways to help individuals function more effectively and more fully meet their own needs. It is an open and developing system of thought, constantly integrating compatible ideas from other treatment models, combining knowledge and insights from other disciplines with its own content and perspectives in a unique way. Psychoanalytic theory has been particularly valuable in enlarging our understanding of the complexities of human personality, including an understanding of the strength of the ego and its coping abilities. There is now considerable optimism about the extent to which people can change and find better ways of handling their lives in response to an interviewing process—or communication process—in which the emphasis is on enhancing the ego's ability to deal with current life pressures. As the cumulative writings of psychosocial casework demonstrate, this approach has been explicit about engaging the ego in greater understanding of other people and of their situation as well as of conscious and preconscious aspects of the self. It stresses the client's growth through understanding of others and of himself or herself, through a meaningful, ego-nourishing relationship, through encouragement to change and fully use the environment, and to try out new ways of functioning in real life, so that the client will experience the reinforcement that reality itself can provide. In coordination with this goes intervention in the environment by the worker as it is called for on the client's behalf. This is a multifaceted, reality-based approach.

## WHOM DO WE SERVE?

To what extent is psychosocial casework class-bound? In the 1930s we set out to demonstrate that interpersonal and social problems were not a monopoly of the poor and near poor, but were experienced by people of all degrees of income and education and that all these groups could and would use casework help. By the 1960s this had been so well established that a hue and cry arose to the effect that casework was a middle-class therapy unsuitable for work with low-income families. Some urged that it readapt itself to work with the poor. Others thought it could have nothing to offer the poor. In actuality, casework as a field has never stopped serving the poor even though it has also served families of average and above-average income. In medical and psychiatric clinics, in child placement agencies, in agencies serving youth, relatively few of the affluent have been treated by caseworkers. Even in child guidance clinics and family services agencies, many clients were —and still are—from low-income families.[2]

True, it is harder to help people who are beset with the host of problems that accompany lack of income—poor housing, poor schooling, crime-infested neighborhoods, unemployment, poor medical facilities, inadequate and often undignified public assistance, public contempt. These are things that cannot be treated by casework alone. Some progress can be made on an individual basis, but these are total community problems and must be tackled by community and government action, which social work must help mobilize. But must these disadvantaged families also be deprived of skilled individualized effort to help them secure as decent a life as they can in spite of these handicaps? The poor can also have family relationships that go awry; they also have to cope as best they can with illness and handicap and loss through death. They also have aspirations for themselves and their children.

Caseworkers have fought to make financial help free of the possibility of interference in personal matters. We must now put equal effort into seeing that first-rate service is easily available to those who lack money but do want help with family and individual problems in social functioning. Structures must be developed and publicly supported to make clinical social work services of good quality readily available to families securing financial assistance, expecially to families with children and to the aged, where such service is so frequently and urgently needed.

## Private Practice

There has been resistance among many social workers to the idea of the private practice of clinical social work on the grounds that we should primarily serve people who cannot afford private fees and should not take strength away from agencies set up for this purpose.

The authors differ with this point of view and believe the current development of private practice is in the main a positive step. It makes no more sense for clinical social work to be class-bound by excluding those who are financially secure than by excluding the poor. We also believe that the ideal of private practice should be to divide one's time between agency practice and independent work, thus insuring that all experienced practitioners will devote part of their time to consultation, field instruction, or direct service with nonpaying or low-fee-paying clients. Most of today's private practitioners do so divide their time. Many have sliding fee scales to accommodate lower income clients.

A further advantage in the spread of private practice for social work itself is the fact that, as we become better known as independent clinicians, our profession will be more widely recognized as the challenging and personally rewarding work that it really is. This, in turn, will bring a greater number of well qualified candidates for professional study.

A justified concern about private practice is that such practitioners may have fewer supports than those employed in agencies of high standards, where various types of information and consultation can be readily available and where the agency vouches for the competence of its workers. People served by private practitioners deserve the equivalent of this protection. Through licensing, or other standard setting devices, it can be required that caseworkers qualifying for private practice have advanced training and experience in clinical social work, are continuing their education, and are making use of peer consultation.

## EDUCATIONAL ISSUES

The seventies saw many changes in education for social work. Chief among them were the development of widespread undergraduate training and a move in a number of schools toward "generalist" education, which trains for beginning performance as caseworker, group worker, and community worker at the master's level. Certainly, many tasks in the field of social welfare are well done by BSWs and by "generalists." Furthermore, BSW training can provide a good underpinning for graduate work leading to clinical social work practice. Some generalists may be better prepared for certain types of social work activity than are those who concentrate primarily on learning clinical theory and skills. These are not the issues. Rather, we are concerned here with the need for intensive concentration in *casework* in the education of social work clinicians.

We have referred many times to the great expansion over the years of the body of knowledge now needed for the practice of clinical social work. To review this for emphasis: Skill is needed in family treatment and in work with formed groups as well as in work with individuals. Knowledge of crisis treatment, short-term treatment, and task-centered treatment, as well as open-ended and long-term treatment, is important. Content concerning personality theory, systems theory, communication theory concerning various types of psychological disturbances, and various types of interpersonal problems is constantly increasing. Knowledge of the social environment has expanded greatly and all workers are now expected to understand the nature of agencies, institutions, and social factors much more fully than formerly. Some knowledge of various theoretical approaches is useful. Increasingly, competent practitioners are also expected to be informed about, and often to participate in, research with its modern complexities.

A beginning understanding of some parts of these requirements can be secured in undergraduate work, and also in the generalist form of study in master's work. But to prepare for even beginning practice as a clinical social worker, making use of the full range of psychosocial treatment, in the opinion of the writers, requires a two-year concentration in casework at the master's level.[3]

Individuals are so unique that in social work, despite well developed practice knowledge and skill, we are constantly confronted by difficult choices! Again and again, decisions about treatment have to be made without knowing for sure what is best. Probably this is better than that, so we do this. Therefore, the worker must have sufficient personal and professional security to act on his or her own best judgment, without undue anxiety. The worker must also be flexible, alert to indications that some other course might be better, ready to modify an approach in the light of new understanding.

No blueprint of treatment can ever be given, any more than a skier can know each twist and turn he or she will have to take on a steep, unknown course. Like the skier, the worker knows the general direction, but the worker, too, may be able to see only a little way ahead and have to quickly adapt technique to the terrain. To do this, it is necessary to be a skilled practitioner, who knows what to do to accomplish what, and when a given procedure is necessary.

It is an essential part of good practice not only to find time to read professional journals and other publications, but also to find ways of keeping in direct touch with the experiences and opinions of colleagues. We must be both open-minded and hard-headed. This means we must study and exchange ideas and, above all, *think*.

A great contribution can be made to the quality of social work practice by the clinical doctorate as such programs become more widely available. We hope and expect that increasing numbers of clinical social workers will undertake this advanced study, preferably after a period of clinical practice in an agency of good standards. Such doctorates could produce advanced practitioners and clinicians with sophisticated research skill, which is so sorely needed today and cannot be acquired in MSW training. It would also make a great contribution to the teaching of clinical social work and research at the master's and doctoral levels. University teachers in direct service courses need not only to have studied theory and practice in depth, but also to be well versed in research methods appropriate to their subject and—most important of all—they should be skilled in the *application* of the theory and knowledge that they will be teaching at both master's and doctoral levels.

## TOWARD WHAT ENDS?

Social casework seeks to strengthen individuals through helping them deal with current dilemmas, find answers to these dilemmas insofar as possible, and emerge from periods of stress with greater competence, more self-confidence, increased self-respect, and greater ability to respond positively to life. In working toward these ends, the clinical social worker seeks first to establish a positive and often warm human relationship so that honest communication can take place and trust can develop. A common ground for work together must be found, with clarity about the client's goals and wishes to proceed along lines that the person or the worker may propose. The client-in-his-situation must be understood in full individuality to make possible help geared to the needs and capacities of the individual and to the modifiability of the situation.

Casework is not an agent of social control. Our effort is distinctly *not* to bend the client to the social system but rather to increase his or her ability to deal with the complexities of modern organizations, enhancing rather than diminishing his or her autonomy. It is often the worker's responsibility to attempt to modify rather than to reinforce social institutions, either in the short run for a particular client or in the long run for the good of us all.

Social work can become a great profession if it matches its opportunity to serve and to release human potential with a quality of professional education equal to its responsibilities. Social workers must be well prepared to work toward the end of helping troubled people achieve their own goals whether these be to resolve particular dilemmas, to cope with particular pressures, to reach for a better balance between their own needs and those of others, or to achieve greater realization of their capacities and greater satisfaction in their lives.

Now more than ever, with the centralization of power in the modern state and in modern industry, and with the mechanization of so much of our lives, society needs a profession that is not aligned with these impersonal or oppressive forces but rather with the well-being of persons, of people—for individualization, and against depersonalization in all its forms.

The essence of psychosocial casework is concern for individual human beings—for their relationships with others, their well-being in a grossly imperfect society, their achieving an enhanced sense of their own value and increased competence in dealing with the vicissitudes of living. In a world where distrust is rampant, alliances and loyalties constantly shifting, values in flux, and bureaucracies ever more powerful and remote, individuals must develop strength and skill to meet their needs and to effect changes in the external world without surrendering autonomy. They must learn to assess their situations realistically and to stand up for themselves. They must use their capacity for love to build islands of refuge and strength in families, with friends, and with neighbors, so that they and their children may be nourished and may come to value, respect, and trust themselves and one another. This is what social work is all about.

## NOTES

1.  For an excellent introduction to many of these approaches, see Francis J. Turner, ed., *Social Work Treatment: Interlocking Theoretical Approaches,* 2nd ed. (New York: Free Press, 1979).
2.  For a picture of family service agency clients, see Dorothy Fahs Beck and Mary Ann Jones, *Progress on Family Problems: A Nationwide Study of Clients' and Counselors' Views on Family Agency Services* (New York: Family Service Association of America, 1973).
3.  The case for this was very well stated by the late Helen Pinkus et al., in a recent position paper, "Education for the Practice of Clinical Social Work at the Master's Level: A Position Paper," *Clinical Social Work Journal,* 5 (Winter 1977), 253–273. In the same issue, see also Shirley Cooper's excellent article, "Reflections on Clinical Social Work," 303–315, and John D. Minor, "An Assessment of Social Work Education and Family Agency Practice," 336–341; both are concerned about the quality of education for clinical social work practice.

    Richard M. Grinnell, Jr., and Nancy S. Kyte, in "The Future of Clinical Practice: A Study," *Clinical Social Work Journal,* 5 (Summer 1977), 132–138, conclude that their findings "appear to provide a strong measure of support for recent predictions of a swing in social work toward clinical practice." Of 1,582 graduate and undergraduate social work students studied, 53.2 percent designated casework, psychotherapy, or private practice (31.9%, 15.9%, and 5.4%, respectively) as their ideal employment choice. It is our hope that the schools of social work will endeavor to provide students who choose to train for direct practice with a clinical curriculum of depth and substance (see Pinkus et al., "Education for Practice of Clinical Social Work," and Cooper, "Reflections on Clinical Social Work"). Nothing less is required for specialization in the complicated work of helping the individuals and families who will be turning to graduate clinical social workers, and counting on them to be experts in their field.

# Appendix

# A Note on the Reliability of the Classification*

Before using a research tool in formal study it is, of course, most important to know the degree of its reliability. Preliminary figures on the reliability of the classification when two judges are coding the same data are encouraging. Several reliability tests were run during the course of developing and experimenting with the typology. In the early stages a running record of agreement percentages was kept. There were times when we were greatly encouraged to find agreement rates in many of the categories that stayed above 80 per cent and sometimes reached 90 per cent or more for a series of three or four interviews. Then suddenly the agreement rate for an interview would drop to 70 per cent, or even lower, either because the dictation was obscure or because it was particularly hard to decide whether the client was really reflecting. Such sudden drops revealed several pitfalls in reliability testing into which it is easy to slip. If reliability had simply been checked until a desirable level was reached, as is sometimes done, a high agreement rate could have been reported fairly early. But this would really have meant that we had stopped playing when we were winning.

A high rate could also have been established, as is sometimes done, by setting up an experiment in which examples of the different types of material are typed on cards that are then coded. This is a useful device to show at least that the system is conceptually clear, but it tells nothing about the borderline instances that are the real cause of disagreement between coders. To avoid these pitfalls, in the two reliability tests 19 and 20 interviews were used, respectively, and coded over an arbitrarily selected time span.

The principal measure of reliability used in the tests was the Spearman Rank Order Correlation Coefficient.[1] John Dollard and Frank Auld have pointed out the error introduced by relying, as is sometimes done, on a simple percentage agreement, the significance of which is so strongly influenced by the number of alternative choices available.[2] When only two choices are possible in a dimension, chance alone would yield 50 per cent agreement even if the coding were completely unreli-

*Taken by permission of *Social Casework* from "The Coding and Application of a Typology of Casework Treatment," *Social Casework*, 48 (October 1967).

able. With each addition to the choices, however, the probability of chance agreement lessens. It is reduced to 33 per cent when there are three possible choices, and to only 20 per cent when there are five choices (assuming equal distribution over all alternatives). In other words, an agreement rate of 60 per cent in the first instance would represent only 20 per cent better than chance, while in the second it would be almost twice as good as chance, and in the third three times as good.

With this in mind it was decided not to use percentage agreement but, instead, to use rank order correlations over a sample comparable in number of cases to the size of sample for which the classification was likely to be used. In this kind of test the number of alternatives available in a given dimension does not have a bearing on the significance of the score. If one assumes that errors are randomized, this test gives a guide to the extent to which, in an actual study of the same number of cases, errors of judges in a given category may obscure differences or similarities that can be located with a more exact research tool.

Reliability scores can be reported on the major means categories and on subject matter categories 1, 2, and 3 used in the exploratory-descriptive-ventilative material and on the change context categories.[3] For the most part, as the accompanying tables show, the Spearman test was used. Three of the major categories were used so rarely that they could not be tested by the Spearman formula. For these Fisher's Exact Probability Test was used, basing the test on the simple presence or absence of the given procedure in the respective interviews.[4]

The figures in Table I represent the average of the two reliability tests done in the next to the last and the last year of the study. The figures in Table II were obtained in the later test. In some categories there was substantial progress in reliability between the first and second tests. For example, the analyses on the average score of .69 given for client C3 represents a rise from .60 to .79 between tests, the score of .36 for worker C3 represents a rise from .03 to .70, the .56 for client d represents a rise from .46 to .67.

The chief categories remaining in difficulty at the time of the second test were client b and worker d. These tables give a minimum estimate of the present reliability of the typology, however, since work was done subsequently to further define the weaker categories.

Though it is hoped that, eventually, all items can be brought up to a reliability score of .80, a score of .70 represents a substantial improvement not only over chance but also over judgments arrived at in a global way. For greatest reliability, two judges should be used on all material, the average of the two sets of coding being used in the analysis. When this averaging method is used, an agreement level of .80 between coders gives a reliability level of .88; agreement of .70, a

reliability of .82; agreement of .65 gives .79. (Using the Spearman–
Brown formula,[5] inter-rater r X 2 divided by 1 + inter-rater r.) If double
coding is not possible because of financial limitations, as is often true of
doctoral dissertations, the author may be consulted concerning measures that should be taken to safeguard reliability as much as is possible
with a single coder.

Table I.
Agreement Between Judges as Measured by Spearman $r$

| CATEGORY | CLIENT | WORKER |
|----------|--------|--------|
| A | — | .83* |
| C | .82* | .87* |
| D | .76* | .75* |
| C1 | .89* | .86* |
| C2 | .78* | .74* |
| C3 | .69† | .36 |
| $a^6$ | .70† | .70† |
| b | .45 | .65† |
| c | .73* | .84* |
| d | .56 | .30 |

* significance level ≤ .001
† significance level ≤ .005

Table II.
Agreement Between Judges as Measured
by Fisher Exact Probability Test

| CATEGORY | AGREE | | DISAGREE | SIG. LEVEL |
|----------|---------|--------|----------|------------|
|          | Present | Absent |          |            |
| Client E | 1 | 18 | 1 | .10 |
| Client F | 5 | 13 | 2 | .005 |
| Worker B | 4 | 11 | 5 | .05 |
| Worker E | 0 | 18 | 2 | N.S. |
| Worker F | 2 | 16 | 2 | .05 |

## REFERENCES

1.  Hubert M. Blalock, Jr., *Social Statistics,* McGraw-Hill Book Co., New York, 1960, pp. 317–19.
2.  John Dollard and Frank Auld, Jr., *Scoring Human Motives: A Manual,* Yale University Press, New Haven, 1959, p. 306.
3.  Subject matter categories have not been useful and have since been dropped.
4.  Blalock, *op. cit.,* pp. 221–25.
5.  J. P. Guilford, *Fundamental Statistics in Psychology and Education,* 4th ed., McGraw-Hill Book Co., New York, 1965, pp. 457–58.
6.  Small letters correspond to arabic numerals 1, 2, 3, & 4 in text.

# Bibliography

ACKERMAN, NATHAN W. "The Diagnosis of Neurotic Marital Interaction." *Social Casework*, 35 (April 1954), 139–147.

——. "Family Healing in a Troubled World." *Social Casework*, 52 (April 1971), 200–205.

——. "Family Psychotherapy Today." *Family Process*, 9 (1970), 123–126.

——. "The Growing Edge of Family Therapy." In Clifford J. Sagar and Helen Singer Kaplan, eds., *Progress in Group and Family Therapy*. New York: Brunner/Mazel, 1972, 440–456.

——. "Prejudice and Scapegoating in the Family." In Gerald H. Zuk and Ivan Boszormenyi-Nagy, eds., *Family Therapy and Disturbed Families*. Palo Alto, Calif.: Science and Behavior Books, 1969, 48–57.

——. *The Psychodynamics of Family Life*. New York: Basic Books, 1958.

——. "The Training of Caseworkers in Psychotherapy." *American Journal of Orthopsychiatry*, 19 (January 1949), 14–24.

——. *Treating the Troubled Family*. New York: Basic Books, 1966.

——, FRANCES L. BEATMAN, and SANFORD N. SHERMAN. *Expanding Theory and Practice in Family Therapy*. New York: Family Service Association of America, 1967.

——, FRANCES L. BEATMAN, and SANFORD N. SHERMAN, eds. *Exploring the Base for Family Therapy*, New York: Family Service Association of America, 1961.

AINSWORTH, MARY D. "The Effects of Maternal Deprivation: A Review of Findings and Controversy in the Context of Research Strategy." In *Deprivation of Maternal Care: A Reassessment of Its Effects*. Geneva: World Health Organization, 1962.

ALEXANDER, JEANETTE. "Alternate Life Styles: Relationship Between New Realities and Practice." *Clinical Social Work Journal*, 4 (Winter 1976), 289–301.

ALLPORT, GORDON. "The Open System in Personality Theory." *Journal of Abnormal and Social Psychology*, 61 (November 1960), 301–310.

ANDERSON, GARY D. "Enhancing Listening Skills for Work with Abusing Parents." *Social Casework*, 60 (December 1979), 602–608.

ANDERSON, LINDA M., et al. "Training in Family Treatment: Needs and Objectives." *Social Casework*, 60 (June 1979), 323–329.

ANGELL, ROBERT C. *The Family Encounters the Depression*. New York: Scribner's, 1936.

APONTE, HARRY J. "Diagnosis in Family Therapy." In Carel B. Germain, ed.,

*Social Work Practice: People and Environments.* New York: Columbia University Press, 1979, 107–149.

———. "Underorganization in the Poor Family." In Philip J. Guerin, ed., *Family Therapy.* New York: Gardner Press, 1976, 432–448.

APPEL, GERALD. "Some Aspects of Transference and Countertransference in Marital Counseling." *Social Casework,* 47 (May 1966), 307–312.

APPLEBAUM, FLORENCE. "Loneliness: A Taxonomy and Psychodynamic View." *Clinical Social Work Journal,* 6 (Spring 1978), 13–20.

APTEKAR, HERBERT H. *The Dynamics of Casework and Counseling.* Boston: Houghton Mifflin, 1955.

ARIETI, SILVANO. *Interpretation of Schizophrenia.* Second ed. New York: Basic Books, 1974.

ARLOW, JACOB, and CHARLES BRENNER. *Psychoanalytic Concepts and the Structural Theory.* New York: International Universities Press, 1964.

ARONSON, H., and B. OVERALL. "Treatment Expectations of Patients in Two Social Classes." *Social Work,* 11 (January 1966), 35–41.

Attneave, CAROLYN L. "Social Networks as the Unit of Intervention." In Philip J. Guerin, Jr., ed., *Family Therapy.* New York: Gardner Press, 1976, 220–232.

AUSTIN, LUCILLE N. "Dynamics and Treatment of the Client with Anxiety Hysteria." In Howard J. Parad, ed., *Ego Psychology and Dynamic Casework.* New York: Family Service Association, 1958, 137–158.

———. "Qualifications for Psychotherapists, Social Caseworkers." *American Journal of Orthopsychiatry,* 26 (1956), 47–57.

———. "Trends in Differential Treatment in Social Casework." *Journal of Social Casework,* 29 (June 1948), 203–211.

AYERS, ALICE Q. "Neighborhood Services: People Caring for People." *Social Casework,* 54 (April 1973), 192–215.

BAILEY, MARGARET. "Casework Treatment of the Alcoholic and His Family." *Alcoholism and Family Casework.* New York: Community Council of Greater New York, 1968, 67–108.

BALDWIN, KATHERINE. "Crisis-Focused Casework in a Child Guidance Clinic." *Social Casework,* 49 (January 1968), 28–34.

BALL, MARGARET. "Issues of Violence in Family Casework." *Social Casework,* 58 (January 1977), 3–12.

BANDLER, BERNARD. "The Concept of Ego-Supportive Psychotherapy." In Howard J. Parad and Roger R. Miller, eds., *Ego-Oriented Casework: Problems and Perspectives.* New York: Family Service Association of America, 1963, 27–44.

BANDLER, LOUISE. "Casework—A Process of Socialization: Gains, Limitations, Conclusions." In Eleanor Pavenstedt, ed., *The Drifters: Children of Disorganized Lower-Class Families.* Boston: Little, Brown, 1967, 255–296.

BANKS, GEORGE P. "The Effects of Race on One-to-One Helping Interviews." *Social Service Review,* 45 (June 1971), 137–146.

BARNES, GEOFFREY B., et al. "Team Treatment for Abusive Families." *Social Casework,* 55 (December 1974), 600–611.

BARTLETT, HARRIETT. *The Common Base of Social Work Practice.* New York: National Association of Social Workers, 1970.

BARTZ, KAREN W., and ELAINE S. LEVINE. "Child Rearing by Black Parents: A Description and Comparison to Anglo and Chicano Parents." *Journal of Marriage and the Family,* 40 (November 1978), 709–719.

BATESON, GREGORY, et al. "A Note on the Double Bind—1962." *Family Process,* 2 (March 1963), 154–161.

———, DON JACKSON, JAY HALEY, and JOHN H. WEAKLAND. "Toward a Theory of Schizophrenia." *Behavioral Science,* 1 (October 1956), 251–264.

BEATRICE, DORY KRONGELB. "Divorce: Problems, Goals, and Growth Facilitation." *Social Casework,* 60 (March 1979), 157–165.

BECK, DOROTHY FAHS, and MARY ANN JONES. *Progress on Family Problems: A Nationwide Study of Clients' and Counselors' Views on Family Agency Services.* New York: Family Service Association of America, 1973.

BEELS, CHRISTIAN C., and ANDREW S. FERBER. "Family Therapy: A View." *Family Process,* 8 (1969), 280–318.

BEHRENS, MARJORIE, and NATHAN ACKERMAN. "The Home Visit as an Aid in Family Diagnosis and Therapy." *Social Casework,* 37 (January 1956), 11–19.

BELL, JOHN E. *Family Group Therapy.* Public Health Monograph No. 64. Washington, D.C.: U.S. Government Printing Office, 1961.

BELLAK, LEOPOLD, et al. *Ego Functions in Schizophrenics, Neurotics, and Normals.* New York: Wiley, 1973.

———. "Psychiatric Aspects of Tuberculosis." *Social Casework,* 31 (May 1950), 183–189.

BENDER, BARBARA. "Management of Acute Hospitalization Anxiety." *Social Casework* (January 1976), 19–26.

BENEDICT, RUTH. *Patterns of Culture.* Boston: Houghton Mifflin, 1934.

BENNETT, BRUCE B., et al. "Police and Social Workers in a Community Outreach Program." *Social Casework,* 57 (January 1976), 41–49.

BENNY, CELIA, et al. "Clinical Complexities in Work Adjustment of Deprived Youth." *Social Casework,* 50 (June 1969), 330–336.

BERGER, RAYMOND MARK "An Advocate Model for Intervention with Homosexuals." *Social Work,* 22 (July 1977), 280–283.

BERGIN, ALLEN E., and SOL L. GARFIELD, eds. *Handbook of Psychotherapy and Behavior Change: An Empirical Analysis.* New York: Wiley, 1971.

BERGLER, EDMUND. *Unhappy Marriage and Divorce.* New York: International Universities Press, 1946.

BERKOWITZ, SIDNEY. "Some Specific Techniques of Psychosocial Diagnosis and Treatment in Family Casework." *Social Casework,* 36 (November 1955), 339–406.

BERLATSKY, MARJORIE. "Some Aspects of the Marital Problems of the Elderly." *Social Casework,* 43 (May 1962), 233–237.

BERTALANFFY, LUDWIG VON. *General Systems Theory: Foundations, Development, Application.* New York: Braziller, 1968.

BIBRING, GRETE L. "Psychiatry and Social Work." *Journal of Social Casework,* 28 (June 1947), 203–211.

BIESTEK, FELIX. *The Casework Relationship.* Chicago: Loyola University Press, 1957.

BILLINGSLEY, ANDREW. *Black Families in White America.* Englewood Cliffs, N.J.: Prentice-Hall, 1968.

BINTZLER, JANET. "Diagnosis and Treatment of Borderline Personality Organization." *Clinical Social Work Journal,* 6 (Summer 1978), 100–107.

BIRDWHISTELL, RAY L. *Kinesics and Context.* Philadelphia: University of Pennsylvania Press, 1970.

BISNO, HERBERT. *The Philosophy of Social Work.* Washington, D.C.: Public Affairs Press, 1952.

BITTERMANN, CATHERINE. "Marital Adjustment Patterns of Clients with Compulsive Character Disorders: Implications for Treatment." *Social Casework,* 47 (November 1966), 575–582.

———. "Multimarriage Family." *Social Casework,* 49 (April 1968), 218–221.

BLANCK, GERTRUDE and RUBIN. *Ego Psychology: Theory and Practice.* New York: Columbia University Press, 1974.

———. *Ego Psychology II.* New York: Columbia University Press, 1979.

BLANCK, RUBIN. "The Case for Individual Treatment." *Social Casework,* 47 (February 1965), 70–74.

———. "Countertransference in Treatment of the Borderline Patient." *Clinical Social Work Journal,* 1 (Summer 1973), 110–117.

BLIZINSKY, MARLIN J., and WILLIAM J. REID. "Problem Focus and Change in a Brief Treatment Model." *Social Work,* 25 (March 1980), 89–93.

BLOCH, DONALD, ed. *Techniques of Family Psychotherapy: A Primer.* New York: Grune & Stratton, 1973.

BLOCH, JULIA. "The White Worker and the Negro Client in Psychotherapy." *Social Work,* 13 (April 1968), 36–42.

BLOOM, MARTIN. "Social Prevention: An Ecological Approach." In Carel B. Germain, ed., *Social Work Practice.* New York: Columbia University Press, 1979, 326–345.

BLOS, PETER. *The Adolescent Passage.* New York: International Universities Press, 1979.

BOATMAN, LOUISE. "Caseworkers' Judgments of Clients' Hope: Some Correlates Among Client–Situation Characteristics and Among Workers' Communication Patterns." Doctoral dissertation, Columbia University School of Social Work, New York, 1974.

BOIE, MAURINE. "The Case Worker's Need for Orientation to the Culture of the Client." *Proceedings of the National Conference of Social Work.* Chicago: University of Chicago Press, 1937, 112–123.

BONNEFIL, MARGARET C. "The Relationship of Interpersonal Acting-Out to the Process of Decompensation." *Clinical Social Work Journal,* 1 (Spring 1973), 13–21.

———. "Therapist, Save My Child: A Family Crisis Case." *Clinical Social Work Journal,* 7 (Spring 1979), 6–14.

BORNSTEIN, BERTA. "On Latency." In Ruth S. Eissler et al., eds., *The Psychoanalytic Study of the Child,* Vol. 6. New York: International Universities Press, 1951, 279–285.

BOSZORMENYI-NAGY, IVAN, and GERALDINE M. SPARK. *Invisible Loyalties.* New York: Harper & Row, 1973.

BOWEN, MURRAY. "The Use of Family Theory in Clinical Practice." In Jay Haley, ed., *Changing Families: A Family Therapy Reader.* New York: Grune & Stratton, 1971, 159–192.

BOWLBY, JOHN. "Grief and Mourning in Infancy and Early Childhood." In Ruth S. Eissler et al., eds., *The Psychoanalytic Study of the Child,* Vol. 15. New York: International Universities Press, 1961.

——. *Maternal Care and Mental Health.* Second ed. World Health Organization Monograph Series No. 2. Geneva: World Health Organization, 1952.

BRAGER, GEORGE A. "Advocacy and Political Behavior." *Social Work,* 13 (April 1968), 5–15.

——, and STEPHEN HOLLOWAY. *Changing Human Service Organizations.* New York: Free Press, 1978.

BRENNAN, WILLIAM, and SHANTI KINDUKA. "Role Discrepancies and Professional Socialization: The Case of the Juvenile Probation Officer." *Social Work,* 15 (April 1970), 87–94.

BRIAR, SCOTT M. "Use of Theory in Studying Effects of Client Social Class on Students' Judgments." *Social Work,* 6 (July 1961), 91–97.

——, and HENRY MILLER. *Problems and Issues in Social Casework.* New York: Columbia University Press, 1971.

BRIARD, FRED K. "Counseling Parents of Children with Learning Disabilities." *Social Casework,* 57 (November 1976), 581–585.

BRIGGS, DEAN. "The Trainee and the Borderline Client: Countertransference Pitfalls." *Clinical Social Work Journal,* 7 (Summer 1979), 133–145.

BRITTON, CLARE. "Casework Techniques in Child Care Services." *Social Casework,* 36 (January 1955), 3–13.

BRODEY, W. M. "Some Family Operations and Schizophrenia." *Archives of General Psychiatry,* 1 (1959), 379–402.

BRONFENBRENNER, URIE. "Socialization and Social Class Through Time and Space." In Eleanor E. Maccoby, Theodore M. Newcomb, and Eugene L. Hartley, eds., *Readings in Social Psychology.* New York Rinehart & Winston, 1958.

BROWN, CAREE ROZEN, and MARILYN LEVITT HELLINGER. "Therapists' Attitudes Toward Women." *Social Work,* 20 (July 1975), 266–270.

BROWN, JOHN A. "Clinical Social Work with Chicanos: Some Unwarranted Assumptions." *Clinical Social Work Journal,* 4 (Winter 1979), 256–266.

BRUCH, HILDE. "The Sullivanian Concept of Anxiety." In William E. Fann, ed., *Phenomenology and Treatment of Anxiety.* New York: Spectrum, 1979, 261–270.

BRUNO, FRANK J. *Trends in Social Work: 1874–1956.* New York: Columbia University Press, 1957.

BRYT, ALBERT. "Dropout of Adolescents from Psychotherapy." In Gerald Caplan and Serge Labovici, eds., *Adolescence: Psychosocial Perspectives.* New York: Basic Books, 1969, 293–303.

BURGESS, ERNEST W., and LEONARD S. COTTRELL, JR. *Predicting Success or Failure in Marriage.* New York: Prentice-Hall, 1939.

BURNS, CRAWFORD E. "White Staff, Black Children: Is There a Problem?" *Child Welfare,* 50 (February 1971), 90–96.

CALIGOR, LEOPOLD, and MILTIADES ZAPHIROPOULOS. "Blue-Collar Psychotherapy: Stereotype and Myth." In Earl G. Witenberg, ed., *Interpersonal Explorations in Psychoanalysis.* New York: Basic Books, 1973, 218–234.

CAMERON, J. DONALD, and ESTHER TALAVERA. "An Advocacy Program for Spanish-Speaking People." *Social Casework*, 57 (July 1976), 427–431.

CANCRO, ROBERT, et al. *Strategic Intervention in Schizophrenia*. New York: Behavioral, 1974.

CAPLAN, GERALD, and SERGE LABOVICI, eds. *Adolescence: Psychosocial Perspectives*. New York: Basic Books, 1969.

CAVAN, RUTH SHONIE, and KATHERINE HOWLAND RANCK. *The Family and the Depression*. Chicago: University of Chicago Press, 1938.

CHAMBERLAIN, EDNA. "Testing with a Treatment Typology." *Australian Journal of Social Work*, 22 (December 1969), 3–8.

CHAPMAN, MARGERY. "Salient Need—A Casework Compass." *Social Casework*, 58 (June 1977), 343–349.

CHIANCOLA, SAMUEL P. "The Process of Separation and Divorce: A New Approach." *Social Casework*, 59 (October 1978), 494–499

CLOWARD, RICHARD A. "Illegitimate Means, Anomie and Deviant Behavior." *American Sociological Review*, 24 (April 1959), 164–175.

——, and FRANCES FOX PIVEN. "Notes Toward a Radical Social Work." In Roy Bailey and Mike Brake, eds., *Radical Social Work*. New York: Pantheon 1975, vii–xlviii.

COHEN, JEROME. "Social Work and the Culture of Poverty." *Social Work*, 9 (January 1964), 3–11.

COHEN, PAULINE, and MERTON KRAUSE. *Casework with Wives of Alcoholics*. New York: Family Service Association of America, 1971.

COLLINS, ALICE H., and JAMES R. MACKEY. "Delinquents Who Use the Primary Defense of Denial." In Francis J. Turner, ed., *Differential Diagnosis and Treatment in Social Work*. Second ed. New York: Free Press, 1976, 64–75.

——, and DIANE L. PANCOAST. *Natural Helping Networks: A Strategy for Prevention*. Washington, D.C.: National Association of Social Workers, 1976.

COLLIS, JOHN STEWART. *The Vision of Glory*. New York: Braziller, 1973.

COMPTON, BEULAH ROBERTS, and BURT GALAWAY. *Social Work Processes*. Homewood, Ill.: Dorsey Press, 1975.

COOPER, DAVID C. *The Death of the Family*. New York: Pantheon, 1970.

COOPER, SHIRLEY. "A Look at the Effect of Racism on Clinical Work." *Social Casework*, 54 (February 1973), 76–84.

——. "Reflections on Clinical Social Work." *Clinical Social Work Journal*, 5 (Winter 1977), 303–315.

CORMICAN, ELIN. "Task-Centered Model for Work with the Aged." *Social Casework*, 58 (October 1977), 490–494.

CORMICAN, JOHN D. "Linguistic Issues in Interviewing." *Social Casework*, 59 (March 1978), 145–151.

COUCH, ELIZABETH H. *Joint and Family Interviews in the Treatment of Marital Problems*. New York: Family Service Association of America, 1969.

CRANE, JOHN A. "The Power of Social Intervention Experiments to Discriminate Differences Between Experimental and Control Groups." *Social Service Review*, 50 (June 1976), 224–242.

DAVIS, INGER P. "Advice-giving in Parent Counselling." *Social Casework*, 56 (June 1975), 343–347.

————. "Use of Influence Techniques in Casework with Parents." Doctoral dissertation, University of Chicago, March 1969.

DAVIS, KINGSLEY. "The Changing Family in Industrial Society." In Robert C. Jackson and Jean Morton, eds., *Family Health Care: Health Promotion and Illness Care.* Berkeley: University of California Press, 1976, 1–16.

DECKER, NORMAN. "Anxiety in the General Hospital." In William E. Fann et al., eds., *Phenomenology and Treatment of Anxiety.* New York: Spectrum, 1979, 287–298.

DE LA FONTAINE, ELISE. "Cultural and Psychological Implications in Case Work Treatment with Irish Clients." *Cultural Problems in Social Case Work.* New York: Family Welfare Association of America, 1940, 21–37.

DEYKIN, EVA Y., et al. "Treatment of Depressed Women." In Francis J. Turner, eds., *Differential Diagnosis and Treatment in Social Work.* Second ed. New York: Free Press, 1976, 288–301.

DUEHN, WAYNE D., and NAZNEED SADA MAYADAS. "Starting Where the Client Is: An Empirical Investigation." *Social Casework,* 60 (February 1979), 67–74.

DUNCAN, STARKEY. "Non-verbal Communication." *Psychological Bulletin,* 72 (1969), 118–137.

EDWARD, JOYCE. "The Use of the Dream in the Promotion of Ego Development." *Clinical Social Work Journal,* 6 (Winter 1978), 261–273.

EHLINE, DAVID, and PEGGY O'DEA TIGUE. "Alcoholism: Early Identification and Intervention in the Social Service Agency." *Child Welfare,* 56 (November 1977), 584–592.

EHRENKRANZ, SHIRLEY M. "A Study of Joint Interviewing in the Treatment of Marital Problems." *Social Casework,* 48 (October and November 1967), 498–502, 570–574.

————. "A Study of the Techniques and Procedures Used in Joint Interviewing in the Treatment of Marital Problems." Doctoral dissertation, Columbia University School of Social Work, New York, 1967.

EPSTEIN, IRVIN. "Social Workers and Social Action: Attitudes Toward Social Action Strategies." *Social Work,* 13 (April 1968), 101–108.

EPSTEIN, NORMAN. "Techniques of Brief Therapy with Children and Parents." *Social Casework.* 57 (May 1976), 317–324.

————, and ANNE SHAINLINE. "Paraprofessional Parent-Aides and Disadvantaged Families." *Social Casework,* 55 (April 1974), 230–236.

ERIKSON, ERIK. *Childhood and Society.* New York: Norton, 1950.

————. *Identity and the Life Cycle.* New York: International Universities Press, 1959.

EWALT, PATRICIA L. "The Crisis-Treatment Approach in a Child Guidance Clinic." *Social Casework,* 54 (July 1973), 406–411.

————, and JANICE KATZ. "An Examination of Advice Giving as a Therapeutic Intervention." *Smith College Studies in Social Work,* 47 (November 1976), 3–19.

FANN, WILLIAM E., et al., eds. *Phenomenology and Treatment of Anxiety.* New York: Spectrum, 1979.

FANSHEL, DAVID, and EUGENE B. SHINN. *Children in Foster Care: a Longitudinal Investigation.* New York: Columbia University Press, 1978.

FANTL, BERTA. "Preventive Intervention." *Social Work*, 7 (July 1962), 41–47.

FARBER, LAURA. "Casework Treatment of Ambulatory Schizophrenics." *Social Casework*, 39 (January 1958), 9–17.

FARRIS, CHARLES E. "American Indian Social Worker Advocates." *Social Casework*, 57 (October 1976), 494–503.

FEDERN, PAUL. "Principles of Psychotherapy in Latent Schizophrenia." *American Journal of Orthopsychiatry*, 1 (April 1947), 129–144.

———. "Psychoanalysis of Psychoses." *Psychiatric Quarterly*, 17 (1941), 3–19, 246–257, 470–487.

FEINSTEIN, SHERMAN C., and PETER L. GIOVACCHINI, eds. *Adolescent Psychiatry: Developmental and Clinical Studies.* Chicago: University of Chicago Press, 1978.

FELDMAN, YONATA. "A Casework Approach Toward Understanding Parents of Emotionally Disturbed Children." *Social Work*, 3 (July 1958), 23–29.

FENICHEL, OTTO. "The Psychoanalytic Theory of Neurosis. New York: Norton 1945.

FERMAN, LOUIS A., ed. *Poverty in America.* Revised ed. Ann Arbor: University of Michigan Press, 1968.

FERREIRA, A. "Family Myths and Homeostasis." *Archives of General Psychiatry*, 9 (1963), 457–463.

FIBUSH, ESTHER, and BEALVA TURNQUEST. "A Black and White Approach to the Problem of Racism." *Social Casework*, 51 (October 1970), 459–466.

FIEDLER, FRED E. "The Concept of the Ideal Therapeutic Relationship." *Journal of Consulting Psychology*, 14 (August 1950), 239–245.

FINCH, WILBUR A., Jr. "Social Workers Versus Bureaucracy." *Social Work*, 21 (September 1976), 370–374.

FINK, ARTHUR E. *The Field of Social Work.* New York: Holt, 1942.

FISCHER, JOEL. "Is Casework Effective? A Review." *Social Work*, 18 (January 1973), 5–20.

FOGARTY, THOMAS F. "Systems Concepts and the Dimensions of Self." In Philip J. Guerin, ed., *Family Therapy.* New York: Gardner Press, 1976.

FOLEY, VINCENT D. *An Introduction to Family Therapy.* New York: Grune & Stratton, 1974.

FONTANE, ARLENE S. "Using Family of Origin Material in Short Term Marriage Counseling." *Social Casework*, 60 (November 1979), 529–537.

FOREN, ROBERT, and BAILEY ROYSTON. *Authority in Social Casework.* New York: Pergamon Press, 1968.

FORTUNE, ANNE E. "Communication in Task-Centered Treatment." *Social Work*, 24 (September 1979), 390–396.

FOSTER, MARION G., and WILLIAM A. PEARMAN. "Social Work, Patient Rights, and Patient Representatives." *Social Casework*, 59 (February 1978), 89–100.

FOX, EVELYN, MARION NELSON, and WILLIAM BOLMAN. "The Termination Process: A Neglected Dimension in Social Work." *Social Work*, 14 (October 1969), 53–63.

FRAIBERG, SELMA. *Every Child's Birthright: In Defense of Mothering.* New York: Basic Books, 1977.

———. *The Magic Years.* New York: Scribner's, 1959.

FRAMO, JAMES L. "Rationale and Techniques of Intensive Family Therapy." In Ivan Boszormenyi-Nagy and James L. Framo, eds., *Intensive Family Therapy.* New York: Harper & Row, 1965, 143–212.

FRANK, JEROME D. "The Dynamics of the Psychotherapeutic Relationship." *Psychiatry,* 22 (February 1959), 17–39

———. "The Role of Hope in Psychotherapy." *International Journal of Psychiatry,* 5 (May 1968), 383–395.

FREED, ANNE O. "The Family Agency and the Kinship System of the Elderly." *Social Casework,* 56 (December 1975), 569–586.

———. "Social Casework: More Than a Modality." *Social Casework,* 58 (April 1977), 204–213.

FREEMAN, HENRY, et al. "Can a Family Agency Be Relevant to the Inner Urban Scene?" *Social Casework,* 51 (January 1970), 12–21.

FREUD, ANNA. *The Ego and the Mechanisms of Defense.* New York: International Universities Press, 1946.

FREUD, SIGMUND. "Analysis of Phobia in a Five-year-old Boy." In James Strachey, ed., *The Complete Works of Sigmund Freud,* Vol. 10. London: Hogarth, 1964, 5–148.

———. "The Unconscious" (1915). In *Collected Papers,* Vol. 4. London: Hogarth Press, 1949, 98–136.

FULLER, JENNIE S. "Duo Therapy Case Studies: Process and Techniques." *Social Casework,* 58 (February 1977), 84–91.

GARCIA, ALEJANDRO. "The Chicano and Social Work." *Social Casework,* 52 (May 1971), 274–278.

GARFIELD, SOL L., and ALLEN E. BERGIN. *Handbook of Psychotherapy and Behavior Change: An Empricial Analysis.* Second ed. New York: Wiley, 1978.

GARRETT, ANNETTE. "Historical Survey of the Evolution of Casework." *Journal of Social Casework,* 30 (June 1949), 219–229.

———. *Interviewing: Its Principles and Methods.* New York: Family Service Association of America, 1942.

———. "Modern Casework: The Contributions of Ego Psychology." In Howard J. Parad, ed., *Ego Psychology and Dynamic Casework.* New York: Family Service Association of America, 1958, 38–52.

———. "The Worker–Client Relationship." In Howard J. Parad, ed., *Ego Psychology and Dynamic Casework.* New York: Family Service Association of America, 1958, 53–72.

GEISMER, LUDWIG L. "Family Disorganization: A Sociological Perspective." *Social Casework,* 59 (November 1978), 545–550.

———. "Thirteen Evaluative Studies." In Edward J. Mullen, James R. Dumpson, et al., eds., *Evaluation of Social Intervention.* San Francisco: Jossey-Bass, 1972.

———, et al. *Early Supports for Family Life: A Social Work Experiment.* Metuchen, N.J.: Scarecrow Press, 1972.

GEIST, JOANNE, and NORMAN GERBER. "Joint Interviewing: A Treatment Technique with Marriage Partners." *Social Casework,* 41 (February 1960), 76–83.

GELMAN, SHELDON R. "Esoterica: A Zero Sum Game in the Helping Professions." *Social Casework,* 61 (January 1980), 48–53.

GERMAIN, CAREL B., and ALEX GITTERMAN. "The Life Model of Social Work Practice." *Social Service Review,* 50 (December 1976), 601–610.

GHALI, SONIA BADILLO. "Culture Sensitivity and the Puerto Rican Client." *Social Casework,* 58 (October 1977), 459–468.

GILBERT, NEIL, and HARRY SPECHT. "Advocacy and Professional Ethics." *Social Work,* 21 (July 1976), 288–293.

GILLIAND, ROBERT M. "Anxiety: A Psychoanalytic View," in William E. Fann et al., eds, *Phenomenology and Treatment of Anxiety.* New York: Spectrum, 1979, 251–260.

GIOVACCHINI, PETER L. *Psychoanalysis of Character Disorders.* New York: Aronson, 1975.

GITTERMAN, ALEX. "Social Work in the Public School System." *Social Casework,* 58 (February 1976), 111–118.

———, and ALICE SCHAEFFER. "The White Professional and the Black Client." *Social Casework,* 53 (May 1972), 280–291.

GLASSER, PAUL and LOIS, eds. *Families in Crisis.* New York: Harper & Row, 1970.

GLICK, IRA D., and JAY HALEY. *Family Therapy and Research: An Annotated Bibliography.* New York: Grune and Stratton, 1971.

GOIN, MARCIA K., et al. "Therapy Congruent with Class-Linked Expectations." *Archives of General Psychiatry,* 13 (August 1956), 133–137.

GOLAN, NAOMI. "Crisis Theory." In Francis J. Turner, ed., *Social Work Treatment: Interlocking Theoretical Approaches.* Second ed. New York: Free Press, 1979, 499–534.

———. *Treatment in Crisis Situations.* New York: Free Press, 1978.

GOLDBERG, GALE. "Breaking the Communication Barrier: The Initial Interview with an Abusing Parent." *Child Welfare,* 54 (April 1975), 274–282.

GORDON, WILLIAM. "Basic Constructs for an Integrative and Generative Conception of Social Work." In Gordon Hearn, ed., *The General Systems Approach: Contributions Toward a Holistic Conception of Social Work.* New York: Council on Social Work Education, 1969.

———. "Knowledge and Value: Their Distinction and Relationship in Clarifying Social Work Practice." *Social Work,* 10 (July 1965), 32–35.

GOTTESFELD, MARY L., and FLORENCE LIEBERMAN. "The Pathological Therapist." *Social Casework,* 60 (July 1979), 387–393.

GOTTLIEB, WERNER, and JOE H. STANLEY. "Mutual Goals and Goal-Setting in Casework." *Social Casework,* 48 (October 1967), 471–477.

GOULD, ROBERT. "Dr. Strangeclass: Or How I Stopped Worrying About Theory and Began Treating the Blue-Collar Worker." *American Journal of Orthopsychiatry,* 37 (January 1967), 78–86.

GRANITE, URSULA. "Foundations for Social Work on Open-Heart Surgery Service." *Social Casework,* 59 (February 1978), 101–105.

GRAY, WILLIAM, FREDERICK J. DUHL, and NICHOLAS D. RIZZO, eds. *General Systems Theory and Psychiatry.* Boston: Little, Brown, 1969.

GREENACRE, PHYLLIS. *Affective Disorders: A Psychoanalytic Contribution to Their Study.* New York: International Universities Press, 1953.

GREENBERG, GEORGE S. "The Family Interactional Perspective: A Study and Examination of the Work of Don D. Jackson." *Family Process,* 16 (December 1977), 385–412.

GREENBERG, LOIS I. "Therapeutic Grief Work with Children." *Social Casework,* 56 (July 1975), 396–403.

GRIMM, JAMES W., and JAMES D. ORTEN. "Student Attitudes Toward the Poor." *Social Work,* 18 (January 1973), 94–100.

GRINNELL, RICHARD M., JR., and NANCY S. KYTE. "Environmental Modification: A Study." *Social Work,* 20 (July 1975), 313–318.

————, and————. "The Future of Clinical Practice: A Study." *Clinical Social Work Journal,* 5 (Summer 1977), 132–138.

GROSSER, CHARLES. "Local Residents as Mediators Between Middle-Class Professional Workers and Lower-Class Clients." *Social Service Review,* 40 (March 1966), 56–63.

Group for the Advancement of Psychiatry. *The Field of Family Therapy.* Report No. 78. New York: GAP, March 1970.

GURMAN, ALAN S., and DAVID P. KNISKERN. "Research on Marital and Family Therapy: Progress, Perspective, and Prospect." In Sol L. Garfield and Allen E. Bergin, eds., *Handbook of Psychotherapy and Behavior Change.* New York: Wiley, 1978.

HAAS, WALTER. "Reaching Out—A Dynamic Concept in Casework." *Social Work,* 4 (July 1959), 41–45.

HADLEY, TREVOR R., et al. "The Relationship Between Family Developmental Crisis and the Appearance of Symptoms in a Family Member." *Family Process,* 13 (June 1974), 207–214.

HALEY, JAY. *Problem-Solving Therapy.* San Francisco: Jossey-Bass, 1976.

HALLOWITZ, DAVID. "Counseling and Treatment of the Poor Black Family." *Social Casework,* 56 (October 1975), 451–459.

HALLOWITZ, EMANUEL. "Innovations in Hospital Social Work." *Social Work,* 17 (July 1972), 89–97.

HALLUM, KENNETH C. "Social Class and Psychotherapy: A Sociolinguistic Approach." *Clinical Social Work Journal,* 6 (Fall 1978), 188–201.

HAMILTON, GORDON. "Basic Concepts upon Which Case Work Practice Is Formulated." *Proceedings of the National Conference of Social Work.* Chicago: University of Chicago Press, 1937.

————. "Basic Concepts in Social Casework." *The Family,* 18 (December 1937), 263–268.

————. "Basic Concepts of Social Casework." *The Family,* 18 (July 1937), 147–156.

————. "Psychoanalytically Oriented Casework and Its Relation to Psychotherapy." *American Journal of Orthopsychiatry,* 19 (1949), 209–223.

————. *Psychotherapy in Child Guidance.* New York: Columbia University Press, 1947.

————. "The Role of Social Casework in Social Policy." *Social Casework,* 33 (October 1952), 315–324.

————. "A Theory of Personality: Freud's Contribution to Social Work." In Howard J. Parad, ed., *Ego Psychology and Dynamic Casework.* New York: Family Service Association of America, 1958, 11–37.

————. *Theory and Practice of Social Casework.* Second ed. Columbia University Press, 1951.

————. "The Underlying Philosophy of Social Casework." *The Family,* 22 (July 1941), 139–148.

HAMMER, EMANUEL F. "Interpretive Technique: A Primer." In Hammer, ed., *Use of Interpretation in Treatment: Technique and Art.* New York: Grune & Stratton, 1968, 31–42.

HANKINS, FRANK. "Contributions of Sociology to Social Work." *Preceedings of the National Conference of Social Work.* Chicago: University of Chicago Press, 1930.

HARDCASTLE, DAVID A. "The Indigenous Non-professional in the Social Service Bureaucracy: A Critical Examination." *Social Work,* 16 (April 1971), 56–63.

HARDGROVE, GRACE. "An Interagency Service Network to Meet Needs of Rape Victims." *Social Casework,* 57 (April 1976), 245–253.

HARDMAN, DALE. "The Matter of Trust." *Crime and Delinquency,* 15 (April 1969), 203–218.

HARTMANN, HEINZ. *Ego Psychology and the Problem of Adaptation.* New York: International Universities Press, 1958.

———, ERNST KRIS, and R. LOEWENSTEIN. "Comments on the Formation of Psychic Structure." In Ruth S. Eissler et al., eds., *The Psychoanalytic Study of the Child,* Vol. 2. New York: International Universities Press, 1946, 11–38.

HAVINGHURST, ROBERT J. "Social and Psychological Needs of the Aging." *The Annals,* 279 (January 1952), 11–17.

HELLENBRAND, SHIRLEY. "Client Value Orientations: Implications for Diagnosis and Treatment." *Social Casework,* 42 (April 1961), 163–169.

———. "Main Currents in Social Casework, 1918–36." Doctoral dissertation, Columbia University School of Social Work, New York, 1965.

HENRY, JULES. *Pathways to Madness.* New York: Random House, 1971.

HEPWORTH, DEAN H. "Early Removal of Resistance in Task-Centered Casework." *Social Work,* 24 (July 1979), 317–323.

HERZOG, ELIZABETH. "Is There a Breakdown of the Negro Family?" *Social Work,* 11 (January 1966), 3–10.

HEYMAN, MARGARET M. "Some Methods in Direct Casework Treatment of the Schizophrenic." *Journal of Psychiatric Social Work,* 19 (Summer 1949), 18–24.

HIRSOHN, SID. "Casework with the Compulsive Mother." *Social Casework,* 32 (June 1951), 254–261.

HO, MAN KEUNG. "Social Work with Asian Americans." *Social Casework,* 57 (March 1976), 195–201.

———, and EUNICE McDOWELL. "The Black Worker–White Client Relationship." *Clinical Social Work Journal,* 1 (Fall 1973), 161–167.

HOCH, PAUL H., and JOSEPH ZUBIN, eds. *The Diagnostic Process in Child Psychiatry.* New York: Grune & Stratton, 1953.

HOFFMAN, DAVID L., and MARY L. REMMEL. "Uncovering the Precipitant in Crisis Intervention," *Social Casework,* 56 (May 1975), 259–267.

HOLLINGSHEAD, AUGUST B., and FREDERICK C. REDLICH. *Social Class and Mental Illness.* New York: Wiley, 1958.

HOLLIS, FLORENCE. "Analysis of Two Casework Treatment Approaches." Unpublished paper, read at Biennial Meeting of Family Service Association of America, 1956.

——. *"Casework In Marital Disharmony."* Doctoral dissertation, Bryn Mawr College, 1947.

——. "Casework and Social Class." *Social Casework,* 46 (October 1965), 463–471.

——. "Continuance and Discontinuance in Marital Counseling and Some Observations on Joint Interviews." *Social Casework,* 49 (March 1968), 167–174.

——. "Environmental (Indirect) Treatment as Determined by Client's Needs." In *Differential Approach in Casework Treatment.* New York: Family Welfare Association of America, 1936.

——. "Principles and Assumptions Underlying Casework Practice." *Social Work* (London), 12 (1955), 41–55.

——. *Social Casework Practice: Six Case Studies.* New York: Family Welfare Association of America, 1939.

——. "A Study of Joint Interviewing in the Treatment of Marital Problems." *Social Casework,* 48 (October & November 1967), 498–502, 570–574.

——. "The Techniques of Casework." *Journal of Social Casework,* 30 (June 1949), 235–244.

——. *A Typology of Casework Treatment.* New York: Family Service Association of America, 1968.

——. "And What Shall We Teach?: The Social Work Educator and Knowledge." *Social Service Review,* 42 (June 1968), 184–196.

——. *Women in Marital Conflict.* New York: Family Welfare Association of America, 1949.

HOLMES, SALLY A., et al " Working with the Parent in Child-Abuse Cases." *Social Casework,* 56 (January 1975), 3–12.

HOWE, MICHAEL W. "Casework Self-Evaluation: A Single-Subject Approach." *Social Service Review,* 48 (March 1974), 1–23.

HUNTER, DAVID. "Social Action to Influence Institutional Change." *Social Casework,* 51 (April 1970), 225–231.

INKELES, ALEX. "Some Sociological Observations on Culture and Personality Studies." In Clyde Kluckhohn, Henry Murray, and David Schneider, eds., *Personality in Nature, Society, and Culture.* New York: Knopf, 1959.

ISAACS, SUSAN. *Social Development in Young Children.* New York: Harcourt, Brace, 1937.

JACKSON, DON D. "Family Interaction, Family Homeostasis and Some Implications for Conjoint Family Psychotherapy." In Jackson, ed., *Therapy, Communication, and Change: Human Communication, Vol. 2,* 185–203.

——. "The Question of Family Homeostasis." In Jackson, ed., *Communication, Family, and Marriage: Human Communication, Vol. 1.* Palo Alto, Calif.: Science and Behavior Books, 1968, 1–11.

JACOBSON, EDITH. *Depression: Comparative Studies of Normal, Neurotic, and Psychotic Conditions.* New York: International Universities Press, 1971.

JANZEN, CURTIS. "Family Treatment for Alcoholism: A Review." *Social Work,* 23 (March 1978), 135–141.

JEFFERS, CAMILLE. *Living Poor.* Ann Arbor, Mich.: Ann Arbor Publishers, 1967.

JOLESCH, MIRIAM. "Casework Treatment of Young Married Couples." *Social Casework,* 43 (May 1962), 245–251.

JONES, MARY ANN, RENEE NEUMAN, and ANN W. SHYNE. *A Second Chance for Families*. New York: Child Welfare League of America, 1976.

JOSSELYN, IRENE. "The Family as a Psychological Unit." *Social Casework*, 34 (October 1953), 336–342.

KADUSHIN, ALFRED "The Racial Factor in the Interview." *Social Work*, 17 (May 1972), 88–98.

———. *The Social Work Interview*. New York Columbia University Press, 1972.

KANTOR, DAVID, and WILLIAM LEHR. *Inside the Family*. San Francisco: Jossey-Bass, 1975.

KAPLAN, DAVID M., and EDWARD A. MASON. "Maternal Reactions to Premature Birth Viewed as an Acute Emotional Disorder." *American Journal of Orthopsychiatry*, 30 (July 1960), 539–547.

KAPLAN, LILLIAN, and JEAN B. LIVERMORE. "Treatment of Two Patients with Punishing Superegos." *Journal of Social Casework*, 29 (October 1948), 310–316.

KARDINER, ABRAM. *The Individual and His Society*. New York: Columbia University Press, 1939.

KASE, HAROLD M. "Purposeful Use of Indigenous Paraprofessionals." *Social Work*, 17 (March 1972), 109–110.

KAUFMAN, IRVING. "Understanding the Dynamics of Parents with Character Disorders." *Casework Papers, 1960*. New York: Family Service Association of America, 1960, 5–15.

KEEFE, THOMAS. "The Economic Context of Empathy." *Social Work*, 23 (November 1978), 460–465.

———. "Empathy: The Critical Skill." *Social Work*, 21 (January 1976), 10–14.

KEITH-LUCAS, Alan. *The Giving and Taking of Help*. Chapel Hill: University of North Carolina Press, 1971.

KELLER, GORDON N. "Bicultural Social Work and Anthropology." *Social Casework*, 53 (October 1972), 455–465.

KEMPE, HENRY, and RAY E. HELFER, eds. *Helping the Battered Child and His Family*. Philadelphia: Lippincott, 1972.

KENDALL, KATHERINE, ed. *Social Work Values in an Age of Discontent*. New York: Council on Social Work Education, 1970.

KERNBERG, OTTO. *Borderline Conditions and Pathological Narcissism*. New York: Aronson, 1975.

———. "The Structural Diagnosis of Borderline Personality Disorganization." In Peter Hartocollis, ed., *Borderline Personality Disorders*. New York: International Universities Press, 1977, 87–121.

KHINDUKA, S. K., and BERNARD J. COUGHLIN. "A Conceptualization of Social Action." *Social Service Review*, 49 (March 1975), 1–14.

KILEY, MARY-LOU. "The Social Worker's Role in a Nursing Home." *Social Casework*, 58 (February 1977), 119–121.

KING, CHARLES. "Family Therapy with the Deprived Family." *Social Casework*, 48 (April 1967), 203–208.

KIRSCHNER, CHARLOTTE. "The Aging Family in Crisis: A Problem in Living." *Social Casework*, 60 (April 1979), 209–216.

KLEIN, EMANUEL. "The Reluctance to Go to School." In Ruth S. Eissler et al., eds., *The Psychoanalytic Study of the Child*, Vol. 1. New York; International Universities Press, 1945, 263–279.

KNIGHT, DANIEL. "New Directions for Public Welfare Caseworkers." *Public Welfare*, 27 (1969), 92–94.

KNOLL, FAUSTINA RAMIREZ. "Casework Services for Mexican Americans." *Social Casework*, 52 (May 1971), 279–284.

KOEHLER, RUTH T. "The Use of Advice in Casework." *Smith College Studies in Social Work*, 23 (February 1953), 151–165.

KOGAN, LEONARD S. "The Short-Term Case in a Family Agency." *Social Casework*, 38 (June 1957), 296–302.

KOHN, MELVIN L. *Class and Conformity: A Study in Values*. Chicago: University of Chicago Press, 1977.

KOHUT, HEINZ. *The Restoration of the Self*. New York: International Universities Press, 1977.

KOMAROWSKY, MIRRA. *Blue-Collar Marriage*. New York: Random House, 1964.
———. *The Unemployed Man and His Family*. New York: Dryden Press, 1940.

KOSS, MARY P. "Research on Brief and Crisis-Oriented Therapies." *Handbook of Psychotherapy and Behavior Change*. Second ed. New York: Wiley, 1978, 725–767.

KOUNIN, JACOB, et al. "Experimental Studies of Clients' Reactions to Initial Interviews." *Human Relations*, 9 (1956), 265–293.

KRAMER, PHILIP. "The Indigenous Worker: Hometowner, Striver, or Activist." *Social Work*, 17 (January 1972), 43–49.

KRUG, OTILDA. "The Dynamic Use of the Ego Functions in Casework Practice." *Social Casework*, 36 (December 1955), 443–450.

KUBLER-ROSS, ELIZABETH. *On Death and Dying*. New York: Macmillan, 1969.

LaBARRE, MAURINE. "The Strengths of the Self-Supporting Poor." *Social Casework*, 49 (October 1968), 459–466.

LAING, L. P. "The Use of Reassurance in Psychotherapy." *Smith College Studies in Social Work*, 22 (February 1952), 75–90.

LAING, RONALD D. "Mystification, Confusion, and Conflict." In Ivan Boszormenyi-Nagy and James L. Framo, eds., *Intensive Family Therapy*. New York: Harper & Row, 1965, 343–363.

———, and A. ESTERSON. *Sanity, Madness and the Family*. Second ed. New York: Basic Books, 1971.

LANCE, EVELYN A. "Intensive Work with a Deprived Family." *Social Casework*, 50 (December 1969), 454–460.

LASSERS, ELIZABETH, et al. "Steps in the Return to School of Children with School Phobia." *American Journal of Psychiatry*, 130 (March 1973), 265–268. Reprinted in Francis J. Turner, ed., *Differential Diagnosis in Social Work*. Second ed. New York: Free Press, 1976, 658–665.

LAZLO, ERVIN, ed. *The Relevance of General Systems Theory*. New York: Braziller, 1972.

LEADER, ARTHUR L. "Current and Future Issues in Family Therapy." *Social Service Review*, 43 (January 1969), 1–11.

———. "Family Therapy for Divorced Fathers and Others Out of the Home." *Social Casework*, 54 (January 1973), 13–19.

———. "Intergenerational Separation Anxiety in Family Therapy." *Social Casework*, 59 (March 1978), 138–144.

———. "The Notion of Responsibility in Family Therapy." *Social Casework*, 60 (March 1979), 131–137.

LEE, JUDITH A., and CAROL R. SWENSON. "Theory in Action: A Community Social Service Agency." *Social Casework*, 59 (June 1978), 359–370.

LESOFF, REEVA. "What to Say When . . ." *Clinical Social Work Journal*, 5 (Spring 1977), 66–76.

LEVANDE, DIANE I. "Family Theory as a Necessary Component of Family Therapy." *Social Casework*, 57 (May 1976), 291–295.

LEVINE, A. "Treatment in the Home." *Social Work*, 9 (January 1964), 19–28.

LEVINSON, HILLIARD. "Communication with an Adolescent in Psychotherapy." *Social Casework*, 54 (October 1973), 480–488.

———. "Termination of Psychotherapy: Some Salient Issues." *Social Casework*, 58 (October 1977), 480–489.

LEVY, CHARLES S. "Advocacy and the Injustice of Justice." *Social Service Review*, 48 (March 1974), 39–50.

———. *Social Work Ethics*. New York: Human Services Press, 1976.

LEVY, LORRAINE POKART. "Services to Parents of Children in a Psychiatric Hospital." *Social Casework*, 58 (April 1977), 204–213.

LEWIS, HELEN BLOCK. *Shame and Guilt in Neurosis*. New York: International Universities Press, 1971.

LEWIS, HYLAN. "Child Rearing Among Low-Income Families." In Louis A. Ferman, ed., *Poverty in America*. Ann Arbor: University of Michigan Press, 1965, 342–353.

———. *Culture, Class and Poverty*. Washington, D.C.: Cross Tell, 1967.

LEWIS, MARIAN F. "Alcoholism and Family Casework." *The Family*, 18 (April 1937), 39–44.

LIDE, PAULINE. "Dynamic Mental Representation: An Analysis of the Empathic Process." *Social Casework*, 47 (March 1966), 146–151.

———, "An Experimental Study of Empathic Functioning." *Social Service Review*, 41 (March 1967), 23–30.

LIDZ, THEODORE. *The Person: His Development Throughout the Life Cycle*. New York: Basic Books, 1968.

LIEBERMAN, FLORENCE. *Social Work with Children*. New York: Human Services Press, 1979.

———, and MARY L. GOTTESFELD. "The Repulsive Client." *Clinical Social Work Journal*, 1 (Spring 1973), 22–31.

LIEBOW, ELLIOT. *Tally's Corner*. Boston: Little, Brown, 1967.

LOEWENSTEIN, SOPHIE. "Inner and Outer Space in Social Casework." *Social Casework*, 60 (January 1979), 19–29.

———. "An Overview of the Concept of Narcissism." *Social Casework*, 58 (March 1977), 136–142.

LOWENSTEIN, RUDOLPH M. "The Problem of Interpretation." *Psychoanalytic Quarterly*, 20 (January 1951), 1–14.

LUTZ, WERNER A. *Concepts and Principles Underlying Social Casework Practice*. Washington, D.C.: National Association of Social Workers, Medical Social Work Section, 1956.

MAAS, HENRY S. "Socio-cultural Factors in Psychiatric Clinic Services for Children." *Smith College Studies in Social Work*, 25 (February 1955), 1–90.

MACRAE, ROBERT H. "Social Work and Social Action." *Social Service Review*, 40 (March 1966), 1–7.

MAHLER, MARGARET S., et al. *The Psychological Birth of the Human Infant: Symbiosis and Individuation.* New York: Basic Books, 1975.

MAILICK, MILDRED D. "A Situational Perspective in Casework Theory." *Social Casework,* 58 (July 1977), 401–411.

MALTSBERGER, JOHN, and DAN BUIE. "Countertransference Hate in the Treatment of Suicidal Patients." *Archives of General Psychiatry,* 30 (May 1974), 625–633.

MALUCCIO, ANTHONY N. *Learning from Clients: Interpersonal Helping as Viewed by Clients and Social Workers.* New York: Free Press, 1979.

———, and WILMA D. MARLOW. "The Case for the Contract." *Social Work,* 19 (January 1974), 28–36

MANN, JAMES. *Time-Limited Psychotherapy.* Cambridge, Mass.: Harvard University Press, 1973.

MARCIANO, TERESA DONATI. "Middle-Class Incomes, Working-Class Hearts." In Arlene S. Skolnick and Jerome H. Skolnick, eds., *Family in Transition.* Boston: Little, Brown, 1977, 465–476.

MARCUS, ESTHER S. "Ego Breakdown in Schizophrenia: Some Implications for Casework Treatment." In Francis J. Turner, ed., *Differential Diagnosis and Treatment in Social Work.* Second ed. New York: Free Press, 1976, 322–340.

MARCUS, LOTTE. "Communication Concepts and Principles." In Francis J. Turner, ed., *Social Work Treatment: Interlocking Theoretical Approaches.* Second ed. New York: Free Press, 1979, 409–432.

———. "The Effect of Extralinguistic Phenomena on the Judgment of Anxiety." Doctoral dissertation, Columbia University School of Social Work, New York, 1969.

MARINE, ESTHER. "School Refusal: Review of the Literature." *Social Service Review,* 42 (December 1968), 464–478.

———. "School Refusal: Who Should Intervene? (diagnostic and treatment categories)" *Journal of School Psychology* (1969), 63–70.

MARMOR, JUDD, ed. *Homosexual Behavior.* New York: Basic Books, 1980.

MASSERMAN, JULES, ed. *Depressions: Theories and Therapies.* New York: Grune & Stratton, 1970.

MASTERSON, JAMES F. *Psychology of the Borderline Adult.* New York: Brunner/ Mazel, 1976.

MAVOGENES, NANCY A., et al. "But Can the Client Understand It?" *Social Work,* 22 (March 1977), 110–112.

MAYER, HERTA, and GERALD SCHAMESS. "Long Term Treatment for the Disadvantaged." *Social Casework,* 50 (March 1969), 138–145.

MAYER, JOHN E., and NOEL TIMMS. "Clash in Perspective Between Worker and Client." *Social Casework,* 50 (January 1969), 32–40.

———, and ———. *The Client Speaks: Working Class Impressions of Casework.* New York: Atherton, 1970.

McCORMICK, MARY J. "Social Advocacy: A New Dimension in Social Work." *Social Casework,* 51 (January 1970), 3–11.

McCULLUM, AUDREY T. "Mothers' Preparation for Their Children's Hospitalization." *Social Casework,* 48 (July 1967), 407–415.

McDERMOTT, F. E., ed. *Self Determination in Social Work.* London: Routledge & Kegan Paul, 1975.

McKamy, Elizabeth Herman. "Social Work with the Wealthy." *Social Casework*, 57 (April 1976), 254–258.

McMillan, Sylvia. "Aspirations of Low-Income Mothers." *Journal of Marriage and the Family*, 29 (May 1967), 282–287.

Mead, Margaret. *Male and Female: A Study of the Sexes in a Changing World.* New York: Morrow, 1949.

———. *Sex and Temperament in Three Primitive Societies.* New York: Morrow, 1935.

Meier, Elizabeth. "Social and Cultural Factors in Casework Diagnosis." *Social Work*, 41 (July 1959), 15–26.

Mencher, Samuel. "The Concept of Authority and Social Casework." *Casework Papers, 1960.* New York: Family Service Association of America, 1960, 126–138.

Mendes, Helen A. "Countertransferences and Counter-culture Clients." *Social Casework*, 58 (March 1977), 159–163.

Meyer, Carol. "Complementarity and Marital Conflict: The Development of a Concept and Its Application to the Casework Method." Doctoral dissertation, Columbia University School of Social Work, New York 1957.

———, ed. *Preventive Intervention.* Washington, D.C.: National Association of Social Workers, 1975.

Miller, Roger R. "Disappointment in Therapy." *Clinical Social Work Journal*, 5 (Spring 1977), 17–28.

———. "Student Research Perspectives on Race in Casework Practice." *Smith College Studies in Social Work*, 41 (November 1970), 10–23.

Miller, S. M., and Elliot Mishler. "Social Class, Mental Illness, and American Psychiatry: An Expository Review." *Milbank Memorial Fund Quarterly*, 37 (April 1959), 174–199.

Milloy, Margaret. "Casework with the Older Person in the Family." *Social Casework*, 45 (October 1964), 450–456.

Mindel, Charles H., and Robert W. Habenstein. *Ethnic Families in America.* New York: Elsevior, 1976.

Minor, John D. "An Assessment of Social Work Education and Family Agency Practice." *Clinical Social Work Journal*, 5 (Winter 1977), 336–341.

Minuchin, Salvador. *Families and Family Therapy.* Cambridge, Mass.: Harvard University Press, 1974.

———, et al. *Families of the Slums.* New York: Basic Books, 1967.

———, and Braulio Montalvo. "Techniques for Working with Disorganized Low Socio-Economic Families." *American Journal of Orthopsychiatry*, 37 (October 1967), 880–887.

———, Bernice L. Rosman, and Lester Baker. *Psychosomatic Families: Anorexia Nervosa in Context.* Cambridge, Mass.: Harvard University Press, 1978.

Mishne, Judith. "Parental Abandonment: A Unique Form of Loss and Narcissistic Injury." *Clinical Social Work Journal*, 7 (Spring 1979), 15–33.

Mitchell, Celia. "The Therapeutic Field in the Treatment of Families in Conflict: Recurrent Themes in Literature and Clinical Practice." In Bernard Reiss, ed., *New Directions in Mental Health.* New York: Grune & Stratton, 1968.

MITTLEMANN, BELA. "Analysis of Reciprocal Neurotic Patterns in Family Relationships." In Victor Eisenstein, ed., *Neurotic Interaction in Marriage.* New
York: Basic Books, 1956, 81–100.

MIZIO, EMELICIA. "Commentary." *Social Casework,* 58 (October 1977), 469–
474.

———. "White Worker–Minority Clients." *Social Work,* 17 (May 1972), 82–86.

MOLYNEUX, I. E. "A Study of Resistance in the Casework Relationship." *Social
Worker,* 34 (November 1966), 217–223.

MONTGOMERY, MITZIE I. R. "Feedback Systems, Interaction Analysis and Counseling Models in Professional Programs." Doctoral dissertation, University
of Edinburgh, 1973.

MOSTWIN, DANUTA. "Multidimensional Model of Working with the Family."
*Social Casework,* 55 (April 1974), 209–215.

———. "Social Work Intervention with Families in Crisis of Change." *Social
Thought,* 2 (Winter 1976).

MOYNIHAN, SHARON K. "Home Visits for Family Treatment." *Social Casework,*
55 (December 1974), 612–617.

MUDD, EMILY. *The Practice of Marriage Counselling.* New York: Association
Press, 1951.

MULLEN, EDWARD J. "Casework Communication." *Social Casework,* 49 (November 1968), 546–551.

———. "Casework Treatment Procedures as a Function of Client Diagnostic
Variables." Doctoral dissertation, Columbia University School of Social
Work, New York, 1968.

———. "Difference in Worker Style in Casework." *Social Casework,* 50 (June
1969), 347–353.

———. "The Relation Between Diagnosis and Treatment in Casework." *Social
Casework,* 50 (April 1969), 218–226.

MURDOCK, GEORGE PETER. "The Universality of the Nuclear Family." In Norman W. Bell and Ezra F. Vogel, eds., *A Modern Introduction to the Family.*
Revised ed. New York: Free Press, 1968, 37–47, 97–101.

MURPHY, ANN, et al. "Group Work with Parents of Children with Down's Syndrome." *Social Casework,* 53 (February 1972), 114–119.

MURRAY, HENRY A. *Explorations in Personality.* New York: Oxford University
Press, 1938.

NADEL, ROBERT. "Interviewing Style and Foster Parents' Verbal Accessibility."
*Child Welfare,* 46 (April 1967), 207–213.

National Association of Social Workers, Ad hoc Committee on Advocacy. "Champion of Social Victims." *Social Work,* 14 (April 1969),
16–22.

NELSEN, JUDITH C. *Communication Theory and Social Work Practice.* Chicago:
University of Chicago Press, 1980.

———. "Dealing with Resistance in Social Work Practice." *Social Casework,* 56
(December 1975), 587–592.

———. "Treatment Issues in Schizophrenia." *Social Casework,* 56 (March
1975), 145–151.

NEUGEBORE, BERNARD. "Opportunity Centered Social Services." *Social Work,*
15 (April 1970), 47–52.

NICHOLI, ARMANDO M., JR., ed. *The Harvard Guide to Modern Psychiatry*. Cambridge, Mass.: Harvard University Press, 1978.

NICHOLLS, GRACE K. "Treatment of a Disturbed Mother–Child Relationship: A Case Presentation." In Howard J. Parad, ed., *Ego Psychology and Dynamic Casework*. New York: Family Service Association of America, 1958, 117–125.

NORMAN, JENNIE SAGE. "Short-Term Treatment with the Adolescent Client." *Social Casework*, 61 (February 1980), 74–82.

NORTHEN, HELEN. "Psychosocial Practice in Small Groups." In Robert W. Roberts and Helen Northen, eds., *Theories of Social Work with Groups*. New York: Columbia University Press, 1976, 116–152.

———. *Social Work with Groups*. New York: Columbia University Press, 1969.

NOVICK, JACK, and KERRY KELLY. "Projection and Externalization." In Ruth S. Eissler et al., eds., *The Psychoanalytic Study of the Child*, Vol. 25. New York: International Universities Press, 1970, 69–95.

OFFER, DANIEL, and EVERT VANDERSTOEP. "Indications and Contraindications for Family Therapy." In Max Sugar, ed., *The Adolescent in Group and Family Therapy*. New York: Brunner/Mazel, 1975, 145–160.

OLSEN, KATHERINE and MARVIN. "Role Expectations and Perceptions for Social Workers in Medical Settings." *Social Work*, 12 (July 1967), 70–78.

OLSON, DAVID H. "Marital and Family Therapy: Integrative Review and Critique." *Journal of Marriage and the Family*, 32 (1970), 501–538.

OPPENHEIMER, JEANETTE. "Use of Crisis Intervention in Casework with the Cancer Patient and His Family." *Social Work*, 12 (April 1967), 44–52.

ORADEI, DONNA M., and NANCY S. WAITE. "Admissions Conferences for Families of Stroke Patients." *Social Casework*, 56 (January 1975), 21–26.

ORCUTT, BEN A. "Casework Intervention and the Problems of the Poor." *Social Casework*, 54 (February 1973), 85–95.

———. "Family Treatment of Poverty Level Families." *Social Casework*, 58 (February 1977), 92–100.

———. "Process Analysis in the First Phase of Treatment." In Pauline Cohen and Merton Krause, eds., *Casework with Wives of Alcoholics*. New York: Family Service Association of America, 1971, 147–164.

ORMSBY, RALPH. "Interpretations in Casework Therapy." *Journal of Social Casework*, 29 (April 1948), 135–141.

OSTBLOOM, NORMAN, and SEDAHLIA JASPER CRASE. "A Model for Conceptualizing Child Abuse Causation and Intervention." *Social Casework*, 61 (March 1980), 164–172.

OVERTON, ALICE. "Establishing the Relationship." *Crime and Delinquency*, 11 (July 1965), 229–238.

———. "Serving Families Who Don't Want Help." *Social Casework*, 34 (July 1953), 304–309.

OXLEY, GENEVIEVE. "The Caseworker's Expectations and Client Motivation." *Social Casework*, 47 (July 1966), 432–437.

———. "Involuntary Clients' Responses to a Treatment Experience." *Social Casework*, 58 (December 1977), 607–614.

———. "Short-Term Therapy with Student Couples." *Social Casework*, 54 (April 1973), 216–223.

PALMORE, E., ed. *Normal Aging* and *Normal Aging II*. Durham, N.C.: Duke University Press, 1970, 1974.

PALUMBO, JOSEPH. "Perceptual Deficits and Self-Esteem in Adolescence." *Clinical Social Work Journal,* 7 (Spring 1979), 34–61.

———. "Theories of Narcissism and the Practice of Clinical Social Work." *Clinical Social Work Journal,* 4 (Fall 1976), 147–161.

PANTER, ETHEL. "Ego-Building Procedures That Foster Social Functioning." *Social Casework,* 48 (March 1967), 139–145.

PARAD, HOWARD J., ed. *Crisis Intervention: Selected Readings.* New York: Family Service Association of America, 1965.

———, ed. *Ego Psychology and Dynamic Casework.* New York: Family Service Association of America, 1958.

———, and R. MILLER, eds. *Ego-Oriented Casework: Problems and Perspectives.* New York: Family Service Association of America, 1963.

PARKES, COLIN MURRAY. *Bereavement: Studies of Grief in Adult Life.* New York: International Universities Press, 1974.

PARSONS, TALCOTT. "The Stability of the American Family System." In Norman W. Bell and Ezra F. Vogel, eds., *A Modern Introduction to the Family.* Revised ed. New York: Free Press, 1968.

PATTI, RINO J. "Limitations and Prospects of Internal Advocacy." *Social Casework,* 55 (November 1974), 537–545.

———, and HERMAN RESNICK. "Changing the Agency from Within." *Social Work,* 17 (July 1972), 48–51.

PAVENSTEDT, ELEANOR, ed. *The Drifters: Children of Disorganized Lower-Class Families.* Boston: Little, Brown, 1967.

PELLMAN, RENEE, et al. "The Van: A Mobile Approach to Services for Adolescents." *Social Casework,* 58 (May 1977), 268–273.

PERLMAN, HELEN HARRIS. *Relationship: The Heart of Helping People.* Chicago: University of Chicago Press, 1979.

———. *Social Casework: A Problem-Solving Process.* Chicago: University of Chicago Press, 1957.

PETRO, OLIVE, and BETTY FRENCH. "The Black Client's View of Himself." *Social Casework,* 53 (October 1972), 466–474.

PIAGET, JEAN. *The Child's Conception of the World.* New York: Harcourt, Brace, 1929.

PIERSON, ARTHUR. "Social Work Techniques with the Poor." *Social Casework,* 51 (October 1970), 481–485.

PILIAVIN, IRVING, and ALAN E. GROSS. "The Effects of Services and Income Maintenance on AFDC Recipients." *Social Service Review,* 51 (September 1977), 389–406.

PINKUS, HELEN. "Casework Techniques Related to Selected Characteristics of Clients and Workers." Doctoral disertation, Columbia University School of Social Work, New York, 1968.

———, et al. "Education for the Practice of Clinical Social Work at the Master's Level: A Position Paper." *Clinical Social Work Journal,* 5 (Winter 1977), 253–272.

PITTMAN, FRANK S., III. "The Family That Hides Together." In Peggy Papp, ed., *Family Therapy: Full Length Case Studies.* New York: Gardner Press, 1977.

———, and KALMAN FLOMENHAFT. "Treating the Doll's House Marriage." *Family Process,* 9 (June 1970), 143–155.

POLANSKY, NORMAN A. *Ego Psychology and Communication.* New York: Atherton Press, 1971.

———. "Powerlessness Among Rural Appalachian Youth." *Rural Sociology,* 34 (June 1969), 219–222.

———, and JACOB KOUNIN. "Clients' Reactions to Initial Interviews: A Field Study." *Human Relations,* 9 (1956), 237–264.

POLLAK, OTTO. *Social Science and Psychotherapy for Children.* New York: Russell Sage Foundation, 1952.

———. "Systems Theory and the Functions of Marriage." In Gertrude Einstein, ed., *Learning to Apply New Concepts to Casework Practice.* New York: Family Service Association of America, 1968, 75–95.

POWELL, THOMAS J. "Negative Expectations of Treatment: Some Ideas About the Source and Management of Two Types." *Clinical Social Work Journal,* 1 (Fall 1973), 177–186.

PRAY, KENNETH. "A Restatement of the Generic Principles of Social Casework Practice." *Journal of Social Casework,* 28 (October 1947), 283–290.

PRICHARD, ELIZABETH R., et al., eds. *Social Work with the Dying Patient and the Family.* New York: Columbia University Press, 1977.

PRODIE, RICHARD D., BETTY L. SINGER, and MARIAN R. WINTERBOTTOM. "Integration of Research Findings and Casework Techniques." *Social Casework,* 48 (June 1967), 360–366.

PRUNTY, HOWARD E., et al. "Confronting Racism in Inner-City Schools." *Social Work,* 22 (May 1977), 190–194.

RAPAPORT, DAVID. *Organization and Pathology of Thought.* New York: Columbia University Press, 1951.

RAPOPORT, LYDIA. "The Concept of Prevention in Social Work." *Social Work,* 6 (January 1961), 19–28.

———. "Crisis Intervention as a Mode of Brief Treatment." In Robert W. Roberts and Robert H. Nee, eds., *Theories of Social Casework.* Chicago: University of Chicago Press, 1970, 265–311.

———. "Social Casework: An Appraisal and an Affirmation." *Smith College Studies in Social Work,* 39 (June 1969), 213–235.

RED HORSE, JOHN G., et al. "Family Behavior of Urban American Indians." *Social Casework,* 59 (February 1978), 67–72.

REDLICH, FREDERICK C., AUGUST B. HOLLINGSHEAD, and ELIZABETH BELLIS. "Social Class Differences in Attitudes Toward Psychiatry." *American Journal of Orthopsychiatry,* 25 (January 1955), 60–70.

REGENSBURG, JEANETTE, and SELMA FRAIBERG. *Direct Casework with Children.* New York: Family Service Association of America, 1957.

REID, KENNETH E. "Nonrational Dynamics of Client–Worker Interaction." *Social Casework,* 58 (December 1977), 600–606.

REID, WILLIAM J. "Task-Centered Treatment." In Francis J. Turner, ed., *Social Work Treatment.* New York: Free Press, 1979, 479–498.

———, and LAURA EPSTEIN. *Task-Centered Casework.* New York: Columbia University Press, 1972.

———, and ———. *Task-Centered Practice.* New York: Columbia University Press, 1977.

———, and BARBARA SHAPIRO. "Client Reactions to Advice." *Social Service Review,* 43 (June 1969), 165–173.

————, and ANN W. SHYNE. *Brief and Extended Casework.* New York: Columbia University Press, 1969, 82–93.

RESNICK, HERMAN. "Effecting Internal Change in Human Service Organizations." *Social Casework,* 58 (November 1977), 546–553.

REYNOLDS, BERTHA CAPEN. "A Study of Responsibility in Social Case Work." *Smith College Studies in Social Work,* 5 (September 1934).

REYNOLDS, ROSEMARY, and ELSE SIEGLE. "A Study of Casework with Sado-Masochistic Marriage Partners." *Social Casework,* 40 (December 1959), 545–551.

RHODES, SONYA L. "Contract Negotiation in the Initial Stage of Casework Service." *Social Service Review,* 51 (March 1977), 125–140.

————. "The Personality of the Worker: An Unexplored Dimension in Treatment." *Social Casework,* 60 (May 1979), 259–264.

RICHMOND, MARY E. *Friendly Visiting Among the Poor: A Handbook for Charity Workers.* New York: Macmillan, 1899.

————. *The Long View.* New York: Russell Sage Foundation, 1930.

————. *Social Diagnosis.* New York: Russell Sage Foundation, 1917.

————. *What Is Social Casework?* New York: Russell Sage Foundation, 1922.

RIESSMAN, FRANK, JEROME COHEN, and ARTHUR PEARL, eds. *Mental Health of the Poor.* New York: Free Press, 1964.

RIGBY, B. D., ed. *Short-Term Training For Social Development: The Preparation of Front-Line Workers and Trainers.* New York: International Association of Schools of Social Work, 1978.

RIPPLE, LILIAN, ERNESTINA ALEXANDER, and BERNICE POLEMIS. *Motivation, Capacity and Opportunity.* Social Service Monographs. Chicago: University of Chicago Press, 1964.

ROBERTS, ROBERT W., and ROBERT H. NEE, eds. *Theories of Social Casework.* Chicago: University of Chicago Press, 1970.

ROBINSON, VIRGINIA. "An Analysis of Processes in the Records of Family Case Working Agencies." *The Family,* 2 (July 1921), 101–106.

————. *A Changing Psychology in Social Case Work.* Chapel Hill: University of North Carolina Press, 1930.

RODMAN, HYMAN. "Lower-Class Family Behavior." In Arlene S. Skolnick and Jerome H. Skolnick, eds., *Family in Transition.* Second ed. Boston: Little, Brown, 1977, 461–465.

ROGERS, CARL. "Client-Centered Therapy." In C. H. Patterson, ed., *Theories of Counseling and Psychotherapy.* New York: Harper & Row, 1966.

————. "The Therapeutic Relationship: Recent Theory and Research." In Floyd Matson and Ashley Montagu, eds., *The Human Dialogue.* New York: Free Press, 1967, 246–259.

ROSENBERG, BLANCA N. "Planned Short-term Treatment in Developmental Crises." *Social Casework,* 56 (April 1975), 195–204.

ROTH, FREDERICK. "A Practice Regimen for Diagnosis and Treatment of Child Abuse." *Child Welfare,* 54 (April 1975), 268–273.

ROWLAND, S. JAMES, JR. "Ego-Directive Psychotherapy in Limited Treatment." *Social Casework,* 56 (November 1975), 543–553.

RUBIN, JULIUS. "Drug Addiction." In George Wiedeman, ed., *Personality Development and Deviation.* New York: International Universities Press, 1975.

RUE, ALICE W. "The Casework Approach to Protective Work." *The Family*, 18 (December 1937), 277–282.

RUEVENI, URI. *Networking Families in Crisis.* New York: Human Services Press, 1979.

RYAN, WILLIAM. *Blaming the Victim.* Revised ed. New York: Random House, 1976.

SALOMON, ELIZABETH. "Humanistic Values and Social Casework." *Social Casework*, 48 (January 1967), 26–32.

SALZMAN, LEON. *The Obsessive Personality.* New York: Science House, 1968.

SANTA-BARBARA, JACK, et al. "The McMaster Family Therapy Outcome Study: An Overview of Methods and Results." *International Journal of Family Therapy*, 1 (Winter 1979), 304–323.

SATIR, VIRGINIA. *Conjoint Family Therapy.* Revised ed. Palo Alto, Calif.: Science and Behavior Books, 1967.

SCANLON, PAULINE L. "Social Work with the Mentally Retarded Client." *Social Casework*, 59 (March 1978), 161–166.

SCHEFLEN, ALBERT E. "Human Communication: Behavioral Programs and Their Integration in Interaction." *Behavioral Science*, 13 (1968).

————. "The Significance of Posture in Communications." *Psychiatry*, 27 (1964), 316–331.

SCHERZ, FRANCES H. "Family Interaction: Some Problems and Implications for Casework." In Howard J. Parad and Roger R. Miller, eds., *Ego-Oriented Casework: Problems and Perspectives.* New York: Family Service Association of America, 1963, 129–144.

————. "Family Treatment Concepts." *Social Casework*, 47 (April 1966), 234–240.

————. "Theory and Practice in Family Therapy." In Robert W. Roberts and Robert H. Nee, eds., *Theories of Social Casework.* Chicago: University of Chicago Press, 1970, 219–264.

————. "Treatment of Acting-out Character Disorders in a Marital Problem." In Casework Papers, 1956. New York: Family Service Association of America, 1956.

SCHORR, ALVIN S. "Editorial Page." *Social Work*, 11 (July 1966), 2.

SCHUERMAN, JOHN R. "Do Family Services Help?" *Social Service Review*, 49 (September 1975), 363–375.

SCHULMAN, GERDA L. "Treatment of Intergenerational Pathology." *Social Casework*, 54 (October 1973), 462–472.

————, and ELSA LEICHTER. "The Prevention of Family Breakup." *Social Casework*, 49 (March 1968), 143–150.

SCHWARTZ, MARY C. "Helping the Worker with Countertransference." *Social Work*, 23 (May 1978), 204–209.

SCHWARTZ, WILLIAM. "Private Troubles and Public Issues: One Social Work Job or Two?" *Social Welfare Forum.* New York: Columbia University Press, 1969, 22–43.

*Scope and Methods of the Family Service Agency.* Report of the Committee on Methods and Scope. New York: Family Service Association of America, 1953.

SEABURY, BRETT A. "Arrangement of Physical Space in Social Work Settings." *Social Work,* 16 (October 1971), 43–49.

———. "Communication Problems in Social Work Practice." *Social Work,* 25 (January 1980), 40–44.

———. "The Contract: Uses, Abuses and Limitations." *Social Work,* 21 (January 1976), 16–21.

SHANNON, BARBARA. "Implications of White Racism for Social Work Practice." *Social Casework,* 51 (May 1970), 270–276.

SHATTUCK, GERALD M., and JOHN M. MARTIN. "New Professional Work Roles and Their Integration into a Social Agency Structure." *Social Work,* 14 (July 1969), 13–20.

SHEA, MARGENE M. "Establishing Initial Relationships with Schizophrenic Patients." *Social Casework,* 37 (January 1965), 25–29.

SHERMAN, SANFORD N. "Family Therapy." In Francis J. Turner, ed., *Social Work Treatment.* Second ed. New York: Free Press, 1979.

———. "Family Treatment: An Approach to Children's Problems." *Social Casework,* 47 (June 1966), 368–372.

———. "Intergenerational Discontinuity and Therapy of the Family." *Social Casework,* 48 (April 1967), 216–221.

SILVERMAN, PHYLLIS R. "A Reexamination of the Intake Procedure." *Social Casework,* 51 (December 1970), 625–634.

SIMOS, BERTHA G. "Grief Therapy to Facilitate Healthy Restitution." *Social Casework,* 58 (June 1977), 337–342.

SIPORIN, MAX. "Social Treatment: A New–Old Helping Method." *Social Work,* 15 (July 1970), 13–25.

SKOLNICK, ARLENE S., and JEROME H. SKOLNICK, eds. *Family in Transition.* Second ed. Boston: Little, Brown, 1977.

SMALDINO, ANGELO. "The Importance of Hope in the Casework Relationship." *Social Casework,* 56 (July 1975), 328–333.

SMALL, LEONARD. *The Briefer Psychotherapies.* New York: Brunner/Mazel, 1971.

SMITH, LARRY L. "Crisis Intervention in Practice." *Social Casework,* 60 (February 1979), 81–89.

———. "A Review of Crisis Intervention Theory." *Social Casework,* 59 (July 1978), 396–405.

SMITH, RUSSELL. "In Defense of Public Welfare." *Social Work,* 11 (October 1966), 90–97.

SMITH, VEON, and DEAN HEPWORTH. "Marriage Counseling with One Partner: Rationale and Clinical Implications." *Social Casework,* 48 (June 1967), 352–359.

SOBEY, FRANCINE. *The Non-Professional Revolution in Mental Health.* New York: Columbia University Press, 1970.

*Social Casework, Generic and Specific: An Outline.* A Report of the Milford Conference. New York: American Association of Social Workers, 1929.

SPECHT, HARRY. "The Deprofessionalization of Social Work." *Social Work,* 17 (March 1972), 3–15.

———. "Disruptive Tactics." *Social Work,* 14 (April 1969), 5–15.

SPECK, ROSS V., and CAROLYN L. ATTNEAVE. "Social Network Intervention." In Clifford J. Sager and Helen Singer Kaplan, eds., *Progress in Group and Family Therapy.* New York: Brunner/Mazel, 1972, 416–439.

SPIEGEL, JOHN P. "Conflicting Formal and Informal Roles in Newly Acculturated Families." In Gertrude Einstein, ed., *Learning to Apply New Concepts to Casework Practice.* New York: Family Service Association of America, 1968, 53–61.

———. "Some Cultural Aspects of Transference and Counter-Transference." In Jules Masserman, ed., *Individual and Familial Dynamics.* New York: Grune & Stratton, 1959, 160–182.

———. "The Social Roles of Doctor and Patient in Psychoanalysis and Psychotherapy." *Psychiatry,* 17 (November 1954), 369–376.

STAMM, ISABEL. "Ego Psychology in the Emerging Theoretical Base of Casework." In A. J. Kahn, ed., *Issues in American Social Work.* New York: Columbia University Press, 1959, 80–109.

STAPLE, ROBERT. "Towards a Sociology of the Black Family: A Theoretical and Methodological Assessment." *Journal of Marriage and the Family,* 33 (February 1971), 119–135.

STEMPLER, BENJ. L. "Effects of Adversive Racism on White Social Work Students." *Social Casework,* 56 (October 1975), 460–467.

STEWART, JAMES C., JR., et al. "The Poor and the Motivation Fallacy." *Social Work,* 17 (November 1972), 34–37.

STIERLIN, HELM. "The Dynamics of Owning and Disowning: Psychoanalytic and Family Perspectives." *Family Process,* 15 (September 1976), 277–288.

———. "Group Fantasies and Family Myths." *Family Process,* 12 (June 1973), 111–125.

STILES, EVELYN, et al. "Hear It Like It Is." *Social Casework,* 53 (May 1972), 292–299.

STREAN, HERBERT S. *Clinical Social Work: Theory and Practice.* New York: Free Press, 1978.

———. "Role Theory." In Francis J. Turner, ed., *Social Work Treatment.* Second ed. New York: Free Press, 1979.

STUDT, ELIOT. "An Outline for Study of Social Authority Factors in Casework." *Social Casework,* 35 (June 1954), 231–238.

———. "Worker–Client Authority Relationships in Social Work." *Social Work,* 4 (January 1959), 18–28.

SUESS, JAMES F. "Short-Term Psychotherapy with the Compulsive Personality and the Obsessive-Compulsive Neurotic." *American Journal of Psychiatry,* 129 (1972), 270–275.

SUNLEY, ROBERT. "Family Advocacy from Case to Cause." *Social Casework,* 51 (June 1970), 347–357.

SWENSON, CAROL. "Social Networks, Mutual Aid, and the Life Model of Practice." In Carel B. Germain, ed., *Social Work Practice.* New York: Columbia University Press, 1979, 213–238.

TAYLOR, SHIRLEY S., and NORMA SIEGEL. "Treating the Separation–Individuation Conflict." *Social Casework,* 59 (June 1978), 337–344.

TERMAN, LEWIS N. *Psychological Factors in Marital Happiness.* New York: McGraw-Hill, 1938.

THOMAS, EDWIN. "Selected Sociobehavioral Techniques and Principles: An Approach to Interpersonal Helping." *Social Work,* 13 (January 1968), 12–26.

THOMPSON, JANE K., and DONALD P. RILEY. "Use of Professionals in Public Welfare." *Social Work,* 11 (January 1966), 22–27.

THURZ, DANIEL. "The Arsenal of Social Action Strategies: Options for Social Workers." *Social Work,* 16 (January 1971), 27–34.

TOWLE, CHARLOTTE. *Common Human Needs.* Revised ed. New York: National Association of Social Workers, 1957.

———. "Factors in Treatment." *Proceedings of the National Conference of Social Work, 1936.* Chicago: University of Chicago Press, 1936, 179–191.

———. "Social Work: Cause and Function." In Helen H. Perlman, ed., *Helping: Charlotte Towle on Social Work and Social Casework.* Chicago: University of Chicago Press, 1969, 277–299.

TROESTER, JAMES D., and JOEL A. DARBY. "The Role of the Mini-Meal in Therapeutic Play Groups." *Social Casework,* 57 (February 1976), 97–103.

TRUAX, CHARLES B., and ROBERT R. CARKHUFF. *Toward Effective Counseling and Psychotherapy: Training and Practice.* Chicago: Aldine, 1967.

TURNER, FRANCIS. "A Comparison of Procedures in the Treatment of Clients with Two Different Value Orientations." *Social Casework,* 45 (May 1964), 273–277.

———, ed. *Differential Diagnosis and Treatment in Social Work.* Second ed. New York: Free Press, 1976.

———. "Ethnic Difference and Client Performance." *Social Service Review,* 44 (March 1970), 1–10.

———, ed. *Social Work Treatment: Interlocking Theoretical Approaches.* Second ed. New York: Free Press, 1979.

———. "Social Work Treatment and Value Differences." Doctoral dissertation, Columbia University School of Social Work, New York, 1963.

ULLMANN, ALICE. "Teaching Medical Students to Understand Stress in Illness." *Social Casework,* 57 (November 1976), 568–574.

VAN LAWICK-GOODALL, JANE. *In the Shadow of Man.* New York: Houghton Mifflin, 1971.

VESPER, SUE. "Casework Aimed at Supporting Marital Role Reversal." *Social Casework,* 43 (June 1962), 303–307.

VONTROSS, CLEMMONT. "Cultural Barriers in Counseling Relationships." *Journal of Counseling Psychology,* 18 (January 1971), 7–13.

WALKER, PHILIP W. "Premarital Counseling for the Developmentally Disabled." *Social Casework,* 58 (October 1977), 475–479.

WALLER, WILLARD. *The Old Love and the New.* New York: Liveright, 1930.

WALZ, THOMAS H., and HARRY J. MACY. "The MSW and the MPA: Confrontation of Two Professions in Public Welfare." *Journal of Sociology and Social Welfare,* 5 (January 1978), 100–117.

WALZER, HANK. "Casework Treatment of the Depressed Parent." *Social Casework,* 42 (December 1961), 505–512.

WASSER, EDNA. "Family Casework Focus on the Older Person." *Social Casework,* 47 (July 1966), 423–431.

WASSERMAN, HARRY. "The Moral Posture of the Social Worker in a Public Agency." *Public Welfare,* 25 (1967), 38–44.

WASSERMAN, HENRY. "Some Thoughts About Teaching Social Casework Today." *Smith College Studies in Social Work*, 43 (February 1973).

WASSERMAN, SYDNEY. "The Middle-Age Separation Crisis and Ego-Supportive Casework Treatment." *Clinical Social Work Journal*, 1 (Spring 1973), 38–47.

WATSON, ANDREW. "Reality Testing and Transference in Psychotherapy." *Smith College Studies in Social Work*, 36 (June 1966), 191–209.

WATTIE, BRENDA. "Evaluating Short-Term Casework in a Family Agency." *Social Casework*, 55 (December 1973).

WATZLAWICK, PAUL. *The Language of Change: Elements of Therapeutic Communication*. New York: Basic Books, 1978.

————, JANET BEAVEN, and DON JACKSON. *Pragmatics of Human Communication*. New York: Norton, 1967.

WEISBERGER, ELEANOR B. "The Current Usefulness of Psychoanalytic Theory to Casework." *Smith College Studies in Social Work*, 37 (February 1967), 106–118.

WEISMAN, AVERY D. *On Dying and Denying: A Psychiatric Study of Terminality*. New York: Behavioral, 1972.

WEISMAN, IRVING. "Offender Status, Role Behavior, and Treatment Considerations." *Social Casework*, 48 (July 1967), 422–425.

WEISSMAN, HAROLD. "The Middle Road to Distributive Justice." *Social Work*, 17 (March 1972), 86–93.

————. *Overcoming Mismanagement in the Human Services*. San Francisco: Jossey-Bass, 1973.

WEISSMAN, MYRNA M., and EUGENE S. PAYKEL. *The Depressed Woman*. Chicago: University of Chicago Press, 1974.

————, et al. "Treatment Effect on the Social Adjustment of Depressed Patients." *Archives of General Psychiatry*, 30 (1974), 771–778.

WELLS, RICHARD A., and ALAN E. DEZEN. "The Results of Family Therapy Revisited: The Nonbehavioral Methods." *Family Process*, 17 (September 1978), 251–274.

WERTHEIM, ELEANOR S. "Family Unit Therapy and the Science and Typology of Family Systems." *Family Process*, 12 (December 1973), 361–376.

————. "The Science and Typology of Family Systems II." *Family Process*, 14 (September 1975), 285–309.

WHITE, ROBERT W. *Ego and Reality in Psychoanalytic Theory*. New York: International Universities Press, 1963.

WICKENDEN, ELIZABETH. "A Perspective on Social Services." *Social Service Review*, 50 (December 1976), 570–585.

WIEDEMAN, GEORGE, ed. *Personality Development and Deviation*. New York: International Universities Press, 1975.

WINEMAN, DAVID, and ADRIENNE JAMES. "The Advocacy Challenge to Schools of Social Work." *Social Work*, 14 (April 1969), 23–32.

WINNICOTT, DONALD W. "Hate in Countertransference." *International Journal of Psychoanalysis*, 30 (part 2, 1949), 69–74.

WISEMAN, REVA S. "Crisis Theory and the Process of Divorce." *Social Casework*, 56 (April 1975), 205–212.

WITMER, HELEN LELAND. *Social Work*. New York: Rinehart, 1942.

WOLBERG, LEWIS R., ed. *Short-Term Psychotherapy.* New York: Grune & Stratton, 1965.

WOLMAN, BENJAMIN B., ed. *Clinical Diagnosis of Mental Disorders: A Handbook.* New York: Plenum Press, 1978.

WOOD, KATHERINE. "The Contribution of Psychoanalysis and Ego Psychology to Social Casework." In Herbert S. Strean, ed., *Social Casework.* Metuchen, N.J.: Scarecrow Press, 1971.

WOODROOFE, KATHLEEN. *From Charity to Social Work in England and the United States.* Toronto: University of Toronto Press, 1962.

WYNNE, LYMAN C. "Some Indications and Contraindications for Exploratory Family Therapy." In Ivan Boszormenyi-Nagy and James L. Framo, eds., *Intensive Family Therapy.* New York: Basic Books, 1965, 289–322.

YOUNG, LOENTINE R. *Wednesday's Children: A Study of Child Neglect and Abuse.* New York: McGraw-Hill, 1964.

YOUNGHUSBAND, EILEEN. "Intercultural Aspects of Social Work." *Journal of Education for Social Work,* 2 (Spring 1966), 59–65.

ZANGER, ALLYN. "A Study of Factors Related to Clinical Empathy." *Smith College Studies in Social Work,* 38 (February 1968), 116–131.

ZBOROWSKI, MARK, "Cultural Components in Response to Pain." *Journal of Social Issues,* 8 (1952), 16–30.

ZENTNER, MONNA. "The Paranoid Client." *Social Casework,* 61 (March 1980), 138–145.

ZIMBERG, SHELDON. "Principles of Alcoholism Psychotherapy." In Zimberg et al., eds., *Practical Approaches to Alcoholism Psychotherapy.* New York: Plenum Press, 1978, 3–18.

ZIMMERMAN, SHIRLEY L. "Reassessing the Effect of Public Policy on Family Functioning." *Social Casework,* 59 (October 1978), 451–457.

ZUK, GERALD H., and DAVID RUBINSTEIN. "A Review of Concepts in the Study and Treatment of Families of Schizophrenics." In Ivan Boszormenyi-Nagy and James L. Framo, eds., *Intensive Family Therapy.* New York: Harper & Row, 1965, 1–25.

# Index